with appreciation
Daphne a Aeyal

D1206089

EXPLORING SOCIAL RIGHTS

Exploring Social Rights looks into the theoretical and practical implications of social rights. The book is organised in five parts. Part I considers theoretical aspects of social rights, and looks into their place within political and legal theory and within the human rights tradition; Part II looks at the status of social rights in international law, with reference to the challenge of globalisation and to the significance of specific regional regulation (such as the European System); Part III includes discussions of various legal systems which are of special interest in this area (Canada, South Africa, India and Israel); Part IV looks at the content of a few central social rights (such as the right to education and the right to health); and Part V discusses the relevance of social rights to distinct social groups (women and people with disabilities). The articles in the book, while using the category of social rights, also challenge the separation of rights into distinct categories and question the division of rights to 'civil' *vs* 'social' rights, from a perspective which considers all rights as 'social'. This book will be of interest to anyone concerned with human rights, the legal protection of social rights and social policy.

Exploring Social Rights

Between Theory and Practice

Edited by
Daphne Barak-Erez and Aeyal M Gross

·HART·
PUBLISHING

OXFORD AND PORTLAND, OREGON
2007

Published in North America (US and Canada) by
Hart Publishing
c/o International Specialized Book Services
920 NE 58th Avenue, Suite 300
Portland, OR 97213-3786
USA
Tel: +1 503 287 3093 or toll-free: (1) 800 944 6190
Fax: +1 503 280 8832
E-mail: orders@isbs.com
Website: http://www.isbs.com

Hart Publishing, 16C Worcester Place, Oxford, OX1 2JW
Telephone: +44 (0)1865 517530 Fax: +44 (0) 1865 510710
E-mail: mail@hartpub.co.uk
Website: http//:www.hartpub.co.uk

British Library Cataloguing in Publication Data

Data Available

ISBN: 978-1-84113-613-4

Typeset by Forewords, Oxford
Printed and bound in Great Britain by
TJ International Ltd, Padstow, Cornwall

Acknowledgements

We are grateful to the Minerva Center for Human Rights and the Cegla Center for the Interdisciplinary Study of the Law at Tel Aviv University for their support of this book. Some of the articles in this book originated in a conference held at the Faculty of Law of Tel Aviv University in May 2001, under the auspices of the Minerva Center for Human Rights. We are particularly grateful to our students who helped us in the editing process. Magi Otsri acted as our deputy editor and offered invaluable help in the various stages of editing. We are grateful for her committed and dedicated work. Olga Frishman, Michal Lev, Itamar Mann, Noa Bar and Dana Efrati also provided crucial assistance in preparing the book for publication. Dana Rothman-Meshulam assisted in editing some of the articles and we are thankful for her excellent work.

Daphne Barak-Erez and Aeyal M Gross
Tel Aviv
May 2007

For Chen, Eran and Yuval, with love

Daphne Barak-Erez

For Ofer; for my dear parents Zvia and Joseph; and for my brother Raz and my sister Vardit and their families, with love

Aeyal M Gross

Contents

List of Contributors

Daphne Barak-Erez is Stewart and Judy Colton Professor of Law at Tel Aviv University.

Upendra Baxi is Professor of Law at the University of Warwick.

Eva Brems is a Lecturer in Law (Docent) at the University of Ghent, Belgium.

Dennis M Davis is a Judge at the Capetown High Court, South Africa.

Aeyal M Gross is a Senior Lecturer in Law at Tel Aviv University.

Jayna Kothari is a practising lawyer in the Karnataka High Court, Bangalore, India.

Patrick Macklem is William C Graham Professor of Law at the University of Toronto.

Frank I Michelman is Robert Walmsley University Professor at Harvard University.

Guy Mundlak is Associate Professor of Law and the Director of the Minerva Center of Human Rights at Tel Aviv University.

Yoram Rabin is a Senior Lecturer in Law at the College of Management, Rishon Lezion.

Kerry Rittich is Associate Professor at the Faculty of Law and the Women's and Gender Studies Institute at the University of Toronto.

Yuval Shany is a Senior Lecturer in Law and Hersch Lauterpacht Chair in Public International Law at the Hebrew University of Jerusalem.

Lucie White is Louis A Horvitz Professor of Law at Harvard University.

Neta Ziv is a Senior Lecturer in Law and the Director of the Clinical Studies at the Faculty of Law of Tel Aviv University.

Table of Cases

Canada

European Committee of Social Rights (ECSR)

European Court of Human Rights

Germany

India

Inter-American Court of Human Rights

Israel

Permanent Court of International Justice

South Africa

UN Human Rights Committee

United Kingdom

United States of America

Venezuela

WTO

Table of Legislation and Legislative Instruments

Canada

China

Croatia

Denmark

Hungary

India

International

Ireland

Israel

Italy

Japan

Latvia

Luxembourg

Macedonia

Malta

Venezuela

1

Introduction: Do We Need Social Rights?

Questions in the Era of Globalisation, Privatisation, and the Diminished Welfare State

DAPHNE BARAK-EREZ AND AEYAL M GROSS[*]

As we approach the sixtieth anniversary of the Universal Declaration of Human Rights ('UDHR'),[1] this book seeks to take stock of social rights as a legal category and of their protection, looking into the theoretical foundations of social rights and the question of their implementation. In the process of this exploration, the discussion throughout the book also invites an inquiry into social rights as a distinct category within the human rights system.

The history of the modern concept of rights has greatly affected the current status of social rights and the role of the UDHR in establishing that status. The roots of our current thinking about human rights can be traced back to the eighteenth century, when the modern notion of rights crystallised in both political philosophy and within the framework of the American and French revolutions. Liberal thought, manifested in the ideas of thinkers such as Locke,[2] advanced the idea of natural rights as a construct that predates the state and whose protection is a primary function of the state. Thus, in the Lockean tradition, the state is prohibited from violating the life, liberty or property of its citizens. This is the concept of rights that lies at the heart of the American constitution.

One of the major critics of this liberal rights approach was Karl Marx, who, in the nineteenth century, made the powerful argument that the

---

* The authors are grateful to Hedi Viterbo and Magi Otsri for their assistance in writing this Introduction and to Dana Rothman-Meshulam for her excellent editing work.
[1] Universal Declaration of Human Rights (adopted 10 December 1948) UNGA Res 217A(III).
[2] See especially J Locke, *The Second Treatise on Government* (Oxford, B Blackwell, 1956).

protection of civil rights does not in fact guarantee human emancipation. Marx pointed out that the eighteenth-century civil rights declarations had not contended with issues of economic inequality, but quite the opposite: one of the major rights of the liberal paradigm, the right to private property, argued Marx, actually perpetuates inequality in the material conditions of living.[3] Thus, in Marx's view, rights promised equality but in fact entrenched inequality. His criticism shed light on the connection between human rights and distributive justice and on the lacunae in the liberal rights ideology in everything pertaining to the material conditions of life. An understanding of rights relating only to the civic sphere, which is focused, in the Lockean spirit, on limiting the power of the state to violate the rights of individuals, is not committed to the material welfare of those individuals and, ultimately, cannot guarantee equal enjoyment of the civil rights themselves. Moreover, such a conception not only excludes any commitment to the individual's material welfare, but can actually hinder actions taken to foster that welfare: because rights, under this paradigm, are understood as restrictions on the state's power to act, the result could be that the civil rights themselves will serve to restrict actions taken by the state to promote welfare. This was the outcome of the US Supreme Court's *Lochner* doctrine during the first third of the twentieth century, under which the Court held various labour and welfare laws to be in violation of the constitutional protection of liberty.[4]

The need to address questions of welfare and material existence within the framework of the rights paradigm has not been limited to thinkers from the Marxist tradition. The UDHR may also be seen as a belated attempt to address these matters. The Declaration crystallised two important developments in the thinking on human rights. The first is the idea of universality, meaning that rights should not be left as a matter within the exclusive domain of states and that their enjoyment should not be dependent upon the individual's membership in a nation-state that, as a matter of fact, protects its citizens' rights.[5] The second development was the emergence of the notion of so-called social rights, which appear in the UDHR alongside civil and political rights. The Declaration recognises not only such rights as the right to life, liberty, equality, freedom of movement and citizenship, but also 'social' rights such as the right to social security, the right to work (encompassing just and favourable working conditions and protection against unemployment), the right of every person to a standard of living adequate for his and his family's health and well-being

---

[3] See especially K Marx, 'On the Jewish Question' in RC Tucker (ed), *The Marx-Engels Reader* (New York, W W Norton, 1972).

[4] See *Lochner v New York* 198 US 45 (1905); C Sunstein, 'Lochner's Legacy' (1987) 87 *Columbia Law Review* 873.

[5] This development may be seen as an attempt to address the problem of the nexus between rights and the nation-state and the question of the 'right to have rights', identified in H Arendt, *The Origins of Totalitarianism* (New York, Meridian Books, 1958) 267–302.

(including food, clothing, housing, medical care, and necessary social services), and the right to education.[6] More generally, the UDHR determines that: 'Everyone, as a member of society... is entitled to realization, through national effort and international co-operation and in accordance with the organization and resources of each State, of the economic, social and cultural rights indispensable for his dignity and the free development of his personality'[7] and that 'Everyone is entitled to a social and international order in which the rights and freedoms set forth in this Declaration can be fully realized'.[8]

TH Marshall, in an influential essay originally published two years after the adoption of the UDHR, offered a theory of citizenship comprising three elements: a civil element composed of the rights necessary for individual freedom, such as liberty of the person, freedom of speech, thought and faith, as well as property; a political element referring to the right to participate in the exercise of political power; and a social element ranging from the right to a modicum of economic welfare and security to the right to live the life of a civilised being according to society's prevailing standards.[9] It was only in the twentieth century, Marshall argued, that social rights attained equal status with the other two elements of citizenship[10]: whereas for civil rights the formative period was the eighteenth century and for political rights the nineteenth century, it was the twentieth century in which the recognition of social rights crystallised.[11] The UDHR includes all three sets of rights. However, the Declaration's historical moment, in which all three elements of citizenship discussed by Marshall acquired equal recognition, was not long-lasting. The covenants that were articulated to translate the UDHR into the binding language of international treaties split the rights into two different types, leading to the birth, in 1966, of two separate treaties: the International Covenant on Civil and Political Rights ('ICCPR')[12] and the International Covenant on Economic, Social and Cultural Rights ('ICESCR').[13] This division stemmed

---

[6] UDHR Arts 22–6.

[7] UDHR Art 22.

[8] UDHR Art 28.

[9] TH Marshall, *Citizenship and Social Class* (New York, Doubleday, 1964) 8. Marshall associated different institutions with the different types of rights: courts of justice with civil rights, parliament and councils of local government with political rights, and the educational system and social services with social rights.

[10] *Ibid* 17. While Marshall's account is a sociological one developed in the British context, the status accorded to social rights within the UDHR attests to the fact that the process he described is not limited to the British context.

[11] *Ibid* 10.

[12] International Covenant on Civil and Political Rights (adopted 16 December 1966, entered into force 23 March 1976) 999 UNTS 171.

[13] International Covenant on Economic, Social and Cultural Rights (adopted 16 December 1966, entered into force 3 January 1976) 993 UNTS 3. On the background to the covenant, see: M Craven, *The International Covenant on Economic, Social and Cultural Rights: A Perspective on its Development* (Oxford, Oxford University Press, 1995) 16–22; K Arambulo,

from controversy over the nature of social rights, which had already arisen at the time of the drafting of the UDHR itself. While agreement was reached to include social rights in the 1948 Declaration, during the years that followed the controversy re-emerged, with the Communist states giving preference to social rights and the United States objecting to any legally-binding status to these rights.[14] The 1966 split was not merely symbolic. The civil and political rights treaty established an international supervision mechanism within the United Nations system that is more developed than the mechanisms created under the social and economic rights treaty. Additionally, the ICCPR imposed on states an immediate duty of implementation, whereas the ICESCR determined that they created a duty upon the state to take steps, to the maximum of their available resources, with a view to achieving progressively the full realisation of these rights.[15] The disparity between the statuses of the different rights was manifested not only in the international treaties. For many years, the major international human rights non-governmental organisations, as well as the United Nation's human rights system itself,[16] focused on civil and political rights and ignored social rights. Moreover, the constitutions of many countries accorded social rights secondary, if any, status. Thus, notwithstanding their equal position in the UDHR, social rights have been relegated to a secondary status in both international law and the national laws of many countries. Often, they are regarded with considerable suspicion and as problematic to implement as full legal rights.

Strengthening the Supervision of the International Covenant on Economic, Social and Cultural Rights: Theoretical and Procedural Aspects (Antwerpen, Intersentia, 1999) 15–23.

[14] The consensus to include social rights in the UDHR was, to a large extent, due to Eleanor Roosevelt's success in persuading the reluctant US State Department. On the inclusion of social rights in the UDHR and the accompanying controversies, see: MA Glendon, *A World Made New: Eleanor Roosevelt and the Universal Declaration of Human Rights* (New York, Random House, 2001) 42–3, 115–17, 155–60, 185–90; J Morsink, *The Universal Declaration of Human Rights: Origins, Drafting, and Intent* (Philadelphia, University of Pennsylvania Press, 1999) 157–238.

[15] Art 2(1). For an influential document on the implementation of the Covenant, which resulted from a meeting of experts under the auspices of the International Commission of Jurists, see The Limburg Principles on the Implementation of the International Covenant on Economic, Social and Cultural Rights, UN Doc E/CN.4/1987/17 (annex, reprinted in (1987) 9 *Human Rights Quarterly* 122). See also 'The Maastricht Guidelines on Violations of Economic, Social and Cultural Rights' (1998) 20 *Human Rights Quarterly* 691 (a document emanating from a meeting of experts convened on the tenth anniversary of the Limburg Principles); and the General Comment adopted by the United Nations Committee on Economic, Social and Cultural Rights, CESCR General Comment 3 on The Nature of State Parties Obligations, Doc E/1991/23 (1990). For a discussion, see Craven, n 13 above, at 106–52.

[16] On the developments leading to the establishment of the Committee on Economic, Social and Cultural Rights within the United Nations (which, unlike the Human Rights Committee established by the ICCPR, was not established by the Covenant itself but only later) and on the operation of the Committee, see Craven, n 13 above, 30–105 and Arambulo, n 13 above, 23–49.

This situation has led to criticism that the civil rights concept associated with Western liberal democracies ignores the harsh social distress typically experienced by much of the world's population, whose lack of access to housing, food, health care and other material living conditions is no less detrimental than violations of rights such as freedom of speech or religion. The international human rights discourse has, to some extent, internalised this criticism, and today there is widespread understanding that social rights are just as important as civil and political rights and often a necessary precondition to the fulfilment of the latter. Since the 1990s, the idea of the interdependence and indivisibility of the different kinds of rights has gained broad recognition.[17] The Declaration adopted by the 1993 second World Congress on Human Rights in Vienna referred to the covenants and the two sets of rights as 'universal, indivisible, and interdependent and interrelated'.[18] This, however, has not meant the end to the controversy over social rights, with many continuing to maintain that they relate to issues of resource allocation, which should not be conceived of in terms of rights. According to those opposing recognition of social rights, binding legal norms should not be set with respect to the allocation of state resources in areas such as education, housing and health, as these are economic policy issues that should not be decided by the judiciary. On the other hand, advocates of social rights argue that the implementation of civil and political rights also entails questions of policy and resource allocation, and hence there is no fundamental difference between the different kinds of rights. An oft-cited example is the right to due process, which, in practice, requires the state to allocate resources for the establishment and operation of the judicial system. The obvious question is: How does this differ from the requirement that states allocate resources

17 For criticisms of the division of rights into two supposedly distinct sets that instead suggest an integrative approach, see, eg: C Scott, 'Toward the Institutional Integration of the Core Human Rights Treaties' in I Merali and V Oosterveld (eds), *Giving Meaning to Economic, Social and Cultural Rights* (Philadelphia, University of Pennsylvania Press, 2001) 7–38; C Puta-Chekwe and N Flood, 'From Division to Integration: Economic, Social and Cultural Rights as Basic Human Rights' in I Merali and V Oosterveld (eds), *Giving Meaning to Economic, Social and Cultural Rights* (Philadelphia, University of Pennsylvania Press, 2001) 39–51; D Otto, 'Defending Women's Economic and Social Rights: Some Thoughts on Indivisibility and a New Standard of Equality' in I Merali and V Oosterveld (eds), *Giving Meaning to Economic, Social and Cultural Rights* (Philadelphia, University of Pennsylvania Press, 2001) 52–67. For a jurisprudential analysis that rejects the idea of an analytical distinction between the two kinds of rights while accepting some structural differences that affect their enforceability but not their status or importance as rights, see R Gavison, 'On the Relationship between Civil and Political Rights and Social and Economic Rights' in JM Coicaud, Michael Doyle and Anne-Marie Gardner (eds), *The Globalization of Human Rights* (New York, United Nations University Press, 2003) 23. For further perspectives on the relationship between the different sets of rights, see A Eide, C Krause and A Rosas (eds), *Economic, Social and Cultural Rights: A Textbook* 2nd revised ed (Dordrecht, Martinus Nijhoff, 2001) 3–130.

18 Vienna Declaration and Programme of Action (adopted 25 June 1993 by World Congress on Human Rights) para 5.

for the establishment and operation of medical services necessary for the realisation of the right to health?[19]

From the debate over the nature and scope of social rights it emerges that distribution and resource allocation issues are not unique to this category of rights and are, in fact, integral to any discussion of rights, including civil and political rights. For example, effective protection of the right to freedom of speech entails not only preventing the state from silencing people through censorship, but also state action fostering people's ability to express opinions. This may take the form of allocation of police resources to protect demonstrators, the maintenance of public media channels, and other measures necessary to guarantee the right. Indeed, in his essay, TH Marshall pointed to the fact that the right to freedom of speech has little substance if, due to a lack of education, people have nothing to say that is worth saying and no means of making themselves heard even if they say it. According to Marshall, these blatant inequalities are not due to flaws in civil rights, but to the absence of social rights.[20] While we agree with Marshall's observation that the right to freedom of speech is abstract and meaningless in the absence of background material conditions, we do not think that these conditions must be addressed only in the context of social rights. Rather, there is a need to think about questions of distribution in regard to all rights and to the lack of a fundamental difference between the various types of rights.

Thus, despite the seemingly renewed consensus regarding the interdependence of rights, the debate over the similarities and differences between the two sets of rights,[21] and the frequent relegation of social rights to a second-class status, persist. It has been argued forcefully that social rights have been systematically neglected and that, notwithstanding their recognition in the UDHR and the ICESCR, they have been more honoured in their breach than in their observance.[22] The disparity between the two sets of rights at both the international and national levels has led scholars to call for a 'reclaiming' of social rights.[23] Hence, at the beginning of the twenty-first century, scholars are still finding it necessary to argue for and justify a constitutional status for social rights,[24] hardly a necessity with

---

[19] For a discussion of the way in which governmental protection of all rights entails funding, see S Holmes and CR Sunstein, *The Cost of Rights: Why Liberty Depends on Taxes* (New York, WW Norton and Co, 1999).

[20] *Ibid* 21.

[21] For an overview of this debate, see H Steiner and P Alston, *International Human Rights in Context: Law, Politics, Morals* (Oxford, Oxford University Press, 2000) 237–320.

[22] D Bilchitz, *Poverty and Fundamental Rights: The Justification and Enforcement of Socio-Economic Rights* (Oxford, Oxford University Press, 2007).

[23] P Hunt, *Reclaiming Social Rights: International and Comparative Perspectives* (Aldhershot, Ashgate, 1996).

[24] See, eg, C Fabre, *Social Rights under the Constitution: Government and the Decent Life* (Oxford, Oxford University Press, 2000) (arguing for constitutional protection of social rights, but maintaining distinctions between civil and social rights that we believe should be questioned).

respect to civil and political rights. Some scholars attribute this state of affairs to the lack of a developed normative justification for socio-economic rights and seek to provide one.[25] While providing normative justification on the philosophical and jurisprudential level is important, we believe that it is an ideological bias that lies at the heart of the distinction between the two sets of rights and, accordingly, affects their differing statuses. The Lockean idea of rights as merely limiting the power of the state to act reinforces the notion that social welfare is a supposedly unique sphere insofar as it involves matters of policy and distribution that belong outside the sphere of rights and judicial enforcement.[26] This bias persists despite the fact that, as mentioned above, the enforcement of civil rights in practice requires positive government action, as well as allocation of resources. All rights, then, have a dimension that entails that the state would refrain from acting and a dimension requiring active state partici-pation for their realisation. The right to health requires that the government would not prevent us from receiving medical care or force medical treatment upon us, but, at the same time, requires that it would act to ensure our access to health care. Similarly, the right to freedom of speech mandates that the state would not use censorship to prevent us from expressing our opinions but, at the same time, requires it to act to ensure our access to effective freedom of speech. Thus, we can see how drawing an artificial line between rights results in more than relegating so-called social rights to the margins of the human rights discourse. Indeed, it also denies the presence of any distributional dimension in the application of the so-called civil rights. Claiming social rights to be unique in addressing resource issues conveys the message that questions of accessi-bility and distribution are not relevant to civil rights and that limiting government censorial power is all that is needed to protect freedom of speech. In other words, questions of distribution are excluded from the rights discourse twice over: by both the exclusion of social rights and the exclusion of distribution concerns from the realm of civil rights.

Thus, although this book focuses on social rights and uses the termi-nology that appears in the UDHR and is anchored in the ICESCR, we query the division of rights into separate categories and take the position that *all* human rights are 'social' by nature. This is based on the contention that no rights have any meaning outside the social context and that we

---

[25] Bilchitz, n 22 above (arguing for a general philosophical theory of fundamental rights that serves as the foundation for both civil and political rights and social and economic rights).

[26] For a discussion of the ways in which the traditional liberal Lockean understanding of rights as individualistic, negative claims against government underlies the argument that social rights are not judicially enforceable, see J Woods, 'Justiciable Social Rights as a Critique of the Liberal Paradigm' (2003) 39 *Texas International Law Journal* 763.

must consider the distributive context of all rights.[27] We maintain that the separation and division between the different sets of rights should be rejected[28] and that all rights are social.[29]

Based on this understanding, we could reach the conclusion that, contrary to the prevailing discourse, which expresses embarrassment at the question of the state's duties in relation to social rights and queries 'social rights' as lacking any clear content, the state's obligations vis-à-vis social rights are in fact far less ambiguous than its duties in the context of civil rights. Returning to the comparison between the right to health and the right to free speech, whereas an accessible public health care system may satisfy many of the requirements of the right to health, it is less apparent what would satisfy the requirements of the right to freedom of speech, when understood as not limited to its 'negative' aspect and entailing also guaranteed access to freedom of speech. Is the state obliged to maintain an accessible public media system? What is the meaning of accessibility in this context? Is it access to all opinions or to all individuals? These are complex questions that, currently, are far more unanswerable than the questions considered in the context of the right to health.

* * *

Against this background, *Exploring Social Rights* engages in a discussion of social rights and examines their implementation, while challenging their classification as a separate category of rights. **Part I** of the book considers theoretical aspects of social rights and their place within political and legal theory and within the human rights tradition. **Part II** inquires into the status of social rights in international law and in the European human rights system, while **Part III** examines various national legal systems of particular interest in this area (India, South Africa, Canada and Israel). **Part IV** analyses the content of central social rights (education, health and work), and **Part V** concludes with a deliberation over the relevance of social rights to distinct social groups (people with disabilities and women). The various chapters in the book echo the concerns outlined above over the division between the two sets of rights, and articulate additional ones.

In the opening chapter of **Part I**, 'The Constitution, Social Rights and Liberal Political Justification', Frank Michelman attempts to define the

---

[27] On the need to give social rights a 'social' dimension, see D Davis, P Macklem and G Mundlak, 'Social Rights, Social Citizenship and Transformative Constitutionalism: A Comparative Assessment' in J Conaghan, R Michael Fischl and K Klare (eds), *Labour Law in an Era of Globalization* (Oxford, Oxford University Press, 2002) 511.

[28] Even scholars who argue for constitutional protection of social rights tend to concede that there are conceptual differences between civil and social rights: see, eg, Fabre, n 24 above.

[29] While this discussion questions the classification of the rights outlined in the UDHR into categories, at the very best, we find 'welfare rights' the more appropriate term to describe the rights set forth in Articles 22–8.

limits of the debate surrounding the constitutionalisation of social rights. Michelman dismisses the standard opposition to this process, which is based on the fear of expanding judicial power. He argues that the fact that social rights entail budgetary expenses or call for government action and not mere forbearance does not differentiate them radically from the constitutionally protected rights to property, to equality before the law and to so-called negative liberties. At the same time, Michelman points to other concerns: first, that adding social rights to the constitution would unduly constrict democracy and, second, that constitutionalising social rights would undermine the constitution's crucial function of legitimising the coercive political and legal orders. He then explains that the first concern can be dealt with in the framework of the formulation of the constitutional social rights and the second concern reflects a specific conception of democracy, which is not the only possible one.

Whereas the first chapter considers the place of social rights within constitutional orders, the two chapters that follow examine the place of social rights in the global context, looking at their role in postcolonial relations. Upendra Baxi's 'Failed Decolonisation and the Future of Social Rights: Some Preliminary Reflections' discusses the second-rate status assigned to social rights in contemporary legal discourse in the context of globalisation and postcolonialism. He presents the traditional arguments raised to support the preference given to so-called civil and political rights, which loom large over social concerns. This tradition, Baxi explains, is anchored in a Hobbesian conception of rights as a means of protection against an over-powering sovereign. He argues that, in the global economy, where multinational corporations have gained awesome powers, this conception has been employed as an active interpretive force to legitimise a global regime in which citizens of the Global South have become practically 'rightless'. In this respect, Baxi continues the line of argument that questions and, in fact, rejects the analytical separation of the two sets of rights and embraces the claim that the distinction between negative and positive rights is misleading since both make substantial claims on state and community resources. Baxi attributes this artificial distinction to the liberal tradition that focuses on rights as constraints on state power and examines the ways in which this division has, in itself, detrimental effects on disempowered populations. The mere expression 'social rights', maintains Baxi, is tautologous, as all human rights make little sense outside human societal frameworks. 'Rights,' he argues, 'are thus *social* or not *at all*'. Accordingly, Baxi proposes historicising the rights discourse in a way that will enable new consideration of the continued legal and ethical responsibilities of the Global North towards subalterns in postcolonial societies. The legacies of colonialism and anti-colonial struggles, as well as the realities of the current global political arena, make this programme an immensely difficult task.

The limits of decolonisation and the status of social rights in the post-colony are further explored by Lucie White in '"If You Don't Pay, You Die": On Death and Desire in the Post-Colony'. White considers the role of 'structural adjustment' as imposing upon states various socio-economic policies in a way that is detrimental to the local population. Drawing on her experience working with American and West-African law students active in the area of health rights in poverty-stricken Africa, White reflects on the limits of liberalism and the human rights discourse. She discusses the ways in which she and her students felt both drawn to what they came to call a 'human rights campaign' and deeply ambivalent about their flirtation with that phrase. Her chapter poses the question of whether human rights can be used in the poor Third World in ways that stretch, and even subvert, liberalism's categorical and, therefore, ultimately conservative notions of justice. The limits of the human rights discourse are illustrated in her suggestion that:

> To voice injustice as a violation of a 'human right,' one buys into a static, atomised notion of the human subject as taking form *before* the law, and outside its constitutive influence.

The hopes embodied in human rights cannot obscure the dangers of this discourse, which will, in White's words, 'train them to think of themselves as good, liberal, rights-consuming subjects as they watch their children die'.

The role of rights in our global world is further explored by the chapters in **Part II**, which examine how social rights play out in the context of the international human rights legal discourse.

Yuval Shany's 'Stuck in a Moment in Time: The International Justiciability of Economic, Social and Cultural Rights' considers the status of social and economic rights in international law. Shany challenges the argument that social rights are not justiciable, by exploring the evolution of available judicial enforcement mechanisms in this area. Addressing the claim that judicial review of social rights involves redistributive decisions that should not be made by the judiciary, Shany highlights the redistributive characteristics of civil and political rights, especially given the emergence of the notion of these rights as entailing positive obligations. The chapter concludes with several guidelines for enforcing social rights. By pointing to the justiciability, enforceability and redistributive effects of social rights, as well as the fact that all rights imply 'positive' duties for states, Shany reinforces the need to question the very separation of the different sets of rights. Acknowledging the open-ended language of the ICESCR, he concludes that the obligations imposed by the Treaty have been significantly concretised by the UN Committee on Economic, Social and Cultural Rights. Shany points to the European Social Charter's review mechanism and to national experience, primarily from South Africa, as proof that social rights, like their civil and political counterparts, are enforceable rights and not mere political aspirations.

The international sphere is also considered by Kerry Rittich in 'Social Rights and Social Policy: Transformations on the International Landscape'. Arguing that '[t]he social is already here', Rittich explores the state of social rights in the contemporary globalised political order. Diverse international organisations such as the International Labour Organization, the Organization for Economic Cooperation and Development, the World Bank, and the World Trade Organization have all purported to have given the highest level of priority to the eradication of poverty. Indeed, social rights have thoroughly permeated the language of human rights in the global sphere. However, on the basis of her survey and analysis of the history of this development, Rittich argues that social rights, even if they have gained recognition as part of the human rights discourse, have been reduced to the most minimal of claims. So, while Shany argues that social rights are justiciable legal rights and not mere aspiration, Rittich shows that, within the current discourse of legal and institutional reform, social rights are barely considered even policy concerns but, rather, met with scepticism. She argues that the combination of elite consensus against universal social entitlements, the erosion of political support for wider redistribution, and the emergence of competitors who have either never recognised extensive social rights or are now prepared to trade them off to attract investment has, in many places, undercut efforts to rescue the foundations of social rights and better calibrate them to the changed social and economic circumstances. Rittich examines the shifts in labour policy and the dominance of the market approach, whereby social protection has transformed into risk management on the individual or household level. She thus identifies a process in which social citizenship is challenged by a world organised to extract the benefits of economic incentives and market forces, where the primary way in which citizens achieve social inclusion and affiliation to the polity is through participation in market activities such as consumption and labour market work.

Eva Brems moves from the global to the regional level in her chapter 'Indirect Protection of Social Rights by the European Court of Human Rights'. Her analysis demonstrates that the European Court uses several techniques to protect social rights, even though the European Convention on Human Rights and its additional protocols do not include these rights (a few exceptions notwithstanding) and the European Social Charter, which does protect certain social rights, is not within the Court's jurisdiction. The chapter distinguishes between three such techniques—interpretation, procedural protection and non-discrimination—and then shows how a court working within the classic paradigm of civil and political rights can nonetheless offer some protection to social rights. This is attributed to the fact that the European Court of Human Rights has long held that civil and political rights entail positive obligations. Through its protection of these rights, the Court has, in fact, in many cases, extended protection to social rights. Brems' analysis illustrates the indivisibility of civil and social rights: often the protection of civil rights such as the right to life entails protection of social rights. However, despite this fact, the Court does limit the extent of its intervention. Thus, while it has held that the right to life also obliges the state to take appropriate steps to safeguard the lives of those within its jurisdiction, the Court refuses to order the funding of necessary medical treatment under either this right or the right to private and family life. It therefore refrained from intervening in issues of access to vital medicines and equipment for the severely disabled essential for their daily functioning. Brems notes, however, that, while the Court refused to intervene in such matters, it did order payment for a gender reassignment operation. This striking inconsistency can be explained, she argues, by, inter alia, the Court's tendency to attach increased importance to issues such as gender identity, which it treats more gravely than physical health and the ability to function independently. The fact that funding for the former is considered a core right but not for the latter illustrates how, despite its explicit recognition of rights as entailing positive obligations, the European Court nonetheless reinforces the distinction between matters pertaining to identity and matters pertaining to material conditions of living, thereby entrenching the arbitrary division betweens the two sets of rights.

Shifting the focus to the protection of social rights within national contexts, **Part III** examines a few countries of particular interest in this regard.

The first chapter in this Part is Jayna Kothari's 'Social Rights Litigation in India: Developments of the Last Decade'. The Indian Constitution does not include social rights as justiciable fundamental rights, but only as directive principles for state policy. Thus, similar to the European context described in the preceding chapter, social rights enjoy only indirect protection derived from other, explicitly protected rights. But in contrast to the European context, the Indian judiciary has shown a marked tendency to take the principle of the interdependence of human rights seriously and to interpret entrenched constitutional guarantees of the fundamental rights in light of the directive principles, in a way that offers expanded protection to social rights. Kothari demonstrates, however, that although the Indian Supreme Court has developed new rights, it has also been ambivalent vis-à-vis well-entrenched socio-economic rights such as the right to housing. The Court had pronounced that this right is part of the right to life as early as 1986, but has since retreated from this position. The chapter focuses on the role of litigation as a strategy for promoting and protecting social rights, mainly in the framework of housing, food and education cases, and sheds light on what has been achieved through social rights litigation and on the potential and limits of this strategy. The success of such litigation is shown to be contingent on external factors as well: social campaigns, research and political will. The chapter thus identifies the ways in which social rights can serve up concrete results in specific cases, as enforceable rights, no less than civil and political rights, but at the same time shows that winning the case in court is not the end of the story, but only one stage on the way to enforcement.

Unlike in India, where the judiciary needed to take an active role in transforming social rights into justiciable ones, in South Africa, discussed by Dennis Davis in 'Socio-Economic Rights: The Promise and Limitation—The South African Experience', the post-apartheid Constitution explicitly includes justiciable social rights. Davis analyses the history of the South African Constitution in the area of social rights and evaluates the fulfilment of the promise of social rights in the South African context. Given the broad explicit recognition of social rights in the Constitution, the South African court judgments regarding these rights have attracted particular attention worldwide. Indeed, South African constitutional law is viewed by many as a test-case or laboratory for the enforcement of constitutional social rights. But as Davis argues, since the Constitution's approval in 1996, tension has arisen between its transformative vision and the macro-economic policy adopted by the South African government, which gives preference to economic growth over social reconstruction as its key objective. It is against this background that Davis analyses the South African Constitutional Court judgments on social rights. These judgments focus on the question of the reasonableness of measures taken by the government rather than on core state obligations. Davis maintains that the Court has failed to outline the contents of the rights in question and has deferred to the political autonomy of the legislature and executive. In his words, the Court has developed a minimalist framework within which to apply social rights by allowing the state the possibility of a full defence against enforcement on grounds of limited availability of resources, except in the context of the development of programmes dealing with the community's poorest. The scope and range of the social rights are left undefined and, to date, the Court has opted to sidestep any adjudication of unqualified socio-economic rights. Davis believes that the South African experience serves as evidence that political organisation remains the primary means of securing different forms of distributional decisions for society's most vulnerable. He further asserts that, even when armed with a progressive text, judges tend to retreat to models of adjudication based on earlier traditions of legal practice, which reduce the potential of the constitutional change. His chapter points to both the achievements and limitations of social rights and reminds us that outcomes in these matters depend less on the recognition of social rights per se and more on the content and interpretation they are given.

Whereas in South Africa social rights are constitutionally entrenched but not de facto enjoyed by many of the poor, in Canada social rights are not part of the Constitution but are also not totally foreign to the legal discourse. In 'Social Rights in Canada', Patrick Macklem focuses on the implementation of rights enshrined in the ICESCR in a country whose Charter of Rights[30] is restricted to civil and political rights. According to Macklem, the domestic implementation of the Convention in Canada occurs on two planes. On the political plane, the legislative and executive branches of government exercise constitutional authority to establish and administer social policy programmes that protect interests typically associated with international social rights. On the juridical plane, domestic implementation is effected through interpretation. The chapter examines these two spheres of implementation and discusses the judicial choices made in this context. Macklem shows how the judiciary has shied away from explicitly relying on Canada's international obligations under the ICESCR when interpreting the Charter and how the constitutional signifi-cance that the judiciary has attached to interests relating to work, social security and health derives more from the limits that the Charter imposes on state action than from the obligations it imposes on the government to promote individual and social well-being. These choices shape, and are shaped by, developments in the political sphere in ways that minimise the domestic significance of Canada's international obligations in this area. Macklem's chapter draws attention to the fact that any examination of the status of social rights should include careful consideration of the actions taken by the different branches of government and the complex relations between the political and juridical fields. His observations about the way the Canadian courts have addressed the issue highlight the persistence of the liberal model of rights as limitations on government action and the hurdles this model places for social rights.

In 'Social Citizenship: The Neglected Aspect of Israeli Constitutional Law', Daphne Barak-Erez and Aeyal Gross examine the weak status accorded to social rights in Israeli constitutional law. Although social rights are not specifically recognised in the basic laws on human rights enacted in 1992,[31] the Israeli Supreme Court has extended them protection, albeit very limited, within the parameters of the general right to human dignity, in the form of a minimal protection associated with avoiding humiliation. However, the chapter points to the fact that, whilst the Court has been willing to read non-enumerated civil rights in their full into the right to human dignity, it has refused to do so when it comes to social rights, beyond the model of minimal protection. Thus, the Court's interpretation has re-erected the artificial divide between civil and social

---

[30] Canadian Charter of Rights and Freedoms.
[31] Basic Law: Freedom of Occupation and Basic Law: Human Dignity and Liberty.

rights. The chapter criticises this partial protection of social rights and exposes its weaknesses, especially against the background of the dwindling welfare state. The Israeli rights discourse seems, for the most part, to reinforce the government's neo-liberal policies rather than protect welfare entitlements.

Shifting the focus from national perspectives to a discussion of specific rights, **Part IV** addresses the protection of a select number of social rights and evaluates international and national experiences with their implementation.

In 'The Many Faces of the Right to Education', Yoram Rabin distinguishes between the different components of this right: the right to receive education, the right to choose education, the right to equal education, and the different aspects of compulsory education. He examines the justifications for protecting the right to education and the kind of protection it should receive and considers the balance that should be struck in protecting the right vis-à-vis the different possible sources of its infringement: the state, the social community (usually a minority group) and the family (mainly the parents).

In 'The Right to Health in an Era of Privatisation and Globalisation: National and International Perspectives', Aeyal Gross examines the right to receive health care and the scope of that right. He considers the extent to which the right to health is protected as a human right, focusing on questions of accessibility and equal distribution as manifested in the scope of the health services provided to eligible recipients and the conditions in which these services are provided. The chapter probes into the tension between the view that treats health 'seriously' as a right and the view that rejects health as a right and, in practice, is increasingly turning health into a commodity. Addressing both the potential and the risks of the 'health and human rights movement', Gross considers whether rights discourse can be a vehicle for more egalitarian access to health care. He illustrates the very real risks of inserting rights analysis into a system of mutual dependency and limited resources and shows that this analysis can actually serve to bolster those already in possession of greater resources. Yet at the same time, commitment to the idea of equal accessibility can turn rights analysis into a tool for reducing existing inequalities. In an era when public health systems are being privatised, the idea of (private) rights may reinforce the commodification of health entailed by this privatisation or, in fact, do the opposite, by reinserting public rights law and public values into the equation.

In 'The Right to Work—The Value of Work', Guy Mundlak examines the different aspects of this right as a social right. Differentiating the right to work from the right to employment and from the duty to work, Mundlak identifies the values underlying the right to work and focuses on the arguments made against its recognition, which sidestep the general arguments for and against social rights. He also examines the risks entailed in turning to rights discourse within the capitalist framework with its income-based disparities, reflecting on the critique that presents the right to work as the right to be exploited. Mundlak considers equality issues in the implementation of the right to work, mainly relating to age and gender, and evaluates the assertion that the right to work is in fact tantamount to the right to a basic income.

Part V sheds light on the different meanings and significances social rights bear for different groups, especially those that historically have suffered from discrimination and social vulnerability.

Neta Ziv's chapter, 'The Social Rights of People with Disabilities: Reconciling Care and Justice', reflects on the struggle of the disabled by using the ethics of care critique of the individual rights-based liberal model. Ziv describes a shift within the disabilities movement from a welfare approach to a liberal-oriented rights approach. She shows the growing role of the rights approach at both the domestic and global levels, pointing to the ways in which the recourse to rights in disability advocacy has promoted a position that underscores choice, autonomy and self-assertion. This stance has been criticised from an alternative standpoint that values care, interdependence and support, which are critical in the lives of the disabled. The chapter queries whether the concept of social rights can accommodate these crucial values: after infusing the rights notion into the world of disabilities in order to move from the welfare model to the autonomy model, the limits and risks of the rights approach itself must now be reckoned with.

Finally, in 'Social Rights as Women's Rights', Daphne Barak-Erez examines the issue of social rights from a feminist perspective. Barak-Erez notes the special importance of social rights for women, who are usually the primary care-providers in their families and who are not fully integrated into the labour market. The chapter reflects on the different needs of women in developed and developing countries, including potential tensions that can arise between women from different social classes.

*   *   *

Read together, the chapters in this book share a commitment to expanding human welfare and reducing socio-economic inequalities. Attracted by the normative and rhetoric power of the rights discourse, they all engage with the idea of social rights, but are simultaneously aware of its limitations, especially in respect to issues of social interdependency. Thus, while none of the chapters shies away from the notion of social rights, they all seek to further understand how the 'social' can be injected into the liberal individual-centred discourse of rights. Much of the discussion in the book reflects on the risk that rights analysis in areas pertaining to the material conditions of living will always be limited to minimal 'tip of the iceberg' cases[32] and may thus obscure the need for broader programmes to address substantial inequalities. A clear picture emerges of how, sixty years after the issuance of the UDHR, social rights, on the one hand, enjoy greater than ever recognition as part and parcel of the human rights tradition, but yet, on the other hand, are often reduced to a minimal concept that cannot seriously contend with current needs, especially given the crisis faced by the modern welfare state. In light of the growing recognition of the positive obligations entailed by civil and political rights, the chapters in this book call into question the distinction between the different types of rights and invite an inquiry into the ideology underlying this division. It is our hope that this book will contribute to the exploration of the hopes and risks entailed in implementing the aspiration embodied in the UDHR to infuse matters of welfare and material existence into the rights paradigm.

---

[32] On human rights as tending to deal with only the 'tip of the iceberg', see D Kennedy, *The Dark Side of Virtue: Reassessing International Humanitarianism* (Princeton, Princeton University Press, 2004) 32.

Part I

Theoretical Perspectives on Social Rights

2

The Constitution, Social Rights and Liberal Political Justification

FRANK I MICHELMAN*

I INTRODUCTION: THE TERMS OF DEBATE

Acountry's written constitutional bill of rights is a high-ranking positive law—a 'statute' regulating 'the relations between the government and the governed'.[1] Granted, the constitution may figure as something more: a 'mirror reflecting the national soul', perhaps; an expression of national ideals, aspirations and values expected, as such, to 'preside and permeate the processes of judicial interpretation and judicial discretion' throughout the length and breadth of the national legal order.[2] Perhaps. But did bills of rights not also and always register as direct, regulatory legislation—as laws to be enforced like other laws—jurists and scholars the world over would not have conducted their debates over the constitutionalisation of social rights in the terms that in fact we have grown used to.

Constitutions, to be sure, are regulatory laws of a special kind, setting terms and conditions for the making and execution of all other laws. Typically, although not necessarily, some of the terms and conditions are cast in the form of a bill of rights: a list of certain interests of persons,

* This chapter was originally published, under the same title, in (2003) 1 *International Journal of Constitutional Law* 13–34. I have omitted one section of the original version and made a few small stylistic changes, but otherwise have left the text as it appeared there. Citations have not been updated, aside from adding a reference to an article by William Forbath responding directly to material that engages his scholarship substantially and directly.

[1] *S v Acheson* [1991] 2 SA 805 (Nm) 813A-B, [1991] NR 1, 10A-B (Mahomed AJ).

[2] *Ibid.* Doubtless Justice Mahomed drew inspiration from the Lüth-jurisprudence of the German Federal Constitutional Court, which has appeared prominently in the nascent constitutional jurisprudence of South Africa. See: *Lüth* [1958] BVerfGE 7, 198; Vicki C Jackson and Mark Tushnet *Comparative Constitutional Law* (New York, Foundation Press, 1999) 1402–35; Case 48/00 *Carmichele v Minister of Safety and Security* [2001] CCT 54 (South Africa)('Our Constitution is not merely a formal document regulating public power. It also embodies, like the German Constitution, an objective, normative value system.') (Ackermann and Goldstone JJ).

upon whom are conferred what are considered to be subjective legal rights, not just background moral claims,[3] to have these interests at least negatively respected,[4] and maybe positively secured and redeemed, by the state's legislative and other actions yet to come.

Among the constitutional-legal rights thus conferred may be rights to satisfaction of certain material needs or wants, or of access to the means of satisfaction. Take, for example, section 26 of the Constitution of South Africa:

(1)   Everyone has the right to have access to adequate housing.

(2)   The state must take reasonable legislative and other measures, within its available resources, to achieve the progressive realisation of this right.[5]

Without a doubt, that declaration of a *right* that everyone has is seriously meant. The surrounding constitutional text makes emphatically clear that section 26 lays down a full-fledged constitutional right, no less a legal right than any other declared by the Bill of Rights—no less intendedly obligatory upon those to whom it is addressed than are legal rights in general and no less intendedly subject to enforcement by whatever means may be available for the effectuation of legal rights in general.[6]

Opinion divides over whether it is a good idea thus to confer full constitutional-legal status upon 'social' rights guarantees of this kind. The division no doubt stems in part from substantive disagreement. You will not support the constitutionalisation of social rights guarantees unless you are convinced, at least provisionally, that the claims for social support of individuals and families for which such guarantees would speak are ones that no morally legitimate or would-be successful political society can ignore. Obviously, not everyone shares that view. Some do, though, and what I have to say here is addressed mainly to them. I want to concentrate on possible non-substantive objections to constitutionalisation. Given what one finds a persuasive *prima facie* moral and practical case for constitutionalisation,[7] are there still reasons for hesitation, rooted in conceptions of the proper workings of constitutional-democratic political and legal institutions?

Those who say yes almost always cite concerns about over-extension of the judiciary. Courts, they fear, will find themselves unable to make convincingly crisp assessments of the government's compliance or non-compliance with social rights guarantees, or to fashion apt and pointed remedial orders in case of non-compliance, without getting

---

[3] See R Dworkin, *Taking Rights Seriously* (Cambridge, Mass, Harvard University Press, 1978) 101–02 (distinguishing between 'institutional' rights and 'background' norms).

[4] See below, Part II.

[5] S 26, Constitution of the Republic of South Africa 1996.

[6] See *ibid*, ss 2, 8(1), 38 and 172(1).

[7] See below, Part IV.

themselves disastrously mixed up in matters beyond their province and their ken as judges of the law. It thus comes to seem a bad idea to invite the judiciary to tussle with the government over material resource allocations and distributions. Of course, there is another side to the debate. Judges who know their business, it is said (drawing lessons from administrative law), can find both properly adjudicative standards for testing claims of social-rights violations and worthwhile, properly judicial remedies for violations when found.[8] Whichever way one tilts, though, it is clear that the debate has been centred on a concern about the place and work of the judiciary in the democratic political order. We seem to think the problem with constitutionalizing social rights comes down mainly, if not solely, to a matter of the separation of powers.

These terms of debate are inadequate. With a view to their modification—not their total transformation—I shall suggest that there is more to the problem of constitutionalized social rights than questions of judicial role and competence, and also less.

There is less in two respects, both of which have received attention in the past. First, courts exercising constitutional review in entirely conventional, non-worrisome ways almost certainly can play a useful, if modest, role, in the promotion of the distributive aims of social rights guarantees.[9] Second, even were that not true and the choice therefore had to be made to bar courts entirely from review of government action for compliance with social rights guarantees, that would not be a good argument against constitutionalisation, in the sight of anyone who believes that a morally legitimate political regime must include a visible, effective commitment to certain forms of positive social support for individuals and families.[10]

Assuming both those points are accepted, the case for the constitutionalisation of social rights is not yet fully made. Two possible grounds for hesitation remain, even for those who are persuaded morally of reasons to go ahead and fear no resulting evil of judicial overreaching. These are, first, a *democratic objection* (as I shall call it) to the effect that adding social rights to the constitution constricts democracy unduly, regardless of whether courts stand ready to enforce such rights; and, second, a *contractarian objection* to the effect that adding social rights to the constitution defeats a crucial function of the constitution-as-law, that of providing legitimacy to coercive political and legal orders. Having put those two possible further objections on the table, I shall suggest that (1)

---

[8] See CR Sunstein, 'Social and Economic Rights: Lessons from South Africa' (2001) 11 *Constitutional Forum* 123. See also the exchange in South Africa between Etienne Mureinik and Dennis Davis: E Mureinik, 'Beyond a Charter of Luxuries: Economic Rights in the Constitution' (1992) 8 *South African Journal on Human Rights* 464; D Davis, 'The Case Against the Inclusion of Socio-economic Demands in a Bill of Rights Except as Directive Principles' (1992) 8 *South African Journal on Human Rights* 475.

[9] See below, Part II.

[10] See below, Parts III and IV.

their force may vary with how sweepingly—or, conversely, how specific-ally—the constitutional social rights guarantees are couched; (2) the contractarian objection is manageable even with a maximally sweeping constitutional guarantee or, at any rate, political liberals cannot deny that it is while upholding in general the practice of constitutionalism; and (3) the democratic objection is grave only if we choose a normative conception of democracy that is not the only one available to us, or the best one.

II SOCIAL RIGHTS AND CONVENTIONAL JUDICIAL REVIEW

As we have noticed, proposals to put positive social and economic guarantees into constitutional law typically are met by an objection linked to the expectation of judicial review. By constitutionalizing social rights, the argument often has run, you force the judiciary to a hapless choice between usurpation and abdication, from which there is no escape without embar-rassment or discredit. Down one path, it is said, lies the judicial choice to issue positive enforcement orders in a pretentious, inexpert, probably vain but nevertheless resented attempt to reshuffle the most basic resource-management priorities of the public household against prevailing political will. Down the other lies the judicial choice to debase dangerously the entire currency of rights and the rule of law by openly ceding to executive and parliamentary bodies an unreviewable privilege of indefinite postponement of a declared constitutional right.

The objection quite obviously is overstated. The constitutionalisation of social-rights guarantees can provide both a prod and a hook for ho-hum forms of judicial action in furtherance of the distributive aims these rights represent. The fact that social rights make budgetary demands, or call for government actions and not just forbearance, does not differentiate them radically from constitutionally protected rights to property, to equality before the law, or to so-called negative liberties.[11] At 'the very minimum', social rights sometimes can be 'negatively protected' by quite ordinary forms of judicial intervention.[12] For example, municipal zoning and land-use laws, insofar as they constrict the local housing supply or escalate

---

[11] See *Ex parte Chairperson of the Constitutional Assembly: In re Certification of the Republic of South Africa Constitution* 1996 (4) SA 744 (CC), 1996 (10) BCLR 1253 (CC) 78; Stephen Holmes and Cass R Sunstein, *The Costs of Rights: Why Liberty Depends on Taxes* (New York, WW Norton, 1999); FI Michelman, 'Welfare Rights in a Constitutional Democracy' (1979) *Washington University Law Quarterly* 659–694; FI Michelman, 'Foreword: On Protecting the Poor Through the Fourteenth Amendment' (1969) 83 *Harvard Law Review* 7, 17–18, 25–26.

[12] See *In re Certification of the Constitution* 1996 (4) SA at 801. See generally FI Michelman, 'Welfare Rights', *ibid*, at 660–664, 686–693.

[13] See above, n 5.

its cost, presumably lie open to challenge under the South African Constitution's guarantee of a right of access to adequate housing for everyone.[13] A court would be expected to test such a law under the standard laid down by section 36 of the Constitution, which permits legislative limitation of rights in the bill of rights, but only by lawmaking that is 'reasonable' as well as 'justifiable in an open and democratic society based on human dignity, equality and freedom'. 'Reasonableness' is not, in any legal discourse known to me, a non-justiciable standard (or are negligence law, general clauses, and proportionality review beyond the pale?), and the remedy for violation, if found, would be a simple prohibitory injunction.

Interestingly, as shown by a recent South African case, a court may act usefully in furtherance of a constitutional social rights guarantee by the most ordinary of all forms of judicial action, namely, dismissal of a case (where relief would have been forthcoming but for the guarantee). In *Minister of Public Works v Kyalami Ridge Association*[14] the government proposed to relocate homeless and destitute flood victims to housing it would cause to be built on state-owned land. Neighbouring homeowners sued for an interdict against this plan on the ground, among others, of *ultra vires*, pointing out that no Act of Parliament authorised the government to build housing for the specific purpose in question. The Constitutional Court allowed the neighbours standing to lodge the *ultra vires* claim. The Court agreed with them that the constitutional conception of the rule of law requires positive-legal authorisation for any government activity that disturbs the interests of others, and further agreed that no Act of Parliament answered the need in this instance. The Court, however, denied the plaintiffs the relief they sought. It found authorisation for the government's action in section 26 of the Constitution, as construed in *Government of the Republic of South Africa v Grootboom*,[15] to place the government under a duty to make provision within its housing plans for short-term aid to persons blamelessly in conditions of housing crisis.

'The government', wrote the Court in *Kyalami*, 'contends that these obligations require it to come to the assistance of the victims of the flooding throughout the country, ... and that in doing so it cannot be said to be acting contrary to the rule of law'.[16] The Court apparently agreed. Like other owners of land, the government has, in general, the right to build on land it owns. Standing by itself, that general property-owners' right cannot satisfy the rule-of-law demand for positive-legal authorisation for government action that trenches upon others' interests, but the Court found that it can do so in combination with section 26 of the Constitution

---

[14] *Minister of Public Works v Kyalami Ridge Association* (2001) (7) BCLR 652 (CC), SACLR LEXIS 36 (2001).
[15] *Government of the Republic of South Africa v Grootboom* (2001) (1) SA 46 (CC); 2000 (11) BCLR 1169 (CC).
[16] *Ibid*, para 40.

as construed in *Grootboom*. If the government asserts its property-owner's building right 'within the framework of the Constitution and the restrictions of any relevant legislation', the Court concluded, 'it acts lawfully'.[17]

III LAWS AND REMEDIES

Suppose we have a constitutional norm, N. Maybe, for some reason, we do not expect or wish our judiciary to get too much mixed up with enforcing compliance with N. But still we do want to say that N is meant to be fully binding, obligatory, on those state officials to whom it is addressed. Indeed, we want to say N is binding in just the ways—whatever they may be—that laws in general are understood to be binding even at moments when they are not being externally enforced.[18] We want to say not only that the addressees are not meant to have a free choice about heeding N, but further that an addressee who consciously disregards N, without special excuse or justification, is blamable for contempt of the rule *of law* in the same way that anyone who flouts the law is blamable. How can we say these things, if we cannot call N a law?

And yet we may not do so, if the judicial-involvement-based objection to the constitutionalisation of social rights is sound. The objection's unstated premise is that to classify an obligation as one of constitutional law is ipso facto to make the obligation one that the judiciary is responsible to enforce to the hilt against a recalcitrant government—that by naming something a constitutional right you also name it a legal right and so willy-nilly make the judiciary responsible for its effectuation. The objection thus conflates the question of a norm's status as constitutional law with the question of its availability for judicial enforcement.

But why must we take this view?

IV THE CONSTITUTIONAL-CONTRACTARIAN CASE FOR SOCIAL RIGHTS

For anyone who does not—for anyone who simply severs the conceptual bond tying the constitutionalisation of a social-rights guarantee to a demand for direct judicial enforcement[19]—judicial-role concerns no longer

---

[17] *Ibid*, para 41.

[18] Lawrence Sager, most prominently among American constitutional-legal scholars, has explained at length the reasons for taking this combination of positions. See: L Sager, 'The Domain of Constitutional Justice' in L Alexander (ed), *Constitutionalism: Philosophical Foundations* (New York, Cambridge University Press, 1998) 235–70; L Sager, 'Justice in Plain Clothes: Reflections on the Thinness of Constitutional Law' (1993) 88 *Northwestern University Law Review* 410.

[19] On the possibility of indirect modes of judicial vindication, see above, Part II.

can support opposition to constitutionalisation. We shall consider soon whether either the democratic or the contractarian objection still supports it. But in order to appraise objections to a practical proposal, you must first have in mind at least the broad outlines of some general case in its favour. Here the proposal is to confer the status of a constitutional-legal right on claims of individuals to certain forms of support and provisioning by the state. I shall now sketch out a general affirmative case for this proposal. This will be a Rawlsian sort of case, a political liberal's sort of case, indeed a contractarian liberal's sort of case—no doubt not the only sort that may be fashioned, but one that you won't find outlandish and one that sets up most clearly both the majoritarian and the contractarian objections to giving social rights a place in the constitution.

The general case I shall present for constitutional social rights is quite specifically limited to the question at hand. It is not a case for a general moral obligation on the part of every separate person having the means to do so to come to the aid of sundry others who find themselves in need. It is only and strictly a case for including social rights in a country's constitutional bill of rights. I suggest there exists at least one appealing argument to the conclusion that a *constitution* ought, as a moral matter, to affirm the claims of individuals to be assured of satisfaction of certain material needs, by the state if necessary, on reasonable conditions of effort and cooperation. I suggest the argument holds regardless of whether we believe there exists any other sort of moral right to succour from one's neighbour. I suggest, in other words, that there is something about the particular moral point or purpose of constitutions, from which it follows that a *constitution*, in particular, is morally defective—it fails of its moral purpose—by reason of its lack of social-rights guarantees; and that this is so regardless of what any of us individually, outside the context of politically governed society, may or may not owe morally to others in the way of aid or support.[20]

The argument I have in mind stands on a certain foundational commitment to positive legal ordering. It simply is a fact, I say—and I don't think you'll deny it—that the societies we're concerned with are committed, irrevocably and without significant dissent, to the practice of social ordering by positive legislation. In our societies, people wake up each day to find in place effectively compulsory regulations of social life—we call them 'laws'—with which the publicly supported authorities in the land predictably will demand everyone's compliance and, in doing so, predictably will have almost everyone's support. No-one who is thus subject to the laws of a country has chosen these laws for himself. In a democratic country, the laws normally will have been decided in voting

---

[20] Compare with C Fried, *Right and Wrong* (Cambridge, Mass, Harvard University Press, 1978) ch 5.

procedures by which majorities rule over dissenters. Whatever may be the precise history of how a democratically governed country's laws came to be what they are, it will not be that any law effectively was chosen by the actions of any single one of the individuals who are called upon to abide by it.[21]

Thus arises the question of political justification or legitimacy. The challenge is to supply a moral warrant for the application of collective force in support of laws produced by non-consensual means, against individual members of a population of presumptively free and equal persons. For countries under democratic rule, this means, as John Rawls has expressed it, to explain how 'citizens [may] by their vote properly exercise their coercive political power over one another'—to explain how your or my exercise of our share of political power may be rendered 'justifiable to others as free and equal'.[22]

Rawls has offered in response what he calls the 'liberal principle of legitimacy':

> Our... political power is... justifiable [to others as free and equal]... when it is exercised in accordance with a constitution the essentials of which all citizens may be expected to endorse in the light of principles and ideals acceptable to them as reasonable and rational.[23]

That exemplifies perfectly what we may call a constitutional-contractarian approach to the question of political justification. At its core stands an uncompromising moral concern with the freedom and equality of each and every individual. From that concern flows the demand that potentially coercive political acts be acceptable from the standpoints of *each* (not 'all', in some collectivised sense of 'all') of countless persons among whom rational conflicts of interest and vision abound. Acceptable, that is, in principle. Acceptable in all reason; acceptable in the sight of whoever applies the test of acceptability.

In Rawls's formulation, political coercion is justified when it is exercised in support of laws issuing from a constitutional regime, on condition that the regime is one that all may be expected to endorse, assuming everyone to be not only rationally self-interested but also 'reasonable'. 'Reasonable' here means three things. First, a reasonable person accepts the inevitability of positive legal ordering. He or she doesn't pretend we are somehow going to get along without lawmakers making laws that have to bind everyone regardless of who in particular likes each law and who does not. Second, a reasonable person accepts the fact of deep and enduring conflicts of interests and ethical visions within his or her society—what Rawls calls

---

21 See FI Michelman, *Brennan and Democracy* (Princeton, Princeton University Press, 1999) 14–16, 31–33.
22 J Rawls, *Political Liberalism* (New York, Columbia University Press, 1993) 217.
23 *Ibid.*

the fact of reasonable pluralism.[24] Third, he or she is imbued with the liberal spirit of reciprocal recognition by persons of each other as free and equal individuals. It results that a reasonable person stands ready to accept the laws as long as (a) he or she sees everyone else generally supporting and complying with these laws, and (b) he or she sees how these laws are ones that merit mutual acceptance by a competently reasoning group of persons, all of whom desire, and suppose each other all to desire, to devise and abide by laws reflecting fair terms of social cooperation in conditions of deep and enduring but reasonable disagreement over questions of the good.[25]

But wait a minute. No matter how reasonable we ask each other to be, surely none of us really expects that every discrete act of lawmaking could pass a test of rational acceptability to every supposedly reasonable inhabitant of a modern, plural society. Realistically, our hope is more modest, and more procedural. It is that an aptly designed *general system or regime* for lawmaking—or call it a constitution—might be able to pass such a test. Maybe we can imagine some such regime, about which we'd be prepared to say that *it* ought to be found acceptable, as a regime, by every rational person who also is reasonable. If so, then we might further maintain that the rational acceptability to you, as reasonable, of the constitutional regime commits you to acceptance of whatever specific laws may issue from the regime.[26] That, after all, is exactly the point of Rawls's claim, in his 'liberal principle of legitimacy', that exercises of political coercion are justifiable insofar as they issue from '*a constitution*, the essentials of which all citizens may be expected to endorse'.

In effect, we have arrived at the idea of a *sufficient, legitimating constitutional agreement*.[27] Four terms compose this idea, as follows:

First, what is supposed to be 'legitimated' (in the sense of justified morally) by this agreement is some specific practice of *positive legal ordering*—of the coercive exercise of collective power, through lawmaking, by and among citizens considered as individually free and equal.

---

[24] See Rawls, above, n 22, 36–37.

[25] See Rawls, *ibid*, 226–27; J Rawls, 'The Idea of Public Reason Revisited' in Samuel Freedman (ed), *Collected Papers* (Cambridge, Mass, Harvard University Press, 1999) 573, 576–79, 581, 605–06.

[26] See S Freeman, 'Original Meaning, Democratic Interpretation, and the Constitution' (1992) 21 *Philosophy and Public Affairs* 26 f, 36 f, cited approvingly in Rawls, above n 22, 234. Cf J Rawls, *A Theory of Justice* (Cambridge, Mass, Harvard University Press, 1993) 195–201 (on 'the four-stage sequence'). This means that your finding particular ordinary laws unjust gives you no ground for resort to unlawful force, not that it gives you no ground for denunciation, civil disobedience or conscientious refusal.

[27] I develop and examine this idea at greater length in FI Michelman, '*The Problem of Constitutional Interpretive Disagreement: Can 'Discourses of Application' Help?*' in M Aboulafia, M Bookman and C Kemp (eds), *Habermas and Pragmatism* (London, Routledge, 2002) 113–38.

Second, what is supposed to have the desired legitimating effect is *agreement* by each person affected. Not, however, actual agreement but hypothetical (what some would call 'counterfactual') agreement—the 'acceptability' of the political practice among persons affected by it, envisioning those persons not only as rational but also as reasonable.

Third, the legitimating hypothetical agreement is a *constitutional* agreement. We don't apply the universal-reasonable acceptability test to each and every specific law that crops up in a country's politics. Rather, we apply it to the country's system for lawmaking.

Lastly, then, 'sufficiency'. In order to meet the test of rational acceptability to every reasonable person, a lawmaking system has to include a principle or guarantee affecting every topic for which a rational person, responding reasonably, would demand a guarantee as a condition of willing support for the system as a whole. (For present purposes—and here I depart a little from Rawls's usage of the term—we may say that the set of 'constitutional essentials' is equivalent to the set of minimally required principles and guarantees.[28]) The set must be extensive enough to comprise a system for political decision-making about which every affected, supposedly reasonable person rationally can say:

> A system measuring up to these principles and terms—all of them—is suffi- ciently regardful of my and everyone's interests and status as free and equal persons that I ought in all reason to support it and its legislative products, pro- vided everyone else does.

Can we not easily now see taking shape the general contractarian case for inclusion in the constitution of some social-rights guarantees? It may well seem that we cannot reasonably call on everyone, as reasonable but also as rational, to submit their fates to the tender mercies of a democratic-majoritarian lawmaking system without also committing our society, from the start, to run itself in ways designed to constitute and sustain every person as a competent and respected contributor to political exchange and contestation and furthermore to social and economic life at large.[29] If so, it seems that social rights guarantees of some kind must compose an essential part of the liberal-democratic constitutional contract.

V THE DEMOCRATIC OBJECTION

We may leave the affirmative case for the constitutionalisation of social rights resting just there for the time being, while we now take up for

---

[28] For Rawls's discussion of 'constitutional essentials,' see Rawls above, n 22, 227–30.

[29] The argument can be cast as well in parallel terms of membership, commitment and identity. See WE Forbath, 'Constitutional Welfare Rights: A History, Critique and Reconstruction' (2001) 69 *Fordham Law Review* 1821, 1875–1876.

consideration the democratic objection. It is raised in dramatic form by a proposal from William Forbath.[30] Forbath asks us to conceive of constitutionalized social rights not as what he calls 'welfare rights' but as what he calls 'social citizenship' rights. Roughly, his idea is this: we assume the general affirmative case for constitutionalized social rights to be something like the one I have suggested, in which the motivating moral ideal is that of a society committed to run itself in ways designed to constitute and sustain every person (at least every person who so chooses on fair terms) as a competent and respected contributor to political, social and economic life. Accordingly, argues Forbath, the key universal right of persons—at any rate the key universal *interest* of persons—would be assurance that one can make a respectable living through forms of social participation that are themselves a source and support of satisfaction, energy, pride and social respect.[31]

This would be, then, a conception in which a central concern would be interests related to *work*: the availability and terms of work, the character of work and the organisation and governance of work.[32] Corresponding to such a conception of a universal interest would be what Forbath calls a 'social citizenship' conception of constitutionally guaranteed social rights,[33] to be contrasted with a 'welfare right' conception focusing on guarantees of money income or of access to specifically listed, basic material necessities regardless of work.[34] Section 26 of the South African Constitution exemplifies a somewhat amphibian constitutional social right that Forbath probably would classify as predominantly a welfare right, not a social-citizenship right.[35]

The two forms of imaginable constitutional guarantees differ drastically in the apparent breadths of their respective, potential applications to the policy choices of legislatures. Consider again the South African Constitution's mandate to the government (laid down by section 26(2)) to take reasonable measures, within available resources, to achieve progressive realisation of the right of every South African (declared by section 26(1)) to have access to adequate housing. In *Government of Republic of South Africa v Grootboom*,[36] the Constitutional Court found that the state's

---

[30] Forbath, *ibid*; WE Forbath, 'Caste, Class, and Equal Citizenship' (1999) 98 *Michigan Law Review* 1. See also Forbath's later response to this essay in WE Forbath, 'Not so Simple Justice: Frank Michelman on Social Rights, 1969-Present' (2004) 39 *Tulsa Law Review* 597.

[31] See, for example, Forbath, above n 29, 1875–76.

[32] See, for example, *ibid* 1824, 1833.

[33] See, for example, *ibid* 1826, 1876.

[34] See, for example, *ibid* 1854, 1871–72.

[35] Following my cue, Forbath has called it a welfare right pure and simple. See *ibid* 1880, but we both may have spoken too soon. A right 'to have access to adequate housing' seemingly is honoured as long as work is available on fair terms, including pay sufficient for procurement of adequate housing that is reasonably available and suitable. See *Government of the Republic of South Africa v Grootboom*, above n 15, 36–37.

[36] See above, n 15.

housing measures failed to be 'reasonable', as required by section 26(2), specifically because of their virtually total inattention to the matter of emergency relief of persons blamelessly placed in conditions of housing crisis. The Court demanded submission of revised plans to judicial scrutiny for their reasonableness, while making clear that no court would try to dictate solutions. This outcome may pose stern tests to judicial skill and wisdom in future cases, but it does not, as it stands, seem shockingly pre-emptive of legislative and executive policy choice.[37] Certainly it does not when compared, say, with the American Constitution's guarantee of freedom of expression, which has been construed to restrict quite sharply a remarkable—in a world-wide view an amazing—range of legislative policy choices respecting such varied and weighty matters as fomentation of group hatred,[38] civil rights legislation aimed at public civic equality,[39] the flow of money in politics[40] and the legal protection of reputation and persona.[41]

Matters seemingly would be different under a Forbath-style constitutional guarantee of social citizenship. To see why, one need only take in Professor Forbath's approving summary of the lawmaking topics that a social-citizenship right was thought to cover by its late nineteenth-century proponents in the United States:

> freeing [labour] from 'the iron rule of the Money power' through public credit and support for cooperative enterprise;… nationalizing the railways;… ensuring for industrial workers the 'right to a remunerative job' through public works and countercyclical spending and, through an end to the repressive common law constraints on workers' collective action…, encouraging robust unions and industrial cooperation; and through these agencies… enabling workers to exercise the rights and responsibilities of control over collective property.[42]

To which we in our own times may add: tax laws and policies; publicly guaranteed education and training for all, of adequate quality; infant, child and elderly care; workplace health and safety, fair employment, wage and hour laws; global trade issues, the WTO and so forth; immigration laws; macroeconomic policy and controls; public oversight of industrial organisation, including antitrust and other legal counters to restraints of trade;

---

[37] See Sunstein, above, n 8. The Court's focus on 'reason' as a justiciable standard of review was prefigured by Mureinik, above, n 8. See F Michelman, 'The Constitution, Social Rights, and Reason' (1998) 14 *South African Journal on Human Rights* 499 at 500–501.

[38] See: *RAV v City of St Paul* [1992] 505 US 377; *American Booksellers v Hudnut* 475 US 1001 (1986).

[39] See *Boy Scouts of America v Dale* 530 US 640 (2000).

[40] See, for example, *Buckley v Valeo* 424 US 1 (1976).

[41] See, for example, *Hustler Magazine v Falwell* 485 US 46 (1988). See generally PD Carrington, 'Our Imperial First Amendment' (2001) 34 *University of Richmond Law Review* 1167.

[42] Forbath, above, n 30, 49.

anti-plutocratic political institutions and practices including campaign finance regulation; and I'm sure I've left a lot out.

In sum, it looks as though a constitutional social-citizenship right has tentacles reaching in a hundred directions, into the deepest redoubts of the common law and the most basic choices of political economy a modern society can make. Abortion aside—if it *is* aside, which it very arguably is not[43]—I can think of no leading issue on the current American political calendar that a constitutional right of social citizenship would leave untouched.

Now suppose you think that a constitution's list of guaranteed rights is also its demarcation of the respective zones of supremacy of the judicial and other branches of government. In other words, you think that constitutional rights are for courts and always for courts to apply or put into action. Legislatures, you think, are supposed to make their policy choices more or less oblivious of constitutional law, then courts come along and police their actions for constitutional compliance. Every proclamation of a constitutional right thus invites the judiciary to add some further sphere or spheres of public decision-making to the ones in which it already feels licensed to take a sometimes heavy hand. If that is how you see matters, you very well may think that constitutionalizing a right of social citizenship, as Forbath conceives it, is a way of turning over to an unelected judiciary a share of control over policymaking that is far too extensive to be tolerable in a democracy.

We do not have to accept the view that a norm can't be constitutional law, can't count as constitutional law, without its being turned over to judges for enforcement. Many of us indeed will be primed to deny that constitutional law enforced by judges has to be all the constitutional law there is or that matters.[44] We maintain that constitutional law outside the courts can figure importantly in the conduct of public affairs. We insist that contention outside the courts over constitutional-legal meanings and obligations very possibly can be a politically cogent activity, a site for democracy in action.[45] Is there any reason why we, taking this view, should hesitate to embrace a social-citizenship conception of constitutional social rights in preference to a welfare-right conception, assuming we find

---

[43] See, for example, *Planned Parenthood v Casey* 505 US 833 (1992), 927–28 (Blackmun J, concurring in the judgment in part and dissenting in part: 'The decision to terminate or continue a pregnancy has no less an impact on a woman's life than decisions about contraception or marriage... Because motherhood has a dramatic impact on a woman's educational prospects, employment opportunities, and self-determination, restrictive abortion laws deprive her of basic control over her life. For these reasons, "the decision whether or not to beget or bear a child" lies at "the very heart of this cluster of constitutionally protected choices".')

[44] See above, Part III.

[45] See generally MV Tushnet *Taking the Constitution Away From the Courts* (Princeton, Princeton University Press, 1999).

[46] Forbath, above, n 29. Forbath makes a stirring and persuasive case for the moral superiority of the social-citizenship conception.

the former to be morally the more appealing conception?[46] If we don't think constitutional law enforced by judges is or need be all the constitutional law that there is or that matters, then why should fears for democracy dictate acceptance of what we deem a morally inferior, constitutional formulation of social rights? We can both constitutionalise a social-citizenship right and tell courts to take no part in enforcing it. We can follow that course at no cost in suppression of democracy. Is all that not so?

My answer for the moment is: not obviously. Such a copiously expansive constitutional right as a right of social citizenship conceivably could call forth a democracy-protective objection even if we assume that courts will abstain totally from trying to enforce it.

Because suppose they do abstain. Then there are two possibilities. Either the legislature will, or it will not, be conscientious about compliance with constitutional law—either it will or it will not feel constrained to comply—even in the absence of judicial enforcement. If it will not, then what would be the point of writing the social citizenship right into the constitution? What would be the point of naming something a constitutional right that we don't mean and expect to be seriously taken, by public officials presumed conscientious? But if we do suppose that a law-abiding legislature really would feel itself constrained to heed a constitutional conferral of social citizenship rights on everyone, would that not subject the legislature to serious curbs on its policymaking discretion? How can we honestly name social citizenship a constitutional right without intending a far-flung constraint on policy choice by majority rule, *even if we assume the courts will make no attempt to enforce the right thus named*?

A different example may help make the point clear. Imagine that some country adds to its constitution what we may call the Libertarian Amendment. It reads:

> The regulatory state is hereby abolished. Parliament shall make no law attaching liabilities, penalties or burdens of any kind to conduct that would not be actionable at common law.[47]

Imagine also that in this country there is no practice of judicial constitutional review. Constitutional law is left to be made effective on its direct, official addressees through self-discipline aided by constituency pressures. The Libertarian Amendment would nevertheless be seen by everyone, supporters as well as detractors, as profoundly counter-democratic. Putting

---

47 See R Epstein, 'Takings, Exclusivity and Speech: The Legacy of *PruneYard v Robins*' (1997) 64 *University of Chicago Law Review* 21, 22–28; cf *Lucas v South Carolina Coastal Comm'n* 505 US 1003 (1992), 1029–30 (Scalia J) (making actionability under prior 'background law', of the uses of property prohibited by a new regulatory enactment, the test of the state's duty to pay compensation as if for a 'taking' of property).

shackles on democracy would be exactly the point and aim of the amendment.

Viewed in such a light, the majoritarian objection to constitutionalisation of a social citizenship right may look formidable, even assuming 'enforcement' of such a right would occur wholly outside the courts, through political and moral pressure. Is the objection as formidable as it may look? I wish to leave that question hanging for a bit, while I now take us through what I've called the contractarian objection to constitutionalised social rights.

VI THE CONTRACTARIAN OBJECTION

Constitutional contractarians, concerned about political legitimacy within a given country, will ask whether the country's basic or constitutional laws—the ones that shape, organise, direct and limit the country's political and legal practice—compose in toto a sufficient, legitimating constitutional agreement. In order to do so, those laws must include a guarantee affecting every topic for which a rational person, responding reasonably, would demand a guarantee as a condition of willing support for the lawmaking system as a whole.[48]

Suppose this constitutional set right now consists of twenty-five clauses, *A* to *Y*, the wording of which is canonical and undisputed. The bill of rights comprises clauses *P* to *Y*. *P* to *Y* say things like 'no search or seizure shall be conducted without a warrant, and warrants shall not issue without probable cause', 'death is hereby prohibited as a punishment for crime' and 'freedom of the press is hereby guaranteed'. There is currently no guarantee of social rights. Prompted by the constitutional-contractarian aim of filling out a complete, legitimating constitutional agreement, the country just now is debating the addition of a twenty-sixth clause, *Z*. *Z* would provide, and I quote,

> Everyone has the right of social citizenship as described in the collected works of William Forbath. Within available resources, the state must direct and conform its legislative and other measures to the progressive realisation of this right.

Suppose it is widely agreed that the *goal* of *Z*—effective social citizenship on fair terms for all who seek it—indeed is one to which the country's governmental operations must visibly be committed in practice, in order that the total governance system may be one that meets the constitutional-contractarian standard of universal reasonable acceptability. Such a moral fact—so to call it—might seem to pose a fatal difficulty for constitu-

---

[48] See above, Part IV.

tional-contractarian political legitimacy. The apparent difficulty lies in the further fact that almost always it will be impossible for anyone to say decisively whether Z is or is not being pursued in earnest. Let's say Parliament this year has done all of the following: replaced welfare with workfare, increased by one half the budget allocation for job training, reduced the minimum wage by one third, extended the collective bargaining laws to cover employers of as few as ten workers, abolished rent control, budgeted an annual sum of 30 billion crowns for housing allowances and job training, increased income tax rates by five per cent, reduced the prime lending rate by two percentage points, doubled the size of the employment discrimination mediation corps and approved a new tariff schedule, somewhat less protective than its predecessor, in exchange for reciprocal concessions from abroad. Are they complying with clause Z? Who decisively can say yes? Who decisively can say no?

Raging indeterminacy of this sort seems to disqualify a clause like Z from figuring as a required component in a complete and legitimating constitutional agreement. Remember how the constitutional-contractarian argument goes. I freely can accept the daily run of coercive acts from a constituted political regime, including acts I judge to be pernicious or unjust, because and only because (i) I regard this regime *qua* regime as rationally acceptable by everyone who is being reasonable, and (ii) *I see my fellow citizens and their government abiding by this regime*. In order for the regime to merit my willing compliance, one of the conditions is that I can know at all times that the commitments that make it universally reasonably and rationally acceptable are actual, not fake. I have to be able to observe my fellow citizens and their government really complying with the principles. And how can I, if Z is one of the principles? Just because I can't, it seems that Z cannot be deemed an indispensable part of any constitution meant to do the political-justificatory work that constitutions morally have to do, in a constitutional-contractarian view.

So there you have the contractarian objection to the idea that social rights belong in a constitutional bill of rights. Because social rights lack the trait of transparency, as we may call it—the trait of more-or-less detectably being realised (or not) at any given moment—we seem barred from regarding them as required parts of the essential constitution, lacking which the constitution would fail to meet the Rawlsian, liberal standard for political legitimacy; lacking which, in other words, the constitution would fail to provide an acceptable basis for political rule, in the sight of every rational person responding reasonably.[49] (And then what *would* be

---

[49] A consideration of this kind may have entered into John Rawls' own conclusion that social-rights guarantees are not among the 'constitutional essentials'. See Rawls, above, n 22, 224–28; FI Michelman, 'Justice as Fairness, Legitimacy, and the Question of Judicial Review: A Comment' (2004) 72 *Fordham Law Review* 1407.

the affirmative case for the constitutionalisation of social rights guarantees?)

VII CONSTITUTIONAL CONTRACTARIANISM IN A BIND: THE MOVE TO PUBLIC REASON

At this point, we must question seriously the cogency and coherence of the constitutional contractarian's answer—his deeply, normatively individualist answer—to the question of political legitimacy. It may, after all, *be true* that a constitutional system without a social-citizenship guarantee—by which I mean a credible guarantee of constant, good faith pursuit by the powers that be of assurance of social citizenship to all who seek it on fair terms—fails to provide every rational and reasonable person with sufficient reason to accept whatever specific laws may issue out of the system from time to time. Believing exactly that, Rawlsians are not free just to shuck the belief if it happens to become theoretically inconvenient.[50] How, then, can a political regime possibly, in their sight, be legitimate?

A regime, they believe, is not legitimate if its basic law does not include a social rights guarantee, but it also is not legitimate if any of its basic-law guarantees, required for legitimacy, are such that citizens cannot judge whether those guarantees are in fact being kept, or at least at all times being pursued in good faith. If a social-citizenship guarantee fails the latter test, then, by constitutional contractarian lights, it cannot form an indispensable part of a sufficient, legitimating constitutional agreement—and yet it does. That looks like a contradiction. If so, the constitutional contractarian theory of political justification through a complete, legitimating constitutional agreement must be a mistaken theory of political justification. If it is mistaken, and if there is in sight no other liberally acceptable theory of political justification for modern, plural, law-governed societies, then, for liberals concerned with such societies, political justice apparently lies beyond the possibility of coherent definition, let alone achievement.[51]

Rawlsian thought offers a way out of this bind. We see it in proposals to give social rights a constitutional status of 'directive principles' rather than 'rights', as well as in John Rawls's ideas about what he calls public

---

[50] To be exact, Rawlsians believe that such a guarantee is a 'matter of basic justice' covered by a 'constraint of public reason'. See Rawls, *ibid*, 224–28.

[51] The problem is graver than my text discloses. The bind I have described is not, in fact, restricted to social-rights guarantees. It extends to all the 'basic liberties', all the members of the standard list of constitutional negative liberties. See FI Michelman, 'Postmodernism, Proceduralism, and Constitutional Justice: a Comment on van der Walt and Botha' (2002) 9 *Constellations* 246; FI Michelman, 'Relative Constraint and Public Reason: What Is "The Work We Expect of Law"?' (2002) 67 *Brooklyn Law Review* 963.

reason and 'matters of basic justice'. The point for Rawls is this: a sufficient, legitimating constitutional agreement has to provide fully firm, strict and reliable substantive guarantees of compliance with what he calls the central ranges of the basic negative liberties—freedoms of conscience and expression, for example. Regarding the rest of social citizenship, the requirement is a looser one. What we need, and all we need, is assurance that, whenever political and legislative choices bear upon the basic structural conditions of social citizenship, those choices will be approached by all who take part in them under what Rawls calls a constraint of public reason. Participants in such decisions must stand ready to explain the consonance of their positions with *some* conception of a complete, legitimate constitutional agreement that—they sincerely maintain—deserves acceptance by every affected person who is rational and reasonable.[52]

The move to public reason eases the strain on constitutional contractarians who honestly believe that a political commitment to the state's constant, good faith pursuit of social citizenship for all must be a term of any universally-reasonably acceptable constitution. The case in which every parliamentarian and, indeed, every voter stands ready, in all sincerity, to explain and defend all their votes, on matters affecting the structural conditions of social citizenship, as expressions of their honest best judgments about which choice is most conducive to assurance of social citizenship for all, is exactly the case of what Rawls would call full compliance with the constraint of public reason. If citizens could have sufficient confidence that public reason in that sense prevails in public decision-making over matters affecting the structural conditions of social citizenship, then that confidence (combined with strict guarantees of everyone's enjoyment at all times of the core, basic negative liberties) would give every reasonable person a sufficient basis for accepting the legislative outcomes, whatever they turn out to be, of a democratic constitutional regime. So Rawls maintains. And notice, then, the converse of his proposition: if the facts on the ground are such that citizens *cannot* reasonably maintain confidence in the effective constraint of public reason on political choices affecting the structural conditions of social citizenship, then the extant system of positive legal ordering is unjust. It fails to measure up to the moral demand for justice in politics, as political-liberal, constitutional-contractarian thought conceives of that demand.

---

[52] Rawls, 'The Idea of Public Reason Revisited' above n 25.

VIII PUBLIC REASON AND DEMOCRACY

Let us now return to the democratic objection to a constitutionalised right of social citizenship. As we left it, the objection was this: to name social citizenship a constitutional right is to impose a far-flung drag on democracy, even assuming that courts are kept out of the picture. We are in a position now to see how this objection trades on a particular, contestable, and indeed poor, conception of democracy.

If a so-called right of social citizenship would be as loose—as indeter-minate—as we have said, if it would lack mechanical applicability to any hard or contested question of public policy, then exactly how does anyone think it will hamper democracy? The case, as we now can see, is very different from that of the Libertarian Amendment. To remind you: the Libertarian Amendment provides that

> Parliament shall make no law attaching liabilities, penalties or burdens of any kind to conduct that would not be actionable at common law.

This provision, while it may leave some room around the edges for good-faith dispute over exactly what conduct is and is not 'actionable at common law', really leaves—surely it is intended to leave—an honest parliamentarian with very little to decide in the way of regulatory law. By contrast, a constitutionally declared right of everyone to the enjoyment of social citizenship would leave just about every major issue of public policy still to be decided. Its maximum (but maybe not trivial) effect on democratic decision-making (the courts being kept away) would be a certain pressure on the frame of mind in which citizens and their elected representatives would approach the sundry questions of public policy always waiting to be decided. In Rawlsian language, the point of naming social citizenship a constitutional right would be to give a certain inflection to political public reason. Across a very broad swathe of public issues, such a naming would amount to a demand that those issues be approached as occasions for exercises of *judgment*—which choice will be conducive to the social citizenship of everyone, on fair terms?—rather than as invitations to press and to vote for one's own naked interests and preferences.

Of course, to call these matters of judgment is to see that they are matters on which opinions can and will differ markedly, reasonably and sincerely, and very probably not independently of people's particular social situations and related interests. (In today's United States, factory workers doubtless will tend on average to see some of them differently from how bond traders will, young mothers differently from senior corporate personnel managers, blacks from whites, etc.) But surely no harm to democracy lies there. Why should not disagreements over constitutional-interpretive judgment make as good a seedbed for democracy, or better, than do raw conflicts of interest and preference? 'Democracy', then, would name the practice by which citizens communicatively form, test, exchange, revise and pool their constitutional-interpretive judgments, only *counting* them as required to obtain, from time to time, the institutional settlements a country needs in order to get on with the tolerably orderly conduct of life.[53]

Granted, that is a pretty idealistic view of what democracy is and how it works. I'm sure it is a minority view, too, by comparison with the view that democracy means, quite strictly, that a country's people are free to treat their political agenda as a series of free-for-all contests of normatively unregulated preferences. On it, however, seems to depend the idea of liberal justice or liberal legitimacy within any possible system of positive legal ordering.

---

[53] See FI Michelman, 'Why Voting?' (2001) 34 *Loyola of Los Angeles Law Review* 985, 1001–1004. On 'the principle of institutional settlement' see HM Hart, Jr and AM Sacks 'The Legal Process: Basic Problems in the Making and Application of Law' in WN Eskridge, Jr and PP Frickey (eds), *The Legal Process* (Westbury NY, Foundation Press, 1994) 1–9.

3

Failed Decolonisation and the Future of Social Rights: Some Preliminary Reflections

UPENDRA BAXI

I PREFATORY

'Philosophers', wrote Emmanuel Levinas, 'have ended up worrying about the meaning of history in a way a shipping company worries about the weather forecasts. Thought no longer dares take flight unless it can fly straight to the heaven of victory.'[1]

I come to reflect on social rights, which may by definition go beyond commercial weather forecasts, in reading some future histories of contemporary human rights norms, standards and values, although it takes considerable courage to foster dialogue concerning social rights in these halcyon days of headlong and heedless globalisation of the world.

In some contexts, the discussion of social rights and justice calls into mind the contrast 'between those who seek to have a State in order to have justice and those who seek justice in order to seek the survival of the State'.[2] But even without this recourse to the audacious Levinasian contrast, it seems to remain possible to talk about social rights only in a most impoverished sense of human rights as grammars and languages of governance.[3]

Levinas, through his notion of 'difficult freedom', implicitly summons us to relate the discourse of *rights* to that of *justice* conceived as a solicitous ethical regard for the other. This task in turn invites further meditation concerning different notions of justice. Conceptions of justice as order collide with those that insist on justice as good order. The

---

[1] E Levinas, *Difficult Freedom: Essays on Judaism* (Baltimore, Johns Hopkins University Press, 1997; Sean Head trs) 226.

[2] *Ibid* 218.

[3] See, generally, U Baxi, *The Future of Human Rights*, 2nd edn (Delhi, Oxford University Press, 2006), hereafter cited as Baxi (2006).

question never was, since Aristotle, how to achieve the 'compossible' (here to evoke Leibniz) ordering of the tasks of 'justice' with the pursuit of order—that is, some regard for basic collective human security, and peaceful conditions of human and social development, both within and across nations. However, the question has always concerned the establishment of 'good' or 'just' national and world orderings. That 'good' or 'just' remains always a contested terrain. The colonised peoples did not regard the Euro-American visions of global orderings as 'good' or 'just'. Nor did the victims of slavery or women yoked to regimes of universalising capitalist forms of patriarchy (still a contemporary reality, despite the motto: 'Women's Rights are Human Rights'). It remains unnecessary to add further examples to demonstrate the truth that conceptions of 'good' order, or of social peace, emerge differently in the lived experience of domination, and stubborn resistance to it.

Increasingly, the languages, logics and paralogics of contemporary human rights and fundamental human freedoms remain poignant sites for the various hegemonic as well as counter-hegemonic conceptions of 'good' and 'just' social orderings. These authorise us all to name the production of unnameable human/social suffering and the constant reproduction of human rightlessness for the despised 'other' as orders of radical evil.

II THE 'SOCIAL'

Even before one addresses the relationship of the dominant discourse to conceptions about the future of social rights, we need to ponder the tautologous nature of the expression 'social rights'. By definition, it would seem obvious that all human rights are social in the minimal sense that recognition, enunciation, enforcement, enjoyment and realisation of rights define and describe social/societal processes; human rights make little sense outside human societal frameworks or networks of meaning and interaction. Rights are thus *social* or not *at all*.

Further, human rights provide salient languages through which individuals and groups increasingly construct and negotiate their conceptions, conditions and relations of social existence, identity, cultural belongings, authority, solidarity, struggle and resistance. In a sense, then, human rights norms and standards impact upon notions of self, society, state and the world at large. It is in this sense that one grasps the gestalt of contemporary human rights as constitutive of an *astonishing* fact of human social life, one that marks a revolution in human sensibility to, and imagination of, freedom.

Despite this, the conventional terminologies continue to contrast individual human rights and freedoms from those compendiously named as 'social, economic and cultural rights'. As is rather well-known, this *depecage* arises from the Realpolitik of the Cold War in which the values and visions underscored by the Universal Declaration of Human Rights underwent distinctive appropriations. What initially marks this division is, of course, the equally well-known difficult passage of the 'classical' liberal human rights notions in which the corpus of constraints on the powers of the Leviathan state constituted the 'essence' of human rights. Social human rights (here used as an abbreviation for social, economic and cultural rights) in contrast signify patterns of re-empowerment of the state, howsoever conceived as a counter-factual moral community which recognises and affirms the respect for equal dignity and concern for all its citizens, and somehow even the stateless persons, under its sovereign jurisdiction.

However, many recent forms of neoliberal/neocon incarnations seem to reinforce the classical liberal human rights message, one in which state respect for the sacrosanctity of the right to property and contract begins to redefine, all over again, the logics and paralogics of human rights.[4] If social human rights ever constituted a promise, it now remains again celebrated by further logics of betrayal.[5]

The tensions, even contradictions, latent in this liberal (and libertarian) dichotomous logic of rights have spawned an enormous amount of extraordinary philosophical labour. Alan Gewirth,[6] for example, in a remarkable endeavour to 'bridge' the antithesis between 'community' and 'rights', has demonstrated the conditions under which rights may be said to be related to community or society: instrumentally, 'being a member of a supportive community helps one to be more effective in achieving one's purposes'. But rights are constitutive of community in the sense that 'one can develop one's full humanity only by and in association with other humans in a stably regulated order'. In making the 'basic structure of society' a discursive object of moral reflection, the celebrated corpus of John Rawls also directs attention to the inescapably 'social' nature or roots of all human rights.[7]

Why are such ethical labours necessary? And what do they achieve, at the end of the day or of a very long deliberative night? What they achieve, or seek to achieve, is a non-reductionist construction of the 'social'. Rights discourse is thought to be meaningful only when the notion of being human, even when embedded within the 'social,' draws bright lines between individual autonomy and social control. A 'stably regulated order'

---

[4] See Baxi (2006) chapters 7–9.

[5] See U Baxi, 'What May the Third World Expect from International Law?' (2006) 27 *Third World Quarterly* 713–25; U Baxi, 'A Report for All Seasons? Small Notes towards Reading *In Larger Freedom*' in CR Kumar and D K Srivastava (eds), *Human Rights and Development: Law, Policy and Governance* (Hong Kong , Lexis-Nexis, 2006) 495–514.

[6] A Gewirth, *The Community of Rights* (Chicago, University of Chicago Press, 1996) 15–16.

[7] See, generally, J Rawls, *A Theory of Justice* (Cambridge, Mass, Harvard University Press, 1971).

is just if and only if it sets limits to the power of the collectivity over the individual human being. Forms of social regulation that set limits to the development of 'one's full humanity' ought to be probelmatised at the bar of human rights and justice. Taken out of context, Rousseau's observation concerning the primacy of 'social order as a sacred right which serves as a foundation of all other rights'[8] makes ethical thought concerning human rights almost impossible.

At least in the juridical discourse the problem of limits stands presented in terms of 'rights' and 'duties'. On this register, human rights enunciations emerge as non-absolute, that is, each human rights enunciation itself carries regimes of exception; the declaration of freedoms guaranteed by civil and political rights also authorise political conduct that may regulate these freedoms. Further, the recognition of 'group' or 'collective' rights remains complicated by a co-equal regard of individuals comprising the collectivity. As concerns duties corresponding to rights, duties stand conceptualised as 'perfect' or 'imperfect'. All this raises further questions concerning the legibility of the rights and duties, and their content and scope. Thus arise some marked interpretive communities possessed of two kinds of power which may determine approaches to meaning and implementation: the *biophilic* power (giving the kiss of life to human rights norms, standards and values) and the *necrophilic* power (of putting these to sleep.)

One principal way in which the problem of limits has been tackled focuses on the 'social' as the political organisation of society.[9] The classical liberal conception of rights celebrates human rights as a just, even when voluminous, corpus of constraints on the Old or the New Leviathan. Powers of the state end, so the storyline runs, when my rights begin. This is the sense of 'negative rights', in Professor Sir Isaiah Berlin's famous enunciation, as *freedom from* the power of the state, which at the same time speaks to a normative conception of governance. The state itself stands, as it were, socialised by the languages of rights.

The hallmark of rights in liberal conceptions is that they mark *state-free* spaces, in which individual human beings may autonomously pursue their life projects, defining reflexively as moral agents their own conceptions of good life or human flourishing. But the state-free spaces remain at the same time state- law-filled places, if only for the reason that when exercise and enjoyment of rights by individuals conflict inter se, the state agencies and apparatuses remain at hand to enable exercise of equal rights to

---

[8] E Barker (ed), *Social Contract: Essays by Locke, Hume, and Rousseau* (Oxford, Oxford University Press, 1962) 240.

[9] The task is relatively uncomplicated; St Augustine asked, 'What is state without justice [and, we may add, human rights as indicators of justice] if not a band of robbers?' Social predation, unlimited aggression against the other, is the hallmark of an unjust order, which may, but ought not to, thrive against demands of minimal justice and rights because *ought* not to equal *right*.

freedoms of all.[10] Regulation of individual human rights in conflict always bears the burden of justification which remains extraordinarily complicated. This may be shown, to name a few examples, by the discourses on 'hate speech', 'sedition', 'free choice' (reproductive rights) and pornography. In an important sense, to reiterate, the state-free spaces that characterise human rights discursivity are at the same time also substantially state-filled spaces.

But increasingly in a genomic and digitising world culture, the distinction between state-free and state-occupied human realms is wearing thin. Much of social theory of human rights predates the emergence of the predatory social relations of production, arising from global capitalism.[11] All these summon a new order of re-imagining the diverse and contradictory relationships between the global and international social.

Ethical dilemmas of regulation stand aggravated by the new modes of production. The famous 'harm' principle, enunciated by John Stuart Mill, now stands incredibly complicated, in our posthuman times of germ line therapies, use of foetal tissue and body parts in biotech research tainted by uninformed consent, advanced possibilities of human cloning, and computational futures which even suggest the uploading of human consciousness onto a computer. Not merely the 'natural' but also that which we might call 'social' stands reconstituted by technoscience. Contemporary rights-talk has already an obsolescent odour. So has the post-Isaiah Berlin language that has reproduced itself endlessly in contrasts between:

— 'Liberty' rights and 'welfare' rights[12]
— 'Legal' rights and 'programme' rights[13]
— 'Civil and political' rights and 'social, economic and cultural' rights
— Rights emplaced within the shorthand distinctions summating the 'generation' of rights enunciation (the four generations of human rights)
— Basic 'material needs' rights and 'non-material' 'autonomy' rights

---

[10] In an ideal world, this won't be necessary because, for example, all moral agents ought to agree with the proposition that my right to smoke ends where your nose begins. Under non-ideal conditions, however, the state and the law may intervene only to the extent that equal liberties of all stand preserved. Smokers have since discovered a world overcrowded with noses.

[11] See especially: D Haraway, *Modest_Witness@Second_Millennium.FemaleMan©_Meets_ OncoMouseTM* (London, Routledge, 1997); NK Hayles, *How We Became Posthuman: Virtual Bodies in Cybernetics, Literature, and Informatics* (Chicago, Chicago University Press, 1999); and U Baxi, *Human Rights in a Posthuman World* (Delhi and Oxford, Oxford University Press, 2007.)

[12] D Kelly, 'A Life of One's Own: Individual Rights and Welfare State' in P Alston and H Steiner (eds), *International Human Rights in Context: Law, Politics, and Morals* (Oxford, Oxford University Press, 2000) 257.

[13] See United Nations, *Annotations on the Text of Draft International Covenants on Human Rights*, UN Doc A/ 2929 (1955).

Each of these divisions, expressing a hierarchy of human rights, now stands re-enunciated in aggravated modes, and remains problematic. The distinction between 'negative' and 'positive' rights, as we know from insufficiently acknowledged experience, is misleading. Both make substantial claims on resources of the community and the state; the so-called negative rights require a great deal of public investment for their promotion and protection.[14] Besides, even social rights may be 'negative rights', in the important sense that the state may not unreasonably interfere with an individual's access to rights to education or health, for example.

The distinction between 'liberty' and 'programme' rights suggests that the former have a sort of priority over the latter, at least in terms of implementation. This is an inaccurate distinction, at least in terms of the positivity of international human rights. Many cherished civil and political rights still remain programmatic.[15] Only a few preferred freedoms (such as the right to freedom of speech and expression, association, conscience and religion, non-discrimination on grounds of race, religion or sex) within the ensemble of 'civil and political rights' constitute here-and-now duties and forms of compliance. And the distinction between the two kinds of rights overlooks the fact that many social, economic and cultural rights remain integral and indispensable to the realisation of civil and political rights. Finally, without being exhaustive, deprived peoples all around the world have yet to grasp why housing, food, health and education are 'needs rights' compared with rights to freedom of speech and expression, association, physical and psychic integrity and well-being.

III DIFFERENT POSITIONINGS

One may identify at the outset at least four principal positions that dominate many a theoretic language game of social rights. The first emerges, as already noted, in the dominant discourse that distinguishes, as it were, between here-and-now enjoyable civil and political rights contrasted with *deferred* rights—'social' (including economic and cultural) rights. The latter, marked by the languages of 'progressive realisation' are often, as already noted, represented as 'manifesto' or 'programme' rights, as compared with civil and political human rights that cast, more or less, comparatively clear-cut enforcement obligations. The justification of the

---

14 S Holmes and CR Sunstein, 'The Cost of Rights: Why Liberty Depends on Taxes' in *Human Rights in Context,* above n 12 at 260–61.

15 As, for example, the right to immunity from capital punishment under the International Covenant on Civil and Political Rights, or the right to immunity from torture, cruel and unusual punishment or treatment. The CEDAW enshrining women's human rights thus remains entirely programmatic.

distinction between the two regimes of human rights is a central issue in this discourse.

Second, in terms of a pragmatic conception of human rights, offering the second or third best world of human rights, the task is how to further develop the best possible ways and means to improve the observance of social rights, regardless of an ethical lament concerning this state of affairs. The real-life struggles of impoverished billions of human beings speak to us of the urgency of action; for these suffering peoples the retarded or deceptive time for the realisation of social human rights talk emerges as a rather cruel form of hoax.

The third positioning stresses the crucial significance of civil and political rights as providing development gateways for the attainment of lived social rights. The basic argument here is that the full protection of the former set of rights is of strategic significance for the eventual attainment of the latter. This argument is elaborated in many complex ways. At issue here, simply put, is the relationship between 'basic needs' (material as well as 'non-material') and normative articulations of human rights. The argument made famous by Amartya Sen's germinal work concerning famines is that, without assurances and actual exercise of civil and political rights, people's basic material needs fail disastrously even to articulate themselves.

The fourth related mode seeks to mutate the hierarchy of human rights by chasing interconnectedness and interdependence of the two kinds of human rights. From this perspective, too sharp a dichotomy between two kinds of human rights is equally destructive of their futures: they need to be read together and as a whole, always bearing in mind the reciprocal connection. To take an example, this perspective maintains that many assurances of the right to life in civil and political rights enunciations remain unintelligible outside the frame of social, economic and cultural rights. The former remain, in Laclau's fecund phrase, 'empty signifiers'.

These four positionings require understanding of different ways of politics *of* human rights and politics *for* human rights.[16] The former represent deployment of human rights languages and logics for the ends of management of power, and governance, national, regional or global. The distinction, for example, between *legal* rights and *programme* rights[17] in United Nations prose is relevant for the administration of international human rights within the United Nations system. So remain the distinctions between civil and political in contrast to social and economic rights for national governance, international development aid and assistance, and the policies and programmes of international financial institutions. Politics *of* human rights also entails the veneration of the doctrine of sovereign

---

[16] See Baxi, 80–85, 152–6 (2006).
[17] See Baxi, above, n 5.

equality of states, an order of deference that diminishes the prospect of compliance with not just civil and political rights but also social, economic and cultural human rights. Politics *for* human rights contests the very notion that rights languages and logic should remain the preserve, the eminent domain, of governance.

To these one may further add a wider quotient of a somewhat 'elevating', prudential (in a Thomist sense) message: certain forms of socially instituted orders of human suffering and deprivation remain, for the time being, and *somehow*, legitimate. The implicit presumption is that 'fulfilment', howsoever fragmented, of civil and political rights is a *necessary*, though not a *sufficient*, condition for overall progress towards the realisation of social, economic and cultural rights. It is true that 'our conceptualisation of economic needs depends on open public debates and discussions, and that guaranteeing of these debates and discussions requires an insistence on political rights'.[18] But it is also equally true that this insistence nowhere marks any sustained, let alone any dramatic, amelioration of the plight of the human rights-violated 'wretched of the earth'. Underlying this instrumentalist perspective on the insistence on political and civil rights remain unelaborated notions concerning the political time and space for the unfolding of human rights.

IV THE 'GLOBAL SOCIAL'

More important, in my opinion, is the way in which this spacetime/horizon stands configured. How may we construct that spacetime of the global social, within which social rights are to have, as it were, their being? The preferred construction of the contemporary global social stands almost wholly emptied of histories of violations of human rights even when the duties to affirm, respect, implement and fulfil social rights are said to extend to all state parties to the International Covenant on Social, Economic and Cultural Rights and other related social rights international instruments. The global social is at once thus *emptied* and *filled*: it is emptied of state capabilities to fulfil these rights while filled by normative obligations. I do not, in saying this, deny the importance of social rights imperatives; I do wish to suggest, however, that these imperatives entail labours of construction of global justice that concretise duties of aid and assistance to ex-colonial nation societies enabling them to fulfil the mandate of the internationally enunciated regime of social rights.

For my part, I wish to begin addressing social rights in the contexts of 'failed decolonisation'. I do so because, to vary a Rawlsian metaphor

---

[18] A Sen, 'Freedom and Needs' (1994) 31 *The New Republic* 32. See also: A Sen, *Development as Freedom* (Oxford, Oxford University Press, 1999) and U Baxi, above n 11, chapter 2.

concerning the circumstances of justice, circumstances of rights do matter for all, but especially for the rightless.

If the nationalist project aiming at the overthrow of colonial and imperial domination made any ethical sense, it did so by the aspiration to move rightless peoples (to use Hannah Arendt's evocative phrase) into a world of human rights. Decolonisation struggles gave birth to contemporary human rights enunciations and movements by striking at the very roots of domination that caused comprehensive rightlessness. These struggles (still continuing in different forms in conditions of postcolony and self-determination situations in the contemporary world) established the authorship and ownership of human rights in cultures and among peoples supposedly devoid of human rights conceptions or praxis.

Although a history of human rights in these terms is still to be written,[19] it is clear (at least from the perspectives of the impoverished and suffering masses) that many a 'new' nation began its journey in independence with a clear commitment to human—social, economic and political—rights in ways that highlight a very different itinerary of human rights from that of Euro-American state formative processes.

All the same, it remains true that many ex-colonial states have failed to deliver on the agenda of human rights, including social and economic rights. This shows the failure of decolonisation, as signifying a complex configuration of global politics of domination and the ethical incoherence of the postcolonial ruling classes and power elites. By the term 'failed decolonisation'[20] I refer to this complex of causative factors. Indubitably, the normative impoverishment of global human rights discourse also plays a decisive role.

No doubt the histories of critical events (to invoke Lyotard's phrase) in colonialism and imperialism, as also embodied in the histories of the Cold War, have come to an end. But their various inheritances live on to constitute the global social into two very distinct worlds: a world *with* human rights and a world *without* human rights. It remains a constitutive global social fact that in their bulk and generality that the rightless peoples overwhelm those who fully exercise and enjoy their rights.

Contemporary constructions of social rights remain founded on practices of politics that so successfully organise global amnesia of colonialism, imperialism and the Cold War, as to make politically incorrect to use such phrases. At the plane of the constructions of the global social, there is little room for ethical enunciation of duties of reparation, rehabilitation and restitution for the horrid acts of colonialism and the Cold War. At the same time, all postcolonial and post-Cold War societies are obliged

---

[19] See Baxi (2006) chapter 2.
[20] I borrow this notion from GC Spivak, *A Critique of Postcolonial Reason: Towards a History of Vanishing Present* (Cambridge, Mass, Harvard University Press, 1999).

to affirm, recognise and respect internationally enunciated political and civil rights as well as social, economic and cultural rights. This *ought* to be so. But the problem of resourcing rights is left severely to the postcolonial and post-Cold War economies and states, without any acceptance of the legitimacy of the claim that the erstwhile beneficiaries of the politics of global predation owe any duties to victimised state-societies and their peoples. Nor is there at hand as yet even a pre-theory of global justice, which coherently articulates an ethic of duties of aid and assistance to postcolonial and post-Cold War peoples of the world.[21]

This lack becomes even more cruelly conspicuous when we recall that the contemporary formations of rights-talk do not usually address the issue whether concentrations of economic and techno-scientific power owe any responsibilities for human rights violations (including violations of social rights). It is now widely recognised that such responsibilities extend beyond the politically organised society (state) to institutions in civil society: family and religious institutions, for example. The women's rights convention (CEDAW) marks the most spectacular advance in this regard.[22] However, this recognition still falls short of attribution of human rights duties to corporations, including transnational enterprises. These formations of techno-science power wield enormous powers over human social futures. The processes of contemporary economic globalisation augment these powers in ways that summon Herculean practices of people's resistance as the archetypal violated peoples from Bhopal to Ogoniland know intergenerationally in their blood and bones.[23] Ulrich Beck has, rightly, described these processes as institutionalising 'organised irresponsibility' and 'organised impunity'.[24] The 'de-centring' of the 'nation-state', entailed in the globalising processes, signifies the end also of the redistributionist polity in ways that diminish the futures of social rights.

It is in this world-historic context, animated by the poverty of justice-theorising, that the 'failure' of the postcolonial is measured by the ahistorical spacetime of contemporary human rights, outside the lived and embodied histories of collective hurt and human violation in the killing fields of postcolonies and the post-Cold War states. This raises the

---

[21] See U Baxi, 'The Failure of Deliberative Democracy and Global Justice,' in Okwui Enwezor *et al* (eds) *Democracy Unrealized: Documenta 11_Platform 1* (Ostfildern-Ruit, Hatje Cantz Publishers, 2001) 113–32.

[22] So does the Convention on the Rights of the Child.

[23] These powers are of *no* avail when confronted with international financial markets, which cause capital flights and stock and currency market crashes in ways that confiscate, beyond redress, wages and savings of individual households. Currency crashes, and measures of devaluation, thus caused lie in the arcane realms of fiscal and monetary policies, dictated by the international financial institutions, in ways that remain obscure in human rights discourse.

[24] U Beck, *The Risk Society* (London, Sage, 1992). See also Baxi (2006) chapter 9 concerning human rights obligations of the multinational corporations and other business entities.

question of the future of social rights in conditions of failure of post-colonialism.

V 'FAILED DECOLONISATION' AND SOCIAL RIGHTS

How may we construct the narratives of 'failed decolonisation'? It is indeed clear that injustices and violations of the right to be and remain human are writ large in the postcolony world. But any understanding of the causative structure of human misery and suffering in the postcolony world raises many questions.[25] Even when the recognition of postcolonial agency is crucial, we need to grasp the national and global etymologies of this failure and indeed to have some benchmarks, which may measure the 'degrees' of failure. I present below a few questions to indicate the intimidating complexity of tasks of understanding and judgment.

The first imponderable is provided, in these postmodern times, by the rejection of 'essentialism'. How may we construct the notions of colonisation and colonialism, other than by making legible and intelligible an homogenous telos of subjugation and repression, planned economic ruin and reign of terror? Perhaps an anti-essentialist stance guides us to the fact that even when considered as an integral aspect of the combined and uneven Western capitalist development, 'colonisation' has not *one* but *many* diverse histories. These histories inevitably shape the itinerary of anti-colonial struggles, and indeed their overall social character. These, too, distinctively define the spacetime of the postcolonial. Anti-essentialism guides us to specific histories and legacies of the colonial experience, opening up space for diverse articulation of modes of power and resistance. 'Failed decolonisation', then, speaks to us concerning the combined and uneven modes of international economic division of labour as well as of the modes of production of global politics of domination and of resistance to them. It is indeed a weighty conception.

Second, we need to understand the nature of class forces that impart a sense of telos to anti-imperialist struggles; it is not clear how this may be best accomplished, given the multiform/multilayered character of nationalist projects. Beyond the minimal assertion of the injustice of colonisation / imperialism, and of the justice of struggles for self-determination in these contexts, arise multiple narratives, defying any privileged teleological narration of the nationalist projects. The diversity and heterogeneity of the 'postcolonial' furnishes a constant reminder of the ways in which the agenda of 'social rights' may be constructed, and ways in which it historically miscarries, or betrays itself.

---

[25] But see now A Dixit, 'Predatory States and Failing States: An Agency Perspective', CEPS Working Paper 131, August 200.

Third, 'decolonisation' at once entails processes of 're-colonisation'. The beginnings of the end of decolonisation also mark the beginnings of various forms and phases of the Cold War. Indeed, a large number of decolonised societies came to birth in the spacetime of the Cold War. The varieties of Cold War imperialism, whether socialist or capitalist, profoundly affect socio-economic futures, and within these the futures of social rights. The 'spheres of influence' theories and practices mark the advent of new forms of neo-colonisation. The killing fields of many a postcolony become the cemeteries of human rights. Resurrection of social rights in such contexts remains inconceivable outside the constant reiteration of the memory of crucifixion.

Fourth, re-colonisation occurred through acts of Cold War diplomacy sanctioned by the two super-powers that endowed tyrannical regimes and cliques with both legitimacy and longevity, at an unconscionable cost of human rights. Sponsored military regimes flourish and all manifestations of dissenting leadership, in politics and civil society, stand cruelly liquidated by gulag politics of the two super-powers and their satellites. Multinational corporations, both defence and extractive (natural resource based) industries, emerge as major governance partners in the catastrophic practices of 'making the world safe for democracy'. National comprador elites attain a high order of immunity and impunity during the various phases of the Cold War and now even in a globalising world economy.

Fifth, development aid by the 'Western' nations, and international financial institutions, remains fraught with variegated impact on the national potential to respect, promote, fulfil and realise social rights. Arturo Escobar has shown how the regimes of representation concerning 'development' have sought to re-colonise the subjects of development discourse.[26]

Sixth, neo-colonialism aids and abets the politics of severely divided societies. Kwame Nkrumah defined neo-colonialism memorably as:

> the worst form of imperialism. For those who practice it, it means power without responsibility and for those who suffer from it, it means exploitation without redress.[27]

Contemporary globalisation exemplifies neo-colonialism precisely in this sense, in ways that awesomely complicate our social rights talk. The great problems of the life and times of social rights, and our sense of their futures, are also constituted by the political production of ethnicity.[28]

---

[26] A Escobar, *Encountering Development: The Making and the Unmaking of the Third World* (Princeton, Princeton University Press, 1995).

[27] Cited in R Young, *Postcolonialism: An Historical Introduction* (Oxford, Blackwell, 2001) 44.

[28] D Horowitz, *The Deadly Ethnic Riot* (Berkeley, University of California Press, 2001) and *Ethnic Groups in Conflict* (Berkeley, University of California Press, 1985).

Ethnicity emerges as much as an aspect of reversion to primordial identity politics as a function of national and global public policy constructs. The politics of 'ethnic' assertion also serve the interests of geopolitical global domination and arms traffic and industries and the ends of the New Military World Order.[29] Contemporary ethnic wars take, as is well known, many forms; but in each of these they inflict unconscionable harm on the future of social rights.

Seventh, and to the extent (rarely) that decolonisation resulted in social reproduction of Western liberal democratic governance in the postcolony, the languages and logics of human, social, rights translate here as forms of protest against failed decolonisation. Even on this historic register, forms of politics *of* human rights often overcome those of politics *for* human rights.

Eighth, the 'ethical' foreign policy of the 'liberal' and 'well-ordered' peoples normativised in an exemplary way by John Rawls's active conceptual advocacy of intolerance by the law of peoples against 'outlaw states'[30] furnishes a real-life justification for both abstention and aggression. On the one hand, abstention stands 'justified' on various grounds when states/societies/peoples become outlaws by their failure to protect human rights to their peoples but even when they engage in massive, ongoing and flagrant denial of the minima of human rights entitlements. On the other hand, the 'out-lawness' summons outright aggression when the overwhelming concern is phrased in terms of intent and capacity of an outlaw state/regime to endangerment of the 'well-ordered societies'. Their protection from the 'outlaw societies' now becomes the principal aim of the law of the peoples, with episodic and incidental achievement of a modicum of respect for social rights for states/ regimes that may be said after all to succeed the vanquished 'outlaws'.

Ninth, decolonisation fails the aspirations of self-determination of the First Nations peoples, at least in terms of autonomy movements aspiring to forms of 'stateness'. In a sad commentary on the state of the art concerning human social rights, the rights of First Nations peoples constitute the last frontier of our 'Age of Human Rights'; as yet, these have to find a coherent, internationally acceptable, enunciation through a Declaration on the Rights of Indigenous Peoples and Populations. From their standpoint, all our talk concerning social rights, and their futures, constitutes a new human rights hoax. If colonialism and imperialism deprived them of their right to be, and to remain, human, contemporary globalisation processes achieve more of the same, often in cruelly aggravated modes and forms.

---

[29] A Giddens, *The Consequences of Modernity* (Cambridge, Polity Press, 1990).
[30] J Rawls, *The Law of Peoples* (Cambridge, Mass, Harvard University Press, 1999).

Tenth, and related, it equally fails the neo-colonial disinherited diasporic peoples: from Palestinian peoples to the Roma and varieties of 'forced' ecological exiles and migrant workers. To name the horrendous orders of human and social suffering failed decolonisation itself constitutes unconscious ways of complicity in human rights violation.

A theoretical approach that ignores the *endogenous* causes of state failure is not wholly worthy of respect. Failed decolonisation is indubitably a consequence of Third World elite political betrayal of many a promise of self-determination movements. At the same time, it is also a function of global politics. In the absence of Swiss bank accounts (protected, no doubt, by the 'insistence on political freedoms' in the North) many a Third World tyrant would not have survived a day in power. In the absence of generous North grant of asylum to deposed Third World tyrants, the loot and plunder of societal resources would have resulted in repatriation of resources in ways that would serve the cause of social rights in these regions. Had the North developed stringent legal regimes against overseas Third World corruption by its defence contractors, resources would have been available to service the future of social rights in these regions. Had the North recognised at least the same order of human rights reparations (as it did for post-War Europe) for acts of colonisation and the Cold War, the future of social rights would have been more secure than it is today and for many suffering tomorrows to come.

Failed decolonisation is a field of cultural production[31] that summates, and encodes, narratives concerning endeavours to theorise justice in its global reach and significance. Typically, even as enormous advances mark the articulation of the place of justice in national governance, we (epistemic communities) yet stumble in the moral quagmire of global justice.[32] We have yet to enunciate cogently the justificatory modes even of talking about ethical duties of the historically advantaged states and peoples to those who these histories deprived of even minimal capabilities to perform the tasks of social rights and justice. And yet this remains a paramount task if we are to take the itineraries of human social rights seriously.

---

[31] For this fecund notion see P Bourdieu, *The Field of Cultural Production* (Cambridge, Polity Press, 1993).

[32] The remarkable post-Rawlsian articulation concerning the possibility of global justice has yet to inform the mainstream human rights discourse. See, especially, C Jones, *Global Justice: Defending Cosmopolitanism* (Oxford, Oxford University Press, 1999) and the literature cited therein.

VI TOWARDS AN UNEASY 'CONCLUSION'

This no doubt is a complex and daunting task, not helped by the mantras of contemporary international human rights movements and markets worshipping at the altar of the indivisibility, inalienability and interdependence of all human rights. At best, these incantations seek to construct a non-material global human rights culture. This is no doubt enormously symbolically significant. But so, if not more, are the tasks of creating a material culture of human rights, forms that entail the creation of international social cooperation crystallising *perfect* obligations directed at combating, without standardless use of military force, the structures and practices deeply violative of social rights. If the cultural production of the fields of social rights signifies an aspect of such cooperation, so do the itineraries of enunciative regimes of duties of envisioning a just international order. The future of social rights remains tethered to our ability to articulate conceptions of global justice, for social rights depend very much on how we choose to conceptualise the global social. The ways in which we construct the global social *determines*, not just *conditions*, the cultural production of the future of social rights everywhere.

In these post-Cold War times, the construction of the 'social' resolutely ignores the problem of ethical and moral agency (and responsibility) of transnational corporations and international and regional financial institutional regimes. The 'social' is still astonishingly constructed in terms of ethical individualism, almost altogether undemanding of an ethic of care and responsibility by transnational actors and agents who now inherit the former estates of sovereignty of states, now also being 'progressively, decentred'.

For all these, and related reasons,[33] I insist that taking the future of social rights seriously requires that we decipher the genealogy of failed decolonisation. I doubt whether this task may ever be done outside a Marx-like grasp of structures of global injustice and new approaches to global justice.

---

[33] These include pre-eminently the two 'terror' wars—the wars *of* and *on* 'terror.' See concerning this, U.Baxi, ' The War *on* Terror and the "War *of* Terror": Nomadic Multitudes, Aggressive Incumbents, and the "New International Law"' (2005) 43 *Osgoode Hall Law Journal* 7–43.

4

'If you don't pay, you die': On Death and Desire in the Postcolony

LUCIE WHITE*

From March 1999 through to the present, I have worked with law students from the United States and a West African university on a 'health rights campaign' in a very low-income area at the centre of the nation's capital city. I'll call this sector 'Nima'. Our African colleagues call it an 'urban slum'. We are working with a grassroots human rights group founded in 1997 by African law students to bring 'human rights' consciousness into Nima, in order to help its residents secure basic life necessities such as clean water, basic health care, adequate food and a primary education for all of Nima's children.

Nima is located in a nation with a much more robust economy than many of its neighbours. Yet in our project we are working with people who can expect to die before their fortieth birthday, even if they beat the odds. We are working with women whose babies are dying not because they can't afford fancy protease-inhibiting drugs, but because they can't afford a fifty-cent mosquito net or oral rehydration kit. We are working with teenagers who are sick all the time because their local district council can't raise the cash to connect their taps to clean water. We are working with people who would die to get onto the sidewalks of Amsterdam or London or New York—even for a day—to work in those cities' thriving underground economies for enough dollars in a week to feed their extended families for a year. Nima's land is becoming more and more valuable as the central city begins to develop in First World style, with two skyscrapers and a mid-town shopping mall just completed and a five-star hotel slated for construction along the still wild coastline that borders the city's financial district.

Soon after the Second World War, the colonial authority gave the land that is now Nima to a group of elite Muslim leaders from the North, as a

* An earlier version of this paper was presented at the 'Law and Disorder in the Postcolony' conference at the Radcliffe Institute of Advanced Study in May 2003.

gesture of thanks for the service they gave to the Crown during the Second World War. Nima seems a world away from the city that surrounds it. It is almost entirely Muslim, in a city that is predominantly, and with increasing fervour, of the Christian faith. Nima's women squat over coal fires to cook. They make do without electric power, sewage treatment, wastewater drainage or rubbish pick-up. Yet their community is ringed by recently upgraded expressways that bring suburban commuters into the city's centre.

Their improvised homes back up onto these highways. The women hang their laundry along the highways' iron guardrails. Their most agile children, watched over by shrewd, determined sisters, gather at the freeway interchanges at dawn and dusk, clambering up businessmen's car-door windows to beg for change. Most of these drivers—the nation's emerging, upwardly mobile, increasingly cosmopolitan, but still quite fragile, upper middle class—curse these children at their windows and move on.

Nima's population mushroomed during the 1980s and 1990s, when natural disasters, political unrest and cutbacks on agricultural subsidies forced small cocoa farmers in the North to go south to the cities for work. Most of these recent arrivals rent shelter from the 'Big Men' who acquired the land from the Crown or, increasingly, from the real estate speculators who are buying it up from them.

Gentrification has already started to creep into the fringes of Nima. One of the city's most exclusive restaurants—reportedly the favoured site for lip-sealed deals between foreign investors and local government officials—is located on a dusty cul-de-sac on Nima's outer edge. Recent arrivals design their housing out of tarpaper, rusted metal and discarded cargo containers from merchant ships. When you look out across Nima from the second-floor balcony of the Legal Resources Centre—that's the grassroots group we work with—you see a counterpane of metal spread out across Nima's hills and the ravine that cuts between them.

The backdrop for our work is a set of domestic legal reforms, popularly known as 'structural adjustment', that were imposed upon poor nations by the United States and international development agencies in the 1980s and 1990s. The intention of these policies was to rescue those nations from bankruptcy, social disorder and political disintegration, and thus to ready them for a long-delayed entry into the global economy.

As a prelude to this reform, international development agencies financed infrastructure improvement projects—the building of roads and dams, the dredging of harbours and rivers—in the nations targeted for structural adjustment. These improvements upgraded the 'hardware' for the new development programme. They would ready poor nations for the cargo boats, long-haul trucks, fibre optic cables and five-star hotels that foreign investment driven development would require. Structural adjustment programmes would then provide the 'software'. These legal reforms were geared to change the institutions, behaviours and beliefs of the poor nations' own peoples, to make them more receptive to the new life-ways that global integration would demand.

The first of the hardware for the new development agenda came to Nima in the early 1980s. A big loan from the World Bank helped pay for dredging the creek that ran through Nima's ravine and for paving the sector's only two-track pathway. The creek carried wastewater from the hills above the city, through Nima, to the sea. During the rainy season the creek tended to flood, causing cholera among Nima's residents. The disease tended to spread as Nima's residents went into the city's affluent households, restaurants and hotels to work. Episodes of cholera in a nation's capital city get in the way of an investment-driven development programme.

The project that paved the road and dredged the creek made no improvements in sanitation or wastewater disposal for Nima's own residents, who lived on the hills above the creek. Without any sewage disposal except a scattering of clogged public toilets, Nima's residents had learned to defecate as infrequently as they found to be humanly possible, and then only in plastic bags. In our survey of the health issues most on the minds of Nima's residents, we learned that some of the young men and women, with iron wills and flat stomachs, had learned to limit their urge to defecate to once every three or four days. It was harder for the more 'vulnerable sectors' of the population—as the nation's social legislation refers to pregnant women, old people and small children—to learn so well.

After the creek was dredged, the people of Nima started calling it the 'Big Gutter'. When we talked to them about it, they would thread these words—'Big Gutter'— into the rhythms of Hausa, like a braid. Only a couple of the law students who work on the project speak Hausa. Most of the African students speak the tribal languages of the dominant tribal group, whose home base is on the plateau that rises above the coastal plain. That group cut the best deals with the former colonial power and has dominated its postcolonial politics for a half century. All of the law students—both African and American—share a high level of fluency in English and a passion for human rights.

The students listen quietly as the residents of Nima, whose woes they seek to witness, repeat the words 'Big Gutter' in their face. Later, in the safety of the Legal Resources Centre's conference room, some of these students confess to feeling shame, or fear, at these moments. The words sound too hard, more like a threat than a gesture of connection.

Part of structural adjustment's 'software' was to impose user fees that made people pay cash at public hospitals and clinics before they could get any treatment. People without money were supposed to be exempted from paying this fee. But these exemptions were rarely made available,

especially to recent migrants from the North who had no clout with the
nurses and doctors in the government clinics. When we met with them, the
nurses said that they were afraid that these Hausa-speaking migrants were
going to overwhelm the city. They had so many children and they seemed
so poor. If they let these people into the clinic, they would run out of
bandages and medicines and would have to work all the time.

After user fees were imposed, public hospitals began to keep patients in
the ward after their medical discharge until their bills were paid. Some of
these patients told us that they felt afraid that the hospital's armed security
guards would shoot them if they tried to leave. Each day that such people
stay in the hospital after their medical discharge, the hospital charges them
15,000 cedi. Families in Nima know about this practice and tend to think
twice before sending their kin to the hospital in the first place, especially
women stuck in labour, whose obstetrical bills are likely to be very high.

I ON POSTCOLONIAL LAWMAKING

The backdrop for the structural adjustment programme was a consensus of
formerly imperial states that was reached in Washington in the early 1980s.
The motives that compelled this consensus were grand: to halt the
economic and social decline of the Third World and then turn it on a path
towards economic prosperity, democratic governance and global
integration. The need for it, according to its backers, was clear: to rescue
Third World nations from the brink of disaster. Their social indicators—
infant mortality and life expectancy—were in rapid decline. They were
nearly bankrupt. They were usually ruled by crooks, backed up by thugs,
who had hidden their nations' natural wealth in Swiss bank accounts. Their
scary downward spiral was threatening to jeopardise the prosperity of the
entire global economy.

The programme of structural adjustment that followed from the
Washington consensus was as harsh as the name implies. The patient
would have been wise to bite on a leather strap as the cure was delivered.
It came in two distinct phases.

The first phase was aimed to correct Third World nations' fiscal insta-
bility. This phase was intended to curb inflation, revalue Third World
currencies, and make Third World governments seem 'credit worthy' to
First World investors. Thus it would rescue Third World economies from
self-inflicted economic ruin. And by taking those economies by the hand, it
would walk them, step by step, towards the economic sovereignty that
their liberation promised.

This phase of structural adjustment called on Third World governments
to enact 'shock' policies that would devalue their currencies and then to
peg them to a floating exchange rate fixed on global currency markets. In

retrospect, most economists agree that this shock was delivered too fast, causing destitution for the poor and a sharp decline in well-being for the urban middle classes.

The second phase of structural adjustment was aimed at the social sector of Third World states. It sought to pare down the public sector, so as to cut costs and improve service quality. It included measures like selling off or reorganising state-owned enterprises, firing state-funded civil servants, withdrawing subsidies from small farmers who produced export crops and 're-inventing' the organisational practices of core, public sector services in more market-oriented ways. By forcing Third World governments to off-load many of their public sector operations, these reforms sought to reduce domestic budget outlays and leave more revenue to pay off foreign loans. These policies would be painful in the short term, but the theory taught that they were the only way to plug Africa into the global economy, and finally liberate Africans to buy Western goods and get real jobs.

In the social sector, handouts like health care for the asking would be replaced by consumer-driven service options. Through this simple innovation, the system would greatly improve. Consumers would finally be in charge. They could choose for themselves which services to use, or whether to use a particular service at all. They could 'vote with their feet'. Thus, Zagat-like, each service would feel heavy pressure to improve. And those that didn't would be driven out of business. A further innovation would make cash the currency through which consumers would exercise these powers. Making consumers pay for what they wanted would ensure that they made their decisions with care. And since the rich would buy more 'luxury' services, at higher mark-ups, their dollars could be folded back into the sector, to help foot the bill for services for the poor.

There was hope that this market-based reform of social services would have spill-over benefits in the political sphere. First, these reforms would erase the lingering traces of failed socialist experiments from Third World statute books. Second, learning to act in a market, even for basic health care, would prepare Third World peoples to enter global labour markets, urban shopping malls and voting booths. It would prepare them for the new world of poverty alleviation, universal democracy and human flourishing that the liberal development paradigm promised.

In the face of all of these rose-coloured hopes for structural adjustment, there were also the critics. They saw structural adjustment as the replay of an old story: a return to colonial domination. Structural adjustment meant a covert US invasion of African legal systems, to 'harmonise' those systems, like it or not, with the global capitalist order. Just like the First World urban renewal schemes of the 1950s, structural adjustment would bulldoze away what was left of nationalist hope and replace it with mean-spirited utilitarian calculation. This round of imperial occupation would come through the subtle coercion of the dollar, rather than overt violence. Specifically, its critics made four claims.

First, structural adjustment would unravel what was left of the postcolonial states' eroding social fabric. Its withdrawal of agricultural subsidies would impoverish subsistence farmers. Its 'marketising' of basic social services would erode public infrastructure. Its fiscal policies would displace large numbers of civil servants and other formal sector workers. Thus, at the same time that structural adjustment promoted a cash culture, its critics feared that it would undermine civil society and thus stifle any ground for democratic social movement.

Second, structural adjustment-mandated reforms would expand the pool of potential workers with little power to hold their own in imperial economies. Displaced civil servants line up for jobs in hotels, massage parlours and fast food restaurants in coastal cities, and migrate towards sectors like nursing and nannying in the metropole. And new waves of super-exploitable workers—farmers displaced by subsidy withdrawals, landless people locked out of safety net services, the unschooled, the unlucky, those determined not to die—would take great risks to get to global cities, so they could scavenge for dangerous informal sector jobs.

Third, structural adjustment would do violence to the hearts, minds and sovereignty of Third World peoples. Like a computer virus, it would inject imperial legal templates into Third World nations' internal legal order. This intrusion would not be limited to those fields like monetary policy and international trade law that govern a nation's relations with other sovereigns. The penetration would extend into those domains of social law at the very heart of any nation's constitutional covenant with its own people, in areas like health, education, civil service, the distribution of seeds and credit to farmers and the distribution of inherited land to widows and orphans. Those domains of domestic law often carried a deep imprint from the colonial era. Yet citizens still felt those laws to be their own.

And fourth, structural adjustment would lead many people to die.

Structural adjustment's strategy of rewriting the law ordering everyday social practices from the inside out repeated a key colonial strategy of social control. Colonial law rewrote the background rules in key spheres like health, education, trade and marriage. It gave local chiefs and opinion leaders an important role in enforcing those arrangements. By reshaping social interactions, behaviours, preferences and desires in this way, the colonial legal order got inside its subjects. On the surface, it often appeared to do its work well, producing deeply grounded compliance with the colonial order. Yet postcolonial literature suggests that it more often produced deep internal conflict.

Thus colonial law and structural adjustment can be read as enacting similar methods of social control. Yet in the postcolonial era, the imperial powers could no longer march in with their troops and missionaries to impose their enlightened law on the natives—at least not until the recent revival of pre-emptive military intervention. To get around this problem, structural adjustment invades the postcolony with carrots rather than sticks. It works by adding new strings, called conditionalities, to international development loans. If a Third World nation wants to get new international loans, it can choose to change its laws according to structural adjustment's templates. If it doesn't like the strings, it can shop elsewhere for loans.

Attaching illegal strings to essential goods like health care was the legal move that First World social conservatives used to impose values like sexual abstinence on poor women when constitutional law prevented those forces from imposing those values directly on the whole population. Structural adjustment, crafted during the same era, used the same legal instrument to get around the postcolonial sovereignty problem. Does this legal move amount to unconscionable coercion in conditions of unequal power? This question continues to divide First World Supreme Courts and constitutional law scholars.[1]

II SOUNDINGS

We began the health rights campaign by going into the alleyways of Nima to hear what people had to say about the greatest dangers to their health. They told us what it felt like to live beside the Big Gutter, to defecate in plastic bags, to be turned away from the health clinic when they were in pain, or in labour, and afraid that they might die.

> My name is Abdallah Abdul Muman. I am 35 years old. I live in Nima, in house number E 501/15. My house is right next to the Big Gutter. I have lived there for almost eleven years. It is very unhealthy next to the Big Gutter—there is always disease. My three children (aged fourteen, seven and three) play around the gutter, which brings them sickness and disease. They get rashes, fever and colds from the gutter. They also get cut by broken bottles in the gutter. It worries me to live where I do. It affects my mood every day—day and night... I can go into my room, but the wind brings it all in—the diseases and the smell that is so bad that I can't breathe. There are also a lot of flies that come when we eat... The gutter is especially dangerous during the rainy season. This past rainy season has damaged the bridge and made it difficult to cross the gutter. There is also a problem with erosion; houses fall into the gutter when it rains. I think my house is in danger, and I worry about my family. I worry that my house will collapse, and I fear for my children.

[1] For more on structural adjustment see J Yong Kim et al (eds), *Dying for Growth: Global Inequality and the Health of the Poor* (Monroe, Me, Common Courage Press, 2000).

My name is Sahadatu Yunus. I live in house number 2316/232. My house is directly behind the public toilet. At times, the smell is so terrible that my family and I cannot bear to go outside the house. We go inside and hide from the odour, spraying something to cover the smell... To use the toilets, I have to wait in a long line, particularly in the early morning around 5 or 6 am or in the evening around 6 or 7 pm. After using the public toilet, I smell so bad I have to bathe. My skin, my hair, my clothes, they all absorb the odour of the public toilets and I have to wash everything. The toilets are not emptied regularly. Often, the hole is overflowing and when I use the toilet, the waste in the hole splashes up against me. It is filthy.

*   *   *

My name is Saudata Sumaila, and 1 am 36 years old. I live in house number E136/30 in East Nima. My house is a few feet from the Big Gutter. There is a small bridge made out of wooden planks across the gutter in front of my house. On Friday 17 August at around 10 am, I was walking across this bridge when one of the wooden planks broke under my weight. My right leg fell through the hole in the plank. I gashed my leg in two places when I fell, and it began bleeding profusely. I went to the government clinic, where I paid 5,000 cedi for a registration card. Still bleeding, I waited for one hour before a nurse finally looked at my injuries. After examining the serious gashes, the nurse sent me to the theatre. At the theatre, the nurses demanded 50,000 cedi to stitch one wound and 35,000 cedi to stitch the other. I begged for treatment, but the nurses refused to stitch the wounds unless I paid. I was in great pain and very disturbed emotionally, but the nurses sent me home without any treatment. The nurses did not give me any instructions on how to care for the deep cuts or the consequences of leaving the cuts exposed. The nurses only told me that if I could not pay for the stitches, I should return to the Polyclinic once a day and pay 2,000 cedi to have the wound washed and bandaged. I have not gone back because I have no money. I thought about returning to the clinic and asking for free treatment again, but the nurses were so hostile the first time that I am reluctant to return. Now my wounds are infected, my leg is swollen and I feel very sick all the time. I have difficulty walking and my whole body feels weak. I don't bandage the gashes because I can't afford the bandages. I do not know where I will get the money to buy more drugs. I am afraid that I can't get the money.

*   *   *

My name is Zenabu Issaka. I am 31 years old and work as a trader. I have two children who are three and seven years old. For each pregnancy, I paid for all of my costs. Five months ago, I went to the clinic to deliver my third child. I was transferred to the hospital because they decided to do a Caesarian section. The nurse from the clinic who brought me there abandoned me after we arrived. I sat by myself in a waiting room for hours. The doctor walked by, but it was a Sunday morning and he was finishing a long shift and went out to get something to eat. He returned in the evening, but it was too late. My baby died in my stomach. It cost almost two million cedi to remove my fresh dead child. My brothers live in America and they were able to help with the payment. I would not have been able to pay without help from my family.

My name is Mohammed Zakari. I am 62 years old. I am a farmer of seasonal cassava and maize crops. I support my three school-aged children with an income of 500,000 cedi per year. On Friday, November 1, I felt a sharp pain in my stomach. My sister, realising the seriousness of it, took me to the city to seek medical treatment. I was taken to the public hospital where I was admitted. I underwent emergency hernia surgery. Having recovered, I was discharged and handed a bill that totals 2,396,000 cedi. I was told that I could not leave the hospital until the bill was paid and that I would be charged daily for accommodation until the bill was paid.

Between December 12 and January 21 I was detained within the limits of the hospital, which is surrounded by a high fence and guarded by private security. I was only allowed outside the fence to buy plantains to eat, under the supervision of hospital staff. I believed that if I left the grounds of the hospital I would be arrested.

III TACTICS

Eventually, we did more surveys and went on talk radio with the results. We organised public hearings and marches and rallies and press conferences. We held community know-your-rights workshops in which we used theatre games and focus groups to tell Nima residents about human rights. We trained women to demand user-fee exemptions when they went to government clinics and trained youth leaders to monitor the number of times the public toilets and rubbish bins were emptied, for a full year. We drafted petitions to the African Commission on People's and Human Rights, complaints to the World Bank's Inspection Panel and lawsuits that we filed in the nation's constitutional court. We met with Members of Parliament and the Minister of Health and the city's public health director and the local district assemblymen and the Imans and the heads of local women's groups and ambassadors from rich nations and local representatives from big international foundations. We brought our sense of human rights into each of these moves, as best we could. Throughout the work, we felt both drawn to what we came to call a 'human rights campaign' and deeply ambivalent about our flirtation with that phrase.

IV QUESTIONS

In this essay, I use this work in Nima as a basis for reflecting on three related questions.

The first question is about ideology. More specifically, it is about the ideology of liberalism, which is so powerful in global circles that it seems almost impossible to imagine any sensible alternative. Is the concept of ideology of any enduring use to scholars and activists, in this era that, some say, sprang out of its ashes? If so, how?

The second question is about how ideology works its way inside human beings, shaping their preferences and desires. An earlier generation of critical scholars, notably Fanon, thought a great deal about this question in the context of Africa's colonial occupation. How might this work on colonial subjectivity help us to understand how, in the current epoch, a different kind of ideology—no longer explicitly raced—might underwrite the desire of postcolonial subjects? Can we think about the relationship between ideology and desire without holding onto rigid notions, like false consciousness, that understand ideology to shape the subject's inner life in a static, predictable way?

The third question is about human rights. The question presumes that the two prior questions have already been explored. It takes for granted that the concept of human rights, as well as the subjects of human rights claims, express liberal ideas. With that understood, can human rights be used, in settings like Nima, in ways that stretch, and even subvert, liberalism's categorical and, therefore, ultimately conservative notions of justice?

A On Ideology

Four big ideas triumphed in post-World War II thinking about how to shape the social world: modernist development, representative democracy, market economics and liberal universalism. After the demise of communism and the upsurge in ultraconservative social philosophy in the mid-1980s, these four ideas were interpreted in an increasingly formalist way. One consequence of this formalism is that policies motivated by these ideas became increasingly blind to unequal background distributions of power, such as those that persisted in postcolonies after their liberation. Thus legal regimes like structural adjustment had the unintended effect of entrenching those unequal patterns of power distribution into the new century. At the same time, the nexus of ideas that motivated such laws did not appear to be an ideology. Rather, as other ways to organise the political economy fell out of favour, that nexus of four ideas, which I will call contemporary liberalism, began to seem like the only sensible way to make a world.

The challenge thus presented is how to perceive liberalism, and the policies like structural adjustment that it legitimates, as one of many potential ideologies, rather than the way things have to be. For unless the liberal world order can be seen, at least intermittently, in this contingent way, then it remains impossible to imagine alternatives. Can we gain any insight into the limits of liberal ideology by taking the standpoint of Third World peoples who have been hurt by structural adjustment and the assumptions that motivated it?

Perhaps the most basic assumption that motivated structural adjustment was that modernist development is inevitable and a good thing. Development is achieved by increasing the nation's productivity, as measured by conventional formulas, through bringing that nation into a globally integrated market economy. In order to accomplish this, a nation must change its laws and its culture to lay a strong foundation for a market system. This means reforming laws—like those governing contract and property—to facilitate market-based exchange on terms that are good for property-holders.

It also means reshaping the hearts, minds and behaviours of the people so that they will want to take part in a globally integrated market economy, and will also know how to do it. The people of underdeveloped nations have to be taught how to work for money in the venues of low-wage global production. They have to learn how to save. They have to learn to buy the goods that are mass-produced for their consumption. And to motivate all of this learning, they have to learn to desire these changes, in a powerful, passionate way. As 'development' took hold in more and more places, images of this new consumer-subject began to circulate through the backwaters of the Third World. This circulation heated up with the spread of the mass media and new technologies, producing a dazzling, dispersed, postmodern consumer mystique that looked nothing like the tight-lipped discipline of the Protestant ethic. The retraining of Third World peoples to desire Western life-ways took on its own momentum, driving the demand side of modernist development schemes. When an ideology has become so embedded in its subjects' emotions and cognition, how can they possibly find a place from which to critique it?

This is a question that left-leaning critical theorists are starting to revisit, after several decades in which the concept of ideology had gone out of style. This revival of interest in ideology follows on the heels of a deep sense of dismay with the track record of global liberalism in the 1980s and 1990s. Peoples, cultures, species and even the planet itself were said to be dying because of liberal ideology's mindless focus on 'economic growth'. Pandemics of Third World poverty, corruption and disease were raging out of control. The entire continent of Africa was viewed as a disaster zone. Indeed, when projections were made of its disease-related mortality rate, the rhetoric of genocide was regularly invoked.

In response to this loss of faith in the liberal world order, new forms of social movement emerged. These new movements promoted—and created—carnivalesque visions of plural culture, experimentalist visions of legal ordering and lattice-like visions of a sustainable g/local world, as well as the more familiar belligerence of up-tight identity politics. At the same time, new fundamentalisms erupted everywhere, and cynicism became rampant.

It was in the face of these disruptions, and in the shadow of Foucault and Bourdieu more than Marx, that a new generation of left-leaning critical theorists began to revisit the concept of ideology. To contrast it from Marxist notions, the new theorists emphasise three novel themes.[2]

First, they see ideology as enacted and embodied by common people through their everyday practices.

Second, they see domains like the law as wellsprings of ideological force. This does not happen as the law adjudicates disputes and imposes punishments. Rather, it happens as law orders the invisible 'background rules' for commonplace practices like market transactions and family inter-actions. It is through law-scripted performances of everyday activities that law most powerfully exerts its ideological force. That force does not follow a straightforward, one-way vector. Rather, the law works ideologi-cally through a dynamic process in which subjects, constituted by law's force, use that law to constitute its normative and social power.

And third, they see ideology as almost totally hidden from view. In contrast to earlier theories of ideology, the new theorists do not see ideology as a discrete and insular set of political beliefs that are drawn upon to govern society. Rather, 'ideology' seems co-extensive with reality itself: it is simply the way things are. In the face of this overwhelming force of ideology, these theorists turn to French psychoanalyst Jacques Lacan for strategies to critique it.

Lacan is best known for a tripartite theory of the psyche, in which the symbolic, the imaginary and the real interact in a complex tension. When the new theorists apply this Lacanian schema of the psyche to the puzzle of how to recognise contemporary liberal ideology as such, they come up with the following idea.

If you want to recognise ideology as such, you have to be open to upsurges of 'the real'. The real is that 'excess' that the version of reality authorised by the prevailing ideology refuses to deal with. It comes up in moments of human experience that are too much for words. To sense it, you must stay alert to such moments, moments in your encounters with the social world that deeply move you, for these are often 'symptoms' of the limits of ideology. They are often symptoms of the gap between reality according to the prevailing ideology, and that which has come to be.

That gap can potentially be reframed as a normative contradiction within the web of beliefs that comprise the contemporary ideological regime. So framed, the tension can sometimes become the ground for

---

[2] For contemporary theories of ideology see S Zizek (ed), *Mapping Ideology* (London and New York, Verso, 1994).

social movement. Occasionally, when the timing is right, that social movement can invigorate democracy. Even the most robustly democratic social movement will quickly become reformist, however, because the very act of reframing necessarily defers to the ideology's basic norms. Yet while it lasts, that social movement can expose the regime's ideological character, thus subverting its hegemonic power.

In First World contexts, those moments of tension have most often arisen around social exclusions and the injuries to dignity that follow. In a world that promises equal citizenship, how can one bear to be excluded from the full privileges of citizenship because of the person one sleeps with? Some of those moments have given rise to an identity-based social movement that has worked to challenge and invigorate plural democratic projects.

Might an even more powerful kind of ideological unveiling arise from the sorts of tension we hear in the voices from Nima? In that place, people are not so much smarting from social exclusion. Rather, they are swept up in the delights of global culture, chasing down their desire, through plate glass windows and computer screens, with imagined cash. Yet when these people return to their homes on the banks of the Big Gutter, the brutal reality of the neoliberal political economy hits them: 'If you don't pay, you die'.

B On The Shaping of Desire

It has been well documented how global consumer culture has drawn Third World peoples into the 'virtual' enjoyment of high-end consumer goods at the same time that their real fortunes—measured by indicators like life expectancy, infant mortality rates, annual incomes and suicide rates—have often declined. This decline of real fortunes has taken place in the context of an unravelling of the basic public health care system that took place, in part, through the imposition of consumer-oriented health care reforms by the United States and international development agencies.

This disjuncture between the promise of consumer pleasure and the scene of death might be read, in the terms of the new ideological theorists, as a welling up of the real. This welling up does not happen through the sorts of social antagonism, insult and exclusion that lead to identity-based social movement. Rather, it happens through deeply embodied sensations of revulsion, terror and rage.

Such moments expose us, momentarily, to the 'excess' that lies outside the boundaries of what is taken to be the way things are. This excess might be voiced as a contradiction, internal to that ideological order, between the imperative of human survival, on the one hand, and the imperative to organise society according to a market paradigm, on the other. According to that paradigm, basic life necessities become profit-maximising enterprises; citizens become investors and savers; human beings become consumers; and the entire nomos becomes a market backed up by the governance structures that will keep it going.

This scene is a good deal more explosive than the sorts of social antagonism that ground the identity-based social movements that we have come to know in the North. It is the sort of scene that might lead to all kinds of disorder: flamboyant, unimaginable acts of suicidal 'terror,' or global epidemics of suicidal depression and the killer diseases that come in its wake; yearnings for a magical past of indigenous bliss and cultural harmony and the fundamentalist movements dead-set to make it real; half-baked theories of 'alternative development' that talk about hammocks and global convergence instead of exchange rates and bottom lines.

But might this scene, and the contradictions within the prevailing ideology into which it might be translated, also lead to the sort of global social movement that might invigorate democracy in pragmatic ways? How might human rights figure in that possibility? And how might this sort of human-rights-based social movement, within its own culture and performance, replay, rather than undo, the very ideology it seeks to challenge?

In my work in Nima, the people I worked with, particularly the young, had been swept up by 'globalisation'. They wore recycled Levis, tee shirts and jogging shoes. They smoked dope and ate ice cream, when they had the money. They hung out at the city's new shopping mall when they didn't. They read *People Magazine* and watched soap operas and went to palatial temples of worship on their Sabbath. They aspired to work hard and open savings accounts at Barclay's Bank and buy starter houses as soon as they could find steady jobs. They believed in the free market, with a passion. They saw it as the bedrock of democracy. They did not, therefore, object to the idea that they should pay for service at the local health clinic. Indeed, it seemed entirely natural. But, at the same time, they weren't prepared to die.

Consumer culture has repeatedly been identified as a core feature of what I have called liberal ideology, particularly as this ideology has penetrated postcolonial societies. How does such an aspect of ideology work itself inside the intimate parts of the 'self', configuring their very desires in ways that make them willing agents of the ideology's larger political/economic order? What happens to those people in the circumstance—perhaps unthinkable to us, but all too common to people who live in places like Nima—when what they want, in order to be, and what they need, in order to live, seem on a collision course?

How do people who get caught in such a bind deal with the situation? What sense do they make of the policies that give rise to such dilemmas, and the powers behind them? Do they lose faith in themselves, the law or the liberal project itself? Do they dissociate, as the young men who had trained their bowels to be silent for days at a time shared with us as their secret? Do they shoot heroin? Do they give themselves over to suicidal depression? Do they pray for the world, or force their prayers on others? Do they storm the clinic dispensaries, or loot the shopping malls? Do they join Internet chat groups that support global social movement? Do they learn to make bombs? How do these sorts of dilemmas help them, and us, to get some further purchase on the workings of liberal ideology and the subject of resistance to it?

C On Doing Human Rights

The Nima health campaign was posed as an experiment in the use of human rights rhetoric and strategies in community-based social justice activism. Throughout the campaign we looked closely at how what we idiosyncratically called a 'human rights paradigm' was playing out through the work. We took for granted that the use of any 'rights strategy' would inevitably draw upon, and thus reinforce, the syntax and legitimating force of liberal ideology.

To voice injustice as a violation of a 'human right,' one buys-in to a static, atomised notion of the human subject as taking form before the law, and outside its constitutive influence. One is buying-in to a sharp dichotomy between powerless, innocent victims, on the one hand, and all-powerful, evil perpetrators, on the other. One is accepting the notion that justice must be redressed by the unilateral action of patriarchal judges, who divide up social goods into rigidly bounded property entitlements that close other people out at the same time that they compensate for wrongs.

In Nima we were using human rights language and strategies among people from many religious and cultural backgrounds, almost all of whom practised the Muslim faith. Many of us, African and American, did not speak Hausa or people's tribal languages. We had little feel for what the various peoples of Nima would make of the practices and performances that we would take them through in the name of human rights.

And yet, we were increasingly drawn into what we called a 'human rights paradigm' as we felt our way forward in the health campaign. We felt a good deal of danger in using human rights, as if we were playing with fire. Three hopes about the potential of its language and usual practices kept us going.

The first hope has to do with the power of human rights to help common people draw complex maps of power and thus plot out equally complex action strategies. Such complex strategies seemed like a good idea for almost imponderably complex social problems. Thus, the human rights framework helped us to put actions as diverse as negotiations with the local garbage-collection service, petitions to the African Commission on Human and People's Rights and demonstrations at the International Monetary Fund's US headquarters all on the same conceptual page.

The second hope has to do with the power of human rights language to connect us with grassroots groups working on similar social justice issues in 'urban slums' all over the Third World. Such links might promote the sorts of 'cross-learning' that would stretch our own creativity. These links might also invite collaborative social movement action—against the World Bank, for example—when a common issue invited it. The Internet creates the potential for such lateral linkages. Since the mid-1990s, 'human rights' has become a hot concept among large foundations funding grassroots organising work around social and economic inequality. Therefore, given the technological capacities of Internet search engines, it made good sense for us to talk about our work in the same vocabulary that other cyber-linked groups would be likely to use.

Both of these hopes present a common danger. Both might lead us to coach the people of Nima to protest against the violence done to them by the liberal order through the very same scripture and verse that hugely powerful institutions within that order seemed to want them to use. We often saw ourselves as neoliberal missionaries, teaching the natives to wash their hands and kill their mosquitoes in the slums of the capital city, so the European elites would not catch the fever. We played our role with fervour, all the while seeking to disavow the deepest sorts of violence with which we were entangled.

Mainstream human rights principles preach the idea of 'progressive realisation' of their core guarantees, especially in the social and economic rights sphere. Teaching this kind of 'human rights consciousness' to the people of Nima would bind them even more tightly into the tricky net of liberal ideology. Human rights might link them up with Internet buddies and help them target the World Bank as well as domestic courts. Yet it would do so at the heavy cost of keeping their passion in line. Human rights consciousness would train them to think of themselves as good, liberal, rights-consuming subjects as they watched their children die.

V ON ELUDING THE 'REAL'

A third hope that motivated our use of human rights cut against the grain of the first two. I call it the 'face to face'. By that elusive term, I invoke a widespread practice among human rights workers that is motivated more by moral commitments than tactical calculations. This practice puts two ideas into play.

The first idea puts in motion a circle of mutually reinforcing, person-centred norms: dignity, inclusion, voice and the sorts of social and material security that might ground peoples' capacities to take these other values seriously in their social and institutional practices.

The second idea refers to advocacy practices that promote those values—dignity, inclusion, voice, capacity/security—in their methods and their objectives. We were particularly interested in the practices of witnessing, testimony and documentation, in which a human rights worker translates the first-person narrative of an aggrieved person into language that will be moving—indeed, arresting—to a wider global audience. This practice intrigued us for several reasons. It is highly stylised, performative more than instrumental, voice-centred but dyadic. It creates a negative sort of interpersonal space—a gap—around a mutual misrecognition that empathy cannot bridge. Thus the practice arouses powerful, disorienting feelings in the person who purports to witness—guilt, shame, pity, terror, revulsion, awe, passionate commitment, profound rage.

We were well aware that human rights affidavits create Third World victims—'victim pornography', in my students' term. The genre has been persuasively critiqued as one more version of the familiar colonial script: passive, ignorant, long-suffering native subject saved by First World preachers and their God's commandments. And yet, without discounting the plausibility of this script, might this practice also do something different? Might this practice arouse in First World subjects the same sorts of feeling that Third World peoples regularly experience in the grip of the liberal order? Might this practice take us beyond the edge of that ideology, at least for a moment, at the same time that it inevitably holds us securely inside it?

Part II

Global and Regional Perspectives on Social Rights

5

Stuck in a Moment in Time: The International Justiciability of Economic, Social and Cultural Rights

YUVAL SHANY*

I INTRODUCTION

In an Article published in the *American Journal of International Law*[1] the authors—Michael Dennis and David Stewart (both US State Department lawyers)—criticise proposals to introduce a new complaints mechanism to implement the International Covenant on Economic, Social and Cultural Rights (ICESCR).[2] Specifically, they raise a number of objections to the adoption of a new proposed Protocol to the ICESCR (Draft Protocol) that would authorise the UN Committee on Economic, Social and Cultural Rights (CESCR) to exercise quasi-judicial powers of review.[3] Although Dennis and Stewart pay lip-service to the importance of economic, social and cultural rights (hereinafter ESR), they conclude that disputes over compliance of state parties to the ICESCR with their obligations to promote ESR are non-justiciable:

> The rights and obligations contained in the ICESCR were never intended to be susceptible to judicial or quasi-judicial determination. The negotiators and

* The author thanks Ms Nitzan Arad for her assistance in research. He also thanks Prof Frances Raday, Dr Yoram Rabin, Professor Steven Wilf, participants in the Hebrew University law faculty seminar and the editors of this book for their comments on earlier drafts.

[1] MJ Dennis and DP Stewart, 'Justiciability of Economic, Social, and Cultural Rights: Should There be an International Complaints Mechanism to Adjudicate the Rights to Food, Water, Housing, and Health?' (2004) 98 *American Journal of International Law* 462.

[2] International Covenant on Economic, Social and Cultural Rights (adopted 16 December 1966, entered into force 3 January 1976) 993 UNTS 3.

[3] UNSG Note on Draft Optional Protocol to the International Covenant on Economic, Social and Cultural Rights (18 December 1996) E/CN.4/1997/105.

drafters of the Universal Declaration and the two Covenants well understood the differences between economic, social, and cultural rights, on the one hand, and civil and political rights, on the other. Those differences have not disappeared.[4]

Of course, scepticism directed against the potential justiciability of ESR is commonplace, not only in the international law sphere, but also in many domestic law systems. Arguably, ESR, such as the right to 'adequate standard of living'[5] or 'highest attainable level of health'[6] are too vague to be reduced to enforceable legal standards. Furthermore, it has been alleged that even if clear legal standards could be developed, their enforcement would have sweeping redistributive implications, which courts or quasi-judicial committees cannot fully grasp and are, anyway, not competent to decide upon. Instead, decisions on the pace and degree in which ESR should be implemented in a given society should, according to this view, remain in the hands of domestic politicians.

The purpose of the present Article is to support, update and develop the position expressed in part of the existing literature,[7] that ESR are internationally justiciable and can be meaningfully enforced by international courts and tribunals.[8] In particular, I focus on the methodology that could be employed in the adjudication of ESR, ie, on the availability of credible legal methods that could facilitate examination of compliance with international standards. In this regard, I argue that Stewart and Dennis's objections to the development of an ESR complaint mechanism (which also reflect the positions of some states)[9] are lacking in three important respects. First, they largely ignore the multi-faceted nature of ESR and its implications for the feasibility of judicial or quasi-judicial review.[10] Still, the non-binding, yet influential recommendations of the CESR have

---

[4] Dennis and Stewart, above n 1, at 515.

[5] ICESCR, Art 11.

[6] ICESCR, Art 12.

[7] See, in particular, K Arambulo, *Strengthening the Supervision of the International Covenant on Economic, Social and Cultural Rights: theoretical and procedural aspects* (Antwerp, Intersentia, 1999); A Eide, C Krause and A Rosas (eds), *Economic, Social, and Cultural Rights: A Textbook* 2nd edn (Dordecht, Martinus Nijhoff Publishers, 2001); M Pieterse, 'Different Shades of Red: Socio-Economic Dimensions of the Right to Life in South Africa Rights' (1999) 15 *South African Journal on Human Rights* 372.

[8] While the Article focuses on review by international courts or quasi-judicial bodies, analogous arguments could be made with relation to the enforceability of ESR in national courts.

[9] See UNCHR 'Report of the Open-Ended Working Group to Consider Options regarding the Elaboration of an Optional Protocol to the International Covenant on Economic, Social and Cultural Rights on its first session' (23 February – 5 March 2004) UN Doc E/CN.4/2004/44 (2004).

[10] Dennis and Stewart accept that some rights are more capable of implementation than others and that a governmental policy that deliberately inflicts miserable conditions of living upon individuals should entail legal sanctions. Dennis and Stewart, above n 1, at 498, 512. Still, they contest the wisdom of selective enforcement and question the capacity of the CESCR to identify deliberate violations.

endorsed a vision of ESR as comprising different elements, entailing diverse state obligations, with varying redistributive implications.[11] This analytical breakdown of ESR proposed by the Committee could help in identifying some normative elements more prone to judicial scrutiny than others. For example, state measures which directly impede the fulfilment of ESR, such as the regulation of private education institutions or forced evictions of tenants, might be more susceptible to effective international review methods than, say, a general duty to provide health services. Hence a more nuanced approach to the justiciability of ESR is warranted, distinguishing between different normative elements.

Second, Dennis and Stewart offer an 'all or nothing' vision of judicial review—ie, a dichotomist choice between intrusive review by international judicial or quasi-judicial bodies, or no review whatsoever. In reality, however, one may conceive of sophisticated methods of review, which could accommodate many of the concerns of the opposition to judicial review over ESR. For example, courts could supervise the relevant decision-making methods and procedures (eg, transparency, the collection of adequate data), as opposed to reviewing specific outcomes; furthermore, courts may accord state authorities generous margins of appreciation on substantive matters related to the implementation of ESR.[12] Hence many of Dennis and Stewart's arguments could be deflected from objection to judicial review over ESR per se, to a plea for restraint in the application of review powers.

Third, Dennis and Stewart fail to assess the normative and institutional implications of interpretive developments undertaken by the European Court of Human Rights (ECtHR) and other international human rights bodies, which led to identification of 'positive obligation' elements in the first-generation human rights enumerated in the European Convention on Human Rights (ECHR)[13] and the International Covenant on Civil and Political Rights (ICCPR).[14] Arguably, if the ECtHR was able to develop methods for examination of complaints alleging the inadequacy of police efforts to curb crime[15] or the lack of due diligence exercised by welfare agencies in removing children from unfit families,[16] then there would seem to be no a priori bar against the introduction of similar methods for reviewing 'positive' ESR obligations. The growing practice of international

---

[11] See below, Part I.

[12] For analysis of the margin of appreciation doctrine, see Y Shany, 'Toward a General Margin of Appreciation Doctrine in International Law?' (2005) 16 *European Journal of International Law* 907.

[13] Convention for the Protection of Human Rights and Fundamental Freedoms (European Convention on Human Rights, as amended) (ECHR) Art 3.

[14] International Covenant on Civil and Political Rights (adopted 16 December 1966, entered into force 23 March 1976) 999 UNTS 171.

[15] *Osman v UK* (App no 23452/94) ECHR 1998-VIII.

[16] *Z v UK* (App no 29392/95) ECHR 2001-V.

and national courts in exercising review over the fulfilment of ESR-related obligations underscores the feasibility of such a task. Hence the disinclination to apply the same review methods, which were developed to oversee the implementation of civil and political rights, with relation to ESR might suggest a value choice, ie, an objection to the specific redistributive implications of ESR, and not an insurmountable problem of legal methodology.

At the same time, one has to acknowledge that Dennis and Stewart lay down a rather accurate historic narrative which captures the minimalist designs of the drafters of the ICESCR. Indeed, it seems that the drafters of that Covenant never intended to facilitate a judicially enforceable legal text. Still, the question, which Dennis and Stewart do not satisfactorily address, is what weight should be accorded to the original vision of the Covenant drafters, in interpreting the treaty 40 or 50 years later.[17] My position on this question is as follows: although, the intent of the drafters no longer serves as a dominant tool for treaty interpretation projects,[18] there is clearly some mismatch between the modest degree of enforcement originally envisioned by the drafters, and the persistent attempts of CESCR to reinterpret the Covenant in a way which introduces extensive obligations, which are politically and economically onerous. Such mismatch would call for prudence and restraint in the operation of enforcement mechanisms. Hence, as in other areas of international human rights law, development of norms and procedures should go hand-in-hand with legitimacy-enhancing strategies. Still, I argue that the non-mandatory nature of the proposed Protocol (state parties to the ICESCR can choose whether or not to ratify it) and the non-binding character of the Committee's recommendations (or views) thereunder, largely meet the aforementioned legitimacy concerns.

Furthermore, Dennis and Stewart raise important questions of policy pertaining to the *utility* of adjudication as a right-promotion strategy,[19] the institutional capabilities of the CESCR and the overlap between procedures under the proposed Protocol and other international human rights mechanisms.[20] These jurisprudential and practical questions lie beyond the scope of the present Article, although one is inclined to assume that

---

[17] For support of a contrary, 'living document' approach to the interpretation of ESR instruments see, eg, Complaint 14/2003 *International Federation of Human Rights Leagues v France* (ECSR 8 September 2004; hereinafter *FIDH v France*) at para 27: '[the European Social Charter] is a living document dedicated to certain values that inspired it: dignity, autonomy, equality and solidarity'. The decisions of the European Committee of Social Rights (ECSR) on specific complaints can be accessed at: <http://www.coe.int/t/e/human_rights/esc/4_Collective_complaints/List_of_collective_complaints/default.asp#TopOfPage>.

[18] Vienna Convention on the Law of Treaties (adopted 23 May 1969, entered into force 27 January 1980) 1155 UNTS 331 Arts 31–32.

[19] Dennis and Stewart, above n 1, 467.

[20] *Ibid*, 502–11.

individuals or groups interested in utilising an ESR complaints mechanism act in their self-interest, and that, at least in some cases, their actions (combined, no doubt with other social change strategies) are generally beneficial, ie, coincide with notions of general societal welfare.[21] Similarly, I will not deal here with the practical resource constraints, which hinder the efforts of the Committee to meet even its current workload. I will assume, for the sake of the present argument, that the entry into force of a Protocol that would significantly expand the powers of the CESCR would require changes in the Committee's working methods and in the resources made available to it. Furthermore, I will assume that any conflict between the powers of the CESCR under the proposed Protocol and other international agencies (which have, generally speaking, only limited individual complaint adjudication functions) can be accommodated through the introduction of proper jurisdiction-regulation provisions into the proposed Protocol.[22]

This Article will thus focus on the normative and institutional post-1966 developments which underlie the claim that ESR are nowadays internationally justiciable as a matter of legal methodology, in the sense that there exist reasonably clear legal criteria for their implementation, which entail politically acceptable consequences. Part II describes the initial difficulties of extrapolating precise normative prescriptions from the vague and relative provisions of the ICESCR. It then explains the four principal interpretive strategies developed by the CESCR in order to overcome these difficulties and to concretise the obligations of states under the ICESCR: (a) enumeration of specific normative contents; (b) utilisation of indicators and benchmarks to assess and encourage progress; (c) identification of divergent types of state obligations; and (d) identification of different timeframes for implementation of ESR. I argue that these developments facilitate the creation of sufficiently clear legal criteria for judicial or quasi-judicial implementation. Part III addresses the feasibility of judicial review over ESR under the new Protocol in the light of the parallel efforts of international and national judicial and quasi-judicial bodies. Part IV draws links between the question of justiciability of ESR and the growing acceptance of the proposition that first-generation human rights also entail 'positive state obligations' with largely open-ended redistributive implications. Part V concludes by offering guidelines for international quasi-judicial review over the implementation of the ICESCR and by addressing the legitimacy of the exercise of such quasi-judicial powers.

---

21 For discussion of the utility in adopting a new Protocol, see MCR Craven, *The International Covenant on Economic, Social and Cultural Rights: A Perspective on its Development* (Oxford, Clarendon Press, 1995) 100–102.

22 See, generally, Y Shany, *The Competing Jurisdictions of International Courts and Tribunals* (Oxford, Oxford University Press, 2003).

II CONCRETISING ECONOMIC AND SOCIAL RIGHTS: THE INTERPRETIVE EFFORTS OF THE COMMITTEE ON ECONOMIC, SOCIAL AND CULTURAL RIGHTS

A The Challenge of Concretising the ICESCR

There is little question that the language used by the ICESCR in describing the scope and nature of the obligations imposed upon its member states raises formidable challenges for any norm-application project, which cast serious doubts over the justiciability of ESR. In particular, one can identify the following features, common to all or many of the rights enumerated in the ICESCR, that complicate attempts to deduce meaningful legal guidance from the provisions of the Covenant:

— *Loose formulations* — some ESR are defined by way of flexible legal standards, which provide member states with limited conduct guidance. For example, Article 9 of the Covenant protects 'the right of everyone to social security, including social insurance'; Article 11 covers 'the right of everyone to an adequate standard of living for himself and his family, including adequate food, clothing and housing, and to the continuous improvement of living conditions'[23]; and Article 12 encompasses 'the right of everyone to the enjoyment of the highest attainable standard of physical and mental health'.[24] While, admittedly, some first generation rights are also formulated in ambiguous language, the intensive practice of national legal systems in implementing them has improved their clarity.

— *Freedom to choose means of implementation* — Article 2(1) of the ICESCR provides that the full realisation of the Covenant ought to be achieved by 'all appropriate means'. Similar open-ended language is also used with relation to some specific ESR provisions.[25] According to the CESCR, these formulations imply that member states retain wide discretion in deciding how to implement the Covenant.[26]

— *Relativity* — all ESR identified in the ICESCR are subject to Article 2(1) of the Covenant, which links between the state parties' duty to

---

[23] While ICESCR, Art 11(2) provides some guidance on the method of implementing the right to food, there is no similar guidance on the implementation of other specific components of the right to an adequate standard of living.

[24] One should note that ICECR, Art 12(2) contains some specific obligations related to the right to health. However, this list of specific obligations is clearly not exhaustive of the general right laid out in Art 12(1).

[25] ICESCR, Arts 6(1), 11(1), 13(2)(b), 13(2)(c) and 14.

[26] UN Committee on Economic, Social and Cultural Rights 'General Comment 3: The Nature of States Parties Obligations' (14 December 1990) UN Doc E/1991/23, annex III at 86, at para 4 ('each State party must decide for itself which means are the most appropriate under the circumstances with respect to each of the rights').

implement ESR and the availability of adequate resources, and to Article 4, which permits limiting ESR in order to promote the general welfare in a democratic society. Additional limitation provisions exist vis-à-vis the special needs of developing countries[27] and some of the specific rights enumerated in the Covenant.[28]

— *Progressive implementation* — Article 2(1) of the ICESCR allows states to gradually implement the ESR enumerated in the Covenant. Additional 'progressive realisation' prescriptions are found in some other provisions protecting specific ESR.[29]

This combination of flexible terms, broad powers of discretion, generous limitation provisions and uncertain timetable for implementation has led some observers to regard the ICESCR as a programmatic or aspirational text, entailing no genuine legal obligations.[30] In the same vein, the inability to deduce precise legal standards from these open-ended formulations has encouraged the view that ESR are non-justiciable.[31]

B The Principal Interpretive Moves Adopted by the CESCR

The CESCR is an 18-member expert body established in 1985 by the UN Economic and Social Council to monitor, on its behalf, the implementation of the ICESCR by the member states (as of today, 156 states are parties to the Covenant).[32] Given its expertise, mandate and cumulative experience in assessing national compliance with international ESR standards, the Committee is particularly well-situated to devise interpretation strategies which could flesh-out the obligations under the Covenant in ways which

---

[27] ICESCR, Art 2(3).

[28] ICESCR, Arts 8(1)(a), 8(1)(c), 8(1)(d), 8(2), 10(1), 13(2)(d) and 13(3).

[29] ICESCR, Arts 13(2)(b), 13(2)(c) and 14.

[30] For discussion see, eg: P Harvey 'Aspirational Law' (2004) 52 *Buffalo Law Review* 701, 709; JK Mapulanga-Hulston, 'Examining the Justiciability of Economic, Social and Cultural Right' (2002) 6 *The International Journal of Human Rights* 29; Dennis and Stewart, above n 1, 464.

[31] Dennis and Stewart, above n 1, 464; AL Bendor, 'Are There Any Limits to Justiciability? The Jurisprudential and Constitutional Controversy in Light of the Israeli and American Experience' (1996–97) 7 *Indiana International & Comparative Law Review* 311.

[32] UN Economic and Social Council Res 1985/17 'Review of the composition, organisation and administrative arrangements of the Sessional Working Group of Governmental Experts on the Implementation of the International Covenant on Economic, Social and Cultural Rights' (28 May 1985) UN Doc S/RES/1985/17. It is interesting to note that, unlike other treaty bodies (such as the Human Rights Committee or the Committee against Torture) which had been created by the relevant treaties enumerating the rights monitored by them, the ICESCR invested monitoring powers only with the UN Economic and Social Council. Still, the Council established the CESCR in order to assist it in carrying out its responsibilities under the Covenant. This configuration of authorities is perhaps indicative of the ICSECR drafters' reluctance to subject ESR to intrusive monitoring procedures. See Dennis and Stewart, above n 1, 477. Still, in practice, it is difficult to identify significant differences between the method of operation or influence of the CESCR and the other treaty monitoring bodies.

could be politically acceptable to the member states (note that the CESCR cannot issue binding decisions and mainly relies on dialogue, persuasion and subtle pressures).[33]

In its work, since 1987, the Committee has developed four principal interpretive strategies aimed at elucidating the specific obligations introduced by the ICESCR. While some of these interpretive moves may be open to criticism, they have been generally accepted by the member states (or, at least, not openly challenged by them).[34] At all events, the very existence of these methods of interpretation underlines the feasibility of developing workable methodologies for implementing ESR and exercising judicial or quasi-judicial review over them. In other words, the putative need to fine-tune the interpretive moves developed by the CESCR does not negate the proposition that such moves *can* be developed.

C Enumerating Specific Normative Contents

One avenue pursued by the CESCR was to identify, in the eighteen General Comments[35] it has issued to date, some specific normative contents of the Covenant, ie, specific obligations deriving from the general standards introduced by the Covenant. The elaboration of these specific requirements helps to overcome some of the problems associated with the vagueness of the ESR covered by the Covenant.

For example, in General Comment 4 on the right to adequate housing (which comprises part of the right to adequate standard of living provided in Article 11), the Committee identified seven tests of adequacy, which facilitate the review of whether member states have fulfilled their obligation to recognise that right: legal security of tenure, availability of services, materials, facilities and infrastructure, affordability, habitability, accessibility, location and cultural adequacy.[36] The Comment then offers more precise guidelines on the application of these specific standards to the domestic housing conditions of the member states (eg, access to water, protection from weather hazards, proximity to schools, etc).[37] In the same

---

[33] See Craven, above n 21, 91.

[34] *Ibid*, 91–2.

[35] General Comments are non-binding interpretive statements periodically issued by the CESCR (as well as other UN human rights treaty bodies). They serve an important function in elucidating the scope and nature of the member states' obligations under the ICESCR. M Nowak, *UN Covenant on Civil and Political Rights: CCPR Commentary* (Kehl, NP Engel, 1993), XXIV.

[36] UN Committee on Economic, Social and Cultural Rights 'General Comment 4: The Right to Adequate Housing' (13 December 1991) UN Doc E/1992/23, annex III, 114, para 8.

[37] *Ibid*. General Comment 7 has elaborated upon the application of the right to adequate housing in forced eviction cases: UN Committee on Economic, Social and Cultural Rights 'General Comment 7: Forced Evictions, and the Right to Adequate Housing,' (25 May 1997) UN Doc E/1998/22, annex IV, 113.

vein, General Comment 14 on the right to the highest attainable level of health (Article 12) identified four more specific parameters for ascertaining the propriety of the health services existing in a particular member state: availability, accessibility, acceptability and quality.[38] Once again, the Comment provided more precise guidelines on the application of the enumerated parameters (eg, availability of essential drugs identified by the WHO and skilled health personnel, proximity of health facility to all population sections, adherence to codes of medical ethics).[39] Similar enumerative exercises have been undertaken by the CESCR in relation to other Covenant rights[40] and the application of Covenant rights to particular groups of individuals with special needs (eg, persons with disabilities or old persons)[41] or to special circumstances (eg, economic sanctions).[42]

D Utilisation of Indicators and Benchmarks

Another important method utilised by the CESCR to assess the status of implementation of the Covenant by the member states has been the development of indicators and benchmarks.[43] Indicators use measurable and processed data, and purport to reflect some aspects of the domestic conditions which ESR regulate. For example, the CESCR has examined during its inspection of state reports on the implementation of the Covenant existing poverty rates,[44] unemployment rates,[45] levels of participation

[38] UNCESCR, 'General Comment 14: The Right to the Highest Attainable Standard of Health' (11 August 2000) UN Doc E/C.12/2000/4, para 12.

[39] *Ibid.*

[40] UNCESCR, 'General Comment 11: Plans of Action for Primary Education' (10 May 1999) UN Doc E/C.12/1999/4; UNCESCR, 'General Comment 12: Right to Adequate Food' (12 May 1999) UN Doc E/C.12/1999/5; UNCESCR, 'General Comment 13: The Right to Education' (8 December 1999) UN Doc E/C.12/1999/10; UNCESCR, 'General Comment 15: The Right to Water' (20 January 2003) UN Doc E/C.12/2002/11; UNCESCR, 'General Comment 16: The Equal Right of Men and Women to the Enjoyment of all Economic, Social and Cultural Rights' (11 August 2005) UN Doc E/C.12/2005/4; UNCESCR, 'General Comment 17: The Right of Everyone to Benefit from the Protection of Moral and Material Interests resulting from any Scientific, Literary or Artistic Production of which he is the Author' (12 January 2006) UN Doc E/C.12/GC/17); UNCESCR, 'The Right to Work' (6 February 2006) UN Doc E/C.12/GC/18.

[41] UNCESCR, 'General Comment No 5: Persons with Disabilities' (9 December 1994), UN Doc E/1995/22, 19; UNCESCR, 'General comment No 6: The Economic, Social and Cultural Rights of Older Persons' (8 December 1995) UN Doc E/1996/22, 20.

[42] UNCESCR, 'General Comment 8: The Relationship Between Economic Sanctions and Respect for Economic, Social and Cultural Rights' (12 December 1997) UN Doc E/C.12/1997/8.

[43] See generally, Craven, above n 21, 117–20.

[44] See, eg, UNCESCR 'Conclusions and Recommendations of the Committee on Economic, Social and Cultural Rights: Estonia' (19 December 2002) UN Doc E/C.12/1/Add.85, para 22.

[45] See, eg, UNCESCR 'Conclusions and Recommendations of the Committee on Economic, Social and Cultural Rights: Denmark' (14 December 2004) UN Doc E/C.12/1/Add.102, para 15.

in the workforce,[46] salary charts disaggregated on the basis of gender,[47] costs of the monthly 'food basket',[48] annual per capita spending on public health, HIV prevalence rate,[49] infant mortality rate,[50] life expectancy, adolescent pregnancy figures,[51] illiteracy rates,[52] school drop-out rates[53] and other indicators. The Committee also urged states on a number of occasions to develop additional indicators which could assist in measuring their progress towards the full implementation of the Covenant.[54]

Even more significant had been the Committee's effort to develop, together with member states, benchmarks, ie, measurable targets which should be achieved, as a rule, within a designated period of time, and plans of action designed to facilitate movement towards the benchmarks. For example, Ireland was requested by the Committee in 2002 to make good on its undertaking to solve the housing needs of families residing in improvised 'traveller community' camps by 2004[55]; Italy was required in 2004 to include 'in its next periodic report, specific benchmarks in relation to chronic diseases, old age and disability, supplemented by disaggregated data, and on a comparative basis for the entire reporting period, to enable the Committee to assess how the right to health, in line with the Committee's general Comment No. 14, has been realised'[56]; Jamaica was urged in 2001 to develop benchmarks on teenage pregnancy[57]; the Republic of Korea was requested in 2001 to provide the CESCR with 'a reasonable timetable for specific actions for the introduction of free and compulsory secondary education'[58]; Russia was asked in 2003 to provide the

---

[46] UNCESCR 'Conclusions and Recommendations of the Committee on Economic, Social and Cultural Rights: Malta' (14 December 2004) UN Doc E/C.12/1/Add.101, para 14.

[47] See, eg,: UNCESCR 'Conclusions and Recommendations of the Committee on Economic, Social and Cultural Rights: Colombia' (30 November 2001) UN Doc E/C.12/1/Add.74, para 16.

[48] UNCESCR 'Conclusions and Recommendations of the Committee on Economic, Social and Cultural Rights: Mexico' (8 December 1999)UN Doc E/C.12/1/Add.41, para 20.

[49] UNCESCR 'Conclusions and Recommendations of the Committee on Economic, Social and Cultural Rights: Republic of Moldova' (12 December 2003) UN Doc E/C.12/1/Add.91, para 26.

[50] See, eg, UNCESCR 'Conclusions and Recommendations of the Committee on Economic, Social and Cultural Rights: Italy' (14 December 2004) UN Doc E/C.12/1/Add.103, para 9.

[51] See, eg, UNCESCR 'Conclusions and Recommendations of the Committee on Economic, Social and Cultural Rights: Honduras' (21 May 2001) UN Doc E/C.12/1/Add.57, para 27.

[52] See, eg, UNCESCR 'Conclusions and Recommendations of the Committee on Economic, Social and Cultural Rights: Canada' (10 December 1998) UN Doc E/C.12/1/Add.31, para 38.

[53] See, eg, UNCESCR 'Conclusions and Recommendations of the Committee on Economic, Social and Cultural Rights: Georgia' (19 December 2002) UN Doc E/C.12/1/Add.83, para 27.

[54] See, eg, UNCESCR 'Conclusions and Recommendations of the Committee on Economic, Social and Cultural Rights: Iceland,' (23 May 2003) UN Doc E/C.12/1/Add.89, para 27.

[55] UNCESCR 'Conclusions and Recommendations of the Committee on Economic, Social and Cultural Rights: Ireland' (5 June 2002) UN Doc E/C.12/1/Add.77, paras 32–33.

[56] CESCR, Conclusions on Italy, above n 50, para 49.

[57] UNCESCR 'Conclusions and Recommendations of the Committee on Economic, Social and Cultural Rights: Jamaica' (30 November 2001) UN Doc E/C.12/1/Add.75, para 30.

[58] UNCESCR 'Conclusions and Recommendations of the Committee on Economic, Social and Cultural Rights: Republic of Korea' (21 May 2001) UN Doc E/C.12/1/Add.59, para 42.

Committee in its 2008 report with 'updated statistical information on a comparative basis on the results of the efforts undertaken to reduce the number of people living below the subsistence minimum to 28-30 million by 2006'[59]; and Zambia was urged to 'strengthen its National Strategic Plan to ensure that its objective of providing 9 years of free and compulsory basic education by 2015 would be reached' and 'to set up both intermediate goals and concrete and measurable benchmarks in this regard'.[60]

The introduction of an ever-increasing number of indicators and benchmarks helps to overcome much of the ambiguity associated with the text of the ICESCR and enables the Committee to assess the actual degree to which the Covenant has been successfully implemented by particular member states. Furthermore, this development circumvents many of the interpretive problems arising out of the progressive nature of the obligations under the Covenant: states are prodded to meet specific objectives in specified time frames, or at least to report within fixed time periods on their progress towards meeting these objectives. The encouragement of member states to undertake to execute specific plans of actions designed to meet the mutually developed benchmarks further erodes the scope of discretion retained by member states over the manner of implementing the Covenant, and commits states to specific targets and measures.

E Identifying Divergent Types of State Obligations

The third interpretive strategy adopted by the CESCR has been to break down the obligations imposed upon member states by the ICESCR into three principal types of obligations: duties to respect, duties to protect and duties to fulfil. The latter duties have been subsequently divided into three more specific obligations: the duty to facilitate, the duty to promote and the duty to provide.[61] The analytical elaboration and classification of different types of state obligation, set out below, not only increases legal certainty: it also provides useful tools for assessing the justiciability of ESR. This is especially so because parallel types of classifications have been developed by international courts and tribunals with relation to the first-generation

---

[59] UNCESCR 'Conclusions and Recommendations of the Committee on Economic, Social and Cultural Rights: Russian Federation' (12 December 2003) UN Doc E/C.12/1/Add.94, para 53.

[60] UNCESCR 'Conclusions and Recommendations of the Committee on Economic, Social and Cultural Rights, Zambia' (23 June 2005) UN Doc E/C.12/1/Add.106, para 54.

[61] *Minister of Health & Others v Treatment Action Campaign & Others* 2002 (10) BCLR 1033 (CC) 43 (S. Afr.) (hereinafter *TAC*): 'Sections 27(1) and 27(2) [of the South African Constitution, providing for the right to health] must be read together as defining the scope of the positive rights that everyone has and the corresponding obligations on the State to "respect, protect, promote and fulfil" such rights'.

obligations of states parties to instruments such as the ICCPR and the ECHR. Consequently, comparisons can be made between the manner of implementing the two generations of rights and the feasibility of exercising judicial or quasi-judicial review over them.

—Duty to respect

According to the CESCR, all ESR entail a negative obligation on the part of government to refrain from preventing the enjoyment of these rights by individuals protected by the Covenant. For example, states should not prevent the delivery of food aid to conflict regions,[62] they should normally refrain from closing private schools,[63] they should not engage in pollution-generating activities with adverse health or access to water implications[64] and nor should they bar contraceptives designed to prevent sexually transmittable diseases.[65]

—Duty to protect

In addition to the duty to respect ESR, member states are also required to protect these rights from infringement by third persons, eg, commercial enterprises, religious organisations, private persons, etc. For example, states should ensure that parents do not bar their girls from attending school,[66] that traditional female genital mutilation practices are abolished,[67] and that business practices of drinking water-supplying private companies are regulated.[68]

—Duty to fulfil

Finally, states should take a variety of implementation measures needed to effectively fulfil their ESR obligations. These include acts designed to ensure access of individuals and communities to ESR (duty to facilitate), such as the creation of medical insurance programmes[69] and monitoring the affordability of water prices[70]; acts designed to create general conditions for the enjoyment of ESR (duty to promote), such as national immunisation programmes,[71] treatment of environmental risks,[72] adequate teacher training[73] and the sustainable utilisation of water

---

[62] CESCR, General Comment 12, above n 40, paras 15, 19.

[63] CESCR, General Comment 13, above n 40, para 50.

[64] CESCR, General Comment 14, above n 38, para 34; CESCR, General Comment 15, above n 40, para 21.

[65] CESCR, General Comment 14, above n 38, para 34.

[66] CESCR, General Comment 13, above n 40, para 50.

[67] CESCR, General Comment 14, above n 38, para 35.

[68] CESCR, General Comment 15, above n 40, para 24. For a more general discussion of the application of ESR to private actors, see Craig Scott, 'Multinational Enterprises and Emergent Jurisprudence on Violations of Economic, Social and Cultural Rights' in Eide, above n 7, 563.

[69] CESCR, General Comment 14, above n 38, para 36.

[70] CESCR, General Comment 15, above n 40, para 27.

[71] CESCR, General Comment 14, above n 38, para 36.

[72] *Ibid*, para 36.

[73] CESCR, General Comment 13, above n 40, para 50.

sources[74]; and direct provision of essential services if all other strategies of fulfilling ESR fail (duty to provide). The latter group of obligations might include provision of food to victims of natural disasters,[75] the provision of free primary education[76] and the provision of basic health and sanitation services in all areas of the country.[77]

The analytical identification of different types of state obligations has significant implications for assessing the justiciability of ESR. Surely, negative obligations raise fewer objections to judicial or quasi-judicial oversight, inter alia, because their redistributive implications are usually negligible. Furthermore, as Part IV indicates, human rights courts are already well accustomed in reviewing state's omissions to protect individuals from right-infringing conduct perpetrated by third parties.[78] Hence the exercise of review over, at least, some types of ESR-related obligations does not seem to exceed the capacities of current review methodologies employed by international human rights bodies.

F Identifying Divergent Time Frames for Implementation

The fourth and last interpretive strategy embraced by the CESCR addresses the ambiguities caused by the progressive nature of the Covenant. In its 1990 General Comment No 3, on the nature of the member states' obligations, the Committee proposed the following legal construction:

—The progressive nature of the ICESCR requires states to start taking concrete steps towards the full realisation of ESR within a reasonably short time after ratification.[79] Hence, the Covenant imposes a duty to 'move forward', and retrogressive measures create a rebuttable presumption of inconsistency with the progressive obligations it introduces.[80]

—Some core elements of ESR, which are essential for ensuring minimal level of rights enjoyment, should be implemented immediately, and failure to do so would constitute a prima facie violation of the Covenant.[81] These core elements include the availability to the vast majority of the population of 'essential foodstuffs, of essential primary health care, of basic shelter and housing, or of the most basic forms of

---

[74] CESCR, General Comment 15, above n 40, para 28.
[75] CESCR, General Comment 12, above n 40, para 15.
[76] CESCR, General Comment 13, above n 40, para 48
[77] CESCR, General Comment 14, above n 38, para 36; CESCR, General Comment 15, above n 40, para 29.
[78] See below, part III.
[79] CESCR, General Comment No 3, above n 26, para 2.
[80] *Ibid*, para 9.
[81] *Ibid*, para 10.

education'.[82] Here too, the burden would rest with the member states to demonstrate that their failure to meet core obligations derived from the inadequacy of the resources they possess (including inability to shift resources from non-core expenditures and failure to secure international support).[83]

—Some other elements of ESR, which do not entail significant resource expenditure, are capable of immediate application, and their inapplicability would be 'difficult to sustain'.[84] These include some legislative arrangements (eg, non-discrimination provisions), regulation of relations between private individuals (eg, labour conditions and the right to unionise), negative obligations (eg, the right to establish private schools and the respect of scientific freedom) and judicial review over the implementation of these elements.[85]

The result of these four developments is that the CESCR has been able to significantly concretise the obligations incurred by member states upon ratification of the ICESCR. The contents of ESR (ie, the end result of the progressive implementation process) and the nature of the obligations appertaining to different normative elements have been elaborated; a methodology for gauging the degree of fulfilment has been developed; and the latitude granted to states with respect to the pace and manner of implementation has been considerably narrowed down. The greater clarity produced by these developments provides potential background conditions for exercising judicial or quasi-judicial review over the implementation process.[86] This last conclusion is further underscored by recent developments in regional human rights bodies and some domestic courts, which demonstrate the possibility of monitoring compliance with ESR obligations in what seems to be a politically acceptable manner.

III COMPARATIVE ASSESSMENT I: RECENT DEVELOPMENTS IN THE JUDICIAL OR QUASI-JUDICIAL ENFORCEMENT OF ESR AT THE REGIONAL AND NATIONAL LEVEL

A Regional Developments

The move towards greater justiciability of ESR, ie, norm elucidation and proposals to create a complaint-based mechanism, are certainly not unique to the CESCR. Indeed, comparable developments can be identified in recent

---

[82] *Ibid*. This list has been expanded upon and developed in subsequent General Comments.
[83] CESCR, General Comment No 3, above n 26, paras 10 and 13; Craven, above n 21, 144–45.
[84] *Ibid*, para 5.
[85] *Ibid*.
[86] See Craven, above n 21, 101–102.

years in regional human rights frameworks; furthermore, some national courts are also showing a greater inclination to engage in the judicial enforcement of ESR.

With the exception of the right to education, which has been incorporated in Article 2 of the First Protocol to the ECHR, ESR are generally protected by the Council of Europe's human rights mechanism through its 1961 Social Charter,[87] a treaty that is roughly parallel in its contents to the ICSECR. Significantly, the Charter is enforced not through the ECtHR, but rather through a weaker body, the European Committee of Social Rights (ECSR), a 13-member committee of independent experts, which oversees the state parties' reports and issues its recommendations. Still, in 1998 a Protocol to the Charter, facilitating the establishment of a complaint mechanism,[88] entered into force (the Protocol has been ratified to date by 17 member states).[89] According to the Protocol, international employers or trade union organisations, or other international non-governmental organisations enjoying a consultative status with the Council of Europe (more than 60 eligible NGOs have registered to date with the Council), may lodge a complaint with the ECSR against a member state that has allegedly breached its obligations under the Charter.[90] The complaints are then reviewed by the Committee, which may issue its recommendations to the state complained against and to the other member states.[91]

Between 1997 and 2005, the ESCR has received 32 complaints (a rather impressive figure, given the limited number of ratifications of the Protocol and the stringent admissibility conditions), 29 of which were found admissible. In these cases, the Committee found a violation of the Charter on 15 occasions and held in eight other cases that no violations had been proved. The other complaints were still pending in late 2006.

Review of the 23 complaints cases that were decided, by 2006, on the merits (grouped into 14 categories of cases) demonstrates, by and large, the workability of the European ESR complaint mechanism:

1. In *International Commission of Jurists v Portugal,* the ECSR held that Portugal has violated its obligation under the Charter to curb child

---

[87] European Social Charter.

[88] Additional Protocol to the European Social Charter Providing for a System of Collective Complaints (hereinafter Complaints Protocol).

[89] Member states to the 1995 Protocol include: Belgium, Croatia, Cyprus, Finland, France, Greece, Ireland, Italy, The Netherlands, Norway, Portugal and Sweden. Seven additional Council of Europe member states signed the Protocol but have not yet ratified it.

[90] If member states agree, representative national employers or trade unions may also lodge complaints under the mechanism. However, until now, only one member state, Finland, has authorised the ECSR to receive complaints from national NGOs.

[91] Complaints Protocol, above n 88, Art 8. For an overview of the Collective Complaints Procedure under the Social Charter, see DJ Harris and J Darcy, *The European Social Charter* 2nd edn (Ardsley, Transnational Publishers, 2001) 354–70.

labour, after it had been shown that thousands of children under the age of 15 work in various places of employment, including dangerous industries, and that efforts by the Portuguese Labour Inspectorate to improve upon the situation have been meagre.[92]

2. In three cases brought by the European Federation of Employees in Public Services, the Committee held that restrictions in France, Italy and Portugal upon the organisation of military personnel were compatible with the relevant right to organise provisions of the Charter.[93] In a fourth case, the Committee confirmed the reasonableness of certain restrictions imposed upon trade unions representing the Portuguese Public Security Police.[94]

3. In *Syndicat national des professions du tourisme v France*, the Committee held that restrictions on access to historic and cultural sites that were placed upon non-accredited French tour guides were discriminatory in nature.[95]

4. In *International Federation of Human Rights Leagues v Greece*, the Committee found three provisions of Greece law, pertaining to the mobilisation of the civilian population in times of emergency and the inability of military personnel to resign their posts, to violate the Charter's prohibition against forced labour.[96]

5. In *Quaker Council for European Affairs v Greece*, the ECSR found that the legal requirement that conscientious objectors serve in civic service for a period of time longer by 18 months than their counterparts who report for compulsory military service represents an excessive restriction on the objectors' freedom of employment.[97]

6. In *Confédération française de l'Encadrement v France*, the Committee held that French legislation does not adequately guarantee a reasonable weekly cap on the working hours of individuals in managerial positions, or a reasonable payment of overtime salary.[98] Two subsequent procedures reviewing amendments in the relevant French legislation concluded that the new legislation did not remove the inconsistencies between French labour law and the Charter. Furthermore, the ECSR

[92] Complaint 1/1998 *International Commission of Jurists v Portugal* (ECSR 9 September 1999).

[93] Complaint 2/1999 *European Federation of Employees in Public Services v France* (ECSR 4 December 2000); Complaint 4/1999 *European Federation of Employees in Public Services v Italy* (ECSR 4 December 2000); Complaint 5/1999 *European Federation of Employees in Public Services v Portugal* (ECSR 4 December 2000).

[94] Complaint 11/2000 *European Council of Police Trade Unions v Portugal* (ECSR 21 May 2002).

[95] Complaint 6/1999 *Syndicat national des professions du tourisme v France* (ECSR 10 October 2000).

[96] Complaint 7/2000 *International Federation of Human Rights Leagues v Greece* (ECSR 5 December 2000).

[97] Complaint 8/2000 *Quaker Council for European Affairs v Greece* (ECSR 25 April 2001).

[98] Complaint 9/2000 *Confédération française de l'Encadrement v France* (ECSR November 2001).

held that the designation of 'on-call' time in the new legislation as rest time violates the Charter's reasonable work and rest hour provisions.[99]

7. In *STTK Ry v Finland*, the Committee held that the refusal by the Finnish government to provide for reduced working hours for hospital personnel exposed to ionizing radiation violates its obligations under the Charter to ensure safe working conditions.[100]

8. In *Confederation of Swedish Enterprise v Sweden*, the ECSR held that toleration of pre-entry closed shop collective agreements (agreements granting preference in hiring to unionised workers) violates Sweden's obligation to respect the workers' right not to organise.[101]

9. In *International Association Autism—Europe v France*, the Committee found French policies regarding the education of autistic children to be inadequate given the very low percentage of their integration in the ordinary and special education systems. The Committee also characterised the definition of autism employed by the French government as overly restrictive.[102]

10. In *International Federation of Human Rights Leagues v France*, the Committee held that the exclusion of illegal immigrants from health coverage programmes (other than treatment in emergency or life-threatening situations) violates France's obligations under the Charter to guarantee the provision of care and assistance to children and young adults.[103]

11. In *European Roma Rights Centre v Greece*, the ECSR held that the substandard conditions of housing in which an excessive number of Roma families reside, combined with the lack of diligence on the part of the Greek government in designating appropriate encampment sites and the widespread practice of forced evictions of Roma settlements, all constitute a violation of Article 16 of the Charter, which requires social, legal and economic protection of the family. The Committee also criticised the Greek government's failure to assess the size of the Roma population and to provide information on the scope of its forced eviction practices. [104]

12. In *World Organisation against Torture v Greece*, the Committee held that Greek law does not provide adequate guarantees for children against corporal punishment at home and in schools, and is thus

---

[99] Complaint 16/2003 *Confédération française de l'Encadrement v France* (ECSR 12 October 2004); Complaint 22/2003 *Confédération générale du travail v France* (ECSR 7 December 2004).

[100] Complaint 10/2000 *STTK Ry v Finland* (ECSR 17 October 2001).

[101] Complaint 12/2002 *The Confederation of Swedish Enterprise v Sweden* (ECSR 15 May 2003).

[102] Complaint 13/2002 *International Association Autism – Europe v France* (ECSR 4 November 2003).

[103] *FIDH v France*, above n 17.

[104] Complaint 15/2003 *European Roma Rights Centre v Greece* (ECSR 8 December 2004).

incompatible with Article 17 of the Charter (protection of children and young adults).[105] Similar decisions had been issued by the ECSR in relation to corporal punishment at homes and foster homes in Ireland and Belgium.[106] However, in other cases the Committee found the legal prohibition on corporal punishment in Italy and Portugal to be adequate.[107]

13. In *Syndicat occitan de l'éducation v France*, the Committee held that the requirements of representativity introduced in the French legislation governing eligibility to serve in public consultative bodies are reasonable and conform to Articles 5 and 6 of the Charter (the rights to organise and to collective bargaining).[108] Similarly, it was held that the election process of trade union representatives to the French National Council for Higher Education and Research falls within the wide margin of appreciation afforded to states in determining the composition of consultative bodies, not directly related to collective bargaining.[109]

14. In *Centrale générale des services publics v Belgium*, the ECSR held that Article 6(1) of the Charter, which requires consultations between workers and employers, cannot be read so as to require legislatures to consult with trade unions over legislative amendments, stating that the legislative process was found to be within 'the prerogative of sovereign States'.[110]

These decisions of the ECSR are instructive for several reasons. First, they clearly support the view that ESR are jusiticiable, ie, that clear legal standards can be developed to effectively examine the degree and propriety of their implementation.[111] Second, review of these decisions indicates that the Committee is most effective in evaluating the compatibility of legislation with the requirements of the Charter (eg, in the French working hours case, the Greek forced labour case and the corporal punishment cases). Still, it has also not shied away, on occasion, from critically evaluating social conditions on the ground (eg, in the Greek Roma and the Portuguese child labour cases). In other words, the Committee is capable of reviewing implementation both in law and in fact. Third, the jurisprudence of the ECSR reveals important methodological choices which facilitate the

---

105 Complaint 17/2003 *World Organisation against Torture v Greece* (ECSR 7 December 2004).

106 Complaint 18/2003 *World Organisation against Torture v Ireland* (ECSR 7 December 2004); Complaint 21/2003 *World Organisation against Torture v Belgium* (ECSR 7 December 2004).

107 Complaint 19/2003 *World Organisation against Torture v Italy* (ECSR 7 December 2004); Complaint 20/2003 *World Organisation against Torture v Portugal* (ECSR 7 December 2004).

108 Complaint 23/2003 *Syndicat occitan de l'éducation v France* (ECSR 7 September 2004).

109 Complaint 26/2004 *Syndicat des Agrégés de l'Enseignement Supérieur v France* (ECSR 15 June 2005).

110 Complaint 25/2004 *Centrale générale des services publics v Belgium* (ECSR 9 May 2005).

adjudication of ESR claims: the use of statistical information (eg, in the Portuguese child labour and the French autistic children case), the shifting of burdens of proof (eg, in the Greek Roma and the Finnish radiation workers cases) and the grant of the margin of appreciation to member states (in the French union election cases).

Significantly, the reaction of the Committee of Ministers of the Council of Europe to the decisions of the ECSR demonstrates the political acceptability of this line of jurisprudence. For example, in Resolution ChS (99) 4, the Committee (which includes representatives of all 39 state parties to the Charter, including states not parties to the Complaints Protocol) required Portugal to report on the application of the ECSR's recommendations regarding the eradication of child labour.[112] Similar decisions, calling upon states to comply with the recommendations of the ECSR, were adopted in relation to most other cases where the ESCR found state measures to fall short of the requirements of the Charter.[113] Furthermore, a cursory examination of the record of state parties in actually implementing the

---

[111] But see Dennis and Stewart, above n 1, 506. According to Dennis and Stewart, the selective nature of the regional ESR complaints procedures underlines their problematic nature and, at all events, renders the attempts to create an additional procedure at the global level redundant.

[112] Council of Europe Committee of Ministers (692nd meeting) Resolution ChS (99) 4: on Collective Complaint No 1/1998 (15 December 1999). Resolutions and Recommendations of the Committee of Ministers concerning specific decisions of the CESCR can be accessed via: <http://www.coe.int/t/e/human_rights/esc/4_Collective_complaints/List_of_collective_complaints/default.asp#TopOfPage>.

[113] See, eg: Council of Europe Committee of Ministers (738th meeting) Recommendation RecChS (2001) 1: on Collective Complaint No 6/1999 (30 January 2001), addressing the French tour guides claim; Council of Europe Committee of Ministers (749th meeting) Resolution RecChS (2001) 6: on Collective Complaint No 7/2000 (5 April 2001), addressing the Greek forced labour claim, and noting Greece's undertaking to implement some recommendations and to challenge others; Council of Europe Committee of Ministers (786th meeting) Resolution RecChS (2002) 3: on Collective Complaint No 8/2000 (6 March 2002), addressing the Greek conscientious objectors case, and noting that Greece has undertaken to comply with the recommendations; Council of Europe Committee of Ministers (853rd meeting) Resolution RecChS (2003) 1: on Collective Complaint No 12/2002 (24 September 2003), addressing the Swedish closed shops case; Council of Europe Committee of Ministers (875th meeting) Resolution RecChS (2004) 1: on Collective Complaint No 13/2002 (10 March 2004), addressing the French autism case, and noting that France has undertaken to comply with the recommendations. Note, however, that, in some cases, the recommendations of the Committee of Ministers seem to grant the relevant states considerable discretion in deciding on the pace and manner of implementation; see, eg: Council of Europe Committee of Ministers (790th meeting) Resolution RecChS (2002) 4: on Collective Complaint No 9/2000 (26 March 2002), addressing the French working hours case, and noting that France had already brought its laws in line with the recommendations; Council of Europe Committee of Ministers (784th meeting) Resolution RecChS (2002) 2: on Complaint No 10/2000 (21 February 2002), addressing the Finnish radiation case, and noting that Finland has undertaken to continue and reduce the risk to hospital workers exposed to radiation; Council of Europe Committee of Ministers (925th meeting) Resolution RecChS (2005) 6: on Collective Complaint No 14/2003 (4 May 2005), addressing the French health coverage hours case; Council of Europe Committee of Ministers (929th meeting) Resolution RecChS (2005) 11: on Collective Complaint No 15/2003 (8 June 2005), addressing the Greek Roma case; noting that Greece has taken several measures to improve the situation, and rejecting the recommendation to reimburse the petitioner's costs.

recommendations of the ECSR under the collective complaints procedure indicates that some member states (though certainly not all of them) have introduced legislative or administrative changes in response to the ESCR's recommendations.[114] While this record of compliance is imperfect, it is suggestive of the procedure's potential for generating some degree of compliance-pull and enforceability.

The feasibility of international monitoring over the manner of implementation of ESR is further confirmed by the long-standing practice of the ECtHR in addressing education,[115] labour association[116] and environmental cases,[117] all matters covered, explicitly or implicitly, by the provisions of the ICESCR and amenable to the jurisdiction of the CESCR under the proposed Protocol.[118] The possibility and political acceptability of the exercise of judicial or quasi-judicial review over ESR is also acknowledged in the 1981 African Charter on Human and Peoples'

---

[114] European Committee of Social Rights, *European Social Charter: Conclusions XVII-2* (Strasbourg, Council of Europe, 2005) 85, noting the failure by Belgium to implement the Committee's recommendations on corporal punishment; *ibid*, 326–27, noting the introduction of new legislation and administrative procedures by Greece following the Committee's recommendation on corporal punishment; European Committee of Social Rights *European Social Charter: Conclusions XVII-2* (Strasbourg, Council of Europe, 2005) 667–68, noting the introduction of new legislation and administrative procedures by Portugal following the Committee's recommendation on child labour; European Committee of Social Rights *European Social Charter: Conclusions XVII-1* (Strasbourg, Council of Europe, 2004) 238, noting the introduction of new legislation and administrative procedures by Greece following the Committee's recommendation on forced labour in the military; European Committee of Social Rights *European Social Charter (Revised): Conclusions 2004* (Strasbourg, Council of Europe, 2004) 210–211, noting failure by France to implement the Committee's recommendations on discrimination among tour guides; European Committee of Social Rights *European Social Charter (Revised): Conclusions 2004* (Strasbourg, Council of Europe, 2004) 564, noting the failure by Sweden to implement the Committee's recommendations on the unlawfulness of closed shop arrangements; European Committee of Social Rights *European Social Charter: Conclusions XVI-2* (Strasbourg, Council of Europe, 2003) 250, noting the failure by Finland to implement the Committee's recommendations on the conditions of health workers exposed to radiation. The annual conclusions of the ECSR are available via: <http://www.coe.int/t/e/human_rights/esc/3_reporting_procedure/2_recent_conclusions/2_by_year/default.asp#TopOfPage>.

[115] See, eg: *Certain Aspects of the Laws on the Use of Languages in Education in Belgium* Series A no 6 (1968) 1 EHRR 252; *Kjeldsen v Denmark* Series A no 23 (1976) 1 EHRR 711; *Campbell v UK* Series A 48 (1982) 4 EHRR 293; *Efstratiou v Greece* (App no 24095/94) ECHR 1996-VI; *Sahin v Turkey* (App no 44774/98) ECHR 10 November 2005; *Eren v Turkey* (App no 60856/00) ECHR 7 February 2006; *DH v Czech Republic* (App no 57325/00) ECHR 7 February 2006.

[116] See, eg: *Swedish Engine Drivers' Union v Sweden* Series A no 20 (1976) 1 EHRR 617; *National Union of Belgian Police v Belgium* Series A no 19 (1975) 1 EHRR 578; *Young v UK* Series A no 44 (1981) 4 EHRR 38; *Gustafsson v Sweden* (App no 15573/89) ECHR 1996-II; *Wilson v UK* (App no 30668/96) ECHR 2002-V; *Sørensen v Denmark* (App no 52562/99) ECHR 11 January 2006.

[117] See, eg: *Lopez Ostra v Spain* Series A no 303-C (1994) 20 EHRR 277; *Guerra v Italy* (App no 14967/89) ECHR 1998-I; *Hatton v UK* (App no 36022/97) ECHR 2003-VIII; *Gomez v Spain* (App no 4143/02) ECHR 2004-X; *Taskin v Turkey* (App no 46117/99) ECHR 2004-X; *Fadeyeva v Russia* (App no 55723/00) ECHR 9 June 2005.

[118] See E Brems, chapter 7 of this volume.

Rights[119] and in the 1988 San Salvador Protocol to the Inter-American Convention on Human Rights (which entered into force in 1999), which explicitly authorised the Inter-American Court of Human Rights to supervise compliance with the right to education and the right to unionise.[120]

B National Developments

The feasibility of judicial supervision over the fulfilment of ESR, including rights entailing redistributive effects, can also find support in some recent developments in domestic constitutional law. The close affinity in object and style between many constitutional law provisions and international human rights law[121] enables one to draw analogies from one body of jurisprudence to the other. Hence the ability of domestic courts to accord specific remedies for alleged breach of a constitutional 'right to health', 'right to education' or 'right to adequate standard of living' underscores the potential justiciability of ESR.

Three of the most notable decisions of the new South African Constitutional Court,[122] demonstrate the potential justiciability of ESR. In *Soobramoney v Minister of Health*, the Constitutional Court considered a claim that the constitutional right to health requires the government to fund an expensive dialysis treatment programme. The Court's judgment granted, in effect, a broad margin of appreciation to the local authorities:

---

[119] African Charter on Human and Peoples' Rights (adopted 27 June 1981, entered into force 21 October 1986) (1982) 21 ILM 58 (African Charter), arts 15–18, 22 and 24. For discussion, see SC Agbakwa, 'Reclaiming Humanity: Economic, Social, and Cultural Rights as the Cornerstone of African Human Rights' (2002) 5 *Yale Human Rights & Development Law Journal* 177.

[120] Additional Protocol to the American Convention on Human Rights in the Area of Economic, Social and Cultural Rights (Protocol of San Salvador) (entered into force 16 November 1999) OAS Treaty Series No 69 (1988), Art 19(6). Fourteen OAS member states have ratified the Protocol to date. The Inter-American Commission has also reviewed in the past issues relating to ESR. See, eg: *Yanomani v Brazil*, Case 7615, Inter-Am CHR Report No 12/85, OEA/ser L/V/II.66, doc 10 rev 1 (1985).

[121] For discussion, see Y Shany, 'How Supreme is the Supreme Law of the Land? Comparative Analysis of the Influence of International Human Rights Treaties Upon the Interpretation of Constitutional Texts by Domestic Courts' (2006) 31 *Brooklyn Journal of International Law* 341.

[122] The jurisprudence of the South African Constitutional Court in the field of economic and social rights has attracted considerable academic attention. See, eg: E de Wet, *The Constitutional Enforceability of Economic and Social Rights: The Meaning of the German Constitutional Model for South Africa* (Durban, Butterworths, 1996); SBO Gutto, 'Beyond Justiciability: Challenges of Implementing/Enforcing Socio-Economic Rights in South Africa' (1998) 4 *Buffalo Human Rights Law Review* 79; MS Kende, 'The South African Constitutional Court's Embrace of Socio-Economic Rights: A Comparative Perspective' (2003) 6 *Chapman Law Review* 137.

The provincial administration which is responsible for health services in KwaZulu-Natal has to make decisions about the funding that should be made available for health care and how such funds should be spent. These choices involve difficult decisions to be taken at the political level in fixing the health budget, and at the functional level in deciding upon the priorities to be met. A court will be slow to interfere with *rational decisions* taken in *good faith* by the political organs and medical authorities whose responsibility it is to deal with such matters.[123] (emphasis added)

Having satisfied itself that the government's decision was rational and was adopted in good faith, the Constitutional Court rejected the petition.[124]

In *Grootboom,* the Constitutional Court confirmed the margin of appreciation afforded to the government:

In any challenge based on section 26 in which it is argued that the State has failed to meet the positive obligations imposed upon it by section 26(2), the question will be whether the legislative and other measures taken by the State are reasonable. A court considering reasonableness will not enquire whether other more desirable or favorable measures could have been adopted, or whether public money could have been better spent. The question would be whether the measures that have been adopted are reasonable. It is necessary to recognise that a wide range of possible measures could be adopted by the State to meet its obligations. Many of these would meet the requirement of reasonableness.[125]

Still, the Constitutional Court held that the government's housing policy failed to meet the aforementioned reasonableness standard by reason of its omission to address the plight of the hundreds of thousands of homeless persons in South Africa. Specifically, it was held that the policy executed in the Cape Metro region had been unreasonable:

[S]ection 26 does oblige the State to devise and implement a coherent, co-ordinated programme designed to meet its section 26 obligations. The programme that has been adopted and was in force in the Cape Metro at the time that this application was brought, fell short of the obligations imposed

---

[123] *Soobramoney v Minister of Health, KwaZulu-Natal,* 1997 (12) BCLR 1696 (CC), para 29 (S Afr).

[124] For other cases, adopting a similar 'margin of appreciation' approach, see *TAC,* above n 61, 42 ('The Constitution contemplates rather a restrained and focused role for the courts, namely, to require the State to take measures to meet its constitutional obligations and to subject the reasonableness of these measures to evaluation.'); *Minister of Health and Another v New Clicks SA (Pty) Ltd and Others (Treatment Action Campaign and Innovative Medicines SA as Amici Curiae)* 2006 (1) BCLR 1 (CC) 552 (S Afr)('the Pricing Committee and the Minister exercise some discretion in the determination of the appropriate dispensing fee. But they must remain within the range of what is appropriate and observe the limits for the exercise of discretion.').

[125] *Government of the Republic of South Africa & Others v Grootboom & Others* 2000 (11) BCLR 1169 (CC) 64 (S Afr).

upon the State by section 26(2) in that it failed to provide for any form of relief to those desperately in need of access to housing.[126]

Finally, in *Minister of Health v TAC*, the Constitutional Court decided to proclaim the non-constitutionality of the government's health policy with regard to HIV positive mothers and children.[127] Significantly, however, the Court's decision entailed limited redistributive implications. The proceedings mainly challenged a restriction, ie, a negative measure, imposed by the government on the distribution of Nevirapine (a drug designed to prevent transmission of the HIV virus from nursing mothers to their children); and it was demonstrated that the government had sufficient resources to progressively introduce the required treatment.

In sum, the South African experience, which is corroborated by the experience of other jurisdictions that have incorporated ESR into their constitutional orders,[128] also demonstrates the feasibility of implementing ESR through judicial means. The cumulative effect of this growing body of international and national precedents suggests that politically acceptable legal standards may derive from ESR, notwithstanding the vagueness of many provisions and their redistributive implications.

IV COMPARATIVE ASSESSMENT II: THE REDISTRIBUTIVE IMPLICATIONS OF FIRST GENERATION RIGHTS

The reluctance to address ESR through judicial or quasi-judicial means becomes even less defensible from a theoretical point of view, when one compares it to the increasingly 'positive' contents given to first generation rights by international human rights bodies. Since the implementation of civil and political rights increasingly entails redistributive implications, which were most probably unforeseen at the time at which the 1966 Covenant was drafted,[129] the unwillingness to acknowledge that similar developments may take place with relation to second generation rights warrants a degree of criticism.

Since the late 1970s, the ECtHR has held on numerous occasions that the duty incumbent upon member states to the ECHR to 'secure' the rights

---

126 *Ibid*, para 95.

127 *TAC*, above n 61.

128 See, for instance, discussions of the constitutionalisation of ESR in Poland, India and Israel: R Cholewinski, 'The Protection of Human Rights in the New Polish Constitution' (1998) 22 *Fordham International Law Journal* 236, 269–76; R Swaminathan, 'Regulating Development: Structural Adjustment and the Case for National Enforcement of Economic and Social Rights' (1998) 37 *Columbia Journal of Transnational Law* (1998) 161, 209–14; Y Rabin and Y Shany, 'The Israeli Constitutional Revolution: Has the Time Come for Protecting Economic and Social Rights?' (2004) 37 *Israeli Law Review* 299.

129 See eg, R Singh, *The Future of Human Rights in the United Kingdom: Essays on Law and Practice* (Oxford, Hart Publishing, 1997), 51–4.

enumerated in the Convention[130] also entails 'positive obligations'.[131] Significantly, some of these 'positive obligation' decisions have had considerable redistributive implications[132]: for example, in *Osman v UK,* the Court held that the state must apply all police measures that could reasonably be expected in order to prevent risk to the lives of individuals from other individuals.[133] Clearly, such legal standards could entail considerable expenses for the state in question.

Furthermore, the ECtHR has applied the 'positive obligations' doctrine in situations involving the promotion of Convention rights which have significant economic and social implications.[134] For example: in *Airey v Ireland,* the ECtHR required Ireland to provide legal aid in situations when such assistance is 'indispensable' for effective access of individuals to court[135]; in *Z v UK,* the Court held that the failure of British social services to extricate four children from the custody of patently negligent parents resulted in violation of their positive obligations to prevent inhumane and degrading treatment of individuals[136]; in *Roche v UK,* where an army veteran alleged that the government failed to provide him with information on his exposure to chemical weapon tests during military service, the Court found that the state in question 'ha[d] not fulfilled the positive obligation to provide an effective and accessible procedure enabling the applicant to have access to all relevant and appropriate information which would allow him to assess any risk to which he had been exposed during his participation in the tests'[137]; and in *Moldovan v Romania* it was held that the Romanian state failed, inter alia, to promptly and adequately

---

130 ECHR, above n 13, Art 1.

131 See, eg: *Marckx v Belgium* Series A no 31 (1979) 2 EHRR 330, para 31; *Airey v Ireland* Series A no 32 (1979) 2 EHRR 305, para 25 (1979); *X v Netherlands* Series A no 91 (1985) 8 EHRR 235, para 23; *Plattform 'Ärtze für das Leben' v Austria* Series A no 139 (1988)13 EHRR 204, para 32. See generally, AR Mowbray, *The Development of Positive Obligations under the European Convention on Human Rights by the European Court of Human Rights* (Oxford, Hart Publishing, 2004).

132 See Mowbray, above n 131, 230.

133 Osman, above n 15, para 116 ('it must be established… that the authorities knew or ought to have known at the time of the existence of a real and immediate risk to the life of an identified individual or individuals from the criminal acts of a third party and that they failed to take measures within the scope of their powers which, judged reasonably, might have been expected to avoid that risk').

134 On the impossibility of totally separating civil and political rights and ESR, see Airey, above n 131, para 26 ('Whilst the Convention sets forth what are essentially civil and political rights, many of them have implications of a social or economic nature. The Court therefore considers, like the Commission, that the mere fact that an interpretation of the Convention may extend into the sphere of social and economic rights should not be a decisive factor against such an interpretation; there is no water-tight division separating that sphere from the field covered by the Convention.').

135 Airey, above n 131, para 26; *D v UK* (App no 30240/96) EHCR 1997-III (deportation of an AIDS patient would deprive him of continued medical service and amounted, in the circumstances of the case, to inhuman treatment).

136 Above 16; *E v UK* (App no 33218/96) ECHR 26 November 2002.

137 *Roche v UK* (App no 32555/96) ECHR 19 October 2005, paras 139–69.

reconstruct houses belonging to Roma dwellers, which were destroyed in a mob attack, and thus exposed the dwellers to prolonged inhumane living conditions.[138]

The methodology applied by the Court in reaching these conclusions is also worth noting: in a number of 'positive obligation' cases, the ECtHR confirmed that states retain wide discretion in deciding which measures satisfy the need to secure the covered rights,[139] stating that the margin of appreciation afforded in cases pertaining to complex social policy issues should be particularly wide.[140] Furthermore, review of the ECtHR case law reveals the influence of procedural and methodological factors upon the Court's determination of the propriety of the member state's 'positive' efforts: for example, in *Roche*, the Court emphasised the non-comprehensive and unstructured nature of the information disclosure policies of the UK[141]; in *Zawadka v Poland*, the Court noted that unmotivated refusals to assist individuals in upholding their right to parental visits are incompatible with the positive obligation to secure the rights[142]; in *Adali v Turkey*, the promptness and expediency of the state's response were identified as important factors in assessing the reasonableness of its effort in conducting a criminal investigation[143]; in *Öneryildiz v Turkey*, the Court alluded to the inconsistent policies of the Turkish government vis-à-vis dwellers in illegal slums, as indicative of the unreasonableness of the measures in question[144]; and, finally, in *Hatton v UK*, a case challenging the government's failure to adequately regulate night flights to and from Heathrow airport, the ECtHR Grand Chamber held that: 'a governmental decision-making process concerning complex issues of environmental and economic policy such as in the present case must necessarily involve appropriate investigations and studies in order to allow them to strike a fair balance between the various conflicting interests at stake'.[145]

The acknowledgement that positive obligations entail wide margins of appreciation and the utility of examining decision-making procedures lends itself to possible judicial or quasi-judicial supervision of ESR under the proposed Protocol: arguably, states should retain significant margins of appreciation in adopting general policy decisions; however, more intrusive

---

138 *Moldovan v Romania* (App no 41138/98) ECHR 12 July 2005, paras 107–13.

139 See, eg: *Airey*, above n 131, para 26; *Lopez Ostra*, above n 117, para 51; *Glaser v UK* (App no 32346/96) ECHR 19 September 2000, paras 63–64; *MC v Bulgaria* (App no 39272/98) ECHR 2003-XII, paras 154–55; *Öneryildiz v Turkey* (App no 48939/99) ECHR 2004-XII, para 107.

140 See, eg: *James v UK* Series A no 98 (1986) 8 EHRR 123, para 46; *Powell and Rayner v UK* Series A no 172 (1990) 12 EHRR 355, para 44; *Hatton*, above n 117, paras 97–100; *Öneryildiz*, above n 139, para 107.

141 *Roche*, above n 137, para 166.

142 *Zawadka v Poland* (App no 48542/99) ECHR 23 June 2005, para 63.

143 *Adali v Turkey* (App no 38187/97) ECHR 31 March 2005, para 224.

144 *Öneryildiz*, above n 139, para 128.

145 *Hatton*, above n 117, para 128.

supervision can be expected vis-à-vis the procedural adequacy of the policy determination process—eg, its factual basis, transparency, promptness, comprehensiveness and consistency.

One should also note that the ECtHR's position on the incorporation of positive obligations within first generation rights now represents the mainstream of international human rights theory and practice. Indeed, the Inter-American Court of Human Rights (I/A CHR) has stated in its landmark *Velásquez Rodriguez* case that:

> The State has a legal duty to take reasonable steps to prevent human rights violations and to use the means at its disposal to carry out a serious investigation of violations committed within its jurisdiction, to identify those responsible, to impose the appropriate punishment and to ensure the victim adequate compensation.[146]

The same position was also taken by the HRC in several of its general comments.[147] For example, in General Comment 6, on the right to life, the Committee opined that the right entails positive obligations:

> The expression 'inherent right to life' cannot properly be understood in a restrictive manner, and the protection of this right requires that States adopt positive measures. In this connection, the Committee considers that it would be desirable for States parties to take all possible measures to reduce infant mortality and to increase life expectancy, especially in adopting measures to eliminate malnutrition and epidemics.[148]

The creeping extension of civil and political rights from negative to positive obligations, and the growing overlap between first and second generation rights, underscores the anachronism in maintaining that ESR cannot and should not become internationally justiciable. If the human rights movement has moved in recent decades, in the field of civil and political rights, from negative right formulations to the language of positive obligations entailing significant costs, there seems to be little reason for freezing in time the parallel development of the positive (and negative) obligations imposed by ESR. Of course, the increased acceptance of the notion of

---

[146] Inter-American Court of Human Rights, *Velásquez Rodriguez v Honduras* (1988) 28 ILM 291, para 174.

[147] See, eg: UN Human Rights Committee 'General Comment 31: Nature of the General Legal Obligation on States Parties to the Covenant' (26 May 2004) UN Doc CCPR/C/21/Rev.1/Add.13, para 6; Human Rights Committee, General Comment 28, Equality of rights between men and women (Article 3), UN Doc CCPR/C/21/Rev.1/Add.10 (2000), para 3; UN Human Rights Committee 'General Comment 21: Replaces general comment 9 concerning humane treatment of persons deprived of liberty (Art. 10)' reprinted in 'Note by the Secretariat, Compilation of General Comments and General Recommendations Adopted by Human Rights Treaty Bodies' (10 April 1992) UN Doc HRI/GEN/1/Rev.1, para 3.

[148] UN Human Rights Committee 'General Comment 6: the right to life' reprinted in 'Note by the Secretariat, Compilation of General Comments and General Recommendations Adopted by Human Rights Treaty Bodies' (30 April 1982) UN Doc HRI/GEN/1/Rev.1, para 5.

indivisibility,[149] ie, that first generation rights cannot be adequately protected without adequate protection of ESR and vice versa, lends policy support to the ESR justiciability-enhancing project represented by the proposed Protocol.[150]

V CONCLUSIONS: LEGITIMACY CONSIDERATIONS AND PRAGMATIC GUIDELINES

So, the human rights movement is evolving—first generation rights have acquired, over time, 'positive obligation' features, which often entail redistributive implications; second generation rights have become more specific, and, hence, amenable to implementation through judicial or quasi-judicial mechanisms; and the borderlines between the two generations of rights have tended to fade away. Still, the problem, which Steward and Dennis correctly identify, is that these developments, actively countenanced by international human rights bodies such as the ECtHR, HRC, ECSR and CESCR, engender a potential legitimacy gap: states are held up nowadays to more demanding standards than the ones they had bargained for when acceding to the relevant international instruments. Specifically, the expectation that international human rights treaties would impose minimal monitoring obligations explains many states' willingness to adopt these treaties in the first place and to agree to the expansive language used therein.[151]

While the interpretive and procedural development of international human right treaties, including the ICESCR, is undeniable (and probably inevitable), Dennis and Stewart should demonstrate that this development systematically fails to enjoy the ex post facto support of the states parties to these specific treaties (as opposed to states, such as the US who refuse till this day to ratify the ICESCR). This they try to do, but the examples they give, which mostly pertain to the refusal of some UN bodies to single out specific elements identified by the CESCR, and the treatment of some ESR elements as development goals and not legal obligations,[152] are ultimately unconvincing, as they do not present a direct challenge to the Committee's recommendations.

At the same time, a number of indicators suggest the endorsement by a good number of states of the position that ESR are justiciable. First, very

---

[149] See 'Vienna Declaration, World Conference on Human Rights' 14–25 June 1993, UN Doc A/CONF.157/24, para 5.

[150] See, eg: Open-ended Working Group Report, above n 9, para 70; R Pejan, 'The Right to Water: The Road to Justiciability' (2004) 36 *George Washington International Law Review* 1181, 1193.

[151] See, eg: AF Bayefsky, *The UN Human Rights Treaty System: Universality at the Crossroads* (Ardsley, Transnational Publishers, 2001).

[152] Dennis and Stewart, above n 1, 495–96.

few member states have publicly protested against the general comments of the CESCR, which seek to concretise the obligations of the member states and to render them more amenable to monitoring. In fact, the record of the dialogues between the Committee and the member states indicates that states have been generally cooperative with the concretisation project. Furthermore, the regular adoption of the annual reports of the CESCR by the UN Economic and Social Council (ECOSOC) demonstrates the broad international support its legal constructions enjoy.[153] In the same vein, the regular adoption on the part of the Council of Europe's Committee of Ministers, which represents the vast majority of European states, of the recommendations of the ECSR confirms the political acceptability of the outcome of the review process. Finally, the increased willingness of states to engage in similar ESR justiciability-enhancing strategies within their domestic constitution laws demonstrates that international developments also reflect parallel national political and legal processes, which are supportive of the justiciability of ESR per se.

What's more, Dennis and Stewart's 'legitimacy gap' argument hardly holds water in the case of the proposed Protocol to the ICESCR. The Protocol (like other protocols appended to human rights treaties) is non-mandatory—ie, state parties to the ICESCR can freely decide whether to join it or not.[154] This opt-in mechanism ensures that quasi-judicial supervision would not be imposed on unwilling states, which review with suspicion ESR or the possibility of quasi-judicial monitoring of compliance with them.[155] In addition, the need to exhaust local remedies and the non-binding character of the 'views' of the CESCR under the proposed Protocol[156] serve as an additional safeguard against excessive intrusion by the Committee in national policy-making.[157] Simply put, states are not formally obliged to follow the recommendations of the CESCR under the Protocol.

In fact, the optional and non-binding nature of the process counsels in favour of prudence on the part of the CESCR. It should proceed with

---

[153] Craven, above n 21, 92.

[154] Dennis and Stewart point out that there is a lack of consensus as to whether the establishment of an ESR complaints mechanism would be beneficial (Dennis and Stewart, above n 1, 475). To my mind, inconclusiveness of the debate cannot justify inertia, but rather, in accordance with the long-standing practices of the international community in a host of issues, the creation of elective procedures. Had we insisted on consensus as a prerequisite for creating new procedures, courts such as the ICC and procedures such as the complaints procedures under the ICCPR, would not have come into existence.

[155] See, eg, Open-ended Working Group Report, above n 9, para 19.

[156] Draft Protocol, Art 7(5). See also CESCR Report on the Optional Protocol, above n 3, para 47. Oddly enough, Dennis and Stewart criticise the introduction of a 'legally binding adjudicative mechanism' under the Optional Protocol (Dennis and Stewart, above n 1, 466 and fn 32).

[157] For expression of fears of intrusiveness on the part of the CESCR, see Open-ended Working Group Report, above n 9, para 22.

caution in the examination of specific complaints (referred to in the proposed Protocol as 'communications')[158] in order to preserve the credibility and legitimacy of the review process. Expediency consideration—ie, the overwhelming work burden of the Committee, its limited resources,[159] and the potential conflict between the Committee's adjudicative and non-adjudicative functions[160]—also militate in favour of deferential standards of review.[161] Such an approach is generally consistent with the position taken by the ECSR in reviewing complaints under the Social Charter, the ECtHR in reviewing 'positive obligation' cases and some domestic courts in the course of constitutional adjudication of ESR.

Hence, I propose that if the proposed Protocol comes into force, the CESCR should adopt the following principles of quasi-judicial supervision:

—The Committee is better situated to address 'negative obligations' (duties to respect) than 'positive obligations' (duties to protect and duties to fulfil), and more limited margins of appreciation should be afforded to states in cases falling under the first category, where states actively interfere with the enjoyment of ESR.

—When reviewing the implementation of positive obligations, the Committee should distinguish between core rights and non-core rights. The margin of appreciation afforded to states over non-core rights should be, as a rule, wider than in core-right cases. In non-core issues, intervention in substantive decisions should be generally restricted to review of the procedure, methodology and rational basis of the policy and its good faith application.

—When reviewing positive obligations, the Committee should focus on procedure and methodology, rather than on substantive evaluation of outcomes. Hence, it should concentrate on factors such as the comprehensive nature of the governmental policy (eg, the breadth of the legislative framework), its consistency, the adequacy of the process of formulating the challenged policy (eg, its scientific basis, transparency, time of formulation, etc), and the existence or lack of good faith efforts on the part of the government to promote the progressive implementation of ESR and to abstain from retrogressive measures.

—In formulating its recommendations in 'positive obligation' cases, the Committee would be well-advised to recommend the development of

---

158 Draft Protocol, Art 2.

159 See Dennis and Stewart, above n 1, 507–11. Review of the experience of the ECSR suggests that the fears of opening the floodgates may be overblown. In all events, strict rules of admissibility could minimise such concerns.

160 UNCHR 'Report of the Independent Expert on the Question of a Draft Optional Protocol to the International Covenant on Economic, Social and Cultural Rights' (12 February 2002) UN Doc E/CN.4/2002/57, paras 39–44.

161 Above n 12.

indicators and benchmarks by the reviewed states, in order to promote the concretisation of ESR in a mutually accepted manner.

While these review strategies are admittedly vague and uncertain, it would be incumbent upon the CESCR to put them into use with great care in order to gradually build confidence in its ability to review compliance. Still, the willingness on the part of states to go in that direction would indicate that ESR are no longer frozen in time—ie, in their 'cold war' era image of non-justiciable principles.

6

Social Rights and Social Policy

Transformations on the International Landscape

KERRY RITTICH

I INTRODUCTION

Social rights are intrinsically related to social policy. The social entitlements that an individual may claim against the state are typically connected to the breadth, depth and health of the social entitlements, programmes and institutions that exist in society at large. For this reason, any analysis of social rights can usefully pay attention not only to the state of these entitlements, programmes and institutions, both in general and in specific jurisdictions, but to the direction of change and the forces that are driving them in one direction or another.

Right now, social rights and social policy are in flux and in question. The central reason is that social rights are linked, semantically, institutionally, normatively and politically, with the most central and contested projects in the international order. To list but a few, social rights are implicated in debates about the character and legitimacy of global economic integration, the nature and demands of development, and the realisation of democratic transformation. In these debates and projects, social rights often play an ambivalent role: they are figured both as the antidote to our problems and the source of our crises.

It is not difficult to find contemporary references to the need for a 'fair globalisation'. To cite but one example, it is the title of the 2004 report of the ILO Commission on the Social Dimension of Globalization.[1] But worries about the 'social deficit' in the emerging international order are

---

[1] ILO, *A Fair Globalization: Creating Opportunities for All*, Final Report, World Commission on the Social Dimensions of Globalization available at: <http://www.ilo.org/public/english/wcsdg/index.htm>.

not limited to the ILO, nor are they new. For well over a decade, the United Nations has been grappling with the perceived tilt in the global institutional framework. Whether articulated in terms of the neglect of social development and workers' rights,[2] the persistent disadvantage of women,[3] the lagging cadre of the global poor,[4] or the difficulty of successfully integrating the nations of the global South into the global trade regime and ensuring that they benefit from economic growth,[5] there is demonstrable convergence around the idea that the social dimension of globalisation should now take a more central place in the international order.

In response to pressure on this front, some of the principal architects of global economic integration, such as the World Bank, have now formally embarked on a modified approach to development and market reform. This 'second generation' path complexifies the singular focus on economic growth that marked the first phase of global market integration, and aims to mitigate its harshest effects through, inter alia, greater attention to the 'structural, social and human' side of development.[6] What form that attention should take, and what is to be done in terms of a changed programmatic or institutional agenda in particular, remains both uncertain and contested. Proposals range from a changed substantive focus, emphasising issues such as gender equality, the environment, health and education, to normative and procedural shifts through the introduction of a human rights or public law lens to the international economic order.

Yet it is useful to observe that despite the calls to 'include' the social in the agendas and activities of the global economic institutions,[7] whether through campaigns to include a social clause in the WTO,[8] by subordinating the international economic regimes to public international law norms,[9] or by reading human rights norms and values into the existing

---

    [2] United Nations, World Summit for Social Development, Copenhagen Declaration on Social Development, UN Doc A/Conf. 166/9, available at: <http://www.un.org/esa/socdev/wssd/agreements/index.html>.

    [3] United Nations, Fourth World Conference on Women, Beijing Declaration, 15 September 1995, available at: <http://www.un.org/womenwatch/daw/beijing/platform/declar.htm>.

    [4] See the United Nations Millennium Development Goals, described at: <http://www.un.org/millenniumgoals>.

    [5] World Trade Organization, Doha Ministerial Declaration 2001, 14 November 2001, available at <http://www.wto.org/English/thewto_e/minist_e/mino1_e/mindecl_e.htm>.

    [6] JD Wolfensohn, *A Proposal for a Comprehensive Development Framework (A Discussion Draft)*, January 1999 <http://www.worldbank.org/cdf/cdf-text.htm>. For a discussion, see K Rittich, 'The Future of Law and Development: Second Generation Reforms and the Incorporation of the Social' in DM Trubek and A Santos (eds), *The New Law and Economic Development: A Critical Appraisal* (Cambridge, Cambridge University Press, 2006) 203.

    [7] ILO, above n 1.

    [8] World Trade Organization, Singapore Ministerial Declaration, Doc WT/MIN(96)/DEC/, reprinted in (1997) 36 *International Legal Materials* 218, 221.

    [9] J Pauwelyn, *Conflict of Norms in Public International Law: How WTO Law Relates to Other Rules of International Law* (New York, Cambridge University Press, 2003).

trade regimes,[10] it is clear that the social is already there. A wide range of policies, assumptions, rules and institutions in the international order already exercise a profound impact on social objectives and the distribution of income, so much so that we could say that much of economic policy is really social policy too. Viewed from this vantage point, it is clear that we are already immersed in a profound transformation of social rights on the international plane.[11]

II SITUATING SOCIAL RIGHTS

A The Task of Social Rights

I want to argue, somewhat against the direction of change, that social rights remain fundamentally about distributive justice. They are concerned not simply with the provision of basic needs or a safety net for the most destitute: they serve as a proxy for values such as social cohesion, solidarity and inclusion and they operate as a metric of our commitment to relative social equality.

While it runs against prevailing trends, this view of social rights is old rather than new. In Marshall's words, social rights are designed to give individuals claims on collective social resources.[12] The conventional mechanism for the realisation of social rights has been the redistributive state. Whether via the Keynesian and New Deal welfare states of the industrialised market economies or through the planned economies of the socialist states, the active refashioning of market transactions, and sometimes their complete displacement by the centralised administration of resources, has been central not simply to the realisation of social and economic rights but to their conception.

A central aim of social rights is to decommodify labour, that is, to make citizens less subject to raw market forces to ensure their basic welfare and

---

10 R Howse and M Mutua, 'Protecting Rights in Global Economy: Challenges for the World Trade Organization' (Rights and Democracy, 2000), available at: <http://www.ichrdd.ca/english/commdoc/publications/globalization/wtoRightsGlob.html>.

11 A caveat is in order. There is an extensive literature, political and legal, beginning at least with the writing of Marx, analysing the weaknesses and limits of reliance upon rights claims simpliciter as instruments of transformative social change. Although the following account might be taken as evidence of the relative weakness of social rights in the face of powerful countervailing political and ideological forces, I do not engage with this issue here. The aim is merely to draw attention to the currents of change, both ideological and institutional, in the realm of labour and social policy, something that should be of deep interest to those interested in social rights in and of themselves, as well as to those interested in the fate of the values and projects with which social rights have traditionally been associated.

12 TH Marshall, 'Citizenship and Social Class' in TH Marshall, *Class, Citizenship and Social Development* (Chicago and London, University of Chicago Press, 1963).

survival. In liberal market orders, a wide array of regulatory and institutional mechanisms at the disposal of the state can be, and has been, deployed to pool risk and redistribute income, change the terms and conditions under which parties transact in markets for labour, and ensure the wide availability of basic goods and services.

The genealogy of social rights suggests why the concern with redistribution and the enduring preoccupation with reducing the commodification of labour are neither accidental nor peripheral. Social rights arose to remedy, to varying degrees and in a variety of ways, the detrimental consequences of market-centred economic activity. These consequences are recurring, foreseeable and, at this point, even predictable. They range from the outright exclusion of some groups from markets to the participation of others under disadvantageous terms. Such exclusions and disadvantages may result from social or cultural norms and barriers to markets on ascriptive bases such as gender, ethnicity, race or caste; the presence of non-market duties or tasks such as obligations of care that impinge on people's ability to engage in market activity; persistent disparities in bargaining power leading to systematically disadvantageous contract terms for classes of market actors such as workers; or simply unequal access to the resources and capital with which to bargain in the first place. Finally, social rights address the periodic inability of even the relatively well-positioned to insulate themselves from cyclical downturns in markets.

The first effort to organise all of economic life according to market principles and to subordinate social life to its demands generated the first of what is a now predictable oscillation towards demands for protective regulation and redistribution.[13] But social rights arose not only to blunt the harsh edge of market forces on the fabric of social life. Because markets themselves are socially embedded, social rights mitigate the effects of forces which, if left unrestrained, arguably destroy the conditions upon which markets themselves depend to operate.[14]

Yet if constraints upon market forces are the very function and raison d'etre of social rights, this objective is now in question. And if the collective assumption of risk and reliance upon the redistributive state are the means by which they have traditionally been achieved, in many quarters these mechanisms represent an exhausted programme for the pursuit of social welfare, the remnants of a paradigm that has now been superseded at the level of both norm and fact.

This partly explains a paradox surrounding social rights: this is the discontinuity between the discursive or ideological commitment to human rights and the actual status of social rights, at least as reflected in institu-

---

[13] K Polanyi, *The Great Transformation* (Boston, Beacon Press, 1944).
[14] F Block, 'Towards a New Understanding of Economic Modernity' in C Joerges, B Strath and P Wagner (eds), *The Economy as a Polity: The Political Constitution of Contemporary Capitalism* (London, UCL Press, 2005) 3.

tional and programmatic commitments. Human rights, in theory, now enjoy unprecedented normative status in the international order. Since the Vienna Declaration on Human Rights, it has been repeatedly said that social rights form an integral part of the world of human rights. In addition, the claim is that human rights are indivisible and interdependent, such that the realisation of one right is dependent on the recognition and protection given to another. Human rights are now increasingly linked to development as well; in one of the most popular contemporary formulations, human rights, including those rights basic to the development of human capabilities, are integral to reconceptualising development as freedom.[15] Yet at the same time, the mechanisms by which social rights have traditionally been advanced are either threatened or are currently being dismantled across a wide variety of states. Where the language of social rights is retained, the values of solidarity, cohesion and equality underlying them are disappearing. At the same time, the meaning of social inclusion is also undergoing transformation, as citizenship is reconceived in terms of consumption and participation in markets.

We can point to three factors behind this development. The first is the emergence of a narrative that locates the path to human welfare in broad participation in markets. The second is a specific institutional and regulatory programme to promote economic growth through greater market integration, the facilitation of market transactions, and the easing of regulatory burdens for investors. The third is the rise of a vision of human rights that is centred around the protection of individual entitlements, and substantially de-linked from the commitment to collective empowerment and shorn of aspirations to guarantee widespread economic security.

All are visible developments across the international order; all are expressed in the research and policy commitments of the international institutions, the economic, financial, development institutions in particular; and all ultimately lie behind the current reforms to social rights and social policy.

B Historicising Social Rights

Social rights are latecomers in the field of rights: in TH Marshall's famous formulation, they represent the third phase in the evolution of modern citizenship, a project that began with the recognition of civil rights in the liberal revolutions of the eighteenth century, continued with the extension of the franchise to previously excluded groups in the nineteenth and early twentieth centuries, and expanded yet again after the Second World War to

[15] Amartya Sen, *Development as Freedom* (New York, Anchor Books, 1999).

encompass economic entitlements provided under the aegis of the welfare state.[16]

If civil rights were defended as a set of necessary protections for the individual against the arbitrary predations of the state, and political rights proclaimed as the means to hold it accountable and democratise its decision-making processes, then social rights represented an assault on the remnants of the feudal order, a concession that all social classes are entitled to a share of the wider resources of the society.

Yet it would be a mistake to think of social rights in purely functional or evolutionary terms, or to assume that they are safely entrenched elements of liberal democratic orders. Social rights are also artefacts of political struggles, the product of a time- and place-specific consensus about the requirements of social peace and economic progress. For example, the consolidation of the social contract that emerged across the liberal states in the post-World War II order owes much to the perceived role of social rights in re-establishing the internal peace and security that was disrupted in the pre-war order.[17] In the United States, the New Deal legislation and programmes which forged a new social contract were the product of a lengthy social, political and legal struggle dating back to the turn of the last century.[18]

The post-war social contract was also underpinned at theoretic and ideological levels: first, by the widespread acceptance of Keynesian economic arguments and models and second, by the consensus borne out of the 1930s and its aftermath that entitlements to economic security and inclusion were of interest not just to those who directly benefited from them, but were instead a broad social and political concern. In Western Europe, social rights played yet another role: the extension of basic social security and benefits to all citizens, common to the political platforms of parties across the ideological spectrum in the post-war era, helped dampen the appeal of alternative economic and political orders, thereby staving off threats to the liberal market polities by the communist regimes on their doorsteps. [19] Social rights were so entrenched, and so normalised, in Europe by the mid-1960s that they could be described as 'no longer so much a politics as a way of life'.[20]

It is worth recalling these historical and ideological roots and moments, if only to remain alert to the possibility that as political conditions change and dominant norms are challenged, the social rights that are their product

---

[16] TH Marshall, above n 12.

[17] See JG Ruggie, 'International Regimes, Transaction and Change: Embedded Liberalism in the Postwar Economic Order' (1982) 36 *International Organization* 379.

[18] M Horwitz, *The Transformation of American Law, 1870–1969: The Crisis of Legal Orthodoxy* (Oxford, OUP, 1992).

[19] T Judt, 'The Social Democratic Moment' in T Judt, *Postwar: A History of Europe Since 1945* (New York, Penguin, 2005) 360.

[20] Ibid 363.

may also undergo transformation. Even where path dependence and political resistance insulates them from easy or immediate change,[21] social rights can hardly be expected to remain untouched.

C The Erosion of the Post-War Model

> From an overall perspective, welfare states may be distinguished by whether or not they grant extensive social rights.[22]

Since the beginning, state policies, institutions and regulations have been central to the delivery of social rights. In the industrialised liberal democracies of the post-World War II order, social rights have almost always been realised through a combination of modifications to labour market institutions on the one hand and programmes, benefits, insurance and public goods provided by the state on the other. However, it is critical to comprehending social rights to realise that they have in fact been secured through broader social welfare regimes: thus, social rights effectively touch on not only the state and its institutions and policies, but regulate the activities of market actors as well. Because the state's role in directly delivering goods and resources can be relatively modest, ultimately, the shape and strength of social rights may have a great deal to do with the background legal norms and entitlements, designed and enforced by state practices and institutions, in which the nominally 'private' parties operate.

In addition, all state entitlements, policies and institutions both imply and construct assumptions about the identity of the normative or ideal worker; they also reflect and generate a set of related norms and expectations about the roles of firms in securing the well-being of workers. Although originally missing from the debate about social rights and social welfare, it is now recognised that households and families are the implicit third party to this social contract, and that unpaid work in the household, usually performed by women, is critical to its overall functioning.[23]

The precise division of labour among the institutions of the state, the market and the family or household in the social contract varies considerably among the welfare regimes in market-based societies. As Esping-Anderson describes in his well-known taxonomy, some regimes repose considerable responsibility in the family while others provide

---

[21] W Korpi and J Palme, 'New Politics and Class Politics in the Context of Austerity and Globalization: Welfare State Regress in 18 Countries, 1975–1995' (2003) 97 *American Political Science Review* 425.

[22] U Becker, 'The Challenge of Migration to the Welfare State' in E Benvenisti and G Nolte (eds), *The Welfare State, Globalization, and International Law* (Berlin and Heidelberg, Springer, 2004) 6.

[23] For a discussion, see K Rittich, 'Equity or Efficiency: International Institutions and the Work/Family Nexus' in J Conaghan and K Rittich (eds), *Labour Law, Work and Family: Critical and Comparative Perspectives* (Oxford, OUP, 2005) 43.

extensive social support for the care of individuals; some regimes, especially those common to the Anglo-American world, are highly individualistic while others are more solidaristic, relying to a greater extent on the state both for residual economic security and as a mechanism for redistribution.[24] Whatever the nature of the welfare regime in question, realising economic security and well-being is a joint project, achieved through reconstructed rights at work and the provision of social goods, social protection and social insurance by the state. To the extent that these measures fail to achieve their objective, the task devolves to the individual or family and the aspirations behind social rights are effectively abandoned.

The obligation of the state to perform its role and secure the bases of economic well-being, whether directly or indirectly, is reflected in the entitlements guaranteed by social rights charters and covenants. For example, the International Covenant on Economic, Social and Cultural Rights (ICESCR)[25] lists myriad rights at work, from limitations and controls on working conditions to the entitlement of workers to form unions; it also specifies rights to social security and social insurance.[26] The ICESCR also contains entitlements to goods and services which, in addition to their intrinsic worth, are deeply interconnected with labour market participation. Like guaranteed access to health services,[27] some social rights reduce the degree to which workers are subject to raw market forces and under pressure to accept work on any terms. Or like the right to education, some entitlements are intimately bound up with future labour market prospects, especially in a skill-based economy.[28]

On the one hand, we can see these social rights reflected in the array of social benefits and legal entitlements either provided or backstopped by the state. In the industrialised world, broad segments of the citizenry normally have access to them, while in the developing world they may be much thinner in content and typically reach only a narrow segment of the citizenry, for example, workers in the formal labour market. Yet anyone familiar with the contemporary discourse of legal and institutional reform is likely to experience at least some of these rights as artefacts of a time and place that has already passed. The right to social security? An adequate standard of living for himself and his family? To just and

---

[24] G Esping-Anderson, *The Three Worlds of Welfare Capitalism* (Cambridge, Polity Press, 1990).

[25] International Covenant on Economic, Social and Cultural Rights (entered into force 3 January 1976) 993 UNTS 3 (ICESCR).

[26] ICESCR, above n 25, Arts 7, 8 and 9.

[27] *Ibid*, Art 12.

[28] Similar rights at work are listed in some regional charters too. The first ten articles of the European Social Charter, for example, are devoted to rights at work: see European Social Charter (Turin, 3 May 1961, entered into force 26 February 1965), available at <http://conventions.coe.int/Treaty/en/Treaties/Html/035.htm>.

favourable conditions of work?? To rest, leisure and reasonable holidays with pay??? You must be dreaming. However relevant, even central, they may still be to economic security and other values and objectives such as solidarity and equality, it is hard to make the case that they are generally recognised as 'rights': constraints upon rule making and institution building; objectives with foundational legal and constitutional status; obligations assumed by states and recognised as such by other actors and institutions. Indeed, it is becoming hard to make the case that they are even still recognised as dominant policy concerns. Instead, they seem increasingly reduced to the status of claims, claims that at one time may have met with widespread assent but which are now often met with scepticism.

Whatever their legal or normative status, social rights do not map easily on to the current vectors of change at the level of rules, policies and institutions, whether international or domestic. The objectives and assumptions that underpinned the rights that are articulated in the ICESCR and other social charters have been challenged; in some jurisdictions, and within influential institutions in the international order, the international economic and financial institutions in particular, they appear to have been decisively rejected. For example, as the concerns that animated the post-war social contract have receded, it is no longer taken for granted that the state has an obligation to maintain full employment; it is no longer clear that citizens' claims for economic security will meet a receptive hearing from the state; it is no longer uncontested that the state has a role to play in ensuring the justice and fairness of conditions at work. At a minimum, the state's direct role in ensuring particular welfare outcomes is under reconsideration. Where the state's responsibility for its citizen's welfare has not been repudiated, the principal mechanisms by which it has traditionally done so—labour market regulation, universal social entitlements, social insurance and social benefits adequate to sustain a basic standard of living—are increasingly questioned and discredited. The actual erosion or dismantling of social rights seems most pronounced in the liberal welfare states of the Anglo-American world. However even where, as in most states in Europe, the commitment to social objectives endures, it is not difficult to find a new emphasis on flexibility and competitiveness and a shifting set of terms and reference points in respect of social rights and economic security.[29]

The fate of social rights is tied to a transformation in the imagined role of the state in social and economic life. In the classical human rights formulation, the state is responsible for respecting, promoting, protecting, and ensuring the fulfilment of a wide range of rights. While this language

[29] See, for example, the debates on 'flexicurity' in Europe: <http://www.euractiv.com/en/socialeurope/social-partners-agree-flexicurity-disagree-definition/article-158980>.

remains intact where property and contract rights are concerned, elsewhere—concerning social development[30] or gender equality,[31] for example—the state's role is often now framed in other terms: merely to create an 'enabling environment'. Entitlements such as education and skills training are just as likely to be defended in terms of their contribution to the human capital of workers or the demands of a knowledge economy as described as fundamental rights or entrenched incidents of citizenship. Even equality norms may be subject to the calculus of efficiency and sold in terms of the demands of growth.[32]

In tandem with these normative shifts is a new regulatory and policy context in which large numbers of persons are losing the possibility of real access to social benefits and services that once were simply incidents of citizenship. In many jurisdictions, access to unemployment insurance has been restricted, and adequate retirement income through public pension schemes is in doubt. Some of this can be attributed to demographic shifts and some is no doubt a function of changes in the wider world of production. But part of it is a result of deliberate policy design, driven by the desire to reduce the fiscal burden on the state and relieve employers and firms of the burden of social costs. Social rights are still formally part of the agenda. But a combination of elite consensus against universal social entitlements, the erosion of political support for wider redistribution, and the emergence of competitors who have either never recognised extensive social rights or are now prepared to trade them off to attract investment has, in many states, undercut efforts to re-secure the foundations of social rights and better calibrate them to the changed social and economic circumstances. For the same reason—the collapse of the established consensus about the role of the modern state in ensuring the welfare of its citizens, and the struggle to consolidate a quite different one in its place—social rights, at least as conventionally understood, do not animate policy and regulatory discussions with respect to the developing world either.

Yet the concerns that lie behind social rights, growing inequality and more intense commodification have not disappeared; if anything, they have increased. A few nations, China and India in particular, have seen economic growth increase at impressive rates in recent years. But the majority of people in both countries have not participated in this growth. There are certainly more fabulously wealthy people in many countries, and there is without a doubt a cadre of professional and high-skill workers who are benefiting from the burgeoning possibilities of newly opened and

---

[30] World Bank, *The World Bank and the Copenhagen Declaration: Ten Years After* (Washington, DC, World Bank, 2004).

[31] World Bank, *Integrating Gender into the World Bank's Work: A Strategy for Action* (Washington, DC, World Bank, 2002).

[32] *Ibid.*

integrated markets. But at the same time, increasing numbers of workers labour under conditions of risk and insecurity, and many find that work is not actually an escape route from poverty.[33]

Even in the wealthiest countries of the world, few workers or their representatives feel in a position to press for revamped entitlements or new social rights that are responsive to the changed structure of risk and reward in the new economy. Instead, their attention tends to be focused on more immediate concerns: preserving the remaining 'good' jobs, preventing further erosion of social entitlements, and resisting the intensification of demands at work.

III GLOBAL ECONOMIC INEQUALITY

A The Current Context

It is hardly news that periods of market integration or rapid market expansion may co-exist with, and even fuel, economic inequality.[34] For example, such events may increase the economic returns to those with access to assets relative to those without, or they may generate market failures that poor people and/or weaker nations are ill-positioned to manage.[35] But it is worth tracing the specific terrain of inequality in the current context.

The first thing to observe is simply that inequality is growing. At the highest level, this inequality is visible in the economic position of states. After a period of convergence in the post-war era, since about 1978 the economic fortunes of states in the international order have been diverging. A recent study tracking trends in global inequality over two broad periods in the post-war era describes the story as one of 'striking downward mobility' for many states.[36] While between 1960 and 1978 many states managed to improve their position within global rankings, between 1978 and 2000 the tale became one of almost unremitting decline. Almost no state managed to join the club of rich countries; those that did are almost

---

[33] S Greenhouse and D Leonhardt, 'Real Wages Fail to Match a Rise in Productivity', *The New York Times* (New York, 28 August 2006).

[34] The economics literature is replete with diverging and overlapping explanations for this phenomenon. See J Antonio Ocampo, 'Globalization, Development and Democracy', Social Science Research Council, 5 *Items and Issues*, available at <http://www.ssrc.org/publications/items/v5n3/globalization1.html>.

[35] N Birdsall, 'The World is Not Flat: Inequality and Injustice in Our Global Economy', WIDER 2005 Annual Lecture, available at <http://www.wider.unu.edu/>.

[36] Milanovic, *Worlds Apart: Measuring International and Global Inequality* (Princeton, Princeton University Press, 2005). Milanovic also sharply distinguishes between three different types of inequality: category (1) inequality among states; category (2) population weighted inequality among states; and category (3) or what he calls 'true' global inequality, which tracks the equality of individuals irrespective of their nationality.

entirely concentrated within East Asia. At the same time, Africa became almost entirely populated with countries of the fourth, most destitute, economic world. The situation in Latin America is also not good; while in 1960 a good number of Latin American countries were either rich or 'contenders'—within realistic striking distance of becoming rich within the next generation—by 2000, there were only five Latin American or Caribbean countries that fell into these categories. The result is not only a tale of economic decline in many regions, but also a tale of the entrenched hegemony and growing dominance of the West in the global economy.[37]

If the equality trends are not good among states, similar trends are emerging even within the states that are 'winners' in the global game: a range of different studies have confirmed that, in the past twenty years, inequality is also growing within nations. The surge in inequality in the last five years has been particularly pronounced: it has been described as 'universal in the transition economies, almost universal in Latin America and the OECD, and increasingly frequent, if less pronounced, in South, Southeast, and East Asia'.[38] The trend towards greater inequality looks even worse when measured in terms of the distribution of global household wealth rather than national or household income.[39]

Part of the inequality within states is a function of the diverging prospects of workers in labour markets. Profound cleavages are emerging in the positions of workers in the new economy.[40] Gross earnings inequality, which had already increased in the previous decade, is increasing at an accelerated pace.[41] Relative poverty rates have risen marginally since 1994,[42] and employment provides no necessary insurance against this fate; during the same time period, there has also been an increase in the proportion of working poor.[43] Part of the story is the concentration of gains at the very top of the income spectrum. The situation in the United States is instructive, particularly as its existing policies and institutions more closely approach emerging global norms than any other state. In the recent economic boom, wages stagnated or even fell for the vast majority of American workers. However, those at the upper end had a very different experience; here, incomes increased

---

[37] For a detailed discussion, see Milanovic, ibid., 'Winners and Losers: Increasing Dominance of the West', 61–81. Milanovic also identifies the disappearance of middle income nations during the same period; this parallels the hollowing out of the middle class and the concentration of people in the upper and lower income deciles that is visible within many states.

[38] GA Cornia, 'Inequality, Growth, and Poverty: An Overview of Changes over the Last Two Decades' in GA Cornia (ed), *Inequality, Growth, and Poverty in an Era of Liberalization and Growth* (Oxford, Oxford University Press, 2004) 8.

[39] JB Davies et al, *The World Distribution of Household Wealth* (Helsinki, UNU-WIDER, 2006).

[40] OECD, *Employment Outlook: Boosting Jobs and Incomes* (Paris, OECD, 2006).

[41] *Ibid* 38

[42] *Ibid* 39.

[43] *Ibid* 40.

handsomely, and in some cases exploded.[44] At the very top, for example among corporate executives, compensation has increased at rates that have been described as indefensible in economic as well as moral terms.[45]

Whether these economic trends indicate a problem seems to be disputed. It seems important to note that growing poverty is not the point of contention. No one defends the presence of poverty *per se*, even if they sometimes contest the direction in which it is moving or defend the policies that seem to be linked to its aggravation; au contraire, everyone, from international human rights bodies to the international financial and economic institutions promoting market reforms, is against it. [46] For example, the Economic, Social and Cultural Rights Committee has stated that poverty is a marker of the denial of social rights.[47] But the World Bank too routinely describes its mission as poverty alleviation.[48]

However, growing inequality is the point at which the common ground gives way. In a statement on the effects of globalisation, the United Nations Economic, Social and Cultural Rights Committee highlighted the adverse effects on economic, social and cultural rights of trends such as: the growing influence of financial markets on national budget priorities; the privatisation of functions previously within the exclusive domain of the state; and the deregulation of activities to facilitate investment and reward individual initiative.[49] While the Committee's concerns were articulated in terms of the effects of such policies on social rights such as collective bargaining rights and access to social security, it is hard to miss the underlying concern about the growing maldistribution of resources and power. By contrast, many of those within the IMF and the Bank are unconvinced that inequality, as distinct from poverty, is a concern, whether among or within states.[50] There is now an active debate about the relationship between equality and growth within the international financial institutions

[44] T Piketty and E Saez, 'Income Inequality in the United States: 1913–1998' (2003) 118 *Quarterly Journal of Economics* 1.

[45] LA Bebchuk and J Fried, *Pay Without Performance: The Unfulfilled Promise of Executive Compensation* (Cambridge, Mass, Harvard University Press, 2004).

[46] See the Millennium Development Goals, described at <http://www.un.org/millenniumgoals/>.

[47] UN, ECOSOC, 'Poverty and the International Covenant on Economic, Social and Cultural Rights', Statement adopted by the Committee on Economic, Social and Cultural Rights, 4 May 2001, UN Doc E/C.122001/10, 10 May 2001, available at <http://www.unhchr.ch/tbs/doc.nsf/oac7e03e4fe8f2bdc125698a0053bf66/518e88bfb89822c9c1256a4e004df048?OpenDocument>.

[48] For a description of the World Bank's mission, see <http://web.worldbank.org/WBSITE/EXTERNAL/EXTABOUTUS/o,,pagePK:50004410~piPK:36602~theSitePK:29708,00.html>.

[49] United Nations, Office of the High Commissioner for Human Rights, Committee on Economic, Social and Cultural Rights, 'Statement on globalization and economic, social and cultural rights', 18th Session, 27 April-15 May 1998, Geneva.

[50] GA Cornia, 'Inequality, Growth, and Poverty: An Overview of Changes over the Last Two Decades' in GA Cornia (ed), *Inequality, Growth, and Poverty in an Era of Liberalization and Growth* (Oxford, Oxford University Press, 2004) 3.

(IFIs). However, redressing inequality, whether through income transfers or alterations to market rules and regulations, remains a controversial project in these institutions because of the supposed growth-impairing effects of income transfers funded through taxation and regulatory 'interventions' that are motivated by concerns other than correcting market failures.[51]

B Inequality and Regulatory Transformation

What makes the issue of compelling interest is the intuition, and the growing evidence, that the increase in inequality is correlated not simply with greater market integration; instead, it tracks the rise of a consensus to enhance the role of market forces in social and economic ordering.

A recent survey of the policy roots of this aggravated inequality implicates a number of standard elements of the governance agenda that has emerged from this policy consensus: macroeconomic stabilisation, in particular the distributive impact of stabilisation-induced recessions; trade liberalisation policies that lead to declines in employment and wages in some sectors whose effects are not offset by increased jobs in the export sector; changes in norms about remuneration as well as policies governing social transfers; financial reforms; and capital account liberalisation in particular. This last factor seems to have contributed to the sharp increase in the rate of return on financial capital, the benefits of which accrue in a concentrated way to an already quite advantaged group.[52] According to Ocampo, 'the combination of the adverse distributive effects of market reforms... and the simultaneous weakening of the institutions of social protection... offers the best explanation' for the rise in inequality.[53] In short, the trajectory of inequality is tied into changed aspirations and assumptions in respect of social and economic policy which have taken concrete, detailed and, by now, familiar regulatory and institutional forms in many jurisdictions.

These comments echo what has been observed elsewhere, which is that the traditional family of macroeconomic policies associated with global economic integration[54] displays a range of biases which tend to empower

---

[51] A classic target are labour market rules that constrain employers' power to unilaterally determine the content of labour contracts: International Monetary Fund, 1999, *World Economic Outlook: International Financial Contagion*. Available at <http://www.imf.org/external/pubs/ft/weo/1999/01/index.htm> ch IV.

[52] A series of papers reviewing the links between these policies and inequality is to be found in GA Cornia (ed), *Inequality, Growth, and Poverty in an Era of Liberalization and Growth* (Oxford, Oxford University Press, 2004).

[53] JA Ocampo, 'Globalisation, Development and Democracy', Social Science Research Council, 5 *Items and Issues*, available at <http://www.ssrc.org/publications/items/v5n3/globalization1.html>.

[54] For a description of these policies, see J Williamson, 'Democracy and the Washington Consensus' (1993) 21 *World Development* 1331.

capital holders at the expense of other social groups, workers and women in particular.[55] Tight control over inflation may protect investments, but sometimes at the expense of jobs and growth. In addition, the preoccupation with fiscal austerity almost invariably compels workers to become more reliant on their own efforts to ensure their well-being, even where, as frequently occurs, market opportunities decline or disappear for reasons, such as economic or trade-related restructuring, that lie entirely beyond their control. Women in particular are likely to bear increased costs in such contexts.[56]

But other governance projects in the international order are also central to social objectives and social outcomes. Enormously important work is done in the course of specifying the concerns and objectives that should motivate state policy and action concerning economic transactions and in setting the regulatory and institutional framework that governs them. For distributive purposes, the relevant changes are not restricted to tax reforms that shift the burden of social costs and result in a more regressive tax structure. Instead, they include reforms to corporate law rules that make it more difficult to take into consideration the concerns of local stakeholders, as well as a broad range of regulatory reforms advanced in the name of 'doing business'; whatever their effects on the level of investment, these reforms also reallocate costs and risks to myriad other parties. Despite the tendency to imagine private law rules as merely the constitutive fabric of a market economy, something that can safely be consigned to the technocracy,[57] important distributive stakes are also disposed here. Enhanced freedom of contract and reforms to property laws may enable firms and investors to operate with greater ease and lower costs, but they also alter the bargaining power of other social and economic actors, often undercutting their capacity to successfully advance their own concerns and interests. In short, distributive justice and social concerns are in play at virtually every level of the economic and regulatory order.

An important part of the story is a set of deeply intertwined changes to labour market rules and institutions and social policy. Both have had a central place in the reform agendas of the international economic and financial institutions during the last ten years.

[55] D Elson and N Cagatay, 'The Social Content of Macroeconomic Policies' (2000) 28 *World Development* 1347.

[56] There is by now a large literature on the gendered effects of macroeconomic reforms and the consequences for women in labour markets of the maldistribution of unpaid work as between men and women. See, for example: L Beneria, 'The enduring debate over unpaid labour' (1999) 138 *International Labour Review* 287; D Elson, 'Labor Markets as Gendered Institutions: Equality, Efficiency and Empowerment Issues' (1999) 27 *World Development* 611.

[57] Study Group on Social Justice in European Law, 'Social Justice in European Contract Law: a Manifesto' (2004) 10 *European Law Journal* 653.

IV TRANSFORMING LABOUR MARKET INSTITUTIONS AND SOCIAL POLICY: THE OECD JOBS STRATEGIES, 1994 AND 2006

A The New Labour Policy

The elements of the current policy consensus around labour market regulation and social policy can be traced to a 1994 report released by the OECD, the *Jobs Study*.[58] A major report analysing the state of labour markets in the industrialised world, the *Jobs Study* detailed the types of structural reforms that were, in the view of the OECD, required to remedy the high levels of unemployment characteristic of the labour markets in Europe at the time. Although labour market issues in Europe were the catalyst for the study, the *Jobs Study* has turned out to be highly influential in respect of the analysis of labour market institutions and social policy in general. Moreover, it is highly representative of the views held within the epistemic community of which the OECD is a part.[59] The essential claims and assumptions upon which the *Jobs Study* is based, as well as the policy and regulatory conclusions that the OECD reached, have been reiterated in myriad different domestic and international fora, and its findings have been incorporated into the labour market and social policy prescriptions of the international economic and financial institutions and beyond ever since.[60] Having entered the realm of regulatory 'common sense', the *Jobs Study* has profoundly influenced both the debate and the direction of labour market institutions and social policy reform across the industrialised and developing world in the intervening time.

The *Jobs Study* was animated by the assumption that poor labour market performance was essentially a function of inadequate labour market flexibility. Echoing longstanding neo-classical arguments about the adverse effects of 'regulation' on growth and competitiveness,[61] the study

---

[58] OECD, *The OECD Jobs Study – Evidence and Explanations; Part I: Labour Market Trends and Underlying Forces of Change; Part II: The Adjustment Potential of the Labour Market* (Paris, OECD, 1994).

[59] For a discussion of the role of epistemic communities in the formation of global social policy, see B Deacon, 'The Politics of Global Social Policy', UNRISD conference on Social Knowledge and International Policy Making: Exploring the Linkages, 20–21 April 2004, Geneva available at: <http://www.unrisd.org/unrisd/website/events.nsf/(httpAuxPages)/4CC501ECF7776561C1256E7B0051D7E8?OpenDocument&category=Presentations>.

[60] See, for example, International Monetary Fund, 2004, *World Economic Outlook: International Financial Contagion*, available at: <http://www.imf.org/external/pubs/ft/weo/1999/01/index.htm>; International Monetary Fund, *World Economic Outlook: Advancing Structural Reforms* (Washington, DC, IMF, 2004); World Bank, *World Development Report 1995: Workers in an Integrating World* (Washington, DC, World Bank, 1995).

[61] The *Jobs Study* did not, however, pay attention to the restrictive assumptions behind neo-classical theory and therefore to the limitations and qualifications on the regulatory and policy uses of such theory. For a recent discussion of this issue in relation to labour market regulation, see S Deakin and F Wilkinson, 'Labour Law and Economic Theory: A Reappraisal' in H Collins, P Davies, and R Rideout (eds), *Legal Regulation of the Employment Relation* (London, Kluwer Law International, 2000) 29.

decisively came down against many of the labour market institutions commonly found across the industrialised world, and suggested that flexibility could be enhanced by weakening or dismantling employment protections in such areas as job security, wage and labour costs and working time, as well as by decentralising collective bargaining.[62] In addition, the study linked these same labour market institutions to distributional disparities among workers. This, in turn, served to undermine the normative basis for workers' rights and labour standards: far from instruments of social justice, this analysis seemed to suggest that labour market institutions simply enhanced the divisions between insiders and outsiders in the labour force.

The *Jobs Study* also contained a series of recommendations on reforms to social policy. These revolved principally around the goal of 'making work pay', largely by foreclosing easy access to alternative sources of income from the state through insurance and other social entitlements and shifting the focus of state policy from passive to active labour market measures. When the OECD revisited the 1994 study in 2006,[63] labour market participation rates had become the main focus, and 'making work pay' took an even more central place in the reform agenda.

In the view of the OECD, increasing labour force participation is now a key priority, given the spectre of an aging population looming on the horizon of virtually all industrialised economies and the growing numbers of dependants who will need to be financed by a diminishing number of active workers. The preferred strategy to forestall the fiscal crises that this shifting ratio of workers to dependants is almost certain to engender is to persuade, induce or coerce those with any capacity to work to enter, or stay in, the labour force. In this vein, the OECD now recommends a range of rule and policy changes that, for example, extend the tenure of individual employment, eliminate early retirement options and facilitate family-friendly arrangements, such as working time flexibility and child care support.[64]

The restated jobs strategy in the 2006 report identifies four policy and regulatory 'pillars': setting appropriate macroeconomic policy; removing impediments to labour market participation; tackling labour- and product-market obstacles to labour demand; and facilitating the development of labour force skills and competencies. As these pillars indicate, much remains of the 1994 approach; indeed, the basic orientation towards labour and social policy remains largely intact. In particular, the report claims that 'too strict' employment protections are 'likely to reduce the

---

[62] For a summary of the recommendations, see OECD, *Employment Outlook: Boosting Jobs and Income* (Paris, OECD, 2006) 24.
[63] OECD, *Boosting Jobs and Incomes: Policy Lessons from Reassessing the OECD Jobs Strategy* (Paris, OECD, 2006).
[64] *Ibid.*

dynamic efficiency of the economy while worsening long-term unemployment and disadvantaging youth and women'.[65] However, the 2006 report places greater emphasis on tightening disciplinary measures to ensure that work does indeed pay.[66] One technique is to cut off routes to what is described as 'benefits dependency', especially the reliance upon disability benefits that has grown in the last ten years as access to unemployment benefits has been restricted.

In 2006, as in 1994, the major route to the creation of jobs remains the promotion of economic growth through appropriate macroeconomic and regulatory policies. Echoing the findings of another influential report series from the World Bank,[67] the report concludes that there must be continuing emphasis on securing private rights while 'competition restraining' control of business on the part of the state should be reduced'.[68] Although the recommendations to 'deregulate' labour markets are supplemented by observations about the need for job training and other active labour market policies, they seem primarily directed towards ensuring that workers are more responsive to changing market demands.

Despite important concessions about the effects of employment standards (it turns out that they don't necessarily lead to higher unemployment[69]), and therefore the viability of different routes to good labour market outcomes, what is consolidated in the 2006 report is what was initially proposed in 1994: fundamentally, a transformation of the social contract and a revolution in the norms concerning employment. No longer is the worker entitled to a measure of job security or even employment security, still less substantial resources from the state when labour markets fail to produce the opportunities that are promised. At best, the goal is employability in a dynamic labour market.

B Reforming Social Policy

The post-war social contract involved a set of inter-related social and economic policies that operated in addition to labour market rules and standards. In most states, it typically rested on: demand-side management of the economy through fiscal and monetary policy; a commitment to the

---

[65] Above n 62, 100.

[66] A number of analysts have noted the tendency to employ increasingly disciplinary measures in the context of labour and social policy reforms: S Deakin, 'Social Rights in a Globalized Economy' in P Alston (ed), *Labour Rights as Human Rights* (Oxford, Oxford University Press, 2005) 25; G Standing, 'Globalisation: Eight Crises of Social Protection' in L Beneria and S Bisnath (eds), *Global Tensions: Challenges and Opportunities in the World Economy* (New York and London, Routledge, 2004) 111.

[67] See, for example, World Bank, *Doing Business in 2004: Understanding Regulation* (Washington, DC, World Bank, 2003).

[68] Above n 63, 22

[69] Above n 62, 96.

maintenance of (relatively) full employment, supported by public employment and public works if necessary; employment and other forms of insurance to compensate workers who were affected by unemployment, whether frictional or structural; additional insurance for those who suffered from disabilities that impaired their capacity to work; income transfers for those either periodically or permanently outside the labour market; state-provided pensions to ensure economic security in old age; and guaranteed universal access to public goods such as health, education and housing.

Central to the new policy and regulatory consensus is a fundamental reconsideration of the Keynesian model and all that it entailed. The effect this reconsideration has exercised on social entitlements is by now well known, as states across the industrialised world have moved to restrict access to income replacement schemes such as unemployment and disability insurance and reduced the levels of benefits to those who still qualify. In a similar vein, the benefits available through need-based entitlements such as welfare have also been reduced. The recurring nature and family resemblance among these policies is not accidental: it is part of a broader strategy to ensure that participation in markets, whether through investment or labour, becomes the primary source of economic security and social inclusion. But labour market participation was key to economic security in the post-war social contract as well. What is different now is the status of social rights and the role envisioned for public goods, social policy and social protection in economic security.

One important difference is simply the range or scope of current social protection and insurance initiatives. Instead of broad-based social provision and social protection, the new social protection paradigm favours a safety net only for the least well-off.[70] Rather than provide universal entitlements to resources and services to citizens at large, states are advised to 'target' resources to the neediest. Even where public resources are indicated, however, support from the state is expected to be not only narrowly targeted but short- rather than long-term to the extent possible. In the process, guarantees of basic services and entitlements to a very wide segment of society and social entitlements that were not merely aspirational but were actually realised to varying degrees in the post-war social contracts of liberal democracies are being discarded.

A key difference lies in the proposed terms of access to social benefits; this in turn reflects a fundamental shift in the purpose of social insurance and income transfers. Rather than merely support workers during periods of unemployment, ensuring the maintenance of at least basic levels of

---

70 B Deacon, 'The Politics of Global Social Policy', UNRISD conference on Social Knowledge and International Policy Making: Exploring the Linkages, 20–21 April 2004, Geneva, available at: <http://www.unrisd.org/unrisd/website/events.nsf/(httpAuxPages)/4CC501ECF7776561C1 256E7B0051D7E8?OpenDocument&category=Presentations>.

income, social policies are being restructured to enhance the possibility that workers will actually relocate and take up new work: hence the new time limits on social benefits and the increased requirements for training and job searches in order to actually obtain benefits that mark the move from 'passive' to 'active' labour market policies.

A number of background assumptions, or claims, lie behind the new paradigm. One is that once the background conditions enabling markets to function optimally are implemented and the disincentives to market participation are removed, markets can be expected to provide employment for the vast majority of citizens. The second is that 'generous' benefits are exactly one of those disincentives to labour market participation that should be avoided; any state that is concerned to enhance market participation must, perforce, scale them back. The third is that economic need arises largely from personal circumstances—for example, individual traits that impair labour market participation, or perhaps personal choice—rather than as a consequence of structural properties or market failures within the economy as a whole.

Arguments that benefits for those outside the market should be sufficient to support an adequate standard of living tend to meet with little sympathy within this frame of analysis. First, such benefits risk placing an unsustainable fiscal strain on the state, particularly in the context of a demographic shift in which a declining number of active workers are funding a growing number of retirees or 'dependants'. Second, the level of benefits is not regarded as a general social concern; instead, it is something of concern to a relatively small contingent of people. Whatever arguments might still be marshalled for greater generosity on the part of the well-off are countered with the claim that they will undermine the efficient operation of labour markets and/or impair growth.

To reiterate, in the new social paradigm there remains scope for a social safety net for the very poorest. But for the vast majority of citizens, those beyond the limited category for whom the safety net is intended, social protection becomes transformed into risk management on the individual or household level.[71] The objective of social risk management departs sharply from the original vision behind social insurance and social protection. It does not involve broad social pooling of risk or significant transfers of resources among citizens. Instead, risk management is focused on objectives such as 'income smoothing', that is, strategies to enable the individual to accommodate and better weather the foreseeable events and needs that occur over his or her lifetime.[72] So, for example, individual retirement accounts might be favoured over publicly guaranteed and managed pensions. Indeed, part of its appeal is the promise of social

[71] G Standing, above n 66, 112.
[72] R Holzmann, L Sherburne-Benz and E Tesliuc, *Social Risk Management: The World Bank's Approach to Social Protection in a Globalizing World* (Washington, DC, World Bank, 2003).

protection that does not involve significant resources transfers or impose burdens on the state. Any wider aspirations to improve the overall economic security of everyone, including many whose labour market position remains precarious, by redistributing resources from those who are doing well, or at least better, to those who are doing worse are drastically scaled back. The extent to which social risk management actually ensures adequate economic security, of course, depends in large part on the prospects of the individual in the market.

V ASSESSING THE JOBS STRATEGY

A Labour Market Security and Empowerment

In both OECD reports, jobs are envisioned as the central, if not sole, source of economic security for the vast majority of citizens. If jobs now effectively 'stand in' for economic security, however, then there are two concerns with the jobs strategy: the first is unemployment, and the second is the problem of precarious work.

It is clear that trade liberalisation may aggravate unemployment levels, particularly in the short to medium term. While it is a submerged element of the overall analysis, the reallocation of labour along with financial and other productive resources in trade-related restructuring is arguably the point of the exercise, as it is an important source of the expected gains from trade. There are inherent risks to workers in the course of trade liberalisation, the main one being that there is no guarantee that the 'replacement' jobs will automatically spring up in any particular place, that they will suit the displaced workers in terms of skill and experience or that, if they do, they will provide roughly equivalent (or better) wages and benefits. Moreover, the risks to workers associated with unemployment, whether trade-related or not, may be exacerbated where regulatory reforms eliminate 'constraints' on the property and contractual rights of investors and employers and allow firms to externalise rather than absorb more of the costs involved in economic restructuring and relocation. Reductions in job security protections, for example, compel workers to bear more of the risk of interruptions to employment. Where employers are released from obligations to pay severance too, workers see less in the way of economic rewards for their work as well. In the face of declining access to social transfers, employment insurance and other services and benefits, the degree of economic hardship experienced may be pronounced.

The upside is supposed to be more, and better, jobs generated by a more dynamic economy. But the downside possibility—job losses accompanied by reduced ability to make claims on the state for adjustment assistance—remains a distinct possibility. In the absence of institutional mechanisms to redistribute trade-related gains, the net result can be worsening inequality as well: high returns for some workers, but declining wages and employment prospects for others.

As the enduring preoccupation with incentives to labour market participation indicates, the jobs strategy rests on the assumption that the question of jobs is primarily a supply-side issue, a matter of inducing workers to take up available labour market opportunities. However, this assumption seriously underplays, if it does not write out of the equation altogether, the structural causes of labour market disruptions, namely, fluctuating or declining demand. The more fundamental problem, however, is that demand-side problems may be actually induced not only by trade liberalisation but by other elements of the policy consensus on good macroeconomic governance too. As a number of analysts have observed, stabilisation measures routinely seem to produce recessions and declining employment;[73] moreover, there are indications that the job losses often remain after the recession itself is over.[74]

But even if trade liberalisation reliably generated new jobs and macroeconomic disruptions to labour markets were put to one side, it remains unclear why a policy simply to generate more jobs should still, in 2006, be enough to garner widespread support. For, in the time between the two studies, it has become clear that higher employment does not necessarily equate to lower poverty or greater economic security; indeed, the 2006 study itself documents the diverging possibilities along precisely these lines. Hence, the task is not just generating jobs but generating 'good' jobs, that is, jobs that are not just marginally more attractive than social benefits, a situation that, in the end, can always be ensured simply by degrading the quality or level of benefits and restricting access to income replacement schemes. However, in light of the conclusion that either road—low labour market standards and regulation accompanied by higher poverty and inequality or lower poverty/higher labour standards along with active labour market policies—can produce 'good' labour market outcomes, it is hard not to conclude that the main concern lies with reducing dependency and simply getting bodies into jobs.

The renewed emphasis on job training and other active labour market policies might seem to be responsive to the concern about 'good' jobs. However, investments in skill may not, on their own, produce matching jobs. Even where a focus on education and training seems appropriate, the complexity of matching skill to the market should not be underestimated, whether in terms of resources or of administrative and institutional infra-

---

[73] A Cornia, above n 38.

[74] R van der Hoeven and C Saget, 'Labour Market Institutions and Income Inequality: What are the New Insights after the Washington Consensus?' in GA Cornia (ed), *Inequality, Growth, and Poverty in an Era of Liberalization and Growth* (Oxford, Oxford University Press, 2004) 197–220.

structure. As the many unsuccessful efforts have underscored, policies to get workers into jobs that are both suitable and provide decent wages typically require sustained effort over the long term and significant amounts of financing, as well as deep and enduring connections between firms and industrial sectors on the one hand and the institutions that are charged with training and education of their workforces on the other. A focus on skill also, of course, implies relatively high base levels of funding for public education. Alas, these elements, or at least some of them, are precisely what tends to be missing in so many jurisdictions, particularly in the Anglo-American world, which has no tradition of coordinated bargaining or labour-management and tripartite consultation over production. Given the concern that is driving the emphasis on increased labour force participation in the first place—namely, alleviating fiscal strain and reducing the scope and ambition of state programmes—there is no reason to think that the financing and administrative structures adequate to these tasks would be warmly embraced, at least where they are not already well entrenched. So it is not surprising that, so far, adequate financing for active labour market policies has received little attention.

Finally, it should be noted that the 2006 study does not assess the influence of policy and regulatory changes on real wages and living standards, even though the report acknowledges that these issues are important to the assessment of labour market performance.[75] Instead, productivity growth is simply identified as a key determinant of real wage growth in the long run. If the gamble is that productivity growth will translate into wage gains for workers in the end, so that a direct focus on supporting wages and improving working conditions by other means is unnecessary, then it is unresponsive to at least one emerging trend: worker productivity gains that are increasingly de-linked from wage gains, as the returns of production shift from wages to income derived from capital. As the evidence indicates, workers' real incomes continue to lag considerably behind the growth in productivity. While the OECD simply characterises the decade after the 1994 study as 'a decade of wage moderation',[76] translated, this observation indicates that most workers have simply failed to benefit economically from the recent economic boom.

The significance of these developments to the jobs strategy would appear to be two-fold. First, they seem to undermine the claim that intensified market participation, on its own, is a reliable route to economic security for workers. Second, they call into question the argument that structural reforms to 'decompress' wages will permit workers' economic rewards to track effort, performance and value to their employers.

---

[75] Above n 62, 23
[76] Above n 62, 20.

B Social Policy and Inequality

This retrenchment in respect of social entitlements undermines economic security in ways that are both obvious and covert. The effects on the individual level are evident: whatever their overall impact on rates of labour market participation, reductions in social transfers and insurance benefits will clearly have adverse effects on those who depend on them for their well-being or survival. And unless the reductions really do reliably generate more jobs, something that as a result of the 2006 study is now clearly in doubt, the net result may be simply diminished economic security and lower levels of social welfare, not only for the affected individuals but in the aggregate as well.

In the scenario that is now unfolding, inequality and social rights may also be related in one of two ways. First, changes to social policy in the direction just described may themselves exacerbate levels of social inequality. Second, growing inequality may itself fuel the erosion of policies and programmes that give life to the concept of social rights. The threat to social rights here is obvious: to the extent that the transformation of social policy increases economic inequality, the risk is a downward spiral, a situation in which it becomes increasingly difficult to hang on to even the more modest ambitions for social rights.

First, changes to the structure and access of social benefits and insurance that may increase inequality. Cuts to benefits available through insurance and income transfers anchor the income of those outside the market at levels significantly below that of market participants, as they are intended to do. In and of themselves, such strategies are likely to increase the dispersion of income across society. However, such policies may well drive more people to accept work on any terms too.

Here we can begin to see how changes to social policies may well have pernicious effects on the quality of jobs as well, thus undermining the capacity of labour markets to deliver economic security as promised. Restricting access to, or suppressing the level of, social benefits may well increase labour market participation as intended. But at the same time, such efforts can be expected to have adverse effects on labour market conditions. All other things being equal, reducing both the possibility and the appeal of alternatives to waged work places downward pressure on wages and working conditions. It also weakens workers' bargaining power vis-à-vis their employers. There is general agreement that workers' bargaining power has already declined in the new economy, for reasons ranging from the reorganisation of production and the enhanced ability of firms to relocate, to regulatory changes, especially those promoted by the *Jobs Study*, that shift costs and risks to workers. In this context, the transformation of social entitlements risks entrenching, even normalising, poor working conditions, diminished worker control and voice at work, and intensifying the extent of the deformalisation and casualisation of work that is already afoot in the new economy.[77] Such results should not be surprising. As Simon Deakin has established in his historical review of social rights in industrialising England, it is already a matter of record that depressing standards inside the workplace and outside can be mutually reinforcing.[78] Rather than a means to 'boost jobs and incomes', reforms to social entitlements strategy may well operate to aggravate the problem of bad jobs.

Second, it seems important to point out that growing economic inequality may itself play a role in undermining social rights, because it undermines the political support that sustains the health of social services and programmes. In tandem with the concentration of wealth at the upper end, increasing numbers of high- and even middle-income earners are defecting from publicly provided services and insurance, detaching themselves from the system after making the calculation that they do not need to pool risk in order to thrive in the current economy. Instead, they are seeking insurance and services privately, and on terms that are sometimes more personally beneficial. As they rely to a larger and larger extent upon privately provided services such as health care and education, they are less inclined to support the public systems from which they no longer directly benefit. This tends to erode the system of public provisioning both financially and politically; the result is that the (many) people who remain very much in need of risk-pooling on a wide basis and benefit from the redistribution of resources from the better-off find themselves in a climate in which such demands are less likely to get a receptive hearing.

This phenomenon too should not be surprising, as it is simply a manifestation of the political economy of targeting. It is an old adage that 'programmes for poor people are poor programmes'. One of the arguments for universal entitlements to insurance schemes and services is that, however much it seems to make sense to target resources to the neediest, middle-class buy-in often turns out to be critical, not only in order to guarantee the quality of services but also to ensure their availability at all. To put it another way, however morally appealing, it may be implausible, if not impossible, in the real world to ensure the well-being of the worst-off without ensuring access to goods and services in general.[79]

Finally, it is worth recalling that the new regulatory consensus involves not only structural reforms to labour markets and the retrenchment of the

---

[77] For a discussion, see J Fudge and R Owens (eds), *Precarious Work, Women, and the New Economy: The Challenge to Legal Norms* (Oxford and Portland, Hart Publishing, 2006).
[78] S Deakin, above n 66.
[79] A Sen, 'The Political Economy of Targeting' in D van de Walle and K Nead (eds), *Public Spending and the Poor: Theory and Evidence* (Baltimore, Johns Hopkins University Press, 1995) 11.

state in respect of social entitlements but extends to the overall structure, delivery and financing of public goods.[80] This development, too, is relevant to questions of equality, economic security and social rights, for the economic prospects of the worst-off may be visibly worsened if we include in the calculus the trend toward privatising services and implementing user fees, not just for social services but for basic infrastructure as well.

For example, user pay arrangements organised by private providers or public-private partnerships may compel citizens to fund costs that, under the old model, were understood to be a collective responsibility funded by the state. Depending on the income levels of consumers and the degree to which rates are regulated, basic services like water can end up beyond the reach of the average consumer or, in the alternative, exact a high level of any available resources. At the same time investors and corporations, whether due to the threat of exit, capital strike or simply because of competition among jurisdictions for investment, are often in a position to extract sizeable concessions in the form of tax breaks or investments in the infrastructure needed to support their economic activity.[81] The result is often regressive redistribution: collective social resources are effectively funnelled to those who already have sufficient bargaining power to tilt regulatory and policy decisions in their favour. Where there is no means of ensuring that that the expected local benefits—whether in jobs, tax revenues or economic spin-offs—actually materialise, this state of affairs can produce results that, from the standpoint of equality, are not simply regressive but perverse.

VI CONCLUSION

In a world organised to extract the benefits of economic incentives and market forces, the primary way in which citizens achieve social inclusion and affiliation to the polity is through participation in market activities like consumption and labour market work. The celebratory attitude held by policy elites toward this state of affairs is evident in a recent anecdote proffered by former World Bank President James Wolfensohn. Describing the reactions of the women in the slums of Rio de Janeiro to the receipt of a bill for their privately provided water services, he had this to say:

> Many of the women I met during my trip to the favelas in Rio were keen to present me with the receipt proving that they had paid their water bill. What they were in fact showing me was the first official document that bore their

---

[80] World Bank, Policy Research Report, *Reforming Infrastructure: Privatization, Regulation and Competition* (Washington, DC, World Bank, 2004), available at: <http://econ.worldbank.org/prr/reforming_infrastructure/>.

[81] J Braithwaite, *Markets in Vice/Markets in Virtue* (Oxford and New York, Oxford University Press, 2005).

names. Having such a document meant that they could go down into Rio and buy a bicycle or apply for a bank loan because, for the first time in their lives, they could offer proof of address. It meant that they were, all of a sudden, recognised members of society...[82]

Whatever else may be said about it, the idea that the opportunity to purchase water and then leverage it to obtain a bank loan might be a marker of social inclusion and citizenship, the entry ticket to society, is a profound challenge to any concept of social rights.[83]

What most distinguishes social rights is the decision to not merely 'abate the nuisance of obvious destitution in the lowest ranks of society'[84] but to intervene in the structure of social and economic inequality. It is this aspiration from which the policy consensus has most clearly retreated, and an emphasis on providing welfare only to the very poorest has been substituted in its place. Although Marshall described social rights as 'creating a universal right to real income which is not proportionate to the market value of the claimant',[85] claims of right in respect of economic security are precisely what is resisted in the imagined new order. But norms of solidarity and equality are also negligible or absent. Whatever social claims the citizens may still have upon the state—for example, the provision of basic education—the dominant policy and regulatory impulse is to reverse the process of decommodification which marked the introduction of social rights, and to increase the extent to which economic and social status tracks market measures, market incentives and market success.

As social policy in the global arena is progressively collapsed into labour market policy, labour policy, in turn, is increasingly merged with considerations of good economic governance. Driven by the perceived demands of competitiveness and efficiency, labour force participation becomes the central preoccupation of states and economic policymakers on the social front, while social entitlements are increasingly geared to ensuring that citizens enter, and stay in, the labour market.

This re-alignment of social, labour and economic policy returns us to the paradox of social rights. Social rights and social policy have traditionally been motivated by the desire to mitigate the effects of market forces on both individuals and society at large. Workers' rights and labour market institutions, too, are rooted in the well-documented limits of freedom of contract for workers. In a context in which global market integration seems to be correlated with growing economic inequality, both

---

[82] JD Wolfensohn, 'The Undivided City' in R Scholar (ed), *The Oxford Amnesty Lectures 2003* (Oxford, Oxford University Press, 2006) 109.

[83] As Aeyal Gross wryly observed, this transforms the 'rights carrying citizen' into the 'bill carrying consumer'.

[84] TH Marshall, 'Citizenship and Social Class', in *Class, Citizenship and Social Development* (Chicago and London, University of Chicago Press, 1963) 106.

[85] TH Marshall, above n 12, 106.

within and among states, we must confront the possibility that labour market institutions and social policy are now symptomatically reflecting, and intensifying, the adverse effects of the wider political and regulatory context for workers, whether measured in terms of bargaining power, economic outcomes or simply the basic elements of citizenship.

7

Indirect Protection of Social Rights by the European Court of Human Rights

EVA BREMS

I INTRODUCTION

Apart from a few exceptions, such as the right to form and join trade unions[1] and the right to legal aid in criminal matters,[2] the European Convention on Human Rights and Fundamental Freedoms ('ECHR') and its additional protocols do not include social rights. Most of the rights encompassed in the Convention can be classified as civil and political rights: for example, the protection of property (Article 1, Protocol 1) is usually classified as an economic right, while the right to education (Article 2, Protocol 1) is classified as a cultural or social right. Under the Council of Europe's human rights protection regime, social rights are protected in a separate treaty instead, namely, the European Social Charter.[3] Complaints regarding violations of the rights protected under the Charter cannot be brought before the European Court of Human Rights ('ECtHR'). Instead, the European Committee of Social Rights monitors the Charter's implementation, mainly through scrutiny of

---

[1] Convention for the Protection of Human Rights and Fundamental Freedoms (European Convention on Human Rights, as amended) (ECHR) Art 11, para 1: 'Everyone has the right to freedom of peaceful assembly and to freedom of association with others, including the right to form and join trade unions for the protection of his interests'.

[2] ECHR Art 6, para 3: 'Everyone charged with a criminal offence has the following minimum rights:... (c) to defend himself in person or through legal assistance of his own choosing or, if he has not sufficient means to pay for legal assistance, to be given it free when the interests of justice so require'.

[3] European Social Charter (Turin, 3 May 1961, entered into force 26 February 1965); Additional Protocol to the European Social Charter (5 May 1988, entered into force 4 September 1992); Protocol Amending the European Social Charter (21 October 1991); Additional Protocol to the European Social Charter Providing for a System of Collective Complaints (9 November 1995, entered into force 1 July 1998); revised Social Charter (3 May 1996, entered into force 1 July 1999). The revised Charter is gradually replacing the original.

state reports. A 1995 protocol to the Charter that entered into force in 1998 provides for a collective complaint procedure for trade unions, employer organisations, and NGOs to appeal to the Committee if they believe that a state has violated one of the rights protected under the Charter.[4] By 1 January 2006, final decisions had been rendered in 27 complaints, and decisions were pending in several other complaints. This mechanism has begun to play an important role in the clarification of the normative contents of social rights and in the development of their justiciability.

This chapter, however, focuses on the European Court of Human Rights.[5] An analysis of the ECtHR case law is obviously crucial for the 46 Council of Europe Member States, as well as being of considerable relevance for human rights lawyers in other countries too. International human rights courts are a rare phenomenon, and the ECtHR is probably the best functioning example or, at the very least, the most experienced such court. In 2005 alone, the Court issued 881 judgments on the merits and 25,451 other final decisions.[6] Through more than 50 years of case law, the Strasbourg court has developed numerous legal techniques that may be useful also for other (national as well as international) courts and supervisory bodies dealing with human rights law. These techniques relate to issues such as interpretation of terms, permissible limitations of rights, conflicts of rights, and the horizontal effect of human rights.

One particularly interesting element in the Court's case law is its broad recognition of positive state obligations,[7] sometimes presented as a distinguishing feature of economic and social rights. The justiciability of these

---

[4] When the Committee finds for a breach of the Charter in its report, the Committee of Ministers of the Council of Europe recommends that the state concerned take measures to remedy the situation (Art 9, Additional Protocol to the European Social Charter Providing for a System of Collective Complaints, 1995).

[5] Studies dealing with the protection of social rights by the ECtHR are scarce. See O De Schutter, 'The Protection of Social Rights by the European Court of Human Rights' in J Vande Lanotte, J Sarkin, T De Pelsmaeker and P Van Der Auweraert (eds), *Economic, Social and Cultural Rights—An Appraisal of Current International and European Developments* (Antwerp, Maklu, 2002) 207–39; M Enrich and I Mas, 'Les droits sociaux dans la jurisprudence de la Cour et de la Commission européennes des droits de l'homme' (1992) 3 *Revue Trimestrielle des Droits de l'Homme* 147–80; JA Frowein, 'Wirtschaftliche und Soziale Rechte in der Rechtsprechung der Strassburger Organe' (1992) 4 *European Review of Public Law* 263–77; M Pellonpää, 'Economic, Social and Cultural Rights' in RS Macdonald, F Matscher and H Petzold (eds), *The European System for the Protection of Human Rights* (Dordrecht/Boston/London, Martinus Nijhoff, 1993) 855–74; F Sudre, 'La protection des droits sociaux par la Cour européenne des droits de l'homme: un exercice de "jurisprudence fiction"?' (2003) 14 *Revue Trimestrielle des Droits de l'Homme* 755–79.

[6] These are decisions of inadmissibility or decisions to strike a case off the list. Statistics are available at <http://www.echr.coe.int/ECHR/EN/Header/Reports+and+Statistics/Statistics/Statistical+Tables>.

[7] The European Court of Human Rights does not make the terminological distinction between obligations to protect, obligations to promote, and obligations to fulfill. It only mentions negative and positive state obligations.

obligations is frequently questioned, despite the compelling arguments made by many leading commentators that the distinction between economic and social rights, on the one hand, and civil and political rights, on the other, is artificial and despite the efforts of the UN Committee on Economic and Social Rights[8] and leading academics[9] to demonstrate the justiciability of economic and social rights. For European human rights lawyers, these debates are sometimes puzzling, for the ECtHR case law has long held that civil and political rights entail positive obligations. In its not-uncommon finding that a state has violated a human right (such as the right to life,[10] the right to privacy,[11] the right to access to court,[12] or freedom of expression[13]) by failing to act in an appropriate manner, the Court frequently demonstrates in practice the justiciability of positive obligations.

This chapter distinguishes three techniques—interpretation, procedural protection and non-discrimination—that are used by the ECtHR to indirectly protect social rights. First, it is important to note that there are numerous cases in which the Court refuses to protect social rights. It regularly reminds applicants that those rights do not fall within the scope of the Convention's protection.[14] The purpose of this chapter, however, is to demonstrate how, without taking a particularly activist approach towards social issues, a court working with classical civil and political rights nevertheless awards in many cases some (at times limited, at times significant) extent of protection to social rights. The cases that are discussed have been selected to illustrate this point. Hence, the image presented is an inevitably partial one.

A significant number of the ECtHR cases examined below are not judgments on the merits but, rather, decisions grounded in points of inadmissibility. In addition to formal admissibility criteria,[15] the Court frequently uses an admissibility test consisting of a summary examination of the merits of the case. Numerous cases are thus dismissed as inadmissible for being 'manifestly ill-founded'. While the reasoning in such

---

[8] See, in particular, CESCR General Comment 3: 'The nature of States parties' obligations' and CESCR General Comment 9: 'The domestic application of the Covenant'.

[9] See, eg, 'The Limburg Principles on the Implementation of the International Covenant on Economic, Social and Cultural Rights' (1987) 9 *Human Rights Quarterly* 122–35; 'Maastricht Guidelines on Violations of Economic, Social and Cultural Rights' (1998) 20 *Human Rights Quarterly* 691–704.

[10] See, eg, *Öneryildiz v Turkey* (App No 48939/99) ECHR 30 November 2004, para 110.

[11] See, eg, *X & Y v The Netherlands* (App No 8978/80) (1985) Series A, No 91.

[12] See, eg, *Airey v Ireland* (App No 6289/73) (1979) Series A, No 32.

[13] See, eg, *Özgür Gündem v Turkey* (App No 231144/93) ECHR 16 March 2000.

[14] See, eg, *Pançenko v Latvia* (App No 40772/98) (Dec) ECHR 28 October 1999: 'The Convention does not guarantee, as such, socio-economic rights, including the right to charge-free dwelling, the right to work, the right to free medical assistance, or the right to claim financial assistance from a State to maintain a certain level of living'.

[15] ECHR Art 35.

decisions tends to be brief, interesting considerations are often put forth, articulating new trends in the Court's case law.

II INTERPRETING THE SCOPE OF CIVIL AND POLITICAL RIGHTS

The French term for indirect protection of social rights through the interpretation of the scope of civil and political rights is 'protection par ricochet'[16]—social rights are, in a sense, interpreted 'into' civil and political rights. This mechanism is not recognised as such by the European Court of Human Rights, nor is it the result of intentional judicial activism. Rather, it seems that the indivisible nature of human rights makes this infusion of social rights into the ECHR inevitable. Indivisibility is more than a dogma of human rights theory: social rights really are inextricably linked to civil and political rights. Hence, in some cases, where this link is particularly strong, it is possible to treat violations of social rights as violations of civil or political rights.

In one of the first cases in which this technique was applied, the Court made the following comment:

> Whilst the Convention sets forth what are essentially civil and political rights, many of them have implications of a social or economic nature. The Court therefore considers... that the mere fact that an interpretation of the Convention may extend into the sphere of social and economic rights should not be a decisive factor against such an interpretation; there is no water-tight division separating that sphere from the field covered by the Convention.[17]

Because there is no such 'water-tight division' separating civil and political rights from economic and social rights, an interpretation of the Convention that is concerned with effective human rights protection and that accepts positive obligations as a corollary of civil and political rights easily moves into the field of social rights.

---

[16] See, eg, M Levinet, 'Recherche sur les fondements du "droit au développement de l'être humain" à partir de l'exemple de la Convention européenne des droits de l'homme' in JY Morin (ed), *Les droits fondamentaux, actes des 1ères Journées scientifiques du Réseau Droits fondamentaux de l'AUPELF-UREF tenues à Tunis du 9 au 12 octobre 1996* (Brussels, Bruylant, 1997) 57; AD Olinga, 'Le droit à des conditions matérielles d'existence minimales en tant qu'élément de la dignité humaine (arts 2 et 3 CEDH)' in JY Morin (ed), para 92; S Priso, 'La dignité par le logement : l'article 1er du Protocole n° 1 de la CEDH et la lutte contre la précarité' in JY Morin (ed), para 117.

[17] *Airey v Ireland*, above n 12, para 26.

A The Right to Legal Aid in Civil Matters

The above passage is quoted from the Court's 1979 judgment in *Airey v Ireland*. The background to the case was Mrs Airey's desire to go to court to obtain a separation from her husband, a violent alcoholic. She had consulted several solicitors, but found no one willing to act on her behalf as she did not have the means to pay, and no legal aid was available for civil matters. In the case law preceding *Airey*, the ECtHR had derived the right to access to court from the right to a fair trial guaranteed under Article 6, Section 1 of the Convention.[18] In this case the Court added that this right to access to court gives rise to positive state duties to ensure effective access for all. Though the state has the freedom to choose the means for realising its duty, sometimes Article 6 may

> compel the state to provide for the assistance of a lawyer when such assistance proves indispensable for an effective access to court either because legal representation is rendered compulsory... or by reason of the complexity of the procedure or of the case.[19]

Thus the Court recognised that whereas the ECHR explicitly includes a right to legal aid only in criminal matters, at times a right to legal aid in civil matters can be derived from the right to a fair trial. It found Ireland in violation of this right in *Airey*.[20]

B The Right to Health or Health Care

The right to health or health care has been indirectly protected by the European Court of Human Rights in several instances on the basis of the prohibition on torture and inhuman or degrading treatment in Article 3 of the ECHR, the Convention's guarantees with respect to detention (Article 5), the right to life guaranteed under Article 2, and the right to protection of private life guaranteed under Article 8.

I The Right to Health Care under Article 3 of the ECHR

a Expulsion of a foreigner in a very poor state of health   There   is   a consistent line of case law that considers the expulsion of a foreigner a possible violation of Article 3 of the Convention if there is a real risk that the person would be subjected to degrading or inhuman treatment or

---

18 The landmark case in this regard was *Golder v United Kingdom* (App No 4451/70) (1975) Series A, No 18.

19 *Airey v Ireland*, above n 12, para 26.

20 This was in spite of the fact that Ireland had registered a reservation to Art 6, para 3(c), of the Convention, which protects the right to legal aid in criminal matters. See *Airey v Ireland*, above n 12, para 26.

torture in the intaking country.[21] In the case of *D v United Kingdom*,[22] this was extended to include a person in a very poor state of health, when no sufficient treatment or family support is available in the intaking country. The applicant in this case was caught with a substantial quantity of cocaine in his possession upon arriving in the United Kingdom. While serving his prison sentence in the UK, he was diagnosed with AIDS. He was to be returned to his home state of St Kitts after his release, which he appealed to the ECtHR. The Court ruled that, based on compelling humanitarian considerations, such deportation would amount to inhuman treatment in violation of Article 3 of the Convention. In the previous case law, expelling states had been held accountable only when the risk of violating Article 3 had emanated from an intentionally inflicted act by public authorities or from the act of a non-state body when the authorities had been unable to afford appropriate protection against this act. In *D v United Kingdom*, however, the Court held that Article 3 may apply also:

> [w]hen the source of the risk... stems from factors which cannot engage either directly or indirectly the responsibility of the public authorities of that country, or which, taken alone, do not in themselves infringe the standards of that article... In any such contexts, however, the Court must subject all the circumstances surrounding the case to a rigorous scrutiny, especially the applicant's personal situation in the expelling state.[23]

Not only was *D* in the advanced stage of a terminal illness, he had no family in St Kitts. The Court stated that:

> The limited quality of life he now enjoys results from the availability of sophisticated treatment and medication in the UK and the care and kindness administered by a charitable organisation.[24] ... The abrupt withdrawal of these facilities will entail the most dramatic consequences for him... There is a serious danger that the conditions of adversity which await him in St Kitts will further reduce his already limited life expectancy and subject him to acute mental and physical suffering. Any medical treatment which he might hope to receive there could not contend with the infections which he may possibly contract on account of his lack of shelter and of a proper diet as well as exposure to the health and sanitation problems which beset the population of St Kitts.[25]

The Court stressed the very exceptional circumstances of the case, emphasising that:

---

[21] See, eg, *Cruz Varas v Sweden* (App No 15576/89) (1991) Series A, No 201; *Chahal v United Kingdom* (App No 22414/93) ECHR 1996-V 1831.

[22] *D v United Kingdom* (App No 30240/96) ECHR 1997-III 777.

[23] *Ibid* para 49.

[24] After the report of the European Commission of Human Rights in his case, he was released from immigration detention and allowed to reside in special sheltered accommodation for AIDS patients provided by a charitable organisation working with the homeless. There, he enjoyed free accommodation, food and services, as well as emotional support from trained volunteers; *ibid* para 19.

[25] *D v United Kingdom*, above n 22, paras 51–2.

Aliens who have served prison sentences and are subject to expulsion cannot in principle claim any entitlement to remain in the territory of a contracting State in order to continue to benefit from medical, social or other forms of assistance provided by the expelling State during their stay in prison.[26]

Yet, in numerous other cases, the ECtHR has ruled that the applicant's situation is not bad enough for his or her expulsion to constitute a violation of Article 3. Cases are rejected—often, in the admissibility stage, for being 'manifestly ill-founded'—on the basis of their being distinguished from *D v United Kingdom*. It is argued that the applicant is not (yet) very ill and/or that treatment and family support are available in his or her home country.[27]

---

[26] *Ibid*, para 54. Following the same line, the European Commission on Human Rights ruled that expelling a Congolese AIDS sufferer from France would violate Article 3 of the ECHR, *BB v France* (App No 30930/96) ECHR 9 March 1998. This case has not come before the Court as the French government made a commitment not to expel the applicant: *BB v France* (App No 30930/96) ECHR 1998-VI 2595. The specific circumstances of the applicant's case as highlighted in the Commission's report were the fact that he was already ill and had received hospital treatment, the non-availability of treatment in the Congo, the numerous epidemics in the Congo that would aggravate the risk of infection, and the absence of family support.

[27] *Karara v Finland* (App No 40900/98) ECHR 7 September 1998 (expulsion of an HIV-positive man to Uganda, when illness had not yet reached an advanced stage); *MM v Switzerland* (App No 43348/98) ECHR 14 September 1998 (expulsion of an HIV-positive man not yet suffering from the illness to the Congo, when Swiss authorities offered to pay his treatment upon his return for one year); *SCC v Sweden*, (App No 46553/99) ECHR 15 February 2000 (refusal of a residence permit to an HIV-infected woman, when early stages of illness and treatment and family support were available in her native Zambia); *Bensaid v United Kingdom* (App No 44599/98) ECHR 2001-I 303 (decision to deport a schizophrenic man to Algeria, where medical treatment was available); *Karagoz v France* (App No 47531/99) ECHR 15 November 2001 (expulsion of a man suffering from a thyroid problem and a gastric ulcer to Turkey, where treatment was available); *Arcila Henao v The Netherlands* (App No 13669/03) ECHR 24 June 2003 (expulsion of an HIV-positive man in a 'reasonable' state of health to Colombia, where treatment was 'in principle available' and there was a 'prospect of family support'); *Nasimi v Sweden* (App No 38865/02) ECHR 16 March 2004 (expulsion of the applicant to Iran against psychiatric advice that the applicant is suicidal and in need of long-term psychotherapy); *Ndangoya v Sweden* (App No 17868/03) ECHR 22 June 2004 (expulsion to Tanzania of an HIV-positive man not yet suffering from HIV-related illness, when treatment was available in Tanzania, albeit at considerable cost and only in urban areas and when the applicant had relatives in Tanzania); *Salkic & Others v Sweden* (App No 7702/04) ECHR 29 June 2004 (expulsion to Bosnia and Herzegovina of a Muslim family of four suffering from post-traumatic stress disorder); *Dragan & Others v Germany* (App No 33743/03) ECHR 3 October 2004 (expulsion of a mother and her children to Romania, where treatment was available); *Amegnigan v The Netherlands* (App No 25629/04) ECHR 25 November 2004 (deportation to Togo of an HIV-positive man whose illness had not yet reached the terminal stage, when medical care was available and there was the prospect of family support in Togo); *Ramadan & Ahjredini v The Netherlands* (App No 35989/03) ECHR 10 November 2005 (expulsion of a couple to FYROM despite their undergoing treatment for depression, when adequate treatment and family support were available in the home country); *Paramsothy v The Netherlands* (App No 14492/03) ECHR 10 November 2005 (expulsion of a man suffering from post-traumatic stress disorder and depression to Sri Lanka, when treatment and family support were available in Sri Lanka); *Rrustemaj & Others v Sweden* (App No 8628/05) ECHR 15 November 2005 (expulsion of a family to Kosovo, even though the mother was suffering from post-traumatic stress disorder); *Hukic v Sweden* (App No 17416/05) ECHR 27 November 2005 (allowing the deportation to Bosnia-Herzegovina of a family whose younger child allegedly

b Medical care for detainees   Another context in which the right to healthcare can fall within the scope of Article 3 of the ECHR is the treatment of detainees. The fact that detainees are in a vulnerable position under the authority of the state makes the latter responsible for their health, including for ensuring appropriate medical treatment.[28] One example of such a case is *Keenan v United Kingdom*,[29] which dealt with the suicide of an imprisoned detainee suffering from mental illness. The Court did not hold the UK responsible for the man's death under Article 2 of the ECHR, but it did find a violation of Article 3 due to the lack of appropriate medical treatment, combined with disciplinary punishment:

> The lack of effective monitoring of Mark Keenan's condition and the lack of informed psychiatric input into his assessment and treatment disclose significant defects in the medical care provided to a mentally ill person known to be a suicide risk. The belated imposition on him in those circumstances of a serious disciplinary punishment—seven days' segregation in the punishment block and an additional twenty-eight days to his sentence imposed two weeks after the event and only nine days before his expected date of release—which may well have threatened his physical and moral resistance, is not compatible with the standard of treatment required in respect of a mentally ill person. It must be regarded as constituting inhuman and degrading treatment and punishment within the meaning of Article 3 of the Convention.[30]

A violation of Article 3 due to a failure to provide adequate medical treatment to a detainee was likewise found in *McGlinchey v United Kingdom*,[31] which revolved around the death of a heroin-addict detainee. The Court pointed to a number of shortcomings in the monitoring of the victim's health in this case: due to a discrepancy in the scales used, the prison authorities had not been able to accurately measure the extent of her weight loss, which would have alerted them to the seriousness of her condition. Moreover, there was a gap in the monitoring of her condition by a doctor over the period of one weekend and a failure on the part of prison authorities to take more effective steps to treat her when she was vomiting continuously, such as hospitalisation to ensure intravenous intake of

would not receive adequate medical care for his conditions—Down's syndrome and epilepsy—if deported, since treatment was available, albeit at considerable cost, and Down's syndrome not comparable to the final stages of a fatal illness).

[28] See, eg, *Kudla v Poland* (App No 30210/96) ECHR 26 October 2000 para 94: '[Under Article 3 of the ECHR] the State must ensure that a person is detained in conditions which are compatible with respect for his human dignity, that the manner and method of the execution of the measure do not subject him to distress or hardship of an intensity exceeding the unavoidable level of suffering inherent in detention and that, given the practical demands of imprisonment, his health and well-being are adequately secured by, among other things, providing him with the requisite medical assistance'.

[29] *Keenan v United Kingdom* (App No 27229/95) ECHR 3 April 2001.

[30] *Ibid* para 116.

[31] *McGlinchey v United Kingdom* (App No 50390/99) ECHR 2003-V 183.

medication and fluids or calling for more expert assistance in controlling the vomiting. Similarly, the Court found the Ukraine responsible for a lack of adequate medical treatment that amounted to degrading treatment in violation of Article 3 when it failed to provide medical follow-up during a detainee's hunger-strike and force-feeding.[32]

In a number of other cases, the Court has found the very detention of a seriously ill person in itself to constitute a violation of Article 3. For example, the UK was found in violation of Article 3 for having held in custody a four-limb-deficient thalidomide victim with numerous health problems, including defective kidneys, for three nights and four days. The Court stated that:

> to detain a severely disabled person in conditions where she is dangerously cold, risks developing sores because her bed is too hard or unreachable, and is unable to go to the toilet or keep clean without the greatest of difficulty, constitutes degrading treatment contrary to Article 3 of the Convention.[33]

France was found to have violated Article 3 for detaining a cancer patient in prison for more than two years.[34] Latvia was found guilty of the same violation for having imprisoned for 21 months a paralyzed 84-year-old suffering from several chronic diseases. The Court noted that making this even more problematic was the fact that he was often left without qualified medical care and was forced to rely on his fellow prisoners for assistance, which he needed for all activities.[35] When the prison is not equipped to deal with the illness, other measures must be taken, such as transfer to a hospital. When evaluating the compatibility of a detainee's health condition with keeping him in detention, the Court takes into account three elements: (a) the detainee's condition; (b) the quality of the treatment he receives; and (c) the desirability of continuing the detention in light of his state of health.[36]

In a number of Turkish cases, the Court held that the re-imprisonment of a person whose prison sentence had been suspended, without evidence of any significant improvement in his or her medical fitness, is in violation of Article 3 of the ECHR. These cases dealt with individuals suffering from Wernicke-Korsakoff Syndrome as a result of a hunger strike in prison.[37]

In other cases, however, the Court found that handicapped or ill detainees were being monitored and receiving adequate care such that their

[32] *Nevmerzhitsky v Ukraine* (App No 54825/00) ECHR 5 April 2005.
[33] *Price v United Kingdom* (App No 33394/96) ECHR 2001-VII 153 para 30.
[34] *Mouisel v France* (App No 67263/01) ECHR 2002-IX 191.
[35] *Farbtuhs v Latvia* (App No 4672/02) ECHR 2 December 2004 para 60.
[36] *Sakkopoulos v Greece* (App No 61828/00) ECHR 15 January 2004 para 39.
[37] *Celik & Yildiz v Turkey* (App No 51479/99) ECHR 10 November 2005; *Gürbüz v Turkey* (App No 26050/04) ECHR 10 November 2005; *Kuruçay v Turkey* (App No 24040/04) ECHR 10 November 2005; *Uyan v Turkey* (App No 7454/04) ECHR 10 November 2005.

situations did not fall within the scope of Article 3 protection.[38] Some of these cases have been dismissed at the admissibility stage, on grounds of being manifestly ill-founded.[39]

ii Psychiatric Care for Detainees 'of Unsound Mind' under Article 5, Section 1 of the ECHR

When persons are held in detention due to their mental illness, their right to psychiatric care is further protected under Article 5, Section 1 of the ECHR. The provision in subsection 1(e) sets forth the conditions for the 'lawful detention' of persons of unsound mind. In this context, the Court ruled that:

> The 'detention' of a person as a mental health patient will only be 'lawful' for the purposes of sub-paragraph (e) of paragraph 1 if affected in a hospital, clinic or other appropriate institution.[40]

The psychiatric wing of the Belgian Lantin prison

> could not be regarded as an institution appropriate for the detention of persons of unsound mind, the latter not receiving either regular medical attention or a therapeutic environment... Moreover, the Government did not deny that the applicant's treatment in Lantin had been unsatisfactory from a therapeutic point of view. The proper relationship between the aim of the detention and the conditions in which it took place was therefore deficient.[41]

iii Health, Health Care and the Right to Life (Article 2 of the ECHR)

Another approach to protecting the right to health is by way of the right to life, protected in Article 2 of the ECHR. For example, in *Cyprus v Turkey*, a grand chamber of the Court observed that:

> an issue may arise under Article 2 of the Convention where it is shown that the authorities of a Contracting State put an individual's life at risk through the denial of health care which they have undertaken to make available to the population generally.[42]

The Court has yet to find for a violation of this negative obligation. Instead, health issues have been dealt with in the context of Article 2 as involving positive obligations. The first sentence of the Article states that

---

[38] *Matencio v France* (App No 58749/00) ECHR 15 January 2004; *Gelfmann v France* (App No 25875/03) ECHR 14 December 2004; *Rohde v Denmark* (App No 69332/01) ECHR 21 July 2005; *Mathew v The Netherlands* (App No 24919/03) ECHR 29 September 2005.

[39] *Sawoniuk v United Kingdom* (App No 63716/00) ECHR 2001-VI 375; *Reggiano Martinelli v Italy* (App No 22682/02) ECHR 16 June 2005.

[40] *Aerts v Belgium* (App No 25357/94) ECHR 1998-V 1939 para 46.

[41] *Ibid* para 49.

[42] *Cyprus v Turkey* (App No 25781/94) ECHR 2001-IV 1 para 219.

'[e]veryone's right to life shall be protected by law'. The ECtHR case law recognises that this

> enjoins the State not only to refrain from the intentional and unlawful taking of life, but also to take appropriate steps to safeguard the lives of those within its jurisdiction.[43]

This obligation to safeguard lives logically extends into the sphere of health protection.

a Medical care for detainees   In *Anguelova v Bulgaria* the Court held that Article 2, Section 1 of the Convention had been violated when a young man in police custody died from injuries as a result of the police's delay in providing him with medical care. When the police officers realised that the victim's condition was deteriorating, instead of calling for an ambulance, they summoned the officers who had made the arrest, who were on patrol. The latter first drove to the police station to verify the situation and then, instead of sending for an ambulance, drove to the hospital to summon an ambulance, which followed them back. The Court noted that:

> It is particularly significant, furthermore, that the case file does not contain any trace of criticism or disapproval of that manner of dealing with a detainee's medical problem... The first medical report and the expert whose opinion was submitted by the applicant found that the delay in providing medical assistance had been fatal... The Court thus finds that the behaviour of the police officers... and the lack of any reaction by the authorities constituted a violation of the State's obligation to protect the lives of persons in custody.[44]

b Prevention   Under Article 2 of the ECHR, state authorities have an obligation to prevent health risks to individuals. This preventive obligation applies when state operations involve health risks. This was recognised in *LCB v United Kingdom*,[45] where the applicant claimed that the UK government was responsible for her disease, leukemia, due to her father's exposure to radiation during the Christmas Island nuclear tests performed by the UK in the 1950s and 1960s. The Court examined whether the authorities had done all that could have been required of them to prevent her life from being avoidably put at risk and thereby recognised a positive state obligation in the sphere of prevention of health risks.[46]

Another example of this preventive obligation is the requirement for both public and private hospitals to set regulations for the protection of

---

[43] *LCB v United Kingdom* (App No 23413/93) ECHR 1998-III 1390 para 36.
[44] *Anguelova v Bulgaria* (App No 38361/97) ECHR 2002-IV 355 paras 128–30.
[45] *LCB. v United Kingdom*, above n 43.
[46] The Court was satisfied that the state had done enough, given the information that was available at the time.

their patients' lives. This obligation was recognised in cases of death resulting from improper medical treatment[47]:

> However, where a Contracting State has made adequate provision for securing high professional standards among health professionals and the protection of the lives of patients, it cannot accept that matters such as error of judgment on the part of a health professional or negligent co-ordination among health professionals in the treatment of a particular patient are sufficient of themselves to call a Contracting State to account from the standpoint of its positive obligations under Article 2 of the Convention to protect life.[48]

c Investigation   In the cases dealing with the preventive obligation, the Court stressed the state's obligation to investigate deaths occurring while the victim is in the care of health professionals and to establish liability for the responsible medical practitioners.[49] In the grand chamber judgment in *Vo v France*, the Court summarised its case law on the matter as follows:

> The positive obligations [under Article 2 of the ECHR] require an effective independent judicial system to be set up so that the cause of death of patients in the care of the medical profession, whether in the public or the private sector, can be determined and those responsible made accountable. Although the right to have third parties prosecuted or sentenced for a criminal offence cannot be asserted independently..., the Court has stated on a number of occasions that an effective judicial system, as required by Article 2, may, and under certain circumstances must, include recourse to the criminal law. However, if the infringement of the right to life or to physical integrity is not caused intentionally, the positive obligation imposed by Article 2 to set up an effective judicial system does not necessarily require the provision of a criminal-law remedy in every case. In the specific sphere of medical negligence, 'the obligation may for instance also be satisfied if the legal system affords victims a remedy in the civil courts, either alone or in conjunction with a remedy in the criminal courts, enabling any liability of the doctors concerned to be established and any appropriate civil redress, such as an order for damages and for the publication of the decision, to be obtained. Disciplinary measures may also be envisaged. [Citation omitted][50]

d State Funding   Finally, the right to life has been invoked—unsuccessfully—in claims for the state to increase its funding of a certain medical treatment. In *Nitecki v Poland*, for example, the applicant, who suffered from amyotrophic lateral sclerosis ('ALS'), also known as Lou Gehrig's disease, was prescribed the drug Rilutek, for which the Public Health Service refunded 70% of the cost. The remaining 30%, however,

---

[47] *Calvelli & Ciglio v Italy* (App No 32967/96) ECHR 17 January 2002 para 47; *Erikson v Italy* (App No 37900/97) 26 October 1999.

[48] *Powell v United Kingdom* (App No 45305/99) ECHR 4 May 2000.

[49] *Calvelli & Ciglio v Italy*, above n 47, para 49; *Erikson v Italy*, above n 47, 7.

[50] *Vo v France* (App No 53924/00) ECHR 8 July 2004 paras 89–90.

constituted a very heavy financial burden for the applicant. As a result, the applicant could not afford the treatment, and his medical situation deteriorated. He argued that the state's refusal to subsidise the entire cost of the life-saving drug violated his right to life. The Court held the complaint to be manifestly ill-founded and not falling within the scope of Article 2. 'Bearing in mind the medical treatment and facilities provided to the applicant, including a refund of the greater part of the cost of the required drug,' the Court ruled that this was not a case in which an omission by the state in the area of health care policy constituted a breach of its responsibility under Article 2.[51]

In another example, *Pentiacova v Moldova*, the applicants were sufferers of chronic renal failure and in need of hemodialysis. Prior to 1997, and then from 2004, the cost of this treatment was fully covered by the health care system in Moldova, but between 1997 and 2004 sufferers had had to pay for part of their treatment due to cuts in government funding for their hospital. The Court stated that the applicants had failed to show that their lives had been put at risk, arguing,

> While it is clearly desirable that everyone has access to a full range of medical treatment, including life-saving medical procedures and drugs, the lack of resources means that there are, unfortunately, in the Contracting States many individuals who do not enjoy them, especially in cases of permanent and expensive treatment.[52]

Since the applicants had had access to the standard of health care offered to the general public, Article 2 of the ECHR had not been violated, and their claims were held to be manifestly ill-founded.

iv Health under Article 8 of the ECHR

a Prevention   Article 8 of the ECHR protects private and family life, with the protection of physical integrity considered part of private life protection. Positive obligations under this Article include certain obligations borne by the state pertaining to health risks, in particular the obligation to provide information about such risks. This was affirmed with regard to hazardous activities engaged in by the government in another case relating to the UK Christmas Island nuclear tests.[53] The applicants in this case had been servicemen during the test and sought access to records of radiation levels. The Court affirmed that:

> Where a Government engages in hazardous activities, such as those in issue in the present case, which might have hidden adverse consequences on the health

---

[51] *Nitecki v Poland* (App No 65653/01) ECHR 21 March 2002.
[52] *Pentiacova & 48 Others v Moldova* (App No 14462/03) ECHR 4 January 2005.
[53] *McGinley & Egan v United Kingdom* (App No 24276/94) ECHR 1998-III 1334.

of those involved in such activities, respect for private and family life under Article 8 requires that an effective and accessible procedure be established which enables such persons to seek all relevant and appropriate information.[54]

This ruling was confirmed by a grand chamber decision in a 2005 case concerning access to information, allowing the assessment of any health risk resulting from participation in army gas tests.[55] In *Guerra v Italy*[56] the same principle was affirmed with regard to a private factory. There, the Court held that the toxic emissions from a chemical factory had a direct effect on the right to respect for the private and family life of the applicants, who lived in a village approximately one kilometre from the factory. The authorities had neglected to give essential information that would have enabled the applicants to assess the risks they and their families might be exposed to if they were to continue to live there and had therefore violated Article 8.

The state's action or inaction in the context of environmental pollution such as air pollution,[57] as well as noise pollution[58] and soil and water pollution,[59] can also be found in violation of Article 8. In many cases, the protection against environmental pollution constitutes protection of the right to health. Yet the Court has explicitly adopted a higher standard in the context of environmental pollution when assessing whether the state has met its obligations under Article 8. Indeed, even without posing serious danger to individuals' health, severe environmental pollution may lead the state to be found in violation of Article 8,[60] with state responsibility in this area extending to the remedies provided to those affected by environmental pollution. In *Fadeyeva v Russia* the Court found that the applicant's health had deteriorated as a result of prolonged exposure to the industrial emissions from a steel plant. Article 8 had been violated, the Court ruled, because the state had not offered the applicant any effective means of helping her move from the dangerous area, nor had it designed or applied effective measures for reducing the industrial pollution to acceptable levels.[61]

b Financial access to medical treatment or assistance   The issue of state funding of medical treatment or assistance that is not strictly life-saving may, in principle, be brought before the ECtHR based on Article 8 of the

---

[54] *Ibid* para 101. In this case, the Court found no violation, because the applicants had not made use of a procedure that had been available to them.

[55] *Roche v United Kingdom* (App No 32555/96) ECHR 19 October 2005.

[56] *Guerra & Others v Italy* (App No 14967/89) ECHR 1998-I 210.

[57] *Lopez Ostra v Spain* (App No 16798/90) (1994) Series A, No 303-C.

[58] *Hatton v United Kingdom* (App No 36022/97) ECHR 2003-VIII 189.

[59] *Taskin & Others v Turkey* (App No 46117/99) ECHR 10 November 2004.

[60] *Lopez Ostra v Spain*, above n 57, para 51.

[61] *Fadeyeva v Russia* (App No 55723/00) ECHR 9 June 2005.

Convention, since the Court has recognised that, under this provision, 'notions of the quality of life take on significance'.[62]

This argument was advanced in the *Sentges* case,[63] initiated by a seventeen-year-old boy suffering from Duchenne muscular dystrophy. The applicant, who uses an electric wheelchair, is completely dependent on assistance from others for every act he needs or wishes to perform, including eating and drinking. His parents submitted a request to their health insurance fund to provide him with a mechanical arm to be mounted on his wheelchair, which would have enabled him to perform many acts unassisted. The total cost amounted to €36,000. The health insurance fund rejected the request on the grounds that the provision of a mechanical arm is not covered by the Dutch statutory health insurance scheme. The applicant argued that the right to respect for his private life encompasses a positive obligation on the part of the state to pay for this medical device. The Court left open the question of whether there was a sufficiently direct and immediate link between the measures sought by the applicant and his private life. It stated that:

> Even assuming that in the present case such a special link indeed exists... regard must be had to the fair balance that has to be struck between the competing interests of the individual and of the community as a whole and to the wide margin of appreciation enjoyed by States in this respect in determining the steps to be taken to ensure compliance with the Convention... This margin of appreciation is even wider when, as in the present case, the issues involve an assessment of the priorities in the context of the allocation of limited State resources.[64]

Since the applicant had access to the standard of health care offered to all persons insured under the statutory scheme, including the provision of an electric wheelchair, the Court held that the Dutch authorities had not exceeded their margin of appreciation, and the complaint was dismissed as manifestly ill-founded.

One month earlier, the Court had held in the *Van Kück* case that a German court's judgment confirming the refusal of a private health insurance company to refund payment for a certain course of medical treatment had violated Article 8 of the ECHR.[65] The distinguishing characteristic of this case is that it revolved around a gender reassignment operation. The European Court of Human Rights considers respect for the gender identity of transsexuals a crucial requirement encompassed in Article 8 and linked to the very essence of the Convention—that is, respect for human dignity and human freedom.[66] The German court had applied

---

62 *Pretty v United Kingdom* (App No 2346/02) ECHR 2002-III 155 para 64.
63 *Sentges v The Netherlands* (App No 27677/02) ECHR 8 July 2003.
64 Ibid 6–7.
65 *Van Kück v Germany* (App No 35968/97) ECHR 2003-VII 1.
66 *Goodwin v United Kingdom* (App No 28957/95) ECHR 2002-VI 1 paras 90–91.

general criteria for reimbursement of medical treatment costs, requiring the applicant to prove the medical necessity of the surgery. The European Court held that in the light of its case law on transsexualism,

> the burden placed on a person to prove the medical necessity of treatment, including irreversible surgery, in the field of one of the most intimate private-life matters, appears disproportionate.[67]

It found that no fair balance had been struck between the interests of the private health insurance company, on the one side, and those of the applicant, on the other.

C The Right to (Adequate) Housing

The right to housing is another social right that enjoys a certain degree of protection under the ECHR. A textual basis for this protection can be found in Article 8 of the Convention, which guarantees not only private life, family life and correspondence, but also 'the home'. In addition, the matter of 'adequate' housing has successfully been linked to the protection of private life. Similarly, some aspects of the right to housing may be linked to the property right safeguarded under Article 1 of the first additional protocol to the Convention. Finally, some cases in the matter of the right to housing have been brought under Article 3 of the Convention.

I The Right to Housing under Article 8 of the ECHR

The text of Article 8 of the ECHR provides a sufficient basis for a number of aspects of a state duty to respect the right to housing (or, in the terminology of the European Court of Human Rights, negative state obligations). The deliberate burning of houses by security forces, for example, would be considered a violation of both the right to respect for the home and the right to respect for family life.[68] Arbitrary eviction of a tenant would likewise constitute a violation of Article 8.[69]

The positive state obligations under Article 8 may, in some cases, relate to the right to adequate housing. As it emerges from the case law, these obligations rest more strongly on the 'private and family life' components of Article 8 than on the provision's reference to respect for the home. The case law on environmental protection, as mentioned earlier, which indirectly protects citizens' right to health (cf above) through the state obligation to protect them from severe pollution, can further extend to ensuring their adequate housing, since housing in a

---

[67] *Van Kück v Germany*, above n 65, para 82.
[68] *Akdivar v Turkey* (App No 21893/93) ECHR 1996-III 1192 para 88.
[69] *Prokopovich v Russia* (App No 58255/00) ECHR 18 November 2004.

severely polluted area cannot be considered adequate. State obligations in this field may, therefore, include the provision of alternative accommodation.[70]

Another context in which health and housing concerns are intertwined is the matter of appropriate housing for disabled persons. This issue was addressed by the Court in *Marzari v Italy*,[71] involving an applicant suffering from a rare illness that had disabled him. The applicant lived in an apartment that he had adapted to his needs; when the apartment was expropriated, he took legal steps as well as other acts of protest against the authorities, who had failed to find him a suitable dwelling to replace his apartment. In its judgment, the Court stated that:

> although Article 8 does not guarantee the right to have one's housing problem solved by the authorities, a refusal of the authorities to provide assistance in this respect to an individual suffering from a severe disease might in certain circumstances raise an issue under Article 8 of the Convention because of the impact of such refusal on the private life of the individual.

A requirement for establishing positive state obligations in this particular area is that there must be 'a direct and immediate link between the measures sought by an applicant and the latter's private life'. In this case, no violation of Article 8 was found, and the complaint was held inadmissible because, in fact, an apartment had eventually been offered to the applicant that had been approved by a medical commission and, although the authorities had been prepared to adapt it, the applicant rejected the offer. The Court ruled that the local authorities could be deemed to have discharged their positive obligations, as there is no obligation 'to provide the applicant with a specific apartment'. Yet the Court's statements in this case opened the door to future claims in contexts where authorities may be less accommodating.

ii Housing and the Right to Property (Article 1 of Protocol 1 to the ECHR)

Like Article 8, Article 1 of the first Protocol to the Convention provides protection against certain violations of the state's duty to respect the right to housing. In particular, it extends protection in cases of expropriation and in cases of state responsibility for the demolition of a house.[72] Furthermore, when a state provides a system of social housing, an individual who is entitled to such housing under domestic law can make a claim based on

[70] *Fadeyeva v Russia* (App No 55723/00) ECHR 9 June 2005.
[71] *Marzari v Italy* (App No 36448/97) ECHR 4 May 1999.
[72] *Akdivar v Turkey*, above n 68. The Court found not only a violation of Article 8 but also of the right to peaceful enjoyment of possessions, protected under Article 1 of the first Protocol.

Article 1 of the first Protocol. When the state fails to provide the type of housing the citizen is entitled to, it violates this provision.[73]

In addition, the provision constitutes the basis for positive state obligations to protect property. An important case in which this was applied in the housing context is *Öneryildiz v Turkey*.[74] A methane explosion in a household refuse tip caused a landslide that engulfed some ten slum dwellings situated below it and killed 39 people. The European Court of Human Rights found that the Turkish authorities had violated both the right to life and the right to property by failing to take protective measures, as well as by failing to properly compensate the victims. It is particularly important to note that the Court extended the concept of possessions in Article 1 of the first Protocol to include slum dwellings that had been illegally erected on state-owned land.[75]

iii The Right to Housing under Article 3 of the ECHR

Article 3 of the ECHR has been applied in the housing context only with respect to negative state obligations. The deliberate demolition of a house by state agents has been labelled in recent case law a violation of Article 3 as well as Article 8 of the Convention and Article 1 of the first Protocol. The cases in point concern the destruction of houses by security forces in Turkish villages suspected of supporting the PKK. The Court noted in particular that the houses had been destroyed in the presence of the applicants, forcing them to leave their village and without receiving any assistance from the state. The Court's ruling that this constitutes inhuman treatment was based on the circumstances of the destruction as well as on the personal circumstances of the applicants.[76]

When individuals are forced to live in appalling housing conditions due to circumstances for which state agents are directly responsible, the Court also may find for a violation of Article 3. The applicants in *Moldovan v Romania*[77] submitted that, over the course of several years,

> they had been forced to live in hen-houses, pigsties, windowless cellars, or in extremely cold and deplorable conditions: sixteen people in one room with no heating; seven people in one room with a mud floor; families sleeping on mud or concrete floors without adequate clothing, heat or blankets; fifteen people in a summer kitchen with a concrete floor... etc.[78]

---

[73] *Teteriny v Russia* (App No 11931/03) ECHR 30 June 2005.

[74] *Öneryildiz v Turkey* (App No 48939/99) ECHR 30 November 2004.

[75] *Ibid* para 129.

[76] See, amongst other cases, *Selçuk & Asker v Turkey* (App No 23184/94, 23185/94) ECHR 1998-II 891; *Bilgin v Turkey* (App No 23819/94) ECHR 16 November 2000; *Dulas v Turkey* (App No 25801/94) ECHR 30 January 2001.

[77] *Moldovan & Others v Romania (No 2)* (App No 41138/98, 64320/01) ECHR 12 July 2005.

[78] *Ibid* para 69.

The applicants were Roma whose houses had been destroyed by a mob incited by the police. After the incident, the Romanian government had allocated funds for the reconstruction of the houses, but only some were actually reconstructed and in such a poor manner that they were uninhabitable, with large gaps left between the windows and walls and roofs left incomplete. Since the actual destruction of the houses had happened before the entry into force of the European Convention with respect to Romania, the case dealt only with the consequences, ie, the subsequent living conditions of the applicants. The Court deemed that the government's responsibility for these living conditions had been activated in 'regard to the direct repercussions of the acts of State agents on the applicants' rights'.[79] It ruled that:

> the applicants' living conditions in the last ten years, in particular the severely overcrowded and unsanitary environment and its detrimental effect on the applicants' health and well-being, combined with the length of the period during which the applicants have had to live in such conditions and the general attitude of the authorities, must have caused them considerable mental suffering, thus diminishing their human dignity and arousing in them such feelings as to cause humiliation and debasement.[80]

Taken together with the racist remarks the applicants had had to endure from the authorities, this amounted, in the Court's opinion, to 'degrading treatment' in violation of Article 3 of the ECHR.[81]

D The Right to Work

The ECtHR's case law grants indirect protection to the right to work when someone is discharged from his or her job or not employed for reasons that violate their rights under the Convention.[82] For example, the Court ruled that the discharge of soldiers from the British Royal Navy due to their homosexuality was a violation of their right to protection of their private life.[83] Likewise, a television director's freedom of expression was deemed to be violated when he was fired after criticising the management in radio interviews.[84] In another case, the dismissal of three British Rail employees who had received termination notices for refusing to join either of the two trade unions that had signed a closed shop agreement with British

---

[79] *Ibid* para 104.
[80] *Ibid* para 110.
[81] *Ibid* para 113.
[82] R Bernhardt, 'L'embauche et le licenciement de travailleurs vus sous l'angle de la Convention européenne' (1991) 2 *Revue Trimestrielle des Droits de l'Homme* 163–165.
[83] *Lustig-Prean & Beckett v United Kingdom* (App No 31417/96, 32377/96) ECHR 27 September 1999; *Smith & Grady v United Kingdom* (App No 33985/96, 33986/96) ECHR 1999 VI 45.
[84] *Fuentes Bobo v Spain* (App No 39293/98) ECHR 29 February 2000.

Rail was determined by the Court to be in violation of their freedom of association.[85]

This line of reasoning applies not only with regard to dismissals but also with respect to access to employment, as illustrated by the case of *Thlimmenos v Greece*.[86] The applicant, a Jehovah's Witness in Greece, was convicted for having refused to do military service on religious grounds. Five years after his conviction, he took a public examination for the appointment of twelve chartered accountants, a liberal profession in Greece. He came second among sixty candidates. However, the Executive Board of the Greek Institute of Chartered Accountants refused to appoint him on the ground that he had been convicted of a felony. The European Court of Human Rights ruled that this had amounted to discrimination on the basis of religion and that the Board should have differentiated among people convicted for ordinary felonies and those convicted for felonies committed as a product of religious conviction.

E The Right to Social Benefits

Where entitlement to a particular social benefit exists under domestic law but, for some reason, is not enforced, or when an entitlement is lost for contestable reasons, Article 1 of the first Protocol to the Convention may be successfully invoked. Attempts to rely on this provision or on Articles 3 or 8 of the ECHR to create a new entitlement to a particular social benefit have, however, failed.

1 Article 1 of the First Protocol to the ECHR

When a claim to a particular social benefit is sufficiently established as enforceable, it is regarded by the Court as a possession in the term's sense in Article 1 of the first Protocol to the ECHR.[87] Moreover, contributing to a pension fund may be deemed, in certain circumstances, as creating a property right and the rights stemming from payments to social insurance systems considered pecuniary rights—and hence property rights—for the purposes of Article 1 of the first Protocol.[88] The right to a pension that derives from employment can also be considered a property right when no special contributions were made by either the employee or employer, but the employer has made a more general undertaking to pay a pension at

---

[85] *Young, James & Webster v United Kingdom* (App No 7601/76, 7806/77) (1981) Series A, No 44.

[86] *Thlimmenos v Greece* (App No 34369/97) ECHR 2000 IV 263.

[87] *Burdov v Russia* (App No 59498/00) ECHR 2002-III 317 para 40; *Teteriny v Russia*, above n 73, para 47.

[88] *Asmundsson v Iceland* (App No 60669/00) ECHR 12 October 2004 para 39.

conditions that can be considered to be part of the employment contract.[89] The Court has also suggested that the pecuniary nature of a given right to a social benefit is sufficient to qualify it as a property right, regardless of the payment of contributions.[90]

The Court has, however, left open the matter of whether Article 1 of the first Protocol guarantees benefits to those who have contributed to a social insurance scheme. Whatever the case may be, the Court has ruled that the Article cannot be interpreted as entitling any such person to a pension in a particular amount.[91] According to the Court:

> An important consideration in the assessment under this provision is whether the applicant's right to derive benefits from the social insurance scheme in question has been infringed in a manner resulting in the impairment of the essence of his pension rights.[92]

In this context, the Court found a violation of Article 1 of the first Protocol in the case of a man who had lost the disability pension he had been receiving for 20 years and which constituted one-third of his gross monthly income, due to legislative changes that had led to a reassessment of his capacity to work. The Court held that there had been a disproportionate interference in the applicant's property right for the reason, amongst others, that the vast majority of disability pensioners had continued to receive disability benefits at the same level as previously, whereas a small minority of disability pensioners had had to bear the most drastic of measures, namely, the total loss of their pension entitlements.[93] As a result, the Court held,

> as an individual, the applicant was made to bear an excessive and disproportionate burden which, even having regard to the wide margin of appreciation to be enjoyed by the State in the area of social legislation, cannot be justified by the legitimate community interests relied on by the authorities. It would have been otherwise had the applicant been obliged to endure a reasonable and commensurate reduction rather than the total deprivation of his entitlements.[94]

When social security legislation is amended for reasons of public policy, which leads to the reduction of social benefits, the Court is less likely to find a violation of Article 1 of the first Protocol. In several instances, it has even gone so far as to dismiss claims in the admissibility stage as manifestly

---

[89] *Azinas v Cyprus* (App No 56679/00) ECHR 20 June 2002 para 34. This ruling was, however, revised by a grand chamber, which held that the case was inadmissible for reason of non-exhaustion of domestic remedies, *Azinas v Cyprus* (App No 56679/00) ECHR 2004-111285.

[90] *Hadžić v Croatia* (App No 48788/99) ECHR 13 September 2001.

[91] *Asmundsson v Iceland*, above n 88, para 39.

[92] *Ibid* para 39.

[93] *Ibid* para 43.

[94] *Ibid* para 45.

ill-founded.[95] This reasoning applies also to the total withdrawal of a social benefit when people with no other means of subsistence can apply for other types of benefits. Accordingly, the Court held as manifestly ill-founded a complaint brought by a disabled woman who had lost the disability benefit she had been enjoying for 16 years after a change in the law, on the grounds that she had not derived any income from work during the year preceding the occurrence of the incapacity. The Court ruled that the withdrawal of her benefit had not been disproportionate since general welfare benefits were available in the Netherlands. The fact that the applicant was not eligible for such benefits given her personal capital did not alter this conclusion,

> since it cannot be regarded as contrary to Article 1 First Protocol that personal savings and other capital are taken into account in the determination of entitlement to general welfare benefits designed to meet basic subsistence needs.[96]

Finally, the Court has ruled that a state's failure to enforce a right to a social benefit that has been established in a final judgment of a domestic court constitutes a violation of Article 1 of the first Protocol. Furthermore, a lack of public funds cannot justify such an omission.[97]

ii Article 8 of the ECHR

Social benefits for the disabled may be linked to Article 8 of the ECHR. The European Court's case law with respect to special provisions for the disabled recognises the existence of positive state obligations where there is a direct and immediate link between the measures sought by the applicant and his or her private and/or family life.[98] In *La Parola and Others v Italy*, the Court deliberated on a complaint resting on Article 8 regarding the denial of a specific benefit to a disabled person, but found that the state had fulfilled its positive obligations under the provision, given the amount of other benefits the applicant had received.[99]

iii Article 3 of the ECHR

In the worst cases, where a state leaves some of its citizens devoid of any means or with a benefit in an amount that is manifestly insufficient to lead a life with human dignity, the Court may hold that the state is in violation

---

[95] See, eg, *Skorkiewicz v Poland* (App No 39860/98) ECHR 1 June 1999; *Domalewski v Poland* (App No 34610/97) ECHR 1999-V 573; *Goudswaard-Van Der Lans v The Netherlands* (App No 75255/01) ECHR 22 September 2005.

[96] *Hoogendijk v The Netherlands* (App No 58641/00) ECHR 6 January 2005.

[97] *Poznakhirina v Russia* (App No 25964/02) ECHR 24 February 2005.

[98] *Botta v Italy* (App No 21439/93) ECHR 1998-I 412; *Zehnalova & Zehnal v Czech Republic* (App No 38621/97) ECHR 2002-V 337.

[99] *La Parola & Others v Italy* (App No 39712/98) ECHR 30 November 2000.

of Article 3 of the ECHR. In its 2002 judgment in *Larioshina v Russia*, the Court opened the door to this possibility. There, it held that a complaint about a wholly insufficient amount of pension and other social benefits 'may, in principle, raise an issue under Article 3 of the Convention which prohibits inhuman or degrading treatment'. This particular case was, however, dismissed as manifestly ill-founded, since there was

> no indication that the amount of the applicant's pension and the additional social benefits has caused such damage to her physical or mental health capable of attaining the minimum level of severity falling within the ambit of Article 3 of the Convention.[100]

II PROCEDURAL PROTECTION

Another technique by which social rights are indirectly protected under the ECHR is through procedural guarantees with respect to the enforcement of the rights in domestic courts. Article 6 of the Convention sets forth extensive guarantees for a fair trial. It does not apply to all court procedures, only to those regarding 'the determination of civil rights and obligations' or a 'criminal charge'. Yet in interpreting these concepts, the Court has given them autonomous meanings that, in many cases, deviate from their meanings in domestic law. In particular, the scope of the concept of civil rights and obligations has been increasingly broadened, so as to include most cases relating to social rights, including social security issues.[101] Hence, the European Convention system guarantees access to court proceedings with all the guarantees of a fair trial vis-à-vis most disputes involving social rights. Procedural justice is an essential element in human rights protection and, in some cases, fair trial guarantees may be the key to preventing or ending violations of social rights.

For example, the right to work is guaranteed, amongst other things, by domestic rules restricting employer discretion to discharge employees. Such rules are toothless, however, if a specific case of dismissal cannot be contested before a court, as illustrated in *Koskinas v Greece*.[102] This case concerned a steward who had been dismissed after a complaint of indecent assault on a passenger had been lodged against him. He challenged his dismissal before the court of first instance, which held that the dismissal had been unfounded as the applicant's guilt had not been established.

---

[100] *Larioshina v Russia* (App No 56869/00) ECHR 23 April 2002.

[101] The main exception is the social security rights of certain categories of public servants. See *Pellegrin v France* (App No 28541/95) ECHR 1999-VIII 207: 'public servants whose duties typify the specific activities of the public service in so far as the latter is acting as the depositary of public authority responsible for protecting the general interests of the state or other public authorities'.

[102] *Koskinas v Greece* (App No 47760/99) ECHR 20 June 2002.

However, this judgment was overturned by the court of appeal, ruling that civil courts do not have the competence to examine the merits of a dismissal decision. The European Court of Human Rights found this decision in violation of Article 6, section 1 of the ECHR, on the grounds that the applicant had been unable to challenge the accusations made against him before any court offering all the guarantees of this provision, including full jurisdiction.

Even some of the more technical or so-called minor guarantees of a fair trial may, in certain cases, be central to the enforcement of social rights. One example is the right to an oral hearing. When a person is denied a disability benefit based on an evaluation of his need for support or assistance and/or of the costs of his disability, he may rightly feel that such an assessment cannot be fairly conducted on the basis of written documents alone. The Court has held that, in such cases, a request for an oral hearing, in which the beneficiary can be heard or can bring witnesses (such as doctors) on his behalf, must be granted.[103]

III NON-DISCRIMINATION WITH REGARD TO SOCIAL RIGHTS

Looking to the future, the most important mechanism for protecting social rights in the European Convention system will be non-discrimination provisions. Article 14 of the Convention already offers some possibilities in this respect,[104] although the entry into force of the twelfth Protocol to the Convention has opened the gates for new types of social rights cases being brought before the Strasbourg Court.

A Article 14 of the ECHR

The non-discrimination clause of the European Convention on Human Rights in Article 14 is not an independent provision. It forbids discrimination only in 'the enjoyment of the rights and freedoms set forth in [the] Convention' and, hence, can only be invoked in conjunction with another article in the Convention or its protocols. As social rights are not as such included therein, it is difficult to bring a claim of discrimination in that area before the European Court of Human Rights.

Yet, in several instances, the Court has applied a very broad interpretation of substantive Convention rights in combination with Article 14.

---

[103] *Lundevall v Sweden, Salomonsson v Sweden* (App No 38978/97) ECHR 12 November 2002; *Miller v Sweden* (App No 55853/00) ECHR 8 February 2005.

[104] SJ Priso Essawe, 'Les droits sociaux et l'égalité de traitement dans la jurisprudence de la Cour européenne des droits de l'homme' (1998) 20 *Revue Trimestrielle des Droits de l'Homme* 721–36.

Although Article 14 is not independent, it is autonomous, which means that a finding for a violation of the substantive right with which it is combined is not necessary for a finding of a violation of Article 14. Rather, it is sufficient that the facts of the case fall within the scope of the substantive provision. The European Court of Human Rights has accepted that the scope of specific Convention rights may be broader when applied in combination with Article 14. It is sufficient that the matter with regard to which discrimination is alleged is linked to the exercise of a right protected in the Convention or constitutes one of the modalities of its exercise.

I Social Benefits

In several cases, discrimination has been alleged under Article 14 with regard to the enjoyment of social benefits. In *Gaygusuz v Austria*,[105] a Turkish man who had worked in Austria for 10 years had been refused the social benefit of an advance on his pension in the form of emergency assistance, because it was available only to Austrian citizens. The ECtHR ruled that this was unjustified discrimination. It arrived at this decision by combining Article 14 with the property right entrenched in Article 1 of the first Protocol and then interpreting this right in a novel way so as to include within its scope the right to social benefits. While the Court did refer to a link to the payment of contributions to an employment insurance fund, this was not the conclusive element in its decision. Rather, the determinative factor in the Court's reasoning was its classification of the right to the social benefit as a pecuniary right, which is protected as a property right under a broad interpretation of Article 1 of the first Protocol. In a later case, *Koua Poirrez v France*, which concerned the denial to foreign nationals of a disability allowance, only the pecuniary nature of the right was retained to support the applicability of Article 1 of the first Protocol in combination with Article 14 of the Convention.[106]

In addition to these cases, which deal with discrimination on the basis of nationality, the Court has deliberated on a number of applications under Article 14 of the ECHR and Article 1 of the first Protocol alleging gender discrimination with respect to social benefits. In *Wessels-Bergervoet v The Netherlands*, for example, the Court found prohibited discrimination in the case of a Dutch woman who had been excluded for 19 years from receiving social insurance under the General Old Age Pensions Act because she was married to a man who had not been insured under the Act during periods of employment abroad. In contrast, a married man in the same situation would not have been thus excluded from the insurance

---

[105] *Gaygusuz v Austria* (App No 17371/90) ECHR 1996-IV 1129.
[106] *Koua Poirrez v France* (App No 40892/98) ECHR 2003-X 45.

scheme. Hence, the facts of the case constituted discrimination on the basis of gender and marital status.[107]

Furthermore, in *Willis v United Kingdom*, the Court considered that:

> the right to a widow's payment and a widowed mother's allowance—in so far as provided for in the applicable legislation—is a sufficiently pecuniary right to fall within the ambit of Article 1 of Protocol No. 1.[108]

Thus, the denial of these rights to a man on account of his gender would constitute discrimination. Yet with respect to the right to a widow's pension, which is another type of benefit, the applicant had not been treated differently from a woman in an analogous situation. For that reason, the Court found it unnecessary to determine whether the right to that benefit fell within the scope of Article 1 of the first Protocol.

In *Van Raalte v The Netherlands*,[109] the Court applied the same combination of articles in finding for discrimination with regard to the obligation to pay social contributions. The applicant was a 63-year-old unmarried and childless man who was objecting to the fact that he had to pay contributions under the General Child Benefits Act, whereas childless women of 45 years and older are exempt from the same obligation. The Court ruled that this constitutes prohibited discrimination, holding that the payment of social contributions falls within the scope of Article 1 of the first Protocol, because the second paragraph of the Article protects the state's right 'to secure the payment of taxes or other contributions'.

Certain claims regarding social benefits may be brought on the basis of a combination of Article 14 and Article 8 of the ECHR. In *Petrovic v Austria*,[110] a claim regarding a right to family allowances was brought grounded on the combined provisions. The applicant complained that as a father he did not have a right to a parental leave allowance, because, until 1989, Austrian legislation had limited this right to mothers. The Court explicitly stated that Article 8 cannot be interpreted to include a positive obligation for the state to provide parental leave allowance.[111] Nevertheless, it did hold that this allowance falls within the scope of Article 8 in combination with Article 14, as it is

> intended to promote family life and necessarily affects the way in which the latter is organised as, in conjunction with parental leave, it enables one of the parents to stay home to look after the children.[112]

---

[107] *Wessels-Bergervoet v The Netherlands* (App No 34462/97) ECHR 2002-IV 239.
[108] *Willis v United Kingdom* (App No 36042/97) ECHR 2002-IV 311 para 36.
[109] *Van Raalte v The Netherlands* (App No 20060/92) ECHR 1997-I 173.
[110] *Petrovic v Austria* (App No 20458/92) ECHR 1998-II 579.
[111] *Ibid.*, para 26.
[112] *Ibid* para 27. The Court did not, however, find that the unequal treatment in this particular context amounted to discrimination.

The denial of a homosexual partner's right to survivor pension was recognised as falling within the scope of Article 8 in *Estevez v Spain*, since 'the applicant's emotional and sexual relationship related to his private life'.[113] Spanish legislation had limited the right to survivor pensions to married couples at a time when Spanish law did not yet allow same-sex marriages. The ECtHR held that this legislation did not amount to prohibited discrimination, since the difference in treatment was proportionate and justified by a legitimate purpose, ie, the protection of the traditional family unit based on heterosexual marriage. This reasoning, however, seems to have been reversed by the Court's decision in *Karner v Austria* (see infra).

ii Housing

Complaints of discrimination in the context of housing can also be brought under a combination of Article 14 of the Convention and Article 8. In *Karner v Austria*,[114] a violation of these provisions was found with respect to Austrian legislation that provides that, after the death of a tenant, his or her 'life companion' has a right to succeed in the tenancy. The Austrian Supreme Court had interpreted this provision in such a way so as to preclude its application to a surviving partner in a homosexual relationship. Overruling earlier case law of the European Commission on Human Rights,[115] the ECtHR held that the objective to protect the traditional sense of the family unit could not legitimise such a distinction.

iii Employment

In certain cases, claims of employment discrimination may be brought under Article 14 of the ECHR in combination with Article 8. In *Sidabras and Džiautas v Lithuania*,[116] for example, the Court found that these provisions had been violated by employment restrictions set in Lithuanian domestic legislation for private sector activities. The relevant legislation stipulated that former KGB employees could not, for a period of 10 years, work as

> public officials or civil servants in government, local or defence authorities, the State Security department, the police, the prosecution, courts or diplomatic service, customs, State supervisory bodies and other authorities monitoring public institutions, as lawyers or notaries, as employees of banks and other credit institutions, on strategic economic projects, in security companies (structures), in

---

113 *Mata Estevez v Spain* (App No 56501/00) ECHR 2001-VI 299.
114 *Karner v Austria* (App No 40016/98) ECHR 2003-IX 199.
115 *Röösli v Germany* (App No 28318/95) ECHR 15 May 1996.
116 *Sidabras & Džiautas v Lithuania* (App No 55480/00, 59330/00) ECHR 27 July 2004.

other companies (structures) providing detective services, in communications systems, or in the educational system as teachers, educators or heads of institutions[;] nor may they perform a job requiring the carrying of a weapon.[117]

The application before the Court concerned only the ban on private sector activities. In its judgment, the Court held that 'a far-reaching ban on taking up private-sector employment does affect "private life"'. Furthermore, the Court stated that it

> attaches particular weight in this respect to the text of Article 1 § 2 of the European Social Charter and the interpretation given by the European Committee of Social Rights... and to the texts adopted by the ILO... It further reiterates that there is no watertight division separating the sphere of social and economic rights from the field covered by the Convention.[118]

The reference to the norms in the European Social Charter and their interpretation by the European Committee of Social Rights, as well as to the ILO texts, relate to their applicability with regard to employment discrimination against former officials of totalitarian regimes. The European Committee of Social Rights and ILO are, however, directly applying social rights, ie, the right to work and the prohibition of discrimination in employment, which makes the Court's reference particularly remarkable.

B The Twelfth Additional Protocol to the ECHR

On 4 November 2000, on the occasion of the ECHR's fiftieth anniversary, the twelfth additional Protocol to the Convention was adopted. This Protocol sets forth a general, independent prohibition on discrimination in the law and by public authorities.[119] The Protocol, which entered into force on 1 April 2005, has currently been ratified by 11 of the 46 Member States of the Council of Europe.[120]

Under the twelfth Protocol, it is no longer necessary to bring a claim of discrimination in combination with a substantive article of the Convention or additional protocols. This innovation may result in large numbers of claims being brought before the Court in many 'new' areas, including the entire field of social rights. Moreover, the number of violations of social

---

[117] *Ibid* para 24.
[118] *Ibid* para 47.
[119] ECHR, 12th Protocol, Art 1: '1. The enjoyment of any right set forth by law shall be secured without discrimination on any ground such as sex, race, colour, language, religion, political or other opinion, national or social origin, association with a national minority, property, birth or other status. 2. No one shall be discriminated against by any public authority on any ground such as those mentioned in paragraph 1.'
[120] This is its status as of 1 January 2006. The ratifying states are: Albania, Armenia, Bosnia and Herzegovina, Croatia, Cyprus, Finland, Georgia, the Netherlands, San Marino, Serbia and Montenegro, and the Former Yugoslav Republic of Macedonia.

rights that can be framed as instances of discrimination under the Convention has been substantially increased by the fact that the ECHR, both in Article 14 and in the twelfth Protocol, prohibits discrimination 'on any ground'. It will thus be possible to contest restrictions on social rights before the European Court of Human Rights not only if based on the 'typical' discrimination grounds, such as gender, nationality and sexual orientation, but also grounded on any of the many other discriminatory distinctions commonly present in social policy and legislation, such as age and state of health. It will be a challenge for the European Court to demarcate the parameters of the states' margin of discretion to differentiate on the latter type of grounds. But there is more: any factor distinguishing one person or group of persons from others can be regarded as a discriminatory distinction. Thus, the twelfth Protocol enables almost all violations of social (or other) rights to be framed as discrimination issues. For example in *Sidabras and Džiautas v Lithuania* (above), discrimination can be read into the distinction between individuals who had worked for the KGB and individuals who had not.

The experience of the Belgian Constitutional Court is also useful in this context. The Court oversees the compatibility of Acts of Parliament with the Belgian Constitution. Until a 2003 reform, only three Constitutional provisions relating to fundamental rights—addressing freedom of education, equality and non-discrimination—had existed for the Court to apply. Nevertheless, the Court (which in no way could be characterised as activist) applied all fundamental rights provisions in the Constitution, as well as those found in international treaties in conjunction with the non-discrimination provisions in the Belgian Constitution. The prohibited discrimination grounds in the Belgian Constitution are open-ended, similar to the ECHR. Thus, instead of arguing that a person's right has been violated, the Belgian Constitutional Court would rule that a person was discriminated against vis-à-vis the exercise of her or his right. The Belgian example thereby shows that general anti-discrimination jurisdiction comes very close to being general human rights jurisdiction. Given this perspective, the indirect protection of social rights by the European Court of Human Rights has only just begun.

IV CONCLUSION

The experience of the European Court of Human Rights shows that the justiciability of civil and political rights leads to what can be termed collateral benefits for social rights. One important yet often ignored way in which such benefits can materialise is by way of guarantees of a fair trial: when social rights are guaranteed in domestic legislation, access to just and fair proceedings is crucial to making these rights enforceable.

Another back-door entrance for social rights is the non-discrimination provisions of the European Convention of Human Rights and Fundamental Freedoms. Due to the accessory nature of Article 14 of the Convention, cases of non-discrimination in the area of social rights have remained scarce. The entry into force of the twelfth Protocol to the Convention, however, may usher in a whole new era of social rights protection in Strasbourg. If the Court wants to prevent a flood of social rights claims through the non-discrimination gate, it will have to set out criteria defining discrimination in a somewhat restrictive manner. As twelfth Protocol cases start coming before the Court during the next decade, it will be interesting to watch the stances taken by the Court in the area of social rights.

In the meantime, applicants' efforts to stretch the scope of both positive and negative state obligations under the ECHR to include some social rights protection remain a fascinating subject of inquiry. Overburdened and with 45 judges presiding in five separate sections, the European Court has not been particularly effective in developing consistent doctrines. Hence it should come as no surprise that since the Court's declaration in *Airey* in 1979 on the lack of a 'water-tight' separation between civil and political rights and economic and social rights, it has not developed a position on social rights as such. Criteria are developed and consistently applied to deal with similar cases (for example, cases of objections to expulsion on medical grounds), but no conscious effort has been made to ensure consistency amongst the different types of social rights cases.

Even though the number of cases in which social rights are indirectly protected is rapidly multiplying, the European Court's basic approach remains a cautious one. This is understandable and correct, in consideration of the fact that, since 1998, a mechanism has existed within the Council of Europe with the specific mandate of adjudicating complaints of violations of social rights, namely, the collective complaints procedure under the European Social Charter. Yet although this mechanism has recently begun to take on an important role, it still has a long way to go before reaching the lofty status enjoyed by the European Court of Human Rights, both in legal circles and among the general public. Moreover, from an individual perspective, the enforcement of social rights under the Social Charter is indirect in a different sense, since only collective complaints can be lodged. Hence, it is to be expected that the indirect protection of social rights by the European Court of Human Rights will remain attractive to individual plaintiffs.

The Court's involvement in social rights is an inevitable result of the genuine indivisibility of human rights. It is obvious that, for example, a failure to protect the right to health care may have consequences in terms of the right to life and that a failure to protect the right to housing may have consequences of inhuman treatment or vis-à-vis the right to protection of family life. There is an inherent tension between this reality of indivisibility, on the one hand, and, on the other, the need for the Court, with its clear mandate to focus on civil and political rights, to draw the line somewhere with regard to its competence to deal with social rights. Obviously, where the line is drawn will be determined not by the logic of the social rights that are indirectly protected, but by the logic of the civil and political rights into which they are incorporated.

Under Article 3 of the ECHR, the main criterion for determining whether a particular treatment is 'inhuman' or 'degrading' is the gravity of the action. Hence, this provision offers a solution to situations that, based on pure instinct, are manifestly unjust and intolerable due to the sheer extent of human suffering involved: the suffering of a seriously ill individual expelled to a country where he or she will die without appropriate medical care or family support; the suffering of people who are left without assistance after the deliberate destruction of their homes by government agents in front of their eyes; and the suffering of families forced to live in atrocious conditions after a racist mob, incited by the police, destroyed their houses and the government failed in its commitment to rebuild their homes. Such instances, in which a violation of the applicants' rights has been found, involve very serious conditions. However, it appears that Article 3 of the ECHR can be interpreted to enable a lowering of the threshold somewhat and the recognition of violations of rights in similar cases where the applicant's condition is somewhat less acute but can still be classified as 'degrading'.

The Court has deemed the indirect protection of the right to health (and health care) under Article 2 of the Convention a matter of positive obligations. In its case law with regard to Article 2 in general, the Court has recognised two types of positive obligations: obligations of prevention (ie, when the state is aware of a real risk to the life of an identified individual, it must do all in its power to prevent the risk from materializing) and obligations of investigation (ie, loss of life due to violence and/or government involvement requires thorough investigation). Yet this framework has emerged as inadequate for dealing with cases (eg, *Nitecki*, *Pentiacova*) in which the saving of lives would require significant government expenditure on medical treatment. From a right to health perspective, economic accessibility of health care is a crucial issue,[121] and retrogressive measures (such as in *Pentiacova*) suspect:

> If any deliberately retrogressive measures are taken, the State party has the burden of proving that they have been introduced after the most careful consideration of all alternatives and that they are duly justified by reference to

---

121 UN Committee on Economic, Social and Cultural Rights, General Comment 14 on the right to the highest attainable standard of health (2000) para 12(b)(iii).

the totality of the rights provided for in the Covenant in the context of the full use of the State party's maximum available resources.[122]

Hence the ease with which the European Court dismisses such cases at the admissibility stage, as manifestly ill-founded, is striking. The Court's cautious approach to social rights issues may explain its reluctance to create an additional category of positive obligations under Article 2 or to adopt a broader interpretation of the preventive obligations. The result might have been different had the Court recognised in its earlier case law an obligation on the part of the government to expend significant amounts on saving lives or, alternatively, had the Court been called upon to consider a case in which the facts were of an extremely serious nature, invoking the same gut sense of intolerability referred to above. In cases involving detainees, however, the Court is more forthcoming, in the context of both Article 3 and Article 2, since detainees are in a particularly vulnerable position, under the total control of the state, which enhances the state's responsibility for their wellbeing.

In claims brought in the framework of Article 8 of the ECHR, the Court has used the criterion of a link to the matters noted in the provision, ie, private life, family life and the home. In this context, direct state interference with the right to housing is relatively easy to deal with, as the protection of the home is explicitly included in the text of Article 8. Other issues related to the right to housing and health care are considered a matter of positive obligation. In this context, the Court has developed a line of case law that requires the state to protect individuals against environmental pollution in their living environments, linking the issue both to the right to enjoy one's home and to the right to protection of family life. The Court has also given strong protection to individuals' right of access to information concerning health hazards, stating in rather vague terms that the matter is 'sufficiently closely linked to their private and family lives within the meaning of Article 8 as to raise an issue under that provision'.[123] In the area of dwellings adapted for disabled individuals, the Court's criterion is, similarly, that there should be a 'direct and immediate link between the measures sought by the applicant and the latter's private life'.[124] Yet it remains unclear in which cases the Court will recognise the existence of such a link and in which it will not. A striking inconsistency appears, for example, between the cases of *Sentges* and *Van Kück*, discussed above. In the former, no violation of Article 8 was found in the state's refusal to oblige a health insurance fund to refund the cost of a mechanical arm that would allow the disabled teenager a certain amount of autonomy. Yet, in the latter case, a violation was found when the state

---

[122] *Ibid* para 32.
[123] *McGinley & Egan v United Kingdom*, above n 53, para 97.
[124] *Marzari v Italy*, above n 71.

had not obliged a health insurance company to reimburse for a gender reassignment operation. Two factors can explain the different outcomes in these cases. The first is the financial aspect, which is always a problematic matter in the protection of social rights. *Van Kück* concerned a private insurance company, whereas *Sentges* dealt with statutory health insurance, wherein the bill is paid by the state. The second factor is the logic underlying Article 8. The Court has recognised many aspects of 'privacy,' including autonomy and social relations (the elements involved in *Sentges*), yet it has also attached increased importance (and offered stronger protection) to certain 'core' matters, including an individual's gender identity[125] (the aspect involved in *Van Kück*).

In this respect, it may be assumed that indirect protection of social rights under civil and political rights provisions will always be unsatisfactory. It does not seem realistic to demand of the European Court of Human Rights that, in such cases, it steer away from its own conceptions of the core of rights and replace them with, for example, those that have been set in the context of social rights (including the right to health) by the UN Committee on Economic, Social and Cultural Rights.[126] This notwithstanding, with the approaching influx of social rights claims arising from the twelfth Protocol, the Court might want to examine which benefits it can draw from the work accomplished by the social rights experts of other entities. In addition to defining the essence of each right, the UN General Comments have, in particular, emphasised issues of availability, accessibility (non-discrimination, physical accessibility, affordability and information accessibility), acceptability and quality. The introduction of some of these concepts into the European Court's case law would add a new dimension to the indivisibility of human rights.

---

[125] *Goodwin v United Kingdom*, above n 66, para 90.
[126] See, eg, General Comment 14, above n 122, para 37.

Part III

National Perspectives on Social Rights

8

Social Rights Litigation in India
Developments of the Last Decade

JAYNA KOTHARI

I INTRODUCTION

The indivisibility of the constitutional social rights of housing, education, food, health and livelihood, with the fundamental rights to life, equality and religion guaranteed in the Indian Constitution cannot be stressed more strongly in India today. In the last decade India has faced some of the world's worst natural disasters and witnessed situations of extreme communal violence. Combined with these, it is during this time that the deleterious effects of globalisation and threats of deprivation of basic social rights have also been acutely felt.

The Indian Constitution does not include social rights as justiciable fundamental rights, but only as directive principles of state policy. The Indian Supreme Court and High Courts, however, have pioneered the movement worldwide for enforcement of social rights as extensions of justiciable fundamental rights through various forms of litigation, most notably public interest litigation. The jurisprudence of the Indian Supreme Court illustrates how the absence of formal constitutional guarantees of social rights does not preclude constitutional protection of certain interests associated with social citizenship through expansive interpretations of civil and political rights.[1]

In examining the protection of social rights in India, this chapter analyses the role of litigation as a strategy to fulfil the social rights laid down in the Indian Constitution focusing specifically on the right to housing, food and education cases over the last decade. The aim is to shed light on what has been achieved through social rights litigation and to

[1] D Davis, P Macklem and G Mundlak, 'Social Rights, Social Citizenship, and Transformative Constitutionalism: A Comparative Assessment' in J Conaghan, M Fischl and K Klare (eds), *Labour Law in an Era of Globalization: Transformative Practices and Possibilities* (Oxford, Oxford University Press, 2004).

extract some insights into the potential and limits of litigation as a strategy for advancing social rights. The emerging new social rights litigation, infused with the principle of interdependence of rights and Supreme Court jurisprudence, from the early 'nineties onwards is especially instructive and positive because it provides factual support for my contention that the judiciary both can and should seek to protect social rights. The recent case law over the last decade on these specific social rights is interesting for a variety of reasons. First, new socio-economic rights such as the basic right to food have been articulated by the Supreme Court with innovative remedies for enforcement. The Court has shown a marked tendency to take the principle of the interdependence of human rights seriously and to interpret entrenched constitutional guarantees of the fundamental rights in light of the Directive Principles. Second, we see that while the Supreme Court has stepped in to enforce new social rights, it has been ambivalent when it comes to well-entrenched socio-economic rights such as the right to housing, which was pronounced as a part of the right to life as early as 1986, and has even gone back on its earlier position. In the third case, ie, the right to education, the litigation in the Supreme Court has spurred the amendment of the Constitution converting the non-justiciable promise of free primary education into a justiciable fundamental right.

Through the discussion and analysis of these specific rights to housing, food and education, I argue that litigation is still an important strategy for making social rights enforceable in India and amenable to judicial implementation. The recent experience, however, shows that enforceability remains the crucial factor, for litigation only succeeds effectively when combined with a variety of factors such as social campaigns, research and political will.

II SOCIAL RIGHTS IN THE INDIAN CONSTITUTION

By 'social rights', or 'socio-economic rights' interchangeably, I refer to rights that protect the necessities of life or that provide for the foundations of an adequate quality of life such as the rights to housing, health care, food, water, social security and education. These social rights have also been defined by Amartya Sen as basic entitlements.[2] The concept of basic human needs involves drawing up a list of foundational human needs of both physiological and social import in order to arrive at a list of the minimum social needs.[3]

---

[2] A Sen, *Development as Freedom* (Oxford, Oxford University Press, 1999).
[3] BB Pande, 'The Constitutionality of Basic Human Needs: An Ignored Area of Legal Discourse' (1989) 4 *Supreme Court Cases (Journal)* 1.

These social rights, or basic entitlements, have been recognised internationally as being as important as other human rights such as the right to equality, the right against discrimination and others which can be termed as civil and political rights generally. As Michelman argues, the fact that social rights make budgetary demands or call for government action and not just forbearance does not in itself differentiate them radically from the standpoint of justiciability from constitutionally protected rights to equality before the law and rights to speech and expression or to so-called negative liberties.[4] At the very minimum, social rights can sometimes even be 'negatively protected' by comfortable forms of judicial intervention, for example when municipal zoning and land use laws, insofar as they constrict local housing, can be open to challenge.

Human rights in the Indian Constitution are divided into two separate parts. Part III of the Constitution houses the 'Fundamental Rights', which include the right to life, the right to equality, the right to free speech and expression, the right to freedom of movement and the right to freedom of religion, among others, which in conventional human rights language may be termed as civil and political rights. Part IV of the constitution contains the Directive Principles of State Policy (DPSPs), which include all the social, economic and cultural rights, such as the right to free primary education (now made into a fundamental right by the Eighty-Sixth Constitutional Amendment Act 2002), the right to livelihood, the right to health and housing, the right to clean environment and others.

While the fundamental rights mentioned in Part III are justiciable under the constitution, the DPSPs are not justiciable rights and their non-compliance cannot be taken as a claim for enforcement against the state. The Directive Principles in Part IV have specifically been made non-justiciable or unenforceable by Article 37 of the Constitution, which states:

> The provisions contained in this Part shall not be enforceable by any court, but the principles therein laid down are nevertheless fundamental in the governance of the country and it shall be the duty of the State to apply these principles in making laws.

The inclusion of the non-justiciable socio-economic rights in Part IV of the Constitution as Directive Principles of State Policy was in order to establish a new social order based on social, economic and political justice. Social revolution was put at the top of the national agenda by the Constituent Assembly when it adopted the Objectives Resolution, which called for social, economic and political justice and equality of status, opportunity and before the law for all people. The DPSPs, it was thought, would make explicit the 'socialist' as well as the social revolutionary content of the

---

[4] F Michelman, 'The Constitution, Social Rights and Liberal Political Justification' (2003) 1 *International Journal of Constitutional Law* 13.

Constitution.[5] In this sense, the vision of the drafters of the Indian constitution was very similar to what the new South African Constitution is imagined to be—a transformative Constitution.

Despite the DPSPs being non-justiciable, it is extremely significant to note that the Indian Supreme Court has been reaffirming that both the fundamental rights and the DPSPs must be interpreted harmoniously—thus laying the foundations for the principle that social rights are complementary, interdependent and indivisible with civil and political rights and therefore also justiciable. The Court has held that there is no disharmony between the Directive Principles and the fundamental rights, because they supplement each other in aiming at the same goal of bringing about a social revolution and the establishment of a welfare state, which is envisaged in the Preamble to the Constitution.[6]

A Social Rights Litigation and Article 21

Socio-economic rights have always been thought of traditionally as being best addressed through policy, campaigns and the democratic political process. Having the courts enforce social rights did not seem viable as it would involve substantial financial expenditure from the government for their enforcement, and many believe that it is not the role of the court to intervene. Also, the judicial process is generally considered efficient in preventing encroachments on rights or liberties. But can it create new rights and enforce positive action in terms of allocation of resources? If we follow the Indian experience of litigation, which started in the late 'seventies and early 'eighties for the enforcement of socio-economic rights, we can see that it has been very positive and has been an important strategy for the enforcement of social rights. Litigation in this area has in many cases successfully ensured that social rights included in the DPSPs have been made enforceable despite them not being included as justiciable fundamental rights in the Constitution. Though initially aimed at providing relief to the most underprivileged sections of society, the Supreme Court and the High Courts have over the years employed this jurisdiction to address a broad and diverse range of issues. In the 1990s the court used its public interest litigation jurisdiction to address several of the concerns of India's burgeoning middle class as well.[7]

---

[5] Mahavir Tyagi from the United Provinces, during the Constituent Assembly Debates said, "… the directive principles accommodate all the revolutionary slogans in a particular form as it is social and economic justice that is demanded by the most radical of the radicals of the world." Constituent Assembly Debates Official Report, 19th Nov. 1948, Vol. No. VII, Book No.2 (New Delhi, Lok Sabha Secretariat, 1999).

[6] *Unni Krishnan v State of AP*, AIR 1993 SC 2178.

[7] V Sripati and A Thiruvengadam, 'India: Constitutional Amendment making the Right to Education a Fundamental Right' (2004) 2 *International Journal of Constitutional Law* 148.

The constitutional social rights or the DPSPs have been enforced or made justiciable by the Supreme Court through an expansion of the fundamental rights in Part III of the Constitution, particularly the right to life guaranteed in Article 21.[8] Right from the late 1970s, starting from the *Maneka Gandhi* case,[9] the Supreme Court has been expanding the guarantee of the right to life in Article 21 to include a whole gamut of social rights.[10] Article 21 has been expanded to include several related rights within its ambit including the rights to a clean environment,[11] food,[12] clean working conditions,[13] emergency medical treatment,[14] free legal aid[15] and release from bonded labour.[16] This strategy of litigation has been widely and continuously used through the years and through the expansion of Article 21 social rights have thus become de facto justiciable and enforceable by the High Courts in the country and in the Supreme Court.

B New Remedies in Social Rights Litigation

That judges are willing to respond to social rights claims is not enough: they must also be able to find adequate legal remedies to repair the violations. The remedies which were intended to deal with private rights situations were simply inadequate, for the suffering of the disadvantaged in social and economic rights violation cases could not always be redressed through the traditional remedies of damages, injunctions, and writs of certiorari, mandamus or prohibition.

In dealing with the huge number of public interest litigation petitions for enforcement of social rights coming before the court, the Supreme Court had to evolve new remedies for giving relief. These new remedies were unorthodox and unconventional and were intended to initiate positive action on the part of the state and its authorities. The range of options that were used by the Supreme Court included 'minimal affirmation', merely requiring the state to *respect* a social right in the negative sense of non-interference; courts ruled that the state has a duty to *protect*

---

[8] Article 21: 'No person shall be deprived of his life or personal liberty except according to procedure established by law'.

[9] AIR 1978 SC 597.

[10] *Francis Coralie Mullin v Union Territory of Delhi* (1981)1 SCC 608; *Chameli Singh v State of UP* (1996) 2 SCC 549.

[11] *Subhash Kumar v Bihar* (1991) 1 SCC 598; *AP Pollution Control Board v MV Nayudu* (1999) 2 SCC 718; *MC Mehta v Union of India* (1987) 4 SCC 463.

[12] *Peoples Union for Civil Liberties (PUCL) v Union of India & Others* WP (Civil) No 196 / 2001, 23 July 2001, unreported.

[13] *Consumer Education & Research Centre v Union of India* (1995) 3 SCC 42.

[14] *Parmanand Katara v Union of India* (1989) 4 SCC 248.

[15] *Khatri v State of Bihar* (1981) 1 SCC 623.

[16] *Bandhua Mukti Morcha v Union of India* (1984) 3 SCC 161.

social rights against encroachment by others; they could order the state to actively *promote* particular social rights by developing policies to this effect; or they could make concrete orders for state agencies to *fulfil* the individual claimants' social rights. Furthermore, court orders may be *declaratory* (stating that laws or actions are in breach of a social rights obligation, but leaving it to the state to devise a remedy), *mandatory* (requiring specific actions to be taken) or *supervisory* (requiring the relevant agency to report back within a set time-frame). Whilst these new remedies were used creatively in socio-economic rights cases, as Gloppen has observed with regard to social rights litigation in South Africa, court performance also depends on the skill and capacity of the judges, and of the jurisprudential resources at their disposal.[17]

The final stage in any litigation is compliance. For public interest litigation to succeed in improving the actual social rights situation, the judgments must be complied with by the relevant authorities and political action taken to implement the ruling. Compliance is again the outcome of a range of factors. The authority of the judgment itself is important. This stems partly from the courts' professionalism, independence and legitimacy. Several aspects of the political contexts are crucial for compliance with social rights judgments: the prevailing political culture; the balance of power between the parties, and, perhaps most important, the political will to follow up and give priority to social rights issues.[18]

Some of these new and creative remedies were taken forward by the Supreme Court in the 'nineties to seek enforcement of some of the newly articulated social rights such as the right to food. By looking at some of the most important constitutional social rights cases of the last decade more closely, specifically the right to food, the right to housing and the right to education, we can see that social rights litigation in India is indeed vibrant and dynamic and has taken a new form in the 'nineties and the twenty-first century.

III THE RIGHT TO FOOD

The right to food in its most basic sense can be understood as freedom from hunger. This can be interpreted in two different ways associated with different readings of the term 'hunger'. In a narrow sense, hunger refers to the pangs of an empty stomach. Correspondingly, the right to food can be understood as the right to have two square meals a day throughout the year. In a broader sense, hunger refers to under-nutrition. The right to food

---

[17] S Gloppen, 'Social Rights Litigation as Transformation: South African Perspectives' (CMI Working Paper WP 2005:3) <http://www.cmi.no/pdf/?file=/publications/2005/wp/wp2005-3.pdf>.
[18] *Ibid.*

(ie, the right to be free from under-nutrition) then links with a wide range of entitlements, not only to food itself but also to other requirements of good nutrition such as clean water, health care and even elementary education.[19] There is also increasing recognition worldwide that food and nutrition is a human right and thus there is a legal obligation to assure that all people are adequately nourished.[20]

While the Indian Supreme Court has reiterated in several of its decisions that the right to life guaranteed in Article 21 of the Constitution in its true meaning includes the basic right to food, clothing and shelter,[21] it is indeed surprising that the justiciability of the specific right to food as an integral right under Article 21 had never been articulated or enforced until 2001![22] This specific right therefore is a newly articulated social right and it is exciting to see how litigation has led to its articulation by the Supreme Court.

A The Right to Food Petition

In 2001 there was a massive drought in several states in India, especially Orissa, Rajasthan and Madhya Pradesh. Due to the drought, which had been going on for months, and the extreme poverty and complete lack of access to food grains, people were starving in large numbers. In this situation, therefore, it was the right to food in the narrow sense that needed attention. The agitation in the country over lack of access to food grains in the drought-hit states of Orissa, Rajasthan, Gujarat and others took rapid momentum after shocking incidents of people in some of the poorest districts of Orissa dying from starvation. Despite these facts, the central government maintained that there were no incidents of starvation

[19] J Dreze, 'Right to Food: From the Courts to the Streets' (2002) 1 Combat Law, <http://www.combatlaw.org/information.php?issue_id=3&article_id=102>

[20] G Kent, 'The Human Right to Food in India' (2002) University of Hawaii, <http://www.earthwindow.com/grc2/foodrights/>. The right to food and nutrition is guaranteed in the international provisions stated in the ICESCR. ICESCR, Art 11.1 provides that the right to adequate food is part of the right of every person to an adequate standard of living, and Art 11.2 recognises the fundamental right of everyone to be free from hunger and states responsibilities for ensuring that.

[21] *Chameli Singh* (above n 10), *Paschim Banga Khet Mazdoor Samity and Others v State of West Bengal* (1996) 4 SCC 37; *Francis Coralie Mullin* (above n 10).

[22] The case of starvation deaths due to poverty in two of the poorest villages of Orissa was brought to the Supreme Court in a PIL in 1989, but the petition did not articulate a violation of the right to food on the part of the State. The Supreme Court in that judgment noted that, on the evidence, 'starvation deaths could not be ruled out', but failed to recognise that the right to food, an integral part of the right to life, was being violated. In this case the court reviewed governmental plans and responses to poverty and starvation in that area and merely ordered increased participation of community members on the Natural Calamities Committee to oversee working of all social welfare measures designed to alleviate poverty. *Kishen Pattnaik and Another v State of Orissa* AIR 1989 SC 677.

deaths.[23] There was an enormous public outcry on this issue since it was openly acknowledged that the granaries of the Food Corporation of India (FCI) were overflowing with food grains, food was rotting and was being wasted and yet in the very same states, people were dying as they had no access to food grains.

Slowly, the agitation over access to food became a fully-fledged right to food campaign in the country with several civil society groups, activists and academics joining the campaign. As part of this campaign, a public interest litigation (PIL) was filed by the People's Union for Civil Liberties (PUCL) in April 2001 in the Supreme Court for enforcement of the right to food of the thousands of families that were starving in the drought-struck states of Orissa, Rajasthan, Chhattisgarh, Gujarat and Maharashtra, demanding that the country's gigantic food stocks should be used without delay to prevent hunger and starvation.[24]

The right to food petition asked three major questions:

1. Starvation deaths had become a national phenomenon while there was a surplus stock of food grains in government granaries. Does the right to life mean that people who are starving and who are too poor to buy food grains should be denied food grains free of cost by the state from the surplus stock of the state, particularly when it is lying unused and rotting?
2. Does not the right to life under Article 21 of the Constitution of India include the right to food?
3. Does not the right to life, which has been upheld by the Supreme Court imply that the state has a duty to provide food, especially in situations of drought, to people who are drought-affected and are not in a position to purchase food?

As relief measures, the petition demanded, among other things, the immediate release of food stocks for drought relief, provision of work for every able-bodied person and the increase in quota of food grains under the Public Distribution Scheme (PDS) for every person. This was the very first time that a distinct right to food was articulated as encompassed within Article 21 and was sought to be enforced in the Supreme Court.

B Enforcement by the Supreme Court

The Supreme Court expressed serious concern about the increasing number of starvation deaths and food insecurity despite overflowing food in FCI storehouses across the country. The bench, comprising Justices Kirpal and Balakrishnan, even broadened the scope of the petition from the initially

---

[23] UNI 'No Starvation Deaths: Minister' *The Hindu* (Bangalore, 3 August 2001), available at <http://www.hinduonnet.com/2001/08/31/stories/01310000e.htm>.
[24] Above n 12.

mentioned six drought-affected states, to include all the Indian states and union territories.

In its hearings, the Court directed all state governments to ensure that all Public Distribution shops are kept open with regular supplies and stated that it is the prime responsibility of the government to prevent hunger and starvation. On 23 July 2001, recognising the right to food, the Court said:

> In our opinion, what is of utmost importance is to see that food is provided to the aged, infirm, disabled, destitute women, destitute men who are in danger of starvation, pregnant and lactating women and destitute children, especially in cases where they or members of their family do not have sufficient funds to provide food for them. In case of famine, there may be shortage of food, but here the situation is that amongst plenty there is scarcity. Plenty of food is available, but distribution of the same amongst the very poor and the destitute is scarce and non-existent leading to mal-nourishment, starvation and other related problems.[25]

C Food Distribution Schemes Made into Entitlements

The Court, in an unprecedented interim order on 28 November 2001,[26] directed all the state governments and the Union of India to effectively enforce eight different centrally sponsored food schemes to the poor.[27] These food security schemes were declared as entitlements or rights of the poor and the Court also laid down specific time limits for the implementation of these schemes with the responsibility on the states to submit compliance affidavits to the Court. Of the eight schemes, the most significant was the Mid-Day Meal Scheme and the Supreme Court directed all state governments to provide cooked mid-day meals to children in all government schools by January 2002. The Supreme Court directed the state governments to:

> implement the Mid-Day Meal Scheme by providing every child in every Government and Government assisted Primary Schools with a prepared mid-day meal with a minimum content of 300 calories and 8-12 grams of protein each day of school for a minimum of 200 days. Those Governments providing dry rations instead of cooked meals must within three months start providing cooked meals in all Govt. and Govt. aided Primary Schools in at least half the districts of the State (in order of poverty) and must within a further period of

25 People's Union for Civil Liberties (above n 12).
26 Unreported order: <http://www.righttofoodindia.org/orders/nov28.html>.
27 These schemes included food distribution schemes and schemes guaranteeing income support in order to gain access to food such as the National Old Age Pension Scheme, the National Maternity Benefit Scheme and the National Family Benefit Scheme.

three months extend the provision of cooked meals to the remaining parts of the State.[28]

In addition to the above Mid-Day Meal Scheme, the Supreme Court also held that, under the Targeted Public Distribution Scheme, the states should commence distribution of 25kgs of grain per family per month (as opposed to the earlier limit of 20kgs of grain per family per month) by 1 January 2002. All state governments were directed to take their

> entire allotment of food grains from the Central Government under the various Schemes and disburse the same in accordance with the Schemes.[29]

Further, the court required that:

> the Food for Work Program in the scarcity areas should also be implemented by the various States to the extent possible.

It is interesting to note that this time the Supreme Court did not merely direct the States to formulate appropriate schemes, as had been done earlier by the Court in several housing rights cases,[30] but it went several steps further in directing strict implementation of already formulated (and modified where considered necessary) schemes within fixed time frames to make them entitlements and to ensure accountability. With a view to ensuring adequate food to the poorest of the poor, the Supreme Court in March 2002 asked all states and union territories to respond to an application seeking the framing of wage employment schemes such as the Sampoorna Gramin Rojgar Yojna (SGRY) ensuring the right to work to adults in rural areas. On 8 May 2002 the Supreme Court agreed on a system of monitoring and also added that the states are to provide a funds utilisation certificate before the money is released for their use.

D Enforcement of the Mid-Day Meal Scheme

Enforcement of the orders of the Supreme Court in the right to food petition has been very varied on the ground. Not all state governments have been implementing the orders, for various reasons.

The most significant implementation was that of the Mid-Day Meal Scheme. Since the beginning of the 2002 academic year, primary schools in Rajasthan started serving mid-day meals in compliance with the Supreme Court orders, and among states that did not already have a mid-day meal scheme Rajasthan was the first to comply. As governments slowly fell in line from then on, media reports highlighted various problems with the

---

[28] Interim Order dated 28 November 2001 in *People's Union for Civil Liberties* (above n 26).
[29] *Ibid.*
[30] *Olga Tellis v Bombay Municipal Corporation* AIR 1986 SC 180; *Ahmedabad Municipal Corporation v Nawab Khan Gulab Khan* (1997) 11 SCC 121.

implementation of mid-day meals. To get an accurate overall picture of the situation, the Right to Food Campaign conducted field surveys in several states. There were areas of genuine concern such as the quality of the meals provided, administrative impediments and meagre financial allocations. However, the surveys also showed that it was possible to implement the scheme well, financial and other constraints notwithstanding. Based on this learning, the campaign lobbied the government for an increase in financial allocations.

Another key element in the enforcement of the Mid-Day Meal Scheme was the intervention of the 'Commissioners' (Dr NC Saxena and Mr SR Sankaran, both retired civil servants) who were appointed by the Supreme Court to monitor the implementation of its interim orders. The Commissioners' reports to the Supreme Court repeatedly highlighted the violation of the order of 28 November 2001 in states such as Bihar, Jharkhand and Uttar Pradesh. These reports, along with lobbying of the central government, resulted in major increases in budgetary allocations in subsequent years.

Today, about 100 million children in India get a cooked meal at school, making this the largest mid-day meal programme in the world. The Mid-Day Meal Scheme is not merely providing nutrition to the school children. In a survey it was found that it resulted in a sharp increase in the enrolment of girls (36 per cent) and a reduction in gender bias in enrolment in schools. Daily attendances of children to the schools had also increased and this was attributed to the mid-day meals.[31] The key to the campaign's success lies in its determination to use all the spaces available in the Indian democratic system—legal action, media advocacy, academic research and street demonstrations among others.[32] However, this battle is far from over: the quality of mid-day meals needs radical improvement in large parts of the country.

Moreover, the implementation of the schemes is by no means perfect, and there remains a lot of scope for further improvement, but in states such as Rajasthan, where the Right to Food Campaign is very strongly asserted, these schemes have been internalised quite quickly by all concerned—school teachers, village administrations, state governments and the communities.

An analysis of this petition shows that Supreme Court orders are extremely useful in strengthening the bargaining power of all those who are working for the realisation of the right to food in India, but it would clearly be naïve to expect these orders to be implemented without further

---

[31] R Khera, 'Mid-day Meals in Rajasthan' *The Hindu* (Bangalore, 13 November 2002) available at: <http://www.hinduonnet.com/thehindu/2002/11/13/stories/2002111300521000.htm>.
[32] R Khera 'India's Right to Food Campaign' (Just For Change, Issue 4, November 2005) <http://www.righttofoodindia.org/links/articles_home.html>

public pressure.[33] The experience in this massive campaign for the right to food has shown that litigation, in order to be successful in social rights cases, cannot work in isolation from other forms of social action and political mobilisation. These orders of the Supreme Court bear great relevance for social rights jurisprudence—it not only shows once again the indivisibility of rights, but also that courts do have the authority to order positive action by the state which has financial / budgetary implications.

IV THE RIGHT TO HOUSING

The Supreme Court of India has elaborated at great length that the right to adequate housing, shelter and livelihood is considered a fundamental right under the right to life under Article 21 of the Constitution. One of the first and most important judgments of the Supreme Court which guaranteed that the right to housing is part of the right to life was the judgment delivered by J Chandrachud in *Olga Tellis v Bombay Municipal Corporation (BMC)* in the mid-'eighties.[34] Following the *Olga Tellis* case, in the 'nineties and early years of this decade, there were several other petitions which went before the Supreme Court seeking a re-iteration of the right to housing as a fundamental right.

Under Part III of the Constitution not only is the right to adequate housing an important component of the right to live with dignity, but also therefore an obvious component of the right to equality. The right to equality is symbiotically linked with social and economic rights, the one set of rights providing some of the context within which the other set can be understood. The Indian Supreme Court has placed great emphasis on guaranteeing the right to shelter as part of the larger goal of achieving social and economic equality, which is also a fundamental constitutional objective and finds form in Article 38 of the Directive Principles.[35] The Indian Constitution, keeping the specific context of extreme poverty in mind, requires the state to constantly work towards achieving these aims. Such an approach acknowledges that people cannot live with a semblance of human dignity where structural inequality prevails and where the state fails to address such inequality and its causes. In this approach, equality

---

[33] 'Right to Food: From the Courts to the Streets' (above n 19).
[34] (1985) 3 SCC 545.
[35] Article 38 states:

> State to secure a social order for the promotion of welfare of the people – (1) The State shall strive to promote the welfare of the people by securing and protecting as effectively as it may a social order in which justice, social, economic and political, shall inform all the institutions of the national life. (2) The State shall, in particular, strive to minimize the inequalities in income, and endeavour to eliminate inequalities in status, facilities and opportunities, not only amongst individuals but also amongst groups of people residing in different areas or engaged in different vocations.

jurisprudence must be based on the understanding that one of the aims of the right to equality is to facilitate the transformation of society and that this cannot be done when the state fails to address the most basic social and economic needs of its citizens, especially the special needs of the most vulnerable section in society. With the equality principle being the backbone of the right to life in India, it gives the right to housing the status of a distinct right. This is evident from some of the judgments of the Supreme Court.

Unlike the development of the other social rights discussed in this chapter, the development of the right to housing in India has not followed a coherent, chronological or principled pattern. The Supreme Court has developed diverse remedies responding to the particulars of the cases coming before it in an ad hoc fashion, at times directing the state to formulate schemes for providing housing for the poor and at times merely directing that persons facing eviction may not be evicted until arrangements for alternative housing have been made for them. However, in none of the major judgments on housing rights has the Supreme Court given concrete positive orders for the enforcement of this right. Very interestingly, litigation strategies for the enforcement of the right to housing have been most contradictory and unpredictable and have even failed in some situations. Litigation around the right to housing has been distinctive from that of other social rights litigation because housing rights cases invariably involve the interests of private non-state parties such as builders and developers. Because of this, housing rights litigation in India has not very often been undertaken in the form of public interest litigation.

In the mid to late 1990s there was a whole spate of litigation that followed the *Olga Tellis* judgment, the most important cases being *Shantistar Builders v Narayan K Totame*,[36] *Chameli Singh v State of UP*[37] and *Ahmedabad Municipal Corporation v Nawab Khan Gulab Khan*.[38] In all these cases the Supreme Court reiterated the right to adequate housing as a distinct constitutional obligation of the state, both under the right to life under Article 21 and under Article 19(1)(e), which guarantees the right of every citizen to reside and settle in any part of the country.

A Remedies Adopted by the Supreme Court

Shantistar Builders v Narayan K Totame[39] was an appeal from a petition filed by Narayan K Totame and others who were members of economically weaker sections of the community. Shantistar Builders in Bombay had been

---

[36] (1990) 1 SCC 520.
[37] (1996) 2 SCC 549.
[38] (1997) 11 SCC 121.
[39] Above n 36.

granted an exemption from the state government for owning land in excess of the Urban Land Ceiling Act, provided certain conditions were followed. One of the conditions laid down was that the builders should construct housing of 17,000 tenements for economically weaker sections of the community at the price and size fixed by the state government in a detailed scheme. The Bombay High Court had ordered that the implementation of this scheme would be monitored by the state authorities. The builders appealed to the Supreme Court against this order of the High Court for monitoring the housing scheme. The applicants from the economically backward group held that the builders were not complying strictly with the scheme and that the builders had increased the prices, and such escalation should not have been approved by the state government. They also alleged that the builders had overlooked the genuine applications for housing made to them by persons belonging to economically weaker sections and were instead allotting apartments to persons not entitled to the benefits and were thus benefiting from this housing racket.

The Supreme Court held that there should be a competent authority appointed by the state government for the proper implementation of the scheme laid down by the state government. The court laid down that, for the sake of clarity, persons with annual incomes of less than Rs18,000 would be persons belonging to economically weaker sections and they would have to show proof of their status at the time of making applications to the builders and the builders would be required to maintain records of applications. The Supreme Court also suggested that a committee may be appointed in every urban conglomeration for overseeing the implementation of these housing schemes.[40] While stating thus, it held:

> Basic needs of man have traditionally been accepted to be three – food, clothing, and shelter. The right to life is guaranteed in any civilized society. That would take within its sweep the right to food, the right to clothing, the right to decent environment and a reasonable accommodation to live in… The constitution aims at ensuring fuller development of every child. That would be possible only if the child is in a proper home. It is not necessary that every citizen must be ensured of living in a well-built comfortable house but a reasonable home particularly for people in India can even be mud-built thatched house or a mud-built fire-proof accommodation.[41]

While in the above case the Supreme Court came up with the remedy of directing the state to appoint a Committee for the proper implementation of a housing scheme for the poor, in another case it directed the municipal corporation to devise special schemes for providing suitable alternative accommodation for evicted pavement dwellers.

---

[40] Above n 36, 531.
[41] *Ibid* 527.

In *Ahmedabad Municipal Corporation v Nawab Khan Gulab Khan*,[42] the main issue was the eviction of 29 pavement dwellers by the Ahmedabad Municipal Corporation as they had constructed huts unauthorisedly on a street in the city. The High Court held that the pavement dwellers could not be evicted from their pavement dwellings without being provided with alternative accommodation. The Ahmedabad Municipal Corporation appealed to the Supreme Court against this order of the High Court.

The Supreme Court held that the right to life has been assured as a basic human right under Article 21 of the Constitution of India. In order to interpret Article 21, it relied upon Article 25(1) of the Universal Declaration of Human Rights and Article 11(1) of the International Covenant on Economic, Social and Cultural Rights, which states that everyone has the right to a standard of living adequate for the health and wellbeing of himself and his family: it includes food, clothing, housing, medical care and necessary social services. The Court also held that the Municipal Corporations Act imposes a statutory duty on the municipal corporation to make provision for accommodation if it is satisfied that within any part of the city it is expedient to provide housing for the poor and that such accommodation can be conveniently provided without making an improvement scheme. This duty to provide housing would be part of its constitutional mandate.

Imposing such a broad constitutional mandate on the municipal corporation to provide housing, the Supreme Court directed the corporation to frame a scheme for providing housing to the pavement dwellers. The municipal corporation, on the directions of the Court, framed three different schemes for providing alternative housing.

The Supreme Court ultimately held that that since the municipal corporation has a constitutional and statutory duty to provide means for settlement and residence of the pavement dwellers by allotting surplus land it has and, if necessary, by acquiring the land and providing house sites or tenements, as the case may be, according to the scheme formulated by the corporation. Interestingly, the Supreme Court held that the financial condition of the corporation would not be a constraint on the corporation to avoid its duty of providing residences/plots to the urban poor and it would therefore be the duty of the corporation to evolve new schemes. The pavement dwellers who were sought to be evicted were given the opportunity to opt for any of the three new schemes framed by the corporation, and if they did not opt for such schemes, they could be evicted with due process.

---

[42] Above n 38.

B Inconsistent Interpretations

Even with the above landmark housing rights cases, the judgment of the Supreme Court in 2000 in *Narmada Bachao Andolan v Union of India*[43] was in complete disregard to the progress made on housing rights prior to it. This petition was filed by the Narmada Bachao Andolan (NBA), a people's movement, against the displacement caused by the construction of the massive Sardar Sarovar dam that had been going on for 15 years. The petition was filed by the NBA against the raising of the height of the Sardar Sarovar dam and the adverse impact it would have on both the environment and the thousands of tribal people in the Narmada valley, who had been displaced with inadequate resettlement and rehabilitation options.

Despite full knowledge of the relevant authorities' failure to determine the total number of people to be displaced or to find adequate land for their resettlement,[44] and the incomplete resettlement of those already displaced, J Kirpal in the Supreme Court ruled that, 'displacement of the tribals and other persons would not per se result in the violation of their fundamental or other rights'.[45] Thus the court permitted the height of the dam to be raised. This single judgment contradicted all previous Supreme Court rulings that have upheld the right to housing and shelter as an integral part of the fundamental right to life.

The decision of the Supreme Court with regard to housing in the October 2000 *Narmada* judgment and the poor and random use of well-developed international law, suggest that the regressive attitude of the courts might well be an indication that social rights litigation may be one of the means, but certainly not the definitive route, to social justice.

V THE RIGHT TO EDUCATION

The journey of the right to education—from being initially enumerated in the Directive Principles to being declared a Fundamental Right as Article 21A—has been a huge struggle and a triumph for activists, child rights advocates and educationists working on the right to education all over the country. Litigation in the Supreme Court has been one major cause of the right to education being declared as a fundamental right in the Constitution by the Eighty-Sixth Constitutional Amendment. This journey, however, has been quite different from that of the other constitutional social rights, the main reason being that Article 45 of the Directive Principles gave a very

---

[43] *Narmada Bachao Andolan v Union of India and Ors* (2000) 10 SCC 664.
[44] Statement by the Madhya Pradesh government that it did not have enough land for resettlement of the displaced persons.
[45] Above n 43.

different promise from the other provisions within the Constitution. Article 45 states:

> The State shall endeavour to provide, within a period of ten years from the commencement of this Constitution, for free and compulsory education for all children until they complete the age of fourteen years.

Article 45 is the only article among all those in Part IV of the Indian Constitution, which speaks of a time limit within which this right should be made justiciable. No other article in Part IV does the same. This in-built time limit makes it clear that the framers of the Constitution were aware that for the realisation of a person's capabilities and for full protection of her rights, education was an important tool. In addition to Article 45, the right to education has been referred to in Articles 41 and 46[46] of the Directive Principles as well, with Article 41, very significantly, stating that:

> The State shall, within the limits of its economic capacity and development, make effective provision for securing the right to work, to education and to public assistance in cases of unemployment, old age, sickness and disablement, and in other cases of undeserved want.

The right to free primary education was first declared as a fundamental right by the Indian Supreme Court and then inserted in Part III by a constitutional amendment. The theory of the complementary nature of rights declared in Part III and Part IV and the harmonious interpretation of these rights has been the foundation for the realisation of primary education being declared a fundamental right today in India.

A The *Mohini Jain* Case and *Unni Krishnan* Judgment

Two crucial judgments of the Supreme Court in the 1990s paved the way for the inclusion of the right to education as a fundamental right and gave full realisation to the interdependence argument of social and civil / political rights. What is surprising is that both of these cases dealt with issues of higher professional education, but resulted ultimately in decisions affecting primary education (ie, education for children up to the age of fourteen).

The case of *Mohini Jain v State of Karnataka*[47] was a petition filed by a medical student in the High Court of Karnataka against the charging of capitation fees in professional medical colleges. When this case went on appeal to the Supreme Court, the bench, while declaring that the charging

---

[46] Article 46 places a duty upon the state to:

> Promote with special care, the educational and economic interests of the weaker sections of the people, and, in particular, of the Scheduled Castes and the Scheduled Tribes.

[47] AIR 1992 SC 1858.

of capitation fees was illegal, categorically held that 'the right to education flows directly from the right to life' as:

> the right to life and the dignity of an individual cannot be assured unless it is accompanied by the right to education

and

> the Fundamental Rights guaranteed under Part III of the Constitution of India, including the right to freedom of speech and expression and other rights under Article 19, cannot be appreciated and fully enjoyed unless a citizen is educated and conscious of his individualistic dignity.[48]

The Supreme Court referred to the principles of the Universal Declaration of Human Rights 1948 and to Article 41 of the Constitution, which recognises an individual's right to education. The Court held that although a citizen cannot enforce the Directive Principles contained in Chapter IV of the Constitution, these were not intended to be mere pious declarations and that the Directive Principles, which are fundamental in the governance of the country, cannot be isolated from the fundamental rights guaranteed under Part III. The Court held that the state is under a constitutional mandate to create conditions in which the fundamental rights guaranteed to individuals under Part III could be enjoyed by all. The Court also relied upon all the Article 21 elaborations and expansions laid down in earlier judgments to uphold the right to education.

The zeal demonstrated in *Mohini Jain* continued in the later very significant Constitution Bench decision in *Unni Krishnan v State of AP & Others*.[49] This case was also challenging capitation fees in professional colleges. It was referred to a Constitution Bench which articulated for the first time that the right to education is a fundamental right which flows from Article 21 and declared the right to free primary education to be a fundamental right, its content being defined by the parameters of Articles 45 and 41 of the Directive Principles. In other words, every child / citizen has a right to free education up to the age of 14 years and thereafter the right would be subject to the limits of the economic capacity of the state.

In *Unni Krishnan*, in dealing with the constitutional status of the right to education, the Supreme Court expressed its frustration at the obvious neglect of Article 45 in the following words:

> It is noteworthy that among several articles in Part IV, only Article 45 speaks of a time-limit: no other article does... Does not the passage of 44 years—more than four times the period stipulated in Article 45—convert the obligation created by the article into an enforceable right? In this context, we feel constrained

---

[48] *Ibid.*
[49] AIR 1993 SC 2178.

to say that allocation of available funds to different sectors of education in India discloses an inversion of priorities indicated by the Constitution.[50]

In *Unni Krishnan* the Court took the support of the right to education as laid down in the Universal Declaration of Human Rights and Article 13 of the International Convention for Economic, Social and Cultural Rights and for the first time articulated it as a 'social' right. This was one of the first judgments where the courts have employed ICESCR language for progressive realisation of the right to higher education while declaring the fundamental right to free primary education. The Court held:

> Many of the articles, whether in Part III or Part IV, represent moral rights which they have recognised as inherent in every human being in this country. The task of protecting and realising these rights is imposed upon all the organs of the State, namely legislative, executive and judicial. What then is the importance to be attached to the fact that the provisions of Part III are enforceable in a court and the provisions in Part IV are not? Is it that the rights reflected in the provisions of Part III are somehow superior to the moral claims and aspirations reflected in the provisions of Part IV? I think not. Free and compulsory education under Article 45 is certainly as important as freedom of religion under Article 25. Freedom from starvation is as important as the right to life. Nor are the provisions in Part III absolute in the sense that the rights represented by them can always be given full implementation.[51]

The argument that the right to life in Article 21 is merely negative in character was rejected by the Court. The question of insufficient resources was also very ingeniously dealt with by J Jeevan Reddy. He stated quite naturally that it is only Article 41 which speaks of the economic capacity of the state, whereas Article 45 does not speak of the limits of its economic capacity and therefore this hurdle would not stand as an obstacle in carving out a fundamental right to primary education from Article 21. Knowing that this would have grave budgetary implications, he went on to hold that:

> We are not seeking to lay down the priorities for the Government—we are only emphasising the constitutional policy as disclosed by Articles 45, 46 and 41. Surely the wisdom of these constitutional provisions is beyond question.[52]

As Upendra Baxi states, this self-effacing timorous or normalising form of activist discourse occurs when judges maintain that they are doing nothing outside their province, or doing nothing new, when everyone knows the situation to be quite frankly otherwise.[53] This form of articulation is pragmatic as it avoids the ethical burden of justification for judicial

---

[50] *Ibid* 2232.
[51] *Ibid.*
[52] *Ibid.*
[53] U Baxi, 'The Avatars of Indian Judicial Activism: Explorations in the Geographies of [In] Justice' in SK Verma and K Kusum (eds), *Fifty Years of the Supreme Court of India* (New Delhi, Oxford University Press, 2000).

activism and paves the way for routine legitimation of judicial innovation. Thus, constructing a fundamental right to education from a long-ignored Directive Principle is presented in *Unni Krishnan* as merely an example of the old idea that the Directive Principles furnish the technology of construction of Part III and now as a swayambhu (self-manifesting) aspect of new judicial power.[54]

B Aftermath of the *Unni Krishnan* Decision

The immediate effect of the *Unni Krishnan* decision was that any child below the age of 14 who was denied facilities for primary education could approach a court for a writ of mandamus directing the authorities to initiate appropriate measures. This became a powerful weapon and the members of civil society and non-governmental organisations began to use this decision as a strategic tool to push the executive and legislature towards serious action on primary education.[55]

Following the *Unni Krishnan* judgment, the declaration of the right to free primary education as a fundamental right has been further upheld and confirmed by an 11-judge Constitutional Bench of the Supreme Court, while deciding on minority rights in *TMA Pai Foundation v Union of India*.[56]

In 1997 the then Indian government (United Front) had proposed an amendment to the Constitution which sought to introduce a change to Article 21 of the Constitution to make the right to primary education for children up to the age of 14 a fundamental right. This sparked off a nationwide campaign spearheaded by civil society organisations working with various aspects of children's rights to pressurise the government into passing the Amendment Act. The Constitutional Eighty-Sixth Amendment Act 2002 was finally passed in December 2002, when the right to free primary education for children between the ages of 6 and 14 was inserted as a justiciable fundamental right into Part III of the Constitution as Article 21A. This constitutional amendment is a huge step forward from Article 45. While Article 45 constantly acted as an ideal for the state to strive for, the insertion of Article 21A into Part III of the Constitution clearly makes the right to free primary education a justiciable social right. Article 21A is different in that it specifies that such a right to free primary education is available only to children between the ages of 6 and 14 years and not for all children up to the age of 14 years, as Article 45 does. This has raised some valid concerns that children up to the age of 6 years would

54 *Ibid.*
55 Above n 7.
56 (2002) 8 SCC 481.

be deprived of schooling and all the added benefits of state-aided education including nutrition provided in the form of mid-day meals.

C Implementation and Enforcement

The question of enforcement of this right to education is a significant part of the entire campaign to declare it as a fundamental right. With the Supreme Court declarations and the recent constitutional amendment, the challenge on the ground which remains to be seen is whether the state machinery is put to work to enforce the right, and also to implement the state-level laws which seek to provide free and compulsory primary education.

In addition to the amendment declaring the right to education as a fundamental right, several states in India have passed laws making primary education compulsory.[57] These statutes have, however, largely remained un-enforced due to various socio-economic and cultural factors as well as administrative and financial constraints. Currently, the present UPA government has proposed a new law to guarantee enforcement of the right to education, called the Right to Education Bill 2005, which is pending approval by Parliament.

With the present situation being that only 53 per cent of all habitations have a primary school, on an average an upper primary school is three kilometres away in 22 per cent of habitations, more than 50 percent of the girls in the country do not enrol in schools, 60 million children are thought to be child labourers, more than 35 million children in the 6-14 age group are out of school and only one in six rural schools having toilets,[58] it remains to be seen whether, with the passing of this new Right to Education Bill 2005, the right to education will really be enforced throughout the country.

VI CONCLUSION

The above narrative suggests a potential role for a creative and sensitive judiciary to enforce constitutional social rights thus re-iterating that litigation still is a strong strategy in India for protection of social rights. The experience of the last decade has shown that the Indian Supreme Court

[57] The states are: Assam, Andhra Pradesh, Bihar, Goa, Gujarat, Haryana, Jammu and Kashmir, Karnataka, Madhya Pradesh, Maharashtra, Punjab, Rajasthan, Tamil Nadu, Kerala, and West Bengal; the union territories are: Chandigarh, Delhi, Pondicherry, and the Andaman and Nicobar Islands.
[58] Statistical data has been compiled from figures provided by CRY, NGO Global March Against Child Labour, and UNICEF.

has refashioned its institutional role to readily enforce social rights and even impose positive obligations on the state. There has been some concern about the legitimacy and accountability of such overt judicial activism in the late 'nineties but the Court continues to justify its interventions by asserting that it is temporarily filling the void created by the lack of strong executive and legislative branches of the government. More importantly, I believe that the recent Indian response opens up new avenues of exploration for the practical application and implementation of social rights in the developing world.

Social rights litigation can play a constructive role—and has done so in South Africa as well as in other parts of the world. But it is demanding. For litigants to succeed several conditions must be present and not all of them are easy to reform at will. These factors may be difficult to replicate elsewhere. We can see that a positive response has been received more often in situations where cases were backed by strong civil society movements and campaigns at the ground level, to push the slow and lethargic administration of the state into action.

The last decade has seen some very innovative directions given by the Indian Supreme Court and creative monitoring and ground level implementation of remedies. For many who subscribe to the generational approach to human rights protection—that civil and political rights are on a higher rung than the social, economic and cultural rights by virtue of being enforceable—and if the above mentioned examples of the Indian experience are any indication, their enforceability is clearly fundamental. In several cases the Supreme Court has rejected the notion of non-enforceability of social rights. There is no reason, therefore, why social rights such as the rights to food, health, education, housing, livelihood and others cannot be made subject to judicial determination. The recent Indian experiment proves that societies can indeed choose to make social rights justiciable and develop appropriate methods for their implementation and enforcement.

9

Socio-Economic Rights: The Promise and Limitation

The South African Experience

DENNIS M DAVIS

Until the late 1980s there had been little thinking in South Africa about the need to include social and economic rights within a constitutional instrument for a democratic South Africa. A few years prior to the un-banning of the African National Congress in February 1990, Albie Sachs published a number of papers, initially drafted for internal circulation within the ANC, which challenged conventional jurisprudential thinking about the role of law in social transformation. In particular, he argued that the South African Constitution needed to provide for an orderly and fair redistribution by means of the establishment of a minimum floor of rights to a series of carefully defined social and economic goods. As he stated:

> The danger exists in our country as in any other, that a new elite will emerge which will use its official position to accumulate wealth, power and status for itself. The poor will remain poor and the oppressed – oppressed. The only difference will be that the poor and powerless will no longer be disenfranchised, that they will only be poor and powerless and that instead of a racial oppression we will have non-racial oppression.[1]

The thrust of Sachs' argument was that substantive equality must be fused with formal equality in order to achieve democracy in South Africa.

[1] A Sachs, *Advancing Human Rights in South Africa* (Cape Town, Oxford University Press, 1992) xii. Albie Sachs was appointed a judge of the constitutional court in 1994. In the late 1950s and early 1960s he had practised at the Cape Bar before being detained without trial and later being exiled. He then taught at Southampton and Maputo Law Schools. Agents of the then South African government attempted to kill him in Maputo, as a result of which he lost an arm and sustained other serious injuries. He continued with his work as a leading member of the ANC's constitutional and legal committee, responsible for the formulation of constitutional proposals for a democratic South Africa.

While Sachs' work was first greeted with caution within legal circles, once negotiations for a democratic Constitution commenced, it became clear that the inclusion of social and economic rights into the body of the Constitution for a democratic South Africa assume central importance. The ANC's draft Bill of Rights published in May 1992 provided for the inclusion of clauses such as: there shall be equal pay for work of equal value and equal access to employment, training and advancement of all men; that women and children have the right to enjoy basic social educational and welfare rights; that legislation shall ensure the creation of a progressively expanding floor of minimum rights in social, educational and welfare spheres for all in the country; that a comprehensive national health service shall be established linking health workers, community organisations, state institutions, private medical schemes and individual medical practitioners so as to provide hygiene education, preventative medicine and health care delivery to all.[2]

This political intervention promoted a vigorous debate in the early 1990s about the wisdom of entrenching social rights in the Constitution. Ranged against the advocates of constitutionalising social and economic rights were both neo-liberals and social democrats. For neo-liberals, the market was seen as the effective agent for the distribution of social capital. Rights which imposed specific duties on the state would legitimise and arguably increase the state's power of interference in the private sphere, thereby minimising individual liberty and the effect of operation of the market.[3] Social democrats who were opposed to the inclusion of these rights contended that the extent and scope to which a court could be entitled to review the legislative output of a democratically elected Parliament and the implementation of policies of an executive could so blur the border line between law and politics as to jeopardise democracy and create a new judicial elite, a new cadre of philosopher kings who would interpret the volksgeist so as to ensure a democratic distribution of wealth, power and status.[4]

These debates notwithstanding, the final Constitution which was passed in 1996 included a range of socio-economic rights, the most important of which were sections 26 and 27. Section 26(1) provides that everyone has

---

[2] See the ANC draft Bill of Rights in Sachs (above n 1) 215.

[3] Those social democrats who opposed the inclusion of socio-economic rights agreed to this extent with neo- liberals that an idealistic set of social standards which were included in a bill of rights could jeopardise the legitimacy of a bill of rights as a whole, particularly were such rights to become idle promises rather than concrete realities.

[4] See DM Davis 'The Case against the Inclusion of Socio-Economic Demands In a Bill of Rights Except as Directive of Principles' (1992) 8 *South African Journal On Human Rights* 475; see the contrary approach by Etienne Mureinik 'Beyond a Charter of Luxuries: Economic Rights in the Constitution' (1992) 8 *South African Journal On Human Rights* 464. For a more generalised treatment of the critical approach to the justiciability of these rights, see A Hutchinson, *It's all in the Game: A Non-Foundationalist Account of Law and Adjudication* (Durham and London, Duke University Press, 2000).

the right to have access to adequate housing. Section 27(1) provides that everyone has a right to have access to (a) health care services, including reproductive health care, (b) sufficient food and water, and (c) social security including, if they are unable to support themselves and their dependants, appropriate social assistance.

In both sections 26 and 27, the right is qualified by the provision that the state must take reasonable legislative and other measures, within its available resources, to achieve the progressive realisation of this right.

This chapter seeks to examine the manner in which the promise of these rights has been fulfilled and the extent to which any of the critics (with the benefit of hindsight) mounted a valid criticism against the inclusion of these rights within the South African constitutional instrument. The analysis is in two parts: first, an examination of the three early cases which laid the foundation for socio-economic rights jurisprudence and, second, a subsequent set of two potentially more expansive decisions. Thereafter the chapter will be in a position to return to the broader consequences of the inclusion of socio-economic rights which were raised in the early debates.

I NATURE OF THE CONSTITUTION

It is perhaps trite that any set of provisions including socio-economic rights cannot be analysed outside the context of the document of which they form a part and, further, the particular history in which that document is located. South Africa's Constitution has been described as a transformative document, one that embraces a long-term vision for the transformation of the country's political and economic institutions and the structures of power. In this regard, the instrument represents essential pillars in the construction of a democratic and egalitarian society.[5] A number of provisions of the constitutional text constitute pointers in this direction. For example, the preamble proclaims that the Constitution was adopted, inter alia, to heal the divisions of the past and establish a society based on democratic values, social justice and fundamental human rights. Section 7(2) provides that the state must respect, protect, promote and fulfil the rights in the Bill of Rights. Section 9 introduces the concept of substantive equality. Sections 26 and 27, as already noted, include social and economic rights. In addition, section 8 of the Constitution provides for the horizontal application of the Bill of Rights so that private power is not left immune from constitutional scrutiny. In section 23, the Constitution entrenches a number of labour rights including the right to form trade unions and the

---

[5] See K Klare, 'Legal Culture and Transformative Constitutionalism' (1998) 14 *South African Journal On Human Rights* 146; P De Vos, 'Substantive Equality after *Grootboom*: The Emergence of Social and Economic context as a guiding value and equality jurisprudence' 2001 *Acta Juridica* 52.

right to strike. Taken together, these rights provide support for the contention that, read as a whole, the text should be read as a social democratic narrative in which, in the words of the preamble, the Constitution seeks to heal the divisions of our past and lay the foundation for a democratic and open society.

Examined in this fashion, the South African Constitution represents an alternative vision to the neo-liberal framework within which the present trajectory of globalisation is analysed. Within the context of neo-liberalism, globalisation entails the call

> Upon governments to relinquish regulatory control over production, trade, and investment, both domestically and across international borders, and to transfer as many state assets and functions as possible to private actors. It also advocates restructuring government so that remaining state operations will emulate private enterprise more closely.[6]

Were the South African government to adopt the kind of economic policy which attained hegemony under Margaret Thatcher and Ronald Reagan, the South African constitutional text would place the courts at war, even of a low intensity kind, with the legislature and the executive. To take an obvious example: the government would have considerable difficulty in removing labour rights which are not only presently contained in statute but are enshrined in the Constitution.[7] The state would have to accept some obligation to provide a basic social and economic infrastructure for the poorest within the South African community, and it would also have to accept some level of control over powerful foci of private power.[8]

---

[6] See L Phillips, 'Taxing the Market Citizen : Fiscal Policy and Inequality in an Age of Privatisation' (2000) 63 *Law and Contemporary Problems* 111,115; see also H Klug, *Constituting Democracy: Law, Globalism and South Africa's Political Reconstruction* (Cambridge, Cambridge University Press, 2000) 24.

[7] Labour Relations Act 66 of 1995.

[8] There has been some discussion as to whether the constitutional entrenchment of social rights would justify judicial review of critical aspects of economic programmes associated with neo-liberalism, such as privatisation. See in this regard D Schneiderman, 'Constitutional Approaches to Privatisation: An Inquiry Into the Magnitude of Neo-Liberal Constitutionalism' (2000) 63 *Law and Contemporary Problems* 83. Also R Malherbe, 'Privatisation and the Constitution: Some explanatory observations' (2001) *Tydskrif vir Suid Afrikaanse Reg* (TSAR) 1. It is doubtful if the South African Constitution could be read so as to proscribe or prevent a specific economic policy from being implemented but, as has been suggested above, policy decisions would have to take account of the constitutional constraints because of the instrument's commitment to social justice and the further obligation imposed upon the state to respect, protect, promote and fulfil all rights in the Bill of Rights which would include the socio-economic provisions contained therein.

II THE ADJUDICATION OF SOCIAL AND ECONOMIC RIGHTS WITHIN THE SOUTH AFRICAN CONSTITUTION: THE EARLY STEPS

In the first case in which it was required to analyse the ambit of social and economic rights, *Soobramoney v Minister of Health KwaZulu Natal,*[9] Chaskalson P, on behalf of a unanimous Constitutional Court, said the following:

> We live in a society in which there are great disparities in wealth. Millions of people are living in deplorable conditions and in great poverty. There is a high level of unemployment, inadequate social security, and many do not have access to clean water or to adequate health services. These conditions already existed when the Constitution was adopted and a commitment to address them, and to transform our society into one in which there will be human dignity, freedom and equality lies at the heart of our new constitutional order. For as long as these conditions continue to exist that aspiration will have a hollow ring.

Notwithstanding this promising exposition of the constitutional commitments contained in the text, the Court in *Soobramoney* adopted a rather timid approach to social and economic rights. The Court concluded that social and economic rights in the South African Constitution were, in effect, to be defined in terms of the availability of resources. Thus Chaskalson P said:

> What is apparent from these provisions is that the obligations imposed on the State by sections 26 and 27 in regard to access to housing, health care, food, water and social security are dependent upon the resources available for such purposes, and that the corresponding rights themselves are limited by reason of the lack of resources.[10]

The second case in which the Court was required to interrogate the scope of socio-economic rights, *Government of the Republic of South Africa and Others v Grootboom and Others,*[11] concerned one of the most pressing of South African social problems, namely the illegal occupation of land by homeless people. The applicants lived under intolerable conditions in an informal settlement outside the major city of Cape Town. A number of the applicants had given up hope that their applications for low-cost housing would be granted by the municipality, conclusions which were not entirely unjustified in that a number of the applicants had been on the waiting list for many years. They moved to vacant land that was privately owned and there constructed shacks and shelters. They were evicted from these premises and their building materials were destroyed. The court a quo relied upon section 28(1)(c), which provides that every child has the right

---

[9] 1997(12) BCLR 1696 (CC) 8.
[10] *Ibid* para 11.
[11] 2000 (11) BCLR 1169 (CC).

to basic nutrition, shelter, basic health care services and social services. As this section did not qualify the right to shelter the court held that the children, among these applicants, together with their parents enjoyed a right to be provided with shelter by the relevant government agency.

The Constitutional Court rejected the finding that the state was in breach of section 28, namely the duty to provide shelter to children, but it did find that the state was in breach of section 26, the right of access to housing.

In a unanimous judgment, delivered by Yacoob J, the Constitutional Court emphasised that both a negative and positive obligation flowed from the social and economic rights contained in the text. Section 26 mandated the state and other entities 'to desist from preventing or impairing the right of access to adequate housing'.[12] A positive duty flowed from these rights to ensure that the state would act decisively in order to provide the basic necessities of life for those living in the most extreme conditions of poverty.

On the basis of this finding, the Court conflated the basic right to housing in terms of section 26(1) with the right to take progressive steps for the achievement of the right in terms of section 26(2). In so doing, the Court employed the concept of reasonableness as the test by which it could assess whether the state was taking measures within its available resources to achieve the progressive realisation of the right.[13] The mandated policy to meet the test of reasonableness had to take account of the fact that '[t]he poor are particularly vulnerable and their needs require special attention'.[14] Thus the state would have failed to take the reasonable steps necessary for the realisation of the right, which were within its available resources, in the event that it failed to meet the needs of those whose ability to enjoy the rights was most imperilled and who were therefore in the poorest and most desperate of financial circumstances.

Although the Court purported to follow international law[15] a number of commentators have observed that the approach adopted differed from that developed in international law. For example, De Vos writes:

> While the idea of the core minimum in international law requires the state to show that every effort has been made to use all resources available to the state to at least provide the core minimum entitlements, the Court argues only that any programme had to show that at least some effort has been made also to achieve the realisation of core minimum entitlements. Thus, any programme aimed at achieving the realisation of the particular right has to be balanced and flexible in order to address the needs of society as a whole – not only the most

---

[12] *Ibid* para 34.
[13] *Ibid* para 33.
[14] *Ibid* para 36.
[15] See United Nations Committee on Economic, Social and Cultural Rights, General Comment No 3 ESC Res. 1985/17 (28 May 1985).

needy and vulnerable. In the context of housing rights this means that any housing policy in measures to implement policy has to take cognizance of short, medium and long term needs.[16]

In the next case which came before the Constitutional Court, *Minister of Health v Treatment Action Campaign*[17] the Court was asked to order that the government provide the antiretroviral drug Nevirapine to pregnant mothers and their children where this was medically indicated and the capacity existed to do so.

The facts of the case made the decision an easier one than was the case with *Grootboom*. In terms of government policy, Nevirapine had been made available in the public sector in a small number of research and training sites throughout the country. The government claimed that this restriction was to evaluate the effectiveness of a future nationwide programme of the provision of the drug in order to combat mother-to-child transmission of HIV.

Following the approach adopted in *Grootboom*, the Court analysed whether the measures taken to confine Nevirapine to a small number of research and training sites was reasonable in the circumstances. In this regard the government raised four fundamental objections to the relief sought by the applicants, being the Treatment Action Campaign, namely that the government accelerate its programme to provide Nevirapine beyond these research and training sites. The government argued, first, that it doubted the efficacy of the drug in the absence of a comprehensive programme. Second, it feared that the development of resistance to Nevirapine would undermine the efficacy of the drug and, third, that there were legitimate doubts as to the safety of the drug. Finally, it contended that the public health sector lacked the capacity to deliver the drug in terms of the relief sought by the Treatment Action Campaign.

The nature of the provision of Nevirapine through the research and training sites, particularly as provided by the Provincial Administrations in the Western Cape and Kwa-Zulu Natal, together with the significant medical evidence put up by the Treatment Action Campaign, overwhelmed these particular objections, making the decision a relatively easy one for the Court, which unlike in the *Grootboom* and *Soobromoney* cases, was not confronted with any sustainable argument concerning distributional questions, in this case the cost of the anti-retroviral drugs.

Following the test adopted in the *Grootboom* case insofar as reasonable measures were concerned, the Court held:

---

[16] De Vos (above n 5) 58.
[17] 2002(5) SA 721(CC) (hereinafter *TAC*).

The policy of confining nevirapine to research and training sites fails to address the needs of mothers and their new-born children who do not have access to these sites.[18]

Unsurprisingly, the Court went on to hold that:

To the extent that government limits the supply of nevirapine to its research sites, it is the poor outside the catchment areas of these sites who will suffer. There is a difference in the positions of those who can afford to pay for services and those who cannot. State policy must take account of these differences.[19]

On this basis the Court concluded that:

Government policy was an inflexible one that denied mothers and their new born children at public hospitals and clinics outside the research and training sites the opportunity of receiving a single dose of nevirapine at the time of the birth of the child. A potentially lifesaving drug was on offer and where testing and counseling facilities were available, it could have been administered within the available resources of the state without any known harm to mother or child.[20]

To the extent that the existing policy of the government to confine the Nevirapine to research sites was inconsistent with the duty to adopt reasonable measures in order to comply with the obligation imposed by section 27(1) read with section 27(2) of the Constitution, being the obligation upon the state to provide health care services in a manner which would achieve the progressive realisation of the right within its available resources, the Court held that the government, without delay, should extend the provision of Nevirapine beyond the research and training sites where this was medically indicated and ordered further that it extend testing and counselling services to hospitals and clinics which were not research sites.

Significantly in the *TAC* case, the Court was faced with arguments by amici curiae to the effect that section 27(2) was not exhaustive of the government's positive duty under this section. On a proper interpretation of the Constitution, section 27 created a free-standing individual right and imposed positive duties on the state to perform in terms of these rights. In other words, section 27(1) contained a minimum core of a right which every individual was entitled to enjoy with immediate effect.

The Court was not prepared to move off its position adopted initially in the *Soobramoney* and later in the *Grootboom* cases. To the arguments of the amici curiae that the content of the right in section 27(1) differed from the content of the obligation in section 27(2), the Court concluded that this approach failed to have regard to the way in which sub-sections (1)

---

[18] *Ibid* para 67.
[19] *Ibid* para 70.
[20] *Ibid* para 80.

and (2) were linked in the text of the Constitution.[21] Thus, a purposive reading of sections 26 and 27 does not lead inexorably to this conclusion. It is impossible to give everyone access even to a 'core' service immediately. All that is possible, and all that can be expected of the state, is that it act reasonably to provide access to the socio-economic rights, identified in sections 26 and 27, on a progressive basis.[22]

In essence, the judgment in the *TAC* case did not represent any development of the approach adopted in *Grootboom*, but rather constituted a confirmation of the approach adopted therein.

In summary, the essential obligation of the state in terms of the socio-economic rights contained in the Constitution was to act reasonably in devising measures and policies that would progressively lead to the realisation of the right in question. In the *Grootboom* case the measures adopted by the government were found not to be reasonable because they did not take account of the needs of the most desperate and vulnerable individuals or groups in society. In the *TAC* case the government's policy with regard to the provision of Nevirapine was held to be unreasonable as doctors of public hospitals and clinics other than research sites were not able to prescribe Nevirapine to reduce the risk of mother-to-child transmission of HIV. Government policy 'failed to make provision for counsels at hospitals and clinics other than research and training sites'.[23]

In this regard the criticism raised by Bilchitz is correct, that the Court was guilty of failing to integrate sub-sections 27(2) and 27(1): it focuses the whole enquiry on sub-section 27(2) without providing a role for sub-section 27(1); that is, the Court failed to give any meaning to the right to health care services and based the 'right' on the obligation of the state to take measures to ensure by way of incremental steps the realisation of a right enshrined in sub-section 27(1) but never defined by the Court. However, sub-section 27(1) is in fact the right, and the obligations flow from what a person is entitled to by virtue of having the right in question. I am thus suggesting that the Court's analysis in each case needs to involve an extra step: first, it should attempt to understand the content of the right, and only then should it engage in the enquiry of determining whether the measures adopted by the government were reasonable measures of progressively realising the right.[24]

Another common feature of these two key cases decided by the Court was the approach taken to the framing of the order. In the court a quo in both *Grootboom* and *TAC*, attempts had been made by these courts to

---

[21] See in particular para 29 of the judgment.
[22] *Ibid* para 35.
[23] See the conclusion of the Court at para 95.
[24] D Bilchitz, 'Towards a Reasonable Approach to the Minimum Core: Laying the Foundations for future Socio-economic Rights Jurisprudence' (2003) 19 *South African Journal On Human Rights* 1, 9.

exercise a form of supervisory jurisdiction in relation to the orders granted. In *Grootboom*, the Court ordered that the government was constitutionally obliged to create a comprehensive and co-ordinated programme designed so as to give content to the right of access to adequate housing. Such a programme should include relief for those who had no access to land, no shelter and who were therefore subjected to the inclement conditions of winter without any physical protection. The Court declared that the existing programme in the Cape metropolitan area did not meet the government's constitutional obligations and it had unreasonably failed to make provision for those who fell within the categories of those in most desperate need. However, the Court desisted from structuring its order so that the successful party could approach the court to determine whether the plan to be implemented in order to give effect to the order met with the test of reasonableness laid down by the court. The supervisory component of the order of the court a quo was not incorporated into the Court's order.

A similar approach was followed by the Court in the *TAC* case. While it had little difficulty in finding that the government's programme was unconstitutional, it desisted from retaining any form of supervision over the implementation of government policy and hence waived the ability to ensure that fresh policy would meet the framework of reasonableness as developed by the Court in its own judgment.

III THE EARLY CASES: AN EVALUATION

Since the introduction of the South African Constitution in 1996, tensions have arisen between its transformative vision and the macro-economic policy adopted by the South African government in which economic growth has been preferred over social reconstruction as the key policy objective. This package of economic policy has vigorously nodded in the direction of the so-called structural adjustment programmes preferred by the World Bank and the International Monetary Fund for developing countries. For the past few years the government's major objective has been to reduce inflation, ensure that the deficit before borrowing is reduced to no more than 3 per cent of GDP and that the tax :GDP ratio does exceed 25 per cent.[25] To the extent that the South African government has adopted a macro-economic strategy containing a number of important neo-liberal elements such as fiscal prudence, privatisation of state assets, deregulation of the market, increased movement towards the abolition of exchange control regulations and a low tax rate for corporations, the earlier rhetoric

---

[25] M Pieterse, 'Beyond the Welfare State: Globalization of neo-liberal culture and the Constitutional protection of social and economic rights in South Africa' (2003) 14 *Stellenbosch Law Review* 3, 11–12.

which embraced a form of social democratic economics has been replaced by a commitment to the centrality of the market.[26]

Accordingly, a dichotomy has began to be created between this growth via the market-oriented policy adopted by the government and the constitutional vision of a democratic society based on a set of social democratic values.

It is arguable that the Constitutional Court's initially cautious approach to socio-economic jurisprudence has taken account of the potential difficulties inherent in this tension. Deference to the policy problems of the legislature and executive, in part, may have been fuelled by the knowledge of South African constitutional lawyers of the experience of the Indian Court and its well-publicised clashes with the Nehru government over property rights.[27] The Constitutional Court appears to have been determined to ensure the development of its institutional integrity, which would not have been possible were the Court to have run headlong into the kind of clashes which the Indian Supreme Court engaged in with the Nehru government.

To recapitulate, the caution shown by the Constitutional Court in the first three socio- economic rights cases can be seen in the manner in which it sought to interpret the core minimum obligation, by conflating the substantive right with the qualification that the state must take reasonable measures within its available resources to achieve the progressive realisation of the particular socio-economic right, together with the cautious approach adopted by the Court to the idea of a supervisory order.

Although the Court developed a concept of reasonableness from international jurisprudence, particularly the interpretation of the International Covenant on Economic, Social and Cultural Rights by the UN Committee on Economic, Social and Cultural Rights, a significant difference exists between the two approaches. Thus in General Comment 3, the UN committee held:

> the fact that realisation over time, or in other words progressively, is foreseen under the Covenant should not be misinterpreted as depriving the obligation of all meaningful content. It is on the one hand a necessary flexibility device, reflecting the realities of the real world and the difficulties involved for any country in ensuring full realisation of economic, social and cultural rights. On the other hand, the phrase must be read in the light overall objective, indeed the raison d'etre, of the Covenant which is to establish clear obligations for States parties in respect of the full realisation of the rights in question. It thus imposes

---

[26] For a compelling account of the manner in which these policy changes have occurred see S Terreblanche, *A History of Inequality in South Africa 1652- 2002* (Pietermaritzburg, University of Natal Press, 2002).

[27] See S Sathe, *Judicial Activism in India: Transgressing Borders and Enforcing Rights* (New Delhi, Oxford University Press, 2002).

an obligation to move as expeditiously and effectively as possible towards that goal.[28]

By contrast, the concept of reasonableness adopted by the Court in *Grootboom* provides far less clarity about the core content to the right. Compare the test in General Comment 3 with this key exposition from the judgment in *Grootboom*:

> To be reasonable, measures cannot leave out of account the degree and extent of the denial of the right they endeavour to realise. Those whose needs are the most urgent and whose ability to enjoy all rights therefore is most in peril, must not be ignored by the measures aimed at achieving realisation of the right. It may not be sufficient to meet the test of reasonableness to show that the measures are capable of achieving a statistical advance in the realisation of a right. Furthermore, the Constitution requires that everyone must be treated with care and concern. If the measures, though statistically successful, fail to respond to the needs of those most desperate they may not pass the test.[29]

When these two dicta are compared, superficially they may appear to achieve the same conclusion. However, General Comment 3 clearly imposes upon the state the obligation to implement components of the right immediately. Thus:

> even where the available resources are demonstrably inadequate, the obligation remains for a State party to strive to ensure the widest possible enjoyment of the relevant rights under the prevailing circumstances.[30]

A related question concerns the absence of an engagement with the core meaning of sections 26(1) and 27(1). When these sections are read together with sections 26(2) and 27(2), there is an expectation that the structure of the provision requires, at the very least, a two-stage enquiry, being an initial determination of the core meaning of the right and thereafter an assessment of the extent to which government has taken reasonable measures to achieve the progressive realisation of that core content as contained in the text and gleaned from the first stage of the enquiry.

In the judgments in neither *Grootboom* nor *TAC* was any significant attempt made to give meaning to the rights as set out in the text of sections 26(1) or 27(1). In terms of precedent, the judgments in *Grootboom* and *TAC* provide meaning to these key socio-economic rights solely in terms of a conflation of the content of the rights as set out in subsection (1) and the realisation thereof in terms of subsection (2). When the treatment of the content of these rights as explicated by the Court is examined, the test of reasonableness is all that remains when the core finding is stripped of its

---

[28] As quoted by M Craven, *The International Covenant on Economic, Social and Cultural Rights* (Oxford, Clarendon Press, 1995) 131.

[29] *Grootboom* (above n 11) 44.

[30] Craven (above n 28) 138.

rhetorical flourishes. The reader will search in vain for a definition of the right to either housing or medical care. Indeed, when the amici curiae laid this particular approach before the Court in the *TAC* case, they were unsuccessful in urging the Court to define the minimum core of the right to health care in section 27(1). [31]

A third defining characteristic of the Court's early jurisprudence relates to the availability of resources.[32] In *Soobramoney*, Chaskalson P observed that

> the obligations imposed on the state by sections 26 and 27… are dependent upon the resources available for such purposes, and that the corresponding rights themselves are limited by reason of the lack of resources.[33]

In *Grootboom*, although the unevenness of the judgment make it more difficult to draw a definitive conclusion about the Court's approach to resources, Yacoob J said 'section 26 does not expect more of the State than is achievable within its available resources'.[34] It would appear that the core content of the right in section 27(1) cannot be defined independently if the Court's assessment of the right is so heavily qualified by the phrase 'available resources' which is contained in section 27(2).

Finally, the cautious approach adopted by the Court to the nature of the order granted to the successful applicant requires critical analysis. In the court a quo in both the *Grootboom* and *TAC* cases, the relief granted included a form of supervisory jurisdiction. In both cases, the Court refused to follow this approach; indeed, in its reasoning in the *TAC* case, it said that there was no reason to believe that the government could not execute the Court order.[35]

Ironically, the evidence points strongly in the direction of the need for a form of supervisory jurisdiction which was rejected by the Court. Research conducted into the aftermath of the *Grootboom* judgment has revealed that, more than two years after the order was granted, there had not been full implementation by any of the relevant government agencies.[36] The experience of the successful litigants in this case has revealed the need for some form of judicial supervision, not because the government expressly refused to abide by a decision of the Court but as a result of a combination of administrative inefficiency, inertia and debilitating demarcation disputes between different levels of government.

These four characteristics of the Court's early socio-economic jurisprudence can be explained in terms of an unstated, inarticulate premise upon which this jurisprudence has been fashioned, namely a concept of

---

[31] *Minister of Health* (above n 17) 26–8.
[32] This issue has been comprehensively analysed by Bilchitz (above n 24) 19–23.
[33] *Soobramoney* (above n 9) 11.
[34] *Grootboom* (above n 11) 46.
[35] *TAC* (above n 17) 129.
[36] K Pillay, 'Implementing *Grootboom*: Supervision Needed' (2002) 3 *ESR Review* 13.

deference to the political autonomy of the legislature and executive. The Court has developed a framework for dealing with socio-economic rights which seeks to maximise the autonomy of the other branches of the state, employing a concept of rationality sourced in international law, fashioned in domestic administrative law and packaged as reasonableness. So long as government is shown to have put in place a plan which is rationally connected to dealing with the least privileged in society as a matter of priority, the Court will not intervene. It will be reluctant to supervise any implementation of the order which is granted to the successful party. It is equally unwilling to develop a set of unqualified socio-economic rights as contained, at least on a literal reading, in section 28(1)(c), being the right of every child to basic nutrition, shelter, health care services and social services.[37] The absence of a qualification concerning resources would mean that a core component of a socio-economic right such as a right to nutrition or shelter would require judicial enforcement, notwithstanding a defence concerning the priority of allocation of public resources. Viewed accordingly, a right to shelter or nutrition would be similar to the right to a fair trial where it is accepted, almost without question, that the state is obliged to find the necessary resources to give content to the core of the right.

In these cases the Court developed a minimalist framework within which to apply these rights by affording the state the possibility of raising a complete defence on the grounds of limited availability of resources save in respect of the development of a programme that deals with the poorest in the community. The scope and range of the rights are left undefined and to date the Court has side-stepped the adjudication of an unqualified socio-economic right.

IV HAS THE CONSTITUTIONALISATION OF SOCIO-ECONOMIC RIGHTS FULFILLED ITS PROMISE?

A The Answer from the Early Cases

The analysis of the development of socio-economic jurisprudence by the Court now permits a return to the primary question posed in this chapter, which concerns the fulfilment of the promise and the aspirations of the initial proponents for inclusion of these rights in the Constitution. This question must be answered in three parts; first, in terms of the early cases which remain the only direct authority for the interpretation of sections 26

---

[37] See, in particular, the Court's rejection of the court a quo's approach in *Grootboom* (above n 11) 70–9.

and 27 of the Constitution; second, by taking account of more recent, halting possibilities for the adjudication of these disputes; and third, within a broader political context.

While the outcome in both *Grootboom* and *TAC* has been welcomed, a number of commentators have urged the Court to go further and establish a firm basis for the enforcement of socio-economic rights; in particular, by way of a more central role for sections 26(1) and 27(1)—the rights of access to housing and to health care.[38] By contrast, the cautious approach adopted by the Court to date would appear to be in keeping with key arguments raised in favour of the inclusion of these rights as developed by Etienne Mureinik in a key paper delivered more than 10 years ago.[39]

The essence of Mureinik's argument was that by means of the inclusion of socio-economic rights in a Constitution, the judiciary would be empowered to ensure that government was held accountable for its performance in fulfilling these constitutional obligations. The employment of concepts sourced in administrative law such as rationality review or review for reasonableness could promote a culture of justification in the implementation of public policy. In terms of constitutional tests framed within the context of these well-established administrative law concepts, the judiciary could compel government to produce evidence to substantiate its claim that policies existed and were being implemented to ensure the fulfilment of socio-economic rights.

This is not only simply a modest framework for a socio-economic jurisprudence. It constitutes an approach which well describes the broad line currently adopted by the Court. Unless the unlikely presumption is accepted that members of the Court are ignorant of the alternative approaches outlined above, which have been enthusiastically endorsed by some academic commentators, the conclusion that the Court has used the justificatory approach to give content to its theory of deference is compelling.

B A New Direction?

Subsequent to the three cases which set the framework for the Court's jurisprudence regarding socio-economic rights, the Court began to hint at the possibility of a socio- economic rights jurisprudence which was not limited to the specific socio-economic rights provisions. In *Khosa v Minister of Social Development*[40] the Court concluded that the exclusion of permanent

---

[38] See for example, Bilchitz, (n 24), De Vos (n 16) and C Scott, 'Social Rights: Towards a Principled and Pragmatic Judicial Role' (1999) 4 *ESR Review* 4.

[39] E Mureinik, 'Beyond a Charter of Luxuries: Economic Rights in the Constitution' (1992) 8 *South African Journal On Human Rights* 464.

[40] 2004 (6) SA 505 (CC).

residents from social security programmes enjoyed by South African citizens had 'a serious impact on [their] dignity' and accordingly found that the applicable legislation violated both the right to equality and the right to social security of permanent residents. The Court went on to hold that these permanent residents

> are part of a vulnerable group in society and, in the circumstances of the present case, are worthy of constitutional protection. We are dealing, here, with intentional, statutorily sanctioned unequal treatment of part of the South African community.[41]

Having so found, the Court considered the financial implications of this decision. Mokgoro J accepted that the concern that

> non-citizens may become a financial burden on the country is a legitimate one and I accept that there are compelling reasons why social benefits should not be made available to all who are in South Africa irrespective of their immigration status.[42]

However, she proceeded to examine the evidence which had been placed before the Court with regard to the financial implications of a decision to extend social benefits to permanent residents. She found that the cost thereof would not place an additional burden upon the State and indeed would constitute 'only a small proportion of the total cost'.[43]

By focusing upon the concepts of dignity and equality rather than the wording of section 27, the Court took a bold decision to extend social benefits to permanent residents. Its approach was unfettered by the reasonableness standard which had dominated the earlier cases brought under sections 26 and 27 of the Constitution.[44]

If *Khosa* represented a hint towards a more progressive approach, the Court pointed expressly to a more fruitful route towards a judicial implementation of the social democratic character of the constitutional text in *Rail Commuters Action Group and Others v Transnet Limited t/a Metrorail and Others*.[45] In this case, the Court was confronted with a group of applicants who contended that the public rail commuter service provided by a state corporation did not pass constitutional muster as the service was extremely unsafe. The Court interpreted the applicable legislation in the light of the values that animate the constitutional rights of dignity, life and freedom and security of the person and accordingly found that the rail corporation was constitutionally obliged to take affirmative

---

41 *Ibid* para 74.
42 *Ibid* para 58.
43 *Ibid* para 62.
44 See, however, the trenchant criticism of the Court's reluctance to extend social benefits to temporary residents by L Williams, 'Issues and challenges addressing poverty and legal rights' (2005) 21 *South Africa Journal On Human Rights* 436.
45 2005(2) SA 359 (CC).

steps to ensure the safety of their commuters. This was the first decision where the Court made no reference to the express socio-economic rights provisions in the Constitution but rather employed the rights of dignity, life and freedom and security of the person to impose a positive obligation upon the rail company, thereby for the first time affirming the concept of a positive right of an individual litigant to claim improved public resources.

V CONCLUSION

As a consequence of our history, structural impediments remain to the achievement of 'dignity, equality and freedom'. Millions of people are still without houses, education and jobs, and there can be little dignity in living under such conditions. Dignity, equality and freedom will only be achieved when the socio-economic conditions are transformed to make this possible. This will take time. In the meantime, government must give effect to its obligations under the Constitution to show respect and concern for those whose basic needs have to be met. The courts must give meaning to, and apply, the Bill of Rights and other provisions of the Constitution in the context of our history, the conditions prevailing in our society and the transformative goals of the Constitution. The manner in which the government and the courts give effect to their constitutional obligations, and in particular the way in which government action is taken and the law developed to promote the values of the Constitution, have important implications for the process of transformation.[46]

The record of socio-economic rights litigation in South Africa during the first decade of constitutional democracy has been criticised essentially on the ground that the model of reasonableness review initially developed in *Grootboom* has generated a deferential approach which fails to provide an effective enforcement of social rights for individuals and groups living in poverty.[47] Sandra Liebenberg has contended, however, that reasonableness review can contribute to the creation of a participatory, dialogical space for adjudicating social rights. This can be achieved, she argues, in three areas of the courts' interpretation of social economic rights. In particular, basic needs claims should receive greater protection within the framework of reasonableness review. In this manner, courts could consider a more rigorous proportionality analysis in circumstances where individuals and groups are deprived of basic subsistence requirements. Second, a court can alter the discourse of rights by emphasising the judicial role in relieving the burden on poor communities and thus strengthening

---

[46] A Chaskalson, 'Human Dignity is a foundational value by Constitutional Order' (2000) 16 *South African Journal On Human* Rights 193, 204–205.
[47] The major critic of the Court's jurisprudence is Sandra Liebenberg: see 'Needs, Rights and Transformation Adjudicating social rights in South Africa' (2005) 6 *ESR Review* 4, 6–7.

the constitutional right to dignity. Finally, social rights can contribute to a deconstruction of the range of private law conceptions which have been produced in the first decade of constitutional democracy, a hierarchical set of legal concepts which support the distribution of resources inherited from apartheid.[48] These suggestions all work within the concept of reasonableness review.

For the reasons already set out in this paper, it is doubtful whether a court will conceive of reasonableness in any other way other than to defer to the decision of a democratically elected legislature and executive. Reasonableness is a standard that judges understand within the context of administrative law, in which deference to the competence and democratic pedigree of the executive authority or the legislature is well established. By contrast, the possibility held out in the *Metrorail* case for a new conception of positive rights which imposes correlative obligations on the part of the state is a potentially far more productive route for the development of a transformative jurisprudence. In particular, a jurisprudence of positive rights forces a court to engage in a far more open-textured proportionality analysis as it seeks to balance these rights against claims built up under apartheid as well as arguments that as a default position majoritarianism should trump any right asserted by an individual litigant against a democratically conceived social policy. In this way, it may be possible for a court to move beyond the traditional approach of judicial deference which leaves the 'Other' vulnerable to the exigencies of the political process.

So much for a micro-analysis of socio-economic rights' jurisprudence in South Africa. There is a broader question which needs to be considered, namely the relationship of rights to democracy and thus the very question of the political process and its alleged less protective role of the vulnerable compared to the judiciary.

Over the past few years, neo-Dworkinians have dominated the debate about socio-economic rights.[49] The debate has been framed as being between neo-liberals who resist the incorporation of socio-economic rights in a constitutional instrument in favour of distribution exclusively through

---

[48] *Ibid*, 6–7. In *President of RSA and Another v Modderklip Boedery (Pty) Ltd* 2005 (8) BCLR 786 (CC) the court was confronted with an application from a landowner for the eviction of some 40,000 squatters from his land. The court sought to achieve a balance between the right to property and the right to housing by refusing to evict the squatters but imposing upon the state an obligation to pay the landowner a market-related rental for the use of his land for effecting the state's obligation to provide land to the squatter community. To an extent the balance struck in this case does reduce the absolute conception of property enshrined in the common law. Its major implication, however, appears to be a further recognition of a positive obligation which can be imposed upon the state.

[49] See inter alia Pieterse (above n 25), Scott (above n 38) and C Scott and P Alston, 'Adjudicating Constitutional Priorities in a Transnational Context: A Comment on *Soobramoney's* Legacy and *Grootboom's* Promise' (2000) 16 *South Africa Journal On Human Rights* 206.

the market and social democrats who fight against neo-liberal globalisation in favour of social rights which will produce social justice. In the latter the courts are elevated to Herculean social engineers and hence the implementers of social policy.

The question which arises is whether the debate has been adequately framed. Are legal rights the source of social democracy? Is social justice achieved by strengthening the state so that it becomes the sole provider of the means to achieve social justice? And are the courts the proper forum for the adoption of key distributional decisions of this nature?

These questions do not admit of easy answers but some cautionary comments can be made on the basis of the South African experience. First, to conceive of social democracy in terms of the provision of goods and services by state apparatuses alone is to fail to learn the lessons of the problems encountered by social democracy over the past fifty years. It reveals an ignorance of the need to strengthen the capacity of the individual to reshape the state through political and economic struggle through civic association as opposed to viewing state institutions as the panacea for the attainment of social justice, thereby building an overwhelming centralised power which is unfettered by the constraints of politics and ultimately of the courts.

Second, the kind of 'rights' approach advocated by the neo-Dworkinians increases the power of one arm of the state, the judiciary, which is now designated to play an active role in key distributional decisions of policy. Litigation is but one, restricted approach to the contestation of distribution. This conclusion does not under-estimate the importance of rights nor dismiss the possibility of progressive promise in the theory of proportionality which can flow from a more coherent adoption of positive rights and obligations, but rather provides a more democratic basis by which the politics of the society should be predicated. As Douzinas has observed:

> Human rights are expressions of the struggle for recognition amongst citizens which presupposes and constructs the political community... many aspects of recognition take the form of rights and all rights are in this sense political; they extend the logic of public access and decision-making to ever-increasing parts of social life... Human rights [are] signs of a communal acknowledgement of openness of society and identity, the place where care, love, and law meet.[50]

Rights can inspire struggle, struggle which may in part take the form of litigation but which ultimately depends on the organisation of those demanding these rights to reshape the state in the image of a social democracy where both the social question and democratic practice are honoured. The South African experience reveals that political organisation

---

[50] C Douzinas, *The End of Human Rights – Critical Legal Thought at the Turn of the Century* (Oxford, Hart Publishing, 2000) 290.

remains the primary means to secure different forms of distributional decisions for the vulnerable within society. It also confirms that, even when armed with progressive texts, judges retreat into models of adjudication which are based on earlier traditions of legal practice and which reduce the potential promise of the text. A jurisprudence which holds a democratically elected government to the distributional consequences of a social democratic constitution is in its infancy in South Africa and may yet be still-born.[51] To convince lawyers that law is deeply imbricated in the political and economic processes of society is a very, very difficult task and not one that has, as yet, succeeded with any clear conviction in South Africa.

---

[51] See the incisive analysis of positive rights viewed comparatively by S Fredman, 'Providing equality: Substantive equality and the positive duty to provide' (2005) 21 *SAJHR* 163. See also K Roach, *Constitutional Remedies in Canada* (Aurora, Ontario, Canada Law Book, 1998) 2–38, where the point is made that Canadian courts have been historically reluctant to order constitutional remedies for a variety of reasons including deference to the executive and doubt as to the precise role of courts within this context. The same reluctance regarding enforcement has been evident in judgements of the South African Constitutional Court: M Swart, 'Left out in the Cold' (2005) 21 *South Africa Journal On Human Rights* 215. Significantly, the TAC were able to use the limited order procured as part of a political strategy to secure anti-retroviral drugs from the state for those in need, notwithstanding the vagueness of the order whereas the homeless litigants in *Grootboom* were literally left in the cold. In fairness to the Court, the litigants in *Grootboom* settled their case at the doors of the Court, leaving the Court to deal only with the question of principle. However, the settlement itself was made an order of Court and the lack of Court supervision and the absence of any political muscle meant the attainment of an illusory victory of a kind that supports the point made about the limitations of litigation when it assumes the primary method of struggle.

10

Social Rights in Canada

PATRICK MACKLEM

I INTRODUCTION

A s a signatory to the International Covenant on Economic, Social and Cultural Rights (ICESCR), Canada is required to implement a wide range of international social rights in its domestic legal order. The focus of this study is on domestic implementation of ICESCR rights that seek to protect interests relating to work, social security and health, and, specifically, the right to just and favourable conditions of work (Article 7), the right to belong to a union, bargain collectively and strike (Article 8), the right to social security, including social insurance (Article 9), the right to an adequate standard of living, including rights to adequate food, clothing and housing (Article 11), and the right to physical and mental health (Article 12). According to the ICESCR, implementation of these rights is consistent with a more general international legal obligation on states under the Charter of the United Nations to 'to promote universal respect for, and observance of, human rights and freedoms'.[1]

Domestic implementation of the ICESCR in Canada occurs on two planes.[2] On the first, political, plane the legislative and executive branches of government exercise constitutional authority to establish and administer social policy programmes that protect interests typically associated with international social rights, including interests relating to work, social security and health. Programmes protecting these and other individual interests of a social—as opposed to civil or political—nature long predated Canada's ratification of the ICESCR in 1976. Such programmes typically were not explicitly designed, promoted or intended to implement Canada's

---

[1] International Covenant on Economic, Social and Cultural Rights (adopted 16 December 1966, entered into force 3 January 1976) 993 UNTS 4.
[2] Implementation, measures taken by the state with a view to its treaty obligations, should not be equated with compliance, that is, whether such measures fulfil a state's treaty obligations. For scholarship criticising Canada for failing to comply with the ICESCR, see B Porter, 'Judging Poverty Rights: Using International Human Rights Law to Refine the Scope of Charter Rights' (2000) 15 *Journal of Law & Social Policy* 117; M Jackman, 'What's Wrong with Social and Economic Rights?' (2000) 11 *National Journal of Constitutional Law* 235.

international legal obligations. Instead, they were and continue to be legislative and regulatory products of domestic political contestation over the appropriate relationship between state and market. Regardless of their domestic origins and purposes, however, social policy programmes in Canada have the effect of implementing international social rights in Canadian law in the form of legislative and regulatory measures that protect certain social interests otherwise threatened by state or non-state action.

On the second, juridical, plane domestic implementation of international social rights occurs through judicial interpretation. Because Canada is a federal state, the judiciary polices the constitutional boundaries between the Parliament of Canada and the provincial legislatures, and thus is responsible for determining which level of government possesses the authority to legislate in relation to social interests. Because Canada also has a written Charter of Rights and Freedoms, the judiciary is responsible for ensuring that the legislative and executive branches of government respect constitutionally entrenched rights and freedoms of individuals and groups. Although international treaty obligations traditionally require implementing legislation to possess domestic legal force, the judiciary is increasingly relying on international legal developments in constitutional and statutory interpretation. As a result, on this second plane, the judiciary possesses the capacity to implement international social rights in Canadian law by interpreting statutory and constitutional provisions in light of Canada's international legal obligations.

Political developments concerning state protection of social interests often generate legal consequences and vice versa, but the relationship between political and juridical event is not simply one of cause and effect. Despite their appellations, each contains elements of the other. The political plane possesses manifold juridical dimensions. Political actors exercise legal authority over social interests, and thus possess the power to enact and administer legislation and regulations that protect or threaten such interests. In exercising this authority, they are responsible for interpreting and applying judicially formulated legal principles and rules. On the juridical plane, constitutional and legislative provisions require substantive normative content to acquire adjudicative significance in specific disputes. Text and precedent underdetermine legal outcomes, producing opportunities for litigation and a politics of judicial interpretation surrounding the distribution of legislative authority, the scope of constitutional rights, and the reach of statutory protection.[3] Judicial choices in each of these contexts frame the location and terms of

---

[3] See R Bahdi, 'Litigating Social and Economic Rights in Canada in Light of International Human Rights Law: What Difference Can It Make?' (2002) 14 *Canadian Journal of Women & Law* 158 for an analysis of litigation strategies.

democratic contestation over the appropriate relationship between market and state. These choices both shape and are shaped by developments on the political plane in ways that minimise the domestic significance of Canada's international obligations to protect interests associated with social rights.

II FEDERAL DISTRIBUTION OF LEGISLATIVE AUTHORITY

At the height of the Depression, in 1937, the Judicial Committee of the Privy Council struck down three statutes concerning the rights of workers enacted by the Parliament of Canada to implement international treaty obligations that Canada had assumed under the auspices of the International Labour Organisation.[4] Drawing a famous distinction between forming and performing a treaty, the Privy Council held that the federal government possesses the authority to form or ratify a treaty and thereby bind Canada at international law, but the performance of a treaty—its implementation into domestic law—requires implementing legislation and thus depends on the distribution of legislative authority between Parliament and provincial legislatures. Relying on precedent established in some of its earlier decisions,[5] the Privy Council held that Parliament does not possess the jurisdiction to enact the legislation in question because labour relations, with the exception of those in enterprises under federal authority, fall within the exclusive authority of provincial legislatures.

Because treaty implementation is subject to the distribution of legislative authority, the Parliament of Canada cannot enact legislation implementing social rights enshrined in the ICESCR except in relation to subject matters that fall within federal legislative competence. And, according to the Supreme Court of Canada, 'human rights'—and, by extension, social rights—do not constitute a distinct subject matter that falls within the exclusive legislative authority of Parliament.[6] The power to enact laws in relation to interests that social rights are designed to protect vests almost exclusively in provincial legislatures.[7] In addition to labour relations, social security and health care are matters that, generally speaking, lie beyond federal legislative authority. As a result, the political capacity to implement social rights is diffused throughout the federation, with democratic contestation over the appropriate relationship between

---

[4] *A-G for Canada v A-G for Ontario* [1937] AC 326 (PC) (Lord Atkin).

[5] *Reference re Regulation and Control of Radio Communication in Canada* [1932] AC 304 (PC); *Toronto Electric Commissioners v Snider* [1925] AC 396 (PC).

[6] *Bell Canada v Quebec (Commission de la santé et de la sécurité du travail)* [1988] 1 SCR 749.

[7] For a critical assessment of this common understanding, see S Choudhry, 'Recasting Social Canada: A Reconsideration of Federal Jurisdiction over Social Policy' (2002) 52 *University of Toronto Law Journal* 163.

market and state in relation to social protection occurring in multiple juris-dictions. The diffusion of regulatory power produced on the juridical plane empowers provincial majorities to tailor social protection to local interests, to engage in regulatory competition with other provinces, and to exper-iment with new forms of economic and social regulation. It also hampers the capacity of the Canadian state to provide for uniform and national levels of protection of interests associated with international social rights.

A Work

A series of industrial clashes during the Second World War, culminating in a wildcat strike of steelworkers early in 1943, led to the introduc-tion of provincial and federal collective bargaining legislation, which provided—and continues to provide—statutory protection of a worker's right to choose a union, bargain collectively with one's employer and strike.[8] In 1967, Parliament extended collective bargaining rights to most federal public sector employees, who responded by unionising in record numbers. Provincial legislatures followed suit, and provincial public sector employees, including those employed in hospitals, schools, day care centres, nursing homes and social service agencies, organised themselves into unions and began to bargain collectively with their employers.

Public and private sector collective bargaining regimes are the primary means by which Article 8 of the ICESCR, which guarantees workers the right to organise, bargain collectively and strike,[9] is implemented in Canadian law. These statutory regimes interlock with federal and provincial employment standards legislation, which provides relatively uniform floor legal entitlements to workers, such as minimum wage and maximum hours requirements, regardless of whether they belong to a union. Employment standards legislation is the primary means of domestic implementation of Article 7 of the ICESCR, which recognises the right to the enjoyment of just and favourable conditions of work, including fair wages and equal remuneration for work of equal value without distinction of any kind; safe and healthy working conditions; and rest, leisure and

[8] See generally I Abella and D Millar (eds), *The Canadian Worker in the Twentieth Century* (Toronto, Oxford University Press, 1978).

[9] The Committee on Economic, Social and Cultural Rights ('CESCR') has consistently held that Article 8 protects the right to join a union, bargain collectively and strike. In its 2001 Concluding Comment on Korea, for example, the CESCR reminded Korea that 'the provisions of article 8 guarantee for all persons the right to freely form and join trade unions, the right to engage in collective bargaining through trade unions for the promotion and protection of their economic and social interests, as well as the right to strike' (E/C12/1/Add59 (09–05–2001) para 39. See generally P Macklem, 'The Right to Bargain Collectively in International Law: Workers' Right, Human Right, International Right?' in P Alston (ed), *Labour Rights as Human Rights* (New York, Oxford University Press, 2005) 61–84.

reasonable limitation of working hours and periodic holidays with pay, as well as remuneration for public holidays. Collective bargaining regimes and employment standards legislation thus constitute measures by which Canada can claim compliance with its international social rights obligations under the ICESCR and other international instruments, notably ILO conventions relating to the rights of workers.[10]

In the 1970s, primarily due to rampant inflation, the federal government came under intense pressures to curtail spiralling labour costs, and responded by introducing mandatory price and wage controls, which empowered federal authorities to monitor and roll back wage increases. Restrictive labour policies continued throughout the 1980s and 1990s, with economic globalisation and debt and deficit reduction replacing inflation as the primary justifications for retrenchment. Private sector unions faced heightened demands to reduce wages in the midst of a dramatic increase in plant closures, most notably in the manufacturing sector.[11] Public sector unions came under attack by federal and provincial governments as they attempted to reduce spending, reduce taxes and balance budgets. Union density began to decline steadily.[12] Legislation was introduced in several jurisdictions restricting the right to organise, bargain collectively and strike with little or no regard to Canada's obligations under the ICESCR or other international instruments to implement rights associated with freedom of association.[13]

British Columbia, for example, introduced legislation in 2002 restructuring the education and health care sectors in the province in ways that dramatically affected the working environment of approximately 100,000 workers.[14] The legislation imposed collective agreements containing pay and working conditions reflecting the employer's position on workers whose collective agreements had expired. It overrode terms and conditions of additional existing collective agreements respecting job security, and contracted out work to non-union employees. It also restricted, and in some cases eliminated, existing rights to strike in the sector. The government defended the restructuring on the basis that changes in the

---

[10] For commentary, see L Swepston, 'Human Rights Law and Freedom of Association: Development through ILO supervision' (1998) 137 *International Labour Review* 169.

[11] Employment in the manufacturing sector continues to decline, decreasing 8.2 per cent between 2002 and 2005: Statistics Canada, *Labour Force Survey* (January 2006).

[12] Union density peaked at 40% in the mid-1980s, declined to 36% in the mid-1990s, and is currently at 30.4%, with most of the decline in the private sector, which shrank from almost 30% in the mid-1980s to less than 20% today: A Jackson, 'Solidarity Forever? Trends in Canadian Union Density' (2004) 74 *Studies in Political Economy* 139.

[13] See generally L Panitch and D Schwartz, *From Consent to Coercion: The Assault on Trade Union Freedoms* 3rd edn (Toronto, Garamond, 2004).

[14] *Health and Social Services Delivery Improvement Act*, SBC 2002, c 2. As of writing, the constitutionality of the Act is before the Supreme Court of Canada: *Health Services and Support-Facilities Subsector Bargaining Association et al v BC*, leave to appeal to SCC granted 21 April 2005.

global economy and public sector expenditure commitments led to unsustainable pressures on its capacity to service its debt and deficit.[15]

British Columbia's actions illustrate how, on the political plane, implementation of ICESCR rights associated with work is a function of political contestation over the appropriate relationship between state and market. The fact that international law requires Canada to implement international rights that protect social interests relating to work rarely influences the ideological character of provincial politics. Framed by a background distribution of legislative authority produced on the juridical plane, contestation primarily occurs within the provincial as opposed to national realm, generated by clashing local interests, yielding variation in levels of worker protection across jurisdictions and over time. Legislative outcomes that have the effect of implementing social rights relating to work enshrined in the ICESCR do so more by coincidence than by design.

B Social Security

In addition to labour relations, provincial legislatures possess exclusive legislative competence to enact laws in relation to most matters that fall within the broad umbrella of social security. However, the Parliament of Canada is not entirely excluded from this legislative role. Employment Insurance (EI), for example, is a federal contributory earnings-related unemployment insurance programme that provides temporary financial assistance for unemployed Canadians while they look for work or upgrade their skills. Under certain conditions, EI is also available in the event of illness and pregnancy, and to assist those caring for a newborn or

---

[15] An earlier version of this legislation was reviewed by the International Labour Organisation's Committee on Freedom of Association (CFA): CFA Cases 1758 Vol LXXVII 1995 Series B No 1 para 227. In strongly worded remarks, the CFA stated that the government was proposing to intervene legislatively in collective bargaining processes, either to put an end to a legal strike, impose wages and working conditions and circumscribe the scope of collective bargaining, or restructure bargaining processes themselves. It acknowledged that public sector collective bargaining requires verification of available resources and that such resources are dependent on the timing and duration of budgets which do not always correspond to collective agreements in the sector. It also acknowledged that it would be not objectionable in certain circumstances for a government to legislate wage ceilings in the face of debt and deficit pressures. It stated that 'the bargaining parties should, however, be free to reach an agreement; if this is not possible, any exercise by the public authorities of their prerogatives in financial matters which hampers the free negotiation of collective agreements is incompatible with the principle of freedom of collective bargaining' (para 209). In such circumstances, the CFA concluded, the government should provide a mechanism to ensure that trade unions and employers are adequately consulted. Any legislated changes 'should be limited in time and protect the standard of living of the most affected workers' (para 209). The CFA recommended that the government repeal certain measures and amend others to enable employees to exercise their rights to bargain collectively and strike, provide appropriate and meaningful consultations in the present and any future dispute, and refrain from resorting to legislatively imposed settlements in the future.

adopted child, as well as those caring for a seriously ill family member.[16] Similarly, the Canada Pension Plan (CPP) is a federal contributory earnings-related social insurance programme which ensures a measure of protection to Canadian workers and their families against the loss of income due to retirement, disability or death.[17] Despite these and other federal legislative programmes, however, provincial legislatures possess the primary authority to implement the right to social security guaranteed by the ICESCR in the Canadian legal order in the form of legislative rights and benefits.

Although its legislative competence is limited, the federal government is said to possess the authority to spend its revenues in areas that fall within provincial legislative competence. By exercising what is known as its 'spending power' and stipulating conditions for provincial receipt of federal funds, the federal government wields extraordinary influence over provincial social policy choices.[18] Beginning in the 1920s, the federal government began to exercise its greater fiscal strength to persuade the provinces, through conditional grants, to provide legislative protection to interests associated with international social rights that met federal standards but which would otherwise have exceeded provincial fiscal capacities.[19] The federal government initially imposed extensive and detailed conditions on the receipt of federal funds. In the face of provincial resistance, most notably from Quebec, it gradually began to reformulate conditions in the form of general principles instead of detailed require- ments, and to permit provinces to 'contract out' of various social programmes and receive a tax abatement in lieu of federal funds. Quebec

---

[16] *Employment Insurance Act* SC 1996, c 23. In *Reference re Employment Insurance Act (Can)*, 2005 SCC 56 the Court upheld the federal provision of income replacement benefits during maternity leave and parental leave as a valid exercise of Parliament's legislative authority to enact laws in relation to unemployment insurance.

[17] *Canada Pension Plan* RSC 1985, c C-8. For a powerful account of the federal politics surrounding the establishment of the Canada Pension Plan, see Richard Simeon, *Federal-Provincial Relations: The Making of Recent Policy in Canada* revised edn (Toronto, University of Toronto Press, 2006).

[18] The constitutional basis and scope of the federal spending power are uncertain. The Supreme Court of Canada affirmed its existence in 1936 in *Reference re Employment and Social Insurance Act* [1936] SCR 427, but the Privy Council in the following year left the issue vague: *A-G for Canada v A-G for Ontario* [1937] AC 355. It was affirmed more recently in passing by a unanimous Court in *YMHA Jewish Community Centre of Winnipeg Inc v Brown* [1989] 1 SCR 1532, at 1549 (L'Heureux-Dubé J). See also *Winterhaven Stables v A-G of Canada* (1988) 53 DLR (4th) 413 (Alta CA), leave to appeal to SCC refused 55 DLR (4th) viii. Scholars who question its merits include A Petter, 'Federalism and the Myth of the Federal Spending Power' (1989) 68 *Canadian Bar Review* 448; and A Lajoie, 'The Federal Spending Power and Meech Lake' in KE Swinton and CJ Rogerson (eds), *Competing Constitutional Visions: The Meech Lake Accord* (Toronto, Carswell, 1988) 175.

[19] Between 1874 and 1937 the costs associated with administering education and public welfare systems rose from $4 billion to $360 billion: Royal Commission on Dominion-Provincial Relations, *Equalisation: Its Contribution to Canada's Economic and Fiscal Progress* (1940), at 244–45.

subsequently opted out of all the major shared-cost programmes. While other provinces did not follow suit, they continued to resist what they perceived as excessive federal conditions attached to the shared-cost programmes.

By the time Canada ratified the ICESCR, in 1975, there were several major social policy programmes established through federal-provincial co-operation that operated to implement at least some international social rights in domestic law. These programmes included equalisation measures, hospital insurance, a publicly funded health care system and post-secondary university education funding. Equalisation measures had been established in 1957 to provide provinces having relatively weak revenue-raising capacities with annual grants to ensure that all provinces could provide citizens with reasonably comparable levels of public services at reasonably comparable rates of taxation. Hospital insurance provided nation-wide coverage for in-patient services in hospitals. Medicare provided a nationwide system of health insurance covering medically necessary hospital care and many outpatient services. In 1967 the federal government also replaced federal grants to universities with a federal-provincial post-secondary education transfer.[20]

The most significant programme in place at the time of Canada's ratification of the ICESCR, however, was the Canada Assistance Plan (CAP), which, in 1966, consolidated earlier programmes and provided a wide variety of social assistance to Canadians, including welfare, work activity programmes, nursing homes and home care, but left provinces free to administer programmes, including the establishment of levels of assistance, eligibility criteria, comprehensiveness and methods of delivery.[21] To be eligible for federal funding under CAP, however, provinces had to meet a number of conditions. Specifically, CAP required: provinces to provide social assistance to any person in need, regardless of the reasons for their need; that levels of assistance take into account the basic requirements of recipients, in terms of food, shelter, clothing, fuel, utilities, household supplies and personal requirements; that welfare services continue to be developed and extended; that provincial residency requirements and waiting periods not be imposed; and that appeal procedures from decisions relating to assistance be made available. Through CAP, the federal government established national standards that sought to ensure that all

---

[20] In 1977, due to provincial dissatisfaction over federal audits and federal concern that its transfers were being determined by provincial spending levels, the federal government introduced Established Programme Financing (EPF) arrangements, as set out in the Federal-Provincial Fiscal Arrangements and Established Programmes Financing Act 1977. The EPF replaced 50/50 conditional grants for hospital insurance, health care and post-secondary education with a combination of block grants and tax points, but retained federal authority to withhold funds where a province failed to meet the criteria set out in hospital insurance and health care legislation.

[21] *Canada Assistance Plan*, 1966, c C-1, repealed, 1995, c 17, s 32.

Canadians had access to a minimum level of income and services on relatively equal terms and conditions in all parts of the country. Together with corresponding provincial legislation, CAP was the major instrument that provided for the domestic implementation of Articles 9 and 11 of the ICESCR, which guarantee, respectively, rights to social security and an adequate standard of living, including adequate food, clothing and housing.

In 1995 the federal government repealed CAP in favour of a new block transfer under the Canada Health and Social Transfer Act, known as the CHST. The stated purpose of the CHST is 'to finance social programmes in a manner that will increase provincial flexibility'. The only national standard with respect to social programmes conditioning receipt of federal funds that survived the repeal of the CAP was a prohibition against provincial residency requirements. The Supreme Court of Canada upheld CAP's repeal, finding there to be no constitutional impediment to its enactment.[22] During the remainder of the 1990s the federal government, in the name of fiscal austerity, significantly reduced overall CHST transfer levels to provincial governments.

Provinces were quick to react. Provincial reforms heightened distinctions between beneficiaries who are deemed to be 'employable' and those who are not, making the former subject to more onerous conditions, and forced beneficiaries in some circumstances to participate in workfare programmes, with reductions in benefit levels. Manitoba introduced cuts of about 10 per cent in social assistance rates for single people. Nova Scotia cut rates for single people by 35 per cent. Ontario cut rates by approximately 20 per cent from families and single people. Reduction of welfare rolls instead of the reduction of poverty became the main objective of most provincial programmes. Landlord-tenant legislation was amended to confer greater power on landlords as against tenants.

In 1993 the UN Committee on Economic, Social and Cultural Rights (CESCR), the treaty body responsible for monitoring compliance with the ICESCR, condemned the level and severity of poverty among vulnerable groups, particularly single mothers, the increasing reliance on food banks, the gap between social assistance rates and the poverty line, and the minimal allocation of resources to deal with homelessness.[23] In 1997 the UN Committee on the Elimination of Discrimination against Women expressed concern about the deepening poverty among women, especially single mothers, aggravated by the withdrawal or weakening of social assis-

---

[22] *Reference Re Canada Assistance Plan (BC)* [1991] 2 SCR 525.
[23] CESCR, *Consideration of Reports Submitted by State Parties under Articles 16 and 17 of the Covenant: Concluding Observations of the Committee on Economic, Social and Cultural Rights (Canada)*, 10 June 1993, E/C12/1993/19.

tance programmes.[24] In 1998 the CESCR noted that the problems it had pointed out in 1993 had grown considerably worse, noted drastic cuts to social programmes, criticised the repeal of the CAP, noted that no progress had been made to alleviate economic and social deprivation among indigenous populations, and criticised the introduction of workfare programmes and social security cuts.[25] In 1999 the UN Human Rights Committee stated:

> The Committee is concerned that many women have been disproportionately affected by poverty. In particular, the high poverty rate among single mothers leaves their children without the protection to which they are entitled under the Covenant... The Committee is concerned that many of the programme cuts in recent years have exacerbated these inequalities and harmed women and other disadvantaged groups. The Committee recommends a thorough assessment of the impact of recent changes in social programmes on women and that action be taken to redress any discriminatory effects of these changes. The HRC also expressed concern that 'homelessness has led to serious health problems and even to death. The Committee recommends that the State party take positive measures required by article 6 (the right to life) to address this serious problem.[26]

International concern did not produce significant domestic reform. In February 1999 the federal, provincial and territorial governments, with the exception of the province of Quebec, signed a Social Union Framework Agreement (SUFA). SUFA affirmed a principle of adequate, affordable, stable and sustainable funding for social programmes, and proposed intergovernmental co-operation, including exchange of information and the monitoring of social policy. Apart from agreeing to the principle of adequate CHST funding, however, SUFA did not reintroduce national standards relating to the quality of provincial social policy, and provinces remain relatively free to spend federal funds in the manner they see fit.[27] To date, SUFA has yielded an early childhood development agreement, an agreement on strengthening Canada's publicly funded health care services,

---

[25] UN Committee on the Elimination of Discrimination Against Women, *Adoption of the Report of the Committee on the Elimination of Discrimination Against Women on its Sixteenth Session: Concluding Observations of the Committee on the Elimination of Discrimination Against Women (Canada)* (29 February 1997) A/52/38/Rev1.

[25] CESCR, *Consideration of Reports Submitted by State Parties under Articles 16 and 17 of the Covenant: Concluding Observations of the Committee on Economic, Social and Cultural Rights (Canada)* (10 December 1998) E/C12/1/Add31.

[26] UN Human Rights Committee, *Consideration of Reports Submitted by State Parties under Article 40 of the Covenant: Concluding Observations of the Committee on Economic, Social and Cultural Rights (Canada)* (7 April 1999) CCPR/C/79/Add105 (1999).

[27] In 2004 the federal government restructured the CHST into two separate transfers, one supporting provincial health care (CHT) and the other a block transfer supporting post-secondary education, social assistance and social services, and early learning and child care (CST). Like its predecessor, the CST continues to require only that provinces not impose residency requirements as a condition of eligibility for social assistance.

and measures designed to improve interprovincial labour mobility. In 2006 the CESCR again expressed concern about the living conditions of aboriginal Canadians, discrimination against First Nations women, lower social assistance benefits, a shortage of affordable housing, and the insufficiency of minimum wages. The Committee also noted 'the absence of any factors or difficulties preventing the effective implementation of the Covenant'.[28]

Although federal government has assumed a more active role in protecting interests associated with social security than those associated with work, it has largely eschewed any international legal obligation to implement ICESCR rights to social security and an adequate standard of living in the name of deficit reduction and provincial regulatory flexibility. The federal government increasingly competes with other jurisdictions, and provinces increasingly compete with each other, to establish regulatory environments that attract and retain direct investment, creating downward pressures on personal and corporate taxation rates. Any efficiency gains produced by jurisdictional competition are tempered by the fact that each level is under an incentive to scale back its social policy commitments to reduce expenditures. In such an environment, the federal distribution of authority leads each level to attempt to locate the responsibility of social protection in the other, blurring political accountability between the two levels of government. And while federal spending in the area alleviates provincial budgetary pressures, federal unwillingness to set uniform national standards attenuates domestic implementation of ICESCR rights relating to social security.

C Health

'Health', like 'human rights', is a subject that, by judicial decision, does not fall within the exclusive legislative authority of either level of government.[29] As a result, neither level possesses exclusive jurisdiction to implement the right to physical and mental health enshrined in Article 12 of the ICESCR. Federal jurisdiction over criminal law authorises Parliament to enact certain laws that protect health-related interests.[30] Provincial legislatures, however, possess primary authority to enact laws in relation to health care by their legislative powers over property and civil rights, hospitals and, more generally, 'matters of a merely local or private

---

[28] CESCR, *Consideration of Reports Submitted by State Parties under Articles 16 and 17 of the Covenant: Concluding Observations of the Committee on Economic, Social and Cultural Rights (Canada)* (22 May 2006) E/C12/CAN/CO/4 – E/C12/CAN/CO/5 para 10.

[29] *Schneider v The Queen* [1982] 2 SCR 112.

[30] *R v Wetmore* [1983] 2 SCR 284; *R v Morgentaler* [1988] 1 SCR 30; *R v Hydro-Quebec* [1997] 3 SCR 213.

nature'.[31] Provincial legislation regulates a vast array of subjects relating to health care, including health care insurance, the prevention and control of disease, health professionals, medical education and hospitals.

Notwithstanding the overwhelming provincial regulatory presence in matters relating to Article 12 of the ICESCR, the federal government possesses the capacity to influence implementation of Article 12 through the exercise of its spending power. The Canada Health Act (CHA) is the most significant instrument in this respect, providing conditional federal funding of provincial health care insurance.[32] The CHA consolidated previous federal health care policy and defined the primary objective of federal policy as 'to protect, promote and restore the physical and mental well-being of residents of Canada and to facilitate reasonable access to health services without financial or other barriers'. The CHA establishes criteria and conditions related to insured health services[33] and extended health care services[34] that the provinces and territories must fulfil to receive federal funding. The aim of the CHA is to ensure that all eligible residents of Canada have reasonable access to insured health services on a prepaid basis, without direct charges at the point of service for such services.

To qualify for the full federal cash contributions, the CHA requires that a provincial health care insurance plan be operated on a non-profit basis by a public authority that is accountable to the provincial government for decision-making on benefit levels and services, and whose records and accounts are publicly audited. It must cover all insured health services.[35]

---

[31] *R v Morgentaler* [1993] 3 SCR 463.

[32] RSC 1985, c C-6.

[33] 'Insured health services' are medically necessary hospital, physician and surgical-dental services provided to insured persons. 'Insured hospital services' are defined under the CHA and include medically necessary in- and out-patient services such as accommodation and meals at the standard or public ward level and preferred accommodation if medically required; nursing services; laboratory, radiological and other diagnostic procedures, together with the necessary interpretations; drugs, biological and related preparations when administered in the hospital; use of operating room, case room and anaesthetic facilities, including necessary equipment and supplies; medical and surgical equipment and supplies; use of radiotherapy facilities; use of physiotherapy facilities; and services provided by persons who receive remuneration therefor from the hospital, but does not include services that are excluded by the regulations. 'Insured physician services' are defined under the Act as 'medically required services rendered by medical practitioners'. Medically required physician services are generally determined by physicians in conjunction with their provincial and territorial health insurance plans. 'Insured surgical-dental services' are services provided by a dentist in a hospital, where a hospital setting is required to properly perform the procedure. Section 22 of the CHA enables the federal government to make regulations prescribing which services to exclude from hospital services. To date, the federal government has not made any regulations in this respect.

[34] 'Extended health care services' as defined in the CHA are certain aspects of long-term residential care (nursing home intermediate care and adult residential care services), and the health aspects of home care and ambulatory care services. Section 22 of the CHA enables the federal government to make regulations defining the services included in the definition of 'extended health care services'. To date, the federal government has not made any regulations in this respect.

[35] These criteria apply equally to territorial health care insurance plans.

All insured residents of a province must be entitled to the insured health services provided by the plan on uniform terms and conditions. Residents moving from one province to another must continue to be covered for insured health services by the 'home' jurisdiction during any waiting period imposed by the new province or territory of residence. Insured persons in a province must have reasonable access to insured services on uniform terms and conditions, unprecluded or unimpeded, either directly or indirectly, by charges (user charges or extra-billing) or other means (eg, discrimination on the basis of age, health status or financial circumstances). Finally, provincial plans must provide reasonable compensation to physicians and dentists for all the insured health services they provide, and payments to hospitals to cover the cost of insured health services.

Although they constitute uniform national standards concerning the provision of health care, these requirements simply condition provincial receipt of federal funds; they do not oblige provinces, under threat of legal sanction, to structure health insurance according to their terms. Provinces are free to authorise physicians to work in for-profit health facilities, foster private health insurance, permit the establishment of private hospitals, and determine which services are to be insured publicly. Provinces bear the lion's share of health care costs even after federal funding is taken into account, and rising health care costs are straining provincial purses. Allegations that the quality of health care is deteriorating are assuming increased political and legal salience.[36] The federal government continues to insist on provincial compliance with national standards enshrined in the CHA as a condition of federal funding, but provincial governments are increasingly experimenting with limited forms of for-profit health care services that would compete with the publicly funded health care system.

III DOMESTIC IMPLEMENTATION OF INTERNATIONAL SOCIAL RIGHTS

The federal distribution of legislative authority is not the only juridical feature of the Canadian state that frames democratic contestation over the nature and scope of protection of interests associated with international social rights. The Constitution of Canada includes the Canadian Charter of Rights and Freedoms, which guarantees a wide range of civil and political rights, as well as linguistic rights and rights pertaining to minority educational institutions. Adopted in 1982, the Charter does not formally guarantee an extensive list of social rights. The Constitution does provide

---

[36] Canada, Standing Senate Committee on Social Affairs, Science and Technology, *The Health of Canadians – The Federal Role* (2002); Canada, Commission on the Future of Health Care in Canada, *Building on Values: The Future of Health Care in Canada: Final Report* (2002); Canada, Department of Finance, *Federal Support for Health Care: The Facts* (2004).

that the federal and provincial governments are 'committed to promoting equal opportunities for the well being of Canadians; furthering economic development to reduce disparity in opportunities; and providing essential public services of reasonable quality to all Canadians', but it also states that these constitutional commitments do not affect the legislative authority of Parliament or the provinces.

Primarily in an effort to accommodate the province of Quebec's demands for greater autonomy, federal and provincial governments have since attempted further amendments of the Constitution. In 1991 a broad coalition of social activists and anti-poverty organisations proposed a Draft Social Charter as part of any future constitutional reform. It sought to affirm Canada's international obligations to respect, protect and promote human rights, and guarantee 'an equal right to well-being', which would include an adequate standard of living, universal and public health care, public education, and access to employment opportunities, as well as the right of workers to organise and bargain collectively.[37]

In 1992 the federal and all provincial governments agreed to a set of constitutional reform proposals known as the Charlottetown Accord. Partly in response to the proposed Draft Social Charter, the Charlottetown Accord proposed a 'social and economic union' clause, setting out a series of non-justiciable policy objectives, including a comprehensive, universal, portable, publicly administered and accessible health care system, adequate social services and benefits to ensure reasonable access to housing, food and other basic necessities, high quality primary and secondary education, protection of the right to organise and bargain collectively, and environmental protection. This proposal was roundly criticised by social activists for its failure to provide for monitoring or enforcement mechanisms. Its merits quickly became moot as the Accord as a whole was rejected by a majority of voters and by voters in a majority of the provinces, in a national referendum.

Adding to the ambiguity surrounding the constitutional significance of interests associated with international social rights is the fact that, unlike the constitutions of some countries,[38] the Constitution of Canada is silent on the domestic legal status of international human rights law. Traditionally understood, Canada is a dualist jurisdiction, whereby an international treaty obligation does not become domestic law unless it has

---

[37] For commentary, see the essays in J Bakan and D Schneiderman (eds), *Social Justice and the Constitution: Perspectives on a Social Union for Canada* (Ottawa, Carleton University Press, 1992).

[38] South Africa's constitution, for example, provides that 'in interpreting the provisions of this Chapter [dealing with fundamental rights], a court of law shall promote the values which underlie an open and democratic society based on freedom and equality and shall, where applicable, have regard to public international law applicable to the protection of the rights entrenched in this Chapter, and may have regard to comparable foreign case law'.

been implemented in domestic legislation.[39] When an international legal obligation is implemented by legislation, its domestic legal force is the product of the statute, not the treaty. The treaty itself creates no domestic legal obligations. The justification for this approach is often said to lie in the fact that the Crown in its executive capacity, by entering into treaties with foreign states, should not be entitled to usurp federal or provincial legislative authority.[40]

This traditional view of the domestic implications of international treaty obligations, however, has gradually but steadily been complemented, if not replaced, by one that sees the boundary between the international and national legal orders in more porous terms.[41] This contemporary approach reflects an increased willingness on the part of the judiciary in democratic societies to look to comparative, regional and international legal developments for assistance and guidance in legal interpretation. It has emerged in Canada in three contexts in which international conventional law serves as an aid in legal interpretation—two of which are relevant to the domestic implementation of international social rights.[42]

A Constitutional Interpretation

First, international law has become a prominent and significant feature of judicial interpretation by the Supreme Court of Canada of the nature and content of rights and freedoms guaranteed by the Charter of Rights and

---

[39] *A-G for Canada v A-G for Ontario*, above n 4. See generally WA Schabas, 'Twenty-Five Years of Public International Law at the Supreme Court of Canada' 79 *Canadian Bar Review* 174, 177 (2000).

[40] See *Capital Cities Communications v CRTC* [1978] 2 SCR 141, 173: 'certainly the convention [the 1937 Inter-American Radio Communications Convention] *per se* cannot prevail against the express stipulations of the Act' (Laskin CJ); *Daniels v White and the Queen* [1968] SCR 517: 'if a statute is unambiguous... its provisions must be followed even if they are contrary to the established rules of international law [specifically, the 1916 Canada-US Migratory Birds Convention]' (Hall J dissenting, but not on this point, and with the concurrence of Ritchie and Spence JJ); *Re Arrow River and Tributaries Slide & Boom Co Limited* [1932] SCR 495, 510 (Lamont J).

[41] See generally K Knop, 'Here and There: International Law in Domestic Courts' (2000) 32 *New York University Journal of International Law & Policy* 501.

[42] The third context is the common law. The judiciary has on several occasions relied on international treaty obligations as a source of common law reasoning. Illustrative of this development is L'Heureux-Dubé J's reasons in *R v Ewanchuk*, a case dealing with statutory sexual assault, where she held that the scope of common law defences should be circumscribed by international legal norms, including those enshrined in a treaty ratified by Canada, the Convention on the Elimination of Discrimination Against Women: *R v Ewanchuk* [1999] 1 SCR 330. See also *Winnipeg Child and Family Services (Northwest Area) v G (DF)* [1997] 3 SCR 925 (Major J): preamble of Declaration of the Rights of the Child relied on in support of a proposed modification of common law protection of unborn children.

Freedoms.[43] In *Reference re Public Service Employees Relations Act (Alberta)*, Dickson CJ, dissenting on other grounds, stated that:

> The various sources of international human rights law—declarations, covenants, conventions, judicial and quasi-judicial decisions of international tribunals, customary norms—must, in my opinion, be relevant and persuasive sources for interpretation of the Charter's provisions.[44]

In the same case, Dickson CJ also stated that 'the Charter should generally be presumed to provide protection at least as great as that afforded by similar provisions in international human rights documents which Canada has ratified'.[45] More recently, the Court made reference to ILO jurisprudence on freedom of association and interpreted the domestic constitutional guarantee of freedom of association as requiring legislative action to secure its protection.[46]

Recent cases have made it clear that the Court is not solely looking to treaties that Canada has ratified for guidance when interpreting the Charter. In *Suresh v Canada (Minister of Citizenship and Immigration)*, for example, the Court relied on at least one international treaty to which Canada is not party to reach the conclusion 'that international law rejects deportation to torture, even where national security interests are at stake' and that this norm 'best informs the content of the principles of fundamental justice under section 7 of the Charter'.[47]

Despite the fact that there are significant textual differences between the two instruments, Canada's international legal obligations under the ICESCR are therefore relevant to the interpretation of domestic constitutional guarantees. In *Canadian Egg Marketing Agency v Richardson*, for example, the Court relied on Article 6 of the ICESCR, which guarantees the right to work, in support of its conclusion that mobility rights enshrined in section 6 of the Charter protect a right to pursue one's

---

43 International treaties are commonly relied on to interpret provisions of the Canadian Charter: see, eg, *R v Keegstra* [1990] 3 SCR 697, 733 (Dickson CJ). International treaties have also provided guidance on whether a subject matter falls within federal and provincial legislative authority: see *R v Crown Zellerbach Canada Ltd* [1988] 1 SCR 401, 436 (Le Dain J). In *Bell Canada v Quebec (Commission de la santé et de la sécurité du travail)* [1988] 1 SCR 749, the ICESCR was cited in support of the proposition that the power to enact human rights legislation is subject to the distribution of legislative authority between Parliament and the provincial legislatures.

44 [1987] 1 SCR 313 para 57. See also *Godbout v Longueuil (City)* [1997] 3 SCR 844 para 69 (La Forest J): art 12 of the ICCPR supports interpreting s 7 as protecting a right to an abode; *R v Jones* [1986] 2 SCR 284 (Wilson J): Art 8(1) of the European Convention supports interpreting s 7 as protecting a right of parents to educate children in accordance with their religious and philosophical convictions.

45 But see *B(R) v Children's Aid Society of Metropolitan Toronto* [1995] 1 SCR 315, 349–50, where restrictive decisions by the Human Rights Committee under the ICCPR were relied on to exclude certain economic interests from the scope of s 7. See, generally, Schabas, above n 37, 187.

46 *Dunmore v Ontario (A-G)* [2001] 3 SCR 1016.

47 [2002] 1 SCR 3.

livelihood across provincial boundaries.[48] In *R v Advance Cutting and Coring* a minority of the Court, dissenting on other grounds, cited Article 8(1)(a) of the ICESCR, which guarantees the right to join a trade union of one's choice, to affirm that freedom of association as guaranteed by the Charter includes a negative right not to be compelled to belong to an association.[49]

In addition, the ICESCR is relevant to determinations of determining what constitute reasonable limits on the exercise of a Charter right or freedom, specifically whether a legislative objective is sufficiently important to justify an infringement of a Charter guarantee. In *Slaight Communications* Dickson CJ, referring to Article 6 of the ICESCR, held that:

> the fact that a value has the status of an international human right, either in customary international law or under a treaty to which Canada is a State Party, should generally be indicative of a high degree of importance attached to that objective.[50]

Similarly, in *R v Sharpe*, Article 10(3) of the ICESCR, which calls on states to protect children 'from economic and social exploitation', was invoked in support of the proposition that legislation criminalising the possession of child pornography possessed an objective sufficiently compelling to justify interfering with freedom of expression guaranteed by the Charter.[51]

B Statutory Interpretation

Second, international treaty obligations are also increasingly used as an aid to statutory interpretation. Because of Canada's traditionally dualist approach to treaty obligations,

> both the federal Parliament and the provincial legislatures may enact statutes that contradict the country's international obligations [and] a statute is not void or inoperative simply because it violates international custom or convention.[52]

But where statutory language permits, courts can and do presume legislatures to have legislated in accordance with international law. In cases where the statute is not in direct conflict, or where the statute is unclear on whether it is in conflict, with international law, the judiciary will interpret

---

48 [1998] 3 SCR 157 paras 58–59.
49 *R v Advance Cutting & Coring Ltd* [2001] 3 SCR 209 para 11 (Bastarache J dissenting).
50 [1989] 1 SCR 1038. For an extensive list of cases that relied on international conventions when applying s 1, see Schabas, above n 39, 187–88.
51 *R v Sharpe* [2001] 1 SCR 45 para 178.
52 *Thomson v Thomson* [1994] 3 SCR 551 at 618, citing PA Coté, *The Interpretation of Legislation in Canada* 2nd edn (Cowansville, Editions Yvon Blais, 1991) 308. See also *Daniels v White and The Queen*, above n 40, 541 (Pigeon J).

the statute to be in conformity with international law. As Justices Iacobucci and Major observed in *Ordon Estate v Grail*:

> Although international law is not formally binding upon Parliament or the provincial legislatures, a court must presume that legislation is intended to comply with Canada's obligations under international instruments and as a member of the international community.[53]

Initially, the presumption that a statute is in conformity with international treaty obligations applied only in cases where the statute in question displayed a 'patent' or 'manifest' ambiguity.[54] Yet the presumption now also applies in cases of 'latent' ambiguities to hold that unless the legislature's intent was to deviate clearly from international treaty obligations, the legislature's intent should be clarified in ways that are consistent with principles and values underpinning relevant international treaties.[55] This is the case regardless of whether or not the statute is designed to implement treaty obligations. In *Zingre v The Queen*, for example, the Court provided a 'fair and liberal interpretation' of the Canada Evidence Act 'with a view to fulfilling Canada's international obligations'.[56] Similarly, in *Delisle v Canada*, a minority of the Court, dissenting on other grounds, stated that federal collective bargaining legislation provides 'the same protections' as those enshrined in Article 8 of the ICESCR, as well as those in Article 22 of the International Covenant on Civil and Political Rights and ILO Convention No 87.[57]

In *Baker v Minister of Citizenship and Immigration* the Court addressed the relevance of unimplemented treaties as an aid to statutory interpretation.[58] At issue was the procedural fairness of the deportation of a woman with Canadian-born children. She had applied for an exemption to the general requirement that an application for permanent residence be made abroad on humanitarian and compassionate grounds, given that her children were born and lived in Canada. The Court held that the power to grant an exemption must be exercised in a way that requires close attention to the interests and needs of her children. In so holding, a majority of the Court also held that the Convention on the Rights of the Child is relevant to the issue, given its commitment to the overriding interests of children.

---

[53] [1998] 3 SCR 437.

[54] See *Schavernoch v Foreign Claims Commission* [1982] 1 SCR 1092, 1098 (Estey J); *Capital Cities*, above n 40, 173 (Laskin CJ).

[55] See, eg, *National Corn Growers Association v Canada (Import Tribunal)* [1992] 2 SCR 1324, 1369; *Canada (A-G) v Ward* [1993] 2 SCR 689; *Pushpanathan v Canada (Minister of Citizenship and Immigration)* [1998] 1 SCR 982 para 51.

[56] [1981] 2 SCR 392, 409–410 (Dickson J); see also *114957 Canada Ltée (Spraytech, Société d'arrosage) v Hudson (Town)* [2001] 2 SCR 241 para 30 (L'Heureux-Dubé J).

[57] [1999] 2 SCR 989 para 71.

[58] [1999] 2 SCR 817.

Of note is that the treaty at issue in *Baker* was ratified by Canada but it had not been incorporated into domestic law by legislation. Strictly speaking, the treaty did not have the force of law in a domestic court and created no binding legal obligations on the state. Nonetheless, a majority of the Court held that the 'values and principles' it enshrines are relevant to interpreting the statute conferring the power to grant an exemption. As a result of *Baker*, international legal obligations that have not been implemented into domestic law by the legislature possess relevance before a domestic court. Specifically, the Court held that

> the legislature is presumed to respect the values and principles enshrined in international law, both customary and conventional, [which] constitute a part of the legal context in which legislation is enacted and read.

Also of note is that the Court in *Baker* reached this conclusion despite the fact that Canada ratified the Convention after, not before, Parliament had enacted the legislation creating the power to grant an exemption and thus Parliament could not be said, strictly speaking, to have legislated with an eye to its international legal obligations.[59]

IV ICESCR AND CONSTITUTIONAL INTERPRETATION

Although international human rights instruments increasingly influence domestic constitutional and statutory interpretation, cases in which the ICESCR has been invoked to this end by the Supreme Court of Canada are few and far between. Since the inception of the Charter in 1982, the Court has invoked provisions of the ICCPR in 31 cases[60] whereas it has invoked

---

[59] For a similar holding, see *Ahmad v Inner London Education Authority* [1978] QB 36 (Eng CA) at 48D. See also *Bloxam v Favre* (1883) 8 PD 101, 107 (Eng CA).

[60] *Kindler v Canada (Minister of Justice)* [1991] 2 SCR 779; *R v Keegstra* above n 43; *Mills v The Queen* [1986] 1 SCR 863; *Edmonton Journal v Alberta (A-G)* [1989] 2 SCR 1326; *B (R) v Children's Aid Society of Metropolitan Toronto*, above n 45; *Reference Re Public Service Employee Relations Act (Alta)*, above n 44; *R v Milne* [1987] 2 SCR 512; *Canada (Human Rights Commission) v Taylor* [1990] 3 SCR 892; *R v Zundel* [1992] 2 SCR 731; *R v Oakes* [1986] 1 SCR 103; *R v Smith (Edward Dewey)* [1987] 1 SCR 1045; *R v Brydges* [1990] 1 SCR 190; *Mckinney v University of Guelph* [1990] 3 SCR 229; *R v Tran* [1994] 2 SCR 951; *United States v Burns* [2001] 1 SCR 283; *Sauvé v Canada (Chief Electoral Officer)* [2002] 3 SCR 519; *R v Big M Drug Mart Ltd* [1985] 1 SCR 295; *R v Prosper* [1994] 3 SCR 236; *Chan v Canada (Minister of Employment and Immigration)* [1995] 3 SCR 593; *R v O'Connor* [1995] 4 SCR 411; *2747-3174 Québec Inc v Quebec (Régie des permis d'alcool)* [1996] 3 SCR 919; *R v Lucas* [1998] 1 SCR 439; *Reference re Secession of Quebec* [1998] 2 SCR 217; *Quebec (Commission des droits de la personne et des droits de la jeunesse) v Montréal (City)* and *Quebec (Commission des droits de la personne et des droits de la jeunesse) v Boisbriand (City)* [2000] 1 SCR 665; *R v Sharpe*, above n 51; *R v Advance Cutting & Coring Ltd*, above n 49; *Suresh v Canada (Minister of Citizenship and Immigration)*, above n 47; *Lavoie v Canada* [2002] 1 SCR 769; *Chamberlain v Surrey School District No 36* [2002] 4 SCR 710; *Canadian Foundation for Children, Youth and the Law v Canada (A-G)* [2004] 1 SCR 76; *Harper v Canada (A-G)* [2004] 1 SCR 827.

the ICESCR in only 12 cases.[61] In only one of these 12 cases has a majority of the Court referred to the ICESCR when determining the nature and scope of a Charter right.[62]

One reason for this discrepancy may be that the Charter does not expressly refer to social rights to housing, social assistance, food, education and the like, whereas it expressly entrenches civil and political rights. As a result, the text of the ICCPR lends itself more readily than that of the ICESCR to the role of an interpretive aid in constitutional adjudication. But the Court has repeatedly affirmed a purposive approach to constitutional interpretation, which analyses rights and freedoms in light of the interests they are to protect.[63] The text of a provision is relevant to, but far from conclusive of, a determination of its underlying interests. The text of the Charter right to security of the person, for example, underdetermines its content, and the interests it is designed to protect require judicial identification and justification. A range of interpretive possibilities presents itself, including the possibility that the right protects certain interests associated with social security. Although not conclusive, the ICESCR, which provides explicit protection of these interests in international law, supports the proposition that they are sufficiently significant to merit domestic constitutional protection. Textual differences between the two instruments do not have the effect of precluding judicial reference to rights enshrined in the ICESCR in Charter interpretation.

Moreover, textual differences between the ICESCR and the Charter do not explain why the Court is relatively reluctant to rely on the ICESCR when interpreting statutes that contain language closely resembling the provisions of the ICESCR, and which protect interests associated with international social rights. Of the 12 cases that referred to the ICESCR since 1982, five were cases in which the Court relied on provisions in the ICESCR to shed light on the meaning of a statute.[64] None of the five relied

---

[61] *Reference Re Public Service Employee Relations Act (Alta)*, above n 44; *Slaight Communications Inc v Davidson*, above n 50; *Bell Canada v Quebec (Commission de la santé et de la sécurité du travail)*, above n 43; *Reference re Secession of Quebec, ibid; Canadian Egg Marketing Agency v Richardson*, above n 48; *Irwin Toy Ltd v Quebec (A-G)* [1989] 1 SCR 927; *Delisle v Canada (Deputy A-G)* [1999] 2 SCR 989; *Quebec (Commission des droits de la personne et des droits de la jeunesse) v Montréal (City)* and *Quebec (Commission des droits de la personne et des droits de la jeunesse) v Boisbriand (City)*, above n 60; *R v Sharpe*, above n 51; *R v Advance Cutting & Coring Ltd.*, above n 49; *Gosselin v Québec (A-G)* [2002] 4 SCR 429; *Quebec (Commission des droits de la personne et des droits de la jeunesse) v Maksteel Québec Inc* [2003] 3 SCR 228.

[62] *Canadian Egg Marketing Agency v Richardson*, above n 48.

[63] *Hunter v Southam Inc* [1984] 2 SCR 145; *R v Big M Drug Mart Ltd*, above n 60.

[64] *Delisle v Canada (Deputy A-G)*, above n 61; *Quebec (Commission des droits de la personne et des droits de la jeunesse) v Montréal (City)* and *Quebec (Commission des droits de la personne et des droits de la jeunesse) v Boisbriand (City)*, above n 61; *Gosselin v Québec (A-G), ibid; Quebec (Commission des droits de la personne et des droits de la jeunesse) v Maksteel Québec Inc*, above n 61.

on the ICESCR in support of an expansive interpretation of the statutory provision at issue.

In *Quebec v Maksteel*, for example, at issue was the precise extent to which non-discrimination provisions in the Quebec Charter of Human Rights and Freedoms, a provincial statute, protected an individual against discrimination on the basis of a criminal record.[65] The Court adopted an interpretation of the Charter that permits an employer to dismiss an employee who is unavailable for work because of incarceration. One of the reasons offered by the Court in support of this interpretation was that the ICESCR did not explicitly prohibit discrimination on the basis of a criminal record.[66] Similarly, in *Gosselin v AG Quebec*, the Court interpreted section 45 of the Quebec Charter, which guarantees the right to 'measures of financial assistance and to social measures provided for by law', as not authorising judicial review of the adequacy of a social assistance regime. It reasoned that had section 45 authorised such assessments, it would have contained language similar to that contained in Article 11(1) of the ICESCR, which guarantees 'the right to an adequate standard of living'.[67]

Despite the fact that the judiciary rarely refers to the ICESCR when interpreting constitutional guarantees, the Charter remains an important avenue for the domestic implementation of ICESCR rights to belong to a union, bargain collectively and strike (Article 8), the right to social security (Article 9), rights to adequate food, clothing and housing (Article 11), and the right to physical and mental health (Article 12). Rights enshrined in the ICESCR protect interests that may possess sufficient constitutional significance, for reasons additional to the fact that Canada is party to the ICESCR, to receive protection by rights guaranteed by the Charter. Yet the Court has not only shied away from explicitly relying on Canada's international obligations under the ICESCR when interpreting the Charter. It has also resisted interpreting the Charter in ways that protect interests associated with rights enshrined in the ICESCR.[68] Any constitutional significance that the judiciary has attached to interests relating to work,

---

[65] *Charter of Human Rights and Freedoms*, RSQ, c C-12.
[66] *Quebec (Commission des droits de la personne et droits de la jeunesse) v Maksteel Quebec Inc*, above n 61, para 44.
[67] *Gosselin v Quebec (A-G)*, above n 61, para 93.
[68] Compare R Hirschl, *Towards Juristocracy: The Origins and Consequences of the New Constitutionalism* (Cambridge, Mass, Harvard University Press, 2004) (constitutional interpretation in New Zealand, Canada and Israel, and South Africa has had a limited impact on advancing progressive notions of social justice in areas such as employment, health, housing and education') with D Davis, P Macklem, and G Mundlak, 'Social Rights, Social Citizenship, and Transformative Constitutionalism: A Comparative Assessment' in J Conaghan, RM Fischl, K Klare (eds) *Labour Law in an Era of Globalization* (Oxford, Oxford University Press, 2002) 511–34 (constitutional interpretation in Canada, Israel and South Africa extends partial constitutional protection to social interests). For European developments, see T Dainith, 'The Constitutional Protection of Economic Rights' (2004) 2 *International Journal of Constitutional Law* 56.

social security and health lies more in the limits that the Charter imposes on state action rather than the obligations it imposes on government to promote individual and social well being. The Court's rulings in these areas frame democratic contestation over social protection on the political plane[69] in terms that separate state power from social and economic inequalities produced by market ordering, obscuring the fact that markets are in fact instruments of state policy. They reinforce a politics of social protection that sidelines debate over the extent to which the state is obliged to take positive measures to ameliorate social and economic disadvantage that its regulatory choices have produced.

A Work

In addition to Article 8 of the ICESCR, numerous international and regional human rights instruments guarantee freedom of association. They provide explicitly, or have been interpreted by relevant international institutions to provide, that such freedom includes not only the right to form a union, but also the right to bargain collectively and the right to strike.[70] Yet a majority of the Court, in the *Alberta Reference*, when faced with determining the scope of protection afforded by the Charter's section 2(d) guarantee of 'freedom of association', held that it does not include a right to strike or bargain collectively.[71] As a result, the federal and provincial governments are under no constitutional obligation to introduce legislative measures to implement Article 8 rights, and indeed possess the constitutional authority to interfere with the exercise of Article 8 rights.

---

[69] On 'framing effects' generally see M Rabin, 'Psychology and Economics' (1998) 36 *Journal of Economic Literature* 11, 36: a 'framing effect' occurs when 'two logically equivalent (but not *transparently* equivalent) statements of a problem lead decision makers to choose different options'. On the effect of constitutional review on Parliamentary decision-making, see JL Hiebert, *Charter Conflicts: What is Parliament's Role?* (Montreal, McGill-Queen's University Press, 2002); on the effect of constitutional review on executive decision-making, see JB Kelly, *Governing with the Charter: Legislative and Judicial Activism and Framers' Intent* (Vancouver, University of British Columbia Press, 2005).

[70] These include the ICCPR, the Constitution of the ILO, ILO Conventions Nos 87 and 98, the 1944 ILO Declaration of Philadelphia, the 1998 ILO Declaration on Fundamental Principles and Rights at Work, the European Convention on Human Rights, the European Social Charter, the European Community Charter of Fundamental Social Rights for Workers and the Charter of Fundamental Rights of the European Union. See generally Macklem, above n 9.

[71] *Reference re Public Service Employees Relations Act (Alta)*, above n 44. The *Alberta Reference* was one of three judgments known as the 'Labour Trilogy'. In *PSAC v Canada* [1987] 1 SCR 424 at issue was the constitutionality of federal legislation that denied the right to strike and the right to bargain collectively to public sector employees for a specified period. In *RWDSU v Saskatchewan* [1987] 1 SCR 460, at issue was 'back-to-work' legislation in the dairy industry. Three years later, in *Professional Institute of the Public Service of Canada v Northwest Territories (Commissioner)* [1990] 2 SCR 367, the Court affirmed that freedom of association does not include a right to bargain collectively.

At issue in the *Alberta Reference* was the constitutionality of several provincial statutes that banned strikes by, and imposed compulsory arbitration on, public service employees, firefighters, hospital employees and police officers in Alberta. The plurality decision by LeDain J held that freedom of association only protects the ability to establish, belong to and maintain an association, and to participate in its lawful activities, not freedom to bargain collectively or strike. In a concurring judgment, McIntyre J held that freedom of association includes the ability to carry out collectively those activities which are lawful for the individual, but not activities which cannot be performed by an individual. Even if such activities are essential to the purposes of the organisation, they cannot come within the scope of freedom of association since a group can only possess the same rights as its individual members. Because there is no individual analogue to striking or bargaining collectively, according to McIntyre J, these actions are not protected as of constitutional right.

In a dissent that has recently received renewed judicial attention, Dickson CJ in the *Alberta Reference* rejected the notion that only those activities which can be performed by individuals fall within the scope of section 2(d). He argued that freedom of association should also protect activities that possess no individual analogue, because of their uniquely social quality. In Dickson CJ's view, freedom of association recognises:

> the profoundly social nature of human endeavours [protects] the individual from State-enforced isolation in the pursuit of his or her ends [and is a vital means of] protecting the essential needs and interests of working people.[72]

Several years later, in *Dunmore v Ontario*,[73] the Court was provided with an opportunity to revisit the normative foundations of its majority opinion in the *Alberta Reference*. At issue in *Dunmore* was the constitutionality of a statutory provision excluding agricultural workers from the protection of a provincial collective bargaining regime. The effect of the exclusion was to render it virtually impossible for agricultural workers to form a union to represent their interests to employers. A majority of the Court, per Bastarache J, held that the collective bargaining regime in question

> provides the only statutory vehicle by which employees in Ontario can associate to defend their interests and, moreover, recognizes that such association is, in many cases, otherwise impossible.

Although the Court was careful to state that freedom of association does not require the state to provide extensive statutory protection of freedom of association, it held that the exclusion from a statutory regime otherwise available to most workers in the province had a chilling effect on the agricultural workers' freedom of association. The Court ordered

---

[72] *Alberta Reference*, above n 44, para 86.
[73] *Dunmore v Ontario (A-G)*, above n 46.

the legislature to provide a statutory framework that secures the right of agricultural workers to form a union and protects freedoms essential to its exercise, such as freedom of assembly, freedom from interference, coercion and discrimination by an employer, and freedom to make lawful representations and participate in the lawful activities of a union.

In so holding, Bastarache J accepted the account of freedom of association offered by Dickson CJ in his dissenting opinion in the *Alberta Reference*. In Bastarache J's view, an association of individuals is 'qualitatively' distinct from the individuals who comprise it: individuals associate not simply because there is strength in numbers, but because a collectivity can embody objectives that individuals cannot. Such objectives include aggregating individual interests into collective representations to an employer and federating with other associations. On this account, the purpose of freedom of association is to protect not simply the collective exercise of lawful individual actions but also actions that are uniquely social—precisely because of their uniquely collective nature.

Bastarache J was careful to pay lip-service to the majority holding in the *Alberta Reference*, noting that the right to bargain collectively was not at issue in the case, and that the legislature is not obliged to provide agricultural workers with the full panoply of statutory protections typically associated with a collective bargaining regime. The logic of his reasons, however, extends well beyond the right to form a union. Given the Court's previous holdings that there is no individual analogue to collective bargaining and striking, *Dunmore* suggests that, in some circumstances at least, the Charter guarantee of freedom of association protects collective actions associated with collective bargaining and striking, a proposition that, if accepted by the Court, would effectively implement Article 8 of the ICESCR in the Canadian legal order. It would also render the constitutional protection of interests associated with work consistent with Canada's obligations under the ICCPR and various ILO conventions.[74] Unless and until the judiciary is willing to revisit its holding in the *Alberta Reference* more generally, however, interests associated with Article 8 of the ICESCR other than those relating to the right to organise will not receive protection under the Charter guarantee of freedom of association.

---

[74] Bastarache J himself refers to Convention (No 87) concerning Freedom of Association and Protection of the Right to Organize, 67 UNTS 17; Convention (No 11) concerning the Rights of Association and Combination of Agricultural Workers, 38 UNTS 153; and Convention (No 141) concerning Organizations of Rural Workers and Their Role in Economic and Social Development (ILO Official Bulletin, vol LVIII, 1975, Series A, No 1, 28).

B Social Security

The Court has displayed deep ambivalence about whether the Charter guarantee of the right to security of the person requires the state to provide social security and an adequate standard of living in ways that might effectively implement ICESCR rights to social security (Article 9) and to an adequate standard of living, including rights to adequate food, clothing and housing (Article 11). Initially, the Court was explicitly open-minded. In *Irwin Toy*, it stated that it would be 'precipitous' to exclude 'at this moment in the history of Charter interpretation,' social rights included in the international covenants, such as 'rights to social security, equal pay for equal work, adequate food, clothing and shelter'.[75]

But then as more precise cases dealing with social interests began to be brought to court, the jurisprudence began to shift towards a less accommodating stance. The first major decision was on the constitutionality of the repeal of the CAP itself. Despite the fact that the federal government is under a constitutional commitment to 'providing essential public services of reasonable quality to all Canadians', the Court upheld the repeal of the CAP, arguing that it was a legislative measure that could be unilaterally altered by subsequent legislation. Subsequently, in several lower court decisions, numerous interests associated with social security were held to fall outside the ambit of the Canadian Charter's section 7 guarantee of the right to security of the person.[76]

The Court has since affirmed that the right to security of the person does not include a right to a minimum level of social assistance. In *Gosselin v Québec (Attorney General)*,[77] at issue was the constitutionality of the level of social assistance to welfare recipients in Quebec. The base amount of money payable to recipients under the age of 30 was one-third of that payable to those aged 30 and older unless those under 30 participated in a designated work activity or education programme designed to encourage young people to get job training and enter the labour force.

---

[75] *Irwin Toy*, above n 61, 1003.
[76] Claims rejected include: a claim to protection against public housing eviction without just cause (*Bernard v Dartmouth Housing* (1988) 53 DLR (4th) 81 (NSCA)); a claim to protection against withdrawal of social assistance upon allegation of living with a spouse (*Conrad v Halifax (County)* (1993) 124 NSR 251 (SC)); a claim to a minimum level of social assistance (*Masse v Ontario (Ministry of Community and Social Services)* (1996) 134 DLR (4th) 20 (Div Ct)); a claim against discontinuance of electricity for failure to pay security deposit when not in arrears (*Clark v Peterborough Utilities Comm'n* (1995) 24 OR (3d) 7 (Gen Div)). Lower courts also rejected s 7 claims to the protection of interests relating to health care, including a claim for access to costly HIV/AIDS medication (*Brown v BC (Minister of Health)* (1990) 66 DLR (4th) 444 (BCSC)); a claim to protection against inadequate care for extended care residents of nursing homes (*Ontario Nursing Home Federation v Ontario* (1990) 72 DLR (4th) 166 (Ont HCJ)); and a claim to an additional allowance for provision of full-time home health care services (*Fernandes v Manitoba (Director of Social Service)* (1992) 93 DLR (4th) (Man CA)).
[77] *Gosselin v Québec (A-G)*, above n 61.

Citing an insufficient evidentiary record, a majority of the Court refused to interpret section 7 as the basis of a 'positive state obligation to guarantee adequate living standards'.[78]

Interests associated with social security have received a measure of protection under section 15 of the Charter, which includes rights to equal protection and equal benefit of the law. The judiciary has staked out a relatively progressive orientation to section 15, mixing formal and substantive models to produce a jurisprudence geared towards the amelioration of economic and social disadvantage. Section 15 is said to express constitutional commitments to the equal worth and human dignity of all persons, and the rectification and prevention of discrimination against particular groups suffering from social, political and legal disadvantage.[79] Courts have interpreted the specific right to equal benefit of the law as a 'positive right' and the Charter's overarching equality guarantee 'as a hybrid of sorts, since it is neither purely positive nor purely negative'.[80] In the context of under-inclusive benefit schemes that impose burdens on disadvantaged groups, the Court has authorised extending benefits to groups otherwise denied a benefit by operation of law. In one case, it held that it was discriminatory to exclude those over the age of 65 from receiving unemployment insurance benefits.[81] In another, it held that excluding chronically disabled workers from a workers' compensation scheme violated their equality rights.[82]

To constitute a violation of section 15, however, the Court has held that an exclusion from a social benefits regime must interfere with a person's dignity by reflecting the view that those excluded are less capable or less worthy than others. In *Law v Canada (Minister of Employment and Immigration)*, a 30 year-old woman was denied spousal survivor's benefits under the Canadian Pension Plan (CPP).[83] The CPP establishes the age of 35 as a threshold age to receive benefits for able-bodied surviving spouses. The Court concluded that the regime's differential treatment of younger people does not violate their dignity as the purpose of the regime was to allocate funds to older persons whose ability to overcome need was weakest.[84] Similarly, in *Gosselin*, a majority of the Court held that Quebec's social assistance regime did not impair the dignity of younger people by providing them with significantly less social assistance than it

---

[78] *Ibid* para 82 (McLachlin CJ). The majority left open the possibility that 'one day s 7 may be interpreted to include positive obligations'.

[79] *Eldridge v British Columbia (A-G)* [1997] 3 SCR 624 para 54.

[80] *Schachter v Canada* [1992] 2 SCR 679, 721.

[81] *Tetréault-Gadoury v Canada (Employment and Immigration Commission)* [1991] 1 SCR 22.

[82] *Nova Scotia (Workers' Compensation Board) v Martin* [2003] 2 SCR 504.

[83] [1999] 1 SCR 497.

[84] See also *Granovsky v Canada (Minister of Employment and Immigration)* [2000] 1 SCR 703.

provided to older recipients because it was attempting to create incentives for younger people to enter the labour force.[85]

C Health

Consistent with the right to health enshrined in Article 12 of the ICESCR, the Court has held that the Charter right to security of the person implicitly encompasses a right to health that in certain circumstances prohibits the state from erecting barriers that prevent individuals from obtaining timely medical care. In *R v Morgentaler* the Court held criminal restrictions on abortions, which required a woman to obtain approval from a therapeutic abortion committee of an approved hospital, to be unconstitutional.[86] A majority of the Court held that these requirements restricted access to the procedure and caused delays in treatment, thereby risking the health of women.

Also consistent with Article 12, the right to health implicit in security of the person includes a right to mental health, which in certain circumstances prevents the state from enacting laws which have a serious and profound effect on a person's psychological integrity. State interference with an individual's physical or psychological integrity need not take the form of criminal sanction to constitute a violation of security of the person. Section 7 extends beyond the criminal law context to 'state action which directly engages the justice system and its administration'.[87] The state action in question, however, must be a direct cause of the psychological stress experienced by the individual.[88] The effects of state interference are assessed objectively, with a view to their impact on the psychological integrity of a person of reasonable sensibility. They need not rise to the level of nervous shock or psychiatric illness, but must be greater than ordinary stress or anxiety.[89]

---

[85] *Gosselin*, above n 61. For the argument that 'claims based upon what the Court considers to be universalistic schemes – schemes which are intended to embrace everyone, including the middle class – are more likely to be successful than are claims seeking access to targeted or means-tested plans, where fundamental distinctions between classes, as emphasized by the Court, are built into the very structure of the programme' see D Schneiderman, 'Universality vs Particularity: Litigating Middle Class Values under Section 15' in S Rodgers and S McIntyre (eds), *Diminishing Returns: Inequality and the Canadian Charter of Rights and Freedoms* (Markham, LexisNexis Butterworths, 2006).

[86] [1988] 1 SCR 30.

[87] *Blencoe v British Columbia (Human Rights Commission)* [2002] SCR 307; *Winnipeg Child and Family Services v KLW* [2000] 2 SCR 519; *New Brunswick (Minister of Health and Community Services) v G (J)* [1999] 3 SCR 46; *B (R) v Children's Aid Society of Metropolitan Toronto*, above n 45; *Reference re ss 193 and 195.1(1)(c) of the Criminal Code (Man)* [1990] 1 SCR 1123.

[88] *Ibid.*

[89] *R v O'Connor*, above n 60; *New Brunswick (Minister of Health and Community Services) v G (J)*, above n 87, 49.

In *Chaoulli v Quebec* the Court was asked to determine whether a provincial law prohibiting individuals from purchasing private health care insurance amounts to a violation of the Charter right to security of the person.[90] At issue in *Chaoulli* was the constitutionality of Quebec legislation prohibiting individuals from purchasing private health insurance to cover services provided by physicians who are not participating in the province's publicly funded health care system when those same services are covered by the public system.[91] A majority of the Court, per Deschamps J, held that the prohibition violates section 1 of the Quebec Charter, which guarantees to 'every human being' the rights to life and personal security. Displaying no deference to the institutional competence of Quebec's National Assembly over the appropriate design of health care delivery, Deschamps J found that, in the case of certain surgical procedures in Quebec, delays that are the necessary result of waiting lists increase the patient's risk of mortality or the risk that his or her injuries will become irreparable, and that many patients on non-urgent waiting lists are in pain and cannot fully enjoy any real quality of life.[92] Prohibiting individuals from purchasing private health insurance, according to Deschamps J, effectively precludes them from obtaining medical services from the private sector which would alleviate these harms.

The Court, however, divided evenly on whether the prohibition against private health insurance violates section 7 of the Canadian Charter.[93] McLachlin CJ and Major J (Bastarache J concurring) concluded that the prohibition violated section 7 of the Canadian Charter as well as section 1 of the Quebec Charter. They accepted that the province has an interest in protecting the public health care system, but were of the opinion that the evidence did not establish that the prohibition properly served this purpose, and that the physical and psychological suffering and risk of death that may result from the prohibition outweigh whatever benefit there may be to the system as a whole. In contrast, Binnie and LeBel JJ (Fish J concurring) were of the view that Quebec's public health care system shares the policy objectives of the federal Canada Health Act, and the means adopted by Quebec to implement federal objectives were not arbitrary. To promote access based on need, not wealth, Quebec sought to discourage the growth of private sector delivery of 'insured' services. For

---

[90] *Chaoulli v Quebec (A-G)* [2005] SCJ No 33. For a collection of essays assessing *Chaoulli* from several perspectives, see CM Flood, K Roach and L Sossin (eds), *Access to Care, Access to Justice: The Legal Debate over Private Health Insurance in Canada* (Toronto, University of Toronto Press, 2005).

[91] *Chaoulli v Quebec (A-G), ibid.*

[92] The unwillingness to defer on institutional competence grounds is especially remarkable given the prominent role that institutional competence concerns have played in the Court's overall jurisprudence on social interests and the Charter. For a comprehensive overview and critique, see D Wiseman, 'Competence Concerns in Charter Adjudication: Countering the Anti-Poverty Incompetence Argument' (2006) 51:2 *McGill Law Journal* 503–46.

[93] Deschamps J expressed no opinion on s 7 of the Canadian Charter.

this reason, they regarded the prohibition as rationally connected to the system's objective and they deferred to the legislature on the appropriate means of accomplishing this objective.

The Court has also sent mixed signals about the extent to which interests relating to health receive constitutional protection under the Charter's equality guarantee. In one case, *Eldridge v BC*, the Court held that equality required the provision of interpreter services for hearing impaired patients in the context of a provincial health care system.[94] Yet, five years later, in *Auton v BC*, the Court held that British Columbia's refusal to fund certain forms of therapy for children with autism was not discrimination based on disability.[95] The Court distinguished its earlier ruling in *Eldridge* on the basis that the failure to provide interpreter services resulted in the deaf population receiving inferior medical care compared to what the hearing population received whereas in *Auton* at issue was a decision not to provide a particular medical service to a particular class of persons.

Constitutional interpretation of interests associated with Article 12 of the ICESCR has thus focused on the negative obligation that security of the person imposes on the state to not erect barriers that prevent individuals from exercising freedom of contract to obtain timely medical care. The judiciary has occasionally required the state, when it decides to exercise legislative authority in an effort to protect interests associated with health, to do so in a manner that is consistent with the Charter's commitment to equality. But it has to date refused to accept the proposition that the state is under a positive obligation to address inequalities of access produced by market power itself.[96]

V CONCLUSION

The implementation of international social rights in Canada occurs through an opaque matrix of interdependent institutional roles and political and juridical possibilities. On the political plane, democratic contestation occurs in multiple jurisdictions over the appropriate relationship between market and state in relation to social protection, which results in jurisdictional variations in levels of protection over time and creates incentives on each level of government to attempt to locate the

---

[94] *Eldridge et al v British Columbia (A-G) et al*, above n 79.

[95] *Auton (Guardian ad litem of) v British Columbia (A-G)* [2004] 3 SCR 657.

[96] The ICESCR is neutral on whether a market is an appropriate regulatory instrument to secure the right to health: CESCR, *The Nature of States Parties Obligations, General Comment No 3* (14 December 1990) ('in terms of political and economic systems the Covenant is neutral and its principles cannot accurately be described as being predicated exclusively upon the need for, or the desirability of a socialist or a capitalist system, or a mixed, centrally planned, or *laisser-faire* economy, or upon any other particular approach').

responsibility of social protection in the other. Legislative outcomes that have the effect of implementing social rights enshrined in the ICESCR relating to work, social security and health do so more by coincidence than by design. On the juridical plane, constitutional interpretation influences not only the political spaces where contestation over social protection occurs but also its very terms. To date, interests associated with international social rights possess constitutional significance in terms that distance the state from social and economic inequality produced by market ordering, and downplay the domestic significance of Canada's international legal obligations under the ICESCR.

11

Social Citizenship

The Neglected Aspect of Israeli Constitutional Law

DAPHNE BARAK-EREZ AND AEYAL M GROSS*

I BACKGROUND: INCREMENTAL CONSTITUTIONAL DEVELOPMENT FROM AN UNWRITTEN CONSTITUTION TO A WRITTEN CONSTITUTION

The legal protection afforded to social citizenship[1] in Israel should be assessed within the more general framework of the recognition and protection of human rights in Israeli constitutional law. For more than forty years after its establishment as a state, Israel lacked constitutional provisions for the protection of human rights, due to social and political disagreements concerning the contents of a future constitution. A political compromise struck in 1950 promised the gradual formulation of Israel's constitution through a process of enacting basic laws that eventually would be consolidated into a full constitution. But until 1992 the existing basic laws had dealt only with the institutional aspects of this constitution and did not include a bill of rights. Thus Israeli constitutional jurisprudence on human rights was based on an unwritten, or judicial, bill of rights developed by the Supreme Court. The rulings that recognised this bill of rights articulated the rights as deriving from the general principles of the Israeli legal system as well as being inspired by the Israeli Declaration of Independence.[2] This method enabled the recognition of a wide range of constitutional rights but, at the same time, judicial review was limited to administrative actions and could not be applied to

* The authors would like to thank Magi Otsri for her assistance and Dana Rothman-Meshulam for her excellent editing work.
1 For the concept of social citizenship, see TH Marshall, 'Citizenship and Social Class' in TH Marshall, *Class, Citizenship and Social Development* (New York, Doubleday, 1964) 71.
2 See D Barak-Erez, 'From an Unwritten to a Written Constitution: The Israeli Challenge in American Perspective' (1995) 26 *Columbia Human Rights Law Review* 309; A Gross, 'The Politics of Rights in Israeli Constitutional Law' (1998) 3 *Israel Studies* 80.

primary legislation.[3] With regard to the latter, the unwritten bill of rights was regarded as having only interpretative force.

The Supreme Court case law that set forth the judicial bill of rights dealt mostly with civil and political rights. The Court played an important role in the recognition of these rights, especially in the early days of the state when, under the Zionist collectivist ideology, the tradition of liberalism was not well-entrenched, on the one hand, while the legislative and executive protection of social rights was broad, on the other hand. Thus judicial recognition of civil and political rights played a crucial role, given the lack of constitutional or statutory text protecting these rights; social rights, in contrast, were mostly maintained not through a rights mechanism but, rather, by way of the legislation and practices that established them.

II THE BASIC LAWS ON HUMAN RIGHTS AND THE NEGLECTED STATUS OF SOCIAL RIGHTS

In 1992, as part of the slow, ongoing constitutional project, the Knesset (Israeli Parliament) passed two basic laws on human rights, Basic Law: Human Dignity and Liberty and Basic Law: Freedom of Occupation. These were originally intended to be the first of a series of basic laws dealing with human rights. The gradual approach to the enactment of basic laws was also supposed to be applied to the process of formulating a bill of rights, with the intention to initially enact only basic laws addressing relatively less controversial human rights and then to incorporate at a later stage rights that are more contentious in the Israeli context.[4] Consequently, Basic Law: Human Dignity and Liberty recognises the right to human dignity and liberty, the right to life and physical integrity, the right to property, the right to privacy and the right to freedom of movement, while Basic Law: Freedom of Occupation guarantees the right to freedom of occupation, traditionally understood in Israeli law as protecting a person's autonomy to choose his or her profession. These two laws were expected to be supplemented by other basic laws, which would encompass more rights. However, the controversy that has emerged around the interpretation of the 1992 Basic Laws and the Supreme Court's review of primary legislation led

---

[3] The only exception to this principle was the availability of judicial review of statutes violating specifically entrenched clauses in the basic laws that dealt with the institutional structure of government. See HCJ 98/69 *Bergman v Minister of Finance* [1969] 23(1) PD 693.

[4] The rights considered controversial were mainly freedom of religion (especially with regard to the application of religious law in matters of marriage and divorce), freedom of expression (with regard to issues such as military censorship) and equality (an issue bearing on both family law and the rights of Israeli Arabs).

to the suspension of the legislation process for other basic laws, and it is doubtful that they will be enacted in the foreseeable future.[5]

III SOCIAL RIGHTS AND QUESTIONS OF CONSTITUTIONAL INTERPRETATION

One of the most significant outcomes of the enactment of the 1992 basic laws was the formation of a two-tiered system of rights. On the one hand, those rights recognised as falling within the scope of the basic laws were now considered of a higher constitutional status and therefore primary legislation affecting those rights became subject to judicial review. On the other hand, other rights, those remaining unwritten and part of the judicial bill of rights, were relegated to secondary status and not protected by judicial review. In other words, the post-1992 constitutional order redefined the contours of the constitutional discourse, with a sharp divide set between rights elevated by the basic laws to the status of supremacy and rights excluded from that status. Thus the question of the interpretation of the basic laws and, especially, the broad and vague right to human dignity became critical. In the context of protecting social rights, the issue was whether the concept of human dignity would be interpreted as incorporating notions of social justice. This has become even more urgent with the gradual adoption over the years of economic policies that cherish competition and restrict social entitlements. The pressures of globalisation, coupled with the particular burdens inherent in the Israeli economy, and the dominance of neo-liberal ideology in the political world have led to significant cuts in social benefits and subsidies to the weaker sectors of the population.

In practice, while the concept of human dignity is sufficiently open-textured to accommodate not only civil and political rights not expressly mentioned in the basic laws but also social rights bearing on human dignity, its hegemonic interpretation by the Supreme Court has shown a bias in favour of civil and political rights. The first prominent writings to address the interpretation of the new basic laws and to suggest that the right to human dignity may serve as a vehicle for rights not enumerated therein were written by none other than Aharon Barak, at the time one of the most influential Supreme Court justices and later the Chief Justice. In a series of articles on the basic laws, Barak suggested that the right to human dignity should be interpreted as encompassing a full set of civil and political rights understood as intertwined with the concept of dignity, including equality, freedom of speech, freedom of religion, freedom

---

[5] For the background to the 1992 basic laws and a detailed discussion of their status, see Barak-Erez, above n 2, and Gross, above n 2.

of art and freedom of association. In Barak's view, at the foundation of Basic Law: Human Dignity and Liberty lies a vision of free individuals. Accordingly, to his understanding, the concept of human dignity includes a protection of the autonomy of free will, and therefore freedom of contract also falls within its scope.[6] Thus, ultimately, Barak's interpretation of the right to human dignity effectively incorporates many civil and even economic rights not expressly mentioned in the two basic laws.

At the same time, the former Chief Justice's conception of the right to human dignity has been less prone to include social rights. Originally, when he first introduced his concept of human dignity, his index of 'non-enumerated' rights did not seem to include any social rights. In later writings, sensitive to criticism of his original position,[7] Barak did, in fact, refer to a right to a minimum material and mental existence as falling within the scope of the right to human dignity. However, this recognition was limited to what are regarded as minimal conditions of existence and did not extend to other social rights, such as the rights to education, health and social welfare.[8] According to Barak, the rights that can be inferred from this minimum approach to the social aspect of human dignity are the rights to temporary shelter, freedom from starvation and access to basic medical care.[9] Barak stressed that he does not dispute the importance of social rights, but merely believes that their recognition must derive from future laws enacted by the Knesset.

IV RIVAL VIEWS IN THE SUPREME COURT'S EARLY JUDGMENTS ON SOCIAL RIGHTS

Early Supreme Court case law on social rights that followed the enactment of the 1992 basic laws reflected the uncertainty that reigned regarding the status of these rights in Israeli constitutional law. In its judgments, the Supreme Court swung from complete rejection of recognition for social rights to stances supporting a certain degree of recognition.

One approach was to reject the idea of constitutional social rights for as long as they are not explicitly recognised in a basic law. The leading judgment representing this line of reasoning was *GILAT*, which dealt with a petition brought against a government decision to stop the funding for

---

[6] A Barak, 'Protected Human Rights: Scope and Limitations' (1993) 1 *Law and Government* 253, 261 [Hebrew].

[7] Concern about Barak's interpretation was first expressed by R Ben-Israel, 'The Effect of the Basic Laws on Labor Law and the Labor Relations System' (1994) 4 *Labor Law Yearbook* 27 [Hebrew].

[8] A Barak, 'Human Dignity as a Constitutional Right' (1994) 41 *Hapraklit* 271, 285 [Hebrew].

[9] A Barak, 'Introduction' in A Barak and H Berenson (eds), *Berenson Book, Volume 2* (Jerusalem, Nevo, 2000) 7–8 [Hebrew].

an education programme for children from underprivileged socio-economic backgrounds. Not only did the Court reject the petition, it also stated, in the majority opinion delivered by Justice Orr, that the right to education cannot be recognised as a constitutional right since it has no foundation in Basic Law: Human Dignity and Liberty.[10] This decision exemplifies the Court's initial tendency to exclude social rights. The petition here revolved around an administrative decision about funding and did not require judicial review of any primary legislation. Thus, as a matter of fact, the Court was not required to invoke the basic laws in the particular circumstances of the case. The petition could have been deliberated in light of an unwritten right to education falling outside the scope of Basic Law: Human Dignity and Liberty but rooted in the Court's tradition of a judicial bill of rights. The Court's judgment, however, failed to distinguish between the question of recognising a right to education in the framework of Israel's unwritten constitution and the question of recognising this right as falling within the scope of the concept of human dignity entrenched in Basic Law: Human Dignity and Liberty. Instead, the Court rejected any notion of a constitutional protection for the right to education as long as it was not specifically recognised by a basic law.[11]

At the same time, another stream in the case law reflected a more positive approach to social rights and social justice. Justice Zamir's dictum in *Kontram*[12] is considered an important contribution to the emergence of social rights in the Supreme Court case law, although it did not directly address the issue. In his opinion, Justice Zamir expressed the view that the state bears a duty to care for its citizens (and, hence, there is a corresponding duty on the part of citizens to act fairly towards the state). In this context, he emphasised the state's role in providing for the well-being of its citizens. Zamir's dictum stated that human rights must not serve the 'satiated person' alone, but should protect all people so that they enjoy de facto and not only de jure human rights.[13] In *Chalamish*,[14] Justice Dorner gave a more concrete support for the view that the right to human dignity encompasses the right to social security. In this case, the petitioner, an Israeli citizen residing abroad, was claiming entitlement to social security

[10] HCJ 1554/95 *Friends of GILAT v Minister of Education* [1996] 50(3) PD 2.
[11] At the same time, it is important to note that, formally speaking, since the dictum on the constitutional status of the right to education was not necessary for the decision, it is possible to argue that it does not constitute binding precedent. Moreover, the two other justices presiding in the case who concurred with the result did not express any stance on this specific matter. In fact, when the Supreme Court was asked to apply to the case its special power to hold a further hearing in a matter dealing with new and controversial legal issues, it declined to do so, explaining that the *GILAT* case did not constitute a precedent in this particular matter. See FH 5456/96 *Itzhak v Minister of Education* (unpublished, 27 November 1996).
[12] HCJ 164/97 *Kontram Inc v Treasury Ministry, Israeli Dep't Customs & VAT* [1998] 52(1) PD 289.
[13] *Ibid* 339–41.
[14] HCJ 890/99 *Chalamish v National Security Institute* [2000] 54(4) PD 423.

payments regardless of his foreign residence. Justice Dorner accepted the petition to the extent that the authorities were ordered to consider a request to enact new regulations in the matter of the social security rights of former residents. However, when the authorities decided, after due consideration, not to expand the entitlement to social security to citizens no longer residing in the country, the Supreme Court refrained from intervening, finding this decision to be reasonable in the circumstances of Israel's economy.[15] As a result, in the end, Justice Dorner's *Chalamish* dictum, like Justice Zamir's dictum in *Kontram*, took on a merely declaratory significance.

The dominant proposition that eventually emerged was the revised view advanced by Barak, which limited the constitutional recognition of social rights to the protection of a minimum level of existence.[16] One of the leading authoritative decisions advancing this position is the *Gamzu* judgment.[17] In *Gamzu* the Court deliberated on a petition brought by a man ordered to pay his alimony and child support debts to his estranged wife and daughter, which he had failed to pay for a number of years. The Court accepted the husband's argument that his right to human dignity and basic human existence should play a role in determining how to spread out the payment of the debt. Justice Barak discussed the necessity of protecting the debtor's human dignity, given his lack of means:

> Human dignity includes... protection of the minimum of human existence... a person living outdoors who has no housing is a person whose dignity has been violated; a person hungry for bread is a person whose dignity as a person has been violated; a person who does not have access to rudimentary medical service is a person whose dignity as a person has been violated; a person who has to live in humiliating physical conditions is a person whose dignity as a person has been violated... this is the case with the dignity of every person; this is the case with the dignity of a debtor who cannot pay his... alimony debt.[18]

Thus the wife's right to alimony and her daughter's right to child support had to be balanced against the need to ensure a minimum standard of living for the estranged husband and father. Accordingly, the Court instructed that the payment of the debt be spread out over a period of time in a way that would ensure respect for the debtor's right to human dignity.

Gamzu was understood by some to be a landmark decision in the protection of social rights. At the same time, it embraced only the minimum approach to social rights, which replaced the former approach

---

[15] HCJ 8313/02 *Eisen v National Security Institute* [2004] 58(6) PD 607. A request for a further hearing in the matter was denied in HCJ 7873/04 *Eisen v National Security Institute* (decision of 19 January 2005).

[16] HCJ 161/94 *Atri v State of Israel* (unpublished, 3 January 1994); CA 7038/93 *Solomon v Solomon* [1995] 51(2) PD 577.

[17] RCA 4905/98 *Gamzu v Yeshaiahu* [2001] 55(3) PD 360.

[18] *Ibid* 375–76.

espousing absolute lack of recognition. In this decision, the Supreme Court did not mention a right to an adequate standard of living and limited its examples to cases in which social rights would be denied in an absolute manner. In addition, the judgment recognised and enforced the right to a minimum level of existence in the context of litigation between private parties and therefore did not address one of the main difficulties entailed in winning recognition for social rights: imposing positive duties on the state. Therefore, although *Gamzu* opened the door to a certain degree of constitutional recognition of social rights, it did so only in a very restricted way, leaving them the 'poor relatives' of civil and political rights.[19]

V THE DEROGATION OF SOCIAL RIGHTS IN LEGISLATION AND THE LIMITS OF JUDICIAL REVIEW

The implications of the minimum approach to social rights became apparent in a few significant cases in which petitioners challenged legislation that derogated from social entitlements. The legislative amendments reviewed in these cases reflected social processes transpiring in Israel that had weakened the legal protection of welfare rights: the erosion of the Israeli welfare state, the privatisation of social services and the waning commitment to provide for disempowered citizens. Against this political and economic background, the safety net that social rights can potentially provide has become especially crucial. In practice, however, the relegation of social rights to a second-class status, excluded from the scope of the constitutional right to human dignity, has reinforced these processes rather than serving as a check on them.

More specifically, the petitions raising the issue of social rights deliberated by the Supreme Court in the early 2000s concerned cuts in welfare programmes. The government countered these petitions with the claim that the Court should not intervene in issues of policy and budget allocation. The social rights issue thus became a bone of contention in the debate over the Court's institutional competence. The Court responded to this by adhering to the minimum approach to the constitutional protection of social rights and rejecting the petitions. In addition to the controversy surrounding the scope of the concept of human dignity, the judicial failure to intervene in these cases can also be explained against the background of the Court's tendency to show greater deference when reviewing primary legislation as opposed to administrative decisions and policies.

---

[19] Other concerns involved in this case related to the adequateness of the protection given to the social rights of a man who failed to provide for his wife and daughter at their expense. For more elaborate critical evaluation of these precedents, see Y Shany and Y Rabin, 'The Israeli Unfinished Constitutional Revolution: Has the Time Come for Protecting Economic and Social Rights?' (2003–2004) 37 *Israel Law Review* 299.

One prominent example is *Manor*,[20] which involved a petition against a cut in social security payments to senior citizens. The petitioners challenged the constitutionality of this cut, arguing that it infringed the right to live in human dignity, the right to social security and the right to property. While the Court did concede that the right to a minimum level of living conditions does fall within the scope of human dignity,[21] it nonetheless dismissed the petition. According to Justice Barak, the petitioners had not succeeded in showing that this right had, indeed, been infringed, given that there had been no cuts in the payments to senior citizens eligible for state-provided income support. Barak was even willing to accept the argument that eligibility for social security payments is a property right that must not be infringed, but added that, in the circumstances of the case, the particular curtailment of the right did conform with the constitutional standards for restricting rights. The other two justices on the panel, Justice Grunis and Justice Rivlin, concurred with the result but refrained from ruling on whether the right to social security should be recognised as a property right.

One year later the parameters of the constitutional protection of human existence in dignity were considered by the Court in a petition that led to the setting of what is still the main precedent in the area of social rights, namely, the *Commitment to Peace and Social Justice Association* judgment,[22] which was decided by an enlarged panel of seven justices. This petition sought to challenge the constitutionality of significant reductions in the level of state income support, which had led to an average reduction in excess of 30 per cent in the level of income support. In addition, some of the benefits and subsidies received by those eligible to income support had been revoked, including discounts on public transportation and exemptions from television and radio fees. The petition rested on the argument that these changes had violated the social component of the constitutional right to dignity. More specifically, the petitioners argued that these cuts had infringed their right to live with dignity. The state, in turn, argued that the cuts had not infringed the constitutional right to live with dignity. Furthermore, it contended that other forms of support provided by the government to the public should be taken into account in the determination of this matter, which should not be based solely on the level of direct payments made in the form of income support.

The majority opinion, delivered by Justice Barak, was based on the same principles that had informed his previous judgments on social rights. Barak stated that the right to human dignity encompasses also a positive right to a minimum level of living, but no more than that. He accepted the

---

[20] HCJ 5587/02 *Manor v Treasury Minister* [2004] 59(1) PD 729.
[21] *Ibid* 736.
[22] HCJ 888, 366/03 *Commitment to Peace & Social Justice Association v Minister of Finance* (decision from 12 December 2005).

state's argument that the right to human dignity is activated only in cases of a material deficiency that prevents a person from subsisting. Accordingly, Barak asserted that it is the state's duty to act in a way that guarantees a safety net which ensures that all people have the sustenance necessary for existence, a place of residence where they can realise their privacy and family life, adequate sanitary conditions and medical services providing access to modern medical facilities. With this definition of the right to human dignity, Barak determined that the petitioners had not met the burden of proof and had failed to show that their rights had been infringed as a result of the reductions in the level of income support, since they had not demonstrated that the state had failed to provide their basic needs at a minimum level. The cut in the income support allowances was not, in itself, a sufficient proof of a violation of the right, because injury to human dignity must be considered in view of the entirety of a person's life conditions and, in the case at hand, the Court had not been presented with sufficient facts to indicate that this right had been violated. While this majority decision did leave the door open to the possibility of someone proving that the state did not ensure him or her the minimal conditions of existence and being awarded a court remedy, it nonetheless attached an exceedingly high burden of proof to any such claim. In addition, it seems unlikely that such individual proceedings could be conducted successfully by disempowered individuals who are burdened with a day-to-day struggle for subsistence. One of the concurring justices, Justice Beinish, who later replaced Barak as Chief Justice, expressed a view more lenient towards potential petitioners in terms of the standard of proof they would have to meet in order to shift the burden onto the state to prove the constitutionality of the legislation in question. In the circumstances of the *Commitment to Peace and Social Justice Association* case, however, Justice Beinish concurred with the majority opinion written by Barak.

A dissenting opinion rendered by Justice Levi in this same case took a very different stance. Levi's view was that the right to human dignity should be interpreted as including a right to adequate conditions of living, as opposed to the minimum approach advocated by Barak. On the facts, Levi was convinced that the data provided by the petitioners proved that the legislative measures in question had violated the right to human dignity. He cited an affidavit submitted to the Court by one of the petitioners that showed how the reduced allowance combined with her other source of income (child allowances) did not cover the cost of her most basic needs. He considered the state's response unsatisfactory because it did not prove, or even attempt to prove, the existence of a safety net that could assure the ability of people with no income to sustain life with dignity.

The importance of the *Commitment to Peace and Social Justice Association* decision cannot be overstated. It is extremely telling of the state of social rights in Israeli law, demonstrating that the rhetoric of social rights is already an integral part of the concept of human rights law in Israel but, at the same time, exposing the different attitudes to these rights in both theory and practice. To begin with, the recognition of these rights as included within the concept of human dignity is limited to the minimum approach. Second, the Supreme Court has adopted a clear policy of extreme restraint with regard to enforcing social rights when there is a clash with legislation that was enacted as a central element in the implementation of government policy. Finally, this case illustrates the discrepancy between the dominant stance, which recognises only a minimal right to exist in human dignity, as expressed by the majority justices, and the dissenting position, which does not relegate social rights to a minimum status and, instead, adopts the idea of adequate standards of living as part of the right to human dignity that should be protected by the Court.[23]

VI   EQUALITY AND SOCIAL RIGHTS

Another possible source of protection for social rights in some contexts has been the principle of equality, traditionally associated with the protection of civil and political rights but, in fact, also important vis-à-vis the equal distribution of social benefits and protections. In *Botzer*[24] the Supreme Court held that schools must make modifications to allow children with disabilities to integrate into the education system on an equal basis, thereby according extensive protection to the social rights of the disabled. In *Danilowitz*,[25] which revolved around the prohibition on discrimination

---

[23] For another case in which the Court refused to intervene in legislation that infringed existing rights, see HCJ 494/03 *Physicians for Human Rights – Israel v Treasury Minister* [2004] 59(3) PD 322. The petition in this case was brought against a legislative amendment aimed at narrowing the definition of the term 'resident' for the purposes of certain social rights entitlements. The new definition was based on a formal test of holding the required visa. The petitioners argued that this amendment had stripped certain people of rights, those who had previously been considered residents because of their attachment to Israel, even though they had not been issued the necessary visa. Accordingly, the constitutional argument made by the petitioners was that the amendment infringed the rights of these de facto residents to social security, understood as part of their constitutional right to human dignity. The petition was dismissed, with Justice Barak ruling that, in general, residency criteria are warranted because they guarantee equality and conserve public resources. More specifically, Barak clarified that not all the entitlements ingrained in current welfare legislation are covered by the constitutional right to social security. In a similar vein, to the extent that the petition was based on the right to health, Barak added that only certain aspects of this right are protected under the right to human dignity. Other limited aspects of the right to health may be protected as part of the right to the protection of the body, but no more than that. At any rate, according to Barak, the right to health does not necessarily mandate an entitlement to be covered by the national medical insurance.

[24] HCJ 7081/93 *Botzer v Macabim-Reut Local Council* [1996] 50(1) PD 19.

[25] HCJ 721/94 *El-Al Israel Airlines v Danilowitz* [1994] 48(5) PD 749.

based on sexual orientation,[26] the Court held that, pursuant to the Equal Employment Opportunities Law from 1988, employers must extend to the same-sex partners of their employees the same spousal benefits offered to different-sex partners.

It is noteworthy, however, that these precedents are limited to cases of deliberate exclusion of groups and are based on opposition to discrimination based on civil, not socio-economic, status. In general, Israeli law does not conceive of poverty as a possible ground for discrimination, although it does, in certain circumstances, leave room for overturning distinctions based on economic ability. In one case the Supreme Court indicated that it might overrule an administrative decision to limit services provided to paying customers only with regard to vital services and when it is impossible for the poor to meet the payment conditions.[27] Potentially, this line of reasoning could have led to effective protection of rights in the social sphere, especially given that the right to equality is usually considered to be encompassed in the constitutional right to human dignity.[28] However, when this issue did arise before the Court in a matter relating to the right to health, it refused to intervene. The particular case involved a woman who was gradually going deaf and an operation to install a cochlear implant in her ear could have saved her hearing. This operation was included in the basket of services provided under Israel's national health insurance scheme, but was subject to a 70 per cent contribution by the patient, which, in this case, amounted to 70,000 NIS (about US$15,500). The petitioner was a teacher and a single parent, earning a low salary with which she could barely care for her family. Her petition was grounded not only on the right to health but also on the right to equality as part of the right to human dignity. The Court, however, refused to intervene, citing the fact that the matter had been considered carefully by the committee authorised to determine the scope of the state-funded health services.[29] It should be noted that, although the petitioner was not

---

[26] For a more detailed discussion of this case, see A Gross, 'Challenges to Compulsory Heterosexuality: Recognition and Non-Recognition of Same-Sex Couples in Israeli Law' in R Wintemute and M Andenas (eds), *Legal Recognition of Same-Sex Partnerships: A Study of National, European and International Law* (Oxford, Hart Publishing, 2001) 391.

[27] HCJ 5394/92 *Hupert v Yad Vashem Memorial Authority* [1994] 48(3) PD 353, 366.

[28] This broad interpretation was suggested by then-Chief Justice Aharon Barak and has gradually gained support. The argument that the right to equality should be inferred from the right to human dignity was eventually adopted by the Supreme Court in HCJ 6427/02 *Movement for Quality Government in Israel v Knesset* (decision from 11 May 2006) and HCJ 7052/03 *Adalah – The Legal Center for Arab Minority Rights v Minister of Interior* (decision from 14 May 2006).

[29] HCJ 2974/06 *Israeli v Committee for the Expansion of the Health Basket* (unpublished, 11 July 2006). This decision can be contrasted with a judgment in which the Supreme Court held that conditioning a demonstration permit on the financing of the expenses of the demonstration's security by its organisers is illegal as it violates the right to freedom of speech: HCJ 2557/05 *Majority Headquarters v Israeli Police* (decision of 12 December 2006). Both cases involved a governmental fee imposed on people wishing to exercise a right. However,

awarded any remedy in this case, the litigation did constitute part of a process that drew attention to the problem of the high patient contribution for this type of operation, which was eventually cancelled by the government.[30]

VII THE RIGHT TO EDUCATION AND THE EVOLVING OPENNESS TOWARDS SOCIAL RIGHTS

In contrast to the path taken by the body of case law described above, other Supreme Court decisions have shown greater openness towards the constitutional protection of social rights. The Court's willingness to accept petitions in matters invoking social rights has been apparent mostly in the context of the judicial review of administrative, rather than legislative, actions. This has been especially so in the context of the right to education, reflecting perhaps the wider consensus within Israeli society regarding the importance of public education.

The leading precedent in this line of case law is *YATED*.[31] Justice Dorner, delivering the Court opinion, recognised the right to education as a basic human right, inspired by and referring to international conventions and constitutional documents from other countries. The approach adopted by Dorner in this case by-stepped the question of whether or not the right to education is included in the right to human dignity and, thus, protected by Basic Law: Human Dignity and Liberty. Because the case involved the review of an administrative and not a legislative action, the Court was able to invoke its unwritten judicial bill of rights and thereby avoid the issue of the scope of the constitutional right to human dignity and refrain from taking a stand on Justice Orr's position in *GILAT*. In *YATED*, the petitioners argued for the right of children with Down's syndrome to receive government assistance for their integration into the regular education system and not merely for special education programmes. The Supreme Court ruled in the petitioners' favour, based on both the general right to education as well as the provisions of the Special Education Law from 1988, which recognises the right of children with disabilities to be integrated into the regular education system. The Court held that the state budget for the ensuing year should take into account the right of children with special needs to be thus integrated. Following this decision, the Knesset amended the Law, giving more express recognition to this right of disabled children to be integrated into the regular education system.

whereas in the context of the right to freedom of speech, such a fee was considered as illegally violating this right, the Court refused to make such a determination in the context of the right to health.

[30] Government Decision 406, 27 August 2006.
[31] HCJ 2599/00 *YATED v Ministry of Education* [2002] 56(5) PD 834.

However, despite the amendment, the Ministry of Finance did not increase the budget designated for integration purposes, forcing the petitioners to bring the matter to the Supreme Court once again. They prevailed the second time as well, with the Court ruling that the law must be interpreted in light of the state's duty to provide education to all its citizens, in accordance with principles of equality and the basic right to education.[32] The recurrence of cases dealing with this matter demonstrates, however, that legal victories do not necessarily lead to actual changes in bureaucratic schemes founded on opposing policies.[33] The Court has invoked the right to education in other cases, as well, when reviewing administrative actions.[34] However, none of its rulings in this matter have challenged the growing inequalities in education in Israel between the rich and poor due to various mechanisms of silent privatisation and the increasing disparities between different municipalities.[35]

Beyond the context of the right to education, there is another significant area in which the Court has intervened to protect social rights while reviewing an administrative action. In the important *Worker Line* case,[36] the Supreme Court accepted a petition challenging the policy of conditioning the work visas issued to foreign citizens on working only for the employer involved in their original arrival in the country. This policy enabled local employers to exploit their foreign workers, who could not leave their positions without losing their visas. The Court's decision in favour of the petition was very significant in terms of securing social rights for work immigrants in Israel. At the same time, it is important to note that the rights underlying the decision were classical liberal rights: individual freedom, human dignity and freedom of occupation. In this case, the Court was called upon to protect people from government regulation that restricted their mobility between employers, something that falls within the paradigm of its case law on freedom of occupation.

---

[32] HCJ 6973/03 *Marzianno v Ministry of Finance* [2003] 58(2) PD 270. A request for a further hearing in the matter was denied in HCJ 247/04 *Ministry of Finance v Marzianno* (decision from 10 May 2004).

[33] For this argument, see D Barak-Erez, 'The Israeli Welfare State: Growing Expectations and Diminishing Returns' in E Benvenisti and G Nolte (eds), *The Welfare State, Globalization and International Law* (Berlin, Springer, 2004) 103.

[34] See, eg, HCJ 7374/01 *Anonymous v Director of the Ministry of Education* [2003] 57(6) PD 529, where the state was required to fund the transfer of a child to another school when the child experienced acute social problems in the original school.

[35] See Y Blank, 'Decentralized National Education: Local Government, Segregation, and Inequality in the Public Education System' (2004) 28 *Tel Aviv University Law Review* 347 [Hebrew]; Y Blank, 'Brown in Jerusalem: A Comparative Look on Race and Ethnicity in Public Schools' (2006) 38(3) *The Urban Lawyer* 367.

[36] HCJ 4542/02 *Worker Line Association v Government of Israel* (decision from 30 March 2006).

VIII THE EQUILIBRIUM OF ECONOMIC RIGHTS AND SOCIAL RIGHTS

The discussion thus far has presented the current reality of the relatively weak protection for social rights within the framework of the two existing basic laws on human rights. The flipside of this coin is the significance assigned to economic rights in these basic laws and their interpretation by the Supreme Court. The term 'economic rights' in this context is used to refer to rights that protect the prevailing regime of possessions. Three rights, protected as constitutional rights since 1992 in Basic Law: Human Dignity and Liberty and Basic Law: Freedom of Occupation, form this protection: the rights to property, freedom of contract and freedom of occupation.

A The Right to Property

The right to property is expressly recognised in Section 3 of Basic Law: Human Dignity and Liberty, a provision that has been the subject of several significant Supreme Court decisions.[37] In fact, the precedent that established the possibility of judicial review under the 1992 basic laws involved the right to property. There, Chief Justice Barak interpreted the right to property in a 'possessive' rather than 'distributive' sense; that is, he adopted a conception of the right to property in the sense of 'keeping', ie, maintaining the status quo of holdings, and not in terms of 'having', ie, requiring that every member of society would possess a minimum amount of property.[38] In Barak's opinion, property is infringed upon by legislation when there is a decline in the value of an interest relative to its value prior to the enactment of the given legislation.[39] This would seem to imply a possessive understanding of the right to property. As Frank Michelman argues, property in its possessive (keeping) sense is used as an anti-redistributive principle, opposed to government intervention in the extant regime of holdings toward distributive ends. This understanding, asserts Michelman, is incomplete without a distributive concern regarding property.[40]

Later case law reflects the ongoing controversy within the Supreme Court regarding the scope and meaning of the right to property. Some

---

[37] See also AM Gross, 'Property as a Constitutional Right and Basic Law: Human Dignity and Liberty' (1997) 21 *Tel-Aviv University Law Review* 405 [Hebrew].

[38] CA 6821/93 *United Mizrahi Bank v Midgal Cooperative Village* [1995] 49(4) PD 221. The distinction between the 'possessive' and 'distributive' senses of the right to property is drawn from FI Michelman, 'Possession *v* Distribution in the Constitutional Idea of Property' (1987) 72 *Iowa Law Review* 1319.

[39] *United Mizrahi Bank*, above n 38, 279.

[40] Michelman, above n 38, 1319–20.

decisions have emphasised the protection of ownership in property,[41] whereas others have stressed the importance of distributive justice in administrative decisions that regulate property.[42]

B Freedom of Contract

Freedom of Contract, with its clear economic implications, is not explicitly mentioned in the basic laws, but it is understood as falling within their scope. As noted, Barak has expressed the opinion, in both his academic writings[43] and his judgments,[44] that the right to human dignity includes protection for the autonomy of free will. Under this approach, freedom of contract is a right protected by Basic Law: Human Dignity and Liberty. By viewing the concept of autonomy as the rationale for protecting freedom of contract, Barak appears to adhere to a will-based understanding of contract law, in a sense that could regard any regulation of contractual relationships as infringing on this freedom. From this perspective, laws on standard contracts and consumer rights could be seen as constricting the constitutional right to freedom of contract. Such restriction would not necessarily be deemed unconstitutional limitations of the rights, as they may be found justified and proportionate in accordance with the constitutional standards set in the basic laws. At the same time, it is somewhat troubling to think of the possibility of social legislation of this sort being considered prima facie 'suspect' for its formal infringement of freedom of contract when conceived as a constitutional right.

C Freedom of Occupation

Freedom of Occupation is entrenched in Basic Law: Freedom of Occupation. As part of Israel's judicial bill of rights, freedom of occupation was traditionally interpreted by the Supreme Court as protecting the right of individuals to freely choose a profession or trade and earn a living from that profession or trade.[45] However, the understanding of the scope of this

---

[41] HCJ 2390/96 *Karasik v State of Israel* [2001] 55(2) PD 625.

[42] FH 1333/02 *Raanana Local Planning Committee v Horowitz* [2004] 58(6) PD 289. See also HCJ 3527/96 *Axelbard v Property Tax Administration* [1998] 52(5) PD 385, 489–98, in which Justice Beinish expressed reservations regarding a broad reading of this right in the context of scrutinising tax legislation. Barak himself, in his academic writings, has left open the question of whether the right to property implies maintaining the status quo or whether it should be understood as a means to protect human dignity. See A Barak, 'The Economic Constitution of Israel' (1998) 4 *Law and Government* 357, 368 [Hebrew].

[43] Barak, above n 8.

[44] CA 294/91 *Hevra Kadisha 'Kehilat Yerushalaim' v Kastenbaum* [1992] 46(2) PD 464.

[45] The classical precedent in this matter is HCJ 1/49 *Bajerano v Minister of Police* [1949] 2 PD 80.

right changed over time, and the Supreme Court began to conceive it as also protecting the individual's freedom to engage in a profession of his or her choice without any limitation or regulation, based on the principle of free competition. The enactment of Basic Law: Freedom of Occupation resulted in a constitutional recognition for this interpretation of the right. A possible ramification of this development is that any legislation that regulates the workplace (ie, all labour and protective legislation) will be perceived as violating freedom of occupation,[46] albeit, again, not necessarily to the point of unconstitutionality if the legislation is found to be justified and proportionate in line with the basic law's criteria.[47]

The constitutional recognition of economic rights in the 1992 basic laws has had a cumulative effect, of which Israel's minimum wage law may serve as an example. The possessive interpretation of the right to property, the notion of freedom of contract based on the will theory, and the free-competition understanding of freedom of occupation could render an understanding of a minimum wage law as violating each one of these rights. Thus such a law could be interpreted as intervening in the employer's privilege to manage his or her property as he or she wishes, as violating the right of parties to enter into contracts regarding wages in accordance with their own free will, and as violating the right to engage in one's profession or trade without limitation or regulation.[48] In the event that the Supreme Court does determine that a minimum wage law generates such violations, it will have to scrutinise it according to the criteria set for judicial review in the basic laws. While the legislation may still be 'saved', the starting point for the constitutional discussion will nonetheless be that the laws violate—rather than embody—constitutionally-protected human rights.[49]

---

[46] See the concern expressed by Ruth Ben-Israel that the rights protected in the 1992 basic laws may serve as vehicles for constitutional attacks on existing and future labour legislation in Ben-Israel, above n 6.

[47] For a more detailed discussion, see A Gross, 'How Did "Free Competition" Become a Constitutional Value? Changes in the Meaning of the Right to Freedom of Occupation' (2000) 23 *Tel-Aviv University Law Review* 229 [Hebrew].

[48] The idea that minimum wage legislation violates the right to freedom of occupation has, in fact, been voiced in Israel: see M Goldberg, *Freedom of Occupation and Its Limits* (Tel-Aviv, Sadan, 1999) 167–68. For a critique of this position, see Gross, above n 47, 252.

[49] For a discussion of problems that may arise even if the Court does uphold social legislation but only by virtue of the basic laws' limitations clauses, see Gross, above n 2, 97–8. There is a danger that any development in this direction may serve as an Israeli 'Lochnerization', that is, pull in the direction taken by the US Supreme Court in the early years of the twentieth century in *Lochner v New York* 198 US 45 (1905), when it interpreted the Constitution as imposing the preservation of the existing distribution of wealth and entitlements according to the current baseline. See: C Sunstein, 'Lochner's Legacy' (1987) 87 *Columbia Law Review* 873; L Tribe, *American Constitutional Law* (New York, Foundation Press, 2000) 1343–46; MJ Horowitz, *The Transformation of American Law 1870–1960: The Crisis of Legal Orthodoxy* (New York, Oxford University Press, 1992) 33–63. This interpretation was grounded in an understanding, much criticised by legal realism, of the economic sphere as a private sphere that should remain free of governmental regulation.

The risks described here can be prevented by certain interpretive moves: the Supreme Court can interpret the right to property as a distributive right, abstain from reading into the basic laws a constitutional right to freedom of contract based on the will theory, and revert to an interpretation of the right to freedom of occupation that focuses on one's right to make a living. Moreover, if this latter path is taken, not only will social legislation such as a minimum wage law not be interpreted as violating the rights protected under the basic laws, it may even be understood as constitutionally mandated—under a distributive interpretation of property which entails that every member of society possess a minimum amount of property or under an understanding of freedom of occupation that rests on the right to earn a living from one's profession. An imbalance arises, however, under the currently prevailing interpretation, which combines broad constitutional recognition of economic rights with minimal constitutional recognition for social rights. Not only have social rights failed to be recognised as constitutional rights, they also have to compete from a disadvantaged position with the constitutionally protected economic rights.

IX SOCIAL RIGHTS AND THE BOUNDARIES OF ISRAELI CONSTITUTIONAL LAW

The discussion above focused on Israeli constitutional law as applied in Israel proper. It is important to note, however, that since 1967 Israel has also occupied territories it conquered in a war with neighbouring Arab countries. In these territories, Israeli law as such does not apply but, rather, local law and applicable international law. The Israeli Supreme Court has held that the actions of the Israeli Army in the Occupied Territories shall be scrutinised according to the basic principles of Israeli public law, but it has yet to make a determination with respect to the application of the basic laws on human rights to the Palestinian population in the Territories.[50] In practice, the activities of the Israeli forces in the Occupied Territories have significant impact not only on the civil and political rights of the local population but also on their social conditions. For example, restrictions on freedom of movement in the Occupied Territories by way of checkpoints and the separation barrier in the West Bank have severe adverse effects on Palestinians' access to medical facilities, schools and workplaces. Indeed, questions relating to the protection of social and economic rights in the

---

[50] The Supreme Court applied the protection extended by the basic laws to the rights of Israeli citizens in the Occupied Territories but left the question of the general applicability of this protection in the area pending. See HCJ 1661/05 *Gaza Beach Regional Authority v Knesset* [2005] 59(2) PD 481 para 80; HCJ 8276/05 *Adalah – Legal Center for Arab Minority Rights in Israel* (decision from 12 December 2006) para 22.

Occupied Territories were intensively discussed in connection with the building of the separation barrier.[51]

Another aspect of this matter that affects non-Israeli citizens is the question of the rights of migrant workers. As non-citizens, the scope of their social rights under Israeli domestic law is more limited, but they may still be protected in extreme cases of exploitation, as determined in the Supreme Court's *Worker Line* decision. In practice, the problems experienced by migrant workers are usually attributable to a de facto absence of access to the legal system due to their lack of information and incapacity to claim rights. However, an extensive discussion of their social rights lies outside the scope of this chapter.

X CONCLUSION

Social rights were not included explicitly in the 1992 Basic Law: Human Dignity and Liberty and Basic Law: Freedom of Occupation, which currently serve as the basis for the protection of constitutional rights in Israeli law. The Supreme Court's initial tendency has been to exclude social rights from the scope of the new basic laws, with the exception of the right to existence with a minimum of human dignity. The exclusion of social rights from the new constitutional order, coupled with the constitutionalisation of economic rights, which has an anti-distributive effect, reinforces the decline of social citizenship in Israel. These processes join the erosion of the Israeli welfare state, the cuts in social welfare, and the privatisation of social services, as well as shifts in the labour market, most notably from collective to individual employment arrangements, which have made employment conditions much more precarious than in the past.

The minimum approach to social rights that has been adopted by the Supreme Court comes into play only in the most extreme cases, in which an individual is denied completely the minimum material conditions of existence and the right to existence with human dignity is violated. This approach may be attributed to the subjection of social rights to the concept of human dignity, which shifts the focus away from questions of distribution and equality to a humiliation-based model. This model protects only persons whose lack of access to welfare, education, health, social security, housing and food humiliates them. Thus it does not allow any discussion of these rights beyond the mere minimum. The implications of this model can be seen in decisions rendered by lower courts on various issues, most notably the right to health, where the minimum model has been applied to reject various claims brought by people who were denied

---

[51] See HCJ 2056/04 *Beit Sourik Village Council v Government of Israel* [2004] 58(5) PD 807, *translated in* (2005) 43 ILM 1099; HCJ 7957/04 *Mara'abe v Prime Minister of Israel* (decision from 15 September 2005).

health rights under the national health insurance scheme.[52] Thus whereas recourse to social rights litigation always carries with it the risk that violations will be recognised only in very extreme, individual cases while the rest of the non-egalitarian and unjust social order is left untouched, the minimum model has actually made this risk a reality. The minimum approach to the protection of social rights is also evident in the judicial reluctance to accept arguments resting on the right to equality with regard to the regulation of access to social services based on economic status. This is the case although the right to equality is widely recognised as a constitutional right and despite the fact that Israel's Declaration of Independence, which is cited in the 1992 basic laws themselves as a source for their interpretation, calls for full 'social and political equality'. The main exceptions to this picture are the Supreme Court decisions on the right to education, reflecting perhaps a broader consensus that exists regarding education issues as well as the fact that these cases did not entail judicial review of primary legislation.

The best way to correct the imbalance described above would be to supplement the current basic laws on human rights with a specific basic law on social rights. Indeed, several proposals for such legislation were submitted and discussed following the enactment of Basic Law: Freedom of Occupation and Basic Law: Human Dignity and Liberty. However, none of the proposals met with any success, both because of a general halt in the legislation of basic laws and because the government was reluctant to support a constitutional amendment that could limit its freedom to pass budgetary cuts and decide economic issues. For the latter reason, the government was willing to support only proposals to enact a basic law that is declaratory in nature with regard to social rights, and not an enforceable social rights bill.

This discussion reveals that Israeli constitutional law, though no longer confined to the recognition of civil and political rights, stops short of fully accepting social rights as human rights on an equal footing with civil and political rights. Social citizenship is still second class to civil and political citizenship. Indeed, it is important to remember that the initial responsibility for these matters lies in the hands of the Knesset in both its constitution-making and law-making capacities and that the primary forum for dealing with issues of social welfare and inequality is the political one. The judiciary, however, is a secondary player that can provide a safety net when the political system neglects its responsibility to social welfare.

---

[52] See A Gross, 'Health in Israel: Between a Right and a Commodity' in Y Shany and Y Rabin (eds), *Social and Economic Rights in Israel* 437 (Tel Aviv, Ramot, 2004) [Hebrew], and A Gross, chapter 13 of this volume.

Part IV

Implementing Specific Social Rights

12

The Many Faces of the Right to Education

YORAM RABIN*

I think by far the most important bill in our whole code is that for the diffusion of knowledge among the people. No other sure foundation can be devised for the preservation of freedom and happiness... preach, my dear sir, a crusade against ignorance; establish and improve the law for educating the common people.[1]

I INTRODUCTION: THE RIGHT TO EDUCATION IN COMPARISON WITH OTHER SOCIAL RIGHTS

In this chapter we deconstruct the constitutional right to education into its various components in order to discuss its character and the problematics related to its application. We do so for the purpose of delineating the dilemmas associated with the realisation of this right. Some of those dilemmas are rooted in the right's definition as a social right while others flow from unique issues related to the right per se; the latter issues are thus dissociated from the conceptual issues surrounding social rights as a distinct, inclusive category. We likewise stress the specific reasons that justify the protection granted to the right to education in many constitutional documents.

Prior to formulating a model capable of contributing to our understanding of the nature of the right to education, we begin by elaborating several of the characteristics that differentiate education from other socio-economic rights. First, contrary to some other welfare rights such as the right to social security, it is impossible to isolate the issue of funding

* The author would like to thank Daphne Barak-Erez, Aeyal Gross, Yuval Shany, Liav Orgad and Shimrit Shahaf for their comments and assistance. The research was supported by a grant from the Research Foundation of the School of Law, the College of Management Academic Studies, Israel.
    1 See F Volio, 'The Child's Right to Education: A Survey' in G Mialaret (ed), *The Child's Right to Education* (Paris, UNESCO, 1979) 19, 22.

from the issue of educational curricula. When individuals demand that the state fund education services for their children, they usually refer not simply to the demand for budgetary support but also to the funding of a specific type of education (educational stream), one reflecting their individual convictions and beliefs. Second, due to the fact that the primary beneficiaries of rights to education are children, the realisation of those rights entails (in most cases) the participation of three parties: the state, the parents and the child. This fact demands that a position be taken not only with respect to the relationships maintained between public authorities and the individual, as with the application of other social rights, but also regarding relationships between parents and children. Indeed, in many cases, parental interests clash with those of the child. Third, the right to education, contrary to other social rights, includes an element of duty and compulsion. That is, although in the majority of cases an individual can refuse to accept state-provided public services, the same does not apply to education.[2]

The right to education is the socio-economic right most commonly acknowledged throughout the world. Rights to education are protected in the constitutions of more than 140 countries[3] and a large number of inter-national covenants.[4] In general, divergent aspects of education are subsumed under the inclusive heading 'education' or 'the right to educa-tion'.[5] The prevalence of this heading continues, even today, to be the source of conceptual confusion. A careful reading of the articles referring to education in constitutions and conventions leads to the conclusion that the right to education encompasses three basic rights that should be distin-guished from one another: the right to receive education, the right to choose (a stream of) education and the right to equal education. These

---

[2] Compulsion is also an element related to the right to health, such as the obligation to inoculate children and the absence of parental right of refusal to do so.

[3] A survey conducted for the purposes of this chapter found that rights in the sphere of education are protected in the constitutions of 148 countries. A number of new constitutions have yet to appear in official English language versions, and other constitutions are still in process of ratification. Therefore, it appears that the final number will be even higher. On the right to education as stipulated in national constitutions throughout the world, see, among others: K Tomasevski, *Free and Compulsory Education for All Children: The Gap between Promise and Performance* (Gothenburg, 2001), 18–19, available at <http://www.right-to-education.org>. For comparative details on constitutional guarantees of the right to education see R Marlow-Ferguson and C Lopez (eds), *The World Education Encyclopedia* 2nd edn (Farmington Hills MI / London, Thomson Gale, 2001).

[4] The most famous of these covenants is the UN's Universal Declaration of Human Rights 1948 (Art 26), and the UN International Convention on Economic, Social and Cultural Rights 1966 (Art 13).

[5] In recent years, several books published have been dedicated to elaboration of the right to education in international law as well as in national constitutional rights; see: K Dieter Beiter, *The Protection of the Right to Education by International Law* (Leiden, Martinus Nijhoff Publishers, 2006); K Tomasevski, *Education Denied* (London, Zed Books, 2003); J Spring, *The Universal Right to Education* (Mahwah, NJ, Lawrence Erlbaum Associates, 2000); D Hodgson, *The Human Right to Education* (Aldershot, Ashgate Publishing, 1998).

rights can either complement or clash, depending on the context. It is therefore incumbent upon us to elaborate quite precisely the conceptual foundations of what we call *the* right to education. Each of the three rights is worthy of a separate discussion.[6]

II THE DIFFERENT FACETS OF THE RIGHT TO EDUCATION

A The Right to Receive Education

The right to receive education is precisely that—the individual's right to receive education and educational services that are funded by the state. This right is a positive right; it assigns to the state the 'duty to perform', to provide and fund education. This positive aspect associates the right to receive education with an entire family of second-generation social rights. The right to receive education thus encompasses three possible avenues of implementation: primary education, secondary education and higher education. The majority of covenants[7] and national constitutions[8] protect the right to receive free basic education (primary and secondary education). In several Western welfare states as well as in those subscribing to the socialist-communist tradition, the right to receive education also includes the right to higher education.[9]

Several justifications for recognising the right to receive education can be listed.[10] The first is that education provides the foundations for individual autonomy, liberty and human dignity. According to this

---

[6] The expression 'the right to education' hereinafter relates to the numerous rights to education subsumed under this title.

[7] See, eg: Art 13(2)(a) (a right to primary education) and Art 13(2)(b) (a right to secondary education), UN Convention on Economic, Social and Cultural Rights 1966.

[8] For examples of national constitutions that grant free elementary and high school education see: Art 29(1), South Africa's Constitution; Art 42(4), Ireland's Constitution; Art 27(4), Spain's Constitution; Art 19, Switzerland's Constitution; Art 24(1), Belgium's Constitution; Art 34(2), Italy's Constitution; Art 16(1), Finland's Constitution; Art 26(3), Japan's Constitution; Art 70(2), Poland's Constitution; Art 23(1), Luxembourg's Constitution; Art 160(1), Taiwan's Constitution.

[9] For examples of constitutions that guarantee free higher education see: Art 13 of the Preamble to France's fourth Constitution 1946; Art 16(4), Greece's Constitution; Art 74, Portugal's Constitution; Art 43(3), Russia's Constitution, 1993; Art 53(4), the Ukraine's Constitution; Art 35, Armenia's Constitution; Art 208, Haiti's Constitution.

[10] Considerations for non-recognition of the right to education also exist, but they lie beyond the scope of this discussion because they emanate from general considerations as opposed to the recognition of social rights; ie, they are not based on criteria for the non-recognition of the right to education per se. For a discussion of this issue see R Gavison, 'On the Relationships between Civil and Political Rights and Social and Economic Rights' in JM Coicaud, MW Doyle and AM Gardner (eds), *The Globalization of Human Rights* (New York, United Nations University Press, 2003) 23.

argument, strong and well-defined interests[11] motivate an individual's right to receive state-provided education because, in modern society, education is essential for the existence of liberty and for its realisation. Without education, liberty declines in value.[12] Education likewise meets two conditions for human dignity. On one level, the right to education relates to human dignity in its extrinsic sense. In meritocracies, such as those found in Western societies, a person's extrinsic dignity is considerably affected by their accomplishments in the field of education because the amount of education obtained represents the primary measure for an assessment of their worth, capabilities and potential to succeed in numerous areas of daily life. The place of education in the construction of a person's status in contemporary society follows from this condition. Moreover, education—and especially the acquisition of higher education—is often the sole hope a person has to leap the barriers of the lowly economic status to which they were born; stated simply, education is a fundamental instrument of social mobility.[13] On the second level, the right to education relates to human dignity in its intrinsic sense. We cannot ignore the decisive contribution of education to personal development and individual self-esteem, to a sense of inner value in addition to individual worth.[14]

The second justification for the right to education is that education is essential to the realisation of basic civil and political rights. This argument has often been raised in US judicial decisions,[15] as it was in a

---

[11] In my attempts to designate rights as interests, I follow in the footsteps of the well-known definition proposed by Raz: 'To give rise to a right an interest must be sufficient to justify the existence of a duty on another person to behave in a way which serves the interest of the right holder' (J Raz, *Ethics in the Public Domain* (Oxford, Oxford University Press, 1994) 35).

[12] I Berlin, *Four Essays on Liberty* (Oxford, Oxford University Press, 1969), at liii, presented a pristine description of this idea: 'If a man is too poor or too ignorant or too feeble to make use of his legal rights, the liberty that these rights confer upon him is nothing to him, but it is not thereby annihilated. The obligation to promote education... is not made less stringent because it is not necessarily directed to the promotion of liberty itself, but to conditions in which alone its possession is of value, or to values which may be independent of it'.

[13] Prof Friedman provides a succinct explication of this idea; see L Friedman, 'Education as a Form of Welfare – Legal and Social Problems' in S Goldstein (ed), *Law and Equality in Education* (Jerusalem, The Van Leer Institution, 1980) 167, 172: 'In a society which rejects distinctions of birth and status, and which only recognizes "merit", it is education which stamps people with the stamp of merit; it is a grading system that affects the life-chances of virtually every child in it'.

[14] J Rawls, *A Theory of Justice* (Cambridge, Belknap Press, 1971) 101; J Rawls, 'Distributive Justice: Some Addenda' in S freeman (ed), *Collected Papers* (Cambridge Mass / London, Harvard University Press, 1999) 154, 166.

[15] See the following judicial decisions: *School District of Abington Township, Pennsylvania v Schempp* (1963) 374 US 203, 230: 'Americans regard the public schools as a most vital civic institution for the preservation of a democratic system of government'; *Wisconsin v Yoder* (1972) 406 US 205, 221 (hereinafter, the *Yoder* case): 'Some degree of education is necessary to prepare citizens to participate effectively and intelligently in our open political system if we are to preserve freedom and independence'; *San Antonio Independent School District v Rodriguez*, (1973) 411 US 1, 63 (hereinafter, the *Rodriguez* case): 'There can be no doubt that education is

crucial decision passed down in Israel on the same subject.[16] For instance, a person has an interest in receiving education because education is necessary to achieve the freedom of expression, another right due them. If freedom of expression is necessary for democracy, the furtherance of truth and the exchange of ideas in 'the free marketplace of ideas', education is a necessary condition for the realisation of all these rights. Education is, after all, the main vehicle for the accumulation of knowledge and the formation of ideas. Without education, the marketplace of ideas characterising democratic regimes would be emptied of its goods.[17] A similar argument can be made with respect to the right to vote: an individual has a strong interest in receiving education because it represents one of the conditions essential to realisation of the basic right to vote. Although it has been suggested that we can train a monkey to drop a slip of paper into the ballot box, the monkey's action has no relationship to the political issues at stake or the issues on the public agenda.[18] Hence, as an essential precondition of the universal right of citizens to vote, we must recognise the citizens' universal right to receive education.

The third justification is embedded in utilitarian considerations: education benefits the individual but also society at large. Considered from this perspective, allocation of funds to education represents an investment in the human resources that promote the nation's economic prosperity as well as its general social well-being, expressed in rising levels of culture, decreased crime rates, prevention of sexually transmitted diseases, such as AIDS, and promotion of the war on poverty, among other social goals. These outputs, despite their diversity, touch the lives of each and every individual. This position has won support among adherents of classical economics who support the model of a free market economy with its 'invisible hand' as propounded by Adam Smith,[19] as well as proponents of

---

inextricably linked to the right to participate in the electoral process'; *Plyler v Doe* (1982) 457 US 202, 221 (hereinafter, the *Plyler* case): 'as... pointed out early in our history... some degree of education is necessary to prepare citizens to participate effectively and intelligently in our open political system if we are to preserve freedom and independence'.

16 See Justice Or on HCJ 1554/95, *Friends of GILAT Association v Minister of Education, Culture and Sport* 50(3) PD 2, at 22–3 (hereinafter, the *Friends of GILAT* case): 'Education is fundamental to the existence of a free, active and functioning democratic society... Education is, without doubt, an important instrument for guaranteeing the rights and freedoms of each and every individual and the realization of fundamental political rights, including the freedom of expression as well as the right to vote and be elected'.

17 See SH Bitensky, 'Theoretical Foundations for a Right to Education under the US Constitution: A Beginning to the End of the National Education Crisis' (1992) 86 *Northwestern University Law Review* 550, 600–1.

18 *Ibid* 603–4.

19 See A Smith, *The Wealth of Nations* (New York, 1991), books 1 (p 90), 2 (p 247) and 5 (ch II).

'The Third Way'[20] and outright social democrats. The assumption shared by this plethora of positions is that an individual without an education not only deprives themselves of their own rights and humanity, but they also jeopardise their community's legitimate interests.

Finally, we can justify the recognition of social rights, especially the right to receive education, based on other, not necessarily liberal perspectives. These entail primarily neo-Aristotelian and communitarian approaches. In order to be part of a community and influence the character of that community, each person must recognise their own inherent capabilities, such as the skills acquired in the course of primary and secondary education. Communitarian approaches express an integrated perspective holding that community membership rests on three levels of rights—civil rights, political rights and socio-economic and cultural rights (especially the right to education)—that are conceived of as complementary.

However, because of the strains it places on the nation's coffers, the right to receive education also raises problems related to eligibility for these rights. We now propose a preliminary delineation of the scope of eligibility for the rights in question.

I Education: A Human or a Civic Right?

Modern theories of the state argue that governments ought to guarantee some basic freedoms to those who enjoy state protection. Regarding the right to receive education, the respective question concerns the appropriateness of making this right available exclusively to a country's citizens. Might not additional groups be considered eligible, too? This question is especially relevant with respect to children of refugees, immigrants or foreign workers. Yet because education is a pre-condition for the exercise of basic human rights—individual autonomy, human dignity and freedom—the right to receive education is a universal human right, not limited to citizens.

The right to receive education consigns to the state certain 'positive duties', specifically, the obligation to bear the cost of each additional person (or student) partaking of the system's services. The courts in many countries have recognised that the right to education is intrinsic, part of the individual's humanity; this right is therefore to be granted to all citizens (especially the poor, prisoners or other persons living on the margins of society) as well as to non-citizens (eg, the children of illegal

---

[20] See A Giddens, *The Third Way – The Renewal of Social Democracy* (Cambridge, Polity Press, 1998) 102–3, 109–11, 125–6. Within the framework of the comprehensive programme that Giddens terms 'the social investment state', investment in education, especially among the poor, plays a central role.

immigrants).[21] We should note here that residents who are not citizens also carry the economic burden of financing the right to education, even if indirectly (eg, by paying taxes). In contrast, occasional tourists, even if they are 'human beings', are not entitled to enjoy the right to education in its positive sense. Eligibility for the right to education hinges, therefore, on a long-term relationship between the state and the individual.

ii The Child's Right to Receive Education

International as well as comparative law has determined that any person can be eligible to receive education. However, the person eligible for this right is usually a child. A recently evolving trend defines the child's right to education within the broader framework of 'children's rights'.[22] A child's right to receive education can thus be conceived as autonomous and self-contained.

iii The Adult's Right to Receive Education

As stated previously, children are generally considered the main parties eligible to receive education; in reality, however, this is not always the case. Recognition of the enduring interest in education and training and the permanent need to update knowledge in order to keep pace with life's changes justify extending eligibility for the right to receive education to adults.[23] A person's interest in receiving the basic education that provides people with the fundamental capacities to survive in modern society is quite powerful, particularly among adults, who, as breadwinners, carry the weight of the responsibility for caring for themselves and their families.

In general, we should differentiate between the two main instances in which an adult (a person more than 18 years of age) is eligible to receive education. The first instance involves adults who were prevented from receiving a basic education when they were children, for example, due to conditions of incarceration.[24] An additional example is that of adults who

---

[21] In a famous case, the US Supreme Court invalidated a law that denied children of illegal immigrants the right to education in the public school system. See the *Plyler* case, above n 15.

[22] JM Eekelaar, 'The Emergence of Children's Rights' (1986) 6 *Oxford Journal of Legal Studies* 161, 172–3.

[23] On the right of adults to receive education in international law see Hodgson, above n 5, 179–81.

[24] See, eg, Art 160(2) of Taiwan's Constitution: 'All citizens above school age who have not received elementary education shall receive supplementary education free of charge and shall also be supplied with books by the Government'.

emigrated from a country that does not provide appropriate basic education.

The second instance of adult eligibility for receiving education arises when adults who did not take advantage of the right to receive a basic education (primary and secondary school) later become interested in receiving state-funded university or other forms of higher education (particularly training beyond vocational high school).[25] Higher education is the key to social integration. Several modern Western states have found access to higher education worthy of inclusion among other constitutional rights to education. This right often includes free higher education.[26] Yet, exceptions notwithstanding, the majority of countries throughout the world are unwilling to recognise the right to subsidised or fully funded higher education.

iv Group Rights

An additional aspect of the right to receive education from the state involves the support given to private schools in general and to private schools run by minority groups in particular. The right to receive support for these schools rests on the right of individuals or groups to influence the educational content transmitted to their children. This feature links the positive right to receive education with the negative right to select and influence the curriculum. The ensuing linkage results from the fact that major aspects of the right to influence the curriculum (dealt with below) are ineffective without state assistance in their implementation. Thus, for example, the right to establish private schools is rarely realised without state financial support. Rights to education granted by law to minority groups on the basis of culture, religion, language or nationality are similarly often meaningless without state support.[27]

---

[25] See, eg, Art XIV, s 2(5) of the Philippines' Constitution: '[The state shall] Provide adult citizens, the disabled, and out-of-school youth with training in civics, vocational efficiency, and other skills'.

[26] See above n 9. However, due to the high costs, opposing trends can also be observed in nations shifting from the model of full state funding of higher education to the model of funding higher education privately or by means of state loans. The state loan model is appropriate to the funding of professions such as law, a field whose graduates are expected to eventually earn high incomes.

[27] See Y Tamir, 'The Chronicle of a Preordained Failure' in D Chen (ed) *Education Towards the 21st Century* (Tel Aviv, Ramot, 1995) 425, 434–5, where the author analyses the relationship between multiculturalism and the requirement that the state defend and support educational institutions run by minority groups.

B The Right to Choose Education

Provisions devoted to education in international covenants[28] and national constitutions[29] include, among other things, arrangements meant to guarantee the individual's right to choose education. This right, negative in essence, belongs to the first-generation family of rights—civil and political rights. That is, whenever the right to choose education is made available to a person (a child or their parents), their exercise of that right denies other entities the power to intervene with that choice or to influence the respective curriculum. Under the broad umbrella of the right to choose education can be found:

—The parental right to choose a school or recognised educational stream available within the state-run public school system.[30]
—The parental right to send their children to private schools and to establish new private schools as alternatives to the state-run public school system.[31]
—The parental right to teach their children at home (home schooling).[32]
—The person's right to obtain higher education (usually resting on capabilities and skills).[33]
—The right to academic freedom in institutions of higher learning.[34] Academic freedom is important because it ensures the variety that expands the individual's range of options within education.

---

[28] See Art 26(3), UN Universal Declaration of Human Rights 1948; and Arts 13(3) and 13(4), UN International Convention on Economic, Social and Cultural Rights 1966.

[29] See, eg: Art 29(2), 29(3), South Africa's Constitution; Art 27(3), 27(6), Spain's Constitution; Art 42(2), Ireland's Constitution; Art 7(2), 7(4), Germany's Basic Law; Art 70(3), Poland's Constitution.

[30] See, eg: Art 27(3), 27(6), Spain's Constitution; Art 37(3), Estonia's Constitution.

[31] For examples of constitutions that guarantee the right to establish private schools, see: Art 7(4), Germany's Basic Law; Art 27(6), Spain's Constitution; Art 45, Macedonia's Constitution; Art 66, Croatia's Constitution; Art 70(3), Poland's Constitution; Art 25(2), Ghana's Constitution.

[32] This right has already been recognised as a constitutional right; see, eg: Art 42(2), Ireland's Constitution of 1990; Art 76, Denmark's Constitution. On the right to home schooling in the US see CJ Klicka, *The Right to Home School* 2nd edn (Durham, Carolina Academic Press, 1998); CJ Klicka, *The Right Choice: The Incredible Failure of Public Education and the Rising Hope of Home Schooling* (Gresham Oregon, Noble Publishing, 1992). On the right to home schooling in Israel see T Meisels, 'Home-schooling: The Right to Choose' (2004) 10 *Israel Affairs* 110. On the right to home schooling in international and comparative law see Hodgson, above n 5, at 181–3.

[33] See, eg: Art 49(3), the Belarus Constitution; Art 70F(2), Hungary's Constitution; Art 35(7), Moldava's Constitution.

[34] See, eg: Art 27(10), Spain's Constitution; Art 70(5), Poland's Constitution; Art 16(3), Finland's Constitution; Art 46(1), Macedonia's Constitution; Art 32(6), Romania's Constitution; Art 79(2), Paraguay's Constitution; Art XIV, s 5(2) of the Constitution of the Philippines.

The right to choose education or influence its curriculum is generally discussed whenever the law fails to establish a duty to provide education. Alternatively, such mention also occurs whenever the law permits flexibility in the application of compulsory education—that is, the duty to send a child to school is stipulated but not the specific educational content to be transmitted. Two major rationales underlie the right to choose education. The first is derived from the centrality of individual autonomy, liberty and human dignity. When dealing with the right to receive education, we indicated that a person has a powerful interest in receiving education. This contention was supported by the argument that, in modern society, education is a major factor in the realisation of individual autonomy, liberty and human dignity. Anyone having a powerful interest in receiving education will also have a powerful interest in determining the curriculum taught. By exercising influence on the curriculum, an individual takes advantage of the opportunity to affect their cultural, linguistic (what languages will be spoken in their community), professional (what profession they will practise in the future) and other environments. This right to affect one of the core mechanisms which construct one's self-identity, prospects and personality, among other things, flows from the constitutional rights of individual autonomy and freedom.

The second rationale for recognising the right to choose education rests on the fact that education is a condition for the perpetuation of those aspects of culture considered necessary for an individual's realisation of their freedom, human dignity and self-identity. The right to choose an educational stream is therefore crucial for a minority group's (eg, religious, linguistic or other) preservation of its culture and uniqueness.

Like other rights, the right to choose education raises issues of eligibility, to which we briefly turn next.

i The Child's Right to Choose Education

The child is the primary subject eligible to enjoy the benefits of education; hence, the child has the strongest natural interest in choosing the type of education they will receive. The right to choose an educational stream and curriculum is nonetheless delegated to parents because children are generally incapable of foreseeing the long-term implications of their decisions. True choice is therefore considered to lie beyond the child's reach. Only in later life will the child be capable of making a forthright account of their own inclinations and wishes. This situation warrants placing the right to choose an educational stream and curriculum with the parents. However, should the child be adamant in their position, parents are obliged to consider their thoughts and preferences.[35] Considering these

---

[35] For an elaboration of the issue see the minority opinion presented by Justice Douglas in the well-known *Yoder* case, above n 15, 241–6.

limitations and the need to maintain educational oversight, the scope of the maturing child's rights is narrower than that of the rights enjoyed by adults. It thus appears appropriate to assign the responsibility for making decisions regarding the educational stream and the curriculum to parents and children in tandem, within the context of mutual consultation and persuasion.

ii The Adult's Right to Choose Education

An adult eligible to receive education, whether basic education which they had never previously obtained or higher education, is assumed to be interested in the type of education they will receive and the curriculum they will be required to learn. After all, education is meant to contribute to the development of the individual. When the person eligible to receive education is an adult and capable of rational decision-making (even if they lack formal education), it is appropriate to grant them the exclusive right to influence the educational curriculum.

iii The Parental Right to Choose Education

Parents' functions as guardians of their children endow them with specific rights and duties. We may nonetheless ask whether any justification exists for awarding parents the right to choose education for their children as opposed to relegating it to the state's purview. The arguments supporting a liberal stance can be presented on two levels.

The first level relates to the child's interests. The child has a powerful interest in obtaining appropriate education, and thus the child also has a strong interest in determining the educational stream and curriculum. However, in the absence of any real capacity to make decisions concerning their own status and future—and thus their educational needs—another entity must take on such tasks. Following the liberal tradition, among all the possible bodies, the child's family (ie, parents) is considered most suitable to fulfil these obligations.[36]

The natural ties of love and concern that exist between parents and children motivate parents to want the best for their children; consequently they are prepared to do their utmost to attain that goal. Parents are not simply stakeholders who see their children as instruments to promote their own objectives (even if those objectives are ideological, such as knowledge, religion or social justice). Stated differently, parents, more than any other persons, will probably be guided by their perception of their children's best interests when choosing an educational framework. This is the position,

---

[36] B Barry, *Culture and Equality – An Egalitarian Critique of Multiculturalism* (Cambridge, Polity Press, 2001) 202. See also the comments made by John Locke in his classic (originally published in 1690) *The Second Treatise of Government* (Indianapolis, Bobbs-Merrill, 1952) 33.

and perhaps the only position, that is commensurate with the basic assumptions at the foundation of the concept of human dignity. Until proven otherwise, this line of argument legitimates awarding this power to parents in the course of their guardianship duties. Freedom of action itself embraces the right of parents to exercise their judgement in all matters pertaining to the child's education: what school to attend, the educational philosophy applied (ie, educational stream) and what will be taught.

The second level addresses the interests of parents. Parents have strong interests, distinct from those of their children, in retaining the right to influence the curriculum taught. The parental right to choose education for their children may be based on the human and material capital they invested when rearing their children. This awards them the right to determine their children's education as they see fit. The extent of this argument is, however, limited because, within the context of the modern welfare state, the public's parallel right to determine the content and structure of education may be recognised on the basis of the public's alleged (economic) contribution—often not less than that of parents—to raising children.

The other factor inspiring this parental right is the need to protect children from state arbitrariness: that is, the parental right to determine their child's future weighed against the dangers arising from the use of education by the state as a medium for indoctrination. Parental rights therefore also reinforce pluralism.

In sum, from a liberal perspective, dividing the obligation to take responsibility for a child's education between parents and the formal state-run education system can be seen as justified. The various arguments we have discussed corroborate the position that parental responsibility for their children's education should be accompanied by the right to choose an educational stream or at least to influence the system's impact through the exercise of influence on the curriculum. From this perspective, the state's role is limited to preventing parental abuse of their power over their children, captured in the prohibition against corporal punishment or the prohibition against choosing an educational stream that will impede the child's integration into the larger society.

iv The Right of (Religious, Ethnic or Cultural) Minority Groups to Influence Curricula

We have shown that the right to choose a child's education generally rests with parents. However, in some instances, realisation of this right is determined by the relationship between parents and the national, religious or cultural minority to which they belong. Minority groups are known to have an interest in establishing private schools in which

a curriculum focusing on the group's distinguishing characteristics—religion, language, culture, customs and so forth—is taught. This
justification for setting up such schools also hinges on the group's desire
to preserve those characteristics. However, from a liberal perspective, a
group has no legal right to act in place of parents with respect to the
decision to send children to these special or any other (public or private)
schools. For this right to be transferred, agreement must be obtained
from the parents. That is, considered from a formal perspective, minority
group rights do not contradict parental rights because parents alone
are entitled to have the last word on the subject. However, formal
parental rights have limited practical impact when confronted with
minority group practices or beliefs. In the majority of cases where
parental preferences contradict those of the group, no genuine choices are
available if parents wish to remain within their natural environment and
familiar cultural framework. In many instances, the only genuine option
available is that of being able to opt out of the group, a costly act from
the standpoint of the family and the individual. Considered in this light,
it soon becomes clear that in the majority of such cases, the effective
balance of power regarding the choice of educational curricula swings
towards the minority group rather than towards the legal-formal rights of
the parents.[37]

C The Right to Equal Education

The right to equal education is derived from the general principle of
equality. Many constitutions stipulate the 'right to equal education' in
addition to universal equality.[38] The reason for this targeted, formal
protection of the right to equal education is that inequality is demonstrably
one of the most common problems to surface within the sphere of
education.[39] The right to equal education—like the principle of universal
equality—is not a mechanical but rather a substantive right. In order to
achieve the goal of equal education, variance must be accepted as a
governing constraint, meaning that more resources should be allocated to
underprivileged, children with special needs requiring special types of

[37] In connection with this argument see Barry, *ibid*, 207.
[38] See, eg: Art 29 of South Africa's Constitution; Art 44(2) of Macedonia's Constitution;
Art 26 of Japan's Constitution; Art 70(4) of Poland's Constitution; Art 24(4) of
Belgium's Constitution; Art 16(1) of Singapore's Constitution; Art 159 of Taiwan's
Constitution.
[39] C De La Vega 'The Right to Equal Education: Merely a Guiding Principle or Customary
International Legal Right?' (1994) 11 *Harvard Blackletter Law Journal* 37.

education[40] and groups formerly suffering historic discrimination in educational institutions.[41]

Substantive equality in education is manifested in the practices employed to award special rights to minority groups for the purpose of preserving their culture and traditions (eg, the study of the minority's language in addition to the study of a country's official language or allocation of additional hours for the study of the minority's traditions).[42] Especially important in this context are the special schemes resulting from a federal structure in which different levels of government award either special/supplemental rights or educational autonomy to specified regions.[43] This phenomenon raises the question of whether the award of supplemental rights to minorities discriminates against the majority culture. This situation may seem paradoxical: democratic states are expected to take a neutral stance towards the majority culture, yet the same authorities are mandated to intervene for the purpose of assisting minorities. The special/supplemental rights awarded to minorities, rights that allegedly introduce inequality, can, however, be justified by the majority culture's capacity—based on its being the majority culture—to sustain a fairly homogeneous environment even without the benefit of special/ supplemental rights. We should recall, however, that in many cases the majority maintains its homogeneity by recourse to other mechanisms, such as immigration and citizenship laws. The outcome of these laws is a situation of inequality that can be rectified, at least partially, through the award of special/supplemental rights to minorities.[44]

---

[40] Regarding the right to special education for those with special needs, see, eg: Art 16(2) of Finland's Constitution; Art 74(2) of Portugal's Constitution; Art 59(1) of Albania's Constitution; Art 45(3) of China's Constitution; Art 63 of Croatia's Constitution; Art 38(3) of Italy's Constitution; Art 81 of Venezuela's Constitution; Art 17(3) of Malta's Constitution; Art 52(2) of Slovenia's Constitution.

[41] See, eg, Art 29(2)(c) of the South African Constitution: 'the state must consider all reasonable educational alternatives, including single medium institutions, taking into account... the need to redress the results of past racially discriminatory laws and practices'.

[42] For constitutions that grant special education rights to linguistic or religious minorities, see, eg: Art 53(5) of the Ukraine's Constitution; Art 26(2) of Russia's Constitution; Art 16(2) of Singapore's Constitution; Art 37(4) of Estonia's Constitution; Art 34(2) of Slovenia's Constitution; Art 30(1) of India's Constitution; Art 75(17) of Argentina's Constitution; Art 77(2) of Paraguay's Constitution.

[43] See, eg: s 23 of the Canadian Charter of Rights and Freedoms, 1982; D Reaume and L Green 'Education and Linguistic Security in the Charter' (1989) 34 *McGill Law Journal* 777.

[44] The famous decision passed down in 1935 by the Permanent Court of International Justice with respect to the schools maintained by the Greek minority in Albania (*Advisory Opinion on Minority Schools in Albania*, PCIJ (1935) Series A/B no 64) should be seen in this light. The Albanian government had closed the special private schools run by the Greek minority, claiming that closing all the country's private schools was egalitarian as it applied to both the Greek minority and the Albanian majority. The court rejected this position by a majority vote and decreed that the closing of all private schools discriminated against the Greek minority, which could continue to study in the Greek language only in private schools. It was also decreed

D Compulsory Education—The Obligation to Attend School

Compulsory education generally refers to two dimensions: first, school attendance for the purpose of receiving education over a fixed period of time (number of years)[45]; second, the specific curriculum determined by the state[46] or other requirements introduced by the educational framework, such as the obligation to wear a school uniform.[47]

Compulsory education allegedly hinders the exercise of individual rights (in this case, the right to receive and the right to choose education). From this perspective, laws that mandate compulsory primary or secondary school education violate the rights of parents (or children) uninterested in school attendance for a stipulated or indeed any period of time. Moreover, compulsory education obliges the individual to learn designated subjects at

---

that even if schools were not crucial to the Albanian majority, they were essential to the Greek minority. Hence, the closing of all private schools operating in the country represented discrimination against the minority. For a discussion of the decision see P Keller, 'Re-thinking Ethnic and Cultural Rights in Europe' (1998) 18 *Oxford Journal of Legal Studies* 29, 50.

[45] See, eg: Art 13(2)(a), the International Covenant on Economic, Social and Cultural Rights 1966; Art 26(1), the Universal Declaration of Human Rights 1948. For national constitutions that have enacted compulsory education, usually primary school education, see, eg: Art 112 of Latvia's Constitution; Art 44(3) of Macedonia's Constitution; Art 27(7) of Spain's Constitution; Art 34(2) of Italy's Constitution; Art 16(3) of the Greek Constitution. We should note here that among all the countries known to us, where compulsory education is not expressly decreed in the constitution, it is mandated within the framework of regular education laws.

[46] International covenants, like various constitutions, do not relate to specific school subjects. Instead, they relate to the curriculum in indirect and general terms. See, eg, Art 13(1) of the International Covenant on Economic, Social and Cultural Rights 1966: 'The States Parties to the present Covenant... agree that education shall be directed to the full development of the human personality and the sense of its dignity, and shall strengthen the respect for human rights and fundamental freedoms. They further agree that education shall enable all persons to participate effectively in a free society, promote understanding, tolerance and friendship among all nations and all racial, ethnic or religious groups, and further the activities of the United Nations for the maintenance of peace'. See also Art XIV s 3 of the Philippines' Constitution.

[47] For instance, in France, it was questioned whether the prohibition enacted by the government against wearing traditional Muslim dress (headscarves or *hija'ab*) when attending public schools does not contradict the constitution and represent discrimination against Muslims in comparison to Christians and Jews. For a discussion see CD Baines, 'L`Affaire des Foulards – Discrimination or the Price of a Secular Public Education System?' (1996) 29 *Vanderbilt Journal of Transnational Law* 303; E Steiner, 'The Muslim Scarf and the French Republic' (1995–96) 6 *King's College Law Journal* 146; see also, in Great Britan: *R (on the application of Begum (by her litigation friend, Rahman)) (Respondent) v Headteacher and Governors of Denbigh High School (Appellants)* House of Lords [2006] UKHL 15. In this case, given in March 2006, the House of Lords decided to allow a maintained secondary school to insist on the wearing of school uniform and to disallow the wearing of the Moslem *hija'ab* (as requested by a pupil at the school, represented by herself and her brother, on the grounds that it concealed to a greater extent the contours of the maturing female body). See also the last important decision on this issue of the European Court of Human Rights: App No 44774/98 *Leyla Sahin v Turkey* (November 2005).

the same time as it limits their freedom to choose the curriculum to be learned.

Compulsory education, however, has become a cornerstone of present attitudes toward education internationally, as indicated by the its incorporation into the national traditions of the majority of the world's countries. This worldwide understanding should inform our search for the grounds to explain the phenomenon. It can be argued that compulsory education is rationalised by reasons of the *general welfare*. We have shown that general welfare can be employed as a reason to award the right to education because, beyond the benefits gained by any particular individual, education benefits all of a nation's citizens and residents. Similarly, the public good also provides grounds for the imposition of compulsory education. To meet society's needs, skills and professions must be inculcated; the same can be said for the common values essential to the creation of social cohesion. In democratic societies, awareness of common values contributes to the maintenance of a democratic régime. Yet, compulsory education contains the potential to violate individual freedom in general and rights to education in particular; it is therefore incumbent upon us to examine this issue from the perspective of *human rights*.

With respect to the right to receive education, compulsory education can be defended on two grounds; the first is paternalism. The right to receive education is so crucial that it justifies imposition of compulsory education. Paternalism is more persuasive as a motive when the subject is a child still unable to make vital decisions. Yet, the paternalism argument dwindles in salience when the person taking advantage of the right to receive education is an adult capable of making decisions.

Second, imposition of compulsory education is also grounded in the need to protect the child from her parents. This argument recognises the child as an autonomous entity, independent of her parents. Viewed from this perspective, compulsory education is meant to protect the child's right to receive education in the presence of shortsighted parents or guardian, who wish to deny the child enjoyment of that right. In other words, recognition of the child's autonomy makes it plain that compulsory education is not targeted at the child, the right's holder, but at her parents (and in some cases, her guardians or employers). By imposing compulsory education, the state institutionalises the parents' duty to guarantee that their child attends school even if doing so contradicts the parents' wishes. Such legislation is therefore positive in character as it ascribes the responsibility to realise the right to specific entities, in this case, a child's parents.

III CHALLENGES TO THE RIGHT TO EDUCATION – FROM OUTSIDE AND WITHIN

Violations of the various educational rights may originate in the behaviour of three main bodies: the state, parents and minority groups. Although the mechanisms of these violation may vary, we briefly focus on those most commonly observed; we likewise illustrate how the courts have confronted them.

A Infringements by the State

The state is the major entity liable to violate the various rights to education, given the dependence of schools, children and parents on the state and its budget. The most common violations inflicted by the state's refusal to budget for education are: first, infringement of an individual's (usually a child's) right to receive appropriate education in a system supported by the state, and, second, violation of an individual's (or a group's) right to equal education. The high costs of education inevitably generate conflict between the need to fund education—which represents only one of society's many needs (such as health, security and so forth)—and attempts to reduce the costs involved.

In response to such political and economic constraints, recognition of the right to receive education (and that right's protection in a constitution or international covenant to which the state is a party) may culminate in the formation of minimal standards. Deviations from those standards are subsequently subject to judicial review. For similar reasons, institutionalisation of the right to equal education can support court attempts to cope with discrimination in education. Recognition of the right to receive education as well as the right to equal education may thus shift education to a higher place on the public agenda.

A notable example of the importance of recognising the right to receive education and the right to equal education in the face of contradictory government policy is provided by an Israeli case decided in 2002–2003.[48] According to the Compulsory Education Law 1949, primary and secondary education in Israel is free. This law has been supplemented by the Special Education Law 1988, which provides for free education in special schools for children with special needs. However, neither law directly addresses the following issue: if parents of children with special needs wish to enrol their children in mainstream schools in the hope that this will facilitate their children's integration into society (following the

---

[48] HCJ 2599/00, YATED – *Association for Parents of Downs Syndrome Children v Minister of Education*, [2002] 56(5) PD 834.

approach of 'inclusion'), who is to incur the additional costs (primarily, individual teaching assistance hours)—the parents or the State? Until 2002, Israel's Ministry of Education required parents of children with special needs to cover some or all of these costs, a policy that resulted in the de facto exclusion from regular schools of children with special needs from families that were not affluent. This policy was the subject of a petition brought before the Supreme Court by a group of parents of children suffering from Down's syndrome who sought to shift the costs of integrating their children in regular schools to the government.

Justice Dalia Dorner, writing for the Supreme Court in the 2002 *YATED* case, accepted the petition and ordered the Ministry of Education to cover the costs of inclusion. The decision is particularly important due to its argumentation. Despite the fact that Israel's basic laws (which are part of the Israeli Constitution in the making) do not specifically mention the right to education, Justice Dorner held that Israeli law does recognise this right. The existence of this right is independent of any basic law and ought to be viewed as part of Israel's (still unwritten) bill of rights.[49] She based this conclusion on a variety of legal sources—international law, comparative law (citing provisions in the Belgian, South African, Spanish, Irish, German and US Constitutions), Jewish law, education legislation and judicial dicta regarding education's importance. Justice Dorner also noted in this regard that the right to education is linked to the principle of equality, given education's potential to close social gaps. After establishing the fundamental right to education, Justice Dorner proceeded to argue that the right to special education derives from this as well as from the right to equality.[50]

In the second part of her decision, Justice Dorner held that the Special Education Law 1988 must be construed in light of the Israeli legal system's fundamental values—the right to education, the principle of equality and the right to special education deriving from both.[51] She further held that the law ought to be construed in accordance with international obligations accepted by the state of Israel—enumerated in Article 13 of the ICESCR and Articles 23, 28 and 29 of the Convention on the Rights of the Child—that specifically deal with the right to education and obligations to address the special needs of disabled children. The Ministry of Education's interpretation of Special Education Law (1988) was thus found to be unlawful.

Violations of a third type concern state infringement of the individual's right to choose education. In general, such events transpire in the absence of any legitimate grounds (eg, arbitrary behaviour or political motives) or due to strict enforcement of standard compulsory education regulations.

---

[49] *Ibid* 843.
[50] *Ibid* 845.
[51] *Ibid* 846.

The ensuing conundrum rests on the fact that strict enforcement of compulsory education can obviate the parental right to choose education for their children. The well-known decision passed down by the European Court of Human Rights regarding sex education in Denmark offers an appropriate illustration of this type of violation.[52]

In the past, public schools in Denmark had offered sex education in special classes; parents who objected to this type of education were entitled to request that their children not participate. In 1970 a compulsory sex education curriculum was introduced into Danish schools. According to the new policy, sex education was to be introduced as early as the third grade within the framework of the compulsory education programme, which included subjects such as the Danish language, religious studies, biology, history and so forth. Three Danish couples presented a petition stating that Denmark's sex education policy violated Article 2 of Protocol No 1 of the European Convention on Human Rights 1950, which protects freedom of education and, among other things, compels the state to respect parental convictions regarding education. The government argued that, in the present circumstances, it had not failed to respect the religious or philosophical convictions of the parents because an alternative educational option existed in Denmark, the system of private schools that enjoyed considerable financial support from the state.

The European Commission, as well as the European Court on Human Rights, rejected the Danish government's argument, which was based on a differentiation between the public and the private school systems. It held that with respect to all practices pertaining to teaching and education, the relevant clause of Article 2 stated that all nation parties to the convention were obliged to guarantee respect for the parents' religious and philosophical convictions in public as well as private schools. A decision was demanded as to whether the sex education curriculum transmitted in Danish public schools violated the parents' beliefs. The European Court responded negatively and rejected the petition. A crucial principle was put forwatd in the judgment according to which the role of the state was to provide education, whether by directly teaching or otherwise transmitting educational information. This role, the court explained, involves, directly or indirectly, the provision of information that necessarily touches on philosophical views or religion. Furthermore, the court ruled, the mandated respect for the parents' convictions can be employed to limit the state's power to provide objective or pluralistic information only in cases when the intent behind transmission of that information is indoctrination:

---

[52] Application No 5095/71 *Kjeldsen, Busk Madsen and Pedersen v Denmark (Danish Sex Education)*, judgment of 7 December 1976, Series A, No 23, p 50.

The state, in fulfilling the functions assumed by it in regard to education and teaching, must take care that information or knowledge included in the curriculum is conveyed in an objective, critical, and pluralistic manner. The state is forbidden to pursue an aim of indoctrination that might be considered as not respecting parents' religious and philosophical convictions. That is the limit that must not be exceeded.[53]

Because Denmark's sex education law was meant to provide Danish children with important information (for example, information regarding abortion, illegitimacy and birth outside marriage as well as contagious sexually transmitted diseases), the curriculum, according to the court's opinion, was acceptable, accurate and scientifically objective. The court stressed that although issues pertaining to sex inevitably penetrate the sphere of values and beliefs, spheres in which the evaluation of facts can readily be transformed into moral judgments, Denmark's sex education curriculum was not intended to indoctrinate or direct students towards any specific types of sexual behaviour. Application of liberal democratic principles, it continued, would lead to the same conclusion.

In sum, this case relates to the fragile balance holding between two contradictory principles: the entitlement of parents to respect for their convictions and state responsibility to provide education appropriate to promoting the general welfare. The same principle, which implies the need to balance state responsibility and authority regarding transmission of education with parental rights, with prohibitions against state indoctrination, also provides the foundations for the negation of those parental rights that prevent the state from imparting indispensable knowledge (in this case, sex education) to the public. At the same time, education authorities are required to act with extreme caution when implementing compulsory education policy without, however, abandoning the objectives of compulsory education. In maintaining the equilibrium between the individual's right to choose education and compulsory education, a certain margin of error must be accepted in order to minimise the likelihood of compulsory education becoming a vehicle for dissemination of the regime's version of the truth. Parents should therefore be granted the option of complying with compulsory education requirements in alternative frameworks, such as private schools or home schooling. At the same time, it should be understood that these frameworks are not amenable to maintaining the same level of state supervision applied in the public school system. Yet such absence of supervision is desirable. If the same degree of oversight were to be applied in private schools and home schooling (both options are very common in the United States), this might lead to duplication of the public school system.

[53] *Ibid* 53.

B Infringements by Parents and Minority Groups

The main right enjoyed by parents in the sphere of education is the right to choose education for their children in conformity with their own convictions. Nonetheless, realisation of this right contains the potential to violate the child's right to receive education, on two levels: first, parental choices may deny education (partially or fully) to the child; second, parental choices may expose the child to an inappropriate, inadequate or worthless curriculum. In a similar vein, realisation of minority group rights to educate children according to the group's culture may violate the right of individual members (usually children) to receive an appropriate or liberal education.

One well-publicised case that illustrates the conflict between the rights of parents and those of children is that of *Wisconsin v Yoder*, decided by the United States Supreme Court.[54] The respondents were members of the Amish Christian community, residing in the state of Wisconsin. Wisconsin's education legislation stipulated that parents were obliged to send their children to recognised public or private schools until they reached the age of 16; it also imposed criminal penalties on parents who failed to comply. In this case, the respondents had refused to send their children, aged 14 and 15, to school beyond the eighth grade, contending that additional education (secondary or high school education) was superfluous for their traditional way of life and would, in addition, expose them to the ills of secular society.[55] The respondents were charged and convicted of transgressing Wisconsin's compulsory education law and fined $5.00.

A review of the evidence presented in the criminal case indicates that the respondents, following traditional Amish strictures,[56] believed that sending their children to secondary school, whether public or private, contradicted their religion and way of life. Attendance at a public high school, they felt, would expose Amish youngsters to spiritually dangerous environments and distance them physically as well as emotionally from the community at a critical stage in their development. Furthermore, such a practice would

---

[54] *Yoder* case, above n 15.

[55] *Ibid*, 210–12. The respondents did not object to their children attending primary school because they believed that their children needed to acquire certain basic fundamental skills, such as the ability to read the Bible, be good farmers and citizens and be capable of negotiating with individuals who did not belong to the Amish community to the degree that this was required in the course of their daily lives. Yet the respondents were convinced that secondary education was undesirable because it contributed to the development of values that distanced individuals from their Creator.

[56] *Ibid* 209–10. The decision in the *Yoder* case sketches the background necessary to understand the community. The Amish arrived in the United States during the eighteenth century from Switzerland. Members of the cult believe in the return to simplicity and early Christianity. According to their traditions, the Amish believe that personal salvation requires a life lived in isolation from materialistic modern industrial society, far from its detrimental influences. The idea of a life antagonistic to modernity and its values lies at the core of its beliefs.

expose their parents to church censure at the same time as it would endanger the spiritual salvation of the respondents and their children. The majority opinion accepted the respondents' position and ruled that the First Amendment of the Constitution, which protects freedom of religion, allows granting the children an exemption from secondary school education. The court also ruled that because the community's objections to formal compulsory education were profoundly anchored in their religious beliefs, compulsory secular secondary education illegally violates parental rights to determine their children's upbringing.[57]

Justice Douglas, representing the minority opinion, opposed the view expressed by the majority opinion. According to Justice Douglas, in cases such as these, the child's rights to receive appropriate education must be considered.[58] In such circumstances, the justice asked, what is the appropriate balance to be achieved between the three parties or stakeholders: the state, parents and children? Justice Douglas was convinced that, in such circumstances, children are entitled to express their own opinions and reveal their views before the court.[59] Thus, Justice Douglas joined the majority in respect of one of the respondents, whose daughter testified to her objections to secondary education but did not agree with the majority's opinion in respect of the other two respondents, in the absence of the opportunity to hear the children express their own views and desires regarding the issue before the court.

The position taken by the court in this case favoured the group (the group's right to freedom of religion) at the expense of the individual (the right of a person—the child—to form their own opinions).[60] Considered

---

[57] Ibid 216. In the majority opinion, Justice Berger stated: 'The record in this case abundantly supports the claim that the traditional way of life of the Amish is not merely a matter of personal preference, but one of deep religious conviction, shared by an organized group, and intimately related to daily living'. And see ibid, 218-19: 'The impact of the compulsory-attendance law on respondents' practice of the Amish religion is not only severe, but inescapable, for the Wisconsin law affirmatively compels them, under threat of criminal sanction, to perform acts undeniably at odds with... their religious beliefs... enforcement of the State's requirement of compulsory formal education after the eighth grade would gravely endanger if not destroy the free exercise of respondents' religious beliefs'.

[58] Ibid. As expressed in the minority opinion: 'Our opinions are full of talk about the power of the parents over the child's education... And we have in the past analyzed similar conflicts between parent and State with little regard for the views of the child... Recent cases, however, have clearly held that the children themselves have a constitutionally protectable interest. These children are 'persons' within the meaning of the Bill of Rights'.

[59] Ibid 244–5: 'While the parents, absent dissent, normally speak for the entire family, the education of the child is a matter on which the child will often have decided views. He may want to be a pianist or an astronaut or an oceanographer. To do so he will have to break from the Amish tradition. It is the future of the student, not the future of the parents that is imperiled by today's decision. If a parent keeps his child out of school beyond the grade school, then the child will be forever barred from entry into the new and amazing world of diversity that we have today. The child may decide that is the preferred course, or he may rebel'.

[60] Again, it should be noted that the right to enjoy the exemption from compulsory secondary education was awarded to the parents and not the Amish as a group. Nevertheless, due to the

from a liberal stance, the court's argument is problematic because it ignored the impact of the decision on the capacity to make real choices, a right granted to minority group members. This point requires clarification: liberal tolerance of minority group positions rests on respect for individual rather than group freedoms. In consequence, liberalism cannot sanction any limitation that violates the right to education, freedom of conscience or other freedoms granted to individual members of minority groups.

Importantly, this critique concurs with international law. Various international covenants recognise the rights of minority groups to establish their own school systems but qualify this right with the requirement that its exercise not violate the rights of the group's individual members. Thus, for example, Article 5(1)(c) of the Convention Against Discrimination in Education, 1960, recognises the right of national minorities to maintain and administer their own school systems under the condition that they do not employ this right as a means to prevent their members from understanding the culture and language of the majority or from participating in public activities, or as a means to violate national sovereignty.

IV CONCLUSION

Within the complex of socio-economic rights, the right to education (in its broadest sense) has won greatest protection in national constitutions, a protection well warranted. This chapter has indicated the importance of education and the justifications for its protection. Constitutional protection endows rights to education with a firm normative status that reinforces the status of education within national political agendas and strengthens its position relative to other competing interests. However, the laconic wording that characterises constitutions cannot release the courts from the necessity of balancing rights in those cases where rights to

---

ties binding the parents to the community, it was rightly decided to view the exemption as awarded to the Amish as a group (although the right would be exercised on an individual basis by the parents of each child) because the parents accept the group's traditions and beliefs. This stance is expressed in the following statement: Barry, above n 36, 208–209: 'In practice, no doubt, any Amish parents who aspired to something better for their children than a one-room schoolhouse with an unqualified teacher educating them for 'farm and domestic work' would pack up and leave. If they stayed and sought to enroll their children in the local high school they would unquestionably be censured and, if they remain obdurate, excommunicated... Regardless of the answer, however, it still remains true that *Yoder* attributed rights to individual parents and not to Amish communities... Although it is the parents who sign up to exercise the right to keep their children out of school after the eighth grade, we may say – rather more appositely than in the case of most of the biblical tags with which the Amish lard their petitions and declarations – 'The voice is Jacob's voice, but the hands are the hands of Esau'.

education either conflict with other constitutional interests or contradict one another. Within this context, the decisions presented here represent crucial illustrations of the range of conflicts arising in the practice of these rights.

13

The Right to Health in an Era of Privatisation and Globalisation

National and International Perspectives

AEYAL M GROSS*

> Inequalities of access and outcome constitute the chief drama of modern medicine. (Paul Framer[1])

I INTRODUCTION: THE RIGHT TO HEALTH AS A HUMAN RIGHT

What is more important to a person than their health? Harm to a person's health, whether the result of illness, accident, or intentional injury by another, is likely to cause pain and suffering and perhaps even death. Emerson's declaration 'The first wealth is health!' expresses well the centrality of health in people's lives. It seems that health is one of the most valuable assets a person possesses and its preservation is of supreme importance.

Any conception of human rights intended to protect the things most vital for a person's existence in the world and their ability to live a life of dignity and equality, free of degradation and with the capacity to make the most meaningful choices in life, will accord health a prominent status.

* The research for this chapter was funded by the Israel National Institute for Health Policy and Health Services Research (Grant R/67/03). Additional funding was provided by the Cegla Center for Interdisciplinary Research of the Law and the Minerva Center for Human Rights, both of the Tel Aviv University Faculty of Law. My special gratitude to Tamar Feldman, Amiram Gil, Liron Halberich, Magi Otsri and Nathan Wise for their dedicated and comprehensive research work and to Dori Spivak for his great assistance. Thanks also to Adi Kronfeld for his assistance at the preliminary stages of the research and special thanks to Dana Rothman-Meshulam for providing her superb language and editing skills. I am grateful to David Bilchitz and Lisa Forman for their comments on an earlier version of this chapter.
[1] P Framer, *Pathologies of Power: Health, Human Rights and the New War on the Poor* (Berkeley, University of California Press, 2005) 164.

Health is crucial for a person to function in the world, to be free of pain and suffering, to fulfil themselves, and even to live. Deprivation of freedom of expression, freedom of religion, or even education can be reversed. In such cases, although later rectification of the violation will not diminish the force of the original injury, it is nonetheless likely to decrease the damage that was caused. In contrast, injury to health is often irreversible, and any obstacle to realising the right to health leads to bodily injury and can even result in death.

In light of this importance of health in a person's life, it could be expected to take a central place in the canon of human rights. But for many years, the right to health has been relegated to the 'stepchild' status generally assigned to social or so-called 'second generation' rights. The traditional development of the conception of human rights as consumed primarily by civil and political rights has not side-stepped the right to health. In the international arena, even though the right to health was defined more than a half- century ago, the different human rights frameworks have been slow to address it, echoing the traditional treatment of other social rights. However, recent years have seen an increase in awareness regarding social rights in general and the right to health specifically. The discussion of the right to health has expanded at the international and national levels. Amongst the most noteworthy developments at the international level are: the comprehensive document released in 2000 by the UN Committee on Economic, Social and Cultural Rights, which sought to infuse the right to health with more concrete substance[2]; the appointment in 2002 of a Special Rapporteur on the right to health by the UN Commission on Human Rights[3]; the extensive use of the notion of a right to health by the World Health Organisation ('WHO'); and the focus on, and recognition of, the relevance of the right in the debate on the crisis over the supply of anti-AIDS drugs in developing countries, particularly in Brazil and South Africa, which has brought to the forefront the tension between intellectual property rights in the drugs and the right to health of those in need of the drugs but unable to pay their high price.[4]

---

[2] See n 30 below.

[3] See P Hunt, 'The UN Special Rapporteur on the Right to Health: Key Objectives, Themes and Interventions' (2003) 7 *Health and Human Rights* 1. See the first report of the Special Rapporteur, 'The Right of Everyone to the Enjoyment of the Highest Attainable Standard of Physical and Mental Health', Report of the Special Rapporteur, P Hunt, Commission on Human Rights, 13 February 2003, E/CN4/2003/58 (hereinafter Rapporteur's Report), and subsequent reports available at <http://www.ohchr.org/english/issues/health/ right/index.htm>.

[4] On the issue of anti-AIDS drugs and the tension between the right to health and intellectual property rights, see 169–207 and accompanying text. For a discussion of the significance of these developments in general for the status of the right to health, see B Loff and S Gruskin, 'Getting Serious About the Right to Health' (2000) 356 (9239) *Lancet* 1453 and P Hunt, 'The Right to Health: From the Margins to the Mainstream' (2002) 340 (9398) *Lancet* 1878.

The constantly expanding discussion of the right to health constitutes part of a broader understanding of the link between health and human rights. This view is not limited only to issues touching on the right to health, but relates also to additional connections between the two subject-matters, such as the ways in which health policy influences human rights other than the right to health, the ramifications for health of various human rights violations and an analysis of the link between health and human rights particularly in the context of socio-economic class and health. The turn to human rights analysis in the sphere of public health is linked to the international AIDS/HIV crisis.[5] In recent years, there has been an appreciable breakthrough in the framework of journals, research institutes and different publications addressing the link between health and human rights, including the right to health itself.[6]

As will be seen, the right to health relates both to the background conditions for health as well as the right to receive medical care. The discussion in this chapter, however, focuses only on the aspect of the right to receive medical care and the scope of that right. It considers the extent to which the right to health is protected as a human right and its accessibility and equal distribution as manifested in the scope of the health services provided to eligible recipients and the conditions in which the services are provided. Moreover, in the context of the treatment of the notion of health in international and comparative law, I argue that, when the right is treated as inconsequential, health becomes a commodity or good—something that is purchased with money by those who wish to and have the means to do so. The chapter thus delves into the tension between

---

[5] See JM Mann et al, 'Health and Human Rights' in J Mann (ed), *Health and Human Rights: A Reader* (New York, Routledge, 1999) 7–20; D Fidler, *International Law and Infectious Diseases* (Oxford, Oxford University Press, 1999) 169–220. In Fidler's words, 'International human rights law has entered into *microbialpolitik*.'

[6] In 1993 a rudimentary research institute on the subject of health and human rights, the François-Xavier Bagnoud Center for Health and Human Rights, was set up at Harvard University. In 1994, the Center began to publish the *Health and Human Rights* journal. In 2002 the *Journal of Law, Medicine and Ethics* devoted a special issue to the subject of health and human rights, 'Symposium: Health, Law, and Human Rights: Exploring the Connections' (2002) 30(4) *Journal of Law, Medicine and Ethics*. See also the attempt at an in-depth analysis of the right from the perspective of international law and at infusing it with substance in this framework in B Toebes, *The Right to Health as a Human Right in International Law* (Antwerpen, Groeningen and Oxford, Intersentia–Hart, 1999). See also the collections of documents in G Alfredsson and K Tomasevski (eds), *A Thematic Guide to Documents on Health and Human Rights* (The Hague, Springer, 1998) and S Marks (ed), *Health and Human Rights: Basic International Documents* (Cambridge, FXB Center for Health and Human Rights, 2006), and the collections J Mann above n 5 and S Gruskin et al (eds), *Perspectives on Health and Human Rights* (New York / London, Routledge, 2005). For an overview of these developments and a look at the relationship between health and human rights, see S Marks, 'The Evolving Field of Health and Human Rights: Issues and Methods' (2002) 30 *Journal of Law, Medicine and Ethics* 739; S Gruskin and D Tarantola, 'Health and Human Rights' in S Gruskin et al (eds), *Perspectives on Health and Human Rights* (New York / London, Routledge, 2005) 3–57.

the view that 'seriously' treats health as a right,[7] and the view that rejects health as a right and, in practice, increasingly turns health into something more closely resembling a commodity. At the same time, I argue that the role that rights can play in the context of health care should be recognised as limited. The turn to rights analysis, in the context of public health systems which are facing the challenges of privatisation and globalisation, raises complex questions about the role of human rights. Within the complex public/private matrix, which is a feature of health systems and of rights themselves, the risk exists that rights analysis, with its focus on the individual, may actually protect private interests in a way that will reinforce rather than counter the inequalities created by privatisation. However, I argue that an understanding of the right to health as requiring equal accessibility to health care may assist in avoiding such risks. This aspect of the discussion rests on the idea of the right to health as deriving from both international law and the national law of various countries and considers whether, when dealing with rights in general and the right to health specifically, there is a need to relate not only to the abstract rights-bearer but also to the concrete individual who bears the needs.

The chapter is divided into four parts. Part II deals with the attempt to infuse substance into the right to health. Relying on international law and theoretical writings on the subject, I will suggest possible concrete, albeit not exhaustive, contents for the right to health as a human right. Part III considers the interaction between public health and human rights in a number of countries, with particular focus on Canada, South Africa, and Israel, reflecting on both the potential and limitations of judicial review of decisions in the public health sphere. Part IV examines the conflict within international law between the right to health and the protection of patents in drugs, and Part V concludes, with observations on the role and limits of the right to health in this era of privatisation and globalisation.

II WHAT IS THE RIGHT TO HEALTH?

A The Development of the Notion of the Right to Health as a Human Right

The notion of a right to health is rooted in two historical developments: first, the public health movement that began in the nineteenth century and, second, the recognition of social rights that crystallised in the twentieth

---

[7] The metaphor of taking rights seriously is borrowed from the title of Ronald Dworkin's well-known book *Taking Rights Seriously* (London, Duckworth, 1977).

century.[8] The starting-point of the discussion on social rights in the twentieth century was the 1948 Universal Declaration of Human Rights. However, even prior to this document, the right to health was mentioned in the 1946 Constitution of the World Health Organisation. Although the 1948 Universal Declaration of Human Rights does not include an independent clause addressing the right to health, its Article 25(1) states that:

> Everyone has the right to a standard of living adequate for the health and well-being of himself and of his family, including food, clothing, housing and medical care and necessary social services, and the right to security in the event of unemployment, sickness, disability, widowhood, old age or other lack of livelihood in circumstances beyond his control.[9]

This general pronouncement was translated into a clause that is far more specific with regard to the right to health in the 1966 International Covenant on Economic, Social and Cultural Rights. Article 12 of the Covenant proclaims:

> 1. The States Parties to the present Covenant recognize the right of everyone to the enjoyment of the highest attainable standard of physical and mental health.
> 2. The steps to be taken by the States Parties to the present Covenant to achieve the full realization of this right shall include those necessary for:
>   (a) The provision for the reduction of the stillbirth-rate and of infant mortality and for the healthy development of the child;
>   (b) The improvement of all aspects of environmental and industrial hygiene;
>   (c) The prevention, treatment and control of epidemic, endemic, occupational and other diseases;
>   (d) The creation of conditions which would assure to all medical service and medical attention in the event of sickness.[10]

As part of a treaty that has been widely ratified across the globe and is legally binding in many countries, Article 12 is currently the foremost international legal document addressing the right to health. Accordingly, the contents of the Article warrant consideration. Of most particular note is the fact that the Article recognises the right to health as encompassing a right to enjoy the highest attainable standard of physical and mental health and mandates creating adequate conditions for ensuring that all receive health services and medical care in the event of illness.

---

8 Toebes, above n 6.

9 UN Universal Declaration of Human Rights, GA Resolution 217 A(III), adopted and proclaimed by the General Assembly 10 December 1948, 183rd meeting available at <http://www.unhchr.ch/udhr/index.htm>.

10 International Covenant on Economic, Social and Cultural Rights, adopted 16 December 1966, entered into force 3 January 1976, 993 UNTS 3.

Subsequent to Article 12, a number of clauses dealing with the right to health appeared in other major human rights treaties. Two additional central documents are the 1978 Declaration of Alma-Ata[11] and the 1998 World Health Declaration,[12] both of which were drafted in the framework of the WHO. The Alma-Ata Declaration sets forth some of the principles that have had considerable impact on the way in which the right to health is conceived. The Declaration emphasises the fact that health constitutes a fundamental human right; it points to the disparities in health conditions amongst states and within states, asserting that these divergences are unacceptable. On the basis of these principles, the Declaration places the emphasis on primary health care, which should be universally accessible. Primary health care, according to the Declaration, should deal with the primary health issues facing the community and should include, amongst other things: education with regard to health problems and their prevention; provision of food, nutrition, water and sanitation; immunisation against major infectious diseases; and supply of essential drugs.

An additional pivotal document is the Doha Declaration, a product of the anti-AIDS drugs supply crisis of recent years. This crisis arose in the wake of the widespread impact of the disease on populations in poverty-stricken nations. In light of the high price of the drugs needed by AIDS patients, various nations, including Brazil and South Africa, asserted a right to sell generic drugs. The drug companies objected to this as a violation of their patent rights. After the matter appeared on the agenda of the World Trade Organization ('WTO'), the Organization adopted a declaration at its Doha Ministerial Conference in 2001, which provided that the patent arrangements in the framework of the WTO that are set forth in the Trade-related Aspects of Intellectual Property Rights ('TRIPS') Agreement do not preclude Organization member states from taking measures to protect public health. The Declaration further provided that the TRIPS Agreement can and should be interpreted and implemented in line with the right of member states to protect public health and, in particular, to promote the accessibility of drugs to all.[13]

In light of the many international human rights treaties and other international documents containing provisions dealing with the right to health, and the more than sixty national constitutions that recognise the right to health (in addition to the forty constitutions that guarantee rights related

---

[11] Declaration of Alma-Ata, International Conference on Primary Health Care, Alma-Ata, USSR, 6–12 September 1978.

[12] World Health Declaration, European Health for All No 5, 1998.

[13] Doha Ministerial Declaration on the TRIPS Agreement and Public Health, adopted 14 November 2001, WT/MIN (01)/DEC/2, Art 4, available via <http://www.wto.org/English/thewto_e/minist_e/min01_e/mindecl_e.htm>. For a discussion of the implications of the Doha Declaration, see nn 189–202 below and accompanying text.

to health),[14] many maintain that the right to health has acquired the status of a universal right and now constitutes customary international law.[15] This has binding legal ramifications manifested in the form of the imposition of an obligation to uphold the right to health also on those few states that are not party to the International Covenant on Economic, Social and Cultural Rights.

B The Contents of the Right to Health and Its Two Components

In discussing the right to health, we must not focus only on the health services in the state providing those services, for the right is not limited to the right to health services. A person's health is affected by many factors. We cannot speak of a right to be healthy or a right not to be ill, if only because it is difficult to conceive of corresponding duties that would not be impossible or unreasonable to meet. Rather, the right to health can and should encompass an array of factors that are likely to affect a person's health. Such factors can include, for example, improvements in water, sanitation, nutrition, or other elements no less vital for ensuring health than medical care.[16] This is the stance adopted by the UN Committee on Economic, Social and Cultural Rights, which is responsible for the Covenant's implementation, as articulated in the Committee's General Comment 14 on the right to the highest attainable standard of health.

The right to health can be divided into two principal components: (1) the background conditions that affect health[17] and (2) medical care.[18] These two components embody two aspects of the right for which there are possible correlative duties—both affirmative and negative—to be borne by the state and other entities. The duties of the state and third parties in the context of the background conditions that affect health are likely to

---

[14] For this figure, see the Rapporteur's Report, above n 3; see also Hunt, above n 3, para 20. Kinney lists 109 states that mention rights related to health in their constitutions. She notes that, even though the right to health is given no mention in the US Constitution, it is recognised in a number of state constitutions: ED Kinney, 'The International Human Right to Health: What Does It Mean for Our Nation and World?' (2001) 34 *Indiana Law Review* 1457. For a comprehensive survey, which shows that 67.5% of the world's constitutions have a provision addressing health or health care, see ED Kinney and BA Clark, 'Provisions for Health and Health Care in the Constitutions of the World' (2004) *Cornell International Law Journal* 285. For a broad survey of the right to health in the constitutions of countries on the American continent, see Fuenzalida-Pulema and Scholle-Connor, n 157 below, at 607–47. For the same regarding the European continent, see Den Exter, France and Hermans, n 44 below.

[15] 'Health' in A Clapham and S Marks, *International Human Rights Lexicon* (Oxford, Oxford University Press, 2005) 197–208; see also Kinney and Clark, above n 14.

[16] K Tomasevski, 'Health Rights' in A Eide et al (eds), *Economic, Social and Cultural Rights – A Textbook* (Boston, Martinus Nijhoff, 1995) 125, 126.

[17] For a discussion of some of the factors comprising the background conditions of health, such as clean drinking water, sanitation, adequate nutritious food, environmental health and occupational health, see Toebes, above n 6, 254–8.

[18] On the right to medical care as part of the broader right to health, see *ibid* 16–19.

include such affirmative duties as the duty to ensure water and sanitation systems and negative duties such as the duty to prevent health-endangering pollution. In the context of medical care, the duties are likely to include affirmative duties such as ensuring an accessible medical system and negative duties such as prohibiting the prevention of medical care, on the one hand, and the coercion of medical treatment, on the other.

When examining the right to health from this broad starting-point, whose purpose is to define the right to health so as to include the factors that affect health and the extent to which the right is implemented, an assessment of the given population's state of health is called for. Assessing the extent to which the right is implemented in a given state does not have to be limited to an evaluation of government policy regarding the background conditions for health and the systems that ensure medical care. Rather, the assessment should also be based on outcomes. The WHO has set indicators based on statistical information that are intended to point to the state of health in any given country. These indicators paint an important, albeit incomplete, picture of the status of the right to health. Any comprehensive discussion of the right, including an examination of the extent to which it is guaranteed in certain countries, must therefore take these indicators into account,[19] since they are likely to be relevant to the right's degree of implementation in countries in general[20] as well as in specific states.[21] The legal discussion—the type of discussion conducted in this chapter—focuses, naturally, on legislation and case law and thus is only a partial description of the degree of implementation of the right to health. Some of the issues to be considered within this framework were addressed in the first report of the UN Special Rapporteur on the right to health. The report focused on the relationship between the right to health and poverty and on the right to health in the context of discrimination and stigmatisation. Thus, for example, it discussed the need to develop strategies for decreasing poverty that are grounded in the right to health and that deal with the improvement of access to health services for the poor, the lessening of the financial burden borne by the poor, and the guarantee of a healthier environment for them.

An additional principle that should be considered in the context of the substance of the right to health is the principle of progressive realisation that is established in international law in general with regard to social

---

[19] For a discussion of these indicators, see P Hunt, *Reclaiming Social Rights: International and Comparative Perspectives* (Aldershot, Ashgate, 1996) 123–30.

[20] *Ibid* 129–30.

[21] For a discussion of the relationship between the health indicators and a human rights approach to health, see the *Annual Report of the Special Rapporteur on the Right of Everyone to the Enjoyment of the Highest Attainable Standard of Physical and Mental Health* (2006), United Nations, Economic and Social Council, E/CN4/2006/48, 3 March 2006, available at <http://www.ohchr.org/english/issues/health/right/annual.htm>.

rights. Article 2(1) of the Covenant on Economic, Social and Cultural Rights provides that each party state will undertake to:

> take steps… to the maximum of its available resources, with a view to achieving progressively the full realization of the rights recognised in the… Covenant by all appropriate means, including particularly the adoption of legislative measures.

When interpreting this principle, we must keep in mind that it does not turn the right to health into a purely abstract, intangible right, for the right is accompanied by specific corresponding duties borne by the states to take steps to implement the right. Moreover, the conventional view is that at the heart or core of the right lie obligations that the states must realise immediately. This view is accepted with regard to social rights in general and, as will be shown in what follows, the Committee on Economic, Social and Cultural Rights detailed in its General Comment some such obligations specifically with regard to the right to health. Furthermore, we can derive from the principle of progressive realisation a significant constraint on the states' power to take retrogressive measures which impair progress in realising the right.

C The Attempt to Circumscribe the Scope of the Right to Health and Some Basic Dilemmas

A problematic aspect to the attempt to give concrete substance to the right to health is, of course, the scope of the right. Much of the literature has tried to contend with the question of the scope of the right, on the one hand, and the state's obligations, on the other.[22] In theory, it is possible to impose maximal duties on the state with regard to both aspects of the right: the duty to ensure conditions that will maximally guarantee the health of the state's citizens and residents and the duty to ensure that all receive the maximum quality and amount of medical care necessary. However, such a maximalist conception of the right is hindered by the limited resources at the state's disposal. Investing all of the state's resources in health would come at the expense of education, housing and other important matters related in part to realising other rights.[23] Thus it is difficult to formulate abstractly precise determinations regarding the state's duty with regard to the right to health. Nonetheless, international law and the theoretical literature on the issue can help in setting some principles that can assist in

---

[22] See, eg: Toebes, n 6 above; V Leary, 'The Right to Health in International Human Rights Law' (1994) 1 *Health and Human Rights* 25; Tomasevski, above n 16; V Leary, 'Implications of a Right to Health' in K Mahoney and P Mahoney (eds), *Human Rights in the Twenty-First Century, A Global Challenge* (Boston, Martinus Nijhoff, 1993); Hunt, above n 19; Fidler, above n 5, at 302–309.

[23] R Dworkin, 'Justice in the Distribution of Health Care' (1993) 38 *McGill Law Journal* 883.

assessing the implementation of the right to health in different countries. However, its concrete implementation will depend on the structure of the health system in the given state and the prevailing conditions there.

In engaging in this discussion, we must devote some consideration to the difficulties entailed in using a rights concept as a tool for determining the issue of health: formulating specific rights in the context of health is a complex matter that touches on the allocation of resources and prioritising. A question arises as to whether the resort to a concept of rights can be relevant in the context of a public health system which is structured around priority-setting against a background of limited resources. How can we articulate a human right that both advances mutual social dependence and guarantees an individual right? Mutual social dependence is not a social ideal in this context but, rather, a reality that is imposed due to the limited nature of the resources. Such questions as who will or will not receive treatment must be answered. But the human rights discourse has difficulty responding to such questions, for it evolved around the individual rights-bearer and is of little avail in matters of how to allocate resources or settle conflicts between rights-bearers. The likely outcome may be the abandonment of the rights discourse for a utilitarian outlook. The challenge here, then, is to consider whether the rights discourse can internalise a concern for the interests of others. Is there an alternative to the individualistic rights discourse that can encompass the questions of mutual dependence?[24] For example, how does the assertion that every person has a right to the highest attainable standard of health further us in determining, as courts in various countries have been called upon to do, which drugs can be given and which not, or which patients will receive drugs covered (or not) by national health insurance? Any such determination would be of a distributive nature, and it is doubtful whether the appeal to individual rights can help in arriving at a solution. Resorting to individual rights may camouflage the distributive nature of the decision and encourage disregard for the needs of others. It probably impedes the social procedures in whose framework distributive social choices are conducted.[25] Moreover, due to the individualistic nature of the rights, resort to them probably encourages decontextualisation of the social

---

[24] These questions were posed by Martha Minow alongside two additional questions regarding the right to health: How can we successfully formulate a human right whose realisation is contingent on material resources? And how can a right be formulated that is both universal and sensitive to divergences amongst human beings in age, sex, cultural tradition, etc.? However, as Minow herself points out, the various questions she raises are not unique to the right to health or to social rights in general. Rather, they arise also in the context of political and civil rights. Minow rejects the distinction between the types of different rights. See M Minow, Participating in an Interdisciplinary Discussion Held at Harvard Law School in September 1993, 'Session I: Applying Rights Rhetoric to Economic and Social Claims' in *Economic and Social Rights and the Right to Health* (Harvard Law School Human Rights Program, 1995) 2–5.

[25] Marks and Clapham, above n 15, at 207.

reality and may come at the expense of considering the overall social context.[26] This is not to imply that the appeal to rights is irrelevant or insignificant in the framework of health. The resort to the rights discourse in no way trivialises the need to set a broad health policy, which entails making choices, setting priorities and reaching decisions of a distributive nature. However, as noted by Susan Marks and Andrew Clapham, the rights discourse should shape health policy and enable insistence on the choices and decisions, including those relating to the structure of the health system, based on certain fundamental principles. These principles, which constitute central elements of the right to health, include: (1) a prohibition on discrimination; (2) the state's duty to take measures, in accordance with the maximum available resources, to increase the accessibility of health for all its citizens and residents, both in the sense of creating background conditions for health and in the sense of providing medical care; and (3) meeting core obligations that, in any event, are binding on the state.[27] In the framework of this discussion, we must recall that rights have normative and rhetorical significance in any discussion of society's responses to human needs. And they should be treated more seriously than mere aspiration: they constitute a commitment to action. Realising rights is not a simple matter; indeed, it is the outcome of complex negotiations between different entities, public and private, and is effected through vigorous political and legal work. These efforts, although universal in scope, must be focused on society's most vulnerable members and those with the least available resources. We cannot ignore disparate allocations in the context of health, and we must consider how the rights tool can be used to draw attention to inequality, pain and suffering, and help diminish them.[28] Using the notion of the right to health, then, manifests the principles of human rights in the sphere of health. Even though it is not a substitute for the need to set policy, the right to health may provide tools that enable critical review of policy decisions. Thus the possibility of addressing the question of health from the vantage-points of justice and rights emerges, and not only from an economic, utilitarian or technical angle. Viewing health as a legal right, and not as a privilege or outcome of altruism or as a good or commodity, is likely to open channels for judicial review that will protect health. Here we can see that conceiving health as a right facilitates legal challenges to inequality in health, whether in the form

---

[26] D Otto, 'Linking Health and Human Rights: A Critical Legal Perspective' (1994) 1 *Health and Human Rights* 273, 277–9.

[27] See Marks and Clapham, above n 15, 208. On core obligations, see also D Bilchitz, 'The Right to Health Care Services and the Minimum Core: Disentangling the Principled and Pragmatic Strands' (2006) 7 *ESR Review* available at <http://www.communitylawcentre.org.za/Projects/Socio-Economic-Rights/esr-review/esr-previous-editions/esr-july-2006.pdf/>.

[28] This discussion is inspired by Minow's words, above n 24, 4–5.

of economic inequality or in disparities amongst different groups, such as women or ethnic minorities.[29]

D Substantiating the Right to Health: General Comment 14

General Comment 14 of the UN Committee on Economic, Social and Cultural Rights[30] is perhaps the most successful attempt to infuse concrete substance into the right to health. The Comment is in fact the official interpretation of Article 12 of the Covenant on Economic, Social and Cultural Rights, which proclaims the right of every person to enjoy the highest attainable standard of physical and mental health. Below, nine chief principles that emerge from the General Comment are listed, in particular those that are relevant to the subjects discussed in this chapter. I pay special note to central parts of the Comment due to its lofty status and the fact that it is the product of profound thought regarding the right to health, but also because its drafters succeeded in accurately identifying certain principles that are likely to be significant in giving concrete substance to the right to health and in applying the right as a tool for scrutinising policy, in a way that may expand access to health.

i General Principle on the Realisation of the Right

Realising the right to health is likely to be achieved in a variety of different and complementary manners. These include the formulation of health policy, implementation of health plans and adoption of specific legal documents. Whatever the case, the right includes elements that are legally enforceable.

ii The Scope of the Right

The right to health is not limited to the right to health care. It is not a right to be healthy but, rather, a right that comprises social and economic components that foster conditions in which human beings are able to lead healthy lives, as well as touching on background conditions for health, such as sustenance and nutrition, housing, accessibility to clean and potable water and sanitation, safe and healthy workplace conditions, and a healthy environment.

---

[29] For a discussion of the advantages to adopting a human rights framework in the debate over health from vantage-points similar to those enumerated here, see Otto, above n 26, 276–7.

[30] General Comment 14: The Right to the Highest Attainable Standard of Health (Article 12), E/C12/2000/4, CESCR (11 August 2000).

iii Inclusiveness of the Right

The right to health includes freedoms and entitlements. Among these freedoms is a person's right to control his or her health and body and to be free from interference in his or her body in the form of non-consensual medical treatment, torture and so on. The positive entitlements include the right to a system of health protection that provides equal opportunity for all people to enjoy the highest attainable level of health. This level is set while taking into account the conditions of the private individual and the state's potentially available resources. While the state cannot ensure the health of all people — that is, cannot guarantee that no one will contract any possible disease — this right does place a duty on the state to ensure a range of facilities, products, services and conditions essential for realising the highest attainable level of health.

iv Four Additional Fundamental Principles

The right to health encompasses four fundamental principles that must be implemented in accordance with the prevailing conditions in the particular state:

a Availability   The state must have an adequate amount of existing health facilities, products, services and programmes. The precise nature of these features will fluctuate in accordance with varying circumstances, including the state's level of development. In any event, they include the background conditions for health, such as water and sanitation, hospitals, clinics, trained medical staff and essential drugs.[31]

b Accessibility   All health facilities, products and services must be equally accessible to all, without any discrimination. There are four overlapping aspects to accessibility: (1) Prohibition on discrimination — accessibility to all, without discrimination, especially to the most vulnerable and marginalised sectors of the population (see the forthcoming discussion on the prohibition on discrimination). (2) Physical accessibility to all sectors of the population, especially vulnerable and marginalised populations, such as minorities, women, children, the elderly and disabled, and HIV and AIDS carriers and patients. (3) Economic accessibility to all. The system of payment for health services, as well as for services related to the background conditions for health, must be based on the principle of equity and must guarantee that these services, whether provided privately or publicly, are accessible to everyone, especially socially underprivileged groups. Equity mandates that the health expenditure burden borne by poor households not be disproportionate to that borne by wealthier households.

---

31 On availability in this sense, see also Toebes, above n 6, 115–16.

(4) Accessibility to information. This is the right to request, receive and provide information and ideas on health issues, subject to the right to personal medical confidentiality.

c Acceptability   All health facilities, products, and services must abide by medical ethics and be sensitive to and respectful of the communities, gender differences, confidentiality and the duty to improve the health status of all those concerned.

d Quality   All health facilities, products and services must be suitable for their purpose and of good medical and scientific quality. To this end, necessary, amongst other things, are skilled medical teams, drugs and scientifically-approved hospital equipment, as well as clean and potable water and adequate sanitation.[32]

v Prohibition on Discrimination

The General Comment reasserts, in accordance with the Covenant on Economic, Social and Cultural Rights, the prohibition on any form of discrimination in access to health services and background health conditions on the basis of race, colour, sex, language, religion, political or other opinion, national or social origin, property, birth, physical or mental disability, health condition (including HIV and AIDS), sexual orientation, or civil, political, social, or other status. The Comment stresses that even countries suffering from a severe deficiency in available resources must protect the most vulnerable members of society. Special emphasis is placed on equality of access to health care and health services: states bear a special obligation to provide those lacking sufficient means with the necessary health insurance and access to health facilities and to prevent any of the prohibited forms of discrimination.

vi The Significance of the Principle of Progressive Realisation

The Comment stresses that, despite the fact that the principle of progressive realisation is embedded in the Covenant, the Covenant also sets obligations that take immediate effect, such as the states' obligations to guarantee that the right to health is exercised without discrimination and to take all steps towards the full realisation of Article 12. The measures must be deliberate, concrete and effective towards the goal of full implementation of the right to health. The obligation of progressive realisation means that the states bear specific and ongoing duties to move as expeditiously and effectively as possible towards the full implementation of Article 12. There is a strong

---

[32] On quality, see also *ibid* 112.

presumption of a prohibition on retrogressive measures with respect to the right to health. In the event that such steps are taken, the state bears the burden of proving that they were adopted only subsequent to extremely cautious consideration of all alternatives and that they can be justified in the context of the full use of the state's maximum available resources.

vii The Obligations Borne by the States

As does every human right, the right to health sets three types of obligations for the states: the obligation to respect, the obligation to protect and the obligation to fulfil.

a The obligation to respect The states are obliged to refrain from impeding the exercise of the right to health.

b The obligation to protect The states are obliged to take all necessary steps to prevent third parties from impeding the guarantee of the right to health. In this context, states must ensure equal access to health care and services provided by third parties and that privatisation of the health system does not impair the availability, accessibility, acceptability or quality of health facilities, products and services.

c The obligation to fulfil This obligation requires the states to take all appropriate measures—including legislative, administrative, budgetary, judicial and promotional—to ensure the full realisation of the right to health. The implications of this obligation are that the states are required to give adequate recognition to the right to health in their political and legal systems, preferably by way of legislation, and to adopt a health policy with a detailed programme aimed at realising the right to health. Amongst other things, the states are obliged to ensure a health system (public, private or mixed) that is economically accessible to all.

viii Core Obligations

According to the Committee on Economic, Social and Cultural Rights, the core obligations of the right to health—namely, those obligations borne by the states related to ensuring the minimal required level of realisation of the right—encompass at least the minimal level of the right, including essential primary health care. In addition, the Committee lists, amongst other things, the following aspects as a partial enumeration of the states' core obligations:

(a) to ensure non-discriminatory access to health facilities, products and services, especially with respect to vulnerable and marginalised sectors;
(b) to provide essential medicines, as defined by the WHO;

(c) to ensure equitable distribution of all health facilities, products and services;

(d) to adopt and implement a national public health strategy based on epidemiological evidence, that addresses the health needs of the entire population;

(e) to ensure access to the minimal essential food that is nutritionally adequate and safe and to ensure freedom from hunger for all; and

(f) to ensure access to basic shelter, housing and sanitation and an adequate supply of clean and potable water.

ix Violations

In considering whether there has been a violation of the right to health, it is necessary to discern whether a state is unable or is unwilling to comply with its obligations. A state that is unwilling to use the maximum of its available resources to realise the right to health is considered in violation of its obligations under Article 12. If resource constraints prevent a state from meeting its duties, then it bears the burden of showing that it took all possible steps to make use of its existing resources. In all events, however, there can be no justification for a state's non-compliance with the core obligations listed above. Adoption of retrogressive measures will be considered, as noted, a violation of the right to health. For example, official repeal or suspension of legislation essential for exercising the right to health or adoption of legislation or policy that is incompatible with preceding legal duties that relate to the right to health will be deemed in violation of Article 12. More broadly, the failure to adopt or implement a national public health policy that is aimed at guaranteeing the right to health, as well as the failure to allocate adequate resources and take steps to reduce distributive inequity with regard to health facilities, products and services, will all constitute such violations.[33]

Thus it is possible to see that the framework of the General Comment leaves a margin of discretion to the states with regard to the structure of their health systems. This notwithstanding, however, the states must take concrete measures to progress steadily towards the realisation of the right to health in all that relates to the four fundamental principles. Analysing General Comment 14 reveals how the right to health can contribute to the formulation of health policy: it cannot be discriminatory; it cannot impede access to health, including economic accessibility for weak sectors; and it

---

[33] When dealing with the matter of violations, it is important to recall that some approaches to social rights, particularly the right to health, propose structuring the discussion around the question of what is to be considered a violation of the right, as opposed to trying to determine the scope and limitations of the right from an abstract perspective. For one such attempt in the context of the right to health, see AR Chapman, 'Conceptualising the Right to Health: A Violations Approach' (1998) 65 *Tennessee Law Review* 389.

must be progressive, not repeal or suspend existing policy or legislation, which would constitute a retrogressive measure for which the state bears the burden of proving as unavoidable.[34]

E Funding Health and the Question of Rights

General Comment 14 demonstrates how the need to give concrete substance to the right to health entails imposing broad obligations on the state. There is no doubt that these obligations, in turn, impose great financial expense, and a fundamental issue in the debate over the right to health is the matter of the funding of the health system. This issue is particularly relevant to the aspect of the right that relates to entitlement to medical care. The funding issue is a significant factor in the extent to which the right to health is realised and in the matter of equity.

Any conception of the right to health as grounded on equal enjoyment of the right must hold that the right to health—specifically, the right to receive medical care—be allocated on a needs-basis. The question of funding is closely linked to this question. If the right to health is recognised as a fundamental right, significant divergences in anything relating to access to health and medical care will be considered a breach of the principle of equality.[35] The way in which the health system is funded affects both accessibility and equality. An egalitarian approach will require that health services be funded and paid for according to ability to pay and be provided according to need and not actual usage of health facilities. While a detailed discussion of the different models of health system funding is beyond the scope of this chapter, it is important to note that many different forms of funding do exist. The two prominent forms, which at times coexist alongside one another, are taxation and direct out-of-pocket payment by patients.[36] Taxation is considered a progressive

---

[34] B Toebes, in her comprehensive study on the right to health, offers a broader list of core obligations than that proposed in General Comment 14. Inspired by the various WHO documents relating to the right to health, Toebes asserts that the core obligations should also include maternal and child health care, including family planning, immunisation against the major infectious diseases, appropriate treatment of common diseases and injuries, provision of essential drugs, adequate supply of clean water and basic sanitation, and the elimination of severe health-endangering environmental threats. Toebes, above n 6, 283–4. Toebes also points to the risks entailed in the core content approach, as the remainder of the right might be considered unimportant. Thus, it should always be kept in mind that states are obliged to take steps towards the full enjoyment of the right. B Toebes, 'The Right to Health' in A Eide et al (eds), *Economic, Social and Cultural Rights* (Dordrecht / Boston / London, Kluwer, 2001) 169–190, at 176.

[35] Leary, above n 22, 483.

[36] For a discussion of various forms of funding, see: A Wagstaff and E van Doorslaer, 'Equity in the Finance of Health Care: Some International Comparisons' (1992) 11 *Journal of Health and Economics* 361; A Wagstaff et al, 'Equity in the Finance of Health Care: Some Further International Comparisons' (1999) 18 *Journal of Health and Economics* 263.

form of funding, though, of course, on the condition that the tax is progressive. In contrast, direct out-of-pocket payment by patients is a regressive form of funding if it constitutes the primary form of funding and, moreover, is a regressive component in systems that include a taxation component. Under a taxation system, the population pays a tax that funds the health system (in conjunction with other sources that do not derive from patients, such as the state budget), and the population receives medical care on a needs-basis. In contrast, the out-of-pocket system, based on need as well as actual use of medical care, without any consideration for patients' financial capabilities, is a regressive collection system, not only because the poor bear a relatively heavier burden, but also because illness and disease are more widespread amongst the poor.[37] Out-of-pocket payment thus widens the gap between the rich and the poor and hampers access to health services.[38] The tension between progressive financing on a taxation basis, which is intended to ensure maximum equity, and direct payments reflects the tension between the view of health as a right whose equal enjoyment must be guaranteed to all members of society and the view of health as a commodity or good that is purchased with money by those willing and able to pay for it.[39] The ramification of a shift between the two approaches is a move away from a rights approach to health towards a 'market' approach.[40] The latter clashes with the conception of health as a right, since it links the enjoyment of health to the ability to pay for it and turns the health system into a forum for the sale of 'products' to 'consumers' rather than for the provision of care to patients.[41]

---

[37] Wagstaff and van Doorslaer, above n 36, 361–4, 384–5.

[38] *European Health Care Reforms, Analysis of Current Strategies* 96 (Copenhagen, WHO Regional Office for Europe, 1996), cited in I Sheiman, 'Excessive State Commitments to Free Health Care in the Russian Federation: Outcomes and Health Policy Implications' in A den Exter, G France and H Hermans (eds), *The Right to Health Care in Several European Countries* (Boston, Kluwer Law International, 1999) 101–13.

[39] See: D Filc, 'The Commodification of Health: The Israeli Health Care System, between State, Civil Society and the Market' (1995) 6 *Theory and Critique* 1, 3 (Hebrew); Framer, above n 1, 175.

[40] On the contradiction between these two approaches, see V Leary, 'Defining the Right to Health Care' in A Chapman (ed), *Health Care Reform, A Human Rights Approach* (Washington, DC, Georgetown University Press, 1994) 87–105. On 'medicine-as-commerce,' see Framer, above n 1, 160–4.

[41] Framer, above n 1, 162.

III RECOGNITION AND PROTECTION OF THE RIGHT TO HEALTH AT THE STATE LEVEL: COMPARATIVE LAW AND THE ROLE OF COURTS

A The Importance of the National Experience

The right to health is recognised as a human right in a number of countries, currently explicitly guaranteed in some sixty constitutions.[42] The experiences of these countries, as well as of countries where the right is not explicitly recognised but their courts deliberate matters regarding access to health, have contributed significantly to the development of thought on what is encompassed in the right. By examining the case law from different countries we can consider what role rights analysis does and can have in the context of health. Critical analysis from the vantage-point of rights, when conducted at the state level, considers existing health systems. It enables us to examine whether the basic structure of an actual given system meets the standards of the right to health and whether the decisions made in the framework of that system are consistent with the right.

The dilemmas that the right to health raises in a world of limited resources have resulted in cases being brought before national courts in ever-increasing numbers.[43] The case law emerging from these courts has yet to offer a clear picture of the right to health, but the considerations weighed by the courts when deliberating these matters are discernible and telling. Indeed, the judicial experience reflects the difficulties entailed in contending with the right to health in conditions of limited resources.[44] As the discussion that follows illustrates, the human rights record in the context of public health is mixed. The idea of the right to health has broad potential to affect judicial decision-making in a way that can increase access and equality in health care; but sometimes infusing public health with rights analysis can in fact generate increased inequality. The ensuing discussion looks at a number of countries where there has been significant litigation around these issues, focusing on Canada, South Africa and Israel, and with a briefer discussion of four other relevant countries. This is by no means intended to be an exhaustive comparative law study, limited both in

---

[42] See above n 14 and accompanying text.

[43] See above n 38. See also the 'Symposium: Legislating and Litigating Health Care Rights Around the World', (2005) 33 *Journal of Law, Medicine and Ethics* 636. This symposium includes discussions of litigation in Canada, Israel, the Netherlands, Norway, South Africa, the UK and the US. For an overview see the introduction to the symposium by CF Flood, L Gable and LO Gostin, *ibid*, 636.

[44] A den Exter and H Hermans, 'The Right to Health Care: A Changing Concept?' in *The Right to Health Care in Several European Countries* (The Hague / London / Boston, Kluwer Law International, 1999) 1, 7.

terms of the countries selected and the scope of the discussion within the framework of each.

B Canada: From a Universal System to a Two-Tier One?

The Canadian Charter of Rights and Freedoms ('Charter of Rights') does not explicitly recognise the right to health; in fact, it omits socio-economic rights altogether. It does include, however, the right to life, liberty and security of the person in Section 7, which has featured in some of the litigation concerning health rights, although the courts have not found the section to entitle Canadians to publicly-funded health care.[45] Also relevant to the right to health is section 15, which guarantees the right to equal protection and equal benefit of the law without discrimination.

In contrast to the Charter of Rights, the Canada Health Act ('CHA')[46] proclaims in its preamble 'that continued access to quality health care without financial or other barriers will be critical to maintaining and improving the health and well-being of Canadians'. Section 3 of the Act determines that:

> the primary objective of Canadian health care policy is to protect, promote and restore the physical and mental well-being of residents of Canada and to facilitate reasonable access to health services without financial or other barriers.

Moreover, under section 7 of the Act, in order for the provinces (which provide the health care services) to qualify for cash contributions from the federal government, they must meet certain criteria, including comprehensiveness, universality and accessibility. The criterion of accessibility is described in section 12 as, inter alia, providing

> for insured health services on uniform terms and conditions and on a basis that does not impede or preclude, either directly or indirectly whether by charges made to insured persons or otherwise, reasonable access to those services by insured persons.

Whilst the CHA sets forth the framework for Canadian health care policy,[47] it does not establish one uniform health system. Rather, the provinces and territories that comprise Canada have individual health systems, which have to comply with the national standards set in the CHA in order to obtain federal funding. As articulated in section 4, the Act's purpose is

---

[45] C Flood, M Stabile and C Tuohy, 'What Is In and Out of Medicare? Who Decides?' in C Flood (ed), *Just Medicare: What's In, What's Out, How We Decide* (Toronto, 2006) 15–41, at 28.

[46] Canada Health Act RS 1985 ch C-6.

[47] See the discussion in P Macklem, chapter 10 of this volume.

to establish criteria and conditions in respect of insured health services and extended health care services provided under provincial law that must be met before a full cash contribution may be made.[48]

The Canadian public health insurance system, known as 'Medicare,' is said to be based on two principles: (1) access to important medical care on a needs-basis rather than ability to pay and (2) general taxation revenues the almost exclusive source of financing for the covered services.[49] However, since neither the CHA nor provincial legislation has provided definitions of what is 'medically necessary' or 'medically required',[50] the question of access to care, of which services should be available to Canadians, has been described as the 'most important issue facing Canadian health care today',[51] involving such critical matters as which health care services should be publicly funded in full, who decides and by what processes.[52] In most provinces, the only recourse when coverage of a particular treatment or service is refused is relief through administrative judicial review or a Charter challenge in the courts.[53] The courts have varied in their responses to challenges to government limitations on Medicare coverage.[54] Due to the interpretation of section 7 of the Charter as not including the right to publicly funded health care, these challenges are usually brought under the equality provision in section 15, with claimants arguing that they are not receiving a benefit (ie, public funding for a medical service) that they assert the government provides to others.[55] Most such challenges have been unsuccessful, although about one-third of the challenges to government health care policy have met with success.[56] The only successful challenge to policies limiting coverage to be upheld by the Supreme Court was in *Eldridge*,[57] brought by hearing-impaired appellants. The appellants claimed they had been subject to discriminatory treatment when the provincial government failed to provide funding for sign-language interpreters for the hearing-impaired when they receive medical services. The Court's decision was based on an infringement of the equality guarantee in section

[48] For a discussion of the Canadian health system, see C Flood, 'The Anatomy of Medicare' in J Downie, T Caulfield and C Flood (eds) *Canadian Health Law and Policy* (Toronto, Butterworths, 2002) 1–54.
[49] Flood, Stabile and Tuohy, above n 45, 15–41, at 15.
[50] *Ibid*, 17.
[51] C Flood, 'Introduction', in Flood, above n 45, 1.
[52] Flood, Stabile and Tuohy, above n 45, 15.
[53] *Ibid* 23–4, 27.
[54] *Ibid* 4, 27.
[55] D Greschner, 'Charter Challenges and Evidence-Based Decision-Making in the Health Care System: Towards a Symbiotic Relationship' in Flood, above n 45, 43.
[56] *Ibid*. See also CM Flood, 'Just Medicare: The Role of Canadian Courts in Determining Health Care Rights and Access' (2005) 33 *Journal of Law, Medicine and Ethics* 669. Flood argues that Canadian courts to date have staked out only a very limited role to help improve the internal fairness and operation of publicly-funded Medicare in Canada.
[57] *Eldridge v British Columbia (Attorney General)* [1997] 3 SCR 624.

15,[58] which explicitly includes disability as a prohibited ground of discrimination. Although the Court emphasised the centrality of communication to the delivery of medical services,[59] it also stressed that the case was about equal access to universally available services and not about a demand for discrete services or products, such as hearing aids, to alleviate their general disadvantage. The Court stated that:

> Their claim is not for a benefit that the government, in the exercise of its discretion to allocate resources to address various social problems, has chosen not to provide.[60]

This reasoning in *Eldridge* resulted in a narrow interpretation of its holding in the later case of *Auton*.[61] In the latter, the claimants were seeking funding for intensive behavioural therapy that they believed to benefit their autistic children. They argued that the failure to fund this service under the health plan amounted to unequal and discriminatory denial of benefits, in violation of section 15 of the Charter.[62] Though the lower courts had ruled in favour of the claimants, the Supreme Court overturned these decisions. It emphasised that the CHA distinguishes between 'core services' (medically necessary services provided by hospitals or physicians) and 'non-core services', and then determined that the therapy in question is not a core service. Only in relation to core services is funding guaranteed for all medically required treatment, whereas funding for non-core benefits is at the provinces' discretion. Thus, the exclusion of particular non-core services from the health plan cannot be viewed per se as adverse distinction; it is actually an anticipated feature of the legislative scheme and does not amount to discrimination. Thus, the province was not required by law to provide the requested treatment, and the refusal to do so did not constitute a violation of the equality provision in section 15 of the Charter.[63] Any other determination, held the Court, would effectively amend the Medicare scheme and extend benefits beyond what it envisions.[64] Here, the Court interpreted *Eldridge* as dealing with unequal access to a benefit that the law confers, in contrast to the matter at hand in *Auton*, which related to a benefit that the law had not conferred.[65] Moreover, the Court went beyond this reasoning to determine that, even if behavioural therapy were a benefit under law, the claimants had not shown that they were being denied a benefit provided to an appropriate comparative group, since the therapy in question was

---

[58] *Ibid* paras 59–61.
[59] *Ibid* paras 70–71.
[60] *Ibid* para 92.
[61] *Auton (Guardian ad litem of) v British Columbia (Attorney General)* [2004] 3 SCR 657.
[62] *Ibid* paras 1–2.
[63] *Ibid* paras 29–37.
[64] *Ibid* para 44.
[65] *Ibid* para 39.

newly emerging and only just being recognised as medically necessary. The Court held that it would be inappropriate to compare funding for experimental non-core therapy to funding for well-established non-core therapies.[66] It refrained from an exhaustive deliberation of the argument that the refusal to fund the treatment had infringed the rights to life, liberty and security of the person guaranteed in section 7 of the Charter, since the issue had been raised only 'fleetingly'.[67]

The Supreme Court's decision in *Auton* has been applauded by some for its careful and adept handling of the issue, for an incautious approach could have entailed a policy of quick funding for every new treatment, something that could bankrupt the system.[68] However, read together with *Eldridge*, the concept of accessibility as developed by the Court can be understood as limited to examining restrictions on accessibility based on such features as disability, but not financial barriers. The outcome is that the treatment deliberated in *Auton* is accessible only to those who can afford to pay for it out of their own pockets. This outcome was reinforced by the third major Supreme Court decision on health rights, *Chaoulli*,[69] in which the Court upheld a challenge to Quebec legislation that prohibited private medical insurance for 'medically necessary' hospital and physician services, which was similar to legislation on the matter in most of the other provinces.[70] The appellants argued that the prohibition deprives them of access to health care services that do not come with the waiting times inherent to the public system[71] in a way that violates their rights to life and security under section 7 of the Canadian Charter and section 1 of the Quebec Charter.[72] The Court's decision to strike down the legislation as infringing these constitutional rights[73] was grounded on the long and unacceptable waiting times.

The implications of *Chaoulli* are still in no way clear.[74] The decision has been described as portending the fall of Medicare, Canada's most cherished social programme, because of its abandonment of the principle that access to care should be allocated according to need alone. It has been claimed that the decision will result in the possible creation of a two-tier

---

[66] *Ibid* paras 48–62. For a discussion, see Greschner, above n 55, 50–51.

[67] *Auton*, above n 61, para 66.

[68] Greschner, above n 55, 51–2.

[69] *Chaoulli v Quebec (Attorney General)* [2005] 1 SCR 791.

[70] M Jackman, 'Misdiagnosis or Cure? Charter Review of the Health Care System' in Flood, above n 45, 59.

[71] *Chaoulli*, above n 69, para 2.

[72] *Ibid* para 14.

[73] The decision was rendered by a 4–3 majority. All four majority justices found the legislation in violation of the Quebec Charter; three of them determined that it also violated the Canadian Charter.

[74] For a comprehensive examination, see C Flood, K Roach and L Sossin (eds), *Access to Care, Access to Justice: The Legal Debate Over Private Health Insurance in Canada* (Toronto, University of Toronto Press, 2005).

Charter rights structure,[75] and that, pursuant to *Chaoulli*, section 7 of the Canadian Charter, rather than guaranteeing a right to publicly funded health care, guarantees a right to buy, if one is able, private insurance covering 'medically necessary' services.[76] This will allow, it is argued, the development of a parallel private insurance system that will have serious adverse consequences for the health care rights of low-income Canadians, both by placing at an advantage those who can purchase private health insurance and care and by draining resources and support from the publicly funded system upon which poor people rely.[77] Indeed, the dissenting justices in *Chaoulli* emphasised that the policy objectives of the Canadian Health Act are the provision of health care based on need not wealth or status; they reasoned that the prohibition against private health insurance is a rational consequence of Quebec's commitment to the CHA goals[78] and that access to private health care based on wealth rather than need contradicts key policy objectives under the CHA as well as the principle of promoting equal treatment of citizens in health care.[79] They deemed the Quebec legislation essential for preventing the deterioration of the health system into a two-tier system.[80] At the same time, others pointed to the fact that *Chaoulli*, despite its portrayal in the press and potential eventual political effects, did not change the face of Medicare nor did it usher in a two-tier system of health care. The decision, it has been claimed, should be read within its limits, especially given that the justices were split, three against three, on whether the Quebec prohibition violated the Canadian Charter. The holding in *Chaoulli* is, thus, limited to the ruling that the legislation violated the Quebec Charter, which would not necessarily affect health care in Canada beyond Quebec.[81]

The Medicare system is a symbol of Canadian values; equal and timely access to medically necessary services based on need is considered a right

[75] Flood, above n 45, 5. See also Andrew Petter's description of *Chaoulli* as possibly implying that Canadians who can afford private health insurance have access to better medical care than those who cannot. A Petter, 'Wealthcare: The Politics of the Charter Revisited' in Flood, above n 45, 116. The decision was also criticised for lacking a serious factual basis that could justify the reasoning that allowing for private health insurance will improve accessibility. See *ibid* 118, and C Flood, M Stabile and S Kontic, 'Finding Health Policy "Arbitrary": The Evidence on Waiting, Dying and Two-Tier Systems' in Flood, above n 45, 296–320.

[76] Flood, Stabile and Tuohy, above n 45, 28. Similarly, the dissenting judges in *Chaoulli* warned of use of the Charter by the wealthy to 'roll back' the benefits of legislative schemes that help the poor: *Chaoulli*, above n 69, para 274.

[77] Jackman, above n 70, 66. In *Chaoulli* the Court did express the view that the prohibition on private insurance would create an obstacle, especially for people with average incomes, as the very wealthy can afford to pay for entirely private services. *Chaoulli*, above n 69, para 55. See also the concurring opinion, *ibid* para 106.

[78] *Chaoulli*, above n 69, para 164.

[79] *Ibid* para 181.

[80] *Ibid* para 166.

[81] See P Russell, '*Chaoulli*: The Political versus the Legal Life of a Judicial Decision' in Flood, above n 45, 6–9; B Dickens, 'The *Chaoulli* Judgment: Less Than Meets the Eye – or More' in Flood, above n 45, 25.

of citizenship, a core and defining feature of the system.[82] Canada, through its provinces, thus has a well-established public health system that is committed in principle to universality and accessibility. But at the same time, as health care spending has risen, social assistance programmes and benefits have been cut across the country.[83] In *Chaoulli*, the Court cited the principles of the CHA, including universality and accessibility, and agreed that they have become 'the hallmarks of Canadian identity'.[84] Yet as we can see, despite its repeated reference to the principle that need should determine access, the Supreme Court jurisprudence, when considered in toto, actually justifies policies that allow for access to be determined by wealth. Although the outcome in *Auton* may have been warranted, its reasoning does not give due consideration to the fact that the treatment in question would become accessible only to those who can pay for it. In *Chaoulli* the idea of access was interpreted so as to in fact reinforce its correspondence with wealth, thereby opening the door to a system where the ability to pay for private health insurance will be the determining factor.

Recognition of a right to health would not, in itself, ensure different results. In fact, such recognition could easily work to provide even more rationales for the reasoning in *Chaoulli*.[85] At the same time, a different result may have been rendered in *Chaoulli* (and possibly *Auton*) had there been recognition of a right to health that encompasses the idea of accessibility as including economic accessibility and focuses, as suggested in the General Comment, on socially underprivileged groups, as well as recognition of equity as mandating that the health expenditure borne by poor households not be disproportionate to that borne by wealthier households.[86] As noted by Bruce Porter,

> if waiting times in the public system violate the right to life and security, what about the plight of the many who cannot afford private insurance or who will not qualify for it because of illness?[87]

And as Sujit Choudhry suggests, it is strange that in *Auton* the Court refused to define 'reasonable health services' but in *Chaoulli* it was willing to define 'reasonable waiting times'. Read in tandem, one may well wonder whether the meaning of these decisions is that 'those who can afford

---

[82] Jackman, above n 70, 58–9 and sources cited therein; Petter, above n 75, 117.
[83] Jackman, above n 70, 65.
[84] *Chaoulli*, above n 69, para 6.
[85] For such possible risks that arise from the recognition of the right to health, see the discussion in text accompanying nn 213–217 below.
[86] See above n 32 and accompanying text.
[87] B Porter, 'A Right to Health Care in Canada – Only if You Can Pay For It' (2005) 6 *ESR Review* available at <http://www.communitylawcentre.org.za/Projects/Socio-Economic-Rights/esr-review/esr-previous-editions/esrreviewnov2005.pdf/>.

private health care have won the right to exit the system, while those trapped in the system without the means to exit get no help at all'.[88]

A commitment to health rights as suggested in this chapter could have allowed the Court to consider, in cases like *Auton*, whether the health policy adheres to these principles as well as the principle of progressive realisation. Similar or different, the outcome would probably have been more convincing. In *Chaoulli*, such a commitment to health rights may have led to the Court requiring the state to take steps to reduce waiting times in a way that would improve access for all within the public system, not just the privileged few.[89] Rights-focused judicial review is not a substitute for policy-making and must be with regard to the existing health system. The Canadian case is a paradoxical one: the principles of the Health Act, which are constantly cited in the case law, emphasise universality and accessibility of health based on need and are a core component of Canadian identity. But at the same time, as the system has to contend with growing needs and limited resources, coupled with the lack of recognition for a right to health, the Supreme Court's decisions in the central health rights cases discussed here seem to stop short of upholding the ideals of the Canadian health scheme.

C South Africa: From a Two-Tier System to a Right to Health?

In Canada the commitment to the principles of comprehensiveness, universality and accessibility is being shaken by the challenges of limited resources and the looming threat of a two-tier system, without any explicit recognition of the right to health. In South Africa, the situation is quite the opposite: the public health care system was not constructed with the aim of providing universal and equitable health services.[90] Indeed, one of the legacies of apartheid is a two-tier health system or, rather, two health systems—a poorly-funded public system serving the majority and a well-funded private system serving the privileged few.[91] Against this background, the post-apartheid Constitution determines in section 27 that everyone has the right to have access to health services and that the state must take reasonable legislative and other measures, within its available resources, towards the progressive realisation of that right amongst others. Moreover, the provision sets forth that no one may be refused emergency

---

[88] S Choudhry, 'Worse than *Lochner?*' in Flood, above n 45, 93–4. For further criticism of *Chaoulli* see Flood, above n 56.

[89] See Petter, above n 75, 117–19.

[90] L Forman, 'Claiming Equity and Justice in Health: The Role of the South African Right to Health in Ensuring Access to HIV/AIDS Treatment' in Flood, above n 45, 80.

[91] J Sarkin, 'A Review of Health and Human Rights After Five Years of Democracy in South Africa' (2000) 19 *Medicine and Law* 287, 288; Forman, above n 90, 83.

medical treatment.[92] Health care reform was high on the new democratic government's agenda. Within its first hundred days in office, it announced that free primary health care services would be provided at state facilities for all South Africans,[93] and in 1997 it issued a policy paper that set the tasks of achieving health equity and meeting the needs of vulnerable groups.[94] Since then, the government has made progress in many areas of health, especially primary health care, but the challenges facing the system are still enormous, with AIDS being a major concern.[95] Approximately 12–15% of the total population is infected with HIV/AIDS, and the government has largely failed to provide access to essential drugs, attributed partly to President Mbeki's subscription to AIDS denialist theories.[96] Various measures taken by the government did not succeed in overcoming serious accessibility and inequity problems. Moreover, it has been argued that the government's neo-liberal policies have translated into decreased investment in health care.[97] Only recently has the government embarked on more serious anti-AIDS measures.[98] Some of the measures taken to increase access to medication were legally challenged by pharmaceutical companies for infringing intellectual property rights, elaborated on in Part D below. Despite the various changes and the government's new efforts, the system remains an essentially two-tier one, with millions subscribing to private medical schemes to bypass the long waiting periods in the public system and to gain immediate access to full or substantial private sector health coverage.[99]

Section 27 of the Constitution provided the basis for two pivotal decisions handed down by the South African Constitutional Court. In *Soobramoney*, the Court rejected a claim to the right to dialysis treatment

---

[92] For a discussion of this Article and social rights in general in South Africa's Constitution as part of the transformative nature of this constitution, see A Gross, 'The Constitution in Reconciliation and Transitional Justice: Lessons from South-Africa and Israel' (2004) 40 *Stanford Journal of International Law* 47, 92–4.

[93] See J A Singh, M Govender and N Reddy, 'South Africa a Decade After Apartheid: Realising Health Through Human Rights' (2005) 12 *Georgetown Journal on Poverty Law and Policy* 355, 360–62.

[94] See South African Department of Health, *White Paper for the Transformation of the Health System in South Africa* (1997) available at <http://www.info.gov.za/whitepapers/1997/health.htm>. See Singh et al, above n 93, 362–6 for a discussion of the White Paper and the subsequent Patient's Rights Charter and National Health Act.

[95] Sarkin, above n 91, 289.

[96] Forman, above n 90, 80–81, 84–6; L Forman, 'Ensuring Reasonable Health: Health Rights, the Judiciary, and South African HIV/AIDS Policy' (2005) 33 *Journal of Law, Medicine and Ethics* 711, 717–18.

[97] See Forman, above n 96, at 715–17; L London, 'Health and Human Rights: What Can Ten Years of Democracy in South Africa Tell Us?' (2004) 8 *Health and Human Rights* 1, 12–13.

[98] R Philips, 'South Africa's Right to Health Care: International and Constitutional Duties in Relation to the HIV/AIDS Epidemic' (2004) 11 *Human Rights Brief* 9.

[99] Singh, above n 93, 368. See also K Pillay, 'Universal Access to Health Care Services: Are We Any Closer to Our Goal' (2002) 3 *ESR Review* available at <http://www.communitylawcentre.org.za/Projects/Socio-Economic-Rights/esr-review/esr-previous-editions/esr-review-vol-3-no-1-july-2002.pdf/>.

and accepted the state's claim that the right to health can be limited in the face of resource constraints, upholding as constitutional the public hospital's exercising of its discretion on how to allocate a limited number of dialysis machines.[100] The Court's reasoning was based on subsection (2) of section 27, which provides that the state must take 'reasonable' measures to achieve the progressive realisation of the right 'within its available resources'. The Court inferred from this provision that the obligations imposed on the state in regard to access to health care are contingent upon available resources.[101] Given that the department of health in the relevant province lacked sufficient funds to cover the costs of services provided to the public, the Court upheld its decision to set guidelines to determine who will receive treatment[102] and accepted that, in preferring patients who suffer from acute renal failure, which can be treated and remedied, over patients, like the petitioner, who suffer from irreversible chronic renal disease, the authorities had opted for a policy more likely to have a beneficial outcome.[103] The Court's decision was rooted in the idea of deferring to rational decisions made in good faith by the political organs and medical authorities, noting that, in the context of limited resources, it may be required to adopt an holistic approach to the broader needs of society rather than focusing on the specific needs of particular individuals.[104] This decision was criticised as overly limited in its conception of the right to health[105] and for the Court's failure to examine the adequacy of the state's health policies[106] and whether they conform to the constitutional obligations.[107] Moreover, it has been argued that the implications of the decision are that express constitutional provision of social rights collapses in the face of limited resources, reducing those rights to mere aspiration.[108] *Soobramoney* is typical of cases that create a difficult dilemma for courts when dealing with questions of resource allocation. The Court failed to provide an adequate health rights analysis, focusing on the 'available resources' part of section 27(2) rather than on the

---

[100] CCT 32/97 *Soobramoney v Minister of Health* [1998] 1 SALR 765 (CC).
[101] *Ibid* para 11.
[102] *Ibid* para 24.
[103] *Ibid* paras 4, 25.
[104] *Ibid* paras 29–32.
[105] See D Davis, P Macklem and G Mundlak, 'Social Rights, Social Citizenship and Transformative Constitutionalism: A Comparative Assessment' in J Conaghan, R Michael Fischl and K Klare (eds), *Labour Law in an Era of Globalization* (Oxford, Oxford University Press, 2002) 511; C Scott and P Alston, 'Adjudicating Constitutional Priorities in a Transnational Context: A Comment on *Soobramoney's* Legacy and *Grootboom's* Promise' (2000)16 *South Africa Journal on Human Rights* 206; D Moellendorf, 'Reasoning About Resources: *Soobramoney* and the Future of Socio-Economic Rights Claims' (1999)14 *South Africa Journal on Human Rights* 327.
[106] See Sarkin, above n 91, 292–3.
[107] C Ngwena, 'The Recognition of Access to Health Care as a Human Right in South Africa, Is It Enough?' (2000) 5 *Health and Human Rights* 27, 33–4.
[108] Davis, Macklem and Mundlak, above n 105, 523–4.

'progressive realisation' part, which would have entailed examining whether the state was taking measures to progressively increase access to health care and whether various policy decisions adhered to the principles of accessibility and equity.

A later Constitutional Court decision on social rights, *Grootboom*,[109] although it dealt with housing and not health rights, can be read as including considerations of policy adequacy in light of constitutional obligations. In this case, the petitioners had been evicted from their homes and had become homeless. The Court held that the state must develop a housing programme that meets the constitutional requirement concerning the right to housing within its available resources, since people in the area in question did not have access to land, or a roof over their heads, and lived in intolerable conditions. The interpretation in this decision was hailed as giving social rights their due, in taking the position of the weakest and most vulnerable members of the community into account when deciding on the constitutional adequacy of measures and policies adopted by the government vis-à-vis social rights.

In its second major health rights decision, *Minister of Health v Treatment Action Campaign* ('*TAC*'),[110] which involved government AIDS policy, the Constitutional Court followed the *Grootboom* decision. Deciding in favour of the petitioner, it ruled that the government must plan and implement, in the framework of its limited resources, a comprehensive and coordinated programme that would gradually provide pregnant women and newborns with access to medical care that would prevent mother-to-child transmission of AIDS. The Court determined that the state must lift restrictions that made Nevirapine (which can prevent mother-to-child transmission) unavailable in public hospitals, except at designated pilot sites.[111] In this decision, the Court gave due weight to the duties imposed on the state under section 27 to give effect to the right to health and to do so progressively in accordance with available resources.[112] It held that:

> The state is obliged to take *reasonable* measures progressively to eliminate or reduce the large areas of severe deprivation that afflicts our society.[113]

---

[109] *Government of the Republic of South Africa v Grootboom* [2001] (1) SALR 46 (CC).

[110] *Minister of Health v Treatment Action Campaign (No 2)* [2002]5 SA 721 (CC) (hereinafter *TAC*). For a discussion of the background to the case, the litigation itself, and its aftermath, see M Heywood, 'Preventing Mother-to-Child HIV Transmission in South Africa: Background, Strategies and Outcomes of the Treatment Action Campaign Case Against the Minister of Health' (2003) 19 *South Africa Journal on Human Rights* 278.

[111] For a discussion of this case, see: G Annas, 'The Right to Health and the Nevirapine Case in South Africa' in Gruskin, above n 6, 497–505; C Ngwena, 'Access to Health Care Services as a Justiciable Socio-Economic Right Under the South African Constitution' (2003) 6 *Medical Law International* 13.

[112] *TAC*, above n 110, at para 29.

[113] *Ibid* paras 36, 71 (emphasis added).

Moreover, an important factor in the Court's analysis and decision was focus on those who cannot afford to pay for services.[114] Although, in this case, the cost of the drug itself was not a factor, as it had been offered for free for a period of five years by the manufacturer,[115] there were costs involved in providing the infrastructure for counselling and testing, as well as other expenses related to treating mothers and children receiving Nevirapine.[116]

The applicants in *TAC* argued that the measures adopted by the government to ensure access to health care for HIV-positive pregnant women were deficient both because they prohibited the administration of Nevirapine at public hospitals and clinics and because they failed to implement a comprehensive programme for the prevention of mother-to-child transmission.[117] The Court engaged in an in-depth analysis of the various arguments adduced by the state, looking at questions of efficacy, quality, risk of resistance, safety and capacity,[118] and determined that the state had failed in its duty to take reasonable measures within available resources to achieve progressive realisation of the right to access to this treatment.[119] The Court noted that, although it was deliberating a question of policy, it must consider whether in formulating and implementing policy the state had fulfilled its constitutional obligations, and if the state had failed to do so, the Court is under a duty to ensure that effective relief is granted.[120] Thus, in the 'relief' section of its judgment, the Court held that it is essential that there be a concerted national effort towards combating HIV/AIDS. Accordingly, it held that the Constitution obliges the government to devise and implement within available resources a comprehensive and coordinated programme to realise progressively the rights of pregnant women and newborns to access to health services to combat mother-to-child transmission of HIV and such a programme must include provision of appropriate treatment. The Court deemed the current policy as falling short of compliance with these requirements, including in its prohibition on prescribing Nevirapine. The government was thus ordered to remove the restrictions on the drug without delay.[121]

The *TAC* decision is promising in terms of both its actual analysis and its potential application. It has been widely criticised for following *Grootboom* and rejecting the idea of minimum core obligations[122] in favour of a 'reasonableness' approach and thereby emptying the right of

---

114 *Ibid* para 70.
115 *Ibid* para 48.
116 *Ibid* para 49.
117 *Ibid* para 44.
118 *Ibid* paras 51–66.
119 *Ibid* para 94.
120 *Ibid* paras 96–114.
121 *Ibid* paras 124–35.
122 On core obligations, see above nn 27, 33 and accompanying text.

much of its contents.[123] But at the same time, the Court's approach in *TAC* did lead to enforcement of the state's duties vis-à-vis health rights, and while this approach may indeed have placed the 'core' of the right at risk, it at the same time opened the door to enforcement of obligations that go beyond that core. Yet notwithstanding the enforcement of section 27 in the *TAC* context of mother-to-child transmission, a significant gap clearly still prevails between the constitutional promise and the reality of substantial inequality in health in South Africa. This gap is the result of entrenched structural inequality, general poverty and the high affliction rate of disease. It has been argued since *TAC* that rights are an effective tool for transforming manifestations of inequality and poverty, as well as unresponsive and irrational governance[124]; at the same time, however, the role of rights and the law in this context is clearly limited, especially if they are not accompanied by socio-economic empowerment of the underprivileged. Moreover, it has been argued that the recognition of the right to access to health care as a constitutionally justiciable right accentuates the crisis created by the gap between the poor majority's expectations of the Constitution in this context and its limited capacity to deliver.[125] Nonetheless, *TAC* is a decision in which the rights discourse was invoked to scrutinise policy, with a commitment to the principles of progressive realisation, reasonableness and concern for the poor. It may also open the door to further scrutiny of health policies to ensure that universal access, while perhaps not immediate, is at least being realised progressively and that the government is working towards this goal by taking steps to lower drug costs and initiating treatment where possible.[126]

Judicial scrutiny of policy raises again the concern that has emerged around Canadian cases like *Auton*, regarding the polycentric consequences of adjudicating social rights. In the South African context, Lisa Forman has argued that this may not necessarily be a bad thing. 'More than ensuring access to a critical health service,' she maintains, 'the Court's decision in *TAC* broke the deadlock on a social struggle where political debates had consistently failed to achieve satisfactory outcomes'. She further argues that the Constitutional Court's firm and thorough review of government health policy in *TAC* sent a powerful message to both the

---

[123] For a discussion of this argument, see M Pieterse, 'Resuscitating Socio-Economic Rights: Constitutional Entitlements to Health Care Services' (2006) 22 *South Africa Journal on Human Rights* 473. For articles that criticise *Grootboom* and *TAC* along this line, see the sources cited in *ibid* fn 3. See also the discussion in DM Davis, chapter 9 of this volume.

[124] Forman, above n 90, 97–8.

[125] C Ngwena, 'Substantive Equality in South African Health Care: The Limits of Law' (2000) 4 *Medical Law International* 111. For the limitations of the notion of the right to health in general and in South Africa in particular for expanding equal accessibility, see L London, 'Human Rights and Public Health: Dichotomies or Synergies in Developing Countries? Examining the Case of HIV in South Africa' (2002) 30 *Journal of Law, Medicine and Ethics* 677. See the discussion in nn 216–217 below and accompanying text.

[126] Forman, above n 90, 92.

government and the public about its willingness to intervene in health policy in the future; this, she says, has had a powerful impact on how the government has subsequently formulated its AIDS treatment policy, manifested in the decision's critical augmentation of public pressure on the government to initiate a national ARV treatment plan, which it announced over a year later. However, concedes Forman, there has been relatively slow and patchy implementation of the *TAC* decision and changes to AIDS policy.[127] Rights discourse, then, while important, remains limited, with the extent of implementation of rights crucial.

The South African experience and *TAC* case specifically exemplify how health rights can be a tool in judicial review of government policy and provide a remedy for inadequate access to health care. Nonetheless, even if a court judgment relates not only to access to a specific treatment (for example, Nevirapine) but also to a need for broad government policy on a general health condition (for example, concerning mother-to-child HIV transmission), it will necessarily be relatively narrow and cannot replace the necessity for devising a comprehensive strategy (for example, concerning the AIDS epidemic), which courts cannot be expected to provide.[128]

D Israel: A Right or a Commodity in a Three-Tier System?[129]

Israel currently lacks a full, comprehensive constitution. Its two basic laws on human rights, which serve as its embryonic and incomplete constitution, do not include explicit recognition of the right to health. The scope of the general right to human dignity guaranteed under Basic Law: Human Dignity and Liberty is contested, and the debate over the more specific rights that derive therefrom and, specifically, whether this can include social and economic rights, remains in full force.[130] The hegemonic position is that the right to human dignity encompasses only the right to a minimal material existence, including 'access to rudimentary medical services'.[131] This minimum approach to social rights casts a shadow on the possibility for judicial review of legislation in the name of the right to health. At the same time, the Israeli legal system has a long-standing tradition of recognising non-written rights in a way that allows for judicial review of at least

---

[127] Forman, above n 96, 718–20.

[128] See Annas, above n 111, 503–504.

[129] In this section, I discuss only questions that came up in the context of Israel's national health insurance and not questions pertaining to the right to health in the Israeli-occupied Palestinian territories, where the right is seriously violated as a result of various circumstances of the Occupation. See, eg, A Stefanini and H Ziv, 'Occupied Palestinian Territory: Linking Health to Human Rights' (2004) 8 *Health and Human Rights* 161.

[130] See D Barak-Erez and A Gross, chapter 11 of this volume.

[131] RCA 4905/98 *Gamzu v Yeshaiahu* [2001] 55(3) PD 360, 375–6.

administrative action although not primary legislation.[132] Moreover, the Basic Law does include explicit references to the rights to life and to body, both of which can have a direct impact on issues of access to health care. The provision of health services in Israel is regulated by the National Health Insurance Law 1994 ('NHIL'). Section 1 of the Law declares that national health insurance in Israel is based upon the principles of 'justice, equality, and mutual assistance'; section 3(a) provides that '[e]ach resident is entitled to health services in accordance with this law'; and section 13(e) states that health services will be provided with respect for human dignity. Under this Law, Israeli residents pay a progressive health tax to the government and, for the most part, the health services are provided by national sick funds.[133]Alongside this public universal health care system a private health system also exists in Israel, which is open to those who can afford it. Moreover, there is a complex mixture of public and private within the public system, in the form of the supplementary insurance offered at an extra charge, in addition to the mandatory universal insurance, and in the form of private services offered by the public hospitals. The latter are usually funded by the supplementary insurance or private insurance and have been highly controversial since their expansion in the mid-1990s. In 2002 the Attorney-General pronounced this practice illegal, and litigation concerning the matter is currently before the Israeli Supreme Court.[134]

Thus the Israeli health insurance system has been described as a three-tier system, composed of the universal national insurance, the supplementary insurance and private insurance.[135] This three-tiered nature aside, the national health scheme is, in theory, a needs-basis system, since the insured pay a progressive health tax to the state and receive services from the sick funds.[136] The NHIL provides that health services included within the health basket will be provided according to medical discretion, in reasonable quality, within reasonable time, and within a reasonable distance from the insured person's place of residence. There is an accompanying proviso, however: 'all in accordance with the financial resources available to the sick funds'.[137] Two basic problems manifest the issue of

---

[132] See Barak-Erez and Gross, above n 130.

[133] National Health Insurance Law, ss 3, 14.

[134] On supplementary insurance, see C Shalev, *Health, Law and Human Rights* (Tel-Aviv, Ramot, 2003) (Hebrew) 255–8, 262–3; on private services in public hospitals, see Y Shuval and O Hanson, *Ha'Ikar HaBriut [Most Importantly, Health]* (Jerusalem, Magnes, 2000) (Hebrew) 307–14.

[135] See G Ben-Nun and G Ofer (eds), *A Decade to the National Health Insurance Law 1995–2005* (Tel-Hashomer, Israel National Institute for Health Policy and Health Services Research, 2006) (Hebrew) 37, 315–75.

[136] For an analysis of the law, see C Shalev and D Chinitz, 'In Search of Equity and Efficiency: Health Care Reform and Managed Competition in Israel' (1997) 20 *Dalhousie Law Journal* 553.

[137] National Health Insurance Law s 3(d).

limited resources and prevent the Law from giving full effect to the right to health. The first problem relates to the increase in additional payments patients are required to make for specific medical services covered under the health plan, which derives mostly from amendments to the original 1994 legislation. The second problem is the exclusion of certain essential services from the 'health basket' and the Law's lack of a mechanism for updating the basket and its cost in light of new technologies and drugs, demographic changes and the overall increased cost of health care. As a result, various services and medicines become available only to those who can pay for them in the form of additional payment for treatments included in the health basket or the full cost of those without any coverage.

Although even in its original form the NHIL included the possibility of charging additional payments for certain covered services and treatments, amendments to the Law, particularly in 1998, expanded this arrangement. These amendments shifted some of the burden of financing the health care system—for which the health tax does not suffice—from the state to patients. Although a limited number of waivers and caps do exist, in principle, the payments are uniform in amount, so that a de facto system of regressive taxation has been created.[138] The Law requires that the payments be 'uniform and non-discriminatory, with no regard to the members' income',[139] yet the supposedly 'non-discriminatory' scheme has a rather discriminatory effect on the poor. Studies have repeatedly shown that the changes to the Law have caused a significant increase in household expenses related to medical services, with a disproportionate effect on the poor. At least one person in ten reported forgoing prescribed medication because of the price, with an even higher proportion amongst the poor, chronically ill and women.[140] Out-of-pocket contributions became a major source of financing for the health system, leading to access to health care becoming contingent on ability to pay, contrary to the principles and spirit of the NHIL.

Considering these changes from the right to health perspective, we can see how conditioning health care on out-of-pocket payments in the way that this has occurred in Israel violates the principle of accessibility articulated in General Comment 14, which declares that the health cost burden for poor households must not be disproportionate to that borne by wealthier households.[141] Making health care financially inaccessible therefore violates the core obligations of the right to health as expressed in

---

[138] For a detailed discussion, see A Gross, 'Health in Israel: Between a Right and a Commodity' in Y Shany and Y Rabin (eds), *Social and Economic Rights in Israel* (Tel Aviv, Ramot, 2004) (Hebrew) 437–531, at 474–81.

[139] National Health Insurance Law s 8(a1)(2).

[140] See Gross, above n 138, 481–9 and the references therein.

[141] See above nn 27, 33 and accompanying text.

the Comment; in Israel's case, this has been effected through retrogressive measures and the adoption of legislation or policy that is incompatible with preceding legal duties that relate to the right to health,[142] in a way that constitutes a violation of the right. However, in the major legal challenge to date brought against additional payments, the *Israeli* case, the Supreme Court rejected arguments that these payments infringe the rights to health and equality. The petitioner was in the process of losing her hearing, which could be reversed with a cochlear implant in her ear. The operation was included in the basket of health services but was subject to a self-contribution of 70 per cent, which, in this case, amounted to 70,000 NIS (about US$15,500). The petitioner, a teacher and single mother, earned a low salary with which she could barely care for her family. Her petition was grounded not only on the right to health but also on the right to equality as included in the right to human dignity. Although the Court expressed concern at how a 70 per cent self-contribution could be regarded as a 'contribution', it refused to intervene, citing the fact that the matter had been carefully considered by the government committee authorised to determine the scope of the health basket.[143] It should be noted that, although the Court did not grant the petitioner a remedy in this case, the litigation was part of a process drawing attention to the problem of the high self-contribution requirement for such operations, which eventually was cancelled by the government.[144] This notwithstanding, however, the *Israeli* decision continues to exemplify judicial deference to the government's discretion in refusing to deliberate questions of accessibility, equality and progressive realisation of the right to health.

Another serious problem with accessibility under the Israeli system is the matter of medications and treatments excluded from the health basket. The health basket currently is updated based on budgetary constraints and is subject to the government's annual budgetary allocation for updates. The Minister of Health can authorise changes to the health basket, but if this entails an increase in the basket's cost, consent from both the Minister of Finance and the government are required, as well as available financial resources.[145] Against this background, dozens of petitions are brought before the Israeli labour courts, the courts of competence in such matters under the NHIL, concerning denial of coverage for prescribed medications

---

[142] See above nn 33–34 and accompanying text.

[143] HCJ 2974/06 *Israeli v Committee for the Expansion of the Health Basket* (6 November 2006) (unpublished).

[144] Government Decision Number 406, 27 August 2006.

[145] National Health Insurance Law, s 8. The Israeli Supreme Court rejected two cases in which the petitioners requested that the Court order the ministers to use their authority under the law to install a regular update mechanism that would take into account changing needs. HCJ 2344/98 *Maccabee Health Services v Minister of Finance* 54(5) PD 729; HCJ 9113/01 *Klalit Health Services v Minister of Health* 56(5) PD 521. For a discussion of these cases, see Gross, above n 138, 497–500.

and services. The challenges faced by the courts can be classified into a few major issues: the question of the scope of the treatments covered under the health basket (eg, how many sessions of physiotherapy is a patient entitled to); eligibility for treatment or medication that are included in the basket but for a different indication from that for which it was prescribed; medications and services completely excluded from the basket; medications that are excluded from coverage but are required as a matter of emergency; and medications and services that are excluded from the basket but have been provided by the sick funds to some patients and, thus, others argue that it is discriminatory to deny them the same.[146]

A few conclusions can be drawn from the case law in these matters, all of which derives from decisions handed down by the regional and national labour courts, as the Supreme Court has not, to date, issued any major decisions in these matters. Generally, the labour courts' position has been that the health basket is limited and there is no pretence that it includes all the medical services required by a person. The health services included in the basket, which the sick funds must provide, are the base; the sick funds can, however, offer additional services or medications beyond what is prescribed by law, in accordance with their financial resources and in light of their commitment to the fulfilment of the NHIL and its principles and their status as a public organ.[147] The lower courts have sometimes relied on the lack of recognition for the right to health as a constitutional right to reject claims made by patients to anything beyond the basic basket components.[148] However, in some cases, the court did hold for the petitioners, based on four different forms of legal justification:

1. Dynamic interpretation of the health basket: in one case, the National Labour Court accepted the argument that the basket must be interpreted in a flexible and dynamic way so as to allow the combination of two treatments that are covered under the basket by treating them as two individual matters and not one combined treatment.[149]
2. The duty to exercise discretion in specific cases: in one case, in which doctors believed that only a medicine indicated for a different type of cancer than she had could serve the patient, the regional labour court noted the

---

[146] For an elabourate discussion of the case law, see Gross, above n 138, at 502–528. For a discussion of litigation concerning health rights in Israel see also C Shalev and D Chinitz, 'Joe Public v. The General Public: The Role of the Courts in Israeli Health Care Policy', (2005) 33 *Journal of Law, Medicine and Ethics* 650.

[147] National Labour Court 5/97–7 *Madzini v Klalit Health Services*, 33 Labour Judgments 193.

[148] District Labour Court 700022/99 *Isaac v Attorney General* (17 June 1999) (unpublished).

[149] National Labour Court 1555/04 *Klalit Health Services v Kaftsan* (29 December 2005) (unpublished). A petition to the Supreme Court against this judgment ended in a settlement where the principle of flexible interpretation was accepted, subject to budgetary considerations. HCJ 3723/06 *Klalit Health Services v Ministry of Health* (24 July 2006) (unpublished).

fact that the sick fund could exercise discretion to provide services beyond those prescribed by law. It further determined that, as a public body, the fund must exercise its discretion and consider the issue, based on four relevant considerations in particular: (1) the treatment in question was necessary for saving the patient's life; (2) her disease was rare; (3) there was no alternative to the recommended medication to save her life; and (4) the fund should have tried to reach a balance between the medical consideration and the economic consideration. The court emphasised that the case involved the patient's right to life, which is explicitly guaranteed in Basic Law: Human Dignity and Liberty, and held that the sick fund's refusal to exercise discretion in this matter was in violation of its duty to give special consideration to specific cases. Accordingly, the court ordered the sick fund to provide the patient the requested treatment.[150] The decision in this case illustrates well how the rights discourse can be used as a tool in judicial review of health policy. In another case, the National Labour Court reviewed the activities of a sick fund's Irregularities Committee, finding them to be flawed not only due to procedural failures, but also because the sick fund sent matters to the committee only as a matter of 'grace' and not rights. The right to health services are a social human right, held the Court, a penumbral right of Basic Law: Human Dignity and Liberty.[151]

3. Judicial review of decisions to exclude services from the health basket: in one case, the regional labour court determined that a government's decision not to include a certain device in the health basket was flawed for failing to take into account the various considerations in favour of including it in addition to the financial considerations. The court held that the government must review the matter again, giving due consideration to matters of human dignity as mandated by Basic Law: Human Dignity and Liberty and the NHIL.[152]

4. The duty to provide emergency care unconditionally: in cases involving the provision of treatment required as a matter of emergency, the courts, instead of adhering to the framework of the NHIL, have sometimes resorted to section 3(b) of the Patient's Rights Law, which provides that 'in a medical emergency a person is entitled to urgent medical care with no

---

[150] District Labour Court 4037/01 *Tabro v Klalit Health Services* 12 Labour District Judgments 205. The decision was appealed before the National Labour Court, in the framework of which the parties agreed that the sick fund would continue to provide the medicine to the patient, but without any admission of the lower court's finding and determinations, which would be nullified. Nonetheless, the lower court's decision remains an important example of the use of rights analysis and is thus discussed in the text.

[151] National Labour Court 1091/00 *Shitrit v Meuchedet Health Services*, 35 Labour Judgments 5.

[152] District Court 5360/01 *Dekel v Klalit Health Services*, 13 Labour Judgments 908. It was later decided, again, not to include the device in the basket of health services.

condition' and have ordered the administration of treatment when convinced the situation was an emergency.[153]

The above examples do not represent all or even the majority of the labour courts' decisions. More often than not, the courts regard the health basket as a reality with which they cannot interfere and reject petitioners' arguments, sometimes on the basis of the lack of constitutional recognition for the right to health. These decisions do not apply a rights analysis. However, in other cases, as the instances described above illustrate, judges have turned to a rights analysis, be they the rights to life and body explicitly recognised in the Basic Law, or the right to health as a penumbral right, or rights to emergency health care guaranteed under the Patient's Rights Law 1996. This application of rights analysis, in conjunction with the principle of flexible and dynamic interpretation, has allowed for judicial intervention in favour of patients in a way that has broadened the protection of the right to health in Israel.

Against this background the Israeli case, too, brings up the question of whether matters of health should be decided from a rights perspective in individual petitions brought before the courts, far away from the context of interdependent decision-making. It could be argued that the courts, which deal with specific, concrete cases, cannot see the general picture of balances, considerations and priorities viewed and considered by the governmental bodies making decisions about the health basket, including the committee that makes the professional recommendations. At the same time, however, the courts make their decisions against the background of a reality in which the state's commitment to health and, specifically, its funding of the health basket have eroded and there is no structural mechanism for properly updating the basket.[154] This seems to justify judicial review from a rights perspective and resort to the rights to life, body, health and equality, in appropriate instances. However, the courts should give careful consideration to the medical opinions and should be convinced that the requested treatment or therapy is warranted by medical need and will significantly improve the quality of life, prolong life or actually save life. Ideally, this would be conducted by the Ministry of Health, but the reality is that the Ministry is part of a governmental system not always sufficiently committed to patients' welfare. Judicial intervention may, therefore, be justified in appropriate instances. This is especially so given the fact that the Israeli Medical Association has cautioned repeatedly that many crucial drugs are excluded from the basket under the existing process and in light of the government's shrinking contribution to financing health care and individual households' increasing

---

[153] District Court 14339/99 *Grundstein v Klalit Health Services* (24 March 1999) (unpublished).

[154] See Ben-Nun and Ofer, above n 135.

share of the burden.[155] The dilemmas involved in examining the concrete case versus viewing the big picture will be further discussed in section F below.

E Other Countries: Case Law from Italy, Venezuela, the UK and India

Courts in many other countries regularly deliberate questions of health rights. In Italy, for example, Article 32 of the Constitution provides that the Republic must protect health as a fundamental individual right as well as a collective interest, and it guarantees the provision of free health care to the poor. The implication is that all citizens have the right to health, but only the poor are guaranteed free treatment. Many court proceedings have been conducted on the basis of this Article, and while the courts did not take a uniform approach with regard to its interpretation, the issue of access to health care is certainly on the judicial agenda.[156]

In Venezuela the right to health is recognised explicitly in Article 76 of the Constitution. Legal proceedings that have revolved around interpretation of this Article have also deliberated on the background conditions for health. In one case the outcome was the prohibition of continuing the construction of a project in a way that was likely to create a risk of chemical and bacterial pollution and to affect the water supply.[157] In another case the Supreme Court ruled that the right to health imposes obligations on the state in the sphere of public health and, after thoroughly examining the budgets allocated to public health, ordered the state to fund the treatment of AIDS carriers and patients, following a determination as to the need for treatment and the patient's financial condition.[158] It should be noted, however, that despite this ruling the government did very little in practice to increase the accessibility of treatment for AIDS victims, apparently disregarding the Court's decision.[159]

---

[155] Gross, above n 138, 525–7.

[156] G France, 'The Changing Nature of the Right to Health Care in Italy' in A den Exter, G France and H Hermans (eds), *The Right to Health Care in Several European Countries* (Boston, Kluwer Law International, 1999) 39–55.

[157] EJ Sanchez Falcon, 'Venezuela' in H Fuenzalida-Pulema and S Scholle-Connor (eds), *The Right to Health in the Americas, A Comparative Constitutional Study* (Washington, Pan American Health Organisation, 1989) 534–5.

[158] Case No 15789, *Cruz Bermudez et al v Ministerio de Sandida y Asistencia Soacial (MSAS)*, Political-Administrative Division of the Supreme Court of Venezuela, 17 July 1999, reprinted in Fidler, above n 5, 316–26.

[159] MA Torres, 'Public Health and International Law: The Human Right to Health, National Courts, and Access to HIV/AIDS Treatment: A Case Study from Venezuela' (2002) 3 *Chicago Journal of International Law* 105. See also E Gonzalez MacDowell, 'Juridical Action for the Protection of Collective Rights and Its Legal Impact: A Case Study' (2002) 30 *Journal of Law, Medicine and Ethics* 644.

In the United Kingdom, which has no written constitution and no recognition of the right to health as a constitutional right, there is an extensive National Health Service in place. Nonetheless, judicial review has increasingly become an avenue for asserting health claims.[160]

In India the Supreme Court has recognised the right to health as part of the basic right to life protected under the Indian Constitution and has deliberated on many issues related to this subject.[161] The Indian instance is of special interest, because it illustrates the possibility of deriving the right to health, even when not explicitly anchored in the constitution, from other, proximate constitutional rights.

F The Role of National Courts in Adjudicating Health Rights: Between the General and the Concrete Other

As the case studies detailed above show, the right to health or related rights have been employed in different countries in different contexts and are often invoked when governments refuse to provide health care that seems necessary. The cases from South Africa, Venezuela and Israel illustrate how rights analysis may serve as a tool for scrutinising policy and for increasing accessibility to health care. Judicial adherence to the principle of equal accessibility may have resulted in diverging outcomes, or at least diverging reasoning, in the Canadian cases, which were decided not based on the right to health but on other rights. An oft-voiced concern about judicial review in these matters is that whereas health care policy decisions are polycentric, claimants evoke instant sympathy because of their needs; thus, courts have 'telescopic vision' with regard to the cases before them, which may blind them to almost anything else—a troublesome perspective from which to view a system with interlocking components. A further risk involved in judicial review in this context is that it could tilt the system in favour of those with the resources to initiate legal action.[162] Given these concerns, some argue that courts should defer to government decisions in such matters and recognise that these decisions reflect the system's values.[163] It has been suggested that the judiciary should not intervene when choices are made according to the 'Evidence-Based Decision-Making' Model.[164] But even in this framework, judicial intervention is justified if it

---

[160] R Tur, 'Resources and Rights: Court Decisions in the United Kingdom' in R Rhodes et al (eds), *Medicine and Social Justice* (Oxford, Oxford University Press, 2002) 156–68; C Nwedick, 'Accountability for Rationing – Theory into Practice' (2005) *Journal of Law, Medicine and Ethics* 660.

[161] SG Shah, 'Illuminating the Possible in the Developing World: Guaranteeing the Human Right to Health in India' (1999) 32 *Vanderbilt Journal of Transnational Law* 391, 474–84.

[162] Greschner, 'Charter Challenges and Evidence-Based Decision Making in the Health Care System: Towards a Symbiotic Relationship' in Flood, above n 45, 44.

[163] *Ibid.*

can be shown that the requested treatment will be effective for the patient's condition and that there is scientific evidence that the non-funded treatment meets a minimum standard while treatment of the appropriate comparator group has met with lower effectiveness.[165] More generally, as discussed in the South African and Israeli contexts, courts should examine whether states show a commitment to progressive realisation and to ensuring equity and accessibility in health care; if policy decisions fail to adhere to these standards, judicial review should be exercised, especially when the litigation concerns access to medication or treatment that is critical for saving or prolonging life or that has a significant effect on quality of life. While decision-making in individual cases might, indeed, obscure the general picture, sometimes there can be an advantage to seeing the actual person involved.

Carol Gilligan's work resulted in recognition of the importance of ethics of care and responsibility as an addition to the ethics of care and justice. In cases where courts have intervened on behalf of patients, even when the cases were correctly formulated as rights cases, due attention was also paid to care and responsibility towards patients. Often, these were not cases merely revolving around abstract rights principles; rather, the courts faced concrete, actual patients. In Gilligan's classic study two children were asked to consider Kohlberg's moral dilemma of a person weighing whether he should steal medicine necessary to save his wife's life which he cannot afford. Gilligan illustrates the ethics of justice by constructing this dilemma as a clash between the value of property and the value of life. The ethics of care are manifested in an approach that views the dilemma as an ongoing relationship between the different sides and seeks a solution that will properly address all of them; it would thus propose that the husband and pharmacist deliberate the matter to find a solution.[166]

But in the cases that reach the courts in the various countries, the attempt to convince the 'pharmacist' has usually already failed, and thus the courts are called upon to decide. When they hold for patients, they do it based on an ethics of justice and rights, combined with an ethics of care and responsibility, which requires considering the concrete person beyond the formal rules. Hence, in discussing the right to health, we need an approach that combines general conceptions of justice with a perspective of care and responsibility in the context of the specific case. Following Gilligan's approach, Seyla Benhabib has addressed the need to see both the 'general other' (as required from an ethics of justice and rights) and the 'concrete other' (as required from an ethics of care and responsibility). While seeing the general other entails examining the individual in an

---

[164] *Ibid* 45–9.

[165] *Ibid* at 52.

[166] C Gilligan, *In a Different Voice: Psychological Theory and Women's Development* (Cambridge, Mass, Harvard University Press, 1993).

abstract way, considering the concrete other requires looking at each person based on his or her individual needs and concrete circumstances.[167] Thus, in concrete instances, like *Auton* or cases deliberated by the Israeli courts, if there is any value to the human dignity and human rights discourse, the court cannot ignore the person standing before it; analysing the case based on general principles and rights must be combined with considering the concrete person and his or her specific circumstances and whether the general rules offer a satisfactory response to his or her case. Indeed, the general health scheme might not offer a solution to those whose only hope is a drug generally not indicated for their particular condition. In such cases, seeing not only the general other but also the concrete other requires seeking a solution that will effectively guarantee the particular patient's access to health care. From this perspective, the Israeli decision requiring the sick funds to apply discretion in cases not covered in the health basket, along with the judicial review of the decisions made by the sick funds' irregularities committees, are examples of what rights analysis can achieve in the context of health. In conducting rights-based review, courts should keep in mind that rights, as discussed above, are not mere aspirations, and judicial decisions should seek to be both universal in application as well as aware of the specific circumstances of those lacking financial means. The approach advocated here does not ignore the budget issues or the need to set priorities. However, when a right exists, it is the state's duty to find the appropriate resources, and it cannot waive its responsibility based on budgetary arguments alone. The state can set priorities within the existing health system and can prefer one treatment over another if it is more essential, effective or cheap, as long as it upholds the core of the right to health, the principles of accessibility (including economic accessibility) and equality, and demonstrates a commitment to health and progressive realisation of the right.

The risk that those with greater access to the courts will have better access to medical treatment and services is a tangible one, even though they may not be the wealthiest, since the latter can fund treatment themselves. Thus, those with the least access to justice may remain without remedy. Legal aid provided by NGOs is only a partial solution to this problem, which should be addressed by expanding access not only to health care but also to justice.

As shown above, courts may be useful in enforcing specific rights. Yet at the same time, the courts usually address only a narrow aspect of the issue, as the South African HIV/AIDS case illustrates, and are not the forum for setting a comprehensive policy of treatment, care and prevention.[168] Thus while court proceedings can serve a role in guaranteeing health rights, they

---

[167] S Benhabib, *Situating the Self* (New York, Routledge, 1992) 102–48.
[168] See Annas, above n 111, 503–4.

by no means should or can replace political action within the two other branches of government.

IV GLOBALISATION AND INTERNATIONAL LAW: HEALTH RIGHTS VERSUS INTELLECTUAL PROPERTY RIGHTS

Within the domestic legal arena, a major challenge to health rights is the maintenance of a public health system with equal access in the face of the transfer of medical services to private or semi-private processes, where they become available for a fee. In the international legal sphere, health rights face the challenge not only of privatisation of access to health care but also of the effects of globalisation. More specifically, this takes the form of the conflict between the right to health and the protection of intellectual property within international trade law.[169] The background to the conflict is the HIV/AIDS pandemics and the gaping disproportion of the incidence of HIV/AIDS between poor countries and rich countries.[170] The impact of the TRIPS, the intellectual property part of the World Trade Organization Agreement on the availability of life-saving drugs, stands at the heart of the debate around the clash between two different rights recognised in international law. While drug companies have sought protection for their patent rights, certain governments (in countries where patented HIV/AIDS drugs are too expensive for general administration) have asserted their right to produce generic drugs under compulsory licensing schemes or to benefit from parallel importing of drugs.[171] Consequently, the tension between intellectual property rights and health rights is very pertinent to the realisation of the right to health.[172] A human rights approach must consider the existence of what Edwin Cameroon has termed 'avoidable deaths', which highlights inequality in access.[173] Granting patent rights over drugs, with

---

[169] See the symposium on 'The Global Aids Crisis: Human Rights, International Pharmaceutical Markets and Intellectual Property' (2002) 17 *Connecticut Journal of International Law*; J Gathii, 'Rights, Patents, Markets and the Global AIDS Pandemic' (2002) 14 *Florida Journal of International Law* 261; WP Nagan, 'International Intellectual Property, Access to Health Care, and Human Rights: South Africa v United States' (2002) 14 *Florida Journal of International Law* 155; L Ferreria, 'Note, Access to Affordable HIV/AIDS Drugs: The Human Rights Obligations of Multinational Pharmaceutical Corporations' (2002) 71 *Fordham Law Review* 1133; B Loff and M Heywood, 'Patents on Drugs: Manufacturing Scarcity or Advancing Health?' (2002) 30 *Journal of Law, Medicine and Ethics* 621.

[170] See J Joni, 'Access to Treatment for HIV/AIDS: A Human Rights Issue in the Developing World' (2002) 17 *Connecticut Journal of International Law* 273.

[171] Marks and Clapham, above n 15, 203.

[172] For a discussion of these tensions, see K Friedgen, 'Rethinking the Struggle Between Health and Intellectual Property: A Proposed Framework for Dynamic, Rather than Absolute, Patent Protection on Essential Medicines' (2002) 16 *Emory International Law Review* 689.

[173] See E Cameroon, 'Patents and Public Health: Principle, Policies and Paradox' *Script-edn*, Vol 1 Issue 1 (2004) 517, 518–19, available at <http://www.law.ed.ac.uk/ahrb/script-ed/issue4/cameron.doc> and <http://www.law.ed.ac.uk/ahrb/script-ed/docs/cameron.asp#puzzle>

their subsequent exorbitant cost, has a detrimental effect on the ability to manage disease. As a result of the high cost of drugs, most of the sick in the poor regions of the world have little or no access to treatment[174]; indeed, about one-third of the world's population lacks access to basic drugs.[175] Reinforcing patent protection of the pharmaceutical process and products under TRIPS has had the effect of limiting the enjoyment of the right to health as guaranteed under international law. Thus commentators have pointed to the need to interpret TRIPS in a way that reduces the constraints on the enjoyment of the right, noting the potential of certain provisions in TRIPS that already allow for this, including specific clauses that indicate that states may adopt measures necessary for protecting public health.[176] Under TRIPS, then, compulsory licensing and parallel imports are two methods by which states might respond to the issue of affordable access to AIDS drugs.[177] This becomes especially crucial as countries such as India, which refuses to recognise product patents on drugs for the purpose of making them accessible, are being required to conform to TRIPS as members of the WTO.[178] The globalisation of trade law may, therefore, have a detrimental effect on access to health and, consequently, specifically on the right to health. Consider, for example, the case of India, where the drugs have been available for significantly lower prices compared to other countries (even though millions there still could not afford even the basic generic drugs).[179] But as a result of TRIPS, in India and other developing countries, enforcement of patent rights on drugs is expected to have a significant influence on access to drugs.[180] The clash between TRIPS patent rights and the right to health thus requires that the importance of health as a human right be weighed against intellectual property rights, which do not bear the status enjoyed by health, of a core human right necessary for human existence in dignity, equality and autonomy.[181]

This context offers a particular perspective on failed legal challenges to legislation in South Africa and Brazil that sought to provide broad access to health at the expense of strict patent protections. Both the South

---

[174] S Musungu, 'The Right to Health, Intellectual Property and Competition Principles' in T Cottier et al (eds), *Human Rights and International Trade* (Oxford, Oxford University Press, 2005) 301–10, 306–10; J Berger, 'Tripping Over Patents – AIDS, Access to Treatment, and the Manufacture of Scarcity' (2002) 17 *Connecticut Journal of International Law* 157. See generally the symposium on 'The Global AIDS Crisis' (2002) 17 *Connecticut Journal of International Law*.

[175] P Cullet, 'Patents and Medicines: The Relationship between TRIPS and the Human Right to Health' in Gruskin, above n 6, 179–202, 182.

[176] S Musungu, 'The Right to Health, Intellectual Property and Competition Principles' in Cottier, above n 174, 306–10. Cullet, above n 174, 183–6.

[177] Nagan, above n 169, 163.

[178] P Ranjan, 'International Trade and Human Rights: Conflicting Obligations' in Cottier, above n 174, 313–15.

[179] Cullet, above n 175, 182–4.

[180] *Ibid* 189.

[181] *Ibid* 190.

African case,[182] which was brought to the domestic courts, and the Brazilian case,[183] which was brought before the WTO Dispute Settlement Body,[184] culminated in understandings between the parties in 2001. These settlements indicated international acceptance of steps taken by countries to promote access to drugs while curtailing patent rights with regard to major epidemics and gave rise to the expectation that similar measures would not be challenged in the near future, when they do not strictly comply with TRIPS.[185] The contested South African legislation[186] allowed for generic substitutions of drugs and included measures intended to increase the availability of affordable drugs. In Brazil the eventually-permitted measures that facilitated the manufacturing of generic drugs were part of a widespread programme for preventing and treating HIV/AIDS. The complaint lodged with the WTO was pursuant to an indication that Brazil was going to use the compulsory licensing exception of TRIPS.[187]

It is important to note that the drug companies eventually backed down, due in good part to the withdrawal of support from their own governments, the result of activism and international public pressure.[188] Subsequent to the conclusion of these two cases, the WHO adopted the Doha Declaration,[189] which recognises the relevance of public health and universal access to drugs for the implementation of the TRIPS Agreement.[190] The Declaration and ensuing decisions regarding its implementation consolidated the principle that access to drugs should be given due concern in the implementation of TRIPS and strengthened the position

---

[182] *Pharmaceutical Manufacturer's Association of South Africa v President of the Republic of South Africa*, Joint Statement of Understanding (2001) available at <http://www.anc.org.za/ancdocs/anctoday/2001/at13.htm#art2>. For detailed accounts of the case, see: RP Petchesky, *Global Prescriptions: Gendering Health and Human Rights* (London / New York, Zed Books, 2003) 86–94; L Ferreira, 'Access to Affordable HIV/AIDS Drugs: The Human Rights Obligations of Multinational Pharmaceutical Corporations' (2002) 71 *Fordham Law Review* 1133; Nagan, above n 169.

[183] *Brazil: Measures Affecting Patent Protection – Notification of Mutually Agreed Solution* WTO Doc WT/DS199/4 (2001). For a detailed account of this case, see Petchesky, above n 182, 94–104.

[184] For a discussion of this case, see 't Hoen, n 188 below, at 206–8.

[185] Cullet, above n 175. Also of importance in this context is the US executive order that directs that measures taken by countries to promote access to HIV/AIDS medicines should not be challenged. See Cullet, above n 175.

[186] Medicines and Related Substances Control Amendments Act, No 90 of 1997 in 't Hoen, n 188 below, 205–20.

[187] Petchesky, above n 182, 94–104.

[188] E 't Hoen, ' TRIPS, Pharmaceutical Patents, and Access to Essential Medicines: A Long Way from Seattle to Doha' in Gruskin, above n 6, 205–6.

[189] See above n 13 and accompanying text. On the background to this adoption, see: 't Hoen, above n 188; F Abbot, 'The "Rule of Reason" and the Right to Health: Integrating Human Rights and Competition Principles in the Context of TRIPS' in Cottier, above n 174, 279–300; S Sell, 'TRIPS and the Access to Medicines Campaign' (2002) 20 *Wisconsin International Law Journal* 481.

[190] On this issue, see also 't Hoen, above n 188.

of those countries seeking to make use of the existing flexibility within TRIPS itself, thereby confirming the stances of countries like South Africa and Brazil.[191] The Doha Declaration provided that TRIPS should not prevent members from taking measures to protect public health and that the Agreement should be interpreted and implemented in a manner supportive of the right of WTO members to protect public access and promote universal access to drugs.[192] In particular, the Declaration proclaimed the right of member states to grant compulsory licences[193] and provided that solutions should be found for WTO members with insufficient or no manufacturing capacities, which could present difficulties in making effective use of compulsory licensing.[194] In 2005 the WTO decided on an amendment to TRIPS, which, upon entry into force, will make such solutions permanent, by allowing countries that use compulsory licensing to export drugs to countries that cannot produce them.[195] The Doha Declaration did not, however, eliminate the clash between international trade and human rights.[196] As noted by Philippe Cullet, the crux of the problem is generally that health remains an exception to property rights both within Doha and in the other WTO processes.[197] Moreover, the challenge to make the Doha Declaration operational at the regional and national levels remains crucial.[198]

Five years after Doha, an Oxfam International report claimed that little has changed since the Declaration. Patented medicines continue to be priced out of the reach of the world's poorest people and trade rules remain a major barrier to accessing affordable versions of patented medicines. Thus, while the prevalence of debilitating and life-threatening diseases in poor countries is increasing, drugs remain unavailable. The spirit of Doha has been broken. Rich countries, particularly the US, are, in

---

[191] Cullet, above n 175, 190–92. For a timeline of the developments from TRIPS to Doha, with the South African and Brazilian litigation as significant milestones along the way, see Petchesky, above n 182, 82–4.

[192] Doha, above n 13, Art 4.

[193] *Ibid* Art 5.b.

[194] *Ibid* Art 6. Subsequent to this, in 2003, the WTO General Council passed a decision on the 'Implementation of paragraph 6 of the Doha Declaration on the TRIPS Agreement and Public Health' WT/L/540 and Corr. 1 available at <http://www.wto.org/English/tratop_e/trips_e/implem_para6_e.htm>.

[195] 'Amendment of the TRIPS Agreement' WT/L/641, 8 December 2005 available at <http://www.wto.org/English/tratop_e/trips_e/wtl641_e.htm>.

[196] P Ranjan, 'International Trader and Human Rights: Conflicting Obligations' in Cottier, above n 174, 314–15.

[197] Cullet, above n 175, 191–2. For further discussion of Doha and its limits, see H Sun, 'The Road to Doha and Beyond: Some Reflections on the TRIPS Agreement and Public Health' (2004) 15 *European Journal of International Law* 123.

[198] 't Hoen, above n 188, 217–19. For a discussion on international law aspects, see J Crook, 'Balancing Intellectual Property Protection with the Human Rights to Health' (2005) 23 *Berkeley Journal of International Law* 524. For additional scepticism about the Doha solution, see A Sykes, 'TRIPS, Pharmaceuticals, Developing Countries and the Doha "Solution"' (2002) 3 *Chicago Journal of International Law* 47.

Oxfam's words, 'bullying' developing countries into stricter intellectual property rules in order to maintain pharmaceutical monopolies, in a way that is restricting generic competition and keeping prices high. According to the report, there are several elements obstructing the implementation of Doha in the spirit that it was intended, including the following: the US's negotiation of bilateral and regional trade agreements, known as 'TRIPS-plus', that weaken or eliminate the public health safeguards allowed under TRIPS; the non-implementation of the solution conceived for countries with little or no manufacturing capacity; and the litigation initiated by various pharmaceutical companies in certain countries, again challenging measures taken by these countries for the purpose of allowing access to drugs. As a result, 77 per cent of Africans still have no access to AIDS treatment, and 30 per cent of the world's population still has no regular access to essential drugs.[199] In South Africa itself the problem is further exacerbated by a history of AIDS denialism by the government.[200] More generally, the problem of access is indicative of the power of strong governments, especially the US, to limit the practical effects of Doha, mostly through bilateral and regional trade agreements that supersede TRIPS in a way that undermines multilateralism. Moreover, developing countries fear that overly weak patent protection could deter investors and may even, argues Cameron, have endorsed and adopted the claims of the pharmaceutical industry.[201] Thus, Cameron notes, ultimately the Doha process may have resulted in a victory for the patent system.[202]

An exhaustive discussion of intellectual property and patent rights is beyond the scope of this chapter,[203] but the controversy over TRIPS and its impact on the right to health illustrates the tension between rights as a tool to reduce inequality and increase accessibility to health care and rights as a tool that (as in the Canadian *Chaoulli* judgment) can actually entrench ownership in a way that increases inequality and restricts access to health care. In fact, an intellectual property rights approach to health could turn health into a commodity itself. Furthermore, it has been argued that this approach neglects the fact that much of the research for many of the drugs patent-holders market and profit from is conducted at public expense by universities and government agencies,[204] as well as detracting from the human right '[t]o enjoy the benefits of scientific progress and its

---

[199] *Patents vs Patients: Five Years After the Doha Declaration*, Oxfam Briefing Paper No 95, Oxfam International available at <http://www.oxfam.org/en/policy/briefingpapers/bp95_patentsvspatients_061114>. For a discussion of the post-Doha 'inaction' and an analysis of what may be the causes for this, see Cameron, above n 173, 537–43.

[200] Cameron, above n 173, 517, 518–19.

[201] *Ibid* 539–43.

[202] *Ibid* 537.

[203] For a discussion of the meaning of property in this context, see Nagan, above n 169, 183–9.

[204] Petchesky, above n 182, 79–80; Cameron, above n 173, 522.

applications'.[205] In this sense and context, globalisation means privatisation, since public access to drugs becomes restricted through the formulation of the rights in drugs as private rights. This is occurring in an era of booming biomedicine and when the pharmaceuticals are the most profitable of all major industries, while at the same time disparities in access and outcome increasingly dominate the health care arena.[206] It seems, therefore, that further work is imperative to revive the spirit of Doha to increase access to drugs and diminish inequalities.[207]

V CONCLUSION: PUBLIC HEALTH RIGHTS IN AN ERA OF GLOBALISATION AND PRIVATISATION

The discussion throughout this chapter has pointed to the challenges faced by the right to health in the current age of privatisation and globalisation. We can no longer think of health care in detachment from the global context and without addressing the challenges that public health systems face across the globe in the wake of growing privatisation of health care. In contending with these immense challenges, including the problems of limited resources and growing demands for health care, we must recognise the limitations of the legal rights discourse. Paul Framer has pointed to the need to rethink health and human rights in a way that will not place all hope on the legal battle approach, which could actually obscure the nature of the violations of this right; rather, we must work through cooperation between disciplines and shift the paradigm to one of solidarity with victims of structural violence (defined broadly as a host of offensives against human dignity, such as poverty and social inequality) and the provision of pragmatic services to those in need. As Framer notes, passing more human rights legislation is not a sufficient response to human rights challenges, and there is currently no lack of international instruments, including the right to health that are regularly breached.[208] Realising the right to health, he argues, requires that the human rights community cross the line from a rights activism of pure principles to one involving transfer of money, food and drugs.[209] Human rights in the sphere of health should not be a matter left only to lawyers.[210] Biomedicine and public health, unlike law, do not

---

[207] ICESCR, Art 15.

[206] Framer, above n 1, 162, 173–4.

[207] For various case studies on the way international trade agreements affect public health, see the symposium on 'How Do International Trade Agreements Influence the Promotion of Public Health?' (2004) 4 *Yale Journal of Health Policy Law and Ethics* 339.

[208] P Framer and N Gastineau, 'Rethinking Health and Human Rights: Time for a Paradigm Shift' in Gruskin, above n 6, 73–94; P Framer, *Pathologies of Power: Health, Human Rights and the New War on the Poor* (Berkeley, University of California Press, 2003) 213–46.

[209] Framer, above n 1, 9–10.

[210] *Ibid* 7.

ask whether an event or process violates an existing rule, but rather whether they have adverse effects on a patient or a population and whether such events can be prevented or remediated.[211] While Framer works within the human rights discourse and asks us to rethink rights outside the legal box, others choose to point to the inadequacy of the rights discourse in the context of public health, especially with respect to AIDS/HIV, in, inter alia, being too ambiguous and lacking an enforcement mechanism, making it 'more facade than fact'.[212]

These challenges force us not only to consider carefully the contents of the right to health, but to think broadly about the relationship between the individual and the collective and the implications of that relationship for the complex relations between human rights and public health, given

---

[211] *Ibid* 235–6.

[212] On the fusion of human rights and public health in the HIV/AIDS context as being more 'facade than fact,' see also Fidler, above n 5, 218. See in this context Rhianna M Fronapfel's critique of the usefulness of the health human rights discourse in the context of AIDS in Burma (Mynamar), when compared to other discourses, such as national security or national economy. Fronapfel argues that the Burmese government is unlikely to be swayed by the ethical call of the health-and-human-rights approach, and international human rights law lacks the enforcement mechanisms or binding power necessary to compel Burma's compliance with international HIV/AIDS prevention agreements. Moreover, argues Fronapfel, it is unclear which HIV/AIDS prevention measures a state must implement or allow in order to comply with its duties in guaranteeing the right to health. The ambiguity inherent in the right-to-health concept, bolstered by the principle of progressive realisation, inhibits the articulation of clear HIV/AIDS prevention duties on the part of states under the right to health: RM Fronapfel, 'AIDS Prevention and the Right to Health Under International Law: Burma as the Hard Case' (2006) 15 *Pacific Rim Law and Policy Journal* 169. For an argument that the right to health is too vague and unenforceable to make a difference, see G Smith, 'Human Rights and Bioethics: Formulating a Universal Right to Health, Health Care, or Health Protection?' (2005) 38 *Vanderbilt Journal of Transnational Law* 1295. Contrast with Jonathan Mann's proposal to focus on human rights in the context of the AIDS pandemic in J Mann, 'Human Rights and AIDS: The Future of the Pandemic' in Mann, above n 5, 216–26. For a discussion of the limits of the right to health and the need to think within the market frameworks to advance accessibility to drugs, within the TRIPS system, see also Gathii, above n 169. For this approach, see also J Gathii, 'Construing Intellectual Property Rights and Competition Policy Consistently with Facilitating Access to Affordable AIDS Drugs to Low-End Consumers' (2001) 53 *Florida Law Review* 727. Based on a survey of 11 states, Amanda Littell concluded that a constitutional right to health does not guarantee universal public coverage or improved health rights, since no correlation exists between constitutional status and universal public coverage for health care services and health outcome indicators and since a right to health is unlikely to be enforceable due to the reluctance of courts to treat positive rights as justiciable: A Littell, 'Can a Constitutional Right to Health Guarantee Universal Health Care Coverage or Improved Health Outcomes?: A Survey of Selected States' (2002) 35 *Connecticut Law Review* 289. Although a comprehensive critique of Littell's methodology, as well as an examination of her determination that some states with constitutional health rights do not have universal or near universal coverage, is beyond the scope of this chapter, it should indeed be noted that recognition (or the lack thereof) of a constitutional right to health should not be expected to determine a state's overall health policy. As we have seen, rights can serve as a tool for scrutinising existing health policies and systems according to certain principles, and in that context they can become enforceable, but they cannot be expected to replace the policies and choices themselves.

privatisation and globalisation.[213] There is a critical need to understand that health issues are global issues[214] and to conceive of how the right to health can be integrated into a global perspective[215] in a way that helps ensure accessibility and equality. This can be accomplished by considering the limits of the health and human rights framework in realising public health objectives. Can traditional public health approaches integrate rights-based approaches to promoting health, or do they instead allow vocal and better-organised lobby groups to gain access to scarce resources in a way that may increase rather than decrease inequality? Does a human rights approach promote selective primary health care in the sense that, in the long run, it only reinforces the services given to those already enjoying access to good health services? Indeed, the need to prevent the co-option of human rights requires the development of rights in a way that maximises access to those most in need[216] as well as prevents the risks entailed in resorting to the rights discourse with its individualistic bent.[217] The Canadian *Chaoulli* judgment illustrates these risks, even though it was based not on the right to health per se, demonstrating that even the idea of accessibility can be turned on its head in a way that may increase inequality. It is important to be aware also of the risk that resort to rights will lead to isolated and minimal solutions so as to actually entrench inequality by not engaging with structural societal inequality and shifting the discourse on health care to a private interests discourse, as in *Chaoulli* and in the context of drug patent rights cases. These processes may lead to access becoming something enjoyed only by those who can pay rather than being universally equal.

These are some of the pertinent risks involved in injecting human rights into the public health sphere. But public health has already been at least partially privatised. A rights approach that focuses on inequality and on society's weakest, as discussed throughout this chapter, may serve to reduce disparity. Resorting to rights in this time of privatisation and

---

[213] BM Meier and LM Mori, 'The Highest Attainable Standard: Advancing a Collective Right to Public Health' (2005) 37 *Columbia Human Rights Law Review* 101. On the need to think of the right to health in the context of globalisation, see O Aginam, 'Global Village, Divided World: South-North Gap and Global Health Challenges at Century's Dawn' (2000) 7 *Indian Journal of Global Legal Studies* 603.

[214] L Chen et al, 'Health as a Global Public Good' in I Kaul et al (eds), *Global Pubic Goods* (Oxford, Oxford University Press, 1999) 284–304. See LC Chen, TG Evans and RA Cash, 'Health as a Global Public Good' in I Kaul et al (eds), *Global Public Goods* (New York, Oxford University Press, 1999) 284–304; D Fidler, 'International Law and Global Public Health' (1999) 48 *Kansas Law Review* 1; O Aginam, *Global Health Governance: International Law and Public Health in a Divided World* (Toronto, University of Toronto Press, 2005).

[215] Fidler, above n 212.

[216] L London, 'Human Rights and Public Health: Dichotomies or Synergies in Developing Countries? Examining the Case of HIV in South Africa' (2002) 30 *Journal of Law, Medicine and Ethics* 677.

[217] See P Jacobsom and S Soliman, 'Co-opting the Health and Human Rights Movement' (2002) 30 *Journal of Law, Medicine and Ethics* 705.

globalisation will not abolish inequalities, but it may narrow them if the rights are interpreted in a distributive egalitarian way. In a world where private property and private health care create two-tier health systems in most if not all countries, the least that can be done through the rights discourse and, specifically, by invoking the right to health, is to attempt to decrease the inequality of such systems and work towards guaranteeing essential health care at a good level for all. If we do not treat health as a right in this sense, then it will turn into a property right or commodity available only to those who can pay for it. This will augment the type of inequality referred to in a declaration which is attributed to Martin Luther King, 'Of all the forms of inequality, injustice in health care is the most shocking and inhumane'. Battling this injustice is a noble goal, and the right to health should be directed at achieving it.

14

The Right to Work — The Value of Work*

GUY MUNDLAK

I INTRODUCTION

The right to work is one of the economic and social rights listed in the International Covenant on Economic, Social and Cultural Rights (ICESCR), and different variations of it also appear in national constitutions and regional human rights instruments.[1] At the same time, it seems to be one of the rights that has received the least judicial attention worldwide. In the few instances in which it has been drawn

---

* This chapter stems from a broader project on the right to work that was funded by the EU's FP6 Marie Curie Intra-European fellowship programme.

[1] In the international sphere, cf: The Universal Declaration of Human Rights (adopted and proclaimed by General Assembly resolution 217 A (III) of 10 December 1948); Declaration on Social Progress and Development, GA Res 2542 (XXIV) (11 December 1969); International Covenant on Economic, Social and Cultural Rights, GA Res 2200A (XXI) (16 December 1966), entry into force 3 January 1976) 993 UNTS 3 (ICESCR); UNGA Convention on the Elimination of All Forms of Discrimination against Women, UN GAOR Supp No 46 UN Doc A/34/46 (1979); Declaration on the Right to Development, UN GAOR Supp No 53 UN Doc A/41/53 (1986); Declaration on the Rights of Disabled Persons, GA Res 3447 (XXX) (9 December 1975); see also: Constitution of the International Labour Organisation, adopted by the peace conference (April, 1919); ILO Convention No 122 concerning Employment Policy, adopted by the General Conference of the International Labour Organisation (9 July 1964); ILO Recommendation No 169 on Employment Policy (26 June 1984). Charter of Fundamental Rights of the European Union, 2000 OJ (C 364) 1 (7 December 2000); European Social Charter (revised) Strasbourg, 3 May 1996.

In state constitutions and bill of rights, cf (a partial list): Art 19, Netherlands's Constitution; Art 23(3), Belgium's Constitution; Art 18, Finland's Constitution; Art 58, Portugal's Constitution; Art 22(2), Greece's Constitution; Art 14, Argentina's Constitution; Art 75, Denmark's Constitution; Art 45(2), Ireland's Constitution; Art 35(1), Spain's Constitution; Art 41, India's Constitution. Constitutional texts were derived from the following websites: <http://www.constitution.org/cons/natlcons.htm> and <http://www.oefre.unibe.ch/law/icl/index.html>.

See also the survey of state-constitutions in: Jean Mayer, 'The Concept of the Right to Work in International Standards and the Legislation of ILO Member States' (1985) 124 *International Labour Review* 225. It should be noted that not all constitutions guarantee the right to work in the simple sense of ensuring work for every one who needs it. Some simply provide a guarantee against coerced work, discrimination or inadequate rights at work.

upon, it has usually been joined to another right, such as the right to livelihood, but has not served as a stand-alone right on which the outcome
solely depends. The discrepancy between acknowledgment of the right in
statute or constitution and its weak implementation can be attributed to
two types of concerns. The first, which is common to all social rights, is
the problem of administering them. Arguments against social rights in this
vein suggest that social rights are positive, boundless, vague and
unjusticiable. These arguments have elicited much academic response,
denying the over-simplistic dichotomy between civil liberties and social
rights.[2] The right to work, however, seems to present yet another challenge, for it appears to be of inferior status even among the social rights
themselves. It has not yet received the attention accorded to other social
rights. What additional burden, then, is carried by the right to work?

On the one hand the right to work is an obvious member of the roster
of social and economic rights. Work is important as a source of income, as
an act of self-expression and self-fulfilment, and as a venue for socialisation. At the same time the critics of the right to work claim that work is
not an end in itself and not something that human rights should strive for.
The claim has been made that the right to work is actually the right to
employment, which is an inherently exploitative relationship. It is a right
to obtain income in an environment where only 'getting a job' matters.
Even if we assume that work is also a source of identity and socialisation,
there is nothing unique about work, and certainly not about employment
(jobs), that requires these traits to be developed at *work*. Identity can be
developed in the family sphere, with friends, in social clubs, in political
activism and through crafts. The myth that work is the setting for the
development of one's identity and forging of friendships is constructed by
economic elites that want to see workers identify with the goal of
corporate profit. Moreover, there is an emerging concern that the *right* to
work is merely a *duty* to work in disguise. The right to work is used to
channel social norms and individual behaviour to the regulated and
governed sphere of wage-earning work, where individuals can submit to a
hierarchy of supervision, earn wages in accordance with market norms,
and remove themselves from the concerns of the state. The right is linked
to the 'third way' ideology, according to which it is assumed that work
offers a way out of social exclusion, but is also a growing barrier between
the poor and state aid. The current growth of work activation programmes

---

[2] C Fabre, *Social Rights Under the Constitution* (Oxford, Clarendon Press, 2000); D Davis,
P Macklem, G Mundlak, 'Social Rights, Social Citizenship and Transformative Constitution-
alism' in MF Joanne Conaghan and K Klare (eds), *Labour Law in an Era of Globalization*
(Oxford, Oxford University Press, 2001) 511; B Hepple, *Social and Labour Rights in a Global
Context: International and Comparative Perspectives* (Cambridge University Press, Cambridge,
2002); S Liebeberg, 'The Protection of Economic and Social Rights in Domestic Legal Systems'
in A Eide, C Krause, and A Rosas (eds), *Economic, Social and Cultural Rights* (Hague, Kluwer
Law International, 2002) 55–84.

suggests that the boundaries between the right and duty to work are all too fragile.

In this article I identify the values underlying the right to work and focus on three types of arguments made against the right to work, which sidestep the general arguments for and against social rights. This does not imply that there are no problems in the implementation of the right. On the contrary, I believe that the nature of the labour market makes it a challenging arena for structuring the right to work. However, these problems are not qualitatively distinct from those that characterise other social rights that bridge public and private and rest on constructs of social solidarity and responsibility.[3] In my view they can be resolved, and the abundance of literature on the topic addresses the means to promote such a resolution. However, the main concern of this chapter is what makes the right to work unique among the social rights, namely the various arguments claiming that work is hardly a thing to strive for. Despite these arguments, I will argue that the right to work remains a necessary component of the roster of human rights. It may not be a panacea, but its absence does not uphold better social values either. It requires complementary theories on human rights and on labour market regulation, which together can provide a strategic tool to aid in exposing the richer values embedded in work. The more expansive meaning of work may further undermine its practical use for simple judicial review, but it can present a discourse that emphasises the countervailing meanings and values embedded in work, reveal trade-offs, and force a critical deliberation over the social significance of work.

II THE VALUES UNDERLYING THE RIGHT TO WORK

Among the social rights, work occupies a separate side-stage. Like health, education, food and housing, work is something one needs and invests in. At the same time work is also the major source of individuals' income in the world.[4] The two dimensions of work are related yet separate. The value of work as a means for obtaining income to satisfy other needs is different from its value as a need in itself.

If work is considered to be a means for generating income then its value is for the most part instrumental. It affords individuals a sense of economic autonomy and independence in modern society, but these are important merely because society wants individuals to remove themselves from a position of dependency on the community. In itself, the guarantee of work

---

[3] G Mundlak, 'The Right to Work: Reflexive Linking of Human Rights and Labour Policy' *International Labour Review* (forthcoming 2008).

[4] A minority of individuals earns income from welfare benefits or capital investment. Others do not earn income at all. The most common source of income is work in its various forms.

so that individuals will stop being dependent is a right in only a thin sense. Work as the liberty to perform an action in exchange for money is part of the 'content neutral' liberties: say what you like, work as you like, exchange in the market according to the conditions the market mandates. Whether any particular work will pay enough 'to make a living', what constitutes a worthwhile 'living', and what the proper exchange rate between work and wages is—these are all matters that lie outside the domain of the liberty to work. This view holds that human rights are fundamentally a measure to shield individuals from the state, but also to disengage the state from the individual.

The economic-liberty view is in tension with the social dimension of the right to work. This difference is based on two particular points, namely the purpose of *work* and the purpose of *rights*. As to the former, the right to work in its social dimension seeks to promote working as an activity that is a good in itself. Drawing on Hanna Arendt's distinction, it seeks to promote work as an act of externalising one's capabilities and achievements, rather than as labour.[5] The importance of work lies in the externalisation of one's capacity, and not in the fact that labour power is commensurable according to a conversion scale determined by government, collective agreements or contract. The difference between the economic and the social is also observable in the underlying philosophy that is often attributed to social rights (but not limited to them). According to this view, rights not only seek to shield individuals,[6] but are also a measure for linking individuals to the community and recognising a necessary and desirable interdependence. They forge a meaning both for the individuals performing work and for the community in which work is performed.[7] The difference in views therefore boils down to whether work is an activity not to be interrupted, or a good that demands societal intervention and endorsement.

The extent to which the economic and social dimensions of work are separate or overlapping rests on the value of work. If labour power is *merely* a commodity, then the demand and supply of labour dictate its conditions. In this context, a human rights discourse may seem to be necessary only to remedy fundamental flaws in the market allocation of labour. While there may be instances in which there is no market failure but a person is nevertheless out of work, the right to work cannot be a feasible solution. A person without work may be aided by social security

---

[5] H Arendt, *The Human Condition* (Chicago, University of Chicago Press, 1958).

[6] F Michelman, 'Possession vs. Distribution in the Constitutional Idea of Property' (1987) 72 *Iowa Law Review* 1319.

[7] E Phelps, *Rewarding Work: How to Restore Participation and Self-Support to Free Enterprise* (Cambridge, Mass, Harvard University Press, 1997); V Schultz, 'Life's Work' (2000) 100 *Columbia Law Review* 1881; A Khan 'The Dignity of Labor' (2001) 32 *Columbia Human Rights Law Review* 289–382; D Peccoud (ed), *Philosophical and Spiritual Perspectives on Decent Work* (Geneva, International Labour Office, 2004).

(income substitute), or by the provision of end-goods that are deemed necessary for human survival (or even flourishing), such as housing, food stamps and education. All of these are commensurable with work, and therefore from a value-neutral perspective the provision of money rather than work might in fact appear preferable.

By contrast, the statement 'labour is not a commodity'[8] implies that there is something in work that cannot be commodified and is not commensurable. There are various arguments to this effect. A descriptive argument might hold that work is a good with some dimensions that cannot be substituted or measured by income. This appears most clearly in Freud's coupling of work and love.[9] A normative argument might hold that although commensurability is possible, it is morally degrading because it assumes that all human experiences can be valued solely in terms of money. Love, kinship, family, pain, rights, the human body, knowledge and labour are all examples of matters to which a critique of their commodification has been applied.[10] To think about them solely in terms of money strips them of other values that distinguish what humanity is all about.

In the remainder of this article I would like to focus on the problems that lie within the multiple constructs of work and labour: (a) that the right to work is the right to be economically exploited; (b) that the right to work is only a right to wage-earning labour and hence discounts the social dimension of work; (c) that the right to work is the duty imposed on individuals to disassociate themselves from state support, and therefore it is a duty to work. Summarising the three questions, I will ask whether the right to work should be substituted with a guarantee of basic income.

III THE RIGHT TO WORK — THE RIGHT TO BE EXPLOITED

A neo-Marxist critique of the right to work suggests that the right to work in a capitalist economy is nothing more than the right to be exploited. The right to work does not assume that work, even decent work, should be structured so as to allow workers to enjoy the fruits of their own labour. It does not seek in particular to advance democratic work, independence in profit-making, or a sense of control over one's daily activities. Consequently, the right to work is the right to sell one's labour power to others, to be instructed what to do in a hierarchical setting, and to comply with the

---

[8] Universal Declaration of Human Rights (adopted 10 December 1948 UNGA Res 217 A(III) (UDHR)); The International Labour Organization Constitution (adopted by the Peace Conference in April 1919).

[9] N Hale, 'Freud's Reflections in Work and Love' in N Smelser and E Erikson (eds), *Themes of Work and Love in Adulthood* (Cambridge, Mass, Harvard University Press, 1980) 29.

[10] MJ Radin, *Contested Commodities* (Cambridge, Mass, Harvard University Press, 1996).

employer's need for profit. Workers are expected to understand that if their employers fail to make a profit they will be left without work. The human rights agenda of the right to work is therefore not only oblivious to the exploitative nature of all wage-earning labour, but actually creates an incentive to extend exploitation. It requires increasing employment levels, something that can be achieved, among other means, by lowering employment standards.[11] The emphasis on wage-earning labour is based on a vision of autonomy and dignity, but undermines both. To achieve the important values associated with the right to work, it must be prescribed in a manner that truly respects the moral and legal ownership a person must have over his or her labour power and sense of self.

How far we want to take this critique may depend on the extent we subscribe to the Marxist view of exploitation in a capitalist market. When seeking to identify the contours of the right to work, it would seem today to be out of context to adopt a view that holds that capitalism as such does not resonate with human rights, not even if safety nets are integrated into the capitalist state and economy. Nor would it seem to make sense to assume that only a socialist economy can accommodate a just right to work. At the same time it would be too easy to dismiss this critique as a Marxist relic. The right to work in itself justly deserves this critique.

Driven to extremes, people with no work and a grave need for income may compromise themselves in the most degrading jobs. What are the most degrading jobs? One potential answer is slavery, in which case the right to work can be easily extended to prohibit such practices.[12] However, beyond slavery the boundaries are blurred. Consider, for example, the French 'dwarf tossing' case, where short people (ie, dwarfs) filed a petition against a municipality that banned 'dwarf tossing' performances in local nightclubs.[13] In the petition, the participating dwarfs argued that the municipality's intervention infringed their freedom of contract. Although the case itself was adjudicated on the basis of the freedom of contract and human dignity, its implications for the right to work are obvious. Accepting this claim would have denied public agencies the power to impose restrictions on individuals' participation in objectionable occupations. The court denied the dwarfs' claim in favour of the values enshrined in the concept of human dignity. The court thereby removed the dwarfs' claim from the limited liberal construct of the right to work as a morally neutral liberty that allows individuals access to a job. However, embedded within the right to work there remains the precarious possibility that it

---

[11] R Anker, I Chernyshev et al, 'Measuring Decent Work with Statistical Indicators' (2003) 2 *International Labour Review* 142; M Godfrey, *Employment Dimensions of Decent Work: Trade-offs and Complementarities* (Geneva, International Institute for Labour Studies, 2003).

[12] Cf General Comment No 18 on the Right to Work, below n 57, para 9.

[13] The history of this litigation is described in UN Human Rights Commission, *Wackenheim v France* (Case No 854/1999), UN Doc. CCPR/C/75/D/854/1999 (2002).

could be used to recognise any occupational choice that falls short of a slavery arrangement.

Why 'precarious'? A potential response to the Marxist critique is that unless we object to the existence of a market economy en masse, there is no better arrangement to ensure the allocation of work opportunities and working conditions and to encourage individuals to identify opportunities in the marketplace. This liberal response to the Marxist critique merely confirms the critics' suspicions. The right to work is the right of the least well off to settle for the least the market has to offer. It is easy to compile a list of least favourable jobs—prostitution, sponging the blood in a meat-packing factory, scrubbing a floor on all fours, working with dangerous substances in sweatshops, clearing minefields and even the drudgery of inserting endless data into computers.[14] There are many lousy jobs. These are not just low paying, but smelly, dangerous, strenuous, boring and demoralising jobs that have little to do with the development of identity, socialisation and autonomy. Perhaps good and rewarding jobs are only an elitist exception. For most there is a need for a right to have time off from work to develop identity, socialisation and independence in vocations and pastimes that are not rewarded by the labour market. In the words of Bertrand Russell, this is the right to being idle.[15]

How is it possible to identify the middle ground between the argument that all work is worthy, and that which holds that all work is exploitative? An obvious way to mediate between the two extremes is to devise a guideline that is based on consent. However, the few examples outlined here are sufficient to indicate that consent provides a weak moral basis. Clearly, in the absence of consent the right to work is hardly a human right. Being forced into slavery is the most obvious example. Yet what kind of consent lies at the basis of a woman's 'choice' to prostitute herself, or a dwarf's to be thrown around, or a migrant worker's to leave her family for years? What about a secretary who hates her job but does it only because the hours are flexible enough to allow her to pick up her children from

---

[14] Everyone has their own list of least favoured jobs. My own fragments of the list are derived from various sources, including journalist's accounts, such as B Ehrenreich, *Nickel and Dimed* (New York, Metropolitan Books, 2001); accounts in fiction, such as the crude descriptions of T Egolf, *Skirt and the Fiddle* (New York, Grove Press, 2001) and *The Lord of the Barnyard* (New York, Grove Press, 2000). In photography, see S Sagado, *Workers: An Archeology of the Industrial Age* (New York, Aperture, 1993).

The inclusion of prostitution is a thorny issue, as can be seen for example in the multiple views within feminism regarding prostitution as an occupation. For a spectrum of views see: M Nussbaum, 'Whether From Reason or Prejudice: Taking Money for Bodily Services' (1998) 27 *Journal of Legal Studies* 693; K Barry, *The Prostitution of Sexuality* (New York, NY University Press, 1996); W Chapkis, *Live Sex Acts: Women Performing Erotic Labor* (New York, Routledge, 1997).

[15] B Russell, *In Praise of Idleness* (London, George Allen and Unwin, 1935); V Richards (ed), *Why Work? Arguments for the Leisure Society* (London, Aldgate Press, 1983).

school? It appears the answer to these questions is that some choices are morally justifiable and others are not.

There have been various attempts to sidestep the question of consent and identify the limits of *just* work, which can serve as an appropriate basis for a human rights agenda.[16] Three bodies of thought can potentially be utilised to complement the right to work and distinguish between morally degrading and just work. From the narrowest approach to the broadest, these include the ILO's list of core labour rights, the ILO's broader agenda, clustered under the term 'decent work', and the UN's agenda on the right to human development.

Complementary Theories of Just Work

Prescribed by the ILO in 1998, the *core labour rights* distinguish the right of freedom from forced labour, the prohibition of child labour, and the guarantees of freedom of association and gender equality in the labour market from the other labour standards promulgated by the ILO.[17] As a way of justifying the priority accorded to some standards over others, unlike the ILO's previous approach viewing labour standards as a coherent whole, the selected rights were held to be strongly interrelated to human rights. Although the core labour rights agenda states nothing with regard to the right to work in terms of increasing access to employment, or achieving full-time employment, the coupling of labour standards with a human rights agenda suggests it may be the perfect match for adding an objective and substantive standard to the qualitative aspect of the right to work.

Despite its promise, the overall project of core labour rights, and the selection of the four rights in particular, has also been criticised for being overly narrow.[18] On the one hand, a reduction of the relationship between work and human rights to these four particular rights omits other rights that are crucial to the values underlying the agenda of socio-economic rights — health and safety, for example, as well as a right to leisure (the right to being idle) and a more generalised right to dignity at work. On the other hand, the reductionist agenda is not really compensated by an

---

[16] On the concept of just work see: R Muirhead, *Just work* (Cambridge, Mass, Harvard University Press, 2004).

[17] See   <http://www.ilo.org/dyn/declaris/DECLARATIONWEB.static_jump?var_language= EN&var_pagename=DECLARATIONTEXT>.

[18] For the critique see P Alston, 'Core Labour Standards and the Transformation of the International Labour Rights Regime' (2004) 15 *European Journal of International Law* 457; G Mundlak, 'The Transformative Weakness of Core Labour Rights in Changing Welfare Regimes' in E Benvenisti and G Nolte (eds), *The Welfare State, Globalisation and International Law* (Berlin, Springer, 2004) 231; J Unni, 'Globalisation and Securing Rights for Women Informal Workers in Asia' (2004) 5 *Journal of Human Development* 335–54; For a defence of the 'core labour rights' project see B Langille, 'The True Story (Reply to Alston)' (2005) *16 European Journal of International Law* 409.

effective enforcement mechanism. The core labour rights agenda mainly reflects a political compromise, a procedural view of advancing workers' rights that actually remains anchored in consent. The underlying assumption seems to be that if individuals are working under conditions that do not amount to slavery (which negates free will), are not children (as these are not assumed to have a well-developed free will) and enjoy the possibility of union protection (which presumes to correct a power imbalance in the labour market), then the employment contract will be just. While the controversy surrounding the adequacy of the core labour rights need not be resolved here, their limitation as a guide to just work is that they do not sufficiently steer clear of the limits of consent. There is a need for a more expansive agenda.

The *decent work* agenda of the ILO in part has emerged in response to the reductionist list of rights promoted by the core labour rights. While the decent work agenda continues to uphold the reduced list of labour rights as human rights, it seeks to complement the short-list with three other *pillars*, namely—promoting widespread access to jobs and income, strengthening social protection, and strengthening social dialogue.[19] Thus, the decent work agenda seeks to place the problem of employment policy beside the human rights issue, presenting them as interrelated pillars that must be advanced concomitantly. The emphasis lies not merely upon improving the bargaining process or the number of jobs, but on 'the creation of jobs of acceptable quality'.

Like the core labour rights, the decent work agenda has not been unequivocally accepted among human rights advocates. For example, Philip Harvey argues that the failure to apply the rhetoric of *rights* to the pillar of jobs and employment indicates that this is still a soft policy.[20] This argument is reinforced by observation of the secondary literature that has been produced under the auspices of the decent work project. For example, Jean-Michel Servais of the ILO distinguishes the group of fundamental core labour rights from the right to work (eg, ILO Convention 122), which belongs to the promotional standards.[21] While this classification serves to expose existing distinctions, it is of no help in translating the right to work into a prescriptive human rights agenda. It seems the existing approach of the decent work agenda is not only concerned with

---

[19] Report of the Director General, 'Decent Work' (presented at the 87th International Labour Conference 1999) <http://www.ilo.org/public/english/standards/relm/ilc/ilc89/rep-i-a.htm.>; Report of the Director-General, 'Reducing the Decent Work Deficit: A Global Challenge' (paper presented at the 89th International Labour Conference 2001)

[20] P Harvey, *Benchmarking the Right to Work* in S Hertel, L Minkler and RA Wilson (eds), *Economic Rights: Conceptual, Measurement, and Policy Issues* (Cambridge, Cambridge University Press, forthcoming 2007).

[21] JM Servais, 'Globalisation and Decent Work Policy: Reflection upon a New Legal Approach' (2004) 143 *International Labour Review* 185.

flexibility of means, but also with the 'softening' of values. This might explain Servais' comment that 'the adoption of promotional standards tends to cause little controversy'.[22]

The third context that can shed light on prescribing the idea of just work is the right to human development, a relatively recent entrant in the international human rights discourse. This right prescribes, inter alia, that all people 'are entitled to participate in, contribute to and enjoy economic, social, cultural and political development, in which all human rights and fundamental freedoms can be fully realized'.[23] This approach draws heavily on the theoretical work of Amrtya Sen, who stressed the need to advance both freedom and capabilities.[24] Sen underlines the need to identify ends rather than means and assign a central role to the individual, to people and their well-being. Means must therefore be designed to ensure freedom from discrimination, want, fear and injustice. Furthermore they need to be targeted at developing and realising one's human potential, and securing freedom of speech, association and participation in political and public life. In this context particular attention is also devoted to the need to secure the freedom of decent work without exploitation. Thus, while work arguably could be viewed in the same way as any other means, and limited to that (unlike ends), it is actually one of the basic human capabilities towards which a developmental strategy should strive. More particularly, work without exploitation is the key to securing and understanding the ends of development.[25]

Of the three objective and normative agendas proposed here to complement the quantitative dimension of the right to work, that of the right to human development is the most ambitious and comprehensive. Some actually hold that it should be viewed as the foundation of all current human rights agendas, akin to the general human rights—such as the right to liberty and human dignity. It has the advantage of emphasising work, while viewing work in a general context that responds precisely to the critique of exploitation. At the same time, the right to human development 'suffers' from many of the same problems attributed to the right to work. Like the right to work, it intersects two spheres of international law—that of human rights and that of international development. As in the case of the right to work, the promise of linking the two is also a source of vulnerability.[26] The right to development has been criticised as

---

[22] Ibid 197.

[23] Declaration on the Right to Development, GA res 41/128 (4 December 1986).

[24] J Dreze and A Sen, *Hunger and Public Action* (Oxford, Clarendon Press, 1989); A Sen, *Development as Freedom* (Oxford, Oxford University Press, 1999).

[25] I Ahmed, 'Decent Work and Human Development' (2003) 142 *International Labour Review* 263.

[26] J Donnelly, *Universal Human Rights in Theory and Practice* (Ithaca / London, Cornell University Press, 2003).

being overly broad and too vague.[27] It is difficult to remedy the vagueness and ambivalence attributed to the right to work with an equally vague and ambivalent agenda of a 'third-generation' right.

In conclusion, regardless which of the three alternatives (or others) one prefers, all three represent an attempt to delineate between good and bad, just and unjust work. This question is necessary for the construction of the right to work as a human right. The right to work as a stand-alone agenda can be precarious. It can be used as a justification for forcing workers to make difficult and unattractive life choices under the disguise of consent. Instead of asking why individuals make such life choices and what they stand to gain by making them, the right to work merely holds them responsible for their own actions and absolves the state of responsibility. Not every kind of work is better than being idle, and not every kind of work dignifies the worker. An additional normative agenda is needed to remedy this formulation of the right. I have argued that this cannot be an agenda that is based on consent. Instead it must posit some understanding of rights, of either a minimal or ideal type, which objectively prescribe what kind of work the right to work must promote.

IV THE RIGHT TO WORK OUTSIDE THE LABOUR MARKET – GENDER AND AGE ISSUES

A different type of critique holds that the right to work seeks to integrate workers in the labour market (ie, 'get a job'). Even assuming that the right is constructed so as to emphasise the need to match individuals with decent jobs, this construct of work is still limited to paying jobs. Other types of work are generally excluded. To demonstrate the problem of narrowing the meaning of work to a paid job, two examples will be given: the value of care work within the household (typically and almost exclusively provided by women), and the problem of mandatory retirement and community (volunteer) work of retirees. Both problems demonstrate that the scope of 'work' that is to be promoted by a right to work is difficult to frame for two reasons. First, there is a moral disagreement whether non-wage-earning and wage-earning ('job') should be equally valued. Second, even when the scope of work is broadened, there are strategic policy problems because many familiar choices promote one type of work at the expense of another. Like the solutions suggested with regard to the first critique, I will argue that it is necessary to complement the right to work with additional policy domains that can be of help in identifying partial solutions to these

---

[27] I Bunn, 'The Right to Development: Implications for International Economic Law' (2000) 15 *American University International Law Review* 1425; S Marks, 'The Human Right to Development: Between Rhetoric and Reality' (2004) 17 *Harvard Human Rights Journal* 137.

dilemmas. I will point to the framework of 'social risk management' as one such solution.

The gap between wage-earning work in the labour market and non-wage-earning work at home has been a moving force in the design of labour market regulation, and in the development of production and managerial practices. The distinction between the different types of work has been strongly gendered and has traditionally rested on the dichotomy between the woman's role of staying at home and caring for the family (reproductive work) and the man's role of earning money (productive work). All too often protective labour regulation has adopted this distinction as a basic assumption.[28] Thus laws that appear to promote the right to work and rights at work are not neutral and equal, even when applied universally. They are inclusive for some and exclusionary for others. While it is clear that the relationship between these normative and socially constituted dichotomies must change, the nature and extent of change remains contested. Is the solution to be found in tweaking labour law, or in re-thinking the relationship between the public and private, the market and the family, wage-earning and non-wage-earning work?[29]

One view holds that as long as the right to work is attributed only to market-valued work (wage-earning employment), care work at home will remain unnoticed and unappreciated. Yet working at home is no less 'work' than working at a job. Often it is difficult labour, despite the male-centred social norm that views it as care work, fun, or the economic framing of non-job activities as 'leisure'. Consequently, this view holds that the human right must be constructed as a right that extends beyond wage-earning employment in the labour market. It is also the right to work at home in care work and to be socially appreciated and legally recognised for performing work that is of both economic and social value. This view can be further divided into two additional categories. First, some argue that non-wage-earning work in the household must be commodified, thereby making care work look more like a 'job'. Falling short of requiring the family to pay the wages of the 'inside' care-giver (typically the mother), suggestions on how to commodify women's socially invisible work include allowing pension rights accumulation while working at home or tax credits of different sorts. Alternatively, it can be argued that non-wage-earning work must be held separate from the market, but valued for its social worth. This claim justifies, for example, the argument that welfare-to-work programmes must acknowledge that mothers at home are working, even if they do not receive wages for their work.

---

[28] J Conaghan, 'Time to Dream? Flexibility, Families and the Regulation of Working Time' in J Fudge and R Owens (eds), *Precarious Work, Women and the New Economy: the Challenge to Legal Norms* (Oxford, Hart Publishing, 2006) 101.

[29] See generally, F Olsen, 'The Family and the Market' (1983) 96 *Harvard Law Review* 1497.

Whether choosing an economic or social approach to valuing work at home, others argue that these strategies are misdirected. Women, so the alternative view holds, cannot situate themselves as equals in the labour market if their agenda is to value their work outside the market.[30] In terms of the right to work's scope, the significance of this argument is that instead of seeking to recognise work at home as equal in value to work in the labour market, the right to work should be strictly restricted to wage-earning work. The problem is that the various constructs of work cannot conveniently coexist. The labour-market integration view cannot accept the extension of the right to work to non-wage-earning care work. Similarly, the view that seeks to recognise the value of household work cannot accept a narrow definition of work that excludes the household and non-wage-earning work

The scope of recognised work is similarly challenged by the life cycle division of labour. The debate on compulsory retirement schemes mirrors some aspects of the controversy over the gendered nature of work's scope. Like those who seek to expand work's scope so as to value non-wage-earning activities as well, some claim that a fixed and universal retirement age could help people retire with dignity.[31] Universality downplays any negative connotation that is attached to retirement. People have other ways of self-fulfilment and situating themselves in the mainstream of society without making themselves available to employers. After retirement people have much to contribute to the community, by means of volunteering and providing non-wage-earning work while they are claiming their retirement pensions. Retirement is viewed as a life cycle right that people justly earn over time, but it does not stipulate that they cease engaging in work. Acknowledging the value of non-wage-earning work by retirees also reflects on similar activities by younger people who seek to reach out to the community, particularly when the welfare state is retrenched and solidarity within the community requires the active participation of individuals outside the formal labour market.

By contrast, like those who claim that wage-earning work is the only means of promoting integration and equality, some argue that forcing retirement on people who are still active and productive is an infringement of their right to work. Pensioners who are forced to retire at a compulsory age may claim that emphasising the right to work is merely another mechanism for relegating them to the margins of society. While the ideals of alternative means of self-fulfilment are certainly worthy in rhetoric, they do not reflect prevailing social values. People who have retired are looked

---

[30] See V Schultz (2000), above n 7.
[31] There are also instrumental arguments in favour of one claim or another, for example, that flexible retirement may have the effect of developing targeted testing of employability, may make lifelong incentive schemes difficult to work out to the detriment of workers who seek security, and may impose a heavy burden on the administration of the social security system.

upon in utilitarian terms as having become part of the non-productive sector of society. Of course they can volunteer and remain socially active, but society values people for the economic value that they create and does not know how to value people on the basis of other measures.

In both the gender and life cycle debates, both sides of the debate actually make their arguments in terms of the right to work. On one side there are those who assume that law must address, respect and accommodate existing divisions of labour (women devote more valuable time to non-wage-earning household care; people who are retired are no longer viewed as making a contribution to society). Hence, community work, continuing education and other activities that allow individuals to externalise their talents and reach out to others in the community should be valued as work. On the other side of the debate are those who accept the primacy accorded to wage-earning work and hence seek to amend the existing division of labour (law should 'nudge' women and the elderly to contribute in the labour market). It is difficult in my view to resolve this debate, particularly in the socio-legal sphere of human rights, by assigning a single meaning to the right to work.

Filling the Gaps in the Right to Work—Work as Transition

The problems of gender and ageism presented here can be further extended to the critique that the right to work ignores the problem of a jobless future. There may not be enough jobs for everyone. Such a claim can be supported by those economists who argue for the positive function of unemployment, or sociologists who point to the move away from time spent on work to time spent on leisure.[32] Unlike the first critique, this one does not claim that the employment relationship is intrinsically exploitative, but that there is not enough employment to go around. As demonstrated, the 'end of work' may underscore the need to acknowledge that there are equally important venues of work that are undervalued by the market. Recognising these activities could be an instrumental strategy, given the absence of work, but more importantly it could be used to indicate the moral value of these activities. This requires extending the protections of labour law, social security and social law more generally to groups of workers who do not receive wages for their work. This is particularly important with regard to pensions, health care and other matters of social insurance.[33]

[32] U Beck, *The Brave New World of Work* (Cambridge, Polity Press, 2000); G Akerloff and J Yellen, *Efficiency Wage Models of the Labour Market* (Cambridge, Cambridge University Press, 1986).

[33] A Supiot, 'Governing Work and Welfare in a Global Economy' in J Zeitlin and D Trubek (eds), *Governing Work and Welfare in a New Economy: European and American Experiments* (Oxford, Oxford University Press, 2003) 376.

Just as in the case of the first critique, it is possible to partially remedy the problem by providing a better fit between the moral objectives of the right to work and the type of work that should be promoted. It is possible to move beyond social protection to broader categories, yet to acknowledge and even encourage the integration of, and movement between, various roles—in the house, in the community, in the market and in school. For example, this is the approach taken by the scholars of transitional labour markets.[34]

The transitional labour markets approach seeks to enable individuals to devise their own life cycle, which includes transition between different types of 'work', broadly defined. The traditional distinction between male and female work and between working age and retirement can no longer be sustained, as it neither reflects the reality of the market any longer, nor offers morally acceptable values regarding work. The labour market is more volatile, with a growing number of entries and exits into and out of it. Work schedules have become more flexible; predominantly to accommodate employers' needs, but also in response to the growing need some have for better control over their lives. Individuals want to balance the various types of work over time (allowing time off for education, raising a family, helping their parents, and even taking a mid-life pause—the right to be idle). From a moral point of view, all of these activities should be deemed worthy of attention and social support. From a practical point of view, the analytical framework of transitional labour markets seeks to explore and promote mechanisms that can accommodate and even encourage the transition between different types of work at different stages over time. By identifying the means to make such individualised transitions, the transitional labour markets framework also aids in legitimising diverse life-choices and multiple meanings of work.

There is an affinity between the transitional labour markets approach and the decent work agenda.[35] It has also been suggested that the two can be merged.[36] Like the decent work agenda that was discussed earlier, the transitional labour markets approach evolves from the study of employment policy and does not directly engage in the human rights discourse. Yet the lessons learned in devising employment policy can help filling the gaps in the right to work. Decent work was advocated in

---

[34] ED Gier and AVD Berg, *Managing Social Risks Through Transitional Labour Markets* (Apeldoorn Netherlands, Spinhuis Publishers, 2006); G Schmid, 'Social Risk Management Through Transitional Labour Markets' (2006) 4 *Socio-Economic Review* 1.

[35] See JM Servais above n 21. See also G Schmid and P Auer, 'Transitional labour markets: Concepts and examples in Europe' in European Academy of the Urban Environment (ed), *New institutional arrangements in the labour market: transitional labour markets as a new full employment concept* (Berlin, EAUE, 1998) 11–28.

[36] T Wilthagen and R Rogowski, 'The Legal Regulation of Transitional Labour Markets' in G Schmid and B Gazier (eds), *The Dynamics of Full Employment: Social Integration Through Transitional Labour Markets* (Cheltenham, UK, Edward Elgar, 2002) 233–73.

response to the prevalence of bad jobs, suggesting a need to eliminate various occupations and guarantee the required working conditions to make otherwise precarious and boring jobs 'decent'. The transitional labour markets approach is advocated as a means to ensure the appropriate context for wage-earning labour. The availability of day-care and recognition that parents may want to be with their children or go to school in the middle of their careers might be achieved through rights *at* work, but can also be achieved by emphasising the right *to* work. Instead of telling women that they *must* promote their equality by competing in the labour market on the basis of the market norms, or that they *must* stay at home and be recognised for their contributions there, social norms and human rights should seek to allow individuals to design their own balance. This argument does not suffice with extending choices to individuals, or blindly follow the moral dictates of the market, but encompasses the realisation that there is a more important and fundamental question here—how does the market interrelate with other social spheres, and how can individuals decommodify their own experience so as to make autonomous choices concerning their own development, instead of allowing the market to dictate it?

V THE RIGHT TO WORK AS A DUTY?

A third line of critique holds that although the subject of inquiry is a *right* to work, policy measures aimed at increasing employability and labour market participation are in fact experienced by many individuals as a *duty* to work. The application of a rights discourse is therefore, once again, a mode of justification for imposing social values on individuals and channelling them into the normative social order. The critique regarding the duty to work is particularly acute given the previous two critiques. First, the mere provision of 'work' without further specifying what type and quality of work is not enough, in itself, to promote the values of dignity and autonomy associated with the social dimension of work. Moreover, an exclusive focus on work as wage-earning labour exerts institutional as well as psychological pressure on those outside the labour market to participate in wage-earning labour and depreciates other forms of social contribution.

However, it is not immediately clear how a right can be transposed into a duty. Generally, human rights are—simply stated—rights, and not duties. The right to free speech does not entail a duty to talk. The right to privacy does not prohibit exhibitionism. Freedom of movement does not make travelling mandatory.[37] However, it becomes more difficult to distinguish

---

[37] Arguably there are some exceptions to the rule that severs duties from rights, but the exceptions are controversial and in fact supportive of the general rule. The most pertinent

between rights and duties when we go from the liberties to the rights of solidarity (eg, the right to health).[38] In the case of these rights, it is sometimes the duty of the stronger elements of the population to take part in effectively fulfilling the right of the weaker elements (eg, mandatory national health care systems). However, the right to work is not necessarily a right of solidarity.[39] Consequently, for the critics, an alternative link between right and duty must be identified.

In some countries the *duty* to work appears in the constitution beside the right to work.[40] These uncommon appearances are indicative of the political economy and political regime at the time the constitution was drafted. Their constitutional standing does not indicate their acceptance in the more universal sphere of human rights.

In the absence of an explicit constitutional provision, there may be a *social norm* regarding a duty to work, but it is not part of the human rights discourse. As such, it is like national security. Yet there is no congruence between social norms, such as work and security and human rights. There is an abundance of examples in which security was used as justification to imprison and kill innocent people, and to infringe on the privacy and speech of many. Similarly, conscription or requiring individuals to work is an infringement of liberty.[41] On the one hand, it is permissible for a community to assert a preference for the social norm of work. Work is a valid norm with roots in religious and secular, philosophical and historical writings.[42] Objecting to the moral value of a working society in the name of individual liberty can easily slip into an argument against any social norm. On the other hand, the right to work, as well as other human liberties, must constrain the norm that underlies the sense of social duty. Thus, despite their common emphasis on work, the social norm of duty and the human right must not be confused. Moreover, the prevalence of the social duty emphasises the importance of

---

example that comes readily to mind is the duty in some countries to vote. However, it is most likely that the duty to vote is a social value, like the duty to work is presented in this section.

[38] The term 'rights of solidarity' matches the apt European classification of social rights under the heading of 'solidarity' in the European Charter of Human Rights.

[39] However, the affiliated right of association in a trade union is a clear example of a solidarity-based right. See: S Leader, *Freedom of Association: A Study in Labor Law and Political Theory* (New Haven, Yale University Press, 1992). Rights at work (eg, maternity leave or minimum wage) can also be considered as solidarity- based rights because they extend protection to workers as a class and not only as individuals (and hence usually cannot be waived by individual agreements).

[40] For example Art 42, China's Constitution and Art 35, Spain's Constitution.

[41] See on this issue: Collective Complaint to the European Committee on Social Rights No7/2000 from the International Federation of Human Rights Leagues against Greece (5 December 2000); Collective Complaint No 8/2000 by the Quaker Council for European Affairs against Greece (25 April 2001).

[42] D Peccoud (2004), above n 7.

developing the human right to pursue meaningful and multiple forms of work as a safeguard against overworking the community.

A different problem crops up when the right-duty nexus evolves from the institutional implementation of the right to work. This is most visible in the welfare-to-work schemes. In a nutshell, in these schemes an individualised programme devised to help and pull the unemployed into the labour markets is also used to push and coerce individuals. Thus programmes that are potentially the best example of the state's fulfilment of its duty to fulfil the right to work can easily fall into a trap of duty. It seems that this is the most common reason for identifying the right with the duty. I will refer to this problem as 'institutional coupling', because it is the same institution that promotes two related yet distinct objectives—the right and the duty to work.

Institutional Coupling—Welfare-to-Work Programmes

Since the early 1990s (although examples of such programmes can be traced much earlier), many states have launched various programmes that are aimed at proactive labour market policy and are sometimes referred to as welfare-to-work programmes (hereafter, WTWPs).[43] While the justifications for these programmes are varied, it seems that their central objectives can be clustered under two main headings: to help individuals into the labour market, and to relieve the state of its obligation to provide social security to those who cannot support themselves. In the push and pull between these two rationales the institutional design of such programmes is shaped. Although some shared interests can be identified within each of the rationales, they are polarised by their competing vision of rights. The first view holds that the state is obliged to utilise its resources to help individuals into the labour market. The second view seeks to reduce the state's obligations by securing a place of work for individuals and thereafter holding them responsible for their own actions. These two views can be correlated with the distinction outlined above between the economic and social views of the right to work.

Arguably, WTWPs that promote employment and the employability of previously excluded individuals may seem like a perfect agenda for bridging left and right. It is therefore not surprising to see these programmes play a strong role in the rhetoric of the 'third way'. The third-way ideology, best voiced in the United Kingdom and Germany commencing in the 1990s, and academically theorised by Anthony

---

[43] See generally: J Handler, *Social Citizenship and Workfare in the United States and Western Europe: The Paradox of Inclusion* (New York, Cambridge University Press, 2004); E Sol and M Westerveld (eds), *Contractualism in Employment Services* (Deventer, Kluwer Law International, 2005).

Giddens, seeks to bridge between the prevalence of capitalist markets and the preservation of social values that characterised the social-democratic states of the past.[44] WTWPs have the advantage of conforming with both neo-liberal pressure to reduce the role of the state and social pressure to aid individuals. This is mostly a supply-side policy, which (unlike the Keynesian demand-side theories) is typical of current neo-liberal economic policies because it seeks to fit people into jobs rather than engage in job creation. At the same time, it differs from the neoclassical assumption that markets (including the labour market) should regulate themselves. The state recognises the fact that many individuals and social groups are marginalised in the modern economy and must receive aid for reintegration into the labour market. Theoretically, 'helping people help themselves' is the perfect thing to do—it preserves the active role and responsibility of the state, yet seeks to withdraw the state over time by empowering individuals and their communities.

The potential of WTWPs to bring the right and left together has made them a highly popular instrument since the 1990s. A survey of developed economies suggests that this is an important arena for social and economic convergence across borders. At the same time, upon closer observation of the details of these programmes, different weights are assigned to these objectives, dictating the nature of the specific programme.[45] Among the institutional differences that distinguish various WTWPs from one another, several are particularly instructive. First and foremost there is the matter of consent and compulsion.[46] At one extreme, all welfare recipients are required to participate in such programmes as a condition for continued welfare support. At the other extreme we find the view that such programmes are wholly voluntary and should be made available to individuals who are interested in re-integration into the labour market. A second point of difference concerns the process of matching individuals to workplaces. On the one hand there are programmes that seek to increase individuals' skills towards job opportunities that adequately compensate and satisfy the individuals' needs and interests. On the other hand there are programmes that seek to place individuals in any available job. The question that lies at the heart of the matter is how much the community is willing to invest in the individual. Yet this is not merely a quantitative matter. There is a qualitative difference between the desire to remove individuals as quickly and inexpensively as possible from public support, and the desire to place an individual in a job that fits his or her skills, or to

---

[44] A Giddens, *The Third Way: The Renewal of Social Democracy* (Cambridge, UK, Polity Press, 1998); A Giddens, *The Third Way and its Critics* (Cambridge, UK, Polity Press, 2000).
[45] See above n 43.
[46] I Lodemel and H Trickey 'A New Contract for Social Assistance' in I Lodemel and H Trickey (eds), *An Offer You Can't Refuse: Workfare in International Perspective* (Bristol, Policy Press, 2001) 1.

develop skills that will help an individual realise his or her potential in the labour market. The first option is all about getting people to work as a physical activity and go on a payroll as an economic matter. The second extends a broader horizon, seeking to help individuals lift themselves upwards in the social strata, support themselves with dignity and develop themselves at work. This approach requires not only better adjustment of individuals to the activity of work, but also adaptation of the labour market to employment-seekers.

The difference between the competing objectives colours each and every component of the WTWPs' institutional design. For example, to what extent do individuals receive job placements that offer them some means of progress? To what extent is their economic situation improved once they are placed in work? How is the state involved in job creation, and to what extent does it act to secure rights at work? How are such programmes monitored and assessed: according to short-term placements or long-term earnings and social mobility?

A particularly thorny issue in the design of WTWPs is the matter of work outside the labour market. This problem extends the previous discussion regarding the recognition of non-wage-earning work. It most commonly appears with regard to single mothers. When single mothers are required to work rather than be on welfare, their work at home is discounted and their care responsibility has to be outsourced to another wage earner, or the child/elder remains uncared for altogether. Does the right to work require dividing the allegedly care (non-work) relationship into two jobs, or should it suffice with recognition of multiple forms of work? As explained above, I hesitate to argue that a human rights agenda can settle this dilemma. In the context of WTWPs, however, the right to work should play an important role in emphasising the individual's view of work. Categorically forcing all in-home care providers to engage in wage-earning labour is as problematic as stating that mothers are exempt or, worse, denied from the labour market because they already work at home. Denying mothers' desire to go out to work or refusing to acknowledge their work at home is equally disrespectful of their life choices. The right to work should be used to defy both types of claim.

Admittedly, individualisation of WTWPs may be costly and difficult to manage, but that is a problem only in the context of cutting public spending. The right to work, like all human rights, is costly to maintain. At the same time, like other human rights, it is not absolute and may need to be balanced with other interests (even including the social duty to work) and rights (such as privacy). While this may be a difficult balancing act, there is no substitute for the right to work in its role of clarifying the trade-offs. It prevents WTWPs from being designed only to reduce public spending and disassociate working people from the state. Insisting on the right to work as a safeguard can expose how a right so easily evolves into a duty. The right to work is an important component in exposing institutional coupling. This can only be achieved by observing the internal conflicts embedded in the right to work.

VI SUMMING UP THE PARTS: THE RIGHT TO WORK OR BASIC INCOME?

The various critiques of the right to work presented in this chapter are correct in their formulations, but they do not necessarily imply that the right to work must be rejected. Instead, they add layers of complexity, making it necessary to distinguish between the different meanings and potential consequences of the right to work. The nuanced delineation of the right's contours may also be one of its major sources of weakness. Is there an alternative? To what extent can the values underlying the right to work be substituted for by the provision of money?

A growing network of academics and policymakers across the world is arguing in favour of a basic income guarantee for all.[47] The contours of the basic income scholarship are neither rigid nor precise.[48] In essence, such a guarantee should be free from the constraints of welfare provisions and unconditional in terms of what people must do in exchange for the money. It is therefore a guarantee of a right, which is very different from the poor man's right to social aid. It is somewhat similar to the familiar universal benefits of many welfare regimes, such as basic old-age pension (first tier) and child benefits. Yet its proposed scope extends even category-based universality, most notably including people at the age of labour-market participation. In response to those who argue that individuals who refuse to work are not morally deserving of such a right,[49] the answer is that such an argument has a paternalist 'labourist' thrust that excludes other forms of useful activity, as discussed earlier in this chapter.[50] The guarantee of a basic income has minimal, if any, conditions of eligibility. It is endorsed as an individual right, and not as compensation for publicly valued action (such as attempts to find paid work).

Although at first glance there appears to be very little overlap between the right to work and the basic income guarantee, advocates of basic income have argued that it is a preferable policy measure over right to work policies.[51] To account for this argument, it is important to take a step

---

[47] See <http://www.basicincome.org>.
[48] For a general overview of the basic income principle see G Standing (ed), *Promoting Income Security as a Right: Europe and North America* (London, Anthem Press, 2002).
[49] A Gutmann and D Thompson *Why Deliberative Democracy?* (Princeton, Princeton University Press, 2004).
[50] See G Standing (2002), above n 48, ch 7.
[51] P Harvey, 'The Right to Work and Basic Income Guarantees: Competing or Complementary Goals?' (2005) 2 *Rutgers Journal of Law and Urban Policy* 8–59.

back and discuss the ethical idea at the foundation of the basic income movement. The argument put forward by the basic income advocates is that people lack economic security and need the community's recognition and support to devise and carry out their life-projects. The individual's ability to act freely is not exhausted by the *liberty* to do so, as it also requires the means to make it happen. Furthermore, in recognition of the fact that different individuals have different ideas of the good, the state must not condition its support of life-projects upon compliance with the good prescribed by the state. The state must remain neutral by granting each and every individual the necessary means to make autonomous choices, whatever these may be. The concept of a right to basic income therefore draws on both capitalist precepts of promoting individual choices and socialist ideas of equality and equity.[52] Given the moral foundations outlined by the proponents of basic income, it is interesting to note that the right to work and the right to basic income seem to share many premises. Therefore the rivalry between these two policy strands is curious, albeit helpful in extracting the added value of work.

The proponents of basic-income guarantee claim that the right to work is not attractive because of the shortage of work opportunities, the trade-off between the right to work and rights at work, the likelihood that the right to work will evolve into a duty to work, and the possibility that people will be coerced to take any work for lack of opportunities. I have taken note of all these arguments throughout this chapter. By contrast, basic income guarantees the necessary means for subsistence. Work is undeniably a good, but people will pursue work for precisely the reasons why it should be considered such—because they seek self-fulfilment, socialisation and externalisation of talents associated with work. They will seek work for the right reasons, and not because they have no other alternative. It has been argued that basic income is the real alternative to the liberal-economic portrayal of the right to work. It is not about liberating individuals to do as they please (including working to avoid hunger), but about making individuals truly free and autonomous in the choices they make.

Advocates of the right to work present a two-fold response to the proponents of basic income.[53] First, they argue that to the extent that the two measures should be viewed as substitutes, the outcomes of a right to work strategy are more just, the costs lower, and that it is more politically feasible to move 'from here to there'. More importantly, in the present context, the right to work provides goods that cannot be satisfied by the

---

[52] PV Parijs, *Real Freedom for All: What (if Anything) can Justify Capitalism?* (Oxford, Oxford University Press, 1995); PV Parijs, J Cohen et al (eds.) *What's Wrong With a Free Lunch?* (Boston, Beacon Press, 2001).
[53] See P Harvey, above n 51; P Harvey, above n 20.

guarantee of basic income.[54] This argument can be approached in various ways. It is possible to argue that while basic income creates a common income baseline for all, it does not address the problems of labour market discrimination, nor does it adequately respond to the 'end of work' problem. Individuals will continue to seek work if they want to have an income that is higher than a basic income. Given that individuals often assess their situation in relation to their neighbours, peers and colleagues, the urge to improve one's position will remain.

Another reason for adhering to the right to work is that, despite deterministic claims about the 'end of work',[55] work has been an important component in situating individuals in society, and at present there are no indications that this is changing. It is true that the experience of work can be taken apart and divided into its various components, identifying an alternative for each. Basic income can substitute for the economic aspect; developing identity can be substituted for by rigorous political participation and a lively civil society; socialisation can be attained by participation in social clubs and community networks; and self-fulfilment can be achieved by more active participation in competitive sports. Yet, as a whole, none of these has thus far provided the regularity and totality that is to be found in work. Moreover, some of the problems associated with work are not absent from the alternatives. Hierarchy, drudgery, uncertainty and competition can be found in some of the substitutes as well.

The plethora of arguments raised in the basic income / right to work debate can be reduced to the fact that while the centrality of work is no truism, it is also not just a social contingency. If I had to choose only one right within the basic income / right to work debate, I would place my eggs in the right to work basket. But what is the debate fundamentally about? As noted above, in my view the various rights merge, or as Guy Standing states, 'A basic income would strengthen the right to work, while weakening the obligation to labour'.[56] At a high level of generality, the guarantee of basic income and right to work are two attempts to increase the social obligation to individuals. They both challenge the idea that work is a ticket for the disengagement of the state from the well-being of the citizenry. Both rights can be misconstrued to achieve precisely the opposite effect. The right to work can easily slip into a duty, and the right to basic income's objection to paternalism can merge into the libertarian value of individualism. But we need not discard rights because they can be manipulated. Both rights seek to change the basic premises of markets towards a

[54] P Harvey, 'Income, Work and Freedom' Expresso Preprint Series, Working Paper 413 (2 September 2004).
[55] J Rifkin, *The End Of Work* (New York, GP Putnam's and Sons, 1995); U Beck (2000), above n 32.
[56] G Standing , above n 48, 9.

greater level of egalitarianism, democracy and respect for human interactions within these markets.

VII CONCLUSION—GENERAL COMMENT NO 18 AND THE RIGHT TO WORK

In November 2005, after several years of deliberations, the Committee on Economic, Social and Cultural Rights issued a General Comment on Article 6 of the Covenant (the right to work).[57] Like other General Comments, its purpose is to 'lay down specific legal obligations, rather than philosophical principles'.[58] Like most of the General Comments, it tries to devise solutions to the general problem of administrating social rights. It refers to the need for progressive realisation and for a list of core obligations. It distinguishes between the duty to respect, protect and fulfil rights, and identifies infringements of omission and commission. Most of these distinctions conform to the general jurisprudence of previous General Comments as well as the general guidelines that are used for implementing economic, social and cultural rights.[59] These partial solutions touch on dilemmas that have not been discussed in this chapter. As noted, the discussion here has sought to identify the problems that differentiate the right to work from other social rights. How does the General Comment approach these problems, and what are the values it has associated with work?

First, the General Comment emphasises the social dimension of the right to work, side by side with the economic dimension, holding that '[t]he right to work contributes... to the survival of the individual..., to his/her development and recognition within the community'. Hence, work is not only a commensurable activity that can be substituted for by income support (welfare), but also an activity that is a good in itself.

With regard to the first critique discussed here—that the right to work is the right to be exploited—the General Comment adopts the 'right to decent' work as a complementarity to the right to work itself. On the one hand it emphasises the importance of consent ('work must be freely chosen or accepted') and the perils of slavery. Yet it also requires that the right to

[57] Committee on Economic, Social and Cultural Rights, General Comment No 18, The Right to Work (adopted 24 November 2005, E/C12/GC/18). On the institution of General Comments to the ICESCR see MCR Craven, *The International Covenant on Economic, Social and Cultural Rights: A Perspective on its Development* (Oxford, Clarendon Press, 1995).

[58] Draft optional protocol to the International Covenant on Economic, Social and Cultural Rights (UN Doc. E/CN4/1997/105), and the Report of the open-ended working group to consider options regarding the elaboration of an optional protocol to the Covenant on Economic, Social and Cultural Rights (UN Doc. E/CN4/2004/44).

[59] The Limburg Principles on the Implementation of the International Covenant on Economic, Social and Cultural Rights (UN Doc E/CN4/1987/17), also published at (1979) 9 *Human Rights Quarterly* 122; The Maastricht Guidelines on Violations of Economic, Social and Cultural Rights (1997) 15 *Netherlands Quarterly on Human Rights* 244.

work should be framed as the right to enjoy 'just and favourable conditions of work' as well as 'decent work'. It emphasises that articles 6, 7 and 8 of the ICESCR (right to work, fair working conditions and freedom of association) are interdependent. It further illustrates the fragility of consent-based formulations when noting that 'people living in the informal economy do so for the most part because of the need to survive, rather than as a matter of choice'.

With regard to the second critique—that the right to work is a right to wage-earning work and hence depreciates other forms of work—the General Comment strengthens the critics' argument. It states that the right to work 'encompasses all forms of work, whether independent work or dependent waged work'. Hence, the General Comment does not require that work must be performed as an 'employee', but extends the concept to cover only independent workers (or contractors) whose work is also remunerated according to market valuation. Work at home, community work and artistic expression are not included within the domain of work.

With regard to the third critique, the General Comment avoids the problem altogether. It does not mention the potential for a duty to work, primarily because it justly discusses 'the freedom of the individual regarding the choice to work'. It emphasises the individual's right not to be discriminated against in the labour market and their right to assistance in integration. It holds that the state violates its obligation to fulfil the right in the event of 'insufficient expenditures or misallocation of public funds', but it does not discuss the pressures imposed on individuals to get into the labour market by threatening to remove welfare support altogether.

The different responses offered to the critiques by the General Comment aptly demonstrate its strengths and weaknesses. On the one hand the Comment provides, for the first time, a systemic analysis of the right to work and seeks to justify its inclusion among the economic and social rights. Like other General Comments to the ICESCR, it tries to structure a discourse, a structured jurisprudence for the right, and at the same time to leave a broad sphere of discretion for each state to adapt the right to its political economy. On the other hand, it seems that the attempt to provide practical rather than philosophical guidelines has also led to an over-simplification that may render the General Comment impractical, or worse—unjust. It avoids the difficulty of identifying the narrow boundaries between fulfilling the right and coercing individuals, or between waged and non-waged work, or other problems that have not been discussed in this chapter, such as the potential trade-offs between the right *to* work and the level of rights *at* work. In doing so, it may be signalling that these are not issues that can be settled within the human rights sphere, and that each state must identify its own solutions.

Leaving conflicts and tensions that are embedded in the right to work to the discretion of the state may not be a mistaken strategy. However, this brings the discussion to a conclusion with the question of what human rights are for. Should the right to work suffice with abolishing slavery and prohibiting discrimination at work—two aspects that are covered by other rights as well, and for which a designated right to work is not necessary? Or should it settle the debate among the various currents of feminism regarding the relationship between waged and non-waged work? If we take human rights to designate a discourse, praxis and a strategic space of social transformation rather than a truism from which absolute answers can be derived for each and every problem, then a more expansive approach to the scope of human rights should be applied. At the same time, with regard to some problems the human rights documents must highlight contradictions, trade-offs and dilemmas. When constructing the meaning of a human right, as the General Comment seeks to do, the document must present a discourse for debating solutions, a tool for advocates, and a road-sign for legislators and judges. Consequently, the just attempt to endorse the right to work as a higher norm of the human rights calibre must confront the various objections to the right to work rather than avoid them.

Part V

Social Rights of Special Groups

15

The Social Rights of People with Disabilities

Reconciling Care and Justice

NETA ZIV

I used to be a member of loads of committees fighting for rights and all that...
yeah, and the Disability Movement do some great stuff for other people. But
how's all that stuff on politics going to get me a girlfriend and a job?[1]

I SOCIAL RIGHTS AND HUMAN RIGHTS—NEW DISCOURSES, NEW CRITIQUES

The United Nation's Declaration of Human Rights in 1948 clearly
envisioned social rights to be part of the universal commitment to
human rights. To be sure, the inclusion of social rights in the
human rights order has been debated and contested, both from a neo-
liberal as well as a liberal-positivistic view point.[2] In addition, the enforcement and implementation of social rights has always been secondary in the
West's strive to protect civil liberties and political rights through legislation, treaties and other international bodies and instruments.[3]
Nevertheless, and despite the acclaimed differences between social rights
and civil and political rights, it is now recognised that the two sets of
rights are inseparable and interdependent.[4] Moreover, in the last decade a

---

[1] Tiger Harris (life story) in D Armstrong, 'The Politics of Self Advocacy and People with
Learning Difficulties' (2002) 30 *Policy and Politics* 333, 341.

[2] R Nozick, *Anarchy, State and Utopia* (Oxford, Blackwell, 1974); M Cranston, *What are
Human Rights?* (London, Bodley Head, 1973).

[3] H Dean, 'Human Rights and Welfare Rights: Contextualising Dependence and
Responsibility' in H Dean (ed), *The Ethics of Welfare, Human Rights, Dependency and
Responsibility* (Bristol, The Policy Press, 2004) 8–9.

[4] See P Alston, 'Economic and Social Rights' in L Henkin and JL Hargrove (eds), *Human
Rights: An Agenda for the Next Century* (Washington DC, American Society of International
Law, 1994) 148 and citations therein.

common critique has developed with regards to the new human rights discourse; although this critique mostly pertains to civil and political rights, it is also pertinent to social and economic rights.

The critique focuses on the language expressed in, and the assumptions underlying, contemporary human rights documents, adopted by various international bodies. They reveal an individualist-liberal philosophy, in which rights correspond with fulfilment of responsibilities, personhood is envisioned by way of autonomy and independence, and individuals are assumed to seek maximisation of opportunities through choice and participation. Against these salient qualities, basic human conditions such as need, vulnerability, dependence and insecurity—all ever more present in a globalised world—are absent or at least imperceptible in contemporary efforts to promote the protection of human rights.

On the United Nations front, the UN 2000 Human Development Report, for example, fuses human rights and human development and treats them as inextricably linked.[5] The term 'human development' is closely associated with the concept of human capabilities, developed by Amartya Sen as a theory of justice (in addition to an economic analysis).[6] Sen's capabilities approach focuses on the actual power of a person to do certain things as a measure of well-being. These capabilities include (but are not limited to) 'elementary things as being adequately nourished, being in good health, avoiding escapable morbidity and premature mortality', ie, those areas of life to which social rights pertain.[7]

Despite the emphasis on capabilities of this sort, the UN report is saturated with reference to human rights as a means to secure freedoms.[8] The connection between rights and freedoms permeates the report in relation to civil rights and to economic and social rights. Social rights are in fact termed as freedoms: 'freedom from want for a decent standard of living' or 'freedom for decent work, without exploitation'.[9] Thus the overall approach of the report treats issues of poverty, welfare and subsistence through the freedom paradigm: '[c]apabilities thus reflects the freedom to achieve functioning. In this sense, human development is freedom'.[10] The report continues to set standards for human rights protection in terms that resemble a 'managerial' mindset and doctrine.[11] These include the need to capitalise upon the opportunities of globalisation through participation (rather than the need to be protected from their

---

[5] United Nations Development Programme, *Human Development Report 2000* (New York, Oxford University Press, 2000) 1: 'Human Rights and human development share a common purpose—to secure the freedom, well-being and dignity of all people everywhere'.

[6] A Sen, *Inequality Reexamined* (Cambridge Mass, Harvard University Press, 1992) IX–XI.

[7] *Ibid* 39, 44–5.

[8] Above n 5, 1.

[9] Above n 5, 3, 5.

[10] Above n 5, 17.

[11] Above n 3, 12.

harms), or the need to incorporate human rights standards into global trade rules, for example through the WTO.[12]

The Charter of Fundamental Rights of The European Union[13] too is based on an individual liberal approach to social rights. Though it includes the rights to health care, housing, education and welfare, these rights are articulated in a general manner, with few concrete obligations on the states to implement them. For example, section 34 of the Charter (dealing with social security) is phrased loosely, and states that the Union 'recognises and respects the entitlement for social security benefits and services' in selective situations of need (maternity, old age, dependency). There is no direct assertion of a right to social security, nor any recognition of personal vulnerability and the need for protection as an inherent human condition.

Similarly, the revised version of the European Social Charter, adopted in Strasburg in 1996, is highly occupied with employment rights (the right to work, to vocational training, to just, safe and healthy conditions in work, to fair remuneration and collective organisation rights).[14] The Charter only scarcely recognises the right to social protection (the rights of children and women in the context of maternity). The right to social welfare services,[15] though acknowledged in the Charter, is limited and selective. Social welfare is connected to the notions of participation, adjustment and development, while conditions such as dependence, support and care are absent from the Charter.

As for people with disabilities, the Charter sets out measures states ought to adopt to promote 'independence, social integration and participation in the life of the community' of people with disabilities. These measures underscore access to opportunities and the need to 'overcome barriers'. In the Charter too, however, there is hardly any acknowledgement of life circumstances that require support, or of need and care, that may (or might not) enable such access.

In sum, the critique of the recent human rights/social rights discourse from this end targets dominant visions of personhood and human experience, as well as their implementation in actual policies. The critique relating to personhood is about what is present in, and what is absent from, the language of human rights. The subject of the rights, explains Ellis, assumes an ethic of justice that is 'associated with an individualistic conception of the autonomous self'.[16] This is a responsible, independent individual who seeks to maximise opportunities by obtaining access to the

---

12 Above n 5, 9.
13 EU Charter of Fundamental Rights of the European Union.
14 European Social Charter (revised).
15 *Ibid* Art 14.
16 K Ellis, 'Dependency, Justice and the Ethic of Care' in D Hartley (ed), *The Ethics of Welfare* (Bristol, The Policy Press, 2004) 32.

public sphere. Accordingly, the goal is to remove barriers that hinder attaining this objective.

This conception of personhood stands in tension with an ethics of care, which views people as existing within (and only within) social relations, as interdependent and as giving or receiving support and care throughout their life.[17] Under this latter understanding, social rights can serve as a framework that encompasses fulfilment of basic needs and that enables people to gain capabilities through provision, assistance and care. Viewed in this sense social rights correspond with such notions. They need not be confined to an individualistic ethos under which a person stands alone before the state and is required to show dessert in order to receive assistance.[18]

As for policy implementation, the liberal-individual model strongly privileges productivity, paid labour and other income-generating activity. Those who are not able to meet the work-productivity ethic remain at the peripheries of society. Family relations and commitments, disability, old age and dependency are set at the opposite end of a dichotomy in which the market is the objective for access, and individuals are measured through their abilities to produce revenues. This worldview manifests itself in regimes that guarantee only minimal social rights rather than universal entitlements, in social/support services that remain at the margins rather than in the mainstream and through selective definitions of need as prerequisites for receiving services.[19] The ethic of individual autonomy coincides with participation in the public sphere; it eclipses social values such as support and care, which are left in the devalued private realm.

II THE SOCIAL MODEL OF DISABILITY AND THE RIGHTS DISCOURSE

The critique of rights from a standpoint that values support, dependence and care as central to human experience also pertains to the social struggles of people with disabilities. In order to understand the relevancy of this critique to disability I will briefly describe the most powerful enter-

---

[17] Carol Gilligan's work developed the idea of an 'Ethics of Care' in the context of gender; see: C Gilligan, *In a Different Voice* (Cambridge, Mass, Harvard University Press, 1982); E Kittay, *Love's Labor: Essays on Women, Equality, and Dependency* (New York, Routledge, 1999); S Sevenhuijsen, 'Caring in the Third Way: the Relation Between Obligation, Responsibility and Care in Third Way Discourse' (2000) 20 *Critical Social Policy* 5.

[18] For this understanding of disability state relations see D Stone, *The Disabled State (Health, Society, and Policy)* (Philadelphia, Temple University Press, 1984).

[19] Above n 16, 33; B Fisher and J Toronto, 'Toward a Feminist Theory of Care' in E Abel and M Nelson (eds), *Circles of Care: Work and Identity in Women's Lives* (Albany, State University of New York Press, 1990).

prise—the 'big idea'[20]—forwarded by the disability movement: the social model of disability, and its legal/rights manifestations.

Beginning in the early 1970s, largely through grassroots activities in the UK and the US, people with disabilities forwarded a political, cultural and legal endeavour to change the way disability is conceptualised and addressed.[21] Under this approach—labelled 'the social model of disability'—people with disabilities demanded to appropriate the treatment of disability from the medical and social welfare disciplines. The movement of people with disabilities reclaimed the right to define disability and transform it from a medical-welfare to a socially constructed phenomenon.[22] The monumental document of the Union of the Physically Impaired against Segregation (UPIAS) from 1975 described the medical-model experience in the following words:

> an army of 'experts' sitting on panels which are set up all over the country. These 'experts', armed with the latest definitions and tests for measuring, will prod and probe into the intimate details of our lives. They will bear down on us with batteries of questions, and wielding their tape measures will attempt to tie down the last remaining vestige of our privacy and dignity as human beings.[23]

The crux of the new approach was the refusal to treat disability as an essential and stable medical (or other) category, but to address it through political terms: a product of power relations and non-accommodated structures and environments.[24] According to this viewpoint, impairment may be a personal tragedy, but biological factors are not the primary cause of disadvantage. It is society's response—the actual construction of the physical and social environment—that disables people.[25] Disability is no less the product of power and knowledge than a physical experience of impairment. Through an emphasis on 'people first', this approach aimed to shift the focus to people's abilities rather than their impairments, and pointed to the paternalistic attitudes of 'ableism'—a power structure that

20 A term coined by Hasler: see F Hasler, 'Developments in the Disabled People's Movement' in J Swain, V Finkelstein, S French and M Oliver (eds), *Disabling Barriers, Enabling Environments* (London, Sage Publications, 1993) 278.
21 In England, The Union of Physically Impaired Against Segregation, a progressive group of people with disabilities, published a manifesto describing this approach: see The Union of Physically Impaired Against Segregation, 'Fundamental Principles of Disability' (Summary of the Discussion Held on 22 November, 1975) <http://www.leeds.ac.uk/disabilitystudies/archiveuk/UPIAS/UPIAS.htm>.
22 On the social model of disability see, eg: Fougeyrollas and L Beauregard, 'An Interactive Person-Environment Social Creation' in GL Albrecht, KD Seelman and M Bury (eds), *Handbook of Disability Studies* (London, Sage Publications, 2001) 171–94; S Wendell, *The Rejected Body, Feminist Philosophical Reflections on Disability* (New York, Routledge, 1996).
23 Above n 21, 17–18.
24 On the political meaning and dimensions of disability, see M Oliver, *The Politics of Disablement* (Basingstoke, Macmillan, 1990).
25 See also V Finkelstein, 'Representing Disability' in J Swain, S French, C Barnes and C Thomas (eds), *Disabling Barriers, Enabling Environments* (London, Sage, 2004) 13.

classifies social groups based on their abilities, and considers people with disabilities inferior to the 'able-bodied'. [26]

In the 1990s the influence of the social model intensified and was translated into formal legal directives that required the accommodation of existing surroundings and the removal of structural barriers to enable access in all areas of life, including employment, public services, public accommodations, housing and education. These policies were conceptualised as rights of people with disabilities, entitling them to a particular claim or response.[27] The rights model too asked to shift the paradigm under which law treated people with disabilities: from subjects of legal intervention into active rights bearers.[28]

In the United States the disability rights movement followed the collective memories and ethos of the civil rights movement and built upon its successes. Accordingly, the rights model defined the goal of the struggle as attaining equality. Equality was to be achieved through integration, participation and equal access.[29] The right to equality was elaborated and redefined to include the positive duty to accommodate, alter and modify existing environments, in the broadest terms. Comprehensive legislation was passed to strengthen these obligations, including the Americans with Disabilities Act 1990 in the US, the Australian Disability Discrimination Act 1992 and the Disability Discrimination Act 1995 in the UK.[30] Through this distributive construal, the rights model incorporated the underlying conception of the social model: as disability was stipulated as a product of structural barriers and environmental impediments, their removal through accommodations was imperative to achieve full participation, ie, equality.

From an historical perspective, the social/rights model was born from the Independent Living Movement (ILM), which originated in the UK and in the US in the 1970s.[31] The ILM defined its goals and strategies by underscoring notions of independence, personal choice, freedom of

---

26 On the development of 'ableism' in disability studies, see S Mor, 'Between Charity, Welfare and Warfare: Privileges and Neglect in the Politics of Disability Policy, A Disability Legal Studies Analysis' 18 (2) *Yale Journal of Law and the Humanities* 63.

27 See, eg, H Hahn, 'Academic debates and political advocacy: the US disability movement' in C Barnes, M Oliver and L Barton (eds), *Disability Studies Today* (Cambridge, Polity Press, 2002) 162–89.

28 See below n 36.

29 On the evolvement of disability rights advocacy in the US see J Shapiro, *No Pity: People with Disabilities Forging a New Civil Rights Movement* (New York, Times Books, 1993) and R Burgdorf, 'The Americans with Disabilities Act: Implications of a Second Generation Civil Rights Statute' (1991) 26 *Harvard Civil Rights-Civil Liberties Law Review* 413.

30 See below nn 43,47 and 48.

31 Shapiro, above n 29, 49–54; CW Levy, *A People's History of the Independent Living Movement* (Centre on Independent Living, University of Kansas, 1998), <http://www.independentliving.org/docs5/ILhistory.html>; SE Brown, *Freedom of Movement: Independent Living History and Philosophy* (Institute on Disability Culture, 2000), http://www.ilru.org/html/publications/bookshelf/freedom_movement.html.

expression and movement, freedom from paternalism and domination, as well as the right of self-advocacy. It rejected decades of domination by professionals, and labelled the situation of people with disabilities as oppression. The ILM philosophy, explains Brown, claims:

> [that] all people with disabilities are oppressed and that there is little difference in the big picture of the discrimination against people with disabilities. To paraphrase a well-known quote: oppression is oppression is oppression.[32]

The ILM demanded to shift the paradigm through which state and society related to people with disabilities. Instead of welfare dependence and subjugation to the medical profession, the ILM pressed for self-advocacy and consumer-type control of the services acquired by people with disabilities.[33] A central theme within the ILM was the debate about independence. At its core, independence was conceptualised as being freed from paternalistic attitudes, from a medicalised approach and from institutionalisation, and was seen as a means to live a full life in the community. The term 'independence' correlated with an ability to make one's own choices about what services to receive, from whom, where and when.

Ed Roberts, considered one of the founders of the independent living movement in the US, explained:

> The students... conceived the idea of 'independent living,' which to them meant active participation in society—working, having a home, raising a family, and generally sharing in the joys and responsibilities of community life. Independent living meant freedom from isolation and institutionalisation; it meant the ability to choose where to live, how to live, and how to carry out the activities of daily living that most able-bodied people take for granted. It meant taking the responsibility for political action and charting a new way of life.[34]

Since many people with disabilities need assistance and support, the ideas forwarded by ILM advocates did not preclude this aspect of peoples' lives, and considered disability benefits programmes to correspond with the ILM ideology. In other words, assistance was viewed as a measure to promote independence, if provided in a way that did not compromise the control, choices and preferences of people with disabilities. The possibility to be in charge of one's own life and to make personal decisions—if and how to use cash and in-kind benefits, who to be assisted by and for what purpose—enabled them to reconcile these two seemingly opposing notions. In other words, in many circumstances benefit entitlements are prerequisites to living in a community setting, without which many disabled

---

32 Brown, *ibid*, 5.

33 SR Bagenstos, 'The Americans with Disabilities Act as Welfare Reform' (2003) 44 *William and Mary Law Review* 921, 988.

34 EV Roberts, 'A History of the Independent Living Movement: A Founder's Perspective' in BW Heller, LS Zagans and LM Flohr *Psychosocial Interventions with Physically Disabled Persons* (eds), (New Brunswick, NJ, Rutgers University Press, 1989) 231, 237.

persons would be unable to make the transition into less restrictive living settings.[35]

Despite the acclaimed promise to settle a demand for independence on the one hand, and a policy of welfare and other disability-related benefits on the other, tension between the two notions surfaced. In practice, and over time, the dichotomy between personal independence and welfare benefits and social support emerged. Disability welfare programmes assume that people with disabilities do not need to work if they are incapacitated; that disability may lead to physical dependence on others; that people with disabilities are sometimes more vulnerable and need to be protected from unnecessary risks. In other words, independence in its conventional sense is qualified.

Nevertheless, due to substantive and tactical motivations (such as the need to articulate a lucid and attainable public message), it was necessary to push the idea of independence to its boundaries. The ILM wanted to convey its revolutionary message to the outside world, but its new paradigm was cast against lifelong experiences of oppression and subordination. To overcome this grim reality the ILM needed to adopt a clear and sharp dictum that would transform society's treatment of disability, from a charity-dependency approach to an autonomous-productive ethos. The image of people with disabilities had to be transformed: they had to be portrayed as self-reliant and independent people, who assume personal responsibility and participate in community life, as active contributors to society and not only as passive recipients. Welfare programmes, in this context, stood for the opposite representation.

In addition, there were internal reasons for the scepticism exhibited by ILM activists towards social benefits and income support. Within the movement of people with disabilities the principle of independence was not monolithic. Some carried what Bagenstos calls a social-democratic understanding of welfare and support, and accepted disability welfare programmes as a means to achieve independence and human dignity. Others, however, identified welfare with charity, and saw it as an impediment to independence, not a means for its realisation. They equated welfare and support with subordination and subjugation, and alleged that benefit programmes left people with disabilities 'subject to the control of welfare agencies and "helping professionals" and in an inferior status in society at large'.[36] From this end activists claimed that support programmes were over-protective and barred people with disabilities from assuming risks, failing and overcoming such pains—all experiences that constitute part of conventional human existence.

---

[35] *Ibid* 240.
[36] Above n 33, 995.

Following this line of thought, some activists continued to claim that people with disabilities need to move away from a 'welfare mentality'—equated with exemptions from work requirements, dependency and passivity—to an opposite state of being, namely, productivity, social contribution and remunerative employment through participation in the labour force.[37]

The salience of independence, accompanied by the ethos of income-generating activities, self-reliance and a cost-benefit analysis of disability policies, formed the central principles underlying subsequent activities of the disability movement. These liberal (some would say almost libertarian) themes constituted the main framework through which the disability movement moved towards the era of rights. Throughout the 1990s international human rights documents were negotiated, and a series of domestic laws enacted, recognising the rights of people with disabilities through a variety of legal mechanisms.

As will be illustrated below, these legal arrangements were based on a liberal philosophy and reflected a set of assumptions about preferred societal values. The laws protected independence and autonomy (as opposed to dependence and subjugation); they mandated integration and inclusion (in contrast to exclusion and segregation); they required access to all life spheres and equal opportunities (in place of segregated discriminatory treatment); and they were frequently justified through a logic of sustainability and productivity (rather than needs and want).

Anti-discrimination laws formed the backbone of these legislative initiatives, claiming that elimination of discrimination would enable full participation in all life spheres and that the costs 'invested' in accommodations—those alterations necessary to facilitate inclusion of people with disabilities in all areas of life—would 'pay off' through direct and indirect activities of people with disabilities. People with disabilities would then become tax-paying employees, autonomous market consumers and active participants in communal life.

III THE HUMAN RIGHTS OF PEOPLE WITH DISABILITIES—SALIENCE OF CIVIL AND POLITICAL RIGHTS

Since the 1990s advocacy by and on behalf of people with disabilities has taken place on the international level, as well as through domestic initiatives (constitutional, statutory and the judiciary), as a means to protect the interests of this group.

---

[37] JE Bickenbach, 'Disability Human Rights, Law, and Policy' in GL Albrecht, KD Seelman and M Bury (eds), *Handbook of Disability Studies* (London, Sage Publications, 2001) 565, 576.

A The International Level

During the 1990s the UN and other international bodies (such as the WHO) sponsored a number of initiatives to promote the rights and interests of people with disabilities. These include the Standard Rules for the Equalisation of Opportunities for Persons with Disabilities, and the WHO Revised International Classification of Functions (ICF).[38] In December 2001 the UN General Assembly established an ad hoc committee 'to consider proposals for a comprehensive and integral international convention to promote and protect the rights and dignity of persons with disabilities'.[39] Since then, the process of drafting a comprehensive human rights document—the International Convention on the Rights of Persons with Disabilities—has taken place. The Convention was adopted by the UN General Assembly on 6 December 2006; it was opened for States' signature in March 2007. Article 3 of the Convention lays down its principles:

—respect for dignity and individual autonomy, including the freedom to make one's own choices, and independence of persons;
—non-discrimination;
—full and effective inclusion of persons with disabilities as equal citizens and participants in all aspects of life;
—respect for difference and acceptance of persons with disabilities as part of human diversity and humanity;
—accessibility
—equality of opportunity and equality between men and women.[40]

Notably, these principles reflect a liberal ethic, emphasising personal autonomy, independence, choice, non-discrimination, participation and equal opportunity. This draft differs from earlier human rights documents from the 1970s on the rights of people with disabilities. The former—namely the Declaration on the Rights of Mentally Retarded Persons from 1971 and the Declaration on the Rights of Disabled Persons from 1975—have been criticised as being based on outmoded medical and welfare models of disability. These declarations did speak in the language of human rights, but rights were qualified and carried a paternalistic flavour. The declarations nonetheless explicitly included rights to receive

---

[38] For a summary of these measures see C Barnes, 'Introduction: Disability, Policy and Politics' (2002) 30 *Policy and Politics* 311, 312.

[39] United Nations General Assembly Resolution 56/168 (19 December 2001) UN Doc A/RES/56/168.

[40] The International Convention on the Rights of Persons with Disabilities can be found at: http://www.un.org/esa/socdev/enable/rights/convtexte.htm.

medical care, rehabilitation, vocational training and education, as well as the right to economic and social security and to a decent level of living.

The Convention recognises numerous civil and political rights, and includes extensive rights to freedom of speech, political participation, privacy, independent living and participation in public life. Social rights such as the right to work, education and health—recognised both as positive rights as well as through general duties of provision imposed on the state—are phrased with an emphasis on access, inclusion and personal development. The right to social security, to a decent standard of living (including food and water), to income support and other special services are phrased in terms of 'access rights' (ie, the need to remove barriers to their realisation).

In sum, although the Convention recognises social rights as part of the human rights guaranteed to persons with disabilities, these rights are defined through a paradigm that emphasises personal autonomy and participation, equal access and removal of barriers. The individual with a disability is portrayed as an active rights-bearer before the state. There is little reference to notions such as the need for protection, vulnerability, care or interdependence between human beings.

B Country Legislation

A similar mindset underlies the Americans with Disabilities Act 1990 (ADA).[41] The ADA served as a model for legislation enacted in many countries since the 1990s, and is still hailed as the most prominent civil rights law in the area of disability rights.[42] The ADA, in its entirety, is an anti-discrimination civil rights law. The law begins by describing the problems faced by people with disabilities in the US as rooted in discrimination, exclusion and other forms of unequal treatment. Accordingly, the goal of the law was to realise 'equality of opportunity, full participation, independent living, and economic self-sufficiency for such individuals'.[43] The ADA extended the definition of discrimination to include the refusal to accommodate or alter, among other things, existing employment surroundings and practices, public services and accommodations, medical examinations, telecommunication services and public transportation. A central justification for this demand was that such accommodations will enable people with disabilities to become

---

[41] Americans with Disabilities Act 1990 (US).
[42] R Burgdorf, 'The Americans with Disabilities Act: Implications of a Second Generation Civil Rights Statute' (1991) 26 *Harvard Civil Rights-Civil Liberties Law Review* 413; TM Cook, 'The Move to Integration' (1991) 64 *Temple Law Review* 393.
[43] Above n 41, para 2(a)(8).

independent and self-reliant participants in society, and will reduce their dependence on welfare and other forms of public support.[44]

Similarly, the UK's Disability Discrimination Act 1995 (DDA)[45] established the basic right of people with disabilities to be free from discrimination. The initial part of the DDA, enacted in 1995, prohibited discrimination on the basis of disability in: employment, access to goods, facilities and services; the management, buying or renting of land or property; and education. Subsequently the law was amended, expanding the duties to make 'reasonable adjustments' in services and physical features and to provide auxiliary aids. In 2002 the law was again amended, requiring schools, colleges, universities, and providers of adult education and youth services to ensure that they do not discriminate against disabled people.

Australia followed the same principles when it passed the Disability Discrimination Act in 1992 (Australian DDA).[46] The Australian DDA is a non-discrimination law, protecting people with disabilities from unequal treatment in education, employment, provision of goods and services, land (housing), sport facilities, public transportation and information services. The Act mandated making reasonable adjustments providing they do not impose 'unjustifiable hardship'. In general, the Australian DDA reflects the social model as well, as it demands the removal of physical and attitudinal barriers that create a disabling environment and experience.[47]

In Israel, advocacy on behalf of Israelis with disabilities is a more recent social phenomenon dating from the mid-1990s.[48] The 1998 Equal Rights for People with Disabilities Act (ERPDA) defines its goal as protecting 'the dignity and liberty of people with disabilities' and entrenching the right to 'equal and active participation' in all areas of life (section 2).[49] Even though one of the law's stated objectives is to provide 'an adequate response' to the needs of persons with disabilities, it is not clear if this term means positive support and services or is limited to the requirement of accommodations and alterations. Originally, the law covered only employment and public transportation: it prohibited discrimination in employment (including the duty to make accommodations) and demanded

---

[44] Above n 33; M Diller, 'Dissonant Disability Policies: The Tensions Between the Americans with Disabilities Act and Federal Disability Benefit Programs' (1998) 76 *Texas Law Review* 1003.

[45] Disability Discrimination Act 1995 (UK).

[46] Disability Discrimination Act, 1992 (Australia).

[47] In 2004 the implementation of the Act was reviewed by the Productivity Commission of the Australian government. The report of the committee can be found at <http://www.pc.gov.au/inquiry/dda/finalreport/>.

[48] Prior to that time, the treatment of disability relied heavily on the medical model, and rights consciousness was completely absent from public discourse and policy: see below n 50, above n 26.

[49] Equal Rights for People with Disabilities Law 1998, SH 252.

accessibility to most forms of public transportation.[50] In 2005 the law was expanded to include a right of access to, and non-discrimination in, public services and public accommodations, broadly defined, with an implementation period extending to 12 years.

Legislation in civil law countries has been slow to follow the rights approach, but has nonetheless been moving in this direction in recent years. During the 1970s Scandinavian countries enacted legislation that afforded benefits and services to persons with disabilities, as a means to attain social inclusion. However, this approach has been changing and new legislation is being introduced to include a non-discrimination rights approach to people with disabilities.[51] Until the last decade EU countries lacked comprehensive legislation protecting the rights of persons with disabilities; however, towards the end of the 1990s a new policy has led European countries to approach the issue in terms of 'equal opportunity for disabled people, non-discrimination, mainstreaming, the rights based approach, inclusion, full participation and removal of barriers to full participation and inclusion'.[52] Though this shift has not yet been translated to fully fledged legislation, it is slowly being adopted as the dominant approach in civil law countries. France, for example, enacted a comprehensive law in 2005 that prohibits discrimination in employment on the basis of disability, requires alteration to employment premises, and addressed issues of accessibility and education.[53] The rights paradigm, therefore, is penetrating civil law countries as well, and is not confined to the jurisprudence of common law countries.[54]

On the constitutional level, a number of countries included persons with disabilities within the grounds for constitutional protection. Section 15 of the Canadian Charter of Rights and Freedoms 1982, for example, prohibits discrimination on the basis of mental or physical disability, stating that:

> every individual is equal before and under the law and has the right to the equal protection and equal benefit of the law without discrimination based on... mental or physical disability.

Article 9(3) of the South African Constitution, enacted in 1996, prohibits discrimination on the basis of disability, and in addition the South African

---

[50] S Herr, 'The Americans with Disabilities Act: Reforming Disability Nondiscrimination Laws: A Comparative Perspective' (2001/2002) 35 *University of Michigan Journal of Law Reform* 305.

[51] B Hvinden, 'Nordic Disability Policies in a Changing Europe: Is There Still a Distinct Nordic Model?' (2004) 39 *Social Law and Administration* 170.

[52] *Ibid* 182.

[53] See, for example, *Government actions to help those with disabilities*, (French) Government Portal, Prime Minister, 8 February 2005, <http://www.premier-ministre.gouv.fr/en/information/latest_news_97/government_actions_to_help_52311.html>.

[54] See, generally, D Schiek, 'A New Framework on Equal Treatment of Persons in EC Law' (2002) 8 (2) *European Law Journal* 290–314.

Employment Equity Act prohibits discrimination on the basis of disability in any employment policy or practice.[55]

To summarise this point, during the 1990s a number of common law countries passed comprehensive legislation protecting the rights of persons with disabilities in public and private spheres. Most laws followed the form of an anti-discrimination prototype and embodied the right to equality as a central principle and theme. These legal arrangements emphasise civil rights, personal autonomy, participation and individual inclusion as means for empowerment and for realisation of human rights and human dignity. One reason often expressed to justify such legislation was that enabling social participation—through provision of accommodations, for example—would reduce welfare dependence. Civil rights were thus set as a favourable alternative to benefit and social support programmes. Accordingly, the civil rights ideals—self-reliance, independence, full participation and gainful employment—were strengthened as the preferred values of human and social existence.

C Case Law

As the statutory and constitutional grounds for human rights protection of people with disabilities were being laid out, litigation was utilised to enforce these rights and implement them. For the most part, case law pertaining to disability rights clearly manifests the civil rights agenda and its underlying attitudes, as the following examples show.

In Canada, the first case of principle invoking section 15 of the Canadian Charter in relation to disability dealt with the pension rights of a disabled employee. Though substantively this case involved a social right—pension benefits—its analysis was conducted through a civil rights paradigm.[56] In this case the court reviewed a state pension policy which required that contributions to a pension fund be made by employees over a period of time, as a condition for receiving pension benefits. The plaintiff did not meet this requirement due to his temporary (and relatively moderate) disability and claimed this rule violated his right to equality. The Canadian Supreme Court's decision is a celebration of the social model; the court differentiated between:

> [the] physical or mental impairment, and functional limitation, and on the other hand the other component, namely, the socially constructed handicap that is not located in the individual at all but in the society in which is obliged to go about his or her everyday tasks.

---

55 Employment Equity Act 55, 1998, s 6.
56 *Granovsky v Minister of Employment & Immigration* [2000] SCR 703.

Nevertheless, the court fell short of recognising the right of the plaintiff to pension, since it resorted to the traditional discrimination analysis under section 15: the plaintiff was compared to a gravely disabled person, who was not required to make pension contributions, and the distinction between the two situations was affirmed. Indirectly, the court differentiated between people with disabilities who can work and those who cannot, confirming that only the latter are rightly exempted from the contribution requirement. Through this differentiation the court reinforced the dichotomy between deserving and undeserving recipients of state aid, and the prevalence of the work ethic as demarcating the boundaries of this division.

Another case handled by the Canadian Supreme Court dealt with the legality of a blanket refusal of the Canadian Motor Vehicle Branch to assess the capability of individuals with a certain visual impairment to drive.[57] The court abolished the broad rule as violating the duty to treat each person according to his/her individual abilities and stated that the case 'deals with no more than the right to be accommodated. It does not decide that [the person] had the right to a driver's license. It merely established that he had the right to be assessed...', and that the state agency could not refuse to permit him 'to demonstrate that his situation could be accommodated'. This decision applies a classical due process analysis, based on the individual liberal model entrenched in the civil rights/civil liberties tradition.

The European Court of Human Rights (ECtHR) handles cases on alleged violations of the European Convention on Human Rights and Fundamental Freedoms ('the Convention'). It should be noted that the Convention does not include prohibition on the basis of disability directly. The court thus relied on general clauses (prohibition against discrimination, the right to life and privacy, prohibition on degrading punishment), as its basis for rulings in this area. A sample of decisions, described below, illustrates the kind of cases that have reached the Court regarding disability.

In 2002 the ECtHR handed down a decision in a complaint against the UK, based on Article 3 of the Convention, which states: 'No one shall be subjected to torture or to inhuman or degrading treatment or punishment'. The complaint was filed on behalf of a severely disabled woman (described by the court as 'four-limb deficient as a result of phocemolia due to Thalidomide'), who alleged that she was held in degrading conditions in prison, following a contempt of court order—a violation of her rights under the Convention.[58] The court accepted the petition and based its

---

[57] *British Columbia (Superintendent of Motor Vehicles) v British Columbia* [1999] SCR 868.
[58] *Price v United Kingdom* (App No 33394/96) (2002) 34 EHRR 53.

decision on one of the most well-established protections in human rights/civil rights doctrine: the right to life and the prohibition of torture.

Another case based on Article 3 of the Convention (together with Article 8, which protects the right to privacy and family life) was filed against the Netherlands in 1986. The case involved the failure of the Dutch police to accept and investigate a complaint by a mentally disabled woman and to initiate criminal proceedings against her alleged rapist. The stated reasons for the police's decision were that, due to her mental capacity, the woman could not file a complaint herself, and that her father could not act as her substitute.[59] The court accepted the complaint, found that the rights of the women were violated under the Convention (Article 8), and awarded her damages.

An Italian case from 1998 entailed the inaccessibility of a seaside resort in northern Italy to a plaintiff using a wheelchair.[60] The court considered whether the complaint could be based on Article 8 of the Convention (respect for private life and family life) and Article 14 (prohibition of discrimination). It held that, lacking a specific prohibition on discrimination on the basis of disability, the case had to be dismissed. It is interesting to note that in this case the plaintiffs tried to establish their right of access to the beach through the right to social relations, derived from Article 8. The court rejected the claim, stating that it concerns:

> interpersonal relations of such broad and indeterminate scope that there can be no conceivable direct link between the measures the State was urged to take in order to make good the omissions of the private bathing establishments and the applicant's private life.

The court, apparently, did not associate the right to family and social life (protected in the convention) with the basic right to equal access.

These and other cases brought before the courts illustrate that, for the most part, human rights litigation was employed to protect the bodily integrity, access and equality of persons with disabilities. Since the European Convention on Human Rights does not guarantee social rights directly, human rights litigation was consequentially less beneficial in protecting social rights such as welfare, rehabilitation, personal assistance, health care and other means vital to guarantee the human dignity of people with disabilities.[61]

The resort to the social/rights model was a double-edged sword. On the one hand it relieved people with disabilities from paternalistic attitudes and denominating practices of the welfare/medical model. On the other hand, it dissociated them from the substantive services and entitlements provided through these unwanted practices. This outcome gave rise to the

---

[59] *X & Y v The Netherlands* (App No 8978/80) (1986) Series A No 91.
[60] *Botta v Italy* (153/1996/772/973) (1998) 26 EHRR 41.
[61] See above n 26, at 27.

critique against the prevalence of the social model, and to the search for alternative frameworks to reach beyond the rigid rights/welfare dichotomy.

IV THE CRITIQUE OF THE SOCIAL/RIGHTS MODEL

The overwhelming prevalence of the social/rights model attracted criticism from numerous directions, particularly in relation to the target group of people with disabilities, to the effectiveness of the rights approach and to its underlying ethics and values.

A Target Group—Who Benefits from the Social Model?

People with disabilities are not a homogenous group, and advocacy on their behalf entailed implementing multifaceted strategies to overcome the vast diversity of interests of different disabilities.[62] The benefits of the social model, critics argued, do not reach all people with disabilities, and the model excludes certain sub-groups of people with disabilities from the advantages of the rights model. The rights model does little for those who are impaired in a way that prevents them from enjoying accommodations and alterations of their surroundings; it has benefited the most visible and notable group of the physically impaired, especially those using wheel-chairs.[63]

Carol Thomas maintains that many people with disabilities are occupied with their impairment and its restrictions, not just its social outcomes. The social model offers them no apparent gain, as their interest cannot be reduced to the violation of equality. Daily reality often entails living with severe physical restrictions, pain and want, and this group is concerned with the need for quality care and continuous support, and with the means to ascertain economic security and a decent standard of living. It is perhaps time to redefine impairment and its relation to the social model.[64] Diller has pointed out that the civil rights/participatory approach of the ADA appears to stand in tension with the US's largest benefits programme (Social Security and Disability Insurance) available to persons who are not part of the workforce. This programme is based on the premise that some people cannot work, despite the acclaimed availability

---

[62] On the strategies to reconcile different group interests during the enactment of the ADA, see N Ziv, 'Cause Lawyers, Clients and the State – Congress as a Forum for Cause Lawyering During the Enactment of The Americans with Disabilities Act' in A Sarat and S Scheingold (eds), *Cause Lawyering and the State in a Global Era* (New York, Oxford University Press, 2001) 211.

[63] SD Watson, 'Discrimination on the basis of disability: The need for a third wave movement' (1994) 3 *Cornell Journal of Law and Public Policy* 253.

[64] C Thomas, 'Disability and Impairment', in Swain et al (eds), *Disabling Barriers, Enabling Environments*, above n 20, at 21.

of accommodations and modifications. But the visibility of this group—its needs, interests and rights—is overshadowed by the ADA ethos, as they do not abide by its set of individualistic liberal assumptions.[65]

From a similar direction, Scott-Hill raises a powerful critique of the use of rights and the social model as a vehicle for disability advocacy. Based on the writings of Teubner, she claims that rights are an inappropriate vehicle for social transformation. Law is one-dimensional and self-referring and thus cannot capture the multiple, conflicting and incoherent life experiences of people with disabilities. Reducing the experiences of people with disabilities to a social model will inevitably exclude those whose actual life experience does not abide by its set of assumptions, for example, the 'politics of visibility' or the idea of self-sufficiency.[66] The social model, from this perspective, is mostly relevant to the lives of the least disabled.[67]

B Effectiveness

Most studies that have assessed the effectiveness of the rights model for persons with disabilities have concentrated on employment. To be sure, in other contexts such as public accommodations, public services, transportation and the like, changes are perceptible and apparent and indeed promote participation in public life.

Employment, however, is the most interesting topic for exploration since anti-discrimination laws, such as the ADA, aspire to bring about significant changes in the work-welfare ratios by increasing the number of people with disabilities in the workforce.[68] The research about the real life impact of anti-discrimination laws in relation to unemployment is, at best, ambiguous and inconclusive. Some research points to a negative effect of employment anti-discrimination laws on employment rates of people with disabilities, if measured by the number of weeks employed per year.[69] Other data indicates a positive, albeit limited, impact of the ADA on employment rates (this result is restricted to persons who had been able to work but had some functional limitations rather than those who were

---

[65] Diller, above n 44.

[66] M Scott-Hill, 'Policy, politics and the silencing of "voice"' (2002) 30 *Policy and Politics* 397, 404.

[67] T Shakespeare and N Watson, 'Making the Difference: Disability, Politics, and Recognition' in GL Albrecht, KD Seelman and M Bury (eds), *Handbook of Disability Studies* (London, Sage Publications, 2001) 546, 550–51.

[68] Diller, above n 44; above n 33, 1016.

[69] D Acemoglu and JD Angrist, 'Consequences of Employment Protection? The Case of the Americans with Disabilities Act' (2001) 109 *Journal of Political Economy* 915, cited in Bagenstos, above n 33, 1017; C Jolls, 'Accommodation Mandates' (2000), 53 *Stanford Law Review* 223.

[70] P Blanck, E Hill, C D Siegal and M Waterstone, *Disability Civil Rights Law and Policy* (Thomson West, 2005) 1009.

'work limited' in a broader sense).[70] On the whole, the evidence shows that anti-discrimination laws such as the ADA have not led a sizeable number of persons with disabilities to join the workforce. So far these laws have not met the promise of altering the non-participant and participant work categories. Against this background, and more so in an era of growing unemployment and a globalised competitive market, it is imperative to reassess our attitude towards people who do not and will not meet the productivity/self sufficiency ethos.

C The Ethics Critique

The ethics critique targets the underlying values of the social/rights model which, explains Ellis, 'tended to place the emphasis on independence rather than interdependence'.[71]

The rights model, it is argued, plays into the all too familiar discourse of global capitalism. Its underlying rationale and internal logic tie into ideas such as self-sufficiency (it is better to work than to rely on welfare); it rests upon a cost-benefit analysis (accommodation will be deemed reasonable if the benefits of inclusion exceed its costs); it celebrates productivity (peoples' success is measured through levels of income generation); and it cherishes independence and autonomy rather than relations and support (reduction of welfare eligibility is a primary goal). Other values such as care for dependants or the fulfilment of needs (economic, emotional and personal) remain in the private sphere, downplayed and inferior to the paid work ethic.[72]

The strong reliance on rights and its underlying presumptions mounts to a loss in important values in a society committed to the protection of human dignity. The ethic of care, the recognition of and respect for conditions of dependence, encouragement of human relations and interconnections—are all an integral part of human existence. Under this understanding dependence is not a discarded state of being; it is a common condition of life—at times temporary and at times permanent—through which other aspects of humanity can be revealed: peoples' connection to each other, their need of each other and their ability to provide care.[73]

From a somewhat different angle, Danermark and Gellerstedt are troubled by the politics of recognition that accompany group struggles, including the disability rights movement. The emphasis on recognition tends to neglect matters of distribution, and overlooks questions of need

---

[71] Above n 16, 43.

[72] C Barnes and G Mercer, 'Disability, work and welfare: Challenging the social exclusion of people with disabilities' (2005) 19 *Work, Employment and Society* 527, 536.

[73] F Williams, 'In and beyond New Labour: Towards a new political ethics of care' (2001) 21 *Critical Social Policy* 467.

and support. In order to overcome this problem they suggest using Nancy Fraser's theory of distribution and recognition[74] to capture the delicate and fragile balances between dependence and autonomy, immediate needs and long-term political aspirations, and identity/culture politics as opposed to socio- economic interests.[75]

The critique of the social model thus finds difficulty with the prevailing human rights discourse and points out its long-term costs, both in practical and in ethical terms.

V INITIATIVES TO PROMOTE THE SOCIAL RIGHTS OF PEOPLE WITH DISABILITIES

We have seen that the turn to human rights discourse and advocacy with regard to people with disabilities has yet to embrace social rights as a prominent term of reference. The core of social rights—the right to basic entitlements such as subsistence (food and water), health care, housing, personal assistance, welfare or employment—have remained at the peripheries of the human rights agenda of persons with disabilities.[76] Can the conceptual framework of social rights be used to promote the dignity and the status of persons with disabilities?

A central focus of social rights is distribution, since many social rights entail direct provision of resources. Even though the social model has distributive implications, these are indirect, and are viewed as a means to achieve inclusion and participation. In addition, the idea of removing social barriers is only partially relevant to some social rights such as education, health, housing and welfare. Their fulfilment requires more, rather than less, involvement of the state, the primary body responsible for their implementation. Moreover, realisation of social rights commonly requires interaction with other people as providers or carers. In other words, their relational aspects are prominent and central.

The confinement of the rights discourse to certain experiences of people with disabilities has led states to adopt legislation in areas less benefited by the anti-discrimination paradigm. The type of arrangement states have chosen in these laws informs us about their ideologies: basic assumptions about humanity, human relations and society.

In 1998 the US Congress passed the Workforce Investment Act, establishing a system to provide employment services to economically and otherwise disadvantaged workers, including people with disabilities, to

---

[74] N Fraser, *Justice Interruptus* (New York, Routledge, 1997) 11–39; N Fraser, 'Recognition without ethics?' (2001) 18 *Theory, Culture and Society* 21.

[75] B Danermark and LC Gellerstedt, 'Social Justice: redistribution and recognition – a non-reductionist perspective on disability' (2004) 19 *Disability and Society* 339.

[76] See above n 26.

help them find work. In the UK the Community Care (Direct Payments) Act 1996 created a system of locally based resource offices that offer direct cash payment to persons with disabilities to acquire community care services. In Israel the Knesset passed in 2000 the Community Rehabilitation for the Mentally Disabled Law, which awards a basket of services in community settings.

Each of these laws was enacted to bring people with disabilities closer to the ideal enshrined by the social rights regime. They all reach beyond a civil rights approach, by providing direct resources and services in relation to rehabilitation, employment and personal care. The laws dissociate themselves from the much criticised medical/welfare model, recognising the impact of environmental factors to the construction of disability. These laws represent different models undertaken by legislators to promote the social rights of people with disabilities. I will point out the potential, as well as the shortcomings, of each scheme to achieve this goal.

A United States: The Workforce Investment Act of 1998

In 1998 Congress enacted The Workforce Investment Act (WIA).[77] The purpose of the WIA, as declared in its preamble is 'to consolidate, coordinate, and improve employment, training, literacy, and vocational rehabilitation programs in the United States, and for other purposes'. The WIA creates a streamlined mechanism of federally funded systems—'one stop employment centers'—whose goals are to facilitate and enable employment opportunities of economically disadvantaged or dislocated workers not currently employed. In order to achieve this objective the state delivers employment-related services such as assessment and job training, adult literacy programmes, rehabilitation, job searches, career planning and the like. Though not a disability-specific law, the WIA serves persons with disabilities inasmuch as they are in need of employment-related services.

The WIA is not an anti-discrimination law, and at first blush seems to reach beyond the traditional civil rights approach. However, a glance at its secondary goals immediately reveals that the law—which seemingly provides affirmative services in the context of employment—clearly embodies a neo-liberal mindset, under which employment is viewed as the preferable pathway out of welfare, and individuals are expected to maximise opportunities and choices to engage in employment. Section 106 of the WIA, which creates state and local systems of employment services, declares that the goals of these services are:

---

[77] Workforce Investment Act of 1998 (US).

> To provide workforce investment activities... that increase employment, reten-
> tion and earning of participants... and as a result improve the quality of the
> workforce, reduce welfare dependency, and enhance the productivity and com-
> petitiveness of the Nation.

With regards to people with disabilities, the WIA aims to facilitate access to
employment training programmes and services, in order to increase participation in the workforce, especially in the private sector. The WIA amends
the 1973 Rehabilitation Act and affirms the right of people with disabilities
to employment-related services.[78] Nevertheless, these services too are
supposed 'to empower individuals with disabilities to maximise
employment, self-sufficiency, independence and inclusion and integration in
society...'. Moreover, particular instructions are designed to ensure that
persons with disabilities are not discriminated against in the provision of
employment-related services, that there is access to offices in which services
are granted, that accommodations be made in the provision of the services,
and that employment be offered in the most inclusive setting.[79] In other
words, civil rights aspects found their way into the law and were incorporated as part of this 'affirmative' bill.

The prevalence of the productivity/self-sufficiency work ethic is evident
and pervades the law. Though the WIA shows commitment to promote
and improve social rights by direct provision due to need (rather than
through anti-discrimination instructions) it nonetheless does so through
the traditional liberal individualistic model. This is a bureaucratised,
top-bottom scheme that does not speak of human rights as an underlying
ideology for providing social services. The services granted in the
law—couched in the managerial term of 'investment'—are means to
achieve objectives that are external to the individual: productivity and
competitiveness of the nation, improvement of the workforce and the
reduction of welfare. Although the WIA recognises that services must be
altered and modified to ensure access by people with disabilities, they too
are instrumental in attaining these overarching goals. The WIA thus
cannot be seen as promoting the ideal and values of social rights despite its
distributive and provisionary aspects.

B Israel: The Community Rehabilitation for the Mentally Disabled Law of 2000

Concurrent to the civil rights approach to disability, in 2000 the Israeli
Knesset enacted the Community Rehabilitation for The Mentally Disabled

---

[78] *Ibid*, Title IV.
[79] R Silverstein, *Analysis of WIA Section 188 Methods of Administration Plans from a Disability Perspective* (April 2004), Center for the Study and Advancement of Disability Policy (CSADP), <http://www.onestops.info/article.php?article_id=235>.

Law (CRMDL).[80] In contrast to the ERPDL, this is not a civil rights/ equality law, but a personal entitlement programme, which applies to people with mental disabilities only. This disability-specific format deviates from the method adopted by rights advocates. Disability-specific laws have been left behind by the disability rights movement in previous and recent rights legislation, in preference to an all-encompassing law that includes all types of disabilities. However, in this case the disability-specific model was reinstated, due to the special needs of persons with mental disabilities.

The law entitles each person with a mental disability to receive a 'basket' of rehabilitation/integration services to enable (section 1):

> rehabilitation and integration in the community and to enable them to achieve independence and quality of life to the highest possible degree, while protecting their human dignity in the spirit of the Basic Law: Human Dignity and Liberty.

The services included in the basket pertain to employment (diagnostic, training and placement services in integrated, supported or protected employment settings); housing assistance (financial and support services in independent and other forms of housing arrangement); financial support for secondary education; support for leisure activities (financial assistance and escort to social activities); dental services, respite and other services to families of persons with mental disabilities. The goal of the CRMDL is to ensure that persons with disabilities can enjoy their social rights, including rehabilitation and employment, housing, education, health and leisure.

The CRMDL thus embodies themes from the liberal rights approach—the aspiration to human dignity, community integration, independence and quality of life. These values are considered central and pervasive in the lives of people with disabilities. In other aspects the law recognises particular entitlements and support services (such as home visitation services and financial aid to acquire assets for one's home), necessary to enable persons with mental disabilities to live in the community in the most integrated setting.

However, the law does not grant persons with disabilities the right or power to choose how these services would be provided or to actively participate in constructing their personal basket of services. The mechanism set up for recognising entitlement is a professional committee that makes decisions for the disabled person following a limited procedural right to be heard. This structure is not inclusive and does not consider the person with a disability an active participant in the decision as to how to build their personal rehabilitation or integration programme, who will provide the service, where it will take place and in what manner. The CRMDL model thus amends the shortfalls of the liberal rights approach only partially: though it recognises and acknowledges the need

---

[80] The Community Rehabilitation for the Mentally Disabled Law 2000, SH 231.

to ensure support and direct services to protect the dignity of persons with disabilities, its bureaucratised structure reveals remnants of the patronising medical model.

C The UK: The Community Care (Direct Payments) Act 1996

Colin Barnes, a prominent disability studies scholar, referred to the Community Care (Direct Payments) Act (CCDPA) as 'one of the most significant developments in British social policy since the development of the modern welfare state'.[81] The core idea of the CCDPA is to enable persons with certain disabilities (learning disabilities, mental illness, sensory disabilities, physical disabilities and older people with chronicle needs) to exchange the social services to which they are entitled (through other legal mechanisms such as The National Assistance Act 1948 or the Chronically Sick and Disabled Persons Act 1970) for direct payments, available from their local authority.

Direct payments can be used for a variety of purposes: hiring personal care (assistance for washing, dressing and eating meals), practical help (such as shopping, cleaning, preparing meals), paying for a break for other carers, daytime activities (including assistance at work, help in school or in college) and support in sports or leisure.

Services can be purchased independently or through a care agency, after needs have been assessed and determined. People with disabilities can also receive assistance in how to use the services as well as assistance in making their choices and managing them. There are restrictions, however, on the kind of services that can be purchased following prior determination of need. In this sense the CCDPA resembles a voucher system, which has attracted criticism from a liberal perspective.[82]

The purpose of this scheme is on the one hand to increase choice, control and independence, while on the other recognising that (some) people must have help to be more independent, that they require support to learn how to make choices, and that they need care to enjoy their rights. The CCDPA thus attempts to break the dichotomy between dependence and independence, care and self-sufficiency, professional assistance and self-assertion, control and need of support.[83] It represents a circular kind of reasoning, in which care is considered a valued resource, and receiving care constitutes an opportunity to enhance independence and choice. Provision of care—by the state—is transformed into a means by which a

---

[81] Community Care (Direct Payments) Act 1996 (UK); C Barnes, 'Introduction: Disability, Policy and Politics' (2002) 30 *Policy and Politics* 311, 312.
[82] SR Bagenstos, 'The Future of Disability Law' (2004) 114 *Yale Law Journal* 1, 78–9.
[83] See above n 73.

person can gain more independence, control and self-assertion. In other words, disability benefits are not at odds with liberal ideas of individualised control; rather, the attempt is to harmonise these seemingly conflicting notions by fusing an ethic of care with an ideal of rights. To be sure, this is not an easy task. On the conceptual level, the CCDPA has been criticised as placing too strong an emphasis on individual choice and autonomy, thus surrendering to New Labour values and principles.[84] On the practical front, there have been difficulties implementing the complex notions of care and independence.[85] Notwithstanding, this is an interesting model that attempts to reconcile an ethic of care with an ethic of individual responsibility in the lives of people with disabilities.

VI SOCIAL RIGHTS OF PEOPLE WITH DISABILITIES: BRINGING TOGETHER CARE AND JUSTICE

The turn to rights in disability studies and disability advocacy has advanced a position that underscores choice, autonomy and self-assertion. This stance has been criticised from a standpoint that accentuates alternative values of care, interdependence and support—critical to the lives of persons with disabilities—and which calls into question the ideal of paid work as the prevailing social ambition.

Can the framework of social rights be helpful in reconciling these seemingly incompatible belief systems? Can social rights encompass both the notions of citizenship, equality and participation, enshrined in the first wave of the disability rights movement, and the ideals of interdependence and support, promoted by their contemporary critiques?

Tronto claims that in order to bring values of care and interdependence closer to the goal of social justice, these notions need to be politicised—seen as part of the public sphere and understood as an essential part of human existence.[86] Similarly, Sevenhuijsen advocates incorporating elements of care within citizenship and Williams develops these themes to include the experiences of different groups such as racial minorities and women.[87] However, the growing body of literature that endeavours to

---

[84] Bagenstos, above n 82.

[85] See for example the report of the 1997 survey conducted by the Policy Studies Institute and National Centre for Independent Living <http://www.jrf.org.uk/knowledge/findings/socialcare/430.asp>, which points out some of the implementation difficulties, including 'the lack of fit between community care policies and the principles of independent living'.

[86] J Tronto, *Moral Boundaries: A Political Argument for an Ethic of Care* (New York, Routledge, 1993) 21.

[87] S Sevenhuijsen, *Citizenship and the Ethic of Care* (London, Routledge, 1998); Williams, above n 73.

merge justice and care/support has yet to invoke social rights as a plausible framework in the undertaking of this cause.

Social rights, per se, are obviously not a guaranteed framework to attain an equitable balance between the justice/care ethics. As illustrated above, if posited through an atomist lens, under which personhood is envisioned as an amalgam of individuals entitled to certain basic resources, the framework of social rights will not serve this goal. However, social rights discourse carries the potential to reframe the relationship between personhood, community and state in a way that fuses these values.

To be sure, civil and political rights too often embody relational aspects, and their exercise often depends upon interaction with other persons. Free speech and freedom of association, for example, are liberties that depend on association and contact with others. At their core, however, is a respect for freedom and personal expression rather than a form of social solidarity. Social rights, which are based on human needs and upon the recognition of people's vulnerability, are an expression of a 'social debt' and are translated into a concrete right to receive support and to be protected. Therefore these notions are conceptually closer to ideas of inter-dependence and care than civil and political rights. Second, social rights cover those substantive areas of life—health care, welfare, housing and shelter, employment and education—that require provision through inter-action between people: providers and those who need to be provided for. This relational aspect opens up possibilities to develop the mutuality between rights and relations, as it situates people within personal connec-tions. From the other viewpoint, as human rights, social rights can become a political tool through which citizenship will be promoted. They are debated in the public sphere, they need to be ingrained in legislation, and they enjoy the status of universally recognised basic entitlements.

The legislative models discussed above are manifestations of social rights legislation that pertains to people with disabilities. The US Workforce Investment Act is a scheme that meets the justice/support mutuality only in a limited manner. Although it recognises the need to provide support and services to persons with disabilities in order to further their inclusion in employment, the law abides by a strong preference for a paid-work ethic and views welfare as an unwanted condition that ought to be minimised. The Israeli Community Rehabilitation for the Mentally Disabled Law attempts to fuse notions of justice—equality, dignity and independence—with the provision of resources, services and support. It falls short, however, of ensuring that these support systems themselves will not be disabling, by vesting much power in the hands of the state to regulate their provision. The UK Community Care (Direct Payments) Act attempts to amend this shortfall by instituting broad discretion within the hands of people with disabilities to determine how support services will be provided, recognising the mutuality between support and independence, care and choice.

The potential of social rights to become a platform that embodies such complementary values is discernible when we turn to persons with disabilities. This is so because disability—as a human and social phenomenon—sharpens our understanding of the complexities of human qualities and of the deceptive relationships between the strengths and weaknesses of human existence.

16

Social Rights as Women's Rights

DAPHNE BARAK-EREZ*

I BETWEEN CIVIL AND POLITICAL RIGHTS AND ECONOMIC RIGHTS

Are social rights a special concern of women? The struggle for women's rights has usually been identified with the right to equality, a primary tenet of the scheme of political and civil rights. This was the nature of the suffragist movement that fought for women's right to vote.[1] Still, it would be wrong to associate feminism only with political and civil rights. The struggle for women's rights has always included the aspiration to achieve freedom through economic independence. Important feminist efforts have focused on the rights of women, and married women in particular, to own property,[2] and on the opening of occupations and professions to women.[3] The ability to own property and earn a living independently is a preliminary condition for personal freedom, and therefore constitutes a crucial first step on the long way towards the equality of women. One can compare this to the vision of Virginia Woolf, who wrote many years ago that a basic condition for the evolvement of women's literature is that the writer would have money and a room of her own.[4] The insight for the present context is that the evolution of women's rights depends on their material condition. Similarly, even Catharine

---

* The author would like to thank Daphna Hacker and Revital Goldhar for their comments. More thanks are due to Noa Mishor and Magi Otsri for their assistance.

[1] This struggle, identified with the first wave of feminism, was successful in many countries, due to the social changes brought about by the First World War (during which women provided for their homes and replaced men in various positions). In the United States, for example, the right to vote was granted to women by the 19th amendment that was passed in 1919 and ratified in 1920.

[2] Laws in the matter of the property of married women were enacted throughout the nineteenth century (eg, New York Married Women's Property Act 1848).

[3] See *Bradwell v Illinois* 83 US 130 (1873).

[4] V Woolf *A Room of One's Own* (London, Hogarth Press, 1929). Woolf's argument can serve as a source of inspiration in this context although she herself, belonging to the educated and affluent classes in England, represents an elitist type of feminism of women who never had to work for their living.

MacKinnon, whose feminist work has usually focused on other issues, pointed out that:

> most women can survive only by being connected to a man's income. This fact powerfully structures women's lives... In money economies, income means survival; its treasure and resources also contribute to freedom, human flourishing, enjoyment of life's possibilities.[5]

II BETWEEN ECONOMIC RIGHTS AND SOCIAL RIGHTS

Social rights are aimed at securing the ability to live a life of dignity for everyone, without dependence on others (other than the state), while reasonably fulfilling all basic needs, including welfare rights, rights in the sphere of employment, and rights to education and health. Therefore, the social rights movement and the feminist struggle, which strives to achieve these goals for women, have a great deal in common

In earlier stages, the feminist claim, with regard to the economic sphere, was focused on liberty: aspiring for the recognition of the rights of women to own property and choose their professional occupations. The struggle for social rights developed only later. Even today, in developing countries, the most important struggles are aimed at recognising the rights of women regarding ownership of property and freedom of occupation.[6] These are of special importance in countries that are still unable to guarantee significant welfare rights.

It is indeed evident that although the right to own property and to choose an occupation cannot always secure the goal of dignified life for everyone, it is important to emphasise that the universal application of these rights to women should be considered a preliminary condition. There are still many countries in the world where women are not able to own property and are limited to traditional occupations. In those countries, women are almost inevitably being led to poverty. Another way to put this argument is that in every system where property rights and freedom of occupation are recognised, it is crucial to recognise the equal rights of

---

[5] CA MacKinnon, *Sex Equality* (New York, Foundation Press, 2001) 77.

[6] See MC Nussbaum 'Public Philosophy and International Feminism' (1998) 108 *Ethics* 762. Nussbaum focuses on the needs of women in developing countries, which are completely different from those of women in the western world. In particularly, she refers to the lives of women in different regions of India. Nussbaum points to the importance attached to property rights, the availability of credit, and the possibility to get a job away from home, as prior conditions for the possibility to protect wholeness of the body and the ability to make reasoned choices about one's course of life. Without these pre-conditions, existence becomes dependent only on the good will and mercy of others. See also MC Nussbaum 'International Human Rights Law in Practice: India: Implementing Sex Equality through the Law' (2001) 2 *Chicago Journal of International Law* 35.

women to enjoy these liberties—not only in the name of equality and autonomy, but also for achieving dignified life without poverty. This emphasis is important due to the tendency to perceive economic rights, and especially constitutional property rights, as rivals of social rights. The feminist struggle for indiscriminate application of the right to property and the right to freedom of occupation for women demonstrates the potential ingrained in the interpretation of these rights in light of distributive justice rather than competitive Darwinist ideas. Feminism illuminates the importance of the right to freedom of occupation not for the sake of promoting business competition free from government regulation, but rather as an expression of the natural right to make a living, and the role of the right to property as a source of personal freedom, and not merely as a tool for protecting the wealthy from taxation.

III SOCIAL RIGHTS AS A FEMINIST ISSUE

As economic development in western countries shows, even legal systems that recognise property rights and freedom of occupation do not guarantee a life of dignity for everyone. This understanding has been a source of motivation to promote the concept of social rights. The recognition of social rights is important for various groups, but it is of special importance for groups that are economically vulnerable, for those who are integrated into the job market less successfully and are paid less even when they are employed. Women constitute a group which shares these characteristics, alongside other disempowered groups, such as people with disabilities, minorities and work immigrants. The rate of working women is lower than the rate of working men, and more women than men are working in part-time jobs, mainly because of existing social norms regarding their domestic role. In general, women usually spend less time in the labour market, due to their family responsibilities, whereas the tasks they fulfil in the domestic sphere are not recognised as having economic value (for the purposes of social benefits). In addition, more women than men are employed in temporary jobs, jobs in the informal sector as domestic workers, and jobs that often do not provide social benefits and economic security. On average, the wages of women in the job market are lower, both in terms of their absolute earnings and their earnings per hour. As a result, women are more likely candidates for poverty. The likelihood of being poor is even greater for the numerous women who raise their children alone as single parents. These women are often forced by their circumstances to limit their hours of work, and face a merciless job market, which tends to discriminate against people with parental duties. The result is that welfare recipients are often women and their dependent children.

Indeed, the feminisation of poverty is an increasing phenomenon, particularly when it comes to single parent families headed by women.[7] In addition, the new challenges to the welfare state, deriving from prolonged lifespans, are especially relevant to women, who, on average, live longer and outlive their male partners. From these perspectives, the interest in welfare rights is definitely a feminist issue, because women constitute a group that needs the safety net provided by social rights. In addition, in an environment in which workers' rights continue to deteriorate due to the pressure of globalisation, the difficulties faced by working women are increasing because of the conflict between the long hours they are required to work and their family duties.[8]

Growing awareness as to the importance of social rights was inspired also by critical race feminism, which argued that traditional feminism was focused mainly on the aspirations of middle class white women, women who are relatively well off and often detached from economic needs.

Welfare rights are considered a feminist issue also from the perspective of cultural feminism and its 'ethic of care'.[9] In this context, the argument is that feminism should be committed to the welfare of women who dedicate their lives to caring for their dependants, as many women in fact do. This view inspired the feminist critique of welfare reforms in the United States, which conditioned welfare entitlements on getting a so-called 'real job' outside the home. The criticism focused on the tendency of these reforms to overlook the social and economic value of the work of women in their homes. Poor women who were required to work outside their homes in order to be entitled for welfare payments often worked in the households of other families, taking care of other people's dependants. However, when they did the same job in their own homes, the social value of their work was not acknowledged. Feminist writers condemned this legislative approach for its disregard of the value that should be attributed to dependency work.[10] Similarly, in the international sphere, women who live

---

[7] See, for instance, D Pearce 'Welfare is not for Women: Why the War on Poverty Cannot Conquer the Feminization of Poverty' in L Gordon (ed), *Women, the State and Welfare* (Wisconsin, University of Wisconsin Press, 1990) 265; 'Symposium: the Changing Face of Need: Feminization of Poverty and the Law' (2003) 5 *Journal of Gender Race and Justice* 233.

[8] See K Rittich, 'Feminism after the State: The Rise of the Market and the Future of Women's Rights' in I Merali and V Oosterveld (eds), *Giving Meanings to Economical, Social and Cultural Rights* (Philadelphia, University of Pennsylvania Press, 2001) 95. The consequences of the pressures of globalisation for working class women are demonstrated in Barbara Ehrenreich, *Nickel and Dimed – On (Not) Getting By in America* (New York, Metropolitan Books 2001).

[9] Carol Gilligan presented her thesis regarding the 'ethic of care' which characterises women in her influential book *In a Different Voice – Psychological Theory and Women's Development* (Cambridge Mass, Harvard University Press, 1982).

[10] See, for instance, EF Kittay *Love's Labor* (New York, Routledge, 1999). For feminist criticism on the American welfare reform regarding mothers who are required to work, see: M Minow, 'The Welfare of Single Mothers and Their Children' (1994) 26 *Connecticut Law Review* 817; L White, 'On the "Consensus" to End Welfare: Where are the Women's Voices?' (1994) 26 *Connecticut Law Review* 843. On the other hand, for criticism focusing on payments

in the developing countries benefit less from the economic aid given to these countries for purposes of growth since their work in their houses and rural surroundings is not considered 'productive' (even when it produces most of the food manufactured in their countries).[11]

The complex relationship between feminism and the welfare state derives also from the role of women's caring work as an alternative to welfare rights or as a tool for achieving welfare goals. On one hand, traditional care by family members, usually women, has obscured the need for social rights. On the other hand, in the context of developed welfare states, working class women and immigrants from developing countries are the basis for the mechanism of paid care, which becomes more accessible to middle class families due to the low wages for such work.

Another feminist perspective on the issue of social rights relates to the difficulties in dealing with the bureaucracy of the welfare state. In many cases, poor women are those who carry the burden of dealing with the requirements of the welfare bureaucracy because they are usually responsible for the daily subsistence of their children and families.[12] These difficulties are represented even more clearly with regard to welfare rights given to single parent families, usually headed by women. In other words, women are those who are in the 'front lines' of the battle over the realisation of social rights in practice. They are those who struggle for the recognition of entitlements for their families in terms of welfare payments, housing aid, etc. In doing so they are the first to confront the constant gap between social rights laws and their realisation.[13]

IV WHO ARE THE WOMEN CLAIMING SOCIAL RIGHTS?

The focus on social rights emphasises existing gaps between different groups of women. The distress and needs of women coming from different

for housework (either by the welfare system or through the recognition of equal rights in family property), see V Schultz, 'Life's Work' (2000) 100 *Columbia Law Review* 1881 (arguing for the importance and centrality of work in people's lives—for the development of their personality and self-esteem, sense of belonging, communal support and independence. Focusing on housework payment is a withdrawal towards traditional perceptions of the distribution of roles between men and women, in a way that denies women the advantages of the work, eg, joy, independence, self-esteem, etc); for an answer to this critic, see MM Ertman 'Love and Work: A Response to Vicki Schultz's "Life's Work"' (2002) 102 *Columbia Law Review* 848.

[11] See H Charlesworth, C Chinkin and S Wright 'Feminist Approaches to International Law' (1991) 85 *American Journal of International Law* 613, 639–41.

[12] An article focusing on the tragic encounter of a needy mother with the welfare state bureaucracy is LE White 'Subordination, Rhetorical Survival Skills, and Sunday Shoes: Notes on the Hearing of Mrs G' (1990) 38 *Buffalo Law Review* 1.

[13] D Barak-Erez 'The Israeli Welfare State: Growing Expectations and Diminishing Return' in G Nolte and E Benvenisti (eds), *The Welfare State, Globalization and International Law* (Berlin, Springer, 2004) 103.

backgrounds are not identical, and nor are their aspirations and priorities. As already noted, these differences were emphasised by feminists who dissociated themselves from the pretence of traditional feminism to represent all women and argued that it was actually representing the interests of educated middle and upper class women, and not reflecting the problems of other women (black women, working class women, etc). This critique has special relevance in the context of the debate over social rights. First of all, the priority of the struggle for social rights varies between groups of women according to their social and economic status. Feminist organisations in which middle and upper class women set the agenda tend to fight more for equal opportunities and career options, and less for 'bread and butter' — minimum wages, income security, etc. Second, the struggle for social rights reveals the conflicts of interest that exist between different groups of women. For instance, securing the right to a minimum wage for women who are domestic workers is a central goal for working class women. At the same time, it threatens educated women, who often use a large percentage of their income to pay the salaries of women who work in their households and take care of their children.[14] In a similar manner, public financing for public day care centres is more important for working class women (who cannot hire the services of other women to work in their households) than to career women who can afford a nanny. It is important to note that issues which are not identified with the struggle for social rights also have a social rights aspect when they are applied to protect women with high economic vulnerability. For instance, sexual harassment law has a social rights aspect when it is applied for the protection of women who depend on their jobs due to acute economic need, such as migrant workers.

V SOCIAL RIGHTS OF WOMEN IN INTERNATIONAL LAW

Each country grants social rights to its citizens and residents as it sees fit. In the background, however, there are the standards set by international law. With regard to the social rights of women, there are several conventions to consider. The first among them is the Convention on the Elimination of All Forms of Discrimination against Women (CEDAW),[15] adopted in 1979. Alongside its main reference to equality in the political and public sphere, the Convention dedicates important provisions to the social and economic

---

14 Indeed, paying for help in the household is no less important also for working fathers, but in fact, due to social inequalities regarding the traditional separation of responsibilities in the family, the salaries of care-workers has more impact on the tendency of women to work outside their households.

15 The Convention on the Elimination of All Forms of Discrimination against Women (CEDAW) (adopted 18 December 1979, entered into force 3 September 1981) 1249 UNTS 13.

spheres. Article 3 includes a general commitment to take any means for securing the development and promotion of women, not only in the 'public' sphere, but also with reference to the 'social, economical and cultural' spheres. The Convention refers both to economic rights (the right to property and the right to work) and to guarantees of social rights. Article 15 states that women should enjoy legal capacity identical to that of men, including with regard to contracts and property. Article 16 makes a specific reference to equality in property rights with regard to married women. Article 11 states that women should have the equal right to 'work as an inalienable right of all human beings'. Other provisions deal with securing the rights of women in different social spheres—education, health, social security and work. Article 10 deals with the rights of women to access and equality in the field of education. Article 11, which deals with rights in the sphere of work, adds to the basic right to work, mentioned above, several additional rights: a prohibition on discrimination in employment opportunities and in promotion; a right to equal wages; a right to social security; a right to health and safety at work, including during pregnancy; a prohibition on discrimination on the grounds of pregnancy, delivery and marriage; and a duty to introduce paid maternity leave. It also refers to the encouragement of integrating parents in the job market, including by establishing networks of child-care facilities. Article 12 sets out the right of women for access and equality in the area of medical services, while referring especially to suitable services related to pregnancy, confinement and the post-natal period. Article 13 states that women are also entitled to equal rights in the field of family benefits, mortgages and other forms of financial credit. Article 14 refers especially to the weak population of rural women, and emphasises the need to ensure their right to have access to health care services, social security programmes, education, financial credit, adequate living conditions and employment. Some of the rights are anchored also in other international treaties, which deal with specific issues, such as the right to equal wages addressed by the Equal Remuneration Convention.[16]

The social rights of women have also been recognised in the main international instrument concerning social and economic rights—the International Covenant on Economic, Social and Cultural Rights of 1966.[17] Article 3 of the Covenant determines generally that

> the states parties to the present covenant undertake to ensure the equal right of men and women to the enjoyment of all economic, social and cultural rights set forth in the present covenant.

---

[16] The ILO Convention Concerning Equal Remuneration for Men and Women Workers for Work of Equal Value (adopted 29 June 1951, entered into force 23 May 1953) (No 100).

[17] International Covenant on Economic, Social and Cultural Rights (adopted 16 December 1966, entered into force 3 January 1976) 993 UNTS 3.

Article 7 of the Covenant, which refers to the right to fair and equal wages, emphasises 'in particular women being guaranteed conditions of work not inferior to those enjoyed by men, with equal pay for equal work'. Article 10 of the Covenant refers to the duty to ensure protection to mothers 'during a reasonable period before and after childbirth', during which they should be accorded paid leave.[18] In addition, there are treaties of the International Labour Organization on the rights of pregnant women and mothers (eg the Maternity Protection Convention 2000).[19]

VI SOCIAL RIGHTS OF WOMEN IN PRACTICE: PROBLEMS OF DISCRIMINATION

A separate discussion dedicated to the social rights of women has to focus on areas in which the application of social rights tends to discriminate against women, usually backed by tradition.

In the area of education, there is a relevant distinction between western societies and traditional societies, usually in developing countries. In western states, the right of education is usually not confronted by unique problems, because education of women has become the norm (in contrast to the past, where women were limited in their possibilities, especially in the context of higher education). In developing countries, the case is different when the prevailing social norms do not approve of full access of women, including young girls, to educational opportunities. The result is that girls in areas populated by traditional societies, mainly in rural areas, are not always sent to school.

In addition, even in western countries, some tensions relate to the full accomplishment of education rights. An indirect challenge to the fulfilment of education rights of women is raised by the so-called 'scarf cases', which deal with Muslim girls who insist on wearing traditional headscarves when they attend school. Some countries have adopted an uncompromised negation towards the wearing of headscarves based on several arguments, mainly secularism on the one hand and equality of women on the other (associating the traditional headscarf with non-egalitarian views towards women). In practice, even when the ban is motivated by equality concerns,

---

[18] For discussion concerning the social and economic rights of women in the context of international law see also: K Tomasevski, 'Women' in A Eide et al (eds), *Economic, Social and Cultural Rights* (Dordrecht, M Nijhoff, 1995) 273; P Hunt, *Reclaiming Social Rights – International and Comparatives Perspectives* (Aldershot, Ashgate, 1996) 71–106; E Brems, 'Social and Economic Rights of Women' in P van der Auweraert et al (eds), *Social, Economic and Cultural Rights: An Appraisal of Current European and International Developments* (Antwerp, R Bayliss, 2002) 17.

[19] The ILO Maternity Protection Convention (adopted 15 June 2000, entered into force 7 February 2002) (No 183).

it threatens the opportunities of traditional Muslim girls to receive education.[20]

Another problem, in a completely different setting, is the standard provision included in many welfare laws, which denies entitlements to people who pursue higher education. Such provisions are in general harmful for the chances of getting out of the trap of poverty, but even more problematic for single mothers who try to pursue education programmes and provide for their children at the same time.[21]

The area of health care rights poses even more questions of discrimination against women. First, many legal systems limit access to birth control and abortions.[22] These limitations do not only infringe the autonomy of women but also affect their health, at least in some circumstances. Second, health care plans afforded by the government do not always cover the health problems and needs of men and women to a similar extent.[23]

Another aspect of discrimination in the scheme of the welfare state concerns social security laws that do not benefit home-makers, or assigns to them lesser rights. The other side of the same problem is the tendency of welfare legislation to deny eligibility of single mothers who cohabit with a

[20] The legal debate in this area has led to different results in different countries. In England, a decision forbidding Muslim girls to wear traditional clothes of their choice was overruled: *R (on the application of SB) v Head Teacher and Governors of Denbigh High School* [2006] 2 All ER 487. In contrast, the European Court of Human Rights refrained from overruling a prohibition on headscarves in a Turkish university. The majority decision was founded on the principle of secularism as well as on the identification of the headscarf with the alienation and inequality of women. The minority opinion pointed out that the headscarf should not always be associated with inequality of women and criticised the majority decision as infringing on the right to education of traditional women: *Leyla Sahin v Turkey* [2005] ECHR 44774/98 (10 November 2005). In Germany, the litigation focused on a decision of a public school teacher to wear a traditional scarf. At the same time, religious clothing of students did not seem to pose a problem: C Landgenfeld and S Mohsen, 'Germany: The Teacher Head Scarf Case' 3 *ICON* 86 (2005); Oliver Gerstenberg, 'Germany: Freedom of Conscience in Public Schools' 3 *ICON* 94 (2005).

[21] See, eg, *Clyke v Nova Scotia (Minister of Community Services)* 2005 ACWSJ 218.

[22] The US Supreme Court has ruled against prohibitions on the use of birth control: see *Griswold v Connecticut* 381 US 479 (1965). The well-known precedent of *Roe v Wade* 410 US 113 (1973) professed to guarantee the right of women to choose an abortion. This is still the rule, despite harsh criticism of the decision and partial curtailment of its details in later decisions: see *Planned Parenthood v Casey* 505 US 833 (1992). It is worthwhile adding that according to the rule of *Roe v Wade* abortions in the so-called second trimester were supposed to be available based on considerations regarding the health of the mother. This rule emphasised the clear connection between abortion law and women's rights to health.

[23] See *Geduldig v Aiello et al* 417 US 484 (1974). This judgment dismissed a challenge to a California Health insurance programme which did not cover pregnancy-related problems. The US Supreme Court held that the programme distinguished between pregnant and non-pregnant people, and therefore did not discriminate against women. A similar decision was made in *General Electric Co v Gilbert* 429 US 125 (1976), which dealt with an insurance plan of a private employer. Eventually, this discrimination was abolished by legislation. For a discussion of the problem of scarce resources invested in pregnancy and birth related risks, see RJ Cook 'Advancing Safe Motherhood Through Human Rights' in I Merali and V Oosterveld (eds), *Giving Meanings to Economic, Social and Cultural Rights* (Philadelphia, University of Pennsylvania Press, 2001) 109.

partner, based on the assumption that men are providers and women are dependent on them. While it is understandable that the state should take into consideration the support that welfare recipients may get from family members and partners, it is problematic that the very fact of joint residence is considered a sole arbiter, when in fact the welfare recipient and her children are not being supported by her male partner or when she is simply in the beginning of a new relationship which may or may not last.[24] The enforcement of these norms is often entangled with infringements of the privacy and autonomy of single mothers.[25]

VII SOCIAL RIGHTS OF WOMEN AS WORKERS

The rights of working women relate to different aspects of demands for equality: equal opportunities at work, equal wages, freedom from sexual harassment, and accommodation for pregnant women and parents in the workplace. In the present context, the discussion will focus on problems of working women that have implications for their ability to live a life of dignity, without dependence. The reason for this choice is that a woman, who is discriminated against in the context of promotion, might be a worker who earns sufficient wages allowing her to live in reasonable conditions. In this case, the main problem with her discrimination is the infringement of her equality rights and her full citizenship rather than the impact on her ability to sustain herself and her family, which is at the centre of the struggle for social rights. Accordingly, the analysis will focus on cases of discrimination in which the harm to the rights of working women does not only infringe their equality and status but rather affects their ability to achieve independent existence in fair conditions.

From the perspective of working class women, a major problem is their low wages—not simply in comparison to their male colleagues, but also in absolute terms. Women, as the weaker participants in the job market, can be pushed to low-paying positions, and are sometimes even paid salaries that are lower than statutory minimum wages. In this sense, the enforcement of minimum wage laws is not only a matter of general concern, but also a group interest of women.

Legislative schemes which secure the ability of women to remain part of the world of work during pregnancy and immediately following childbirth are also of utmost importance. The first layer of protection is composed of

---

24 For two Canadian precedents which criticised and interfered with over-broad provisions of this kind, see: *Regina v Rehberg* [1994] 111 DLR (4th) 336; *Falkiner v Ontario (Ministry of Community and Social Services)* 59 OR (3d) 481; OJ No 1771 (Ont CA).

25 For this criticism in the context of American legislation, see T Plank, 'Human Rights, Women's Rights and Welfare Reform: An Analysis of HR 4 from an International Human Rights Perspective' (1996) 17 *Women's Rights Law Reports* 345.

anti-discrimination laws which prohibit discrimination on the basis of pregnancy. The second layer consists of schemes which secure the ability of women to take maternity leaves (as a separate entitlement, not dependent on the ordinary regulation of vacations or sick leaves).[26] Such legislative schemes are considered problematic from the perspective of formal equality, due to fears of a slippery slope effect that would enable discrimination against women. This view should, however, be opposed, based on substantial concepts of equality, since the survival of women in the labour market necessitates that their jobs be kept for them when they choose to have children. Otherwise, women, in contrast to men, will have to make a cruel choice between parenthood and work.[27] A similar concern, relevant to all workers who are parents of children and are interested in involved parenting, is the adaptation of the workplace to workers who are not interested in working long hours.[28] In this context, adaptation means mainly enforcement of laws which limit maximum hours of work per day.[29] These laws are more relevant to low level positions, and are not applied (officially or unofficially) to high-ranking managerial positions. With regard to those, the more relevant norms would be anti-discrimination laws (with an emphasis on the prohibition of discrimination against parents). These norms would not necessarily help in cases of a so-called relevant distinction between workers who are more invested in their jobs and those who are not, unless another approach is adopted, based on a view that long office hours cannot serve as criteria for distinction, but rather actual accomplishments.

Sexual harassment law is also very important in the context of social rights. Indeed, anti-harassment measures are aimed at protecting equality

---

[26] Emphasis should be put on the possibility of taking leave with no effect on the position of the employee upon return: see *Margaret L Prescod v Unemployment Insurance Appeals Board* 57 Cal App 3d 29 (1976). It should be stressed that mandatory long pregnancy leaves in the last months of pregnancy are not an equality-promoting scheme, but rather another form of discrimination: see *Cleveland Board of Education v LaFleur* 414 US 632 (1974).

[27] In American law the current view is that granting privileges concerning pregnancy and delivery do not constitute discrimination. This question was debated in the context of the Pregnancy Discrimination Act 1978, which prohibited discrimination on grounds of pregnancy, in *California Federal v Guerra* 479 US 272 (1987). This case concerned a state law which granted pregnant women unpaid maternity leaves while keeping their jobs. The US Supreme Court dismissed the argument that this law contradicts the federal prohibition on discrimination on grounds of pregnancy.

[28] For the construction of the ideal worker as one who delegates all his family responsibilities, see: JC Williams, *Unbending Gender – Why Family and Work Conflict and What to Do about It* (Oxford, Oxford University Press, 2001).

[29] An emphasis should be put on the legislation and enforcement of laws limiting the hours of daily and weekly work for women and men equally, thus enabling both to function as active parents (or pursue other leisure time occupations). In *Lochner v New York* 198 US 45 (1905) the US Supreme Court invalidated a law which limited weekly employment to sixty hours, thus unofficially declaring the beginning of the so-called *Lochner* era characterised by judicial suspicion towards the regulation of economic activities. At the same time, it was open to uphold a similar law, limiting the daily employment of women in laundries and factories to ten hours: see *Muller v Oregon* 208 US 412 (1908).

and human dignity, but they also protect the ability of women to be part of the world of labour and support themselves. In addition, it is quite clear that working class women who are more dependent on their employment are more susceptible to being used and pressured by methods of sexual harassment.

VIII SOCIAL RIGHTS OF WOMEN AND SOCIAL RIGHTS OF CHILDREN

Social rights of children, such as the rights to free public education and health care, have significant impact on the lives of women, and in this sense indirectly serve women as well, because women are usually the prime carers of their children. At the same time, it would be a mistake to argue that the rights of children and the rights of their mothers always go hand in hand. For example, equal integration of women in the career world may not necessarily be favourable to their children if the norms of this world will continue to be based on unlimited working days.[30]

IX SOCIAL FEMINISM AND SOCIAL RIGHTS OF WOMEN

The discussion so far has demonstrated an argument which was two-fold: first, social rights are especially important to women since they constitute a relatively less well-off segment of society but nevertheless usually serve as the primary care providers for their families; and, second, the application of social rights entitlements to women is not always conducted on an equal footing to the application of the same rights to men. The analysis becomes even more complicated due to the different interests of women coming from various backgrounds and the competing priorities of the feminist struggle (traditionally more associated with civil and political rights). In other words, the social rights of women are contingent, among other things, also on a broader understanding among women as well that the struggle to achieve social rights should be regarded as a prioritised feminist goal.

---

[30] See also the text accompanying above nn 28–9.

Index